Going Global

atsushima
松島
CHAUMET
VENTO
Cartier
Cartier
Cartier
LBION
POLA
中央美術画廊
OSHINOYA
松島

GOING GLOBAL

The Textile and Apparel Industry

SECOND EDITION

Grace I. Kunz
Iowa State University

Myrna B. Garner
Illinois State University

Fairchild Books • New York

Vice President & General Manager,
Education & Conference Division: Elizabeth Tighe
Executive Editor: Olga T. Kontzias
Senior Associate Acquiring Editor: Jaclyn Bergeron
Assistant Acquisitions Editor: Amanda Breccia
Editorial Development Director: Jennifer Crane
Associate Development Editor: Lisa Vecchione
Production Director: Ginger Hillman
Creative Director: Carolyn Eckert
Assistant Art Director: Sarah Silberg
Production Editor: Andrew Fargnoli
Project Manager: Jeff Hoffman
Copyeditor: Ellen Howard
Ancillaries Editor: Noah Schwartzberg
Photo Researcher: Avital Aronowitz
Cover Design: Carolyn Eckert
Cover Art: (*top left, clockwise*) © Richard Hamilton Smith/CORBIS,
Courtesy of WWD, Courtesy of WWD, Courtesy of WWD
Back Cover Art: (*shopper*) © Patrick Sheandell O'Carroll/PhotoAlto/Corbis;
(*flags*) National Geographic/Getty Images/ B. Anthony Stewart;
(*runway*) Courtesy of WWD/Giovanni Giannoni
Opener Art: (*title page*) iStockphoto; (*part 1*) © Laurence Mouton/PhotoAlto/Corbis;
(*part 2*) © Claro Cortes IV/Reuters/Corbis; (*part 3*) Courtesy of WWD/Sean Gallup
Insert Art: (*CP1*) Courtesy Fairchild Books; (*CP2*) www.cottonmadeinafrica.org;
(*CP3*) © Paul Loewen/istockphoto; (*CP4*) © Joerg Boethling / Alamy; (*CP5*) Courtesy
Wal-Mart; (*CP6*) Photograph by Tim Mitchell. www.timmitchellphotography
.co.uk; (*CP7*) © Dreamstime; (*CP8*) REUTERS/Stringer Shanghai; (*CP9*) © Nike;
(*CP10*) Photo courtesy of Patagonia, Inc.; (*CP11*) © Nike; (*CP12*) © Nike; (*CP13*) AP Photo/
Chiang Ying-ying; (*CP14*) © Condé Nast; (*CP15*) Robert Nickelsberg/Getty Images;
(*CP16*) Kristen Luce/*The New York Times*/Redux; (*CP17*) Orhan Çam/shutterstock;
(*CP18*) © AP Photo; (*CP19*) © The Hindu Photo Archives; (*CP20*) David McNew/
GettyImages; (*CP21*) © Port of Los Angeles; (*CP22*) www.wethica.com; (*CP23*) Courtesy
Marks & Spencer; (*CP24*) Courtesy Marks & Spencer
Text Design: Tina Henderson

Library of Congress Catalog Card Number: 2010932256
ISBN: 978-1-60901-106-2
GST R 133004424
Printed in the United States of America

Contents

Extended Contents

Preface

In 2009 and early 2010, while we were planning the second edition of *Going Global*, the most frequently encountered concept in the trade literature was *sustainability of supply chains*. In 2003 and 2004, while we were developing the first edition, social responsibility was a primary concern, and it still is. However, social responsibility is now part of a total concept of global corporate responsibility, with dimensions that are economic, political, environmental, and cultural. Global corporate responsibility is what makes it possible for supply chains to be sustainable. When supply chains are sustainable, all participants benefit. The importance of sustainability in corporate priorities is reflected in the presence of a corporate responsibility component in the current Web sites of almost all textile- and apparel-related firms. Two firms recognized for their globally sustainable supply chains are Walmart and Nike. A quick review of their Web sites makes their sustainability efforts very apparent and reflects the benefits each firm has gained from improving sustainability.

We are using Li & Fung's conceptual model of a global supply chain, presented as a loop that begins and ends with the customer, as our introduction to the global textile and apparel marketplace. Li & Fung, based in Hong Kong, is a world leader in global sourcing and supply chain management for textiles and apparel as well as many other products. Li & Fung's model comprises the primary components necessary for the global sourcing of textiles and apparel. The model involves not only product developers, producers, and distributors, but also logistics operations and government involvement, via customs services. The Li & Fung conceptual model represents the language and processes that are actually being used in the textile and apparel industry at this time. There are other conceptual models of supply chains, for supply chains have always existed, even when the whole process was domestic; however, the process became more complex as global sourcing of textiles and apparel emerged as the dominant form of merchandise development and acquisition.

A conceptual model is an evolving thing, because processes, priorities, technology, and various influences wax and wane. In application, the model is adapted to the product type, the number of firms involved, the number of countries involved, technology, time frames, and so on. Thus, there are hundreds of actual supply chains, some with many subloops, but each one begins and ends with the customer: each process begins with assessment of potential customer demand and ends with customer acceptance or rejection of the products offered.

This text is in three parts. In part 1, we partner the Li & Fung supply chain model with our updated model of the textile and apparel industry matrix to create a more complete visual representation of the complexity of today's global sourcing systems. Part 1 continues with an exploration of the range of choices to be made by ultimate consumers, the textile and apparel supply matrix as an explanation of the components of the textile and apparel industry and how they are classified for sourcing and processing through global supply chains, and the concept of developing sustainable global supply chains. The concept of sustainable global supply chains is further explored in part 1 in an eight-page color photo essay, "Challenges for Achieving Sustainable Supply Chains in the Textile Complex."

Part 2 of this edition begins with a new chapter addressing processes necessary for global sourcing within the textile and apparel industry. This is followed by an exploration of the barriers and regulations inherent to global trade activities, the identification of illegal and unethical trade activities, and the role of politics and political positioning in global trade.

Part 3 looks at the current status of today's four major global trading blocs: Europe and the European Union, the Americas and the Caribbean Basin, Asia and Oceania, and the Middle East and Africa.

Comprehension of the enormity of change that the paradigm shifts in the world dynamic have brought to the textile and apparel business in the past decade may begin with one fact: 95 percent of the apparel sold in the United States, and in most developed countries today, is sourced in developing countries. Because just a few decades ago the percentage of offshore apparel sourcing was minimal, the shift in U.S. apparel acquisition alone exemplifies the need to expose today's textile and apparel students to the complexity of the global textile and apparel

marketplace and the issues that exist in the profession they are preparing to enter.

The overall learning objectives of *Going Global* are as follows:

1. Develop critical thinking and presentation skills
2. Read, listen, observe, think, and discuss
3. Analyze consistency and conflicts in ideas, concepts, and documentation
4. Synthesize responses
5. Explore the process of globalization, considering least developed, newly developing, developing, and developed countries
6. Address the economic and business, political and government, and social and labor perspectives related to globalization of the textile and apparel complex
7. Examine the complexity of textile and apparel supply chains and the benefits and costs global sourcing has brought to the textile and apparel industry
8. Gain appreciation of the reasons for, and the difficulties associated with, sustainable supply chains

Going Global is designed for college and university students in their sophomore or junior years and for graduate students who are beginning their studies in international trade. The approach is the active learner format, in which tables, figures, discussion questions, and activities are placed within the chapters at the points where topics are discussed. Global issues in textiles and apparel are examined from several viewpoints, providing the student with the facts and data needed to consider and weigh the ramifications of trade decisions, without being unduly biased toward any one perspective, be it economic, political, or social. The goal is for students to see overarching principles and connections, while recognizing that there is more than one correct answer to most questions, depending on who you are and the nature of your responsibilities.

This text provides enough information to understand the language and basic concepts of the global textile and apparel trade without overwhelming students with information or data that may become readily outdated. Students are encouraged to seek the latest available information related to numerous topics on the Internet, taking care to visit official sites. The active learner approach to the issues enables students to comprehend and internalize information before they move on to the next issue or perspective. In structuring the text, we have made use of our more than 70 years of combined teaching experience; international travel, in both developed and developing countries; consulting experiences with businesses and various governments; and experiences with international students.

We chose the Central Intelligence Agency's *World Factbook* as the source for our foundation data related to levels of development because it is a continuously updated, comprehensive source for 180 countries that draws on dozens of databases and that is in the public domain. This is a likely source for students to use when developing presentations and papers. It contains a great deal more information than has been incorporated into this text.

ACKNOWLEDGMENTS

Thanks to our students, undergraduate and graduate, domestic and foreign, who participated in global issues–related textile and apparel classes. You considered ideas, raised challenging questions, conducted research, and synthesized ideas to support class discussion, position papers, research papers, and panel presentations. You were essential to the development of the mind-set of the authors of this text. We owe our undying gratitude to Elise Shibles, LLC, for her knowledgeable analysis and articulate feedback related to trade relationships, laws, rules, and regulations, which framed the format of the first edition. Thank you to Dr. Geitel Winakor, Distinguished Professor Emerita at Iowa State University, for developing a course titled "Family Clothing Consumption." Some of the resources that she assembled and economic concepts that she taught provided the foundation for Chapter 2.

Women's Wear Daily and *just-style* provided daily updates on what is going on in the textile and apparel world and are cited many times throughout the text. Mike Todaro, of the American Apparel Producers' Network, provided us a great service by including us in his e-mail list so that we might receive the latest news related to textiles and apparel from across the nation and often beyond. Thanks also to Mike Fralix and [TC]² for your biweekly technology newsletter and to the American Apparel and Footwear Association for including faculty on your committees, providing opportunities for the authors to interact regularly with textile and apparel executives.

Special thanks to our reviewers, selected by Fairchild Books—Lynn Barnes, West Virginia University; Peter Brickman, Marist College; Lizhu Davis, California State University, Fresno; Sally L. Fortenberry, Texas Christian University; Eun Jin Hwang, Indiana University of Pennsylvania; Tricia Johnson, Illinois State University; Elena Karpova, Iowa State University; Natalie Nixon, Philadelphia University; Mijeong Noh, Western Illinois University; Marjorie Norton, Virginia Polytechnic Institute and State University; and John Talbott, Indiana University Bloomington—for your critical analysis of the manuscript and constructive suggestions for improvement. Thank you also to the staff at Fairchild Books who worked with us on *Going Global*—Olga Kontzias, executive editor; Jaclyn Bergeron; Amanda Breccia; Jennifer Crane; Lisa Vecchione; Avital Aronowitz; and Andrew Fargnoli—for your ongoing support and encouragement. Most of all, thanks for technology. We could not have updated this book without the help of the Internet.

1 EMBARKING ON A GLOBAL ADVENTURE

1 Introduction to Globalization

FUN FACT

United States–based firms are importing textile and apparel products from nearly all the more than 200 countries in the world.

TEXTILE AND APPAREL professionals determine the availability of products for their customers by engaging in merchandising, marketing, design, product development, production, and distribution. No other form of commerce can claim to be as pervasive throughout the globe as the textile and apparel business. The textile and apparel business provides employment for more people than any other business segment, directly affording a livelihood to many millions of people in every country in the world, including more than 35 million individuals in India alone (Chandra, 2006). This text explores the complexities involved in where textile and apparel products come from and how these products are distributed in today's global marketplace. The core of the discussion is examination of economic, political, and social issues that textile and apparel professionals face when making decisions.

Investing time, attention, and critical thinking to the topics addressed by this text will optimize the learning process and the opportunity for long-term application of principles gained. Critical thinking is the type of thinking involved in solving problems, formulating inferences, calculating likelihoods, and making decisions. It is useful in all aspects of our lives, and it will be valuable in the reading of this text as well as in making use of the information presented. Concepts

Objectives

- Discuss perspectives for the examination of global issues and the critical thinking required for appropriate understanding of those issues.

- Explore measuring differences among countries that are classified as newly developing, developing, and developed.

- Examine the nature of firms in the textile complex.

- Introduce the concept of a supply chain.

and principles related to globalization of the textile and apparel business are presented in many forms: as main text; in cases; and in pictures, diagrams, and tables. (Tables of numbers can provide amazing insight, but it usually takes a special bit of time and attention to appreciate what they have to offer.) Each form provides a different perspective and emphasis and different food for thought. In addition, learning activities dispersed through each chapter provide the opportunity to think about what has been read, consider what is already known, and assess the overall meaning and importance of the combination of information. Our purpose is to generate long-term retention as well as the ability to transfer what is learned to other scenarios.

At some point during a course using this text, students are often asked to write a position paper that involves identifying an issue, researching multiple perspectives, recognizing and criticizing assumptions, analyzing relationships, and giving reasons to support conclusions. This is critical thinking at its best, because it is direct practice of critical thinking skills that will continue to be useful in many facets of life. We encourage delving into the complexity of the global textile and clothing market and appreciating the challenges that are likely to be a part of a professional career.

Chapter 1 introduces perspectives for examining globalization, presents the global lexicon, explains a system for classifying countries according to levels of development, and examines the nature of firms in the textile complex.

PERSPECTIVES FOR CONSIDERATION OF GLOBALIZATION

Because of globalization, the world's people have become increasingly connected and interdependent in all facets of their lives. For example, in the last 30 years the sources and methods used by textile and apparel professionals for procuring textile and apparel products for their customers have undergone profound changes. In the mid-20th century, the vast majority of textile and apparel products available to consumers in developed countries were produced within the domestic economy of each. As we progressed through the 1980s and 1990s and into the 21st century, however, the source of these products changed from domestic to international to multinational to global as textile and apparel professionals sought the ever-elusive supplies of merchandise that would both satisfy their customers and generate the levels of profit necessary to sustain their businesses. Until the 1990s this shift was primarily viewed from political/government and economic/business perspectives. Now, social/labor perspectives, including environmental and economic sustainability, also must be considered (Figure 1.1).

From the perspective of some consumers, textile and apparel products are simply something they purchase in the marketplace with their monetary resources to satisfy their personal needs. The majority of these

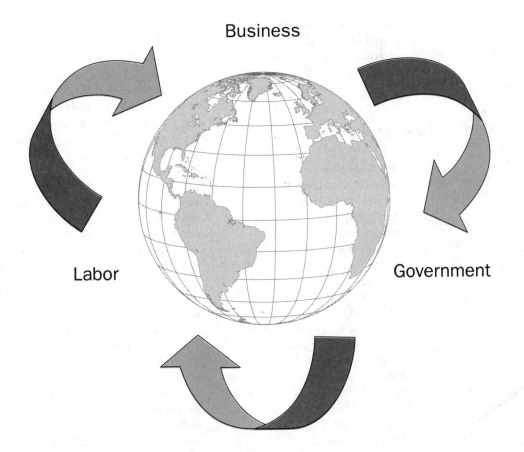

Business

Labor

Government

consumers have little understanding of or particular interest in where these products originate or how they arrive at the consumers' favorite stores. At the opposite end of the consumer continuum are individuals who are concerned about unfair business practices, particularly labor exploitation. These consumers may accuse the textile and apparel professionals of taking unfair advantage of the labor force, both domestically and abroad. Social concerns also include environmental issues, such as chemical dumping. These viewpoints related to labor and the environment are primarily social perspectives of globalization issues. At the same time, every business involved in textiles and apparel must be concerned about economic realities.

Throughout the exploration of any form of global trade, including textiles and apparel, participants and observers use multiple legitimate perspectives to reach diverse justifiable conclusions. The appropriate viewpoint is dependent upon content and context. The synergy among these perspectives is complex, challenging, and constantly changing.

Figure 1.1 Business decisions related to textiles and apparel require consideration from business, labor, and government perspectives. Conflicts arise because of differing priorities among a firm's constituencies.
(*Courtesy Fairchild Books*)

Case 1.1 presents a global trade scenario with an array of different economic, political, and social perspectives. After you have read this case, Learning Activity 1.1 will help you explore it through group discussion.

Learning Activity 1.1
PERSPECTIVES ON GLOBALIZATION

1. Read Case 1.1, and identify the economic, social, and political perspectives that you see involved in this case.
2. Identify the specific issues that are mentioned in the case.
3. How do the social, economic, and political perspectives differ, relative to the issues identified in question 2?
4. If you were an apparel professional importing from Myanmar, how might President Bush's and President Obama's decisions affect your business?
5. From the perspective of the citizens of Myanmar, what are the advantages and disadvantages of the U.S. presidents' decisions to ban imports to the United States?
6. Share group findings with the class to explore the complexity of this global trade scenario.

Global Lexicon

The **textile complex** incorporates firms around the world to accomplish textile fiber production and manufacturing, textile manufacturing, apparel manufacturing, retailing, and product consumption. Examination of the textile complex in the global market involves language drawn from economic, political, and social perspectives. For your convenience, components of a global lexicon (the vocabulary used to examine the concepts presented in this text) are listed and defined at the beginning of each chapter. You are probably familiar with many of these terms in a different context, but reviewing the lexicon before you proceed to read through a chapter is an active learning approach that can speed your progress and enhance your understanding of the topics discussed. Referring back to the lexicon to remind yourself of definitions as you work your way through the chapter is a strategic means of building your vocabulary. Fortunately, the number of terms in the global lexicon tends to decrease from one chapter to the next because of repeated use of established terminology.

In 2009, the U.S. Congress and President Barack Obama reaffirmed a 6-year ban on imports from Myanmar. Kevin M. Burke, the president and CEO of the American Apparel and Footwear Association (AAFA), supported the action, saying, "the global community must join together and implement global sanctions to demonstrate that oppression will not be tolerated in the global marketplace" (AAFA, 2009). Thus, the United States continues not to recognize the government of Myanmar and to ban imports from that nation.

Previously, President George W. Bush had signed *The Burmese Freedom and Democracy Act of 2003*, which banned all imports from the military dictatorship of Myanmar. A large portion of these imports were textile, apparel, and footwear products. In 2002, Myanmar's exports to the United States, the bulk of which were garments, totaled approximately $356 million. Strong bipartisan support for the bill was garnered based on reports of violent crackdowns by the Burmese government on prodemocracy leaders in Myanmar. The bill banned all imports from Burma until it could be determined that the ruling Burmese government had made substantial progress to end its human rights abuses. The passing of the bill also froze Myanmar's assets in the United States and called on other nations, such as China and Thailand, to follow suit. Several U.S. firms had already stopped Myanmar imports, citing human rights concerns and military investments in its garment industry. According to the U.S. government's 2002 Country Reports on Human Rights Practices, the Burmese government had continuously restricted worker rights, banned unions, and used forced labor, despite ordinances outlawing the practice.

In 2002, the AAFA CEO Kevin M. Burke said the ban was supported by AAFA, owing to the Burmese military regime's "persistent and egregious violations of International Labor Organization (ILO) conventions on forced labor, child labor and the overall abhorrent labor situation in Burma. In fact, the situation . . . deteriorated with the economy in ruins and human rights abuses rampant due largely to the inept and corrupt policies of Burma's military rulers" (Ellis, 2003, p. 6). Unfortunately, labor conditions did not measurably improve in the following years.

In 2008 Myanmar suffered from a horrendous cyclone that killed 85 thousand people, with an additional 54 thousand missing and presumed dead. The survivors were starving, with no homes and no jobs. Many agencies and nations offered aid, including the International Monetary Fund, the World Bank, and the Global Fund to Fight Aids, but, despite the desperation of the population, the ruling generals, who feared an invasion by Western powers, refused the help offered. Eventually, some aid was accepted from members of the Association of Southeast Asia Nations. However, reports again surfaced of labor-related child abuse, and these contributed to the Obama decision to continue the ban on imports from Myanmar.

Sources:

AAFA hails Burma import ban renewal. (2009, July 24). Arlington, VA: American Apparel and Footwear Association.

AAFA president and chief executive officer testimony before Senate subcommittee hearing on Burma. (2003, June 19). Arlington, VA: American Apparel and Footwear Association.

Ellis, K. (2003, July 19). Bush bans Myanmar imports. *Women's Wear Daily*, 2, 6.

In brief: Burma ban. (2003, July 16). *Women's Wear Daily*, 2.

apparel firm the term currently used to describe a vertically integrated firm engaged in a combination of product development, sourcing, and retailing

apparel manufacturer traditionally, a firm engaged in the entire process of apparel manufacturing

apparel manufacturing processes involved with merchandising, design, product development, production, and often wholesale marketing

apparel production part of the process of apparel manufacturing that actually converts materials—including fabrics, findings, trims, and usually thread—into a consumable good

apparel production vendor firm that takes orders for apparel products from other firms and that either produce or arrange for the production of those specific garments; historically called production contractors

apparel sourcing identifying appropriate countries of origin and contracting with cost-efficient vendors for services, production, or finished goods, or a combination of these; for delivery of a specified quantity and quality within an identified time frame

brand manager another name for a vertically integrated apparel firm whose business is based on a stable of valuable product names/brands

buying office company that provided sourcing services to retail buyers primarily from the 1950s through the 1980s

CMT (cut-make-trim) apparel contractors who commonly provide apparel assembly as their primary service

conglomerate a business formed when firms serving multiple markets join together with common ownership

contractor a firm that provides services for other businesses; often used for selected apparel manufacturing processes; in today's sourcing language these firms are called vendors

country of origin the location where goods were grown, mined, produced, or manufactured

department store a retailer that provides a variety of product lines, including apparel for men, women, and children; soft goods for the home; and home furnishings, usually at moderate-to-higher price levels

developed country a nation whose gross domestic product per capita and other measures of well-being fall well above the world average

developing country a nation whose gross domestic product per capita and other measures of well-being fall near or slightly below the world average, based on the benefits of industrial growth

domestic trade exchange of goods, services, or both within the boundaries of a specified state or country

e-commerce electronic business transactions conducted by systems such as Internet

e-tailing retailers' providing opportunities for ultimate consumers to purchase products or services, using electronic systems such as the Internet

exports goods shipped to another country for import in exchange for money, other goods, or jobs

findings materials other than face fabric used to construct garments: interlinings, pocket bags, linings, closures, and trims

firm any business, corporation, proprietorship, or partnership

full-package vendor apparel contractor that not only provides production services but also assists with and finances materials sourcing and sometimes some phases of product development

global trade includes the potential interactive participation of many groups, cultures, and nations in the merchandising, design, development, production, and distribution of products

globalization the process whereby the world's people, their firms, and their countries become increasingly interconnected in all facets of their lives

gross domestic product (GDP) the market value of the output of products and services produced within a country in a year

gross domestic product (GDP) per capita gross domestic product (GDP) of a country divided by the number of people in the population after GDP has been adjusted by purchasing power parity (PPP).

gross national product (GNP) the value of the average output produced by domestic residents of a nation as they labor within that nation

gross national product (GNP) per capita gross national product of a country divided by the number of people in the population

horizontal integration joining together under a single management organization, previously competitive enterprises engaged in offering similar goods or services

import and export trading a recently developed type of enterprise that assists textile and apparel firms in satisfying customer demand for goods and services from the global market

imports goods available for domestic consumption or materials available for domestic production because of exports of other countries

international trade any exchange of goods involving two or more countries

lean retailing effective management of inventory, based on accurate and timely information and frequent resupply

least developed country a nation whose gross domestic product per capita and other economic measures are among the lowest in the world; has little involvement in industrial development, which often involves production of apparel

market week calendar time set aside for trade shows featuring manufacturers' and brand managers' lines of textile materials, apparel, or machinery, presented at wholesale to other manufacturers or retail buyers

mass retailer a firm that offers a wide variety of consumer goods in a self-service environment with broad appeal across income ranges, ethnic groups, occupations, and lifestyles

merger combining two business entities into one larger business

newly developing country a nation whose gross domestic product per capita and other measures of well-being fall well below the world average but that is beginning to be engaged in industrial development, probably related to apparel production

nonstore retailer a firm that sells goods to the ultimate consumer without use of traditional "brick-and-mortar" store presentation

origin-conferring operations processes that determine what a label on a product will state as country of origin

outsourcing shifting specific operations outside the country in which the origin-conferring operations are performed; the process of acquiring technical services in foreign countries; sometimes used interchangeably with *sourcing*

outward processing outsourcing non-origin-conferring operations to a country with a lower wage rate

per capita by or for each individual; total is divided by the number of individuals involved; all share equally

politics the methods or tactics involved in managing an organization, business, state, or government; sometimes includes crafty or unprincipled methods, or both

product development the design and engineering of products to be serviceable, producible, salable, and profitable (Glock & Kunz, 1995)

purchasing power parity (PPP) measure that allows comparison of well-being among populations in different countries, as indicated by GDP; determined by adjusting GDP of a country by the buying power of its currency using a system such as the Consumer Price Index

quota method used to restrict quantities of certain types of goods that can be imported or exported; limit on the quantity of products allowed to enter or exit a country

retail product developer an individual or team that creates the product designs and develops the merchandise plans and specifications for a retailer's private brands, which are ultimately sourced from production vendors

retailing sale of merchandise or services, or both, to ultimate consumers

soft goods products made of textiles or other flexible materials: fabrics, apparel, linens, towels, upholstery, and small fashion accessories

sourcing determining the most cost-efficient vendor of services, materials, production, or finished goods, or a combination of these, at a specified quality and service level, for delivery within an identified time frame

specialty stores retailers that focus on specific classes of merchandise to the exclusion of other products

state trading the involvement of governments in the business environment

supply chain a total sequence of business processes involving single or multiple businesses and countries that enables demand for products or services to be satisfied

sustainability corporate responsibility strategy that integrates economic, political, environmental, and cultural dimensions to promote cooperation and solidarity among people and generations

takeover the absorption of a weaker firm into a more successful operation

tariff a tax on imports or exports; duty

textile complex the combination of textile-related industries that supply soft goods to the world population

textile materials sourcing identifying appropriate countries of origin and contracting with cost-efficient vendors of fabric, thread, or findings at a specified quantity, quality, and service level, for delivery within a designated time frame

trade agreement a means of encouraging, regulating, or restricting elements of trade among countries

trade balance the quantitative relationship between exports and imports of a country

trade barriers means of regulating or restricting trade; examples include state trading, tariffs, quotas, and limits on foreign investment

trade deficit a negative trade balance; value of imports exceeds value of exports

trade surplus a positive trade balance; value of exports exceeds value of imports

vertical integration combining firms that perform different stages of the production of the same type of products

World Trade Organization (WTO) an organization with more than 153 countries as members; deals with the global rules of trade among nations

LEVELS OF TRADE

Domestic trade refers to exchange of goods, services, or both within the boundaries of a specified state or country. **International trade** is any exchange of goods involving two or more countries. The concept transcends national and political boundaries, limits, and viewpoints. **Global trade** goes beyond the concept of international trade to include the potential interactive participation of many groups, cultures, and nations in the manufacturing and distribution of products. Although the terms *international* and *global* are sometimes used interchangeably, most people understand *global* to mean a universal, comprehensive perspective that pertains to the whole world. The terms *internationalization* and *globalization* are also sometimes used in relation to these same definitions used above. **Trade agreements** established by governments enhance or control trade. When reading trade literature, critical thinking is required to analyze and interpret the perspectives being reported.

International Trade

International trade in textiles and apparel is not a new phenomenon. Since the centuries-old trade routes brought silk out of China by way of camel caravans that crossed the Middle East to Europe, international trade in textile products has prevailed. The silk trade involved silk fiber, silk yarn, silk fabric, and some silk garments produced domestically in China and transported to Italy for exchange for other goods and services. Ships crossing the Mediterranean Sea from Asia to Europe invariably included textiles in their cargoes. The first ships that arrived in the Americas carried textiles as items for trade with the natives. One of the reasons the South was

unable to win the U.S. Civil War was because of the loss of revenue from the cotton trade with Great Britain.

In today's markets, large and small textile and apparel firms import materials, finished goods, or both through international trade with firms in countries where supplies are available. Many of these same firms are using international trade to export their products and make them available for sale in multiple countries.

A primary driver of the growth of international trade of textiles and apparel into global trade is the sourcing of products by firms based in developed countries from firms based in developing countries with lower labor costs. **Sourcing** is the process of determining the most cost-efficient vendor of services, materials, production, or finished goods, or a combination of these, at a specified quality and service level, for delivery within an identified time frame. Sourcing priorities have contributed to the globalization of trade by driving the apparel manufacturing industry in particular around the world.

Global Trade

Lodge (1995) provided a generalized definition of the **globalization** concept, stating that "globalization is the process whereby the world's people are becoming increasingly interconnected in all facets of their lives—cultural, economic, political, technological, and environmental" (p. 1). In part, this global model of business and economic exchange has resulted from the actions of many developing nations, who, wishing to increase their participation in the Western capitalism model of economics, have relaxed their barriers to trade and investment. This easing of restraints facilitates entry into the interconnected global economy, but it also may produce a homogenization effect whereby individual cultures and beliefs are absorbed, diluted, or lost.

To further explain global business and the process of globalization, we must clarify the nature of global business transactions. Moshe Hirsch argued that they are carried out by enterprises that operate in a world divided by national states, each claiming sovereignty over all the economic activities within their boundaries (as cited in Buckley, 2003, p. xiii). The following three types of integration are occurring in the international business environment:

- financial, which tends to be globally integrated
- trade and investment, which tends to be regionally integrated
- labor, which tends to be nationally regulated (Buckley, 2003)

The globalization of the financial markets was evident early in the recession of the late 2000s, when stock markets dropped dramatically in many countries around the world within a few days of each other.

Regional integration ranges from the narrowly defined free trade area identified by the North American Free Trade Agreement (NAFTA), which is made up of just 3 countries (Canada, Mexico, and the United States) to broader economic and trade arrangements, such as the European Union (EU), which in 2009 included 27 member nations that speak more than 32 languages. The EU is now unified to the extent that trade data for all its member countries are reported in many sources as a single set of numbers, as if the EU were a single country, like the states of the United States.

Businesses involved with the development and distribution of textile and apparel products in a global market potentially deal with a combination of financial, trade and investment, and labor transactions. Seen from a more pragmatic viewpoint, global trade might simply involve 10 thousand pairs of khaki pants. These pants, sold in department stores in towns in the rural and subur-

ban United States, could have been designed and developed in Chicago, made with fabric woven in South Korea out of cotton fiber from Pakistan and polyester fiber from Taiwan, and cut and sewn somewhere in Honduras (Central America). In each country, individuals of different cultural backgrounds are employed; different languages are spoken; diverse tasks requiring different sets of performance skills are performed; and resources, from pesticides and petrochemicals to water and machinery, were required to manufacture the product. This simple pair of pants becomes a microcosm of globalization, involving many complex and potentially problematic issues.

MEASURING LEVELS OF TRADE

International trade and global trade are often described in terms of exports and imports. **Exports** represent goods shipped for import to another country in exchange for money, other goods, or jobs. Exports result in the accruing of revenue to the firms in the countries where the goods originated if the firms operate in a capitalistic system; revenue accrues to the government if the countries operate in a communistic system. **Imports** make goods available for domestic consumption or materials available for domestic production. The goods produced can be consumed domestically or exported, depending on the trade regulations that apply.

The difference between imports and exports for a region or a country is called the **trade balance**. The trade balance is calculated as follows:

trade balance = exports − imports

A **trade surplus** means there is a positive trade balance; the value of exports exceeds the value of imports. A trade

Table 1.1 Trade Balance of Countries Selected from the Top 15 Countries Trading Textiles and Apparel in 2008 in Millions of Dollars

	Country	Textile Exports	Textile Imports	Apparel Exports	Apparel Imports	Trade Balance
1	European Union (27 countries)	80.2	84.0	112.4	177.7	Textile trade deficit Apparel trade deficit
2	China	65.3	16.2	120.0	2.3	Textile trade surplus Apparel trade surplus
3	United States	12.5	23.1	4.4	82.5	Textile trade deficit Apparel trade deficit
4	Hong Kong	12.3	12.3	27.9	18.5	Textile trade deficit Apparel trade surplus
5	India	10.3	—	10.9	—	Textile trade surplus Apparel trade surplus
6	Turkey	9.4	5.7	13.6	2.2	Textile trade surplus Apparel trade surplus
7	Japan	7.3	7.0	—	25.9	Textile trade surplus Apparel trade deficit
8	Indonesia	3.7	3.3	6.3	—	Textile trade surplus Apparel trade surplus
9	Mexico	2.0	5.4	4.9	2.5	Textile trade deficit Apparel trade surplus
10	Canada	2.0	4.4	—	8.5	Textile trade deficit Apparel trade deficit

Source: Based on data from The World Trade Organization (WTO). (2009). International trade statistics 2009: Top 15 countries in textiles and apparel trade in 2008. Retrieved November 14, 2009, from http://www.wto.org/english/res_e/statis_e/its2009

surplus is sometimes regarded as desirable, because, cumulatively, the country in question has gained more revenue from the sale of exported goods than it gave up to other countries for the purchase of imported goods. There is a net gain in revenue that can be invested in domestic resources. It is important to note that a trade surplus does not necessarily mean that more products are available for trade than can be consumed domestically. In developing countries it is common that goods produced for export are not made available to domestic consumers.

A **trade deficit** means there is a negative trade balance; the value of imports exceeds the value of exports. A negative trade balance may be regarded as undesirable, because greater revenue is accrued to foreign countries as the result of trade than to the domestic country in question. Table 1.1 lists the values of imports and exports and resulting trade balances in selected countries ranked in the top 15 in the textile and apparel trade.

The first "country" listed in Table 1.1 is the European Union (EU); as mentioned previously, the EU is not a single country, but rather a group of 27 countries that now report their international trade statistics together, as if they were a single country. Some of the countries in the EU have substantial textile and apparel production, and others, relatively high consumption levels. The result is a very high volume of trade, with a slight trade deficit in both textiles and apparel. However, the addition of several developing countries to EU in the first decade of the 2000s has added to the current apparel production levels and provides opportunities for future increases at reasonable costs. As a result, the EU could soon have an apparel trade surplus.

China (2) ranks second in textile exports and first in apparel exports, with extremely high textile and apparel trade surpluses. Since the early 1990s, China has developed a textile and apparel production industry second to none in efficiency even though it no longer has the lowest labor costs. The net effect is, in 2008 the Chinese economy benefited more from textile and apparel trade than any other country in the world.

The United States (3) ranks second to the EU in both textile and apparel imports, but in contrast to the EU, now has low levels of textile and apparel exports. Manufacturing of textiles and apparel has declined rapidly since the 1980s. Because of high rates of consumption, the United States has dramatic trade deficits in both textiles and apparel.

Hong Kong (4) shows a slight textile trade deficit but a large apparel trade surplus. Hong Kong became an apparel sourcing base for U.S. department stores during the 1970s. At first, textile and apparel production rapidly increased in Hong Kong, but soon demand exceeded what could be produced in a very small country. Thus, Hong Kong was the first country to develop the expertise to offer **apparel sourcing** services, including identifying appropriate countries of origin

and contracting with cost-efficient vendors for services, production, or finished goods, or a combination of these, for delivery of a specified quantity and quality within an identified time frame. To support the apparel production that was taking place in Hong Kong as well as what was being sourced abroad, **textile materials sourcing** services were also developed. This provided a means to acquire necessary fabrics, thread, and findings to support the quantity, quality, and time frames established for apparel. Consequently, Hong Kong developed a negative trade balance in textiles and a positive trade balance in apparel, a situation that was still in place in 2008.

Then during the 1990s Mexico (9) became a primary U.S. apparel supplier. Mexico also did not produce enough textiles to support the sourcing demand for apparel exports, resulting in a textile trade deficit and apparel trade surplus. Industrial development in both Hong Kong and Mexico resulted in increased labor costs, and, since 2000, they have had reduced exports to developed countries. In 2008, India (5), Turkey (6), and Indonesia (8) all show trade surpluses in textiles and apparel. Production of textiles and apparel for the world market makes major contributions to the economies of these countries.

Japan (7) is known for export of high-tech fibers and fabrics, including microfibers, and so textiles have a slight trade surplus. Canada (10), despite its large size, has a relatively small population and economic base. Japan, Canada, and the United States all have relatively high labor rates, high rates of domestic consumption, and declines in domestic apparel production, thus creating a negative trade balance in apparel. The constantly increasing trade deficits are of considerable concern for long-term economic security (Uchitelle, 2004).

Expand your understanding of levels of trade by doing Learning Activity 1.2.

Learning Activity 1.2

LEVELS OF TRADE

1. Identify two primary differences among domestic trade, international trade, and global trade.

2. Why might small firms be more likely to be involved in international trade than global trade?

3. What is the purpose of trade agreements among nations?

4. What is the meaning of a trade surplus?

5. What is the meaning of a trade deficit?

6. How might sourcing of textiles or apparel that creates imports relate to a corresponding trade surplus or trade deficit?

7. Why are developed countries more likely to have trade deficits in apparel?

8. To comprehend the pervasiveness of imported apparel in our marketplace, conduct this class survey:

9. Make a list of all the countries represented in the labels of your clothing, and state the type of garment (e.g., jeans, Mexico; T-shirt, Haiti).

10. Compare your list with those of your classmates, and tally the list of countries and types of garments to see which countries are represented most frequently and what types of garments come from the countries identified.

11. Do some types of garments seem more likely to come from certain countries? Describe your results.

12. Be alert in future chapters to why specific garments may come from certain countries.

MEASURING LEVELS OF DEVELOPMENT

In its discussions of world trade, the **World Trade Organization** (**WTO**) commonly describes differences between "rich" countries and "poor" countries, but it does not define the terms *rich* and *poor*. The World Bank and United Nations use the term **least developed** to describe the world's poorest countries—those countries in which the majority of the population lives in extreme poverty.

Another set of terminology that has been used to indicate differences in levels of development is *First World, Second World, Third World*. After World War II, the *First World* referred to the North American and European Western bloc, and the *Second World* referred to the Soviet-led Eastern bloc. *Western* and *Eastern* referred to two sociopolitical regions in the northern half of the globe's hemispheres. During the last half of the 20th century, the two blocs had the most economic and military power and faced off in an ideological confrontation known as the cold war. The *Third World* referred to countries in the globe's Southern Hemisphere, namely, countries in Asia, Africa, Latin America, and the Pacific that were trying to make their own way in a rapidly developing world. These terms are no longer widely used because of the demise of the Soviet Union, but you may come across them in descriptions of recent history (Ellwood, 2001).

This text defines countries' levels of well-being, in relation to the textile and apparel business, with the classifications *least developed, newly developing, developing,* and *developed* countries The level of development is of particular interest to us because location of different parts of the textile and apparel business is largely determined by level of development of the countries involved. In general, the textile and apparel production industry takes place primarily in countries at the middle levels of development, whereas most of the consumption takes place in countries with high levels of development.

Developed countries are comparatively rich, **developing countries** are comparatively less rich, **newly developing countries** are poor, and least developed countries are very poor. The least developed countries are often very poor because ongoing political disruptions have discouraged development of any kind of industry. The textiles and apparel industry is often the first form of industrial development and therefore is extremely important for growing adequate wealth in least developed countries. Only a few countries in the "least developed" category are discussed in this text, because few of them have embarked on industrialization. Many measures of level of development are presented on a per capita basis. **Per capita** means each measure is presented by or for each individual; the total is divided by the number of individuals involved; all share equally.

A concept traditionally used to measure a country's relative level of development is **gross national product (GNP)**. GNP is the value of the average output produced by domestic residents of a nation as they labor within it. GNP includes the profits made by domestic firms, even if those profits resulted from activities that occurred outside the nation's borders. It does not include the output of foreigners who are producing within the country. **Gross national product (GNP) per capita** is GNP divided by the number of citizens in the population. It shows the relative rate of production per citizen.

The **gross domestic product (GDP)** is an alternative method of measuring the economic activity of nations that is now commonly used. GDP has gained favor, because it represents the market value of the output of products and services produced within a country in a year. Unlike the GNP, GDP includes the contributions of migrant workers and other foreigners employed within a country. GDP does, however, exclude the profits made by domestic firms from activities they completed in other countries. To compare well-being across nations, **purchasing power parity (PPP)** is used to adjust GDP in each country, using a system such as the Consumer Price Index. PPP determines the relative buying power of each currency, making it much easier to do comparisons between countries. The U.S. dollar is often used as the standard for presenting PPP, although the euro has gained considerable economic importance since it was adopted as the common currency among most of the countries in the European Union (EU).

Gross domestic product (GDP) per capita is GDP divided by the number of people in a country's population after GDP has been adjusted by PPP. It provides insight into how total market value of products and services produced in a country relates to the number of individuals in the population. It also provides an understanding of how well off each person in a country's population can be on average. (It is important not to drown in acronyms, so try to get a handle on them from the beginning.)

When comparing the economic well-being of individual nations, it is essential to select the same measures. If the GNP of one nation were compared with the GDP of another, the results would be of little use in understanding the overall economic picture. In addition, the GNP and GDP are inclusive measures of overall production; we would need to extrapolate more specific information from those measures to determine and compare the contribution of textile and apparel. Yet, understanding GDP is a start.

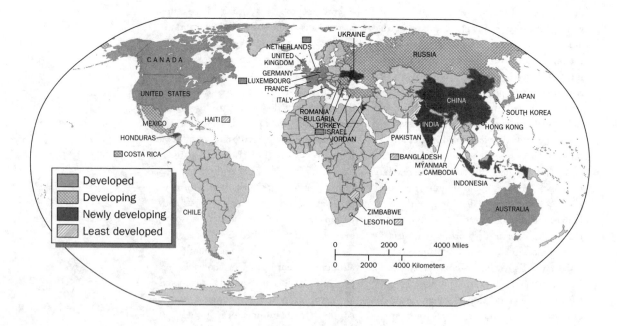

Figure 1.2 World map showing locations of developed, developing, newly developing, and least developed countries.
(Courtesy Fairchild Books)

The map in Figure 1.2 shows the locations of countries classified as developed, developing, newly developing, and least developed, based on per capita GDP. Note how the countries at different levels of development tend to be clustered in different parts of the world.

Table 1.2 reports populations, GDP, and GDP per capita for some of the countries active in the textile and apparel industry and selected for study in this text. The list of countries is arranged from the highest to the lowest in per capita GDP. Two countries not active in the textile and apparel industry are also included—one with very high GDP (Luxembourg) and one with very low GDP (Zimbabwe)—to provide perspective on the total range of relative wealth available in countries around the world. Take a few moments to examine the range in levels of population and GDPs represented by the countries in this table.

Note the great difference in population of the countries listed and the related GDP. Then examine the range of per capita GDP across classes of countries as well as the differences in per capita GDP within each class. Keep in mind that per capita GDP is an average for the population

Table 1.2 POPULATION, GROSS DOMESTIC PRODUCT (GDP), AND PER CAPITA GROSS DOMESTIC PRODUCT FOR SELECTED DEVELOPED, DEVELOPING, NEWLY DEVELOPING, AND LEAST DEVELOPED COUNTRIES, IN ORDER OF PER CAPITA GDP IN 2009*

Countries	Population	GDP (in Billions of U.S. Dollars)	Per Capita GDP (in U.S. Dollars)
Developed			
Luxembourg (EU)	491,775	$ 38.1	$ 77,600
United States	307,212,123	14,250.0	46,400
Hong Kong	7,055,017	301.3	42,700
The Netherlands (EU)	16,715,999	652.3	39,000
Australia	21,262,641	819.0	38,500
Canada	33,487,208	1,287.0	38,400
United Kingdom (EU)	61,113,205	2,165.0	35,400
Germany (EU)	82,329,758	2,812.0	34,200
France (EU)	64,057,792	2,113.0	32,800
Japan	127,078,679	4,141.0	32,600
Italy (EU)	58,126,212	1,756.0	32,200
Israel	7,233,701	205.2	28,400
Korea, South	48,508,972	1,343.0	27,700
Developing			
Hungary	9,905,596	186.4	18,800
Russia	140,041,247	2,103.0	15,200
Chile	16,601,707	244.3	14,700
Mexico	111,211,789	1,473.0	13,200
Bulgaria	7,204,687	90.5	12,600
Romania	22,245,421	256.3	11,500
Costa Rica	4,253,877	48.2	11,300
Turkey	76,805,524	861.6	11,200
Newly developing			
China	1,338,612,968	8,767.0	6,500
Ukraine	46	294.3	6,400
Jordan	6,342,948	33.6	5,300
Honduras	7,792,854	11.6	4,200
Indonesia	240	514.9	4,000
India	1,166,079,217	3,548.0	3,100
Least developed			
Pakistan	176,242,949	448.1	2,600
Cambodia	14,494,293	29.9	1,900
Bangladesh	156,050,883	242.2	1,600
Haiti	9,035,536	11.6	1,300
Burma/Myanmar	48,137,741	56.5	1,200
Zimbabwe	11,392,629	0.3	200

Source: Based on estimates of 2009 data from Central Intelligence Agency (CIA). (2009). *The world factbook*.
Retrieved November 2009 from https://www.cia.gov/library/publications/the-world-factbook/index.html
* Based on purchasing power parity.

of a particular country, based on purchasing power parity. GDPs per capita for developed countries on this table range from $77,600 down to $27,700; developing countries range from $18,800 down to $11,200; newly developing countries range from $6,500 down to $3,100; least developed countries range from $2,600 down to $200. The United States is ranked second here, and yet we know that not everyone who lives in the United States is rich; many are relatively poor. What the per capita GDP indicates is that most of the people in the U.S. population have a chance to be better off than most of the rest of the people in the world but not nearly as good a chance as the people that live in Luxembourg.

Recognizing that Hong Kong reverted to China in 1997, after 100 years of British rule, we have elected to continue to look at Hong Kong and China as separate entities; they are treated as separate entities in the global market, and separate data are available for evaluating their participation. The routes that Hong Kong and China took for entry into global trade were different, and their levels of development are remarkably different. In Table 1.2, Hong Kong is ranked third in the "developed" country class, whereas China is first in the "newly developing" class.

For a closer look at indicators of levels of development, examine Table 1.3. It includes countries that have the highest and the lowest GDP per capita in each classification of countries presented in Table 1.2. This table presents some additional variables to consider when examining how a country's classification relates to its level of development. In general, the variables presented change in a positive direction as counties become more developed. Note also that

women who are 15 years old or older are less likely to be able to read than men in countries at lower levels of development. When looking at data like these, it is important to assess the reliability of the source of data and to read the footnotes, which often explain peculiarities related to the reliability of the numbers.

For example, in Table 1.3, Zimbabwe, the least developed country in the world, has an extremely high unemployment rate but has reported surprisingly high literacy rates. The infant mortality rate is high, with 32 babies dying within the first year of life out of each one thousand live births. However, infant mortality is not as high as might be anticipated, given a life expectancy of 46 years. Infant mortality is about half the number reported for Pakistan. At the same time, life expectancy is reported as 19 years less in Zimbabwe as in Pakistan. This seeming paradox requires additional exploration if seeking to understand more fully the relative well-being of the populations in these two countries. (The source of these data is *The World Factbook*, a publication prepared and continually updated by the U.S. Central Intelligence Agency [CIA]). It is an amazing, incredibly complete resource about nearly every country in the world.)

We will be using demographics and other data like these throughout this text to examine well-being of populations in relation to where the textile and apparel industry is located and how it works. As we move firmly into the 21st century, we discover that the majority of apparel products sold within developed and developing countries are sourced from other, less developed countries around the globe. This trend affects every individual who seeks a career in the field of textile and apparel.

Table 1.3 INDICATORS OF LEVELS OF DEVELOPMENT FOR THE COUNTRIES WITH THE HIGHEST AND THE LOWEST PER CAPITA GROSS DOMESTIC PRODUCT, CLASSIFIED AS DEVELOPED, DEVELOPING, NEWLY DEVELOPING, AND LEAST DEVELOPED IN TABLE 1.2

	Unemployment Rate	Literacy[a] Male	Literacy[a] Female	Infant Mortality (in Thousands of Live Births)	Life Expectancy at Birth (in Years)
Developed					
Luxembourg	7%	100%	100%	5	79
Korea, South	4%	99%	98%	4	79
Developing					
Hungary	8%	99%	99%	8	73
Turkey	15%	95%	80%	27	72
Newly Developing					
China	4%	95%	88%	20	74
India	10%	73%	48%	50	66
Least Developed					
Pakistan	15%	63%	36%	60	65
Zimbabwe	95%	94%	87%	32	46

Source: Based on estimates of 2009 data from The Central Intelligence Agency (CIA). *The world factbook*. Retrieved November 2009 from https://www.cia.gov/library/publications/the-world-factbook/index.html
a. Can read and write at age 15 and older.

Developed Countries

The developed countries listed in Table 1.2 built their economic base primarily on industrialization. Beginning in the late 1700s, with the start of Industrial Revolution, production of textile and apparel products formed the foundation of the economies of these countries. These countries have shifted their primary emphasis from producing textiles and apparel to consuming them. This shift came about in the late 20th century as each nation improved its economic status. In every case, these nations have at one time or another utilized textile and apparel production as a major means of achieving industrial and economic growth. Most still have firms that are involved in some stages of manufactur-

ing significant amounts of these products. However, the major contributions made to the world economy have progressed from full industrial production to other stages, such as **product development** that encompasses the design and engineering of products to be serviceable, producible, salable, and profitable (Glock & Kunz, 2005) or even forms of less labor-intensive endeavors, such as technology, communications, and services. For example, beginning in the 1980s, South Korea moved into this group by readily embracing industrialization and open trade policies as a means of building economic development. As the economy improves, industry evolves from a primary focus on industrial production to creative and technological aspects of business and industry.

Developing Countries

Note that the unemployment rates and most other criteria for developing countries are similar to those of developed countries. Developing countries have significantly improved their overall economic condition beyond those of newly developing countries. Countries in the "Developing Country" class have double, triple, and quadruple the per capita GDP of newly developing countries. The developing nations are those that have embraced the production of textile and apparel products as a way to compete in the global marketplace and in some cases are involved in producing many other products as well. The developing countries shown in Table 1.2 are quite different from one another in their cultural orientation and their approaches to economic modernization. Their populations, according to Western standards, have benefitted from industrial development and achieved a much more comfortable way of living.

However, the developing countries are no longer the lowest-cost labor sources for textiles, apparel, and many other products. Thus, several of these countries have struggled to maintain textile and apparel sales in the face of lower labor costs in newly developing and least developed countries. Generally, developing countries are in a transition phase between focusing primarily on production for export and increasing focus on production for domestic consumption while facing increasing imports from lower-wage countries. The domestic demand for low-to-moderate-priced goods becomes satisfied by low cost imports, but there may still be opportunity for upscale, high-quality goods both in domestic markets and abroad. For example, Costa Rica is no longer one of the lowest wage countries in the Americas, but it has become a successful exporter to the United States and other developed countries of better quality natural fiber sweaters, threads, and other goods. As domestic production costs increased, exporting firms produced fewer units of higher quality goods positioned at better and designer price points to remain profitable.

Newly Developing Countries

Newly developing countries are defined here as those nations whose overall economic conditions fall well below the world average in GDP per capita and other measures. These countries tend to be nations that, for many different reasons, have been slow in changing their way of life from agrarian, or basic sustenance, to industrial age and beyond but that have begun the process and made some progress. Growth has been the result of finding ways to overcome problems such as inadequate basic resources, poor education, and repression caused by internal politics or outside influences.

For newly developing countries, where unemployment and poverty rates are high and wages are low, apparel production continues to be the vehicle that provides employment where unemployment and poverty rates are high and wages are low. Startup costs for apparel production are comparatively low, and training times tend to be short. Because the apparel industry still requires labor-intensive production, newly developing countries can be ideal locations, as one of their most available resources is human labor. Thus, these countries tend to focus more on production for export, which provides jobs for otherwise unemployed workers, rather than on production for domestic consumption. It is not unusual for it to be illegal in such countries for citizens to retain goods that are produced for export but that are often in high demand in black market scenarios.

As shown in Table 1.2, China is the most populous country in the world and has the highest GDP of any country listed except the United States. However, China's GDP per capita puts it in the "newly developing" class. According to the CIA (2010), China reports much of its population-related economic data only for its urban population, which has much higher rates of employment and income than the rural sector. During the first decade of the 2000s, China has made significant changes in its level of participation in the open, or capitalist, model of economic development. As a result, China has significantly enhanced its place in global trade in textiles and apparel as well as many other products. For example, China's successful hosting of the 2008 Olympic Games put it on the world stage for the first time in hundreds of years. According to most criteria, it seems China should be in the "developing country" category, but much of its huge population has not yet benefited from the nation's economic growth.

The second highest ranked newly developing country, Ukraine, became an independent country with the break-up of the Soviet Union in the 1991 but has continued to suffer from a legacy of state control and corruption. After Russia, Ukraine was the most productive member of USSR. This reality is reflected in its literacy rates. But since independence, productivity has fallen to less than half of its previous levels (CIA, 2010). If Ukraine's report of 5 percent unemployment is accurate, then wages in general must be extremely low.

Least Developed Countries

Least developed countries are those that rank the lowest in measures of economic well-being. Countries in this category tend to be those that have suffered from governmental exploitation, ongoing tribal wars, lack of education, and cultural traditions that deny acceptance of change. Commonly, a large portion of the population lives in extreme poverty. The citizens have low levels of income; high levels of unemployment, illiteracy, and infant mortality; and comparatively low life expectancies.

Developing some form of industry to provide employment is usually the first step in improving the well-being of these populations. The textile and apparel business often provides that opportunity. These countries frequently begin to develop when apparel production services for export are initiated. Pakistan, Cambodia, Bangladesh, Haiti, and Myanmar all have some apparel manufacturing but have struggled to develop the support systems that would allow the business truly to thrive.

Pakistan, the highest ranked least developed country, has the lowest literacy rates for both men and women and the highest infant mortality rates of the countries in this table. Life expectancies for both least developed and newly developing countries are noticeably lower than those of developing and developed countries, a strong indicator of levels of well-being within populations.

Now, do Learning Activity 1.3 to broaden your knowledge of levels of development through group discussion.

Learning Activity 1.3

LEVELS OF DEVELOPMENT

1. Select one country from each country category: developed, developing, newly developing, and least developed.
2. Examine the data in Tables 1.2 and 1.3 for the countries you selected.
3. What are the relationships among population, levels of imports and exports, trade balance, levels of GDP, and GDP per capita for each of the countries you selected?
4. Look up each of the countries you selected in *The World Factbook* online (https://www.cia.gov/library/publications/the-world-factbook/). Skim through data available. What additional information supports or disputes the countries' classification as to level of development?

The textile complex is the combination of textile-related business firms that supply soft goods to the world population. A **firm** is any business, be it corporation, proprietorship, or partnership. In the textile complex a firm could be engaged in manufacturing; sourcing; supplying materials, equipment, or technology; retailing; or some combination of these activities; or it may be any other organization that conducts business related to soft goods. **Soft goods** are products made of textiles or other flexible materials, including batting, fabrics, apparel, linens, towels, upholstery, draperies, and fashion accessories. There are three primary end uses for soft goods: apparel, household goods, and industrial products. The primary focus of discussion here is on the apparel component of the textile complex, although textile products, such as bedding, drapes, and towels, and industrial products, such as medical materials, roadbeds, and building materials, are growing components of the textile complex.

In the mid-20th century, textile and apparel firms were frequently small and family owned. As such, some of these companies tended to be slower to confront changes occurring in the overall business environment. Their reticence to modernize, inflexibility, and lack of response to markets condemned some of them to compromising product quality and even to failure (Underhill, 1998). To survive in the changing business climate, many firms found they had to join forces through horizontal integration. **Horizontal integration** is change brought about through **mergers** (firms with similar functions joining forces to form one larger business) and **takeovers** (strong firms absorbing weaker firms to form one larger business).

Another method of change that has proven successful for the survival and growth of textile and apparel businesses is

Table 1.4 RANKING OF THE TOP 15 PUBLICLY TRADED APPAREL COMPANIES WITH AT LEAST $ 100 MILLION IN ANNUAL SALES, BY PROFIT MARGIN, INCLUDING ANNUAL SALES AND NET INCOME, IN MILLIONS

Rank 2009	Rank 2008	Company Name	Sales (in Millions)	Net Income (in Millions)	Profit Margin (Percentage)
1	1	True Religion	$ 270.0	$ 44.4	16.44%
2	New	The Buckle	$ 792.0	$ 104.4	13.18%
3	5	lululemon athletica	$ 353.5	$ 39.4	11.15%
4	8	Urban Outfitters	$ 1,834.6	$ 199.4	10.87%
5	6	Guess?	$ 2,093.4	$ 123.6	10.20%
6	10	Nike	$ 18,627.0	$ 1,883.4	10.11%
7	12	Gymboree	$ 1,000.7	$ 93.5	9.34%
8	4	bebe Stores	$ 687.6	$ 63.1	9.18%
9	11	Cintas Group	$ 3,937.9	$ 335.4	8.52%
10	15	Jos. A. Bank Clothiers	$ 695.9	$ 58.4	8.39%
11	14	Polo Ralph Lauren	$ 5,018.9	$ 406.0	8.09%
12	12	Delia's	$ 215.6	$ 17.2	7.98%
13	17	Aeropostale	$ 1,885.5	$ 149.4	7.92%
14	16	VF	$ 7,642.6	$ 602.8	7.89%
15	3	Abercrombie & Fitch	$ 3,540.3	$ 272.3	7.69%

Source: Based on 2009: The *Apparel* top 50. *Apparel*. (2009, July). Retrieved from http://www.apparelmag.com/ME2/dirmod.asp?sid=&nm=&type=MultiPublishing&mod=PublishingTitles&mid=CD746117C0BB4828857A1831CE70 7DBE&tier=4&id=5758C3BE5F8A40769215BFC6835C3AB5

vertical integration. **Vertical integration** occurs when firms that perform different stages in the planning, design, production, and distribution of products join to form one larger business. Takeovers are also a means used to create a vertically integrated textile or apparel firm, especially if supply of essential material or equipment is involved.

Mergers and acquisitions have been at an all-time high since the 1990s. However, today there are more alternatives to survival than merely increasing in size. One alternative is to have companies concentrate on core competencies and source specific tasks that prove too costly to do in-house from firms that specialize in those activities. Many firms located in developed countries have looked to partnering with or sourcing from offshore firms to support their continued growth.

Apparel magazine (http://www.apparelmag.com) annually publishes a list of the top 50 U.S. publicly traded apparel companies, ranked by profit margin, with at least $100 million in annual sales for the most recent fiscal years. Table 1.4 shows the top 15 companies. You will probably recognize some of the companies as retailers, others as manufacturers, and still others as designers or brands. Many of the companies are horizontally and vertically integrated in some form. The following discussion includes an overview of the functions of companies operating at each level of the textile complex.

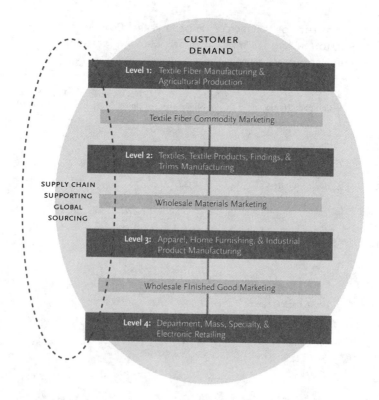

CUSTOMER DEMAND

Level 1: Textile Fiber Manufacturing & Agricultural Production

Textile Fiber Commodity Marketing

Level 2: Textiles, Textile Products, Findings, & Trims Manufacturing

Wholesale Materials Marketing

Level 3: Apparel, Home Furnishing, & Industrial Product Manufacturing

Wholesale Finished Good Marketing

Level 4: Department, Mass, Specialty, & Electronic Retailing

SUPPLY CHAIN SUPPORTING GLOBAL SOURCING

Figure 1.3 The primary components of the textile complex integrated into a global supply chain. (*Developed by Grace Kunz*)

Structure of the Textile Complex

Developed, developing, newly developing, and least developed countries all have roles in the textile complex. At this point in time, developed and developing countries have primary roles in consumption, whereas many developing, newly developing, and least developed countries have primary roles in production. Figure 1.3 presents a conceptual model showing four levels that are primary components of the textile complex. Levels 1 through 4 of this model represent the organizational structure of the textile complex, from fiber and other materials supply through retailing of finished goods. Each of the four levels represents different but related areas of specialization necessary to convert raw materials from producers to finished goods for consumers.

Each of the four levels of the textile complex has multiple categories, subcategories, and auxiliary activities that contribute to the functions in each area of specialization. Between each of the levels is a wholesale marketing function for transferring ownership of goods to the next level in the textile complex.

In the model the four levels are floating over a sea of customer demand that constantly requires redefinition of the products being conceptualized, planned, designed, developed, and produced for the next retail selling period. Ultimate consumers make the final decisions that determine who and what are winners and losers.

Level 1—Textile Fiber Agriculture Production and Manufacturing: Textile Fiber Commodity Marketing
Natural textile fibers derived from plants and animals are two basic types: cellulose and protein. Common examples of cellulose fibers from plants include cotton, flax (commonly called linen), and ramie; examples of protein

fibers are wool (from sheep), cashmere (from goats), and silk (from silk worms). Natural fibers have been used for human protection and comfort for thousands of years. Most manufactured and synthetic fibers were developed during the 20th century. Manufactured fibers, including rayon and acetate, are made from cellulosic sources, such as wood pulp and cotton linters, that contain naturally occurring polymers; rayon and acetate are two examples. Bamboo has recently become a popular source of wood pulp for making rayon. Many synthetic fibers, including nylon, polyester, and acrylic, have polymers made from petrochemicals, so their characteristics differ greatly from those of natural and manufactured cellulosic fibers.

Whether the fibers come from the farm, the forest, or the laboratory, once they are harvested or generated, many are sold in commodity markets, where prices change on a daily basis, depending on supply and demand. Other fibers might be purchased directly from the producer or manufacturer.

Level 2—Textiles, Textile Products, and Findings Manufacturing: Wholesale Materials Marketing Level 2 of the textile complex comprises all the activities related to textile manufacturing, including yarns, fabrics, fabric finishing, and the production of findings. Historically, in the United States, beginning in the mid-1800s as textile production became commercialized, each of the stages of textile production was completed by individual, family-owned businesses. Some companies specialized in yarns, others in weaving or knitting, and still others in fabric finishing. The products were bought and sold in each stage of textile development. Now, many firms are vertically integrated, so they make yarn; weave fabric; and finish fabric by dyeing or printing and applying wrinkle resistance, water resistance, and other finishes so that the fabrics are ready to be cut and sewn. In addition to being vertically integrated, some textile fabric mills are

now also horizontally integrated and perform both weaving and knitting. An example of horizontal and vertical integration within Level 2 of the textile complex would be the merging of smaller mills into a massive textile conglomerate, such as Milliken, one of the largest privately owned producers of textile products in the United States. A **conglomerate** is a business formed when firms serving multiple markets join together with common ownership.

In contrast, China is now a major producer of textiles. China was primarily an agrarian society until the 1930s, when steel mills and other industries began to develop. In the late 1940s, the communist government took ownership of industrial development, with the goal of making China a major industrial power. The textile plants began as integrated manufacturing systems; by the 1970s textile production was China's most important light industry. The textile mills were government owned for much of the 20th century but are now being privatized and developed, via foreign investment.

The industry defines **findings** as all the materials used in apparel products in addition to the face fabrics. Major categories of findings are as follows:

- thread, a special type of yarn that holds pieces of sewn products together for the useful life of the product
- closures, including zippers, snaps, hooks, and buttons
- support materials, including interlining, shoulder pads, adhesives, tapes, sleeve headers, and collar stays
- trims, including ribbon, lace, bindings, edging, and anything else that might be used to ornament or enhance garments
- labels, permanently attached information related to brand names, trademarks, fiber content, care information

Because fabric and findings decisions need to be made very early in the apparel design process, wholesale textile product

Figure 1.4 A designer examines fabrics at a wholesale textile market. She may first order samples that can be used for inspiration during the early stages of garment design. *(Courtesy of WWD)*

marketing must occur early in the apparel product development cycle. Traditionally, fabrics were designed, marketed to product designers and stylists, and produced on a calendar scheduled up to a year in advance of apparel manufacturing. The present trend is to move wholesale markets and textile manufacturers closer to apparel producers in whatever country is most appropriate. Fabrics are more readily available for the finished goods manufacturing process; this shortening and simplifying of the supply chain can cut weeks off the apparel production process, making it possible to respond more quickly to changes in fashion-related customer demand. One of the major international market fairs for textile products is Première Vision, held in Paris, France.

Level 3—Apparel Manufacturing: Wholesale Finished Goods Marketing

Apparel manufacturing encompasses processes involved with merchandising, design, product development, production, and often wholesale marketing. Apparel manufacturing includes three different, but often overlapping, categories of business structure: apparel manufacturers, apparel production vendors, and retail product developers. **Apparel manufacturers**, traditionally, were firms that engaged in the entire manufacturing process, including merchandising (line planning, design, and product development), production, and

wholesale marketing of apparel, using the yarns and fabrics produced in Level 1.

However, in today's global market, few firms engaged in the apparel manufacturing business own all the technology, equipment, and expertise to complete the process from beginning to end. Manufacturers that were formerly vertically integrated may now specialize only in product development and wholesale marketing. The production process itself—those processes actually required to cut materials and assemble and finish garments—is usually sourced from firms called apparel production vendors that, at this point in time, might be located anywhere in the world. Thus, the term *apparel manufacturer* has been replaced by simply **apparel firm** or **brand manager** because of the emphasis on marketing nationally and internationally known brands of merchandise.

Apparel production vendors, historically called **contractors**, are firms that take orders for apparel products from other firms and that either produce or arrange for the production of those specific garments. Firms that participate in activities related to apparel production may be referred to as secondary producers, manufacturers, or even "rag businesses," depending on the person being communicated with. **Apparel production** includes processes required to convert materials into finished garments: cutting, sewing, pressing, inspecting, packaging, and shipping. An apparel vendor can be located anywhere as long as there are transportation and power systems and a relatively low-cost labor supply.

There are two primary forms of production contractors: CMT and full package. **CMT (cut, make, trim)** apparel vendors commonly offer apparel assembly services. CMT vendors are paid to provide machines, labor, and thread to sew specified garments. The sourcing company provides product specifications and fabric. However, because many of the retailers engaged in private brand development depend on vendors for both product development and production expertise, **full-package vendors** are very much in demand. Full package requires that the vendor not only provide and fund production expertise, but also engage in product development and materials sourcing. Apparel vendors in Hong Kong have provided full-package services since the 1970s, and now many contractors in other countries are struggling to do the same. It is common for major apparel firms and brand managers to source finished goods in dozens of countries.

Level 3 also includes **retail product developers**. Retail product developers are individuals or teams who create designs and develop merchandise plans and specifications for retailers' private brands, which are ultimately sourced from CMT or full-package vendors. Retail product developers usually perform the merchandising and design functions of the product development process and therefore avoid the costs of buying finished goods from brand managers.

An example of a firm that has integrated many stages in production, from the manufacturing of fabric in Level 2 to the sale of garments at retail in Level 4, is the brand manager VF Corporation, the world's largest apparel firm. VF now produces major brands of everything from hosiery to jeans, although it has elected to spin off some of its textile production. VF also operates a chain of outlet stores that retails a significant portion of its business. VF is ranked 14 in the list of most profitable firms in Table 1.4.

Wholesale finished goods marketing connects Level 3, apparel manufacturing with Level 4, retailing, when firms are not vertically integrated. In Level 3, two to five times a year, firms engaged in apparel manufacturing plan, design, and develop their apparel product lines. Firms only engaged in apparel manufacturing have sales forces that sell their product lines to retailers either at wholesale markets,

at a retail buyer's office, through sourcing fairs, or on the Internet. An example of the traditional wholesale market method is the prêt-à-porter (ready-to-wear) market weeks in the major cities of Europe. During **market weeks**, formal presentations, such as fashion shows and personal presentations of styles to individual buyers by sales representatives, are made to encourage sales (Figures 1.5a and 1.5b). Most retail buyers view the options among dozens of product lines and return home to examine their merchandise plans and place orders to translate the line plans into styles, sizes, and colors of real merchandise. The product orders put the desired merchandise selections into production.

Figure 1.5a Apparel market runway fashion shows are major venues for promotion of designer goods. Professional models show off the latest styles for a fashion-hungry audience.
(Courtesy of WWD/ Giovanni Giannoni)

Figure 1.5b An apparel market showroom floor is segmented into booths for display of styles offered by each designer or manufacturer. Sales representatives are located at each booth so they can work with retail buyers.
(Courtesy of WWD/ Tyler Boye)

Because textiles and garments were most often sold at wholesale based on samples before they are mass-produced, market weeks were traditionally scheduled several months before the selling period in retail stores. However, with current technologies, the time between order placement and receipt of merchandise can now be weeks instead of months for some products, depending on a firm's supply chain strategies. For example, Tommy Hilfiger moved his traditional March market week for fall delivery of menswear to May, making the retail commitment for merchandise closer to point of sale at retail.

Major apparel market centers in the United States are located in New York, Los Angeles, Atlanta, Dallas, and Chicago. Major offshore apparel market centers include Milan, Paris, and London, in Europe, and Tokyo, Hong Kong, and Singapore, in Asia. One of the major market centers for knitwear is Florence, Italy. Today, global wholesale market activities are found on the calendar year-round, at various times of the year, depending on the categories of products, and in locations that include developing countries, such as India, China, and Turkey.

Level 4—Department, Mass, Specialty, Electronic, and Other Forms of Retailing

Retailing is sale of merchandise or services, or both, to ultimate consumers. The face of retail in the United States and elsewhere has changed significantly in the first decade of the 2000s, and the traditional definitions and recognized classifications of these businesses and their product lines have become blurred. In the United States and some other developed countries, traditional brick-and-mortar-store-type retailing has grown to such an extent that experts believe we are now "over-stored." The United States is confronted with more retail establishments than the consumer market can possibly support. Yet, new stores continue to open, while other retail businesses are closing their doors because of economic failure.

Traditional retailers are being severely challenged by the over-stored scenario as well as by the advent of many nonstore retail sectors, such as direct marketing, including catalog and television sales, and "e-tailing" on the Internet. In 2009, Internet retail sales were only about 5 percent of total retail sales, but the venue is also being used to test new products and product designs as well as to sell aged inventory. Today, many retailers use multiple formats and stores in multiple countries to tap into both store and nonstore clientele.

When the retail environment in one area of the world becomes saturated, retail firms look to other developed countries and to newly emerging economies as a solution to their need for growth. The National Retail Federation (NRF), the largest retail trade association in the United States, created a subsidiary, the International Retail Federation (IRF). The IRF, in association with *Stores* magazine, developed a new publication, which is available on the Internet, titled *Global Powers of Retailing*. It is updated annually, and it lists the 250 largest retailers in the world. Many of these are globalized retail conglomerates that consist of firms involved in unrelated markets but that are joined together because of common ownership.

Retailing has become truly globalized, but, as you can see in Figure 1.6, most global retailers are based in developed countries. The United States (US) (35 percent) dominates, followed by Japan (10 percent), Germany and the United Kingdom (UK) (8 percent), France (5 percent), and "Other European" countries (totaling 18 percent). The multitude of Asian countries only has only 6 percent of the global retailers based there. Canada (Other N. American) has 4 percent. In the following discussion, retailers that were ranked among the top 250 in 2009 are noted.

The major categories of retail stores are specialty stores, department stores, and mass merchandisers. **Specialty stores** focus on specific classes of merchandise to the exclusion of other products. For example, within the moderate-price-point range found in many malls around the world, we find Foot Locker (ranked 150th in *"Global Powers of Retailing* Top 250"), which has 3,641 stores, including those in 20 countries outside the United States, focusing on athletic shoes. An example of the higher-price-point store that

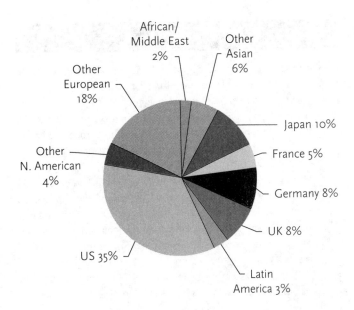

is commonly found in major U.S. cities, but not in other countries, is Nordstrom (ranked 92d) (*Global Powers of Retailing*, 2009).

A primary example of a retail conglomerate within the "specialty store" category is Limited Brands (ranked 87th), with more than 3,000 stores scattered across the United States, including Bath and Body Works, Victoria's Secret, White Barn Candle Company, Henri Bendel, and La Senza. Limited Brands has become successful by developing its own private brand programs, in which it merchandises, designs, and sources production of its own products. To comprehend the magnitude of some of these conglomerates, it is not unusual for a nationwide chain of specialty stores to contract production for up to 100,000 garments in one style.

Specialty store variations include the off-price retailers. Off-price retailers, such as T.J.Maxx (which is owned by TJX Companies, ranked 44th), focus their merchandise mix on distressed merchandise acquired from manufacturers and other retailers, including broken lots, end-of-season goods, and overruns. Distressed goods

Figure 1.6
Regions of the world in which global retailers are based. (*National Retail Federation,* Stores. January 2009. 2009 *Global powers of retailing.* Stores, p. G28. *www.stores.org.* Retrieved October 25, 2009.)

Since 1947, H&M, the Sweden-based vertical retail chain, has made its mark on the apparel industry, mixing the latest trends with fashion classics. Like some of its global competitors, H&M has cut a swath across the supply chain, successfully managing two thousand stores in 35 countries; more than 900 suppliers, half in Europe and half in Asia; and 21 production offices worldwide. Germany is its number one market, with 25 percent of sales.

H&M caters to women, men, teenagers, and children. In addition to streetwear, the majority of H&M stores offer underwear, accessories, and cosmetics. Behind H&M's clothes is a very savvy production environment, with a few middlemen buying large volumes cost consciously. H&M currently buys more than 400 million garments a year.

The firm does not own factories, but it plays an active role in quality assurance through its supplier base. The firm enforces a strict vendor code of conduct. For suppliers, compliance to its code includes "ensuring that products are manufactured under good working conditions; adhering to H&M's strict environmental policies; and delivering goods of high quality at the right price" (H&M, 2009). Sixty percent of the merchandise is made in Asia, the rest in Europe.

Logistically speaking, H&M maintains a tight rein on all aspects of the supply chain, acting as importer, wholesaler, and agent. H&M has 13 distribution centers in Europe and Asia as well as one in the United States. Karen Belva, H&M executive, notes, "It works smoothly—our production, sourcing, and buying," pointing out that the standard delivery time from design to store floor is approximately 12 weeks (Haisley, 2002).

Sources:

Haisley, T. (2002, February). How H&M cooks up success. *Bobbin*, 15–17.
H&M. (2009). H&M in brief. Retrieved from http://www.hm.com/us/abouthm/factsabouthm__facts.nhtml

Read Case 1.2 to see how H&M, of Sweden, grows in the global market.

Department stores provide a variety of product lines, such as apparel for men, women, and children; soft goods for the home; and home furnishings. Products are priced at or near the middle-to-upper-middle price point ranges. Since the mid-1990s, department stores, like the main street specialty stores, have also lost market share. They have been threatened by chains such as Kohl's, which successfully use price promotion and fashion appeal to offer branded merchandise at moderate and lower-moderate price points. U.S. department store groups are trying to maintain their current market share of retail apparel sales by expanding their private label programs to complement their offerings from brand managers and through expansion into non-brick-and-mortar-store activities, such as catalog sales and e-commerce. A primary means of growth for large department store groups has been the use of horizontal integration through swallowing up independent department stores in selected regions. They are also moving toward fewer, but larger, ownership groups, such as the recent merger of Federated (Macy's and Bloomingdale's) (ranked 35th in 2004) and May (Famous-Barr and Marshall Fields) (ranked 42nd in 2004). In 2007 Federated changed its corporate name to Macy's, and in 2007 it was ranked 31st (Figure 1.7a–d).

Two firms that straddle two categories—department stores and mass merchants—are (1) Sears (ranked 13th), which bought Lands' End and was absorbed by Kmart to become Sears Holding in 2005, and (2) JCPenney (ranked 41st), which has centralized its merchandising process. In 2009 Sears had stores in 5 countries; JCPenney had stores in 2 countries. Currently, although both are still formidable forces in the retail environment in terms of sheer volume, JCPenney seems to be more successful in refocusing its primary mission

are purchased for much less than regular wholesale prices, sometimes at a few cents a pound. Specialty stores also make up the majority of thousands of main street, single-unit retailers located around the world. Historically, these stores were the foundation of the community; however, since the 1980s, they have suffered from competition from malls, including chain store organizations (Kosters, Damhorst, & Kunz, 1996).

Figure 1.7a Old Navy is a specialty store chain that is a division of The Gap Stores, Inc., and that is ranked 50th among global retailers. Old Navy targets a younger customer base than does Gap or Banana Republic.

(Courtesy of WWD/Kyle Ericksen)

Figure 1.7b T.J.Maxx is a division of TJX Companies, Inc., a group of off-price retailers, ranked 44th among global retailers. Marshall's is also a division of TJX Companies.

(Courtesy of WWD)

Figure 1.7c Dillard's Inc. ranks among America's largest fashion apparel and home furnishings department stores, with annual revenues exceeding $7.2 billion. The company has more than 320 stores in 29 states, all operating under one name—Dillard's. It was ranked 110th among global retailers.

(Courtesy of WWD)

Figure 1.7d Target is a mass retailer based in Minneapolis, Minnesota. It is ranked 8th among global retailers, with 1,743 stores in 49 states and $64.4 billion in sales. Target is known for its fashion leadership in the mass apparel market. (*Courtesy of WWD*)

within the retail environment to secure its continuing place in the overall market.

Broad line, **mass retailers**, such as Walmart (ranked 1st), with stores in 15 countries, and Target (ranked 8th), dominate the current retail scene, with nearly 10,000 stores between them. These retailers sell in great volume at the lower-moderate and budget price points. They have established significant private label programs, such as the Mossimo and Liz Lange brands. At Target the sheer size of its individual stores and the volume of merchandise that flows through its sales floors daily were almost unheard of until the last two decades. At the same time, Walmart is intent on globalizing its retail empire. You may have noticed that Walmart no longer emphasizes its "Made in America" slogan.

During the first decade of the 21st century, the **nonstore retailer** category of the apparel business has expanded. Catalog sales have increased as consumers select their merchandise directly from printed catalog offerings and order by mail, phone, or Internet. Some business firms, such as Coldwater Creek, Lands' End, and L.L. Bean, have continued to expand into e-commerce activities. Nonstore retailing includes television shopping networks, such

as QVC and the Home Shopping Network, and the Internet, referred to by the business community as **e-commerce** or **e-tailing**. Television shopping depends heavily on impulse purchases and use of the telephone or internet connection to complete the purchase transaction. Product offerings for this venue change with great rapidity. Many consumers, however, use Internet sites for gathering product and pricing information and go to the actual stores to complete their sales transactions. For all forms of nonstore retailing, the issue of sizing and fit remains one of the most significant costs of doing business because of the high rate of consumer returns of ill-fitting garments.

Most forms of retailing have adopted practices now known as lean retailing, a term coined by the Harvard Center for Textile and Apparel Research in 1999 (Abernathy, Dunlop, Hammond, & Weil, 1999). **Lean retailing** is the effective management of inventory based on accurate and timely information. The fundamental goal is to maximize sales and gross margins while maintaining a minimum quantity of inventory in stock. Lean retailing practices have forced suppliers to hold inventory for retailers; replacement shipments are determined by electronically transmitted sales data.

Customer Demand

The purpose and driving force behind the entire apparel business is consumers, as represented by the "sea of customer demand" in Figure 1.3. In today's marketplace the needs and desires of the customer are what fuel the demand for product, keeping the production and distribution cycle moving. Intensive competition for attention drives marketing departments to generate pressure for consumption of products consumers did not even know they wanted or needed—and they respond.

Probably the biggest challenge in the textile and apparel business is forecasting what customers want to buy. Reliable consumer preference forecasts are essential for success at all levels of the textile complex. Major shifts in consumer demographics affect the acceptance of products offered in the marketplace. Recent changes in the cultural makeup of the overall population of the United States include significant growth of the Hispanic population, inclusion of larger and more diverse Asian populations, and a more visible Muslim population. The apparel preferences of these ethnic groups are influencing the styling and sizing of products being made available to all American consumers and increasing the focus on micromarketing by retailers.

One example of an ethnic group's influence on apparel styling in the United States is the opulent and colorful "Bollywood" style being credited to the very visible export movie industry that has sprung up in Mumbai, India (formerly Bombay). These movies are readily available in communities within the United States in which there is a significant Indian population, fueling interest in apparel with the strong colors and lavish embellishment techniques that are rooted in the Indian culture and reflected on the screen. In addition, domestic movies, such as the Academy Award–winning *Slum Dog Millionaire* help create interest in Indian attire in consumers who are not Indian or of Indian descent. Could the recent interest in use of beading be traced to this influence?

Other consumer demographics are creating changes in the marketplace as well. Increased educational levels and higher incomes are influencing the apparel choices and expenditures of these consumers. An increasingly aging demographic is causing a need for changes in product styling. Populations in most countries are living longer because of increases in income as well as more sophisticated medical care. Changes in

lifestyle, such as participation in fitness programs, bring changes not only in physique, but in products desired as well. Conversely, the epidemic of obesity within the United States results in a need for increases in product sizes and in the sheer volume of fabric required for production of individual garments.

The most significant change affecting apparel choices of consumers worldwide may be the greater availability of satellite television and the Internet. Consumers throughout the globe are able to tune into hundreds of channels of television, instantly seeing the dress styles of entertainment and news figures around the world. The days in which a fashion trend takes months or years to disseminate to large groups of consumers is over. A consumer in Jordan can watch an episode of *Desperate Housewives* today, look on the Internet to find a product he or she has seen on the program, and have that product delivered within days. (That consumer can also spend a day flying to Australia and turn on the TV to pick up where his or her favorite soaps left off.)

The results of all these changes are causing something of a dichotomy. On one hand, there are more ethnically diverse ideas of what is beautiful and appropriate or fashionable to wear, and these ideas are made available to more consumers more quickly than at any time in history. However, more cultures are seeing and being influenced by what they see on television from the United States and Europe; much of the business climate worldwide is embracing Western economic methods and being influenced by those conducting business. This increased visibility creates a homogenization of design ideas, with consumers from other cultures beginning to adapt their local choices in order to look and dress like the people they see from the United States and western Europe. A prime example of this homogenization over the last hundred years is the almost universal adoption of the tailored business suit. Another is the acceptance of jeans anytime and anywhere. This dichotomy of cultural differences versus universal sameness presents great challenges to the industry. One reality is—ultimate consumers still determine the winners.

Textile and apparel consumption and the ability of consumers to consume is the topic of Chapter 2. Customer demand is the reason there are supply chains.

Sustainable Supply Chains Supporting Global Sourcing

Beginning in the late 1950s, **buying offices** offered services that involved international business relationships, then mostly with firms based in Hong Kong, to supply U.S. and European apparel retail buyers with finished garments different from or at a lower cost than what was being offered by domestic apparel manufacturers. In the U.S. most of the buying offices for domestic retailers were located in New York, and some of them still are. The buying offices also assisted buyers with the development of merchandise plans and the selection of domestically produced merchandise. Buying offices grew in number and popularity until the late 1980s, when vertical and horizontal mergers concentrated merchandising divisions and merchandisers got involved in product development for private label lines. The race then began in earnest to find lowest-cost labor to make the garments somewhere in the world. This led to the development of the standardized merchandise identification systems essential for processing goods that are transported from one country to another. This is the topic of Chapter 3.

A new category of textile and apparel business developed that is now called **import and export trading**. Based on a contract, import and export trading companies will merchandise, design, develop, source, or distribute textile and apparel products, or a combination of these, for customers anywhere in the world. Part of import and export trading responsibility is to develop and manage supply chains to assure that the desired goods will be delivered in a timely manner, in appropriate quantity and quality, and using sustainable methods. A **supply chain** is a total sequence of business processes within a single or multiple firms and countries that enables demand for products or services to be satisfied. Supply chains for textiles and apparel, more often than not, are global in scope and may involve a few, dozens, or even hundreds of different companies and governments. **Sustainability** involves the corporate, government, and consumer responsibility to integrate economic, political, environmental, and cultural dimensions to promote cooperation and solidarity among people and generations (Birnbaum, 2010). This is the focus of Chapter 4.

The dominant firm involved with supply chains is Li & Fung, based in Hong Kong. The type and quantity of goods to source are commonly determined by a sourcing firm, often a retailer, based in one of the developed countries. Then Li & Fung, or one of many other firms offering similar services, determines where goods will be sourced and how they will arrive at the required destination on time, in the defined quantity and quality, and at a reasonable price.

Figure 1.8 shows a Li & Fung conceptual model of a global supply chain. Carefully examine the figure, noting all the different dimensions of a supply chain process, beginning with customer demand, followed by developing and acquiring goods from the global market and then delivering them to a retailer, who sells the goods to consumers, who immediately develop more, different needs. Import and export trading firms provide services essential to the entire textile and apparel manufacturing and distribution process.

If you turn Li & Fung's model (Figure 1.8) on end, with the consumer end up, you can visualize it in place of the oval in Figure 1.3 labeled "Supply Chain Supporting Global Sourcing"; you can see the complexities of today's supply chains in relation to the textile and apparel trade matrix. The supply chain components listed on the right side of the loop relate to the levels of the textile and apparel complex and the inputs required to plan, design, and make the products desired—elements that make up what we now call sourcing. **Sourcing** is determining the most cost-efficient vendors of services, materials, production, or finished goods, or a combination of these, at a specified quality and service level, for delivery within an identified time frame. This is the topic of Chapter 5.

Again considering Figures 1.3 and 1.8, the factors on the left side of the supply chain loop (that sort of hang out in the air in the combined model you are visualizing) are related to complexities involved in dealing with the global market structure and transport of materials, supplies, and finished goods. Supply chains not only provide procurement, but also navigate the snarl of worldwide transport and governmental interventions inherent in global trade. Transport of equipment, supplies, materials, finished goods, and people from one country to another requires dealing with all manner of import and export policies, laws, and regulations in each country involved.

Trade agreements among governments encourage, regulate, or restrict elements of trade among the respective countries. Governments or political agencies establish agreements unilaterally by a single country, bilaterally between countries, and multilaterally by groups of countries that are involved in trade relationships. Trade is encouraged with favorable terms and simplified processes. According to Hirsch, trade is regulated and restricted by erecting **trade barriers** that include the following:

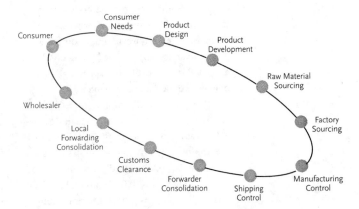

- **state trading**—the involvement of governments in the business environment
- **tariffs**—taxes on imports
- **quotas**—limits on the quantity of products allowed to enter the country
- foreign investment limits placed on in the local economy of participating countries (Buckley, 2003, p. xiii)

Governments establish regulations and trade barriers regarding the transfer of products from one country to another as well as verify their origin, ownership, quality, and safety. This is the focus of Chapter 6.

Trade barriers and regulations of all kinds of activities by governments result in attempts to get around them. Free trade, trade barriers, requirements for customs compliance, intellectual property law, and social responsibility are on-going sources of controversy and illegal activity in the global market. Illegal and unethical activity is rampant in the textile and apparel world. This is the topic of Chapter 7.

Supply chains for textiles and apparel, more often than not, are global in scope and may involve a few, dozens, or even hundreds of different companies and governments. The interaction of all of the components of the supply chain takes place in countries with different political systems and among firms with divergent priorities and methods of making

Figure 1.8 Li & Fung supply chain model.

(www.lifung.com— Li & Fung Limited)

decisions. **Politics** are the methods, or tactics, involved in managing an organization, business, state, or government—sometimes including crafty, unprincipled politics. Politics, as related to the textile and apparel global market, are the topic of Chapter 8.

Chapters 9 to 12 examine countries in four major parts of the world, which we have defined as Europe and the European Union, the Americas and the Caribbean Basin, Asia and Oceania, and the Middle East and Africa. We sincerely hope you find your global adventure challenging, insightful, and rewarding. Put these preliminary concepts in perspective by completing Learning Activity 1.4.

Learning Activity 1.4
NATURE OF FIRMS IN THE TEXTILE COMPLEX

1. Identify the several primary means that firms can use to grow.
2. In what ways have apparel manufacturers and retailers become similar?
3. What has caused firms in the textile complex to be called apparel firms or brand managers instead of manufacturers?
4. What evidence has been presented so far that would explain why one-third of the world's largest retailers are based in the United States?
5. Why has the demand for services related to import and export trading and sourcing companies exploded in the global market?
6. How does the concept of sustainability of supply chains complicate decision making?
7. Considering the Li & Fung model, draw an example of what a supply chain might look like when only domestic sourcing is used to acquire all the products and services necessary to develop and sell to consumers an apparel product line. Explain your thinking about the process.
8. Refer back to Table 1.4. Select three firms from the list, and look them up on the Internet. What country is the home base for each of the firms you selected? Have they acquired any additional companies since the merger listed in the table?

SUMMARY

A primary purpose of this chapter was to introduce perspectives central to the study of the textile and apparel trade from a global perspective. There are many valid ways to view and analyze the operations of global production and distribution. Perspectives include economic and business, political and governmental, and sociological and labor. These viewpoints commonly result in conflicts among options for resolution of issues. The conflicts are part of the context we wish to address.

The countries around the world can be viewed as newly developing, developing, or developed, based on the trade balance of each in relation to textiles and apparel and gross domestic product per capita. Gross domestic product per capita is gross domestic product of a country divided by the number of people in the population. Other related measures include literacy, poverty, infant mortality, and life expectancy. Newly developing and developing countries tend to focus on production and export of textiles and apparel to provide jobs to fuel industrial development. Developed countries have higher production costs, so they focus on product development and consumption of finished products and production of goods that are less labor-intensive and more technology intensive, such as synthetic yarns.

The textile complex incorporates firms around the world to accomplish textile manufacturing, apparel manufacturing, retailing, and consumption of textile products. Import and export trading and sourcing companies are a new type of firm that has responded to the demand for sourcing apparel in many countries around the world. Sustainable global supply chains involve many areas of expertise to navigate successfully and are a current priority in the textile and apparel industry.

REFERENCES

AAFA applauds House passage of legislation banning imports from Burma. (2003, July 15). Arlington, VA: American Apparel and Footwear Association.

AAFA hails Burma import ban renewal (2009, July 24). Arlington, VA: American Apparel and Footwear Association.

AAFA president and chief executive officer testifies before Senate subcommittee hearing on Burma. (2003, June 19). Arlington, VA: American Apparel and Footwear Association.

Abernathy, F. H., Dunlop, J. T., Hammond, J. H., & Weil, D. (1999). *A stitch in time: Lean retailing and the transformation of manufacturing—Lessons from the apparel and textile industries.* New York: Oxford University Press.

Birnbaum, D. (2010, March 9). Comment: Garment sector well-placed to sell sustainability. Retrieved from http://www.just-style.com

Buckley, P. J. (2003). *The changing global context of international business.* New York: Palgrave Macmillan.

Central Intelligence Agency (CIA). (2009). *The world factbook.* Retrieved November 2009 from https://www.cia.gov/library/publications/the-world-factbook/index.html

Chandra, P. (2006, April). *The textile and apparel industry in India.* Vastrapur, Ahmedabad, India: Indian Institute of Management.

Ellis, K. (2003, July 29). Bush bans Myanmar imports. *Women's Wear Daily,* 2, 6.

Ellwood, W. (2001). *The no-nonsense guide to globalization.* Oxford, England: New International.

Global powers of retailing top 25. (2009, January). *Stores,* G7–G24. Retrieved November 22, 2009, from http://www.stores.org/stores-magazine-january-2010/global-powers-retailing-top-250

Glock, R., & Kunz, G. I. (2005). *Apparel manufacturing: Sewn product analysis* (4th ed.). Upper Saddle River, NJ: Prentice Hall.

Haisley, T. (2002, February). How H&M cooks up success. *Bobbin,* 15–17. Retrieved from http://www.hm.com/us/abouthm/factsabouthm__facts.nhtml

H&M. (2009). H&M in brief. Retrieved from http://www.hm.com/us/abouthm/factsabouthm__facts.nhtml

In brief: Burma ban. (2003, July 16). *Women's Wear Daily,* 2.

Kosters, P., Damhorst, M. L., & Kunz, G. I. (1996). Organizational culture of small retail firms. *Journal of Small Business Strategy,* 7(3), 29–52.

Lodge, G. (1995). *Managing globalization in the age of interdependence.* San Diego, CA: Pfeiffer.

2009: The *Apparel* top 50. (2009, July). *Apparel.* Retrieved from http://www.apparelmag.com

Uchitelle, L. (2004, September 18). U.S. and trade partners maintain unhealthy long-term relationship. *New York Times.* Retrieved from http://www.nytimes.com/2004/09/18/business/18trade.html

Underhill, G. (1998). *Industrial crisis and the open economy: Politics, global trade and the textile industry in the advanced economies.* New York: St. Martin's Press.

World Trade Organization (WTO). International trade statistics 2009: Top 15 countries in textiles and apparel trade in 2008. Retrieved November 14, 2009, from http://www.wto.org/english/res_e/statis_e/its2009

2 Consumers, Consumption, and Well-Being

● ●● ●●● ●●● ●●●●● ● ●●● ●●●●● ●●●●●●●●●●●●●●●● ●●● ●●● ●●● ●●●● ●●●● ●●● ●●● ●●●● ●●

LEVELS OF TEXTILE and apparel consumption vary greatly among people in least developed, newly developing, and developing countries, owing in large part to the levels of available income. These countries loom large as potential markets for textile and apparel firms based in developed countries. Unlike with many other manufactured products, consumer use of some form of textiles and apparel is universal. Clothing styles and the materials with which they are made may differ from place to place, but forms of these products are present everywhere and regarded as essential components of the consumption process. The unique nature of textiles and apparel can be attributed to many things, from their seemingly incompatible uses as both protection and adornment to the unpredictability of demand for and acceptance of new styles—the fashion factor. Demand from the world's consumers is the driver of the textile and apparel supply chain.

This chapter examines concepts associated with human well-being and explores common methods of measuring it. One unique thing about this chapter is that many of the citations are more than 20 years old because the authors of the works cited are the originators or early interpreters of the concepts and theories discussed.

Objectives

- Explore foundations of apparel choices.

- Examine the concepts of levels and standards of consumption and living and their relationships to apparel consumption patterns.

- Examine theories of income–consumption relationships.

- Evaluate the meaning of consumption expenditure data representing developed and developing countries.

- Explore the clothing consumption process.

acquisition the act of making garments available for personal use; increases inventory

basic goods tend to be standardized and utilitarian, with infrequent demand for changes in styling

buying power the amount of goods that can be purchased with a given amount of money at a given place and time

complement a product purchased and used along with another; for example, shoes and socks

consumer obsolescence discard of products owing to lack of interest in them rather than lack of their usability

Consumer Price Index (CPI) a measure of the impact of inflation on consumer buying power in the United States

consumption commodities (goods and services), their uses and services consumed

consumption expenditure money used to support the level of consumption during a specified period

current dollars buying power at a specified time, numbers not adjusted to account for inflation

discard the act of giving up possession and ownership of a garment; reduces inventory

discretionary income the amount of money available after all current obligations are covered

disposable income take-home pay; the amount available to an individual or family to support the level of consumption, savings, and investment at a particular time

economic luxury *see* superior good

economic necessity *see* normal good

fashion a style of dress accepted by the majority of a group at a particular time

fashion goods individualized, differentiated by style and color

income elasticity *see* income elasticity of demand

income elasticity of demand determined by relative changes in income and expenditures over a defined time period; percentage change in expenditure ÷ percentage change in income

inferior good a product consumed out of necessity but not preferred according to the standard of consumption; the amount spent decreases when income increases and increases when income decreases

inflation an increase of general price level, causing a decline in purchasing power

inventory the entire stock of garments owned by an individual or group that could be used as clothing at a given time

level of consumption that which is actually experienced, enjoyed, or suffered by an individual or group during a given time period

level of living that which is actually experienced, enjoyed, or suffered by an individual or group during a given period of time

living consumption and other dimensions of life, including levels of remuneration, comfort, job security, and working conditions as well as related factors

minimum needs the essentials of life, defined by levels and standards of consumption and living; vary according to place and time

nonverbal communication uses appearance to communicate perspective, identity, age, sexual orientation, educational level, occupation, economic status, or marital status

normal good spending pattern reflects an economic necessity: the amount spent increases as income increases and decreases when income decreases but at a slower rate than the income increase or decrease

poverty a lack of enough income or resources, or both, to satisfy minimum needs

price elasticity of clothing expenditure inelastic, positive, but less than one; a normal good

price elasticity of demand determined by relative changes in prices and expenditures; percentage change in price ÷ percentage change in income

primary source the most frequent means of clothing acquisition; purchased new ready-to-wear in developed countries, purchased secondhand or handed down in least developed countries

progressive tax has an increase in tax rate as income rises

purchased secondhand garments that have been used by someone else; inferior good in the economic perspective of clothing consumption

purchasing power the amount of goods or services that can be acquired with a specified amount of currency at a particular time

real expenditure outlay adjusted to reflect buying power, considering rate of inflation

real income earnings adjusted to reflect buying power, considering rate of inflation

regressive tax requires lower-income people to pay higher rates than higher-income people

secondary source a means of acquiring clothing other than the primary source; gifts, purchased used, handed down, rental, home sewing, custom-made, and others

standard of consumption or living a level that is urgently desired and strived for, substantial success yielding special gratification, and substantial failure yielding bitter frustration (Davis, 1945).

substitute a product purchased and used in place of another; for example, pants rather than skirts

superior good a preferred product, according to standards of consumption and living; the amount spent increases as income increases and decreases when income decreases but at a faster rate than the income increases or decreases; economic luxury

temporary possession a means of momentary clothing acquisition from sources such as rental, borrowing, and perhaps clothing provided by an employer

total income gross income or personal income

well-being a good or satisfactory condition of existence

THE NATURE OF APPAREL CHOICES

Every human culture uses textiles and apparel for aesthetics, protection, and **nonverbal communication**. But the mystery component of clothing selection is fashion. One definition of **fashion** is the style of dress accepted by the majority of a group at a given time. Fashion is a powerful force in that it influences the types of garments people choose to wear. Textile and apparel products tend to be different from many other consumer products, owing to their perishable desirability. This temporal quality of a garment's acceptance means that many of those who can afford to acquire new garments will continue to seek new and different items, whether it is physically necessary or not. The definition of the need for clothing extends well beyond adequate garments for physical comfort and protection. Fashion makes the textile and apparel business much less predictable than trade in most other consumer products. The factors of unpredictability and ongoing change make trade in textiles and apparel a vital but sometimes fickle field.

Fashion and Basic Goods

Apparel professionals often think of apparel products in two categories: basics and fashion. These two broad classifications of apparel differ in product characteristics, product presentation, inventory control, appeal to customer, and characteristics of firms that specialize in their manufacturing and retailing. Professionals in the field must understand the underlying nature of consumer product choices to make viable business decisions in the marketplace (Table 2.1).

Basic goods tend to be standardized and utilitarian and have infrequent demand for changes in styling. The same styles, sizes, and colors can be sold for a year or longer, with consistent levels of demand. Inventories in basic goods are steady, predictable, and refillable. Automated replenishment based on point-of-sale (POS) data can be used to keep products in stock. **Fashion goods** are individualized, differentiated by style and color. Styles of one brand are distinct from styles of another brand. Fashion goods have demand peaks followed by obsolescence.

Table 2.1 CHARACTERISTICS OF BASIC AND FASHION MERCHANDISE

	Basic	Fashion
Product characteristics	Standard	Individualized (differentiated)
	Utilitarian	Romanced with atmosphere
	Infrequent changes in styling	Frequent changes in styling
	More common in menswear	More common in women's wear
Product presentation	Individual items	Coordinated groups
	Simple presentation	Project a fashion image
Inventory control	Steady, predictable demand	Demand peaks followed by obsolescence
	Predictable selection	Ever-changing stocks
	Automated replenishment	Selection limited by current fashion
	Similar inventory consistently	Zero-to-zero inventory in stock
Selection process	Easy price comparisons	Value difficult to assess
	Comparative shopping	Impulse shopping
Appeal to customer	Logical	Emotional
	Tangible product	Intangible fashion image
	Intrinsic value	Extrinsic; externally created value
	Meeting a need	Creating or directing a need
	Replacement	Adding variety to a wardrobe
	Price is a major factor	Appearance is a major selection factor
Characteristics of the firm	Large	Smaller
	Partially automated	Labor intensive

Merchandisers plan for zero-to-zero inventories in fashion categories. Merchandise is bought, stocked, sold, and cleared from the retail sales floor during each selling period—extended times for basic goods and short periods for fashion goods—and replaced with new styles. It is usually difficult or impossible to restock fashion goods in the middle of a selling period, especially when they come from distant suppliers. The contrasts in the merchandising of basic and fashion goods require not only staying ahead of the fashion cycle, but also different timing and management of the textile and apparel supply chains (Figure 2.1a–c).

The appeal of basic goods tends to be in meeting a need or in replacing a product already owned. Price is often a major selection factor. The appeal of fashion goods is more emotional, as the customer acquires not only the garment, but also its associated fashion image. Appearance is the major selection factor with fashion goods.

The characteristics of firms that produce and distribute basic and fashion products also differ. Basic goods can be manufactured using mass production techniques for large quantities of goods. Mass retailers and department stores can retail basic goods by replenishing similar merchandise on a

Figure 2.1a Successful display of basic goods at retail involves making it easy for customers to identify the styles available and keeping all sizes and colors in stock. "Stock-outs" mean lost sales and reduced profits. (*Courtesy of WWD*)

Figure 2.1b Successful display of fashion goods at retail also involves establishing an environment to enhance the appeal. (*Courtesy of WWD/Lisa Movius*)

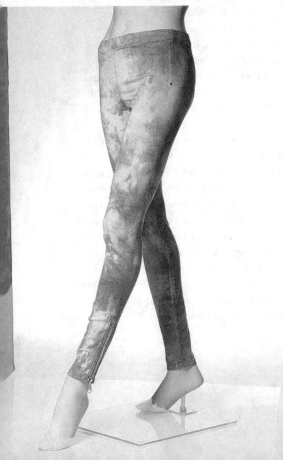

Figure 2.1c Leggings were an important statement fashion product in early 2010. (*Courtesy of WWD/ Thomas Iannaccone*)

During the early 1990s, in the poverty-stricken nation of Malawi, Africa, where 65 percent of the people were living on less than US$1 a day, the fledgling apparel industry was struggling because of scarce private investment and lack of machinery and trained personnel. With little domestic production of apparel, and few skilled home sewers, mainly two types of clothing were available: custom-made garments for the very rich and well-used, secondhand clothing for the very poor (Semu-Banda, 2007).

After the elimination of some trade barriers, via the Africa Growth and Opportunity Act (AGOA), Malawi saw an influx of secondhand, recycled clothing, mostly originating from charities in the United States and Canada. These nonprofit groups sold their excess inventory to for-profit companies, and, after baling the garments, exported the bales to Africa and other undeveloped countries. Most U.S. and Canadian consumers were not aware of the practice of nonprofit charities' selling excess inventory to for-profit companies, but the used-clothing trade became an important source of income and employment in the importing countries (Johns, 2001).

In Malawi, recycled garments continue to be sold in the villages' open, "bend-over markets" (so named because the merchandise is presented on the ground). The garments may be presented four different ways: unopened bales, unsorted piles, sorted piles, or clothing refurbished by laundering and ironing. Profits of a hundred dollars or more can result from buying a bale and reselling the contents in small quantities; profits also increase with refurbished garments (Johns, 2001).

It is common to be able to buy a secondhand blouse for US$1 that would cost US$15 new. In a country with a very low annual per capita income, the used-clothing trade has become an important source of income and employment. Large numbers of people are engaged in the selling, processing, and buying of the recycled garments (Semu-Banda, 2007).

Sources:

Johns, M. J. (2001, November). *The used-clothing market in Malawi.* Paper presented at the annual meeting of the International Textiles and Apparel Association, Kansas City, MO.

Semu-Banda, P. (2007, June 14). Trade-Malawi: Clothing and textiles become unstitched. Inter Press Service News Agency. Retrieved from http://ipsnews.net/news.asp?idnews=38177

daily or weekly basis over long periods of time. However, fashion goods have to be produced by manufacturers or contractors who can produce relatively small quantities of styles, with frequent shutdown and start-up of production lines to introduce new styles. Fashion goods are more likely to be offered by specialty stores for short time periods in smaller quantities, as fashion customers want to see new merchandise every time they enter the store.

With fashion goods, in most economies, **consumer obsolescence** is a factor, because any individual with sufficient **purchasing power** may discard products from lack of interest in them rather than out of need of a replacement. In poorer economies, including those of developing countries, the fashion cycle slows, and items of dress tend to be worn until they have no further useful value to the consumer despite possible awareness of a preference for new fashions.

In developed countries, because of relatively high income levels, both secondhand and distressed new ready-to-wear are exported by charitable organizations and retailers and may become important sources of new clothing to those in less developed nations. However, because of the pervasiveness of communication technology, particularly television, fashions available in developed countries are known to consumers throughout the world. Current fashions not only influence consumers' purchase preferences when they are economically able to acquire new clothes but also guide choices in secondhand clothing markets. The desire for fashion appears to be universal.

Case 2.1 describes the sale of used clothing in one of the less developed African countries. Follow your reading of this case with Learning Activity 2.1.

Levels and Standards of Consumption and Living

Survival of global capitalism as a model of economic exchange depends on the ability of participants to cope with some very real problems. One of these problems is the skewed distribution of economic development among participating nations. Another problem is the deterioration of the environment. A third is the decline of nonrenewable natural resources. A variation of this issue emerges when host governments lack the power to impose rules on the owners of foreign-owned business enterprises. These are fundamental issues in the sustainability of supply chains.

To some, the greatest shortcoming of the Western capitalist model of global business is the ownership advantage provided to some participants to the detriment of others. Critics of capitalism report that the gap between rich and poor is widening across the world. Unfortunately, the measure of how rich and how poor is tricky. To do it well, it is essential to develop a method of measuring consumption so that useful comparisons can be made across countries and across time. Each method introduces different types of biases into the conclusions drawn from the data. This text focuses on basic measures defined by levels and standards of consumption, including consumption expenditure, gross national product, gross domestic product, and purchasing power parity.

The well-being, together with the potential exploitation of citizens living in the countries involved with the textile and apparel trade, is a primary global issue. Levels and standards of consumption and living are commonly used measures of **well-being**. The types and amounts of products that people consume are used as indicators. Although many researchers regard it as too simplistic, consumption expenditure may be the most available measure of rate of consumption. To be effective, however, things like inflation must be accounted for, because inflation reduces **buying power** and distorts comparisons of different places and points in time. To compare across countries, monetary exchange rates also have to be considered.

To understand consumption patterns, the first challenge is developing and understanding a system of language to define concepts and clarify relationships. Joseph Stancliffe Davis (1945) laid out a system of language for describing well-being that is still used today. The four terms he used were *consumption*, *living*, *level*, and *standard*.

The term **consumption** means commodities (goods and services), their uses and services consumed. Consumption includes goods purchased in the market as well as in-kind gifts and those provided through home production. **Living** includes consumption and other dimensions of life, such as levels of remuneration, comfort, job security, and safe working conditions. Living also includes freedom of movement and association, security of personal and financial well-being, and environmental and political atmosphere (Davis, 1945).

In this context, the term **level** implies that which is actually experienced, enjoyed, or suffered by an individual or group. The term **standard** is what "is urgently desired and striven for, special gratification attending substantial success and substantial failure yielding bitter frustration" (Davis, 1945, pp. 3–4). Level is what a person or family actually has, whereas standard is what is desired. Typically, the standard is higher than the level. It is common to want more things or to want things that are different from what we actually have.

Teaming the terms *level* and *standard* with *consumption* and *living* provides additional distinctions and a better understanding of the concepts. A **level of consumption** includes
- the overall amount of food, fuel, and other nondurable goods consumed
- the use of houses, automobiles, clothing, and other durable and semidurable goods
- the services of people used by an individual or group in a given period of time (Davis, 1945)

A decline in the level of consumption means a reduction in the quantity or quality of goods and services consumed. A rise in the level of consumption means an increase in volume or improvement in its quality. The term *standard of living* is sometimes misapplied to the level of consumption as defined above.

A **standard of living** is the level of consumption urgently desired and strived for, as mentioned above, plus the following additional components:
- working conditions
- freedom of movement and association
- safety and security
- political and environmental atmosphere

Standards of living are based on multiple aspects of our lives; the levels of consumption and other aspects of living that we strive for are founded on a variety of sources and experiences. For some people, religious faith or spirituality is first priority. For others, social acceptance is of primary importance—"what would the neighbors think?" For still others, providing evidence of conspicuous consumption (having more, better, newer designer clothes, homes, furniture, pools, TV sets, automobiles, and so on) is the greatest goal.

It seems to be inherent in the human intellect to continually want to improve our state of being, but what we think will make us better off varies with gender, age, culture, weather, income, education, religion, occupation, and life experience. Thus, our individual standard of living, in this sense, is more complex and abstract than our level of consumption and more difficult to measure in its entirety. For this reason, simpler measures are commonly used to determine well-being, such as monetary income.

It is common for standard of living to exceed **level of living** and standard of consumption to exceed level of consumption. Even at high levels of consumption, "more" is commonly perceived as "better." Higher-quality, more fashionable products—products that are regarded as more aesthetically pleasing but more expensive—are commonly included in the level of living to which individuals or families

In 2008, the parliament of Turkey voted to amend the constitution to lift a longstanding ban on wearing Islamic head scarves at Turkey's universities, despite opposition from the secular establishment (Hacaoglu, 2008). The head scarf ban was originally seen as a strong secular statement of separation of church and state.

Secularism assures the neutrality of the state toward religious beliefs. Turkey originally adopted this form of secularism in order to control the place of religion in society and to make extreme changes that would distance it from its Ottoman past. At the same time, Islamic head scarves are required wear for practicing Muslim women when appearing in public; 99.8 percent of Turkey's citizens follow Islam (Hashmi, 2009).

Four months after being lifted, Turkey's top constitutional court reimposed the ban on university campuses, reaffirming the separation of church and state. The government news agency stressed that the style of head scarf legalized in the reimposed ban was not necessarily Islamic. Justice Department officials promised to interpret the measure as allowing only head scarves that tied under the chin, a style seen as traditionally Turkish rather than Islamic. The ban does not allow women to wear more rigidly Islamic attire in public offices, for example, veils that cover all of the hair, neck, and face and cloaks that cover the body (O'Malley, 2008).

In Turkey, women continue to cry out against the head scarf ban. Over the years in which the ban has been in effect, thousands of women have avoided participating in higher education in Turkey. Some who chose to attend classes felt incredibly guilty with their hair exposed; others wore wigs to protect their modesty. Women report that they want the freedom of covering their heads to fulfill their religious duty without giving up their ability to gain an education or have jobs of their choice (Hashmi, 2009).

The decision to reimpose the ban deepened the political crisis brought about by the head scarf issue. The prime minister believes that allowing women to wear the scarf is a question of religious freedom; his own daughters studied in the United States so that they could be free to wear the head scarf (O'Malley, 2008).

Sources:

Hacaoglu, S. (2008, February 10). Turkey lifts long ban on head scarves at colleges. *The Des Moines Register*, p. 5A.

Hashmi, (2009, December 22). Take off my what? Headscarves, hats and history. Today's Zaman. Retrieved from http://www.todayszaman.com/tz-web/news-196211-109-take-off-my-what-headscarves-hats-and-history-2-by-hera-hashmi.html

O'Malley, B. (2008, June 8). Turkey: Headscarf ban re-imposed. *University World News*, issue 0031. Retrieved from http://www.universityworldnews.com/article.php?story=20080606083302196

aspire but are not yet included in their level of consumption because of budget constraints. When income increases, some components of the standard of living may be added to the level of consumption, increasing perceived well-being, but at the same time, *new aspirations are commonly added to the standard of living*. Thus, there is constant pressure to increase levels of consumption and living to achieve an ever-increasing standard of living. The standard and level of living provide a frame work to guide the standard and level of consumption.

Read Case 2.2, and then do Learning Activity 2.2, to explore how import of used clothing and Turkey's head scarf ban affects levels and standards of consumption and living.

Learning Activity 2.2

LEVELS AND STANDARDS OF
CONSUMPTION AND LIVING

1. What are the fundamental differences between level of consumption and standard of consumption?
2. What are the fundamental differences between level of living and standard of living?
3. What is the relationship between a standard of living and a level of consumption?
4. Consider the perspective of Davis's concepts of levels and standards of consumption and living in relation to Case 2.1. Write two statements describing the effect on consumers in Malawi of importing secondhand clothing, one for standards of consumption and one for level of consumption.
5. What might have been the impact on standards of living and level of living?
6. What aspects of the Turkey head scarf issue relate to women's standard of living?
7. What aspects of the Turkey head scarf issue relate to women's level of living?
8. What aspects of the Turkey head scarf issue relate to women's standard of consumption?
9. What aspects of the Turkey head scarf issue relate to women's level of consumption?

Definitions of Income

Based on the assumption that people are better off when income is higher, evaluation of the well-being of citizens of cities, states, and countries is often gauged by levels of income and consumption expenditures. In developed countries, levels of consumption at a given time are primarily dependent on levels of income, because most citizens are employed and purchase rather than produce their own goods and services. However, there are many different definitions of income, and they are used in different ways. For a defined time period, the relationships of four of these income definitions to expenditures are as follows:

total income (gross income) –
income tax and other taxes =

disposable income (take-home pay) –
savings and investment =

consumption expenditures
(consumption level) –
necessary consumption expenditures =

discretionary income =

amount of income that is uncommitted
(Schwenk, 1985)

Total income is sometimes called gross income or personal income. It is the total amount earned in a given period of time. Many people never see or have their total income in hand, because employers deduct income taxes and other taxes and contributions to benefits before paychecks are written. Thus, the amount most people receive on a weekly or monthly basis is disposable income:

disposable income = total income –
income tax and other taxes and contributions

Disposable income is commonly known as take-home pay, the amount available to an individual or family to support the level of consumption, savings, and investments:

consumption expenditure =
disposable income – savings and investment

Consumption expenditure is the money used to support the level of consumption during a specified period. When disposable income exceeds levels of savings, investments, and previously committed and other necessary consumption expenditures, discretionary income is available. If consumption expenditure exceeds disposable income, discretionary income is negative, resulting in obligations against future income:

discretionary income =
disposable income – consumption expenditure

Discretionary income is the amount available about which new decisions can be made when some income remains after all current obligations have been covered with disposable income. Discretionary income can be saved toward future expenditure, invested, or spent as desired. Discretionary income may be used to move the family or household closer to its desired standard of living. This may involve increases in savings or investments, opportunities for impulse purchases, or a vacation, depending on the current standards of consumption and living. Discretionary income is often associated with fashionable clothing purchases, because fashionable clothing may be regarded as desirable according to standards but not necessary according to levels of consumption. Careful applications of these definitions can assist in analyzing past consumption levels and forecasting future consumption expenditures.

When reading and evaluating descriptions of well-being, it is essential to pay particular attention to the measures of income and consumption that are being used. If one study uses disposable income, another uses discretionary income, and a third uses consumption expenditure, their conclusions cannot be directly compared even though each may be valid in its own right. All may be interesting and useful, but remembering the definitions of these terms is essential for interpreting the findings.

Definitions of Poverty

Poverty is the lack of enough income or resources, or both, to satisfy a person's minimum needs. The **poverty line** is the point at which income or resources are inadequate to maintain life and health at a subsistence level. However, minimum needs for subsistence are not the same everywhere. **Minimum needs,** as defined by standards and levels of consumption and living, vary according to place and time. For example, in developed countries, the Internet is used regularly by the majority of people, both personally and professionally. Gaining access to the Internet is likely to be part of the standard of living for people in developed countries who do not have access. In least developed countries, the Internet is unknown to the majority of people and inaccessible to most of those who do know about it. Internet is unlikely to be a part of the standard of living in these least developed nations, because basic necessities are often unavailable, including clean water, adequate food, and medical attention (United Nations Press Release, 2002).

Read Case 2.3 to learn more about definitions of poverty. Follow your reading with Learning Activity 2.3.

The World Bank reported that recent estimates showed there were more poor people around the world than previously thought but also revealed big successes in the fight to overcome extreme poverty: "The new estimates, which reflect improvements in internationally comparable price data, offer a much more accurate picture of the cost of living in developing countries and set a new poverty line of US$1.25 a day. They are based on the results of the 2005 International Comparison Program (ICP), released earlier in 2009" (World Bank News Release, 2009).

The revised estimates of poverty found that "1.4 billion people (one in four) in the developing world were living below US$1.25 in 2005, down from 1.9 billion (one in two) in 1981." The new estimates assess world poverty by the consumption levels of the poorest countries. The new line ($1.25 a day) is the 2005 average national poverty line for the poorest 10 to 20 countries. This is the first major effort to update poverty data using 2005 measures of purchasing power parity (World Bank News Release, 2009).

"'The new estimates are a major advance in poverty measurement because they are based on far better price data for assuming that poverty lines are comparable across countries,' said Martin Ravallion, Director of the Development Research group at the World Bank. 'Data from household surveys have also improved in terms of country coverage, data access, and timeliness'" (World Bank News Release, 2009).

The data show that the number of poor fell by 500 million since 1981, from 52 percent of the developing world's population, in 1981, to 26 percent, in 2005. However, there are marked regional differences in the progress against poverty. For example, poverty in East Asia fell from nearly 80 percent of the population in 1981, to 18 percent, in 2005. The poverty rate in Sub-Saharan Africa remained at 50 percent in 2005, no lower than in 1981 (World Bank News Release, 2009).

For middle-income countries, the poverty line of $2 a day is appropriate with 2.6 billion people living on less than $2 a day in 2005, very similar to 1981. Considering $2 a day for the same time period, poverty fell in Latin America, the Middle East, and North Africa, but not enough to bring down the total number of poor, as the populations had increased (World Bank News Release, 2009).

Source:

New data show 1.4 billion live on less than US$1.25 a day, but progress against poverty remains strong. (2009, December 6). World Bank News Release 2009/065/DEC. Retrieved from http://go.worldbank.org/T0TEVOV4E0

Learning Activity 2.3
Definitions of Poverty

1. The level of consumption is used as a measure of poverty level. Why is that more appropriate than using the standard of living?

2. What is the role of price data in determining poverty level?

3. How does purchasing power parity contribute to accuracy of the level of poverty assessment when multiple countries are involved?

4. Which definition of income does "U.S. $1.25" most closely relate to? Why?

BASIC THEORIES OF INCOME–CONSUMPTION RELATIONSHIPS

From an economic perspective, consumable goods are sometimes classified as superior, normal, or inferior. These terms do not relate to product quality but rather to the standards of living to which consumers aspire.

When products are classified as **superior goods**, the amount spent increases as income increases and decreases when income decreases but at a *faster* rate than the income increases or decreases. These goods are sometimes called economic luxuries. They are part of standards of consumption or living to which people aspire but may not be part of the level of consumption they experience.

When products are classified as **normal goods**, the amount spent increases as income increases and decreases when income decreases but at a *slower* rate than the income increases or decreases. These goods are sometimes called economic necessities. They are a part of the level of consumption and will continue to be regularly consumed, but relatively small increases in consumption will satisfy needs and wants defined by standards of consumption.

Table 2.2 CLASSIFICATION OF GOODS BY INCOME ELASTICITY OF DEMAND

Class	Relationships	Elasticity
Superior goods (economic luxury)	Expenditure increases as income increases and decreases as income decreases but at a *faster* rate than income	Greater than 1
Normal goods (economic necessity)	Expenditure increases as income increases and decreases as income decreases but at a *slower* rate than income	Between 0 and 1
Inferior goods (inadequate income)	Expenditure decreases as income increases and increases as income decreases	Between 0 and 1

When products are classified as **inferior goods**, the amount spent decreases when income increases and increases when income decreases. These goods are being consumed out of necessity; they are not goods that people prefer, according to their standard of consumption. As soon as increases in income allow, more satisfactory goods are consumed.

Purchased secondhand clothing has been found to be an inferior good in economic terms—a measure not related to the quality of the product. In a 1971 study of low-income families in the United States, income elasticity for purchased secondhand clothing was negative. Within the low-income group, lower-income families spent higher proportions of consumption expenditure on secondhand clothing than higher income families. The clothing standards of these lower-income families clearly included new clothing, but they bought secondhand clothing because of economic constraints (Winakor, MacDonald, Kunz, & Saladino, 1971). With the popularity of garage sales, thrift stores, and resale shops, these data may have changed, particularly with regard to children's clothing, which may be less of an inferior good than in 1971. There are no data available, however, to confirm this supposition.

Refer back to Case 2.1. The demand for secondhand clothing in Malawi can be compared with the **purchased secondhand** clothing in the United States. In Malawi it appears that the lowest-quality second-hand clothing is also an inferior good. As

the case indicates, many consumers have very little disposable income and therefore choose "inferior" secondhand because of the incredibly low price. If their economic condition improves, they have the opportunity to move closer to their standards of consumption by moving up to better sec-ondhand and or new garments.

Income and Price Elasticity of Demand

The economic classifications of superior, normal, and inferior goods are based on **income elasticity**, technically known as **income elasticity of demand**. It is determined by relative changes in income and expenditures over a defined time period.

income elasticity of demand =
percentage change in expenditures ÷
percentage change in income

An income elasticity of 1 means elasticity is unitary; that is, both are changing at the same rate and in the same direction. Income and expenditure are changing at the same rate, for example, an increase of 15 percent in income associated with an increase of 15 percent in expenditure for a particular good. Percentage variation in expenditure is the same as percentage variation in income. When elasticity is greater than 1 for a particular product, the relationship is described as elastic. When elasticity is less than 1, the relationship is described as inelastic (Table 2.2).

Superior and normal goods have a positive income elasticity of demand. Inferior goods have a negative income elasticity of demand. The income elasticity of superior goods is greater than 1, income elasticity of normal goods is between 0 and 1.0, and income elasticity of inferior goods is a negative number.

From an income–consumption relationship perspective, clothing (purchased new ready-to-wear clothing, in particular) is described as a moderate luxury. Numerous research studies have shown an income elasticity of demand for clothing of about 1.2. This means the rate of increase in expenditure exceeds the rate of increase in income, suggesting that more or higher-priced clothing tends to be a priority, according to the individual or family's standards of consumption. There is perceived need to upgrade the clothing inventory, and the need is satisfied by increasing expenditure when more income is available. Thus, when forecasting apparel demand for future selling periods, apparel professionals focus on trends in employment and business growth. Customers with income increases will spend more money on apparel. We can think of the formulas as follows:

income elasticity =
percentage change in total expenditure ÷
percentage change in income = 1.20

price elasticity =
percentage change in clothing expenditure ÷
percentage change in price = 0.70

Income elasticity relates to how changes in expenditure impact the consumer's economic condition. Price elasticity of demand relates to how the consumer's income elasticity impacts the profitability of the business supplying the products consumers buy. **Price elasticity of demand** can be examined in a manner similar to income elasticity. Price elasticity is of particular interest when a nation's economy is slowing down and, to a merchant, when merchandise is not selling as fast as planned. The question becomes how much increase in sales will result from price decreases and what will happen to total revenue. In reality an increase in income or a decrease in price can have a similar effect on overall consumer well-being, either can result in increase in consumption as well as in overall well-being.

Multiple studies of U.S. clothing consumption have found that **price elasticity of clothing expenditure** is inelastic—positive but less than 1 (Bryant & Wang, 1990; Cheng, 2000; Houthakker & Taylor, 1970; Mokhtari, 1992; Norum, 1990). The price elasticity for clothing expenditures in these studies ranges from 0.5 to 0.8. The price elasticity of clothing demand of 0.7 suggests that the price reduction increased clothing expenditure but not at as high a rate as the prices were reduced. In general, then, when income or price changes, clothing expenditures will also change in the same direction but proportionally not as much as the income or price changes. This, in economic terms, is what is known as a normal good.

Yet, understanding clothing expenditure alone does not provide adequate information about well-being. Examining trends in consumption expenditures over time by types of goods provides insight to business managers so that they can develop merchandise plans and to politicians so that they can develop national and international policy.

Read Case 2.4 to learn about the eager consumption of luxury goods by China's "one-child" generation. Learning Activity 2.4 will help you further explore income–consumption relationships.

1. Explain the meaning of this statement: a product is a superior good when it is included in an individual's or family's standard of living.

2. Explain the meaning of this statement: a product is an inferior good when it is not included in an individual's or family's standard of living.

3. Explain the meaning of this statement to a consumer: the income elasticity of clothing means that clothing is a normal good.

4. Explain the meaning of this statement to a retailer: price elasticity of clothing is inelastic, thus less than one.

5. Considering Case 2.4, would you say that the parents and grandparents of China's "one-child" generation have different standards of living for their children than for themselves? Explain.

6. Are the luxury goods being consumed by the Chinese youth also superior goods, as defined here? Explain.

7. Given that there are already reports of a marked decline in savings by Chinese citizens, are the children of the Chinese youth likely to be able to sustain the current level of living of their parents? Why or why not?

Case 2.4 LUXURY GOODS DESIRED BY CHINA'S ONE-CHILD GENERATION

"The X factor in China's burgeoning luxury consumption is the country's one-child generation—a group of people who tend to be highly individualistic and perceive luxury goods as a way to set themselves apart" (Seckler, 2009).

According to Patti Pao, the author of a "China Luxury Panel" report, the one-child-per-family population policy, in place for 30 years, has created a value system among these millions of only children, who are "more self-indulgent and self-interested" than their predecessors (Seckler, 2009).

Michael Silverstein, a senior partner at The Boston Consulting Group, observed that the mothers and fathers of these young adults were "prodigious savers," but their children receive funds that propel luxury spending. For most families there are four grandparents and one child, and so a lot of attention and money are lavished on that child (Seckler, 2009). Approximately 75 percent of the luxury goods sold in China are purchased by people under 40.

According to the Hong Kong Trade Development Council, approximately "60 percent of luxury spending stems from existing family wealth, with the rest paid for with earned income." Purchases of authentic foreign luxury brands are made in major cities, such as Beijing and Shanghai: approximately "40 percent in Mainland China, 48 percent in Hong Kong, and the balance are made elsewhere," but the trend is spreading to second- and third-tier cities in China (Seckler, 2009).

"With housing and food available in China at far lower costs than is common in developed nations, annual household income of about $6,000, or 40,920 yuan, allows for savings and discretionary spending that could include luxury goods. . . . Such luxuries encompass $400 Chanel sunglasses as well as $200 Adidas and Nike running shoes, also seen as premium products in the emerging economy" (Seckler, 2009). Young consumers are very brand conscious and buy highly visible things, such as watches bearing large logos, big-screen TVs, high-end bikes, and leather couches (Seckler, 2009).

Thirty eight million Chinese consumers between the ages of 20 and 40 provide a considerable merchandising target for luxury product manufacturers and retailers, including pioneers in China—Louis Vuitton, Hermès, Gucci, Chanel, Prada, Cartier, and Tiffany & Co." (Seckler, 2009).

Source:

Seckler, V. (2009, November 25). China's one-child generation clamors for luxury goods. *Women's Wear Daily.* Retrieved from http://www.wwd.com/business-news/chinas-one-child-generation-clamors-for-luxury-goods-2379885//?full=true

THE MEANING OF CONSUMPTION EXPENDITURE DATA

In general, when income increases, consumption expenditures increase. From the perspective of determining overall well-being or forecasting retail sales, one enlightening aspect is the relative rate of increase for different types of goods. The best known of early theorists of income–consumption relationships is Ernst Engel, who in 1857 proposed the famous law of food consumption: the poorer a family is, the greater the proportion of total expenditure must it use to procure food (Monroe, 1974). When income is lower, total expenditure is lower, but a larger proportion of income is required to have enough food.

Figure 2.2a Chinese shoppers in this store reflect the commonalities of the retail experience throughout the world. (*Jiang ning – Imaginechina/ AP Images*)

For example, in newly developing countries it is not unusual for families to spend 60 to 80 percent of income on food. In the same environment, when income is higher, a smaller proportion is required to buy the same amount of food; there is a small amount of income available for other goods and services.

Expenditure Patterns in Rural China

It is well documented that overall well-being in China is much better in urban areas (as exemplified by Case 2.4) than in rural areas. Well-being in rural areas still includes high rates of poverty and sometimes extreme poverty. According to Lu & Peng (2000), a study of **consumption expenditures** of families in rural China found that in 1978 food expenditures were about 68 percent of total consumption expenditures. In China this represented a starvation level of poverty. But in 1978, China began economic reform in rural areas where farm households became independent production and accounting units. The changes were enthusiastically received by the rural population of nearly 800 million (Figures 2.2a and 2.2b).

Table 2.3 includes total consumption expenditures as well as the proportional changes in expenditure for eight product classes, from 1980 to 2004. Note that for food, clothing, and household operation, the percentages of expenditures became smaller almost every year. It is important to recognize that a percentage decrease can actually represent a monetary increase in expenditure when income is increasing. In fact, all categories of expenditures in yuan increased every year in Table 2.3.

Table 2.3 Consumption Expenditures in Yuan, and Percentage of Total Expenditures, for Types of Items for Chinese Rural Consumer Units (Selected Years: 1980–2004)

	Year					
	1980	1985	1990	1995	1998	2004
Average Annual Expenditures (in Yuan)	162.2	317.4	584.6	1,310.4	1,598.3	NA
Food (Percentage)	61.8	57.8	58.8	58.6	49.1	47.2
Clothing (Percentage)	12.3	9.7	7.8	6.9	5.8	5.5
Housing (Percentage)	13.9	18.2	17.3	13.9	15.5	14.8
Household Operation (Percentage)	9.4	5.1	5.3	5.2	4.5	4.1
Health Care (Percentage)	—	—	3.3	3.2	5.2	6.0
Transportation, Communication (Percentage)	—	—	1.4	2.6	5.6	8.8
Education, Recreation (Percentage)	2.6	3.9	5.4	7.8	11.2	11.3
Other (Percentage)	0.0	5.2	0.7	1.8	3.1	2.2

Sources: Based on The Central Intelligence Agency (CIA). (2009). *The world factbook.*
Retrieved October 2009 from https://www.cia.gov/library/publications/the-world-factbook/index.html
Lu, J., & Peng, A. (2000). Evolution of rural consumption pattern in China. *Consumer Interests Annual, 46,* 222–225.

Table 2.4 Total Consumption Expenditures, and Expenditures for Types of Items, in Yuan for Chinese Rural Consumer Units (Selected Years: 1980–2004)

	Year					
	1980	1985	1990	1995	1998	2004
Average Annual Expenditures (in Yuan)	162.2	317.4	584.6	1,310.4	1,598.3	NA
Food	100.2	183.4	343.8	768.6	849.6	NA
Clothing	20.0	30.9	45.4	89.8	98.1	NA
Housing	22.5	57.9	101.4	182.1	239.6	NA
Household Operation	15.3	16.3	30.9	68.5	85.4	NA
Health Care	—	—	19.0	42.5	NA	NA
Transportation, Communication	—	—	8.4	33.8	NA	NA
Education, Recreation	4.3	12.5	31.8	102.3	159.4	NA
Other	0.0	16.5	31.8	99.5	158.2	NA

Sources: Based on The Central Intelligence Agency (CIA). (2009). *The world factbook.*
Retrieved October 2009 from https://www.cia.gov/library/publications/the-world-factbook/index.html
Lu, J., & Peng, A. (2000). Evolution of rural consumption pattern in China. *Consumer Interests Annual, 46,* 222–225.

Figure 2.2b Chinese customers at an H&M store in Beijing. (*Courtesy of WWD/ Lou Linwei*)

Compare Table 2.3 with Table 2.4. It covers similar years and includes total consumption expenditures that were available for selected years as well as consumption expenditures for each category in yuan for rural Chinese. According to Table 2.4, from 1980 to 1998, total expenditures increased almost 10 times (885 percent). A reminder of the method for calculating percentage change from one period to the next; the basic formula is

percentage change =
difference ÷ original × 100

percentage change =
1998 total expenditures –
1980 total expenditures ÷
1980 total expenditures × 100

885% = 1,593.3 yuan –
162.2 yuan ÷ 162.2 yuan × 100

Expenditures for food (in yuan) increased 8.5 times (748 percent), a fact concealed by looking at the percentage of total expenditures, because the proportion of total expenditure decreased each year, while expenditures were increasing. Clothing increased 4.9 times (398 percent); household operation, 5.3 times (458 percent). While housing percentages were up and down, the increases in actual expenditures increased steadily up to 11 times (965 percent). In 1998, education and recreation expenditures were 37.5 times greater than in 1980. A combined food and clothing expenditure of almost 55 percent of total expenditures has moved rural farmers above the poverty level in China, to "adequate food and clothing" (Lu & Peng, 2000), according to Chinese standards. The percent allocations provide insight into changing priorities, according to the standards of consumption and living, as income increased. Many other Chinese standards and customs are radically different from American expectations.

Critically analyze Tables 2.3 and 2.4, relative to rural Chinese consumption expenditures in percentages of total expenditure and in yuan for individual categories of goods and services. Then read Case 2.5 to learn about cultural differences between Chinese and American workers. Finally, do Learning Activity 2.5 to enhance your learning.

Learning Activity 2.5

EXPENDITURE PATTERNS IN CHINA

1. According to Tables 2.3 and 2.4, which categories of expenditure from 1980 to 2004 would be described as normal goods? Describe why in terms of levels and standards of consumption and living.

2. Which categories of expenditure from 1980 to 2004 would be described as superior goods? Describe in terms of levels and standards of consumption and living.

3. Which categories of expenditure from 1980 to 2004 would be described as inferior goods from a consumption theory perspective? Why?

4. What information does the percentage of expenditures provide that is difficult to discern from expenditures in yuan?

5. Does the increase in clothing expenditure mean the rural Chinese family will have five times as many clothes in 1998 as in 1980? Why or why not?

6. Why might there have been no expenditures for health care and transportation at very low levels of total expenditures?

7. Is it safe to assume that expenditure data are an accurate reflection of income data? Why or why not?

8. How might the cultural practices discussed in Case 2.5 be reflected in rural Chinese consumers' standards of consumption and standards of living?

9. Considering that an income of 6 thousand dollars (about 40 thousand yuan) provides enough money for savings and discretionary spending, including some luxury goods (see Case 2.4), how poor were the rural Chinese families by comparison?

Case 2.5 U.S. MANAGERS CHALLENGED BY CHINESE CULTURE

"Many U.S. managers are learning a hard lesson when they are on assignment in China: the practices they used in America to be successful may very likely bring failure in China. . . .

. . . Chinese culture is so different from what Americans have experienced in life and in the workplace. The nuances often can trip up even the most talented manager. . . .

. . . Chinese workers have a deeply paternalistic culture, which means that their private life is connected to their work life. . . . They expect their colleagues and managers to be part of their lives even after business hours. So if an employee has a family wedding, the manager should expect an invitation—and also should be prepared to make a nice speech about the worker at the wedding" (Bruzzese, 2008).

The culture's indirect communication style often confounds American managers. A priority is saving face, or protecting self-image. It is unusual for Chinese workers to volunteer information. Thus, if feedback is desired, managers have to ask for information (Bruzzese, 2008).

Some other cultural differences:

- asking for help is avoided, because it indicates weakness
- teamwork is not considered natural; orders from the managers are consistent with the paternalistic culture
- gift giving is a normal part of doing business and not considered to be bribery
- loyalty is more important than performance; a job is not lost as long as the employee is "loyal"
- hoarding is common practice, particularly in conditions of poverty; sharing with managers or other workers may inhibit one's own success (Bruzzese, 2008).

These cultural practices are deeply embedded and clearly extend well beyond the workplace. American managers must adjust their behavior patterns to gain what they regard as desirable outcomes (Bruzzese, 2008).

Source:

Bruzzese, A. (2008, July 21). U.S. managers find a world of difference in Chinese culture. *The Des Moines Register*, p. 2D.

Expenditure Patterns in the United States

Food as a proportion of consumption expenditure is sometimes used as a rule of thumb in defining the level of poverty in the United States. Engel's Law—the theory that the proportion of income spent on food decreases as income increases— is applied in analysis of U.S. expenditure patterns. When food expenditure is one third or less of total consumption expenditure, a person's ability to consume may be regarded as adequate for general well-being. When food expenditure is greater than one third of total expenditure, the person is regarded as living in poverty. Clearly, according to U.S. standards, and despite great increases in food expenditure, the rural Chinese were still living in poverty in 1998.

Tables 2.5 and 2.6 show consumption expenditures in the United States for similar categories and years as the Chinese consumption expenditures reflected in Tables

Table 2.5 AVERAGE ANNUAL CONSUMPTION EXPENDITURES, AND PERCENTAGE OF AVERAGE ANNUAL EXPENDITURES FOR CATEGORIES OF PRODUCTS, FOR U.S. CONSUMER UNITS (SELECTED YEARS: 1980–2006)

	Year					
	1980	1985	1990	1995	1998	2006
Average Annual Expenditures (in Dollars)	$ 7,741	$ 11,373	$ 15,237	$ 18,658	$ 21,226	$ 48,398
Food, Tobacco (Percentage)	21.4%	18.4%	17.7%	16.2%	15.5%	12.6%
Clothing, Jewelry (Percentage)	7.5%	7.0%	6.8%	6.4%	6.3%	3.9%
Housing (Percentage)	14.5%	15.0%	15.3%	14.9%	14.7%	33.8%
Household Operation (Percentage)	13.3%	12.7%	11.3%	11.2%	11.0%	10.6%
Education, Recreation (Percentage)	8.5%	8.9%	9.6%	10.4%	10.8%	4.9%
Medical, Transportation, Other (Percentage)	34.9%	38.1%	39.3%	41.0%	41.8%	34.3%

Source: Based on data selected from 2008 National Income and Product Accounts Tables, Bureau of Economic Analysis, U.S. Department of Commerce.

Table 2.6 AVERAGE ANNUAL CONSUMPTION EXPENDITURES, AND CONSUMPTION EXPENDITURES FOR CATEGORIES OF PRODUCTS, FOR U.S. CONSUMER UNITS, IN DOLLARS (SELECTED YEARS: 1980–2006)

	Year					
	1980	1985	1990	1995	1998	2006
Average Annual Expenditures (in Dollars)	$ 7,741	$ 11,373	$ 15,237	$ 18,658	$ 21,226	$ 48,398
Food, Tobacco (in Dollars)	1,655	2,090	2,712	3,013	3,287	6,111
Clothing, Jewelry (in Dollars)	581	790	1,047	1,191	1,331	1,874
Housing (in Dollars)	1,120	1,706	2,343	2,781	3,116	16,366
Household Operation (in Dollars)	1,027	1,443	1,735	2,084	2,330	5,129
Education, Recreation (in Dollars)	660	1,012	1,475	1,938	2,281	2,376
Medical, Transportation, Other (in Dollars)	2,699	4,335	6,018	7,649	8,881	11,274

Source: Based on data selected from 2008 National Income and Product Accounts Tables, Bureau of Economic Analysis, U.S. Department of Commerce.

2.3 and 2.4. Compare the percentage of food expenditure in the United States (Table 2.5) with the percentage of food expenditure for rural China (Table 2.3). These numbers suggest dramatic differences in levels of potential well-being. In the United States, with less than 20 percent of total expenditures committed to food, on average, greater total consumption expenditure is available for other goods and services. One interesting thing to note is the similarity of percentages between rural Chinese and U.S spending on clothing.

The data in these tables are in **current dollars**, meaning that the numbers are not adjusted to account for inflation. Inflation reduces buying power. If **inflation** is 5 percent annually, this means that next year each dollar is worth five cents less or, assuming the same prices, that you will have to spend five cents more each year for every dollar's worth of expenditure to acquire the same amount of goods and services as last year. Inflation in the United States ranged from about 3 percent to 9 percent annually over the years reflected in the tables. Some developing countries experienced 20 percent inflation annually over part of the same time period. Data adjusted for inflation are sometimes called real numbers—**real income, real expenditure** reflecting buying power of the currency. Use of real income provides a much more realistic view of the amount of goods and services that could have been acquired.

In the United States the **Consumer Price Index (CPI)** is used to measure the impact of inflation on consumer buying power. CPI is based on the Consumer Expenditure Survey program, which began in 1979 and was adjusted in 1984 using 1984 = 100 as a foundation for the CPI. The CPI is now about 220, meaning that prices have more than doubled for consumer goods in the United States since 1984. The monthly research to update the CPI provides a continuous flow of data on the buying habits of U.S. consumers. It has two components: (1) an interview panel survey, in which the expenditures of consumer units are obtained in five interviews, conducted every 3 months and (2) a diary, or record-keeping survey, completed by participating households for two consecutive 1-week periods. Each component of the survey queries an independent sample of consumer units representative of the U.S. population. Ten thousand diaries are provided by five thousand consumers each year, and five thousand other consumers participate in panels each quarter. Data are collected in 88 urban and 16 rural areas of the country. Results are published monthly (Bureau of Labor Statistics, 2010, Consumer Price Index frequently asked questions).

The CPI demonstrates that inflation has varied a lot since the 1970s, although the general trend has been toward lower rates of inflation annually:

- 1970s—7.0 percent annually
- 1980s—5.5 percent annually
- 1990s—3.0 percent annually
- 2000s—2.8 percent annually

Since the mid-1990s, medical care and fuel were responsible for a significant portion of price increases. Textile home furnishings increased in price about 8 percent, and apparel decreased in price by 10 percent.

As a consumer, it is unlikely that you are aware that, overall, apparel prices have decreased in recent years, but apparel may be the best bargain in consumer goods right now. Why have apparel prices decreased in the United States? As mentioned previously, the U.S. retail condition is often described as being "overstored" and "overmalled." The availability of apparel at retail has increased at a faster rate than overall retail sales of apparel. Therefore, there are a lot of competitive price reductions. Another major contributor to reduction of retail prices of apparel is the increased level of apparel

Figure 2.3a The Macy's flagship store, in New York City, is a favorite spot for spending discretionary income. *(Courtesy of WWD/John Aquino)*

Figure 2.3b U.S. shoppers looking for good deals to stretch discretionary income. *(Courtesy of WWD/Kyle Ericksen)*

imported from developing countries. The price competition at retail has forced sourcers and vendors of apparel to seek lower-cost goods. Because apparel is a labor-intensive product, a lower-cost labor supply reduces production costs and allows retailers to use lower retail prices and still make the necessary gross margins to achieve profitability and stay in business. However, this business practice has also resulted in many overinventoried retailers and lots of markdowns on excess merchandise.

U.S. consumers have financially benefited from the competition among retailers and the explosion of imports of textiles and apparel. During the first decade of the 21st century, apparel expenditures averaged a modest 3 percent increase a year. In 2002, however, apparel expenditures actually declined for the first time in more than 50 years. But did consumption actually decline? Not necessarily, when the reduction in apparel prices indicated by the CPI is considered (Figures 2.3 and 2.4).

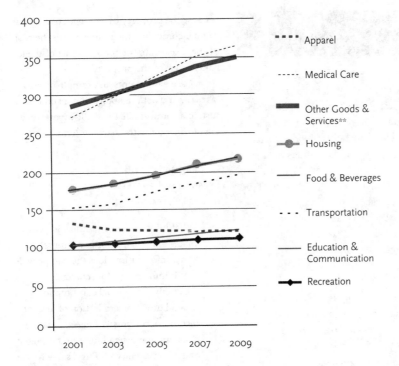

Figure 2.4 Line graph of the relative changes in prices for different categories of goods when prices are adjusted by the Consumer Price Index (CPI), 2001–2008. (*Courtesy Fairchild Books*)

Legend:
- Apparel
- Medical Care
- Other Goods & Services**
- Housing
- Food & Beverages
- Transportation
- Education & Communication
- Recreation

Note that the CPI was set at a base of 100 for each category of goods and services in 1982–1984. Changes in other years were then recorded as a rate of increase or decrease relative to the 100 used for the base. By 2001, the price of medical care went from 100 to 273, nearly triple in about 20 years. By comparison, prices of apparel went from 129 to 119. Apparel is the only category in which prices went down between 2001 and 2009. The other two bargains were education and communication and recreation, which had slight increases. Housing and food/beverages increased at about the same rate as the all-items index, which is the average of all the indexes together. Given that the CPI actually declined for clothing, it was possible, from 2001 to 2009, for U.S. consumers to spend less money per year and to buy more apparel than they did the year before. However, at the end of the decade, they needed almost three times as much money to pay for medical care.

Other Factors Affecting Consumption Expenditure Patterns

Taxes are another factor that can have a profound effect on consumption expenditures. Most of us face taxes in various forms every day: income taxes, sales taxes, excise taxes, real estate taxes, automobile license taxes, city service taxes. Setting and applying tax rates can have a profound effect on how much consumers have available to spend on the goods and services that determine their level of living.

Taxes are often described as being progressive or regressive. **Progressive taxes** have an increase in tax rate as income rises; higher-income consumers pay higher rates than lower-income consumers. The U.S. income tax is an example of a progressive tax. With **regressive taxes,** lower-income people pay higher rates than higher-income people. For example, a sales tax is regressive, because a 6 percent sales tax takes a higher

Des Moines (AP)—A new study finds that low-income Iowans pay a bigger share of their incomes in state and local taxes than do wealthy residents. A study by Iowa Policy Project, a liberal Iowa City–based think tank, said the bottom 60 percent of Iowa taxpayers pay roughly 10 percent of their income in state and local taxes. . . . Those in the top 1 percent, making more than $320 thousand a year, pay 6.3 percent.

Christine Ralston, a research analyst for the group, pointed to a 10 percent cut in income taxes approved in 1998. Since then, Iowa's state sales and cigarette taxes have been increased.

"The state sales tax has doubled in the last 25 years while we made big cuts in the [state] income tax," said Ralstan. "This is not a good trade-off if we want a tax system that better reflects a household's ability to pay."

The group said it was basing its analysis on data from the Washington-based Institute on Taxation and Economic Policy.

For low-income families making less than $16,000 a year, 7.3 percent of the household income goes for sales and excise taxes. Those taxes consume 2 percent of [income for] those with household incomes above $127 thousand.

Source:

Study finds low-income Iowans pay higher share in state taxes. (2008, November 11). *The Des Moines Register*, p. A5.

because the property owner, who usually has more income than the renter, passes the cost of the taxes on to the renter as part of the fee paid for use of the property

Case 2.6 presents an example of how taxes can impact the ability of consumers to sustain a comfortable life. Follow your reading of this case with Learning Activity 2.6.

Learning Activity 2.6
EXPENDITURE PATTERNS
IN THE UNITED STATES

1. What information does the CPI provide that is informative for consumers?
2. What information does the CPI provide that is informative for retailers?
3. Assuming that annual consumption expenditures are a reflection of level of income, according to Table 2.5, are the consumption expenditures in the United States consistent with Engel's Law?
4. According to Table 2.6, would you say the U.S. level of consumption is increasing, decreasing, or staying the same? Explain.
5. When you answered the previous question, did you consider the CPI? Why or why not?
6. Considering Case 2.6, sales tax rates are the same for all consumers, regardless of income level, so how can sales tax have a regressive effect on low-income consumers?

CLOTHING CONSUMPTION PROCESS

The major parts of the clothing consumption process are acquisition, inventory, use, renovation, and discard. **Acquisition** is the act of making garments available for personal use; it provides possession or ownership, depending on the source of clothing. Acquisition increases inventory. Acquisition may or may not involve monetary expenditure (Winakor, 1969).

proportion of a low-income consumer's total income than a high-income person's total income. Low-income individuals and families commonly spend all or even more than all of their current income, whereas for high-income people, only half or less is spent on current consumption, with the rest going into savings or investments. That is why, in some states, sales taxes are not applied to food and sometimes not to clothing as well. For policymakers in these states, food is regarded as a necessity and should not be subject to a regressive tax. This omission lowers the total impact of the sales tax on a low-income consumer's budget. Other regressive taxes include property taxes on rental units

The majority of garments acquired by individuals in developed countries come from one **primary source**, purchased new ready-to-wear. **Secondary sources** of clothing include gifts, purchased used, handed down, home sewing, and others (Britton, 1969). Items acquired for **temporary possession** come from sources such as rental, borrowing, and perhaps clothing provided by an employer. Such items are available for use by the individual, are possessed by the individual, but are not owned by the individual. The intent is that these items will be returned to the owner when the individual no longer uses them (Winakor, 1969).

The majority of garments acquired by individuals in developing countries are likely to come from what are regarded as secondary sources in developed countries. Because of extreme differences in levels of clothing expenditure, purchased used, handed down, and home sewing are likely to be important sources for clothing. Individual ownership of garments may be less defined with garments drawn from a common inventory possessed by the household.

Inventory is the entire stock of garment owned by an individual or group that could be used as clothing at a given time. Items that are temporarily in the possession of another person, such as borrowed or loaned garments, are considered part of the inventory of the owner, not the borrower. Inventory may have two parts, active inventory and inactive inventory. Active inventory may be defined as garments used within a 1-year period (Winakor, 1969). Consumers in developed countries may have large quantities of inactive inventory, because these consumers have the ability to acquire more clothing than they can use at a particular time. Consumers in developing countries may have only a small amount of active inventory.

Discard is the act of giving up possession and ownership of a garment; there is

no longer intent for the item to be used as clothing by that individual or group. Discard reduces inventory. Some garments are destroyed or used as something other than clothing, such as rags. Garments may be cut into parts for a quilt; jeans may be converted into a purse. When items are discarded by handing down or selling, discard becomes a form of acquisition for someone else. Sale of garments at a consignment shop or garage sale can result in monetary gain for the owner. Contributions of clothing to a charitable organization can result in income tax deductions (Winakor, 1969).

The owner's intent for the use of a garment determines the use-life of a garment. For example, a garment that is acquired with the intended use of everyday wear, whether at work or at home, might have a use-life cycle as follows:

1. acquisition
2. frequent interchange of active storage, use, renovation
3. less frequent interchange of active storage, use, renovation
4. continuous inactive storage
5. discard

The movement of a garment through the use–life cycle from steps 2 to 4 may be caused by acquisition of **substitutes** for the garment or lack of suitable **complements** for the garment, or products that can be used along with it (e.g., scarves). For example, acquisition of a shirt may result in the less frequent use of a shirt already owned (substitute) and the more frequent use of a skirt (complement). The more complements a garment has, the slower it may move through the cycle. The acquisition of a complement may move an item back from step 4 into step 2, where it will go through the process a second time.

In contrast, garments that are acquired for special occasions, such as wedding dresses, may have a short or infrequent use-life and a long storage life, as follows:

1. acquisition
2. active storage, one or a few uses, renovation
3. continuous inactive storage

The position of garments in the use-life cycle and the type of use-lives garments have seem to be determined by the following:

- clothing standards of the owner
- intent of the owner toward the garments in inventory
- length of time garments have been owned
- condition of the garments in inventory relative to wear, fashion, and repair
- number of substitutes and complements that are available in inventory (Kunz, 1987)

Analysis of textiles and clothing expenditures and consumption processes provides insight into consumer well-being and opportunities to make comparisons of well-being among populations in different countries.

Expand your understanding of the clothing consumption process with Learning Activity 2.7.

Learning Activity 2.7
CLOTHING CONSUMPTION PROCESS

1. In what aspects of the clothing consumption process would you expect U.S. and rural Chinese consumers to differ the most?
2. In what ways would you expect the clothing consumption process to be the same?
3. Think through the clothing use-life cycle described above. How does the use-life cycle of your clothes compare with use-life as described? How would your parents' use-life cycles compare?
4. How would you expect the rural Chinese clothing consumption process to differ from that of the urban "one-child" generation?

SUMMARY
....

Textiles and apparel are unique consumer goods because of their contributions to both aesthetics and protection in the lives of human beings. Fashion has a powerful influence on clothing consumption. Fashion's influence is commonly described in the form of a fashion cycle. Fashion influences what is selected in the market, when, and by whom. However, not all of apparel is fashion driven. Some apparel products are basics.

Standards of living commonly include desire for increased quality and quantities of textile and apparel products. From an economic perspective, these products are what are sometimes called normal goods, and demand for them tends to be inelastic. That is, when incomes increase, expenditures for soft goods increase; when incomes decrease, expenditures decrease, but the increases and decreases are proportionally less than the change in income. Income elasticity describes the relationship between change in income and the related change in expenditure. Price elasticity describes the relationship between change in price and the related change in demand. Income elasticity is more relevant to the well-being of the consumer; price elasticity is more relevant to the well-being of the retailer.

Proportion of total consumption expenditures on food is sometimes used as a measure of overall well-being of a population. For example, in 2004 in rural China, the proportion spent on food was 47 percent, down from 62 percent in 1980, indicating considerable improvement in well-being. During a similar time period in the United States, the proportion for food went from 21 percent to 13 percent.

In the United States, clothing expenditures are currently close to 4 percent of total consumption expenditures. Clothing expenditures as a percentage of total expenditures has declined about 3 percent over the past 10 years. According to the CPI, clothing prices have declined about 10 percent. Because of the decline in prices, U.S. citizens have been able to increase clothing expenditures even though the proportion of total expenditures has declined.

The clothing consumption process involves different types of use-life cycles, depending on the perceived purpose of a garment.

REFERENCES

Britton, V. (1969, September). Gifts and handed down clothing important in family wardrobes. *Family Economics Review,* 3–5.

Bruzzese, A. (2008, July 21). U.S. managers find a world of difference in Chinese culture. *The Des Moines Register,* p. 2D.

Bryant, W. K., & Wang, Y. (1990). American consumption patterns and the price of time: A time-series analysis. *Journal of Consumer Affairs, 24,* 280–306.

Bureau of Labor Statistics. Consumer Price Index frequently asked questions (FAQs). Retrieved January 5, 2010, from http://www.bls.gov/cpi/cpifaq.htm

Central Intelligence Agency (CIA). (2009). *The world factbook.* Retrieved November 2009, from https://www.cia.gov/library/publications/the-world-factbook/index.html

Cheng, S. (2000). U.S. clothing expenditures: A closer look. *Consumer Interest Annual, 46.* Retrieved September 2003 from http://www.consumerinterests.org/public/articles/clothing.pdf

Davis, J. S. (1945, March). Standards and content of living. *American Economic Review, 35*(1), 1–15.

Hacaoglu, S. (2008, February 10). Turkey lifts long ban on head scarves at colleges. *The Des Moines Register,* p. 5A.

Hashmi, H. (2009, December 22). Take off my what? Headscarves, hats and history. Today's Zaman. Retrieved January 12, 2010, from http://www.todayszaman.com/tz-web/news-196211-109-take-off-my-what-headscarves-hats-and-history-2-by-hera-hashmi.html

Houthakker, H. S., & Taylor, L.D. (1970). *Consumer demand in the United States: Analysis and projections* (2d ed.). Cambridge, MA: Harvard University Press.

Johns, M. J. (2001, November). *The used-clothing market in Malawi.* Paper presented at the annual meeting of the International Textiles and Clothing Association, Kansas City, MO.

Kunz, G. I. (1987). *Clothing consumption process: Use-life of garments.* Unpublished. Iowa State University.

Lu, J., & Peng, A. (2000). Evolution of rural consumption pattern in China. *Consumer Interests Annual, 46,* 222–225.

Mokhtari, M. (1992). An alternative model of U.S. clothing expenditures: Application of cointegration techniques. *Journal of Consumer Affairs, 26,* 305–323.

Monroe, D. (1974, September). Pre-Engel studies and the work of Engel: The origins of consumption research. *Home Economics Research Journal, 3*(1), 43–65

New data show 1.4 billion live on less than U.S.$1.25 a day, but progress against poverty remains strong. (2009, December 6). World Bank News Release 2009/065/DEC. Retrieved from http://go.worldbank.org/ToTEVOV4Eo

Norum, P. S. (1990). Clothing expenditures: A time series analysis, 1929–1987. In Mary Carsky (Ed.), *American Council on Consumer Interests—The Proceedings* (pp. 75-81). Columbia, MO: American Council on Consumer Interests.

O'Malley, B. (2008, June 8). Turkey: Headscarf ban re-imposed. *University World News,* issue 0031 Retrieved from http://www.universityworldnews.com/article.php?story=20080606083302196

Progressive Policy Institute (2004). Retrieved October 5, 2004, from http://www.ppi_admin@dlcppi.org

Schwenk, N. E. (1985). Measurements of family income. *Family Economics Review,* 1–4.

Seckler, V. (2009, November 25). China's one-child generation clamors for luxury goods. *Women's Wear Daily*. Retrieved from http://www.wwd.com/business-news/chinas-one-child-generation-clamors-for-luxury-goods-2379885//?full=true

Semu-Banda, P. (2009, June 14). Trade-Malawi: Clothing and textiles become unstitched. Inter Press Service News Agency. Retrieved from http://ipsnews.net/news.asp?idnews=38177

Study finds low-income Iowans pay higher share of state taxes. (2008, November 11). *The Des Moines Register*, p. A5.

United Nations Press Release TAD/1930. (2002). Report on least-developed countries. Retrieved from http://www.un.org/News/Press/docs/2002/TAD1930.doc.htm

Winakor, G. (1969, October). The process of clothing consumption. *Journal of Home Economics, 61*(8), 629–634.

Winakor, G., MacDonald, N. M., Kunz, G. I., & Saladino, K. B. (1971, April). Development of low-income clothing budgets. *Journal of Home Economics, 63*(4), 256–262.

3 Textile and Apparel Supply Matrix

Eighty billion garments are produced annually worldwide, sixteen billion of which are T-shirts: that's nearly three T-shirts for each man, woman, and child in the world (Speer, 2004).

TODAY'S TEXTILE AND apparel professionals work in a supply chain made up of an interwoven complex of firms, ranging from individual cotton growers to global business conglomerates. Many view the textile and apparel business from a linear perspective, comparing the industry with a pipeline of connected processes from growing or producing fibers used as raw material for textiles to distributing finished apparel products to the ultimate consumer. However, in today's marketplace this linear view is too simplistic. The magnitude and the complexity of the business defy such a singular orientation. Today's global textile complex may be better described as a matrix of interconnected structures and activities that provides multiple venues for designing, producing, marketing, merchandising, and distributing textiles and apparel and that begins and ends with consumers.

In Chapter 3 we introduce the Harmonized System for identifying textiles and apparel products, utilize the NAICS system of industry classification to understand the product flow of the apparel component of the textile complex, move on to the paradox of technology development and demand for low-cost labor, and complete the industry overview with an introduction to trade issues in textiles and apparel.

Objectives

- Examine the classification of textile materials and apparel for the purpose of documenting them as they proceed through the supply chain.

- Identify some of the major textile and apparel producers.

- Examine the technology development and low-cost labor paradox that frustrates supply chain managers.

- Explore trade issues in the textile and apparel business.

apparel knitting mill a manufacturing facility that interloops yarns to produce garments without producing the fabric first; some sweaters, tops, scarves, hats, and underwear

apparent consumption an estimation of domestic consumption based on levels of domestic production, imports, and exports (production + imports - exports)

converters fabric mills that specialize in application of yarn and fabric finishes

cut-and-sew apparel manufacturing an apparel production plant that performs both preproduction and production processes

distressed goods merchandise that is not salable at the intended price; seconds, overruns, samples, last season's goods, retailer returns, and so on

domestic production products made in the home country

dyeing the process of combining fibers, yarns, or fabrics with a coloring substance and creating a bond

fabric finishing processes that convert greige goods into completed fabric

fiberweb fabrics made directly from fibers; traditionally called nonwovens

flexible production system quickly and efficiently producing a variety of styles at low volume per style, with zero defects; often uses single-ply cutters and modular systems with stand-up sewing

floor ready garment producers attach retailer-specified tickets and labels to garments that are ready for display before shipping them out

greige goods fabrics whose fibers are still their natural color and texture; usually require additional processes to improve aesthetics and performance

Harmonized System (HS) the international Harmonized Commodity Description and Classification System, developed by the World Customs Organization

Harmonized Tariff Schedule of the United States (HTS) the classification of goods used to determine tariffs on specific products imported into the United States

import penetration the amount of consumption that is provided by imports (imports ÷ consumption)

knit fabric fabric made by intertwining yarn or thread in a series of connected loops rather than by weaving

knit outerwear sweaters (jumpers), jackets, and coats

layette apparel that is specially designed and produced for children, from birth until they begin walking

logistics the science of moving products through the supply chain to their final destination in a timely manner

manufactured fibers made from chemical compounds; examples include nylon, polyester, acrylic, polypropylene, and spandex; also known as man-made fibers

CLASSIFICATION OF PRODUCTS

Every textile and apparel professional has to communicate information about specific textile and apparel products. This has to be done in a systematic manner for multiple people in multiple countries so that everyone involved in the supply chain understands exactly the quantities and types of garments that are involved, including styles, sizes, and colors. Changes in the methods of doing business, along with the necessity of establishing record-keeping methods that are compatible for all global partners, have precipitated new ways of identifying products and classifying them.

The Harmonized Commodity Description and Code System, generally referred to as **Harmonized System** or **HS,** is a multipurpose international product nomenclature developed by the World Customs Organization (WCO). The system is used by more than 200 countries as a basis for the collection of international trade statistics and as a foundation for their tariff systems. The system is also used for harmonization of customs and trade procedures. The HS is a universal economic language and code for goods and an indispensible tool for international trade. More than 98 percent of the merchandise in international trade, including textiles and apparel, is classified in terms of HS (World Customs Organization, 2010).

The World Customs Organization HS classifies a product by assigning it a six-digit tariff classification number, based on its name, use, or the material used in its construction, or a combination of these. In

mass customization the integration of information technology, automation, and team-based flexible manufacturing to produce a variety of products and services based on individual customer demand

Multifiber Arrangement (MFA) international trade agreement that allowed the quantity of textile and apparel trade to be regulated through quotas established in bilateral agreements between nations

natural fibers cotton, wool, silk, and linen as well as other vegetable and animal fibers

North American Industry Classification System (NAICS) introduced in 1997 to standardize the identification of textiles and apparel for Canada, Mexico, and the United States in a manner consistent with the world market

Office of Textiles and Apparel (OTEXA) a division of U.S. Department of Commerce that monitors textile trade throughout the globe in terms of both quantity and value

printing the localized application of color to the surface of a yarn or fabric

productivity a ratio of the outputs of a production process to the inputs; a measure of performance toward an established goal

radio frequency identification (RFID) a new generation of wireless bar code systems; being used for identifying and tracking products, cartons, and containers

real-time immediately available when data are collected

square meter equivalent (SME) a means of measuring quantities of fabric and garments that are being exported or imported

Standard Industrial Classification System (SIC) replaced by the North American Industrial Classification System (NAICS)

sweatshop a firm with poor working conditions, very low pay, safety violations, and often inhumane treatment of employees

textile mill a manufacturing facility where yarns or fabrics are produced

textile product mill a manufacturing facility that produces fabric and uses it to create consumable goods, including carpets, rugs, curtains, draperies, and bed and bath products

thread a special form of yarn designed for use in sewing cut fabric pieces together to form garments or other products

transparency of information open communication among all participants within a system

underwear and sleepwear knitting mill a manufacturing facility in which products are produced by cutting and sewing knit fabrics

Universal Product Code (UPC) a bar code system for identifying and tracking products or containers

woven fabrics produced by interlocking two or more sets of yarns at right angles

yarn a continuous strand produced by twisting fibers together

---

addition to providing a means of identifying specific products, the HS is used to collect data on country of origin, quantity, and monetary value of specific textile and apparel imports. For the United States, which expands the numbering system to ten digits, the information regarding exports varies significantly from that of imports and is maintained on a separate schedule within the **Harmonized Tariff Schedule of the United States (HTS)**. The HTS is based on the HS and is the primary resource for determining tariff classifications for goods imported into and exported from the United States (Harmonized Tariff Schedule for the United States, 2008).

The HTS is divided into 99 chapters and contains numerous appendices and indexes. Textile products are assigned to Chapters 50 through 60; apparel products are identified in Chapters 61 (knit) and 62 (woven). The system is maintained by The U.S. International Trade Commission (USITC); tariffs on the products are collected by U.S. Customs and Border Protection (CBP), an agency within the Department of Homeland Security. Annual updates of specific information in this system can be found online, and anyone who considers using the schedules for calculating tariff costs is strongly encouraged to make use of these updates.

When the United States, Canada, and Mexico joined to form the North American Free Trade Agreement (NAFTA) in 1994, they had a serious problem documenting the types and quantities of products they produced and traded in the supply chains linking the countries. Mexico and Canada use the metric system, and the United States

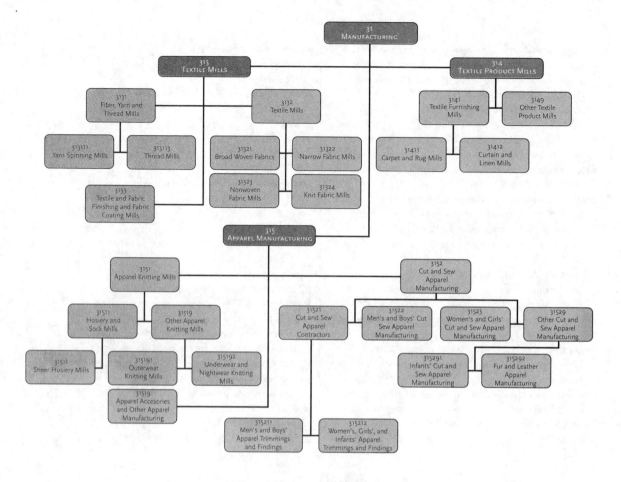

The following chart appears:

31 MANUFACTURING

- **313 TEXTILE MILLS**
  - **3131 Fiber, Yarn and Thread Mills**
    - 313111 Yarn Spinning Mills
    - 313113 Thread Mills
  - **3133 Textile and Fabric Finishing and Fabric Coating Mills**
  - **3132 Textile Mills**
    - 31321 Broad Woven Fabrics
    - 31322 Narrow Fabric Mills
    - 31323 Nonwoven Fabric Mills
    - 31324 Knit Fabric Mills
- **314 TEXTILE PRODUCT MILLS**
  - **3141 Textile Furnishing Mills**
    - 31411 Carpet and Rug Mills
    - 31412 Curtain and Linen Mills
  - **3149 Other Textile Product Mills**

315 APPAREL MANUFACTURING

- **3151 Apparel Knitting Mills**
  - **31511 Hosiery and Sock Mills**
    - 31511 Sheer Hosiery Mills
    - 315191 Outerwear Knitting Mills
    - 315192 Underwear and Nightwear Knitting Mills
  - **31519 Other Apparel Knitting Mills**
  - **31519 Apparel Accesories and Other Apparel Manufacturing**
    - 315211 Men's and Boys' Apparel Trimmings and Findings
    - 315212 Women's, Girls', and Infants' Apparel Trimmings and Findings
- **3152 Cut and Sew Apparel Manufacturing**
  - **31521 Cut and Sew Apparel Contractors**
  - **31522 Men's and Boys' Cut Sew Apparel Manufacturing**
  - **31523 Women's and Girls' Cut and Sew Apparel Manufacturing**
  - **31529 Other Cut and Sew Apparel Manufacturing**
    - 315291 Infants' Cut and Sew Apparel Manufacturing
    - 315292 Fur and Leather Apparel Manufacturing

Figure 3.1 NAICS is an example of an industry classification system used by a trading bloc to identify imported and exported products and production. NAICS is compatible with the Harmonized System (HS), which is used in global trade.

(© *US Census Bureau*)

is the only country in the world that uses the English system of measurement. Therefore, based on HS, the three countries developed the **North American Industry Classification System** (**NAICS**) in 1997 to standardize the identification of textiles and apparel and other products in a manner consistent with the world market. NAICS replaced the 1987 **U.S. Standard Industrial Classification** (**SIC**). Figure 3.1 gives examples of NAICS codes for the manufacturing sector of textiles and apparel.

The NAICS classification system facilitates communication between firms and agencies and provides the record-keeping capabilities needed to make many business decisions, especially those related to measuring productivity levels and unit labor costs. NAICS also explains why some job categories are defined as they are within the industry. For example, because hosiery and sweaters can be produced directly from yarn into finished apparel products, knit goods designers can skip the fabric production level; in fact, they are often hired and trained separately from designers for other apparel product categories. The rationale is that knit products are produced by different methods, in different environments and require business practices that are different from those for other apparel products.

Case 3.1 gives an overview of the development of NAICS. Follow that with Learning Activity 3.1, which extends the discussion of product classification.

The United States began using a new industry classification system on April 9, 1997, when the Office of Management and Budget (OMB) announced its decision to adopt the North American Industry Classification System (NAICS) (pronounced NAYKS) as the industry classification system used by the statistical agencies of the United States. NAICS replaced the 1987 U.S. Standard Industrial Classification (SIC). The SIC was established in the 1930s to promote uniformity and compatibility of data collected and published by agencies within the U.S. government, state agencies, trade associations, and research organizations. The SIC was revised periodically to reflect changes in the economic structure of the United States, the last revision having taken place in 1987. NAICS was designed to accommodate the similar needs of three countries: Canada, Mexico, and the United States. NAICS was updated in 2002 and again in 2007, and an update is in progress for 2012.

NAICS is the first-ever North American industry classification system. Representatives from Canada, Mexico, and the United States collaborated to develop a system to provide comparable statistics across the three countries. NAICS also allows for increased comparability with the International Standard Industrial Classification System (ISIC, Revision 3), developed and maintained by the United Nations.

NAICS has a unique system for classifying business establishments. This production-oriented, industry based system means that statistical agencies produce data that can be used for measuring productivity, unit labor costs, and the capital intensity of production, constructing input–output relationships and estimating employment–output relationships and other statistics. This method reflects the structure of today's global economy, including the emergence and growth of the service sector and new and advanced technologies.

NAICS is a six- to ten-digit system. It provides comparability among the three countries at the five-digit level. Additional digits are used to refine the definition of the industries involved. Ten digits are required to identify individual products. Examples of the meaning of the ten digits include the following:

- 2-digit = manufacturing sector (31)
- 3-digit = subsectors, including textile mills (313), textile mill products (314), and apparel manufacturing (315)
- 4-digit = industry groups, including fabric mills (3132), textile furnishing mills (3141), apparel knitting mills (3151), and cut-and-sew apparel manufacturing (3152)
- 5-digit = industry, including broad-woven fabric (31321), curtain and linen mills (31412), hosiery and sock mills (31511), and cut-and-sew apparel contractors (31521)
- 6-digit = national, including sheer hosiery mills (315111), and infant cut-and-sew manufacturing (315291)
- 10-digit = required to identify individual products

NAICS includes descriptions of more than 20 thousand industries, including manufacturers and retailers. With practice, the logic of the numbering system becomes second nature. Apparel professionals can read numbers as if they were words on the page. Updates are being prepared for implementation in 2012.

Source:

U.S. Bureau of the Census. (2007). *North American Industry Classification System.* Retrieved May 6, 2010 from http://www.census.gov/eos/www/naics/

TEXTILE MILLS (NAICS 313)

Textile mills are manufacturing facilities of different types that process and produce fibers, yarns, fabrics, and finishes. Textile mills are businesses that own their own machinery. The following discussion is organized according to types of production processes and products, as reflected by NAICS codes.

Fiber, Yarn, and Thread Mills (NAICS 3131)

As mentioned previously, the raw material in textiles is fiber (see Chapter 1). Fibers are divided into two basic categories: natural and manufactured. **Natural fibers** include cotton, wool, silk, and flax as well as a number of less widely used fibers, such as ramie, jute, cashmere, and mohair. Natural fibers are grown as vegetable or animal agricultural products and have been important to agricultural trade throughout the globe for centuries; NAICS classifies natural fibers under agriculture rather than manufacturing. Of these fibers, only cotton and wool are produced in significant quantities in the United States, so garments made domestically of other natural fibers are typically made of imported fibers.

Concentrations of agriculture producing natural fiber are found in diverse pockets throughout the globe. For example, significant quantities of cotton are grown in Pakistan, Turkey, China, Egypt, and the United States. Silk fiber is produced in areas such as China and Thailand, where mulberry leaves required for feeding the silk larva are readily available.

Manufactured fibers, both cellulosic (acetate and rayon) and synthetic (nylon, polyester, acrylic, polypropylene, and spandex), are produced in many areas of the world. Production of manufactured fibers requires significant investment of capital and access to technology. These fibers are relatively new to the marketplace; much of their development as consumer products did not occur until the late 1940s, after World War II. The use of these fibers has skyrocketed since their introduction, both in volume and value.

A natural fiber recently introduced into global trade is bamboo. Although bamboo is itself a natural fiber, it is produced as a textile product in the form of manufactured rayon. Therefore, the United States now requires that bamboo be labeled "rayon" or "rayon from bamboo" when used for producing knit shirts and bath towels. The biggest use of bamboo is in disposable diapers. The U.S. Federal Trade Commission has been charging some companies of being deceptive in their claims of bamboo's being environmentally friendly, because some of the processes required to make it usable as a textile product are not.

Among synthetic fiber producers, horizontal integration (mergers between companies with the same target market) has concentrated technical expertise into fewer larger companies. It has also concentrated corporate assets and the ability to do fundamental research for new product development, which has been especially important to the development of synthetic fibers. Mergers among already known global textile companies have produced the largest textile company ever known. DuPont, based in the United States, evolved its textile business into DuPont Textiles and Interiors, focusing on brands such as Cordura, Supplex, and CoolMax products, and fiber products, such as Lycra. These advances were followed by a name change, to INVISTA. Subsequently, the company was acquired by Koch Industries, of Wichita, Kansas, in 2004, and restructuring ensued (Walzer, 2005). Koch also owned KoSa, which purchased the worldwide Trevira polyester business from the German manufacturer Hoechst in 1998, and by forming a consortium between KoSa and Grupo Xtra, of Mexico City, Koch became the world's largest polyester producers (Saba/ Koch, 1998). Koch then merged that consortium business into INVISTA, making it the largest textile firm in the world. INVISTA operates in 20 nations throughout the globe, including China.

Other sizeable global firms that produce synthetic fiber yarns and textiles include Formosa Plastics Group, Far Eastern Textile Ltd., and Hualon Corporation, of Taiwan; Reliance, of Mumbai, India; Huvis Corporation, of Seoul, South Korea; Teijun, of Osaka, Japan; and Sinopec Yizheng Chemical Fibre Company Ltd., in China (*Women's Wear Daily*, 2003).

Now, read Case 3.2, an announcement of INVISTA's agreeement to license its manufacturing technologies for two intermediates (chemical compounds) to the Chinese firm Chongqing Jian-Feng Industrial Group Co.

Case 3.2 INVISTA AND JIAN-FENG SIGN BDO, PTMEG LICENSE AGREEMENT FOR RMB 2 BILLION ($300 MILLION) PROJECT

New York, NY—August 20, 2009—INVISTA, a world leader in chemical intermediates, polymers and fibers, signed a technology licensing agreement with Chongqing Jian-Feng Industrial Group Co., Ltd., to license its BDO and PTMEG manufacturing technologies to the Chinese company.

Jian-Feng is investing RMB 2 billion (approximately $300 million U.S.) in building a manufacturing complex to produce these two products at Chongqing Chemical Industry Park in the Fuling District of the Chongqing Municipality.

Mr. Li Xian Wen, vice general manager of the Jianfeng Industrial Group, and Mr. Jeff Gentry, chairman of the board of directors and CEO of INVISTA, participated in a signing ceremony held here today for the licensing deal. Also present were senior representatives from both companies and senior government leaders from the Chongqing Municipality, including Mayor Wang Hongju.

"We are proud to support Chongqing's continuing technological and industrial development through our licensing of BDO and PTMEG technologies," said Gentry. "We admire the clear vision for Chongqing's continued growth as an industrial center being advanced by Mayor Wang and other Chongqing leaders."

The licensing agreement covers the manufacturing processes, required technologies, product formulations as well as expert engineering services for the two plants with annual capacity of 60,000 tons of BDO and 46,000 tons of PTMEG.

"Our technology licensing organization, INVISTA Performance Technologies, has over 40 years of technology transfer experience and has participated in over 40 projects in China," said Gentry. "We are pleased to provide Jian-Feng with the design and know-how for its manufacturing operation in Chongqing."

Chemical intermediate BDO (1,4 butanediol) is used in making polyester resins and polyurethanes, and PTMEG (polytetramethylene ether glycol) is a polyether glycol used as a building block in high-performance polyurethanes, polyesters co-polymers and other polymers. Typical end uses for PTMEG include spandex fibers, thermal plastic elastomers, and cast elastomers for apparel, automotive, and industrial uses.

INVISTA has been licensing its leading technologies in chemical intermediates and polymers in China since 1990. The total investment of INVISTA's Chinese licensees has now exceeded RMB 32 billion.

Source:

INVISTA and Jian-Feng Sign BDO, PTMEG license agreement for RMB 2 billion ($300 million) project. Retrieved May 13, 2010, from http://www.invista.com/ news_releases/2009/pr_090820_PTMEG.shtml. Reprinted with permission from INVISTA, July 2010.

Figure 3.2 Thread manufacturing at the American & Efird, Inc., facility in Costa Rica.

(Photo by Myrna Garner)

Some fibers are spun into yarns in mills close to where the fibers are produced, but others are shipped in raw form to areas where production machinery is more readily available. Major factors in the determination of where yarns are spun are ease of transport, intended end use, and economic conditions related to technology.

Threads Mills (NAICS 313113)

Thread is a special form of yarn. It is produced by treating and finishing the yarn to make it strong, with a fine diameter that is used in sewing cut fabric pieces together to form garments or other products. Although seemingly insignificant to the outsider, thread is a critical component, related to the quality and durability of finished textile and apparel products.

One major manufacturer of thread products is *American & Efird, Inc.*; its headquarters are located in Mount Holly, North Carolina, and it has manufacturing capacity in Costa Rica and China (American & Efird, 2009–2010). Its supply network currently has 30 manufacturing centers and 70 service centers, located in 44 countries.

This firm manufactures sewing thread for industrial and consumer markets, producing a variety of thread products for use in apparel, upholstery, home furnishings, and footwear. Variations of their thread products are packaged in numerous formats, on bobbins, spools, and cones suitable for commercial production or home sewing use (e.g., Mettler and Maxi-Lock consumer products) (Figure 3.2).

Yarn-Spinning Mills (NAICS 313111)

Yarns are the basic building blocks of woven and knit fabrics and other products. Staple yarn is produced by twisting fibers together; filament yarns are produced by extrusion. Pure, natural fiber yarns are produced to make things like 100 percent cotton fabrics. Natural and manufactured fibers are also mixed together to form blended yarns. The most common blend today is a mixture of cotton and polyester, used extensively in fabrics for apparel and home use.

Another blend in use today is a cotton-and-ramie yarn found in sweaters and woven fabrics. The use of this blend increased during the latter part of the 20th century, when quota limits were set on the amount of cotton that could be brought into the United States from China. Because there were no such limits on ramie at the time, blends of the two fibers were made to avoid going over the cotton quota, so that more sweaters could be imported. The result was the development of ramie as a widely used textile fiber for apparel. Before that time, ramie—a rather stiff cellulose fiber—was rarely seen in the United States.

Fabric Mills (NAICS 3132)

Yarns made of fiber are interlocked by mechanical and chemical means to produce fabrics. **Woven fabrics** and **knit fabrics** constitute a significant portion of fabric production destined for use in apparel, although **fiberweb fabrics,** traditionally called nonwovens, are the fastest growing category of textile materials (Kadolph

& Langford, 2002). Broad-woven fabrics for apparel range in width from approximately 27 inches to 144 inches. Narrow-woven fabrics include laces, ribbons, and braids used for trim. Fiberweb fabrics are now widely used for garment interfacings and for disposable products, such as diapers and single-use hospital gowns and scrubs. Knit-fabric mills often make either filling-knit or warp-knit fabrics, because each requires different types of machinery and yarns.

Since the advent of manufactured fiber products in the mid-20th century, fabrics are produced in more areas of the globe than was possible when the industry was hampered by geographical limitations in agricultural production, transportation, and power sources to run the looms. Over time, fabric production has tended to follow the growth patterns of the industrialization of nations and has contributed heavily to the early growth of many national economies. For example, during the 1700s, England imported cotton and wool from its colonies India and Australia and flax for linen from Ireland, to produce enough fabric not only to supply its own population but also to sell to settlers in the United States and other places. As the United States began to move from an agrarian society to industrialization during the 1800s, the textile industry led the way. At the same time, Italy has long imported silk from China for production of fabrics for apparel and home furnishings that are still highly sought after throughout the world.

More recently, as apparel production has increased in developing countries, fabric production has followed; therefore, there have been decreases in apparel fabric production in developed countries. For example, during the 1990s, much of jeans production moved from the United States to Mexico. Many denim mills followed, including *Cone Mills*, whose goal was to be the largest denim producer in the world (Figures 3.3a and 3b). Today, Cone Mills operates facilities in the United States,

Figure 3.3a Cone Mills moved much of its denim production out of the United States to be closer to where jeans are made. The white filling yarns on spools in the foreground are interlocked in a twill weave with dyed warp yarns by the automated loom to create the ever-popular denim fabric. (*Courtesy of WWD*)

Figure 3.3b Wet processing has become a standard part of finishing denim garments. Bleaches, dyes, and abrasive materials are employed to enhance the fashion appeal of finished garments. (*Courtesy of WWD*)

Mexico, Nicaragua, and China and has joint ventures in India and Turkey. Cone Mills now functions as part of International Textile Group, owned by WL Ross & Co., which also owns Cone's former competitor *Burlington Industries*. In the United States, denim production increased until 1989, when it peaked, and has since declined to below the 1989 level (Conway, 2004).

Textile and Fabric Finishing and Fabric Coating Mills (NAICS 3133)

A majority of fabrics used in apparel tend to be produced as greige goods. **Greige goods** are made up of fibers that are still their natural color and texture and that require additional processes to improve aesthetics and performance. Whereas mills that make yarn and fabric and convert greige goods to finished textiles are considered vertically integrated textile mills, those that specialize in fabric finishing processes only may be referred to as converters. **Converters** buy greige goods from a fabric mill and apply the finishes, such as dyeing and printing.

Dyeing and **printing** produce colors, and **fabric finishing** processes change hand or simplify product care. The transition from natural to chemical dyes and the development of finishes to improve the comfort and ease of care of textile products have contributed heavily to more recent changes within the textile industry. Many finishing processes require complex manufacturing techniques or significant investment of capital in the technology used to produce them, or both. Another consideration is the need for large quantities of fresh water for these processes. For these reasons, more economically developed nations tend to excel in new dyeing and finishing techniques. Countries such as the United States, Germany, and Japan led the way, but Taiwan and South Korea moved into these areas of specialization as their economies improved in the latter part of the 20th century.

TEXTILE PRODUCT MILLS (NAICS 314)

Textile product mills producing home furnishing textiles, including carpets and rugs, curtains and draperies, and bed and bath products, are important components of the textile business. A unique aspect of textile product mills is that they usually produce finished goods instead of materials for other firms to convert into finished goods. For example, a mill producing sheets or towels generally cuts and hems the fabric and then packages the finished goods for sale to the ultimate consumer.

The rates of sale of home furnishing textiles tend to reflect rates of sale of homes. During the 1990s, when textile production was decreasing in developed countries, carpet production increased in the United States by 46 percent. The 1990s was a very active period of home building in the United States. Bedding and bath textile production peaked during the mid-1990s and declined as the country experienced a corresponding increase in imports, making towels and bedding from distant nations more visible in the U.S. marketplace (*Textile Hi-Lights*, 2004). By the late 2000s overall carpet sales were down anywhere from 20 percent to 30 percent as the market faced a weakening economy, with declining new home sales and increasing foreclosures of existing homes. ("Commercial Carpet Report," 2009).

Continue to explore textile mills with Learning Activity 3.2.

1. In the textile sense, what is a mill?
2. Why are manufactured fibers made in a mill but not natural fibers?
3. What is the difference between a yarn mill and a fabric mill?
4. What is the difference between a knitting mill and a weaving mill?
5. What are some of the consumer benefits of fabric finishing mills?
6. How are textile mill products different from products manufactured by a textile mill?

APPAREL MANUFACTURING (NAICS 315)

Yarns and fabrics are the basic materials used in the production of the two major categories of apparel—knit products and cut-and-sew apparel. The NAICS classifications of knit products are "hosiery and socks" and "other" knit apparel, containing the subcategories "outerwear," "underwear," and "sleepwear." Cut-and-sew products reflect the classification of all garments made by cutting knit or woven fabric into garment components and sewing garment components into finished apparel.

Apparel Knitting Mills (NAICS 3151)

Growth in the production and use of knit-apparel products has been fueled by the introduction of new technology. Specialized knitting machines can produce jersey, tricot, or double-knit fabrics or finished knit garments made directly from yarns, such as sweaters and socks. New technology in knitting has sig-nificantly increased the capability of **apparel knitting mills** to produce finished products.

Hosiery-and-Sock Mills (NAICS 31511) and Sheer Hosiery Mills (NAICS 315111)
The line between the two areas of this category, hosiery and socks, seems blurred because of the vocabulary used to define the products. *Hosiery News*, the trade publication from manufacturers of hosiery products, tends to use "hosiery" as an umbrella term for all these products, and "socks" and "sheers" (or "sheer hosiery") as the two subcategories in their discussions of the business.

Within the United States, sales volume for the overall hosiery category has been up in recent years. When production of sheer hosiery is examined separately from the overall figures, it becomes evident that the fashion trend to wear sandals without hose has reduced previous figures for sheers in both volume produced and dollar value, whereas socks have increased enough to produce growth in the overall category (Cohen, 2004). The growing popularity of casual clothing in the office environment has also been a factor in the reduction of sales of sheer hosiery.

The sources of hosiery products are also in a state of flux. Previously, the greatest quantities of socks sold in the United States were produced domestically or in Central America. Today, significantly greater quantities of socks are being imported from China.

Other Apparel Knitting Mills (NAICS 31519)
All other apparel products made by the knitting process tend to fall into this loosely defined and encompassing category. The category includes products knitted directly from yarns and garments made from knitted fabrics.

Figure 3.4a Sock production at a hosiery mill in Costa Rica. (*Photo by Myrna Garner*)

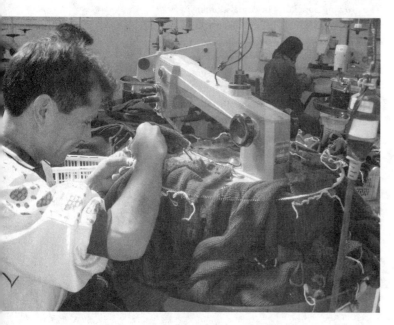

Figure 3.4b Linking alpaca sweaters in a knitting mill in Peru. (*Photo by Sandra Keiser*)

Outerwear Knitting Mills (NAICS 315191)
Knit outerwear might be best identified as sweaters. Britain and its former colonies refer to sweaters as jumpers, which confuses some Americans, because in the United States a jumper is a completely different article of clothing. Therefore, the category for sweaters is "outerwear" so that everyone in the global community is clear on what is being discussed.

The category contains products of diverse styling and value, depending not only on their design but also on the fibers used for the yarns and whether the garment is made by machine or requires many hand operations. Today, the majority of sweaters marketed in the United States are machine made, with yarn composed of cotton, wool, or man-made fiber (such as acrylic), or a combination of these. In smaller quantities we find sweaters made of expensive fibers, such as cashmere and alpaca (Figure 3.4b).

When evaluating the value of knit outerwear products, it becomes clear that the economic value of a large quantity of inexpensive cotton-ramie blend, machine-made (automatic, as opposed to manual) sweaters from China may be similar in dollar value to a small number of very expensive handmade or manually machine-made alpaca sweaters from Peru. When making comparisons of production from different parts of the world, it is critical to have an accurate description of the category and the products involved as well as figures of the overall volume and value of the products.

Underwear and Sleepwear Knitting Mills (315192)
Products made in **underwear and sleepwear knitting mills** are manufactured by cutting and sewing knit fabrics. Because many of the products found in this category today are basic products that are sold year-round and considered staples in the overall wardrobe, they lend themselves well to mass-production

methods, including the significant use of automation to reduce labor costs. The construction methods used to produce T-shirts and shorts or underpants are also quite simple, so these items tend to be relatively inexpensive to produce and market when compared with tailored suits or coats made of woven fabrics.

The three largest producers of branded men's underwear in the United States are *Fruit of the Loom*, *Hanes*, and *Jockey*. The production facilities for these companies are located in the United States and scattered elsewhere throughout the globe, making their products readily available for retail.

Great quantities of this product category are sourced by U.S. retailers and manufacturers from Mexico, Central America, and China and sold by retailers in the United States. The rationale, as with many other products, is that merchandise costs are less if the product is manufactured offshore and shipped to the United States rather than if it is manufactured domestically.

Now, try your hand at Learning Activity 3.3.

Learning Activity 3.3
APPAREL KNITTING MILLS

1. What is the difference between an apparel knitting mill and a fabric knitting mill?
2. What types of garments can be created and finished on knitting machines without cutting and sewing?
3. What is the British name for a popular U.S. form of knit outerwear? What is the commonly used name for this product in the United States?
4. How does this distinction in the name of a globally used product underscore the difficulty of clearly communicating about apparel products across political borders?

Cut-and-Sew Apparel Manufacturing (NAICS 3152)

The remainder of apparel manufacturing is placed in the **cut-and-sew apparel manufacturing** classification in NAICS. The concept of manufactured ready-to-wear may be traced to Elias Howe, who patented the lock-stitch sewing machine in 1846 (The Great Idea Finder, 2004). Some people credit Isaac Singer with this invention, but his activities were related to the development of sewing machines for home use.

Discussion of cut-and-sew apparel manufacturing is further complicated by the issue of whether a firm previously recognized as a manufacturer actually produces the finished products that bear its name now or if it contracts the production to outside contractors. NAICS has separated these two divisions, but the categories are becoming increasingly blurred, as many firms previously recognized as apparel manufacturers in the United States have farmed out so much of their actual production to other contractors that they now might be better identified as brand managers or brand vendors.

Cut-and-Sew Apparel Contractors (NAICS 31521)
As defined previously, CMT (cut-make-trim) and full-package contractors are those firms that provide production services and produce apparel products for other firms, including branded label goods for other manufacturers or private label goods for retailers (see Chapter 1). Typically, contractors of garments are not visible to consumers because contractors are producing products that will carry brands representing other firms. The uniqueness of the position is that contractors are paid for their production by the business that sourced the products, the products carry the sourcing firm's label in them, and the contractor does not bear the responsibility for whether the garments produced actually sell in the retail environment (the sourcing firm bears that responsibility).

One of the larger manufacturers and contractors of apparel in the United States is *Kellwood Company*, headquartered in St. Louis, Missouri. Kellwood became part of Sun Capital Partners, Inc., in 2008; the firm specializes in producing branded and private label apparel products for women in a number of categories. Typical consumers are not aware of Kellwood, yet they would recognize many of the products Kellwood manufactures and contracts production for under a variety of labels, including Baby Phat, Briggs New York, Jax, Jolt girls sportswear, Koret, My Michelle, Phat Farm, Sag Harbor, Vince, and XOXO (Kellwood, 2009).

Men's and Boys' Apparel Trimmings and Findings (NAICS 315211) and Women's, Girls', and Infants' Trimmings and Findings (NAICS 315212)
The other materials needed for construction of garments, beyond fabric and thread, are commonly called trims, trimmings, or findings. This term represents the product category sometimes known as notions in the home sewing business. **Findings** include components constructed of fabric and other materials, such as interfacings, pocket bags, and linings; *closures* include buttons, zippers, Velcro tapes, and snaps; and *trims* and decorative embellishments include lace, beading, and embroidery.

YKK is an example of a global findings manufacturer that was founded in Japan, as a zipper manufacturer, in 1934. YKK now does business in 70 countries worldwide and is considered the world's largest maker of zippers, producing thousands of varieties for use in a multitude of consumer products, from apparel to luggage (YKK, 2009). Zippers are critical to a garment's serviceability; like thread, a zipper can either make a garment functional or render it useless. Among its many products, the firm also makes hook and loop tapes that are used in many applications, from apparel to automobile upholstery, and a large assortment of snap fasteners.

Some firms that supply findings are wholesalers that assemble assortments of closures, support materials, and trims that serve a particular segment of the apparel market, such as children's wear or bras. Most of these products require specialized equipment or processes to be manufactured, because they come in a vast variety of sizes, styles, and volume. Demand for different products in the findings category is based on fashion trends from season to season, so it remains compatible with the most current fabrics and garment designs.

Other firms offering findings are more diverse, providing a variety of materials or findings to manufacturers of finished garments. One of these companies is *QST Industries*, headquartered in Chicago, Illinois, which claims to be a "leading supplier of innovative men's, women's and children's apparel construction components to the international garment industry" (QST Industries, 2010). This firm produces interlining products for use in men's tailored garments, such as pocket bags and curtains for the waistbands of men's slacks, and a variety of products used as closures. QST has also added a line of ecofriendly products that help make garments green (QST Industries, 2010). QST has expanded its business operations into 32 countries in all regions of the world.

Men's and Boys' Cut-and-Sew Apparel Manufacturing (NAICS 31522)
The earliest forms of apparel made in factories were men's garments. Men's apparel products have always been good candidates for assembly-line production, because they are more static in terms of style than women's fashion. For this reason, men's garments also tend to be produced in fewer, larger firms than are women's apparel.

Boys' products are styled and constructed with techniques and fabrics similar to those used for menswear, so they are often made in the same factories. This helps explain why product data for boys' apparel have been kept as a part of men's traditionally.

Tailored apparel, such as suits and coats, were the basis of this classification for many years, but lifestyle changes in American consumers have made sportswear, active sportswear, and uniforms the current growth product categories. The manufacturing techniques for making sportswear and active sportswear tend to be quite different from those of more traditional men's tailored apparel, using a variety of innovative textile materials and encompassing an amazing breadth of end products. Because the production methods required are often the same for both men's and women's products, they are usually manufactured in the same facilities, blurring the distinction between the men's and women's manufacturing categories. *Nike* and the Canadian *lululemon athletica* are two of the most profitable sportswear firms in today's marketplace, but many others in this field are readily recognizable to U.S. consumers, including The North Face, Patagonia, Under Armour, and Columbia Sportswear.

Cintas Corporation and *Red Kap* are two major manufacturers of uniforms in the United States, providing everything from shirts and pants for your local car service personnel, to suits for hotel doormen and airline personnel, to restaurant cook hats and aprons, to nurses' uniforms and hospital scrubs. Cintas is the largest uniform supplier in North America, with 34 thousand employees and 11 manufacturing plants (Cintas, n.d.). Red Kap is a part of VF Imagewear, Inc., a division of VF Corporation, the world's largest publicly owned apparel company (Red Kap, 2006). Both Cintas and Red Kap have developed some unique methods of product distribution, including garment rental programs.

One of the legends in U.S. menswear apparel manufacturing for more than a century was Hart, Schaffner & Marx, of Chicago, Illinois, more recently known as *Hartmarx*. Hartmarx expanded beyond its

Figure 3.5a Worker in a Hartmarx plant in Des Plaines, Illinois. (*Scott Olson/Getty Images*)

Figure 3.5b Quality control operation (checking measurements) as garments come off the production line. (*Courtesy of WWD*)

original focus on men's tailored suits into other areas of production; in 2008 it filed for bankruptcy. The firm was then acquired by Britain's Emerisque Brands and SKNL North America in August, 2009 (Bankruptcy, 2009). Hartmarx employs about three thousand people nationwide, with 600 of them in Des Plaines, Illinois. The firm's most prominent brands include Hickey Freeman (luxury suits), Sansabelt (casual slacks), and Hart Schaffner Marx (suits). The company also produces licensed products for numerous brands, including the Bobby Jones, Jack Nicklaus, and Austin Reed labels (Figure 3.5a).

Women's and Girls' Cut-and-Sew Apparel Manufacturing (NAICS 31523)

Factory production of women's wear developed later than men's, starting its climb in 1917, during World War I. A reason for this delay in production compared with men's products was that women's fashions tend to change more quickly than men's, and prior to the war, women's garments were very complex. Because of diversity of styling choices, firms producing products for women tend to be smaller and produce in shorter runs (fewer garments at a time) than is typical with menswear, thus maintaining the flexibility to produce new fashions as consumers seek them. This smaller production capacity for individual styles still remains true for the highest price points and most fashion-oriented products in women's fashion apparel.

However, in the latter part of the 20th century there was a trend toward consolidation of this market, resulting in mass-volume production and in consumer complaints of uniformity across the marketplace caused by the homogenization of styling inherent to mass production. The volatile nature of the women's fashion business has led to something of a revolving door for brands and labels available in the market over time.

Named after the original designer for the business, *Liz Claiborne, Inc.*, continued to grow after its namesake retired. With headquarters in New York City, the firm had 15 thousand employees in 2008 and sales of more than $3,984 million (Colbert, 2009). However, those figures reflected a downturn from previous years. In 2009, the firm was restructuring and announced that it would exit the department store channel for distribution of its Liz Claiborne New York brand, designed by Isaac Mizrahi, and distribute it only through the shopping channel QVC.

The firm's other brands, Liz Claiborne and Claiborne, will now only be sold in the United States by JCPenney. The design process will be retained by Liz Claiborne, Inc., but the sourcing, production, and distribution of these lines will be the responsibility of JCPenney (Ayling, 2009). The firm will continue its other brands, including Juicy Couture, Kate Spade, and Mexx.

Assembly methods for preschool children's apparel are more similar to women's than to men's apparel. Garments are often constructed in unisex mode, with the only differentiations existing in color, trim, and fabric choices. Although infant apparel is categorized separately, both preschool boys' and girls' apparel volume and financial data are grouped with women's. Boys' products are shifted into the men's category at about the time boys enter school. Products for older girls are styled and produced by methods like those of women's.

Other Cut-and-Sew Apparel Manufacturing (31529)

The remaining categories of cut-and-sew apparel are classified "other." The products in this area are diverse, but each grouping is developed for a very specific target market or specialized product line.

Infants' Cut-and-Sew Apparel Manufacturing (315291)

The infants' category reflects all the apparel specially designed and produced for children from birth until they begin to walk. Products in this category are often referred to in the business as the **layette**. These products are small in size, have very specialized use and care requirements, and are subject to a number of government supervisory safety regulations. The Consumer Product Safety Commission (CPSC), under the U.S. Federal

Trade Commission in the Department of Commerce, oversees many of the products in this division, watching for flammability standards, safety issues related to choking hazards, and lead content in zippers and other closures or trims.

Two of the larger brands found in the infants' product category are *Gerber* and *Carter's*. Great quantities of infant apparel are developed as private label products for specific retailers, such as JCPenney, Sears, Target, and Walmart and are manufactured by contractors throughout the globe.

Fur and Leather Apparel Manufacturing (NAICS 315292)

Both fur and leather products are traditionally made of natural animal skins and are therefore classified together. Today, many synthetic fur and leather apparel products, made of specialized fabrics produced as yardage, are found in the market. Fur products require specialized construction techniques; leather products require equipment that is typically heavier than that used for general apparel construction.

The acceptability of real fur products within the consumer market varies, depending on visibility and emphasis on animal rights. However, there has been a continuing market for fine fur garments with affluent customers for centuries. These consumers tend to see their fur garments as symbols of their success, and the market for them tends to increase when the economy is strong.

Leather apparel products are available in a variety of price points. Inexpensive leather products made from cowhide or synthetic leather are readily available from many countries. Low- to moderate-price leather products are produced in locations such as China, Morocco, Cyprus, and Argentina.

Pigskin is often used for budget-price products and for shoe linings (Kunz, Albrecht, Stout, & Horne, 1992). Finer leather products, such as coats and jackets, are produced at moderate to higher price points out of calfskin and lamb. Fashionable calfskin products found in the United States are often imported from workshops in and around Florence, Italy.

Apparel Accessories and Other Apparel Manufacturing (NAICS 3159)

This catchall classification contains many diverse products, from simple scarves to hats and gloves. The volume of these products seems low when compared with all the other apparel products found in the marketplace. However, many of the items in this category are specialized, and firms that produce them are very viable contributors to the overall apparel business.

Gloves are one of the largest-volume categories in this classification. *Polygenex International, Inc.,* located in Cary, North Carolina, is a vendor for a multitude of glove types. The firm's Web site (www.gloves-online.com) provides an extensive listing of gloves available in the market today. In addition to the typical knit and leather gloves used for cold weather and sports, such as golf and skiing, the list includes clean-room gloves, used for precision handling and assembly work; latex gloves, including the disposable varieties used for medical purposes; rubber gloves, including those used for household cleaning; and grip gloves, including those used for gardening.

Continue your study of cut-and-sew apparel manufacturing with Learning Activity 3.4.

1. Why are cut-and-sew apparel contractors separated from cut-and-sew men's and women's apparel manufacturers in NAICS?

2. Why do manufacturers of women's apparel have a different NAICS code from manufacturers of men's apparel?

3. Why might zippers, snaps, elastic, tape, and other such items have peculiar names, such as notions and findings?

4. Why is boys' apparel classified with men's? Why is girls' apparel classified with women's?

5. Pick one of the major production firms whose names are italicized in the previous discussion. Find its Web site, and write a two- or three-paragraph update on the current status of the company.

TECHNOLOGY DEVELOPMENT AND THE LOW-COST LABOR PARADOX

The rate of change from localized markets to global perspectives increased significantly in the last two decades, owing to innovations in technology and increases in capital investment. Technology has made it possible for trade and supply chains to become more globalized. At the same time, particularly for the labor-intensive apparel production sector, the pursuit of low-cost labor has been driving the textile and apparel industry worldwide.

Technology has profoundly influenced product development, transportation, and logistics, making distant locations viable sourcing partners in the supply chain. New transportation and communication tools and technological improvements in production are also influencing textile and apparel sourcing decisions. Review the Li & Fung supply chain (see Figure 1.8). Note that one side of the loop relates to the previous discussion of

identification of textile and apparel products, whereas the other side relates to decisions involved with methods and timing of moving goods from source to consumer. Technology development has facilitated processes involved on both sides of the supply chain.

Transportation and Logistics

Methods of transporting textile and apparel products evolved from the camel trains out of China to sailing vessels loaded with fabrics and fashion from Europe bound for the American colonies. Today, the majority of textile and apparel products are transported in containers on fleets of steamships and transferred to rail cars or trucks to reach their ultimate destinations (Figures 3.6a and 3.6b). Costs are less when a single shipment fills an entire container, so quantities of products bound for the same port are placed in the same containers for efficiency's sake. A smaller percentage of products is shipped by air cargo to meet critical deadlines for sale on the retail sales floor.

The science of moving products through the supply chain to their final destination in a timely manner is called **logistics**. One of the major tools for coordinating this process is the computer. Use of standardized computer software packages and the Internet for planning and tracking deliveries has compressed transportation time frames and improved efficiency for both textile and apparel firms.

In addition to the use of computer and Internet for scheduling and tracking the status of orders in the pipeline, the sheer volume of business has fostered the development of new technologies, for keeping track not only of containers, but of their contents as well.

Universal Product Code

The **Universal Product Code** (UPC) system developed in the 1970s, recognized by anyone who has examined a label on a package of food at the grocery store, enables the tracking of products, from factory to consumer. The UPC code system can identify individual products for data collection at any stage of the delivery process and is most frequently used for logistics and inventory control. American companies once favored a 12-digit configuration, but to facilitate more consistent global communication, the Uniform Code Council, a nonprofit industry group that oversees bar code standards in the United States and Canada, adopted the global 13-digit configuration, beginning January 1, 2005. It was estimated that the new codes could save 10 percent of the time previously needed to harmonize product data and reconcile invoices internationally.

During transit, the bar code system works adequately on any container on which the label can be seen and scanned. The universal bar code is also very good for tracking individual items at point of sale, but identifying items shipped within another container poses a problem.

Radio Frequency Identification

A newer logistics tool is **radio frequency identification (RFID)**. It was introduced to help identify the location of a transmitter-tagged pallet or case of merchandise within a large shipping container, continuously monitor its location until it reaches a store's distribution center, and communicate where that specific pallet is in the facility when it is needed (Corcoran, 2004). RFID is a tool that can also solve the problem of tracking individual items housed within containers in a retail store.

The cost of RFID technology is relatively large initially, but the long-term savings in inventory and logistics costs are significant. RFID tags improve inventory management by allowing manufacturers to enter new goods into inventory efficiently and to readily track the flow of those

Figure 3.6a Containers—large steel boxes approximately the size of railroad cars—are stacked aboard ships for transport of textiles and apparel to customers. Increases in global trade have created demand for larger and faster cargo ships and more efficient loading and unloading methods. *(Courtesy of WWD)*

Figure 3.6b Off-loading containers on a truck for transport to their ultimate destination. For apparel, it is probably a distribution center where garments are inspected and sorted for shipment to individual retail stores. *(Courtesy of WWD)*

goods. A boxful of goods can be entered into inventory all at once, without having to enter each individual item, because an RFID scanner can pick up the signals from all the individual chips within the box simultaneously, something bar code systems cannot do. The chips themselves are very small, and an RFID scanner sends out a radio signal in the store, and each chip on the specific scanned frequency responds by sending out a return signal. With one scan the retailer can take inventory of all those items in the store without locating and hand counting or scanning them individually. The chips can also be used to find desired items within closed boxes so that products that are needed in stock immediately or that have been misplaced can be located and restocked with ease. RFID tags also facilitate self-checking of merchandise as customers leave retail stores. Walmart requires that its top suppliers use RFID tags on their products.

Communication

Technology may have had its most significant impact on the speed and sophistication of communication. Just 100 years ago, telephone and telex lines enabled the exchange of verbal information between continents via cables strung across the land and laid under the oceans. Within the last four decades, introduction of satellite communications, fiber optic cable networks, and the Internet has significantly changed communications systems and expectations. These new modes of communication facilitate the rapid exchange of written and visual forms of information. Initially, these communications were completed by fax, but now much of the process has been usurped by computer applications on the Internet.

Computer Applications

An apparel design can be created in one country, and patterns and samples can be made for that design on the same day in another country. Style analysis may take place through computer transmission of digital photographs of the prototypes on the firm's fit models (who reside in the country where style development takes place); the samples are then modified by the product development team, and new photos are e-mailed back for approval. Today's newest computer design systems provide the capability of completely bypassing the sample revision process by designing and completing the fitting alterations on a three-dimensional avatar model. Styles may be perfected in a matter of hours instead of weeks, without the need to have samples shipped back and forth or for the product development team to travel to distant factories.

Expansion of computer technology related to every aspect of a business has provided an avenue for transparency of real-time communication among members of supply chains, replacing or integrating electronic data interchange (EDI) with the Internet, featuring interactive computer communications. **Transparency of information** within the system is an issue. Information that previously might have been considered proprietary, or private to an individual company, may of necessity become part of open communication among all participants within a system. **Real-time** communication means that changes in design or tracking of products are instantaneously and continuously available to all individuals involved, whether they are in the next room or across several continents.

Interactive communications have been enhanced by development of software packages dedicated to product data management (PDM) and computer-aided design (CAD) processes. Harnessing the full spectrum of these software components into workable and flexible systems available to all sectors involved in a supply chain for individual product lines has been challenging, but these systems are now being realized. Systems combining data and design components have been devised, providing solutions referred to as product lifecycle management (PLM). These PLM solutions have been instrumental in boosting efficiencies throughout the supply chain, from shortening product lifecycle times by at least half to the addition of the management systems (MMS) and markdown optimization solutions (MOS) to manage inventories.

However, until recently many of these software solutions could only communicate with others within their own dedicated software systems; when a supply chain partner used a different system, there could be no online sharing of information. Now, the focus is shifting to utilizing platforms capable of integrating information from a variety of software systems, thus enabling them to more readily communicate with each other. Fully describing these open-architecture computer solutions is beyond the scope of our discussion, but the development of these systems may be credited with shifts in global sourcing patterns for apparel. Professionals in textile and apparel positions throughout the business find they must be computer literate in many of these areas to do their jobs.

New Methods of Producing Apparel

Mass customization of apparel requires integration of information technology, automation, and team-based flexible manufacturing to produce a variety of styles, based on individual customer demand (Lee, Kunz, Fiore, & Campbell, 2002). Mass customization had been tried by firms such as Lands'

End, but is no longer on that company's Web site. Brooks Brothers can produce customized factory-made items, such as men's sports coats from its flagship store in New York City, using a "Digital Tailor," to scan for measurements. The customer then selects fabric from swatches and decides among design details, via samples; finished garments are delivered to the customer's door in less than 3 weeks. Each stage of this form of product development—determining the customer's size, making the pattern, cutting the fabric, assembling the garment, delivering it to the customer—is dependent upon sophisticated computerization.

Flexible production systems, including single-ply cutters and modular systems with stand-up sewing, make it possible to ship finished garments the same day a style goes into production instead of 3 to 6 weeks later, as with traditional bundle systems. Flexible systems make it possible to respond to customer demand for greater variety of styles with more frequent introduction of new styles on the retail sales floor. "Hot" styles can be resupplied faster, in sizes and colors that complement existing inventory. Garments are shipped **floor ready**, that is, with all the labels and tickets required by the retailer and with appropriate hangars or other display devices. Because of application of technology, time can be reduced in nearly every aspect of merchandising, design, production, and distribution to improve profitability and consumer satisfaction simultaneously.

Clemson University's technical laboratory facilities have been working for more than a decade on no-sew production methods for apparel. The goal of building a seam that does not give way from thread breakage and that provides a barrier to air and pathogens, without being bulky or stiff, has been elusive. Today, wearable garments are indeed being made without sewing the seams.

The use of nanotechnology in textiles and garments is a grow-ing area—but surprisingly there is no widely accepted defini-tion of the term that can be used in legislation on its safe use. In preparation for future EU regulations on nanomaterials, the European Commission's Joint Research Centre (JRC) recommends that size should be the only defining property, with particles ranging from 1nm to 100nm.

It also suggests specific properties and attributes (e.g., state of agglomeration, biopersistance, or whether intentionally manufac-tured) may also be relevant, and that the general definition may need to be adapted to the needs of a specific implementation.

The JRC's reference report on "Considerations on a Definition of Nanomaterial for Regulatory Purposes" also recommends that the term "particulate nanomaterial" should be used in legislation.

Nanoparticles have a range of applications in clothing, rang-ing from stain-resistant finishes to the use of nanosilver particles to reduce the formation of bacteria and associated unpleasant odors.

Yet a number of scientists are uneasy about the rush to embrace nanotechnology. Areas of concern include whether nanofibers can pass into human cells, and whether nanoparticles are lost during the use of a garment or during cleaning.

There are also worries about what might happen to nanopar-ticles washed out during cleaning in the sewage treatment plant.

Source:

EU: Takes steps towards defining nanomaterials. (2010). just-style.com. Retrieved July 26, 2010, from http://www.just-style.com/news/takes-steps-towards-defining-nanomaterials_id108196.aspx

Case 3.3 explores the potential use of nanotechnology in textiles. Follow your read-ing with Learning Activity 3.5.

Learning Activity 3.5
TECHNOLOGY DEVELOPMENT

1. At the time Walmart announced that all its suppliers must use RFID tags, they cost nearly $.50 each, but, as of 2010, some were down to $.05, and others were even less. At $.05 each, a pair of socks that sold for $4.00 would carry an RFID tag that cost the supplier $.05. Assuming 50 percent markup, Walmart paid the producer $2.00 for the socks. If the supplier were to make the typi-cal 5 percent profit on the socks, the profit would be $.10. Thus, adding the tag reduces the supplier's profit by 50 percent. How could Walmart expect the supplier to provide such an expensive convenience?

2. Speed is everything in today's textile and apparel world. Make a list of ways that Internet communications can con-tribute to reducing the time required to move new styles through the supply chain.

3. What does transparency of information mean? How can it be both desirable and undesirable in operating a supply chain?

4. What is the contribution of flexible production systems toward success in the global market?

Low-Cost Labor

Even with the advent of computerization to aid in manufacturing, overall the production of textiles and apparel remains labor intensive. In most production industries, technology has been able to replace labor and therefore reduce labor costs. Significant progress has been seen in the mechanization, automation, and, in some cases, "robotization" of textile production, especially in spinning, dyeing, weaving, and knitting processes. However, these technologies tend to be applied to high-volume basic fabrics that do not satisfy the fashion-minded customer. The challenge is to apply the technologies to short production runs of fabrics that vary in fiber content, yarn type, and fabric structure.

The creative and technical design stages of apparel product development have also benefited from the development of software applications to facilitate these creative and technical design processes. However, apparel assembly remains one of the most labor-intensive manufacturing processes in the entire field of consumer products.

Most cut garment pieces must still be hand fed into sewing machines, and hand control must still be maintained throughout all the remaining stages of production. Because of this heavy involvement of hand labor, the goal of most developers of apparel products has been to seek the location of cheapest labor as a means to controlling the overall costs of finished goods production. It has not yet been possible to develop technology that can control the materials handling processes required for sewing and also have those systems be adaptable to production of new styles six to twelve times a year for fashion goods categories.

One of the major by-products of the low-cost labor quest has been the perpetuation of the historical propensity for hiring women to construct apparel products. As the Industrial Revolution progressed, apparel manufacturers sought women who had sewing construction skills because of their experience in sewing at home. The practice of lower wages for women became prevalent in the textile and apparel business, as generations of women entered the job market by way of working in the sewing industry. As the overall income of a nation has risen, some women have typically moved on to more lucrative positions within the economy, and rather than pay more to keep that workforce, manufacturers have usually looked elsewhere for a population of workers who could be trained easily to do the job for low wages. Many newly developing nations have an eager and hungry potential source of employees, especially women seeking any form of acceptable employment that can provide potential improvement in their families' levels of consumption.

The need for apparel firms to keep costs of labor low has produced some rather diverse phenomena. When a firm contracts labor in a newly developing country, the positives may include improvement in the economy and standard of living for part of the population in that country. The downside is that segments of the population may abandon their traditional livelihood and move to urban areas, where employment is available. In addition, because apparel production equipment is easily transportable, when unanticipated problems arise, the apparel employer may move on to a different city or country, leaving unemployment and great hardship in its wake. This causes disruption in that country's economy and the quality of life of its population.

One of the more unwelcome outcomes of the quest for cheap labor occurs when employees are so desperate for any income that they continue to work for lower wages and in unsafe working conditions, even when the economy around them has progressed to a better level. This results in the phenomenon known as **sweatshops**, in which firms take advantage of employees by maintaining substandard working conditions and below-subsistence wages. This issue will be examined more fully in later chapters.

Necessity of Profits

Worldwide, the textile and apparel industry operates primarily in an environment of capitalism. In a capitalistic system, firms are privately owned and operated for a profit. Firms have to make a profit in order to have funds to invest in the growth of the firm. Growth is essential for staying even, because operating expenses increase every year, even if the firm has the same physical plant, investment in materials, and number of employees. Some small level of inflation is regarded as normal, but the result is loss of buying power.

So, if inflation is 3 percent a year, the firm will have to buy 3 percent fewer materials, survive with 3 percent fewer utilities, and do 3 percent less maintenance, and even though employees are paid the same salaries and wages as the previous year, they will acquire 3 percent fewer goods and services. Thus, the firm has to grow to stay even but it can thrive only if it is able to increase revenue faster than the rate of inflation. Of course, another option is to reduce the cost of inputs when the products could continue to be sold at the same price. These are the economic challenges that every textile and apparel firm faces in today's global market. What is the technology–low-cost labor paradox? Communication and logistics technologies have made globalization possible; in the apparel industry, globalization has made it possible for sourcing firms to chase the lowest labor cost available from country to country. Other realities are now creeping in because of rising fuel costs and pressure to shorten the time line from concept to consumer for many product lines. Keep tuned to the Internet for developments.

Now, extend your understanding of labor costs and profits with Learning Activity 3.6.

Learning Activity 3.6

LABOR COSTS AND PROFITS

1. What is a paradox?
2. Do you agree that the development of technology in the presence of the pursuit of low-cost labor is a paradox? Explain.
3. How does the low-cost labor–development of technology paradox affect operation of a supply chain?
4. What are the advantages and disadvantages of mass customization from a consumer's perspective?
5. What are the advantages and disadvantages of mass customization from a manufacturer's/retailer's perspective?
6. What is the source of the pressure to drive down textile and apparel product costs?
7. Why do firms have to make a profit?

TRADE ISSUES IN TEXTILES AND APPAREL

As shown in the supply chain model, the textile and apparel business is driven by consumer response to fashion and technology. When economies grow, consumer well-being usually improves, and the potential to satisfy consumer fashion wants and needs increases, causing growth for business firms within the soft goods industry. Technology not only creates the demand for styling change through rapid communications of fashion ideas, but also provides some of the tools for satisfying product demands through integration of new computerized production processes.

National economies that have been slower to develop have looked to developed nations and adopted some of the practices that enabled the growth of the stronger industries. In many cases, participation in the textile and apparel industry has provided an avenue for economic growth. The relatively low requirements for capital investment to start up production of apparel and the availability of quantities of low-cost labor provide the climate for developing nations to enter the global market. Shifts in the locations of textile and apparel production and the quantity of that production are tracked carefully as indicators of the economic health of individual nations.

Trends in Trade and Production

The World Trade Organization (WTO) is the only global organization that deals with the rules of trade among nations. The WTO's main purpose "is to ensure that trade flows as smoothly, predictably, and freely as possible" (World Trade Organization, 2010). As of July 2008 WTO had 153 member countries and 30 observer governments, for a total of 183 countries addressing macro- and micro-issues of trade. At the center of the multilateral trading system are the WTO's agreements, negotiated and accepted by participating nations. These agreements are essentially contracts for international commerce among member nations. The system began as a series of negotiations, called rounds, held under GATT (General Agreement on Tariffs and Trade). They dealt mostly with quota and tariff reductions and other areas, such as antidumping. The Uruguay Round led to the WTO's creation, in 1995. New rounds of talks began in 2000, in Doha, Qatar, and appear to be ongoing.

The WTO and the **Office of Textiles and Apparel (OTEXA),** in the U.S. Department of Commerce, monitor textile trade throughout the globe, using both quantitative amounts and dollar value to measure and compare production from country to country and from year to year. The Bureau of Industry and Security (BIS), in the Department of Commerce, also monitors the health and competitiveness of the U.S. textile and apparel business.

Throughout this text, measures of trade and levels of production were selected and rigorously edited to facilitate your comprehension of the magnitude of and the business activity within the textile and apparel complex without throwing an overwhelming volume of data at you. Because these figures are constantly changing and may quickly become outdated, readers are encouraged to seek updated information that is readily available on the Internet, on official Web sites. However, it is important to put on your critical thinking hat before interpreting, applying, or reporting the information. Also, be sure you understand the definitions of terms as they are used in the source so that you can use the data appropriately.

The quantity of trade between nations may be measured in number of units or in monetary value. Number of units may be determined by weight, size, or number of pieces or cartons, depending on the product. The number of units of woven fabrics is usually measured in square yards or square meters, whereas narrow fabrics used for trims, such as ribbon, are measured in linear yards or meters. Square yard or square meter measurements are used rather than linear meters or linear yards to measure woven fabrics, because the width of frequently used fabrics can vary from 27-inch silk brocades, to 72-inch polyester suiting, to 144-inch sheeting and drapery fabrics. Number of units of yarns and knit fabrics may be measured by weight, in pounds or kilograms. Findings, such as buttons, are measured in dozens or by the gross, or they may be sold by weight.

Apparel is measured in units (number of garments) and in monetary value. For many years, apparel was measured in **square meter equivalents (SME)** as a condition of the **Multifiber Arrangement (MFA),** an international trade agreement regulating the quantity of textiles and apparel that can be imported into developed countries. The MFA had a system of converting different types of garments into the number of square meters of fabric required. Since the MFA was phased out, in 2005, the United States has incorporated the use of square meter equivalents into all its trade agreements (E. Shibles, personal communication, March 21, 2005). Data may also report total value or number of garments in a shipment, or both. The only time apparel is likely to be measured by weight is for export of used garments from developed countries for sale in newly developing or least developed countries.

Monetary value is often determined by the cost of the product at the point ownership changes; in the case of international trade, ownership usually changes when it is shipped to the buyer. U.S. dollars have different value from Australian dollars and Canadian dollars, and most other countries also have their own currencies. For reporting purposes, international monetary values are usually converted to U.S. dollars via exchange rates. The reader is cautioned to be vigilant in interpreting data, because there has been some movement toward the use of the euro instead of the U.S. dollar as the base currency by some record-keeping agencies.

Penetration of Imports

The interaction between domestic production and imports on actual consumption within developed countries is of increasing concern. Textile and apparel firms in the United States and other developed countries have sought products from other parts of the world for multiple reasons, including securing products at lower costs and providing consumers with an increased array of product choices. However, the sheer volume of apparel products being imported into developed countries is causing grave concerns for some parts of the textile and apparel complex.

The first concern is that importing products rather than producing them means a reduction in **domestic production** when imports increase more rapidly

than domestic consumption. This puts laborers within a nation out of their jobs, leaving them with no income to purchase any product, let alone apparel. Another concern is that if offshore purchasing continues, the resulting negative trade balance will leave us economically vulnerable. An extreme trade deficit creates an environment within a country with the potential for financial disaster, including bankruptcy of domestic firms, unless other avenues for domestic production can be developed to counterbalance the deficit.

Continue the discussion of trends in trade with Learning Activity 3.7.

Learning Activity 3.7
TRENDS IN TRADE

1. How do newly developing countries benefit from starting an apparel industry?
2. How do developed countries benefit from apparel industries in developing countries?
3. What do developed countries give up when apparel firms move to developing countries?
4. Why will square meter equivalents continue to be used to measure apparel trade?
5. If textile and apparel trade is measured in units, what might actually be measured?
6. If trade is measured in value, what is likely to be measured?

Analyzing Production and Import Statistics

Germany, France, the United Kingdom (UK), and The Netherlands felt the effects of low-cost imports as early as the late 1960s. Between 1965 and 1985, employment in textiles and apparel in these countries declined 51 percent, from 4.1 million to 2 million workers. Japan experienced similar declines, and the United States and Italy had declines between 15 and 20 percent (Cline, 1990).

These declines in employment were not entirely due to imports. In Europe and Japan, textile and apparel firms were increasing **productivity** through additional investment in technology. As a result, workers produced more goods each hour of each day. Productivity was increasing faster than markets were expanding. In contrast, U.S. and Italian consumers continued to increase, supporting ongoing growth in output into the 1990s (Cline, 1990). During the late 1980s the United States also initiated quick response business systems to improve customer service to compensate for higher wage rates.

Considering wages relative to productivity, the United States and Italy were found to be the most competitive with developing countries. At that time, Hong Kong, South Korea, and Taiwan were the "big three" textile and apparel exporters. It is normal for developing countries to be less productive per hour of labor than developed countries, given lower levels of literacy, technology, and infrastructure. Thus, developed countries can compete relative to product cost when higher labor rates are compensated by higher production per hour. The other reality is that level of employment is not necessarily an indicator of the overall health of the industry.

U.S. output of textiles and apparel continued to increase as employment decreased until the mid-1990s, although imports were increasing much faster than domestic production. The textile component of the U.S. industry was regarded as more internationally competitive than the apparel component. It was not until the late 1990s that the textile component suffered declines in production, following dramatic declines in apparel production, beginning in 1995.

Table 3.1a shows U.S. apparel production and imports of apparel in millions of garments for 2001 through 2008 (Trends, 2009). The OTEXA government Web site reports these same figures in SMEs rather

Table 3.1a PROFILE OF U.S. APPAREL PRODUCTION AND IMPORTS, IN MILLIONS OF GARMENTS

	Production	Imports
2001	4,518.3	13,448.5
2002	3,706.4	14,486.6
2003	3,085.2	15,905.1
2004	2,282.1	16,769.9
2005	2,083.2	18,313.6
2006	1,653.1	18,827.4
2007	986.9	19,150.7
2008	582.5	18,925.4

Source: Based on *Trends: An annual statistical analysis of the U.S. apparel and footwear industries.* (2009, August). Arlington, VA: American Apparel and Footwear Association.

Table 3.1b VALUE OF U.S. APPAREL EXPORTS AND IMPORTS, IN MILLIONS OF DOLLARS

	Exports	Imports
2001	$ 6,540.4	$ 56,460.4
2002	$ 5,643.1	$ 56,963.0
2003	$ 5,162.9	$ 61,162.1
2004	$ 4,629.7	$ 64,767.7
2005	$ 4,471.2	$ 68,713.3
2006	$ 4,317.0	$ 71,629.8
2007	$ 3,664.9	$ 73,922.6
2008	$ 3,761.7	$ 71,568.4

Source: Based on Office of Textiles and Apparel. (2009). U.S. imports of textiles and apparel. Retrieved October 9, 2009, from http://www.otexa.ita.doc.gov/scripts/tqads1.exe/catpage

than individual garment numbers. Whatever unit measurement is utilized, however, apparel production numbers reflect meaningful declines for all years, especially in 2007 and 2008. At the same time, imports were increasing steadily until the beginning of an economic downturn in 2008.

The value of U.S. apparel exports to the rest of the world decreased from $6,540.4 million, in 2001, to $3,761.7 million, in 2008. What is of great interest is that although the value of exports decreased by almost half, the number of units produced decreased from 4.5 billion units to fewer than .6 billion units, or more than sevenfold. This means the individual items being exported were increasing in value during this time period even though the overall figures reflect a decrease in the total value of apparel products destined for export. Also the figures reflect the precipitous decline in overall U.S. apparel production. During the same time period the total dollar value of imports increased every year, until 2008, when the global economy began experiencing an economic downturn (Table 3.1b).

Let us consider **apparent consumption** (production + imports – exports). First, the total number of units produced and imported during the time period increased each year even though production declined, indicating that the growing import numbers were significant: consumers were buying more garments. Unfortunately, we cannot accurately state the unit apparent consumption figure, because the actual unit amount for exports is not provided. Nor can we truly see how the consumption value progressed, because the data do not include the actual value of production. However, we do know from other sources that during the same time period, overall prices were going down; this can be confirmed by the CPI. As mentioned previously, apparel is one of the best consumer bargains (see Chapter 2).

With apparent consumption, the assumption is that everything that is produced and imported and is not exported is consumed (that is why it is called *apparent* consumption). This is not likely the case. One of the serious problems in the retail community is excess inventory. That is what keeps offprice stores, such as Marshall's and T.J.Maxx, in business. The source of their inventory is **distressed goods** that were not sold on clearance. Sometimes, the merchandise never even left the distribution center of the original retail owner. The amount of retail inventory that goes unsold to customers is not a published number, but it could be as much as 10 to 20 percent. The excess inventory originates in part from foreign sourcing of garments, in which resupplying is not an option. Many retail buyers believe they are financially better off with excess inventory when the product has a low price per unit than with lost sales because of stockouts.

What about apparent import penetration (imports ÷ consumption × 100)? **Import penetration** is the amount of consumption that is provided by imports. Even with the limited available data, we could estimate the total value of production as well as the number of units of exports. From these calculations, we could extrapolate an estimated figure for import penetration, based either on units or value. Although the results would be different, these figures would be similar enough to report with confidence that apparent import penetration of apparel is now more than 95 percent and has been creeping ever higher each year.

So which number best represents the level of import penetration: the number calculated based on units or the number calculated based on value? Both are mathematically acceptable, but they provide different kinds of information. Either could be useful, depending on the situation. In general, if you want to make a case for the successful survival of domestic industry in the face of import competition, the value figures might suit your purpose. If you want the make a case to Congress for import protection, use the unit-based numbers, because those figures emphasize the magnitude of the import problem. Is it unethical to use data in this way? That is another matter. For now, the point is that a data set can tell many stories, and it is up to the reader and the listener to analyze critically what assumptions are being made, what is being said, and what is being omitted or ignored.

Learning Activity 3.8 will help you further your understanding of penetration of imports.

Learning Activity 3.8
PENETRATION OF IMPORTS

1. What are three effects of low-cost imports on developed countries?
2. Why did some countries in Europe experience declines in demand for domestically produced goods 20 years before the United States and Italy did?
3. How is it possible for production to increase while employment decreases?
4. In Tables 3.1a and 3.1b, why is the term *apparent* used in relation to consumption and import penetration?
5. What trends has the textile industry already faced in the 21st century?
6. What trends has the apparel industry already faced in the 21st century?

SUMMARY

The interconnectedness of business activities between nations is reflected not only in the securing of finished products, but also in the conducting of production processes in diverse locations around the world. The Harmonized Commodity Description and Code Systems, generally referred to as Harmonized System

or HS, is a multipurpose international product nomenclature developed by the World Customs Organization (WCO) and used by more than 200 countries. The Harmonized Tariff System (HTS) for the United States, which is an application derived from the overall HS, focuses on identifying specific products for collection of import duties and data related to quantity of imports.

The North American Industry Classification System (NAICS) is an example of systems based on the HS that are used for categorizing manufactured products and industrial production methods. This six-digit system is used for documenting levels of trade and for assembling trade statistics related to production and labor issues. NAICS was developed to support the North American Free Trade Agreement (NAFTA). Global companies mentioned in the discussion of textile and apparel industry categories include American & Efird, Inc.; Cone Mills; Kellwood Company; QST Industries; Cintas Corporation; VF Corporation; HMX (formerly Hartmarx); Polygenex International; Liz Claiborne, Inc.; and YKK.

Technology development has provided dramatic increases in productivity in textiles, improvements in the creative and technical design of apparel, and changes in transportation and logistics. Improvements in communications and information processing have facilitated development of global companies. Despite implementation of agile business systems for apparel manufacturing, low-cost labor is still regarded as an economic necessity for apparel production.

The result of these changes has been decreases in production of textiles and apparel in developed countries and increases in the number of countries involved and in the quantity of goods produced in developing countries. As a proportion of consumption, imports into the United States continue to increase, but the picture varies somewhat, depending on whether units or values are measured.

REFERENCES

American & Efird. (2009–2010). Global locations. Retrieved October 4, 2009, from http://www.amefird.com/contact/global-locations/

Ayling, J. (2009, October 9). Insight: Liz Claiborne inks "next level" deal with JCPenney. just-style.com. Retrieved from http://www.just-style.com/article.aspx?id=105561

Bankruptcy court OKs sale of suitmaker Hartmarx. (2009, June 29). *The Chicago Tribune*. Retrieved May 5, 2010, from http://www.chicagotribune.com/business/chi-fri-hartmarx-0626jun26,0,3235508.story

Cintas. (n.d.). Facts about . . . Cintas. Retrieved October 5, 2009, from http://www.cintas.com/company/news_media/downloads/company_overview.pdf

Cline, W. R. (1990). *The future of world trade in textiles and apparel*. Washington D.C.: Institute of International Economics.

Cohen, M. (2004, March–April). Hosiery 2003: The year in review. *Hosiery News*, 24.

Colbert, C. (2009). Liz Claiborne, Inc. Hoover's Inc. Retrieved from http://premium.hoovers.com/subscribe/co/factsheet.xhtml?ID=ryskkfcffhstyf.

Commercial carpet report: Modular sales breathe life into sluggish market. (2009, June 4). Retrieved from http://www.floorbiz.com/BizNews/NPViewArticle.asp?ArticleID=4541.

Conway, P. (2004, November 10). The impact of negotiated restraints on U.S. trade in textiles. Retrieved June 26, from http://www.unc.edu/pconway/textiles/textile_quota_pdf

Corcoran, C.T. (2004, June 18). Wal-Mart details RFID to top suppliers. *Women's Wear Daily*, 13.

The Great Idea Finder. (2004). Fascinating facts about the invention of the sewing machine by Elias Howe in 1846. Retrieved from http://www.ideafinder.com/history/inventions/story065.htm

INVISTA and Jian-Feng Sign BDO, PTMEG license agreement for RMB 2 billion ($300 million) project. (2010). Retrieved May 13, 2010, from http://www.invista.com/news_releases/2009/pr_090820_PTMEG.shtml

Kadolph, S. J., & Langford, A. L. (2002). *Textiles* (9th ed.). Upper Saddle River, NJ: Prentice Hall.

Kellwood. (2009). About Kellwood. Retrieved October 5, 2009, from http://www.kellwood.com

Kunz, G. I., Albrecht, J., Stout, S., & Horne, L. (1992). Pigskin as a component of the international leather market. *Clothing and Textiles Research Journal*, 10(1), 40–46.

Lee, S., Kunz, G. I., Fiore, A. M., & Campbell, J. R. (2002). Acceptance of mass customization of apparel: Merchandising issues associated with the preference of product, process, and place. *Clothing and Textile Research Journal*, 20(3), 138–146.

Li & Fung. 2003 annual report. Retrieved June 30, 2004, from http://www.lifung.com

NAICS Codes and Titles. (2007). U.S. Census Bureau. Retrieved October 3, 2009, from http://www.census.gov/eos/www/naics/

Office of Textiles and Apparel. (2009). U.S. imports of textiles and apparel. Retrieved October 9, 2009, from http://www.otexa.ita.doc.gov/scripts/tqads1.exe/catpage

QST Industries. Products. Retrieved April 17, 2010, from http://www.qst.com

Red Kap. (2006). About Red Kap and VF Imagewear. Retrieved October 9, 2009, from http://www.redkap.com/page.asp?SID=6&Page=60009

Saba/Koch Consortium to purchase Hoechst's polyester business. (1998, April 22). Retrieved April 29, 2005, from http://www.kochind.com/articles/templates/article_file_template_print.asp? ID540

Speer, J. K. (2004, April 1). A label-conscious world. *Apparel*. Retrieved from http://www.bobbin.com

Textile Hi-Lights. (2004, March). Washington D.C.: American Textile Manufacturers Institute.

Trends: An annual statistical analysis of the U.S. apparel and footwear industries. (2004). Arlington, VA: American Apparel and Footwear Association.

Trends: An annual statistical analysis of the U.S. apparel and footwear industries. (2009, August). Arlington, VA: American Apparel and Footwear Association.

U.S. Bureau of the Census. (2007). North American Industry Classification System. Retrieved May 6, 2010, from http://www.census .gov/eos/www/naics/

U.S. Textile and Apparel Industries: An Industrial Base Assessment. (2003). U.S. Bureau of Industry and Security and U.S. Department of Commerce.

Walzer, E. (2005, January). INVISTA'S vision. *Sporting Goods Business, 38*(12), 14.

World Customs Organization (2010). Retrieved from http://www.wcoomd.org/home_wco_ topics_hsoverviewboxes_hsoverview_ hsharmonizedsystem.htm

WWD list: The weavers. (2003, December 18). *Women's Wear Daily,* 10.

World Trade Organization. (2010). The World Trade Organization . . . in brief. Retrieved from http:// www.wto.org/english/res_e/doload_e/inbr_e.pdf

4 Developing Sustainable Supply Chains

"Sustainability
is our generation's defining issue"
(Mark Parker, CEO, Nike, Inc. [Parker, 2010]).

M ANY CONSUMERS AROUND the world are accepting social and environmental responsibilities, particularly with regard to protecting basic resources and the environment, by recycling waste products made of paper, plastic, and metal. As a result in part of the world recession of the first decade of the 2000s, many consumers are also taking a serious look at economic responsibility for themselves, their families, and their communities. However, many issues that are global in scope are demanding our attention as well, such as unfair treatment of human beings, global warming, diminishing petroleum resources, shortages of water, pollution/contamination of land and water, and many others. Corporations have always paid attention to economic responsibilities, as how they affect their bottom lines, but now corporations are also tuning in to their social and environmental responsibilities and recognizing that economic responsibilities extend beyond their own bottom lines.

Addressing these responsibilities has been described as "two-faced capitalism" and "one of the biggest corporate fads of the 1990s" ("No sweat," 2004). These corporate responsibilities also have been described as "a crucial element of international efforts to foster sustainable and equitable development worldwide" (World Bank Institute, n.d.). **Corporate social, environmental, political, and**

Objectives

- Discuss the concept of supply chain sustainability.

- Examine the application of business ethics and their role in relation to sustainable corporate social, environmental, and economic responsibilities.

- Explore forms of human exploitation and their relationships to textiles and apparel.

- Analyze the role of selected special interest groups, including social activists, labor unions, legislators, and consumers, in enforcement of corporate responsibilities.

American Apparel and Footwear Association (AAFA) a predominant U.S.-based apparel-related trade association in the Americas

code of conduct a statement of principles and standards by which business decisions are made

corporate social, environmental, political, and economic responsibilities the ethical obligation of businesses to value and support the well-being of their employees, customers, and suppliers and the resources, environments, and laws in countries in which they operate; essential for the sustainability of supply chains

economic responsibility the obligations of an individual, group, or general population for assuming responsibility for the value of materials, services, and resources consumed and for using them efficiently, with a minimum of waste

environmental responsibility the obligations of an individual, group, or general population for the physical conditions, circumstances, and related resources influencing the health and comfort of current and future generations

ethics a system or code of morals of a particular person, group, or profession and its application to decisions or particular problems of conduct

fair trade a trading partnership, based on dialogue, transparency and respect, that contributes to sustainable development by supporting trading conditions that secure the rights of marginalized producers and workers (World Fair Trade Organization [WFTO], 2009)

Human Development Index (HDI) an indicator of well-being, incorporating measures of gross domestic product, life expectancy at birth, and adult literacy

human rights the ability to experience dignity, life, liberty, and security

International Textile, Garment, and Leather Workers Federation (ITGLWF) a global association bringing together unions associated with the textile complex

labor exploitation taking advantage of employees because of poverty, gender, age, or opportunity, or a combination of these

labor union an organization that bargains with employers on behalf of workers about terms and conditions of employment; lobbies for the interests of workers

living wage the level of income that covers a family's basic needs, including maintenance of good health

morals the degree of conformity with generally accepted or prescribed standards of goodness or rightness in character or conduct

social activist a person or organization that endorses a doctrine or policy of taking positive, direct action to achieve an end, especially a political or social end

social responsibility the obligations of an individual, group, or general population for its well-being, including fair treatment of human beings, related resources, and the law

sustainability a corporate responsibility strategy that integrates economic, political, environmental, and cultural dimensions to promote cooperation and solidarity among people and generations

Worldwide Responsible Accredited Production (WRAP) an independent nonprofit corporation dedicated to the promotion and certification of lawful, humane, and ethical manufacturing throughout the world

economic responsibilities include the ethical obligation of businesses to value and support the well-being of their employees, customers, and suppliers and the resources, environments, and laws in countries in which they operate.

Codes of conduct are one corporate response that gives attention to these responsibilities in the supply chain and in business decision-making processes. Most of the current corporate codes of conduct, however, still address primarily exploitation of human beings, with little attention to the interaction of social, environmental, and economic corporate responsibilities. As Figure 4.1 suggests, these interactions are essential for creating systems that are bearable, viable, equitable, and, ultimately, sustainable. Now it is time to delve into the complexity of executing corporate responsibilities to create sustainable supply chains.

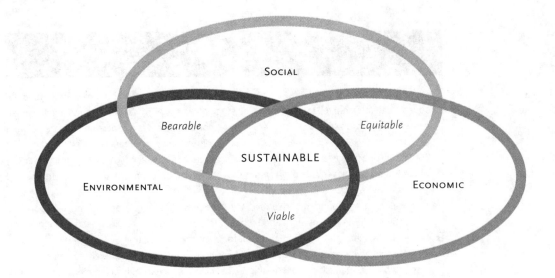

In the Venn diagram:

SOCIAL

Bearable

Equitable

SUSTAINABLE

ENVIRONMENTAL

ECONOMIC

Viable

THE CHALLENGE OF SUSTAINABILITY OF CORPORATE SUPPLY CHAINS

Sustainability is a corporate responsibility strategy that integrates economic, political, environmental, and cultural dimensions to promote cooperation and solidarity among the people and generations in its supply chain. A comprehensive code of conduct is a starting point for supporting sustainability. However, applying a code of conduct consistently throughout the complex supply chains that even small firms now operate in the global market is extremely difficult. Refer back to Figure 1.3, representing the primary components of the global textile complex (see Chapter 1). Even small firms are often involved with individual firms in all five levels of the textile complex, and some levels, especially for large firms, may involve dozens or even hundreds of individual firms. Also, Figure 1.3 does not indicate the dozens of firms outside the textile complex that might be involved in a supply chain. Challenges include multiple languages, cultural traditions, resource availability, and infrastructure limitations facing decision makers pressured to meet quantity and quality deadlines and financial limitations. Dedicating a corporation to addressing these complexities requires strong executive leadership.

Pressure for Corporate Attention to Sustainability

Case 4.1 discusses research that was done by *BusinessWeek* Research Services on corporate sustainability and the use of information analysis to measure outcomes and the success of competitive strategies.

Consumer activist organizations have been primary sources of pressure on corporations to assume more social and environmental responsibility. Case 4.2 looks at the positive response of The Gap Stores, Inc. to pressure from consumer activists regarding working conditions in its factories and the subsequent expansion of its corporate sustainability activities. Follow your reading with Learning Activity 4.1.

Figure 4.1 Model of the fundamental concepts involved in creating sustainable supply chains. To learn more about the challenges of achieving sustainable supply chains in the textile complex, refer to the color photo essay later in this chapter. (*Courtesy Fairchild Books*)

In April 2009, *BusinessWeek* Research Services launched a research program to determine the sources of leadership related to developing sustainable supply chains and improving how businesses make fact-based decisions. More than a hundred business leaders and executives were asked to complete an online survey. This survey found that an organization's ability to meet both its business needs and the larger social and environmental needs of the communities in which it does business was not a top-tier (board of directors) concern at the time but was still a focus of many CEOs and presidents.

Half of the respondents identified the president/CEO as the person most responsible for sustainability initiatives. Half the responding organizations had increased their focus on sustainability, whereas two in five had kept their emphasis the same.

Executives reported a greater demand for both environmental awareness and corporate accountability. Organizations are finding that success is increasingly being measured not only by financial performance, but also by ecological and social accomplishments. The multidimensional sustainability focus on "people, planet, and profit" is motivating firms to find new methods to satisfy multiple types of priorities. "Research suggests that the most forward-thinking enterprises are using analytics to their advantage by applying it to sustainability" ("Emerging Green Intelligence," 2009, p. 3).

Shareholders expect companies to generate profits, but they also want firms to make a contribution to society, while negating environmental impact. However, doing so requires a dual commitment to "analyzing data to achieve goals and challenging the organizational culture to change" ("Emerging Green Intelligence," 2009, p. 3) in addition to "measuring environmental and social outcomes resulting from the nature of an organization's business as well as its management, and competitive strategies ("Emerging Green Intelligence," 2009, p. 4).

Information analysis provides the opportunity to identify opportunities for improvement and to evaluate alternative business scenarios. To do so, information analysis must consistently integrate environmental and social information for sustainability reporting.

Business analytics focuses on extensive use of data and creative analysis to drive business decisions. Half the executives believed that business analytics could have an impact on the area of sustainability. Those who had used analytics had seen improvement in the sustainability-related issues of managing change, sustaining business growth, and risk management.

Nearly all the top companies in the world have a "sustainability officer." Benefits of a sustainability focus include "easier attraction of capital, greater employee productivity and retention of top talent, and increased brand equity. Companies from Wal-Mart to GE are finding that sustainability and profit are definitely not mutually exclusive" ("Emerging Green Intelligence," 2009, p. 5).

Source:

Emerging green intelligence: Business analytics and corporate sustainability. (2009). White paper. *BusinessWeek* Research Services. Retrieved June 15, 2010, from http://hbp.hbr.org/pdf-dep/200810/sas/WP4_Green_Intelligence.pdf

Gap Inc. originated in the 1960s with the simple mission of making it easier to find a pair of jeans. In 2008, Gap Inc. was ranked fifth among global fashion goods retailers, with more than $14.5 billion in sales. The giant retailer contracts with 2 thousand production plants in about 50 countries to supply Gap, Old Navy, Banana Republic, Piperlime, and Athleta brands to 3,100 retail specialty stores located in Canada, France, Ireland, Japan, the United Kingdom, and the United States. Gap Inc. supports 150 thousand employees, a comparable number of factory workers, and millions of customers around the world (Zager, 2009). In addition, Gap Inc. is expanding its international presence with franchise agreements in Asia, Europe, Latin America, and the Middle East.

Gap responded to consumer activists in the mid-1990s by forming a global social responsibility compliance team, creating a vendor code of conduct related to child labor and wage standards, and monitoring suppliers against the code of conduct. To make the code of conduct work, Gap found it had to place people near the factories who knew the language, culture, and local issues. However, negative reports continued to surface over the next decade regarding working conditions in factories contracting to produce Gap merchandise. These reports continued despite formation of an initial inspection system that resulted in refusal to contract with approximately 90 percent of the plants seeking to provide services.

In 2004, an unusual Gap Inc. report conceded that working conditions were far from perfect at many of the factories that made its clothing. The report represented a dramatic change in strategy for a retailer that had long been on the defensive about working conditions at its contractors' factories. In the three years prior to the report, Gap had developed a factory rating system and created a more flexible monitoring plan that devoted the greatest attention to the factories that needed the most oversight. Gap also spent more time on training and on helping factories develop their own compliance programs.

The publication of the report represented a deft strategic move; the 40-page report won praise from some of Gap's most vociferous critics (Merrick, 2004) and became a model for how other major retailers could address social responsibility.

Since then, Gap Inc. has added other dimensions to its corporate sustainability activities. Gap has been recognized by the U.S. Environmental Protection Agency's Climate Leaders program for reducing greenhouse gas emission by 20 percent over 5 years, between 2003 and 2008. The company reduced energy use across its U.S. operations through the installation of energy-efficient lightbulbs at its distribution centers and improved energy performance at its headquarters locations and stores through better management systems and behavior changes. In addition to its energy efficiency efforts, Gap Inc. is participating in several initiatives to demonstrate support for climate and energy policies at the federal and international levels (Press Release, 2009).

Sources:

Company reduces energy use by 20% over 5 years as a part of overall climate action plan. (2009, December 2). Press release. Retrieved on May 4, 2010 from http://www. gap.com/public/Media/Press_Releases/med_pr_ClimateLeaders12022009.shtml\

Merrick, A. (2004, May 12). Gap offers unusual look at factory conditions. *Wall Street Journal*, p. A1. Retrieved May 12, 2004, from http://www.wsj.com

Zager, M. (2009, August 13). Doing well by doing good: Gap Inc's social responsibility program. *Apparel*. Retrieved from http://www.apparelmag.com/ME2/dirmod.asp?sid=&nm=&type=MultiPublishing&mod=PublishingTitles&mid=CD746117C0BB4828857A1831CE707DBE&tier=4&id=83AD30069F4D447092D27E4AED84C87F

1. According to Case 4.1, what are two sources of resistance for moving toward corporate supply chain sustainability?

2. What are two sources of pressure for moving toward corporate supply chain sustainability?

3. In what ways does the concept of sustainability imply changes in the mode of operation for apparel firms?

4. What was unique about the 2004 Gap report that made it a model for other corporations?

5. In what ways has Gap demonstrated the concept of sustainability?

Figure 4.2 Reducing and reusing wastewater at factories can lower costs and environmental impact. (*China Photos/Stringer/Getty Images*)

Implementation of Corporate Supply Chain Sustainability

Social and environmental corporate responsibility involves a wide range of obligations to individuals, groups, or general populations for their well-being, including fair treatment of human beings, related resources, and the law. During the last decade of the 20th century, **social responsibility** became a watchword of business, particularly the apparel business. Reports of unjust labor practices in scenarios of labor-intensive production became common in the daily news. Exploitation was occurring with regard to pay scales below a living wage, sexual harassment, extended work hours, and child labor here and around the world. Exploitation related to assembly of toys and electronic equipment was also reported, but apparel production got the most negative publicity. Some consumers were outraged by the abuses found in the United States and in many other countries, and several nonprofit observer, or reporter, types of organizations were created to combat labor exploitation and other social responsibility–related issues.

Another outcome was the establishment of the *Fair Labor Association (FLA)*, a coalition of companies, universities, and nongovernmental organizations dedicated to improving labor conditions around the world. In 2009, there were 28 brand name companies involved in FLA, including Adidas, Eddie Bauer, H&M, Liz Claiborne, Nordstrom, and Patagonia, plus 180 colleges and universities. These schools require the licensees of their trademarks and logos to participate in the FLA licensee program, which includes implementation of a code of conduct focused primarily on labor exploitation. Case 4.3 is set in 2009, in Honduras, where a combination of social and environmental sustainability organizations challenged Russell Athletic to improve its human rights practices.

Over the past decade, the intense focus on social responsibility in the supply chain has resulted in less attention paid to **environmental responsibility**. However, the environmental issues often pose even tougher ethical challenges than the social issues. Environmental issues include climate change, protecting nature and biodiversity, and resource and waste management. Many of these problems develop over a long timeline, and causes are often camouflaged by acceptance of common practices and multiple sources of contributors (Figure 4.2).

As with social responsibility, environmental responsibility is best tackled through the formation of "joint action" type groups that bring different methods and priorities to the table, for example, apparel or textile firms coming together with common goals; trade associations collaborating with divisions of government; parts of supply chains collaborating to improve the totality of their processes.

A European textile and clothing trade association, Euratex, has been involved in the environmental policy debate for several years, with a number of goals:

- improving the sustainability of supply chains
- insuring a supply of safe textiles and apparel
- integrating environmental strategy into standard operation of government and business
- disseminating environmental information to members
- coordinating actions to safeguard textile and apparel industry interests

For the textile and clothing sector, Euratex identified seven categories of environmental issues: sustainable raw materials, chemical usage, fossil fuel usage, volatile organic compound absorption and emissions, and water usage and waste. The Euratex mission underlines the importance of industry's engaging regulators, policy makers,

Case 4.3 Victory for Workers: Russell Athletic in Honduras

Russell Athletic reached a landmark agreement with the union representing workers of Jerzees de Honduras (JDH). According to the Workers Rights Consortium (WRC), the deal represents one of the most significant advances for workplace rights in the twenty-year history of codes of conduct in the apparel industry.

Among other things, Russell agreed to open a new facility in the area, rehire and provide substantial economic assistance to the former JDH workers, and commit to a position of neutrality with respect to unionization, which will open the door for union representation at all of Fruit of the Loom's Honduran facilities. (Russell Athletic is owned by Fruit of the Loom.)

Fruit of the Loom is Honduras' largest private sector employer. It is a subsidiary of Berkshire Hathaway.

The agreement follows massive efforts by students, unions and labor-rights organizations in Honduras, the U.S., Canada, and Europe. Campaign work of the United Students Against Sweatshops (USAS) resulted in over 90 colleges' and universities' severing or suspending their licensing agreements with Russell. The agreements—some yielding more than $1 million in sales—allowed Russell to put university logos on T-shirts, sweatshirts, and fleeces.

The CCC [Clean Clothes Campaign] collaborated with the union and the Maquila Solidarity Network (MSN) to file a complaint to the Fair Labor Association while Labour Behind the Label (the UK CCC) worked with student campaign group People and Planet to mobilize students to put pressure on Russell.

Certain aspects of these agreements are particularly noteworthy, as they include measures to protect freedom of association that are, to our knowledge, unprecedented in agreements of this type in Central America.

These include (a) union access to, and joint union–management freedom of association trainings in, all of the company's unorganized plants in Honduras; (b) employer neutrality regarding future organizing efforts; and (c) mechanisms for third-party dispute resolution. Importantly, the company also has agreed to phase out existing "solidarista" employee representation systems at its non-union plants to ensure that these do not obstruct workers' exercise of freedom of association.

Source:

Victory for workers: Russell Athletic in Honduras. (2009, November 19). Clean Clothes Campaign. Retrieved from http://www.cleanclothes.org/news/victory-for-workers-russell-athletic-in-honduras

and legislators in supporting its mission. Unlike the United States, China, India, and many other countries, the EU has a battery of legislation that defines and mandates a high level of environmental and consumer safety as well as green production processes ("Meeting the Environmental Challenge," 2009).

Historically, the process of industrialization, as countries develop, has been a source of severe social and environmental harm. Developing countries have suffered through the development process until moderate levels of human well-being are achieved. Now, with thousands of industries operating in the global environment in the presence of consumer activist organizations, attention of big business is becoming focused on corporate responsibilities and sustainability of supply chains. Time and money are now being spent on social and environmental responsibilities that often, to the surprise of some, result in improvement of economic performance.

Now, extend your understanding of corporate supply chain sustainability with Learning Activity 4.2.

Learning Activity 4.2
SOCIAL AND ENVIRONMENTAL
RESPONSIBILITY

1. How would you describe your personal awareness of corporate social and environmental responsibility?
2. Does your understanding focus more on fair treatment of human beings and related resources or on supporting the law? Why do you think you have that perspective?
3. What is the role of college and university membership in the FLA?
4. Are you aware of any social or environmental corporate responsibility–related organizations that are active on your campus? If so, in what aspects of corporate responsibility are they involved in?

5. In paragraph five of Case 4.3, six activist organizations are identified as influential in reaching an agreement that reflects corporate responsibility. Choose three, and find their Web sites by doing an Internet search. Then write a statement for each that reflects the fundamental purpose and the nature of its membership.
6. What aspects of its mission have helped make Eurotex an effective advocate for environmental responsibility?

Corporate Codes of Conduct

Corporations are ethically obligated to value the well-being of their employees, customers, and suppliers as well as the resources and laws in countries in which they operate. One of the ways apparel firms address corporate social and environmental responsibility is through development of codes of conduct for business relationships. A **code of conduct** is a statement of principles and standards by which business decisions are made. In 1996, the U.S. Department of Labor published a report titled "The Apparel Industry and Codes of Conduct: A Solution to the International Child Labor Problem?" The purpose of the report was to satisfy a congressional mandate to examine the status of child labor. The report was based on a voluntary survey of 48 apparel importers and visits to six countries producing garments for the U.S. market. Of the 42 companies that responded to the survey, 36 had established policies prohibiting child labor. The report determined that "codes of conduct can be a positive factor in solving the global child labor problem . . . but codes of conduct are not a panacea" (n.p.).

Box 4.1 is a synthesis of codes of conduct for textile and apparel companies, based on codes used by the FLA and Worldwide Responsible Accredited Production (WRAP). As mentioned previously, the FLA is a coalition of companies, universities, and nongovernmental organizations dedicated to improving labor conditions around the world. In Box 4.1, FLA principles are represented by numbers 2 through 10.

Worldwide Responsible Accredited Production (WRAP), formerly known as Worldwide Responsible Apparel Production, is an independent, nonprofit corporation dedicated to the promotion and certification of lawful, humane, and ethical manufacturing throughout the world. WRAP originated within the American Apparel and Footwear Association (AAFA), but it soon became apparent that it could be more effective if it were independent of the companies it was evaluating. Thus, it eliminated its relationship to AAFA and became an independent company focused on factory operations. WRAP is comprehensive in relation to the concepts of social responsibility, comprising 22 participating organizations from 20 different countries. These organizations are apparel industry associations that have subscribed to WRAP principles and that promote WRAP certification among their members (WRAP, 2009). As seen in Box 4.1 (numbers 1, 11, 12, and 13), WRAP principles extend beyond those of the FLA by addressing more definitively legal issues as well as environmental and safety issues.

WRAP has strategic alliances with two operating partners, Panjiva.com and the textile channel of MFG.com. By leveraging a variety of public and private data sources to collect information needed by supply chain and global production managers, Panjiva became a leading online source of information related to global manufacturers. MFG.com's textile channel is a leading sourcing platform, connecting sourcing managers and merchandisers with sites that have the appropriate expertise and capacity to produce specified types and quantities of apparel, footwear, and home and commercial textiles (http://mfg.com/textiles; panjiva.com).

Box 4.1 CODES OF CONDUCT FOR TEXTILE AND APPAREL FIRMS

1. Compliance with laws and workplace regulations in all places where business is conducted.
2. Prohibition of forced labor—prison, indentured, bonded, or otherwise.
3. Prohibition of child labor under the age of 14, the age interfering with compulsory schooling, or the minimum age established by law, whichever is greater.
4. Prohibition of harassment or abuse or corporal punishment in any form—physical, sexual, psychological, or verbal.
5. Compensation and benefits will pay at least the minimum total compensation required by local law, including all allowances and benefits, or the prevailing industry wage, whichever is higher.
6. Hours of work will comply with hours worked each day, and days worked each week shall not exceed the legal limitations of the country, or 48 hours per week and 12 hours of overtime, whichever is less, with at least 1 day off in each 7-day period.
7. Overtime compensation, in addition to regular compensation, will be paid at the premium rate required by law or at least equal to the regular compensation rate.
8. Prohibition of discrimination in employment, including hiring, salary, benefits, advancement, discipline, termination, and retirement, on the basis of gender, race, religion, age, disability, sexual orientation, nationality, political opinion, or social or ethnic origin.
9. Health and safety will be a priority at work, to prevent accidents and injury, and in housing if it is provided.
10. Freedom of association and collective bargaining will recognize and respect the right of employees to meet and socialize as desired.
11. Environmentally conscious practices will be protected by complying with environmental rules, regulations, and standards applicable to their operations.
12. Customs compliance will support customs laws, particularly regarding illegal transshipment.
13. Safety and security will be assured by maintaining procedures to avoid hazards in and around facilities and to guard against introduction of nonmanifested cargo into outbound shipments—drugs, explosives, biohazards, or contraband.

Sources:

Based on The Fair Labor Association (FLA). (n.d.). Workplace code of conduct. Retrieved December 2, 2009, from http://www.fairlabor.org/about_us_code_conduct_el.html

Worldwide Responsible Accredited Production (WRAP) (n.d.). Retrieved December 12, 2009, from http://www.wrapcompliance.org/ en/wrap-12-principles

WRAP is now the most widely used social and environmental compliance certification program for the apparel industry, with more than 1,700 certified programs in 60 countries (MFG.com/textiles). To become WRAP certified, a five-step process is required that can take several years:

1. Application—the factory submits a completed application form and pays an application fee.
2. Self-Assessment—based on the WRAP Handbook, the factory conducts a 90 day self-assessment and submits it to WRAP.
3. Monitoring—upon approval of the self-assessment, WRAP authorizes factory management to hire an appropriate independent monitor to perform an audit and submit a report to WRAP with a favorable recommendation within six months.
4. Evaluation—the report is evaluated and WRAP notifies the factory that (1) it must correct certain procedures before it can be certified or (2) WRAP recommends to the Certification Board that the factory should be certified.
5. Certification—during the one year certification period, the Certification Board (currently the Board of Directors of WRAP) studies the report, considers the WRAP recommendation and related reports. The Board votes to support certification or to repeat step 4 to improve compliance with WRAP standards (WRAP, 2009).

Fair Trade

The term *fair trade* traditionally was used by WTO, governments, legislators, and industry professionals to describe trade systems and regulations that are less discriminatory in benefits among rich and poor, large and small, and developed and developing countries. However, over the past 35 years fair trade has developed a more specific meaning related to sustainability. To define sustainable fair trade, one must consider who benefits and who is accountable. Fair trade is closely associated with small-scale economic initiatives or partnerships among cultural artisan producers in developing countries with marketers of commercial products in developed countries. The marketers provide education and opportunity to their suppliers that can change peoples' lives and the way they see the world.

Fair trade is supported by many non-profit organizations (each with slightly different definitions of the priorities for fair trade) whose goal is to achieve sustainability through social, environmental, and economic responsibility. In 2009, four of these organizations agreed that "**Fair Trade** is a trading partnership, based on dialogue, transparency and respect, that seeks greater equity in international trade. It contributes to sustainable development for offering better trading conditions to, and securing the rights of, marginalized producers and workers" (World Fair Trade Organization [WTO], 2009).

The organizations contributing to the definition include three umbrella groups to which most fair-trade organizations around the world now belong. *Fair Trade Labeling Organizations International (FLO)* is based in Bonn, Germany. FLO brings together a growing number of fair-trade labels, and, for some time, has been developing closer links with producers. The *International Federation for Alternative Trade (IFAT)* is a global network of 145 fair-trade organizations in 47 countries, many of them producers. It is controlled by its membership. The *World Fair Trade Organization (WFTO)* (formerly known as the Alternative Trading Organization) is the global representative of more than 350 organizations committed to 100 percent fair trade. The WFTO operates in 70 countries, across five regions of the world. FLO, IFAT, and the WFTO have different functions and therefore slightly different standards—not all their members necessarily observe them all, and none of them have direct power over their membership, although peer-group pressure has considerable influence.

"Fair Trade organisations (backed by consumers) are engaged actively in supporting producers, awareness raising and in campaigning for changes in the rules and practice of conventional international trade" (European Fair Trade Association, 2010, n.p.). Two international associations (FLO and WFTO) also agreed in January of 2009 on ten standards of Fair Trade relating to how fair trade business should be carried out. The standards address opportunities for economically disadvantaged producers, transparency and accountability, trading practices, payment of fair prices, child and forced labor, gender equity and freedom of association, working conditions, and the environment. These standards are intended to lead to more consistency of priorities among fair trade organizations in general (WTO, 2009). See Box 4.2. It presents measures of sustainability for fair trade. Then do Learning Activity 4.3 to strengthen your knowledge of corporate codes of conduct and fair trade.

Learning Activity 4.3
CORPORATE CODES OF CONDUCT AND FAIR TRADE

1. What is the fundamental purpose of a corporate code of conduct?
2. Why is there a need for a corporate code of conduct?
3. How do corporate codes of conduct support the concept of sustainability?
4. Describe two different uses for the term *fair trade*.
5. In what ways is fair trade sustainable?
6. Why might fair trade be difficult to sustain?
7. In what ways are the fair trade associations different from WRAP and the FLA?

8. According to the WRAP certification process, it takes years for a factory to become certified. Why might that be a deterrent for factories that want to earn certification? Why might it be appropriate to take that long to determine compliance with code of conduct standards?
9. Why is it important to have measures of sustainability in Box 4.2?

Concepts and Sources of Business Ethics

A business is a commercial enterprise or profession organized and operated for the purpose of making a profit by providing a product or service. Businesses have to make profits to invest in the company's growth and to reward stockholders for their investments. The business must also be able to maintain a payroll that compensates owners and employees for their efforts. Many difficult and sometimes controversial decisions have to be made so that a business can consistently meet its financial obligations. The strength of executive ethics and morals may be tested when attempting to meet all the needs of the firm.

The terms *ethics* and *morals* are often used interchangeably, and they are sometimes used to define each other, but these terms also have multiple definitions. In the business context, and for this text's purposes, the following definitions apply:

- **ethics** is a system or code of morals of a particular person, group, or profession and its application to decisions or particular problems of conduct
- **morals** are the degree of conformity with generally accepted or prescribed standards of goodness or rightness in character or conduct

Historically, moral character of individuals was expected to be shaped by family, religion, and education. However, in today's Western world, two-career families, daily access to television and the Internet, and a more flexible approach to religion have

Box 4.2 MEASURES OF SUSTAINABILITY FOR FAIR TRADE

Human Rights

Fair wages with gender equity—workers are paid at least that country's minimum wage; whenever feasible, workers are paid a living wage.

No child labor—though child labor is a much more complex issue than is sometimes suggested, its use is incompatible with fair trade.

Healthy working conditions—work in clean and safe conditions that sustain physical, psychological, and emotional well-being.

Respect cultural identity—artisans are encouraged to develop and produce products based on cultural traditions adapted for Western markets.

Recognize trade unions—when ownership is vested in others, workers producing for fair trade must have the right to organize and negotiate through free trade unions.

Business Relationships

Fair prices that cover the cost of production—this usually means providing minimum-price guarantees, regardless of world commodity prices.

Financial and technical support for growth—artisans benefit from affordable financing, including prepayments to finance production and technology to support production and marketing.

Long-term relationships—these extend beyond specific contracts to purchase and may involve a much longer-term commitment if mutually agreed conditions are met. This matters to both producers and fair-trade purchases, so that suppliers are available even in the rare boom years when prices are high and the need for fair trade seems less pressing.

Social premiums to improve conditions—fair trade is a different kind of transaction, and in many cases a premium is paid that does not go directly to individual producers, but to their organizations for collective projects.

Democratic, cooperative workplaces—producers must be able to exercise control, by owning the land on which they work, by being organized into cooperative or democratic associations, or in other ways appropriate to particular settings.

Consumer education—promote cross-cultural understanding and help consumers understand the importance of purchasing fairly traded products that support living wages and healthy working conditions.

The Larger Environment

Environmental protection—refrain from reducing future productivity of the environment through degradation or pollution, or destruction of the land, water, and air.

Environmental sustainability—fair trade is becoming increasingly green, in part because prices for greener products (like organic food) are generally better, but primarily because producers themselves prefer it.

Sources:

Based on Fair Trade Federation Principles for the Fair Trade Federation members. (n.d.). Retrieved from http://www.fairtradefederation.org/ht/d/sp/i/8447/pid/8447

Littrell, M.A., & Dickson, M.A. (1999). *Social responsibility in the global market: Fair trade of cultural products.* Thousand Oaks, CA: Sage Publications.

Ransom, D. (2001). *The No-Nonsense guide to fair trade.* Oxford, UK: New International Publications.

Challenges for Achieving Sustainable Supply Chains in the Textile Complex

The Spheres of Sustainability

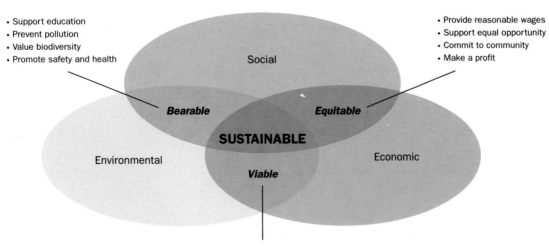

- Support education
- Prevent pollution
- Value biodiversity
- Promote safety and health

Social

- Provide reasonable wages
- Support equal opportunity
- Commit to community
- Make a profit

Bearable

Equitable

SUSTAINABLE

Environmental

Economic

Viable

- Minimize energy consumption
- Preserve natural resources
- Recycle wastes

CP1

CP2. Avery Dennison is a global partner of the Cotton made in Africa project, whose goals are to improve cotton growing through sustainable production, enhance competitiveness, and implement corporate responsibility.

CP3. A field of organic cotton grown using sustainable methods, including no pesticides.

Verantwortlich handeln
A fair deal
Equitable et responsable

www.cottonmadeinafrica.org

Cotton made in Africa

CP2

CP3

CP4. African women working in a field of organic cotton.

CP5. Children's garments made of organic cotton.

CP6. At a commercial textile recycling company, clothing is sorted for the international market. Here, garments are fed into a mutilating machine, which prevents them from being illegally sold as clothing in the destination countries. Used clothing is sold in more than 100 countries.

CP7. Trans-America is one of the largest of about 3 thousand textile recyclers in the United States, processing more than 12 million pounds of postconsumer textiles each year.

CP8. Recycled plastic water and soda bottles.

CP9. National soccer teams from many nations, including Brazil and the United States, wore jerseys made entirely from recycled polyester for the World Cup in 2010. Each jersey is produced from up to eight recycled plastic bottles sourced from Japanese and Taiwanese landfill sites.

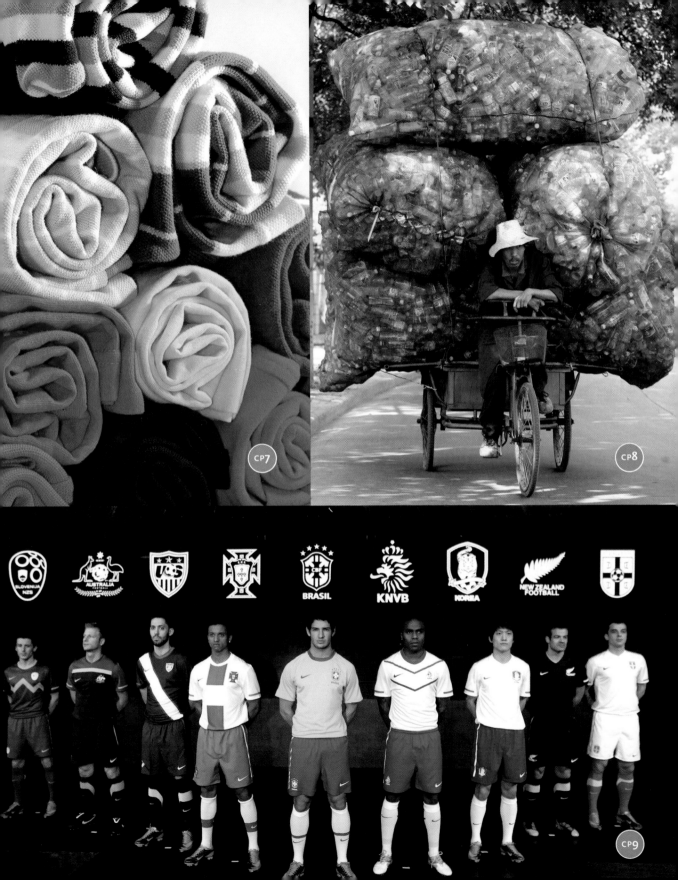

CP7

CP8

CP9

CP10. The retailer Patagonia has been selling fleece clothing made from postconsumer plastic soda bottles since 1993.

CP11. Athletic shoes destined for recycling.

CP12. Playground surfaces made from recycled athletic shoes.

CP13. Shoes made from recycled newspapers.

THIS COULD BE A BASKETBALL COURT.

CLEVER LITTLE BAG ⊕

⊕ WELL IT'S SMARTER THAN AN OLD FASHIONED SHOEBOX BECAUSE IT USES USES 65% LESS PAPER, EVEN BETTER, IT DOESN'T NEED AN EXTRA BAG AND IT CAN BE USED OVER AND OVER. CLEVER HUH? FOLLOW THE PUMA ECO-TABLE. REUSE THIS BAG.

PUMA.COM/ECO-TABLE

CP14. Puma shoes are packaged in boxes made from recycled paper products.

CP14

CP15. Solar panels being installed on the roof of a Kohl's department store in Hillsborough, N.J.

CP15

CP19

CP20

CP21

CP16. Jordan Marsh, an amateur boxer from New York City, trying on boxing gloves at the Modell's Sporting Goods in Times Square. The store received a grant from Consolidated Edison to replace all its lighting with energy-efficient bulbs.

CP17. Wind turbines provide energy for the Bahrain World Trade Center.

CP18. Toxic chemical dyes are frequently used in the textile, printing, and paper industries, badly polluting the water supply in areas where they are used. This example is in China. Fortunately, an inexpensive, recyclable metal oxide cleaning system developed by researchers in the United States and China may significantly reduce this type of pollution of the world's rivers and waterways.

CP19. Dyed clothing produced by textile printers being washed in the Kalingarayan Canal at KAS Nagar, in Erode, India. This clothing is considered a health hazard when added to other textile dyes, tanning effluents, and sewage water flowing into the canal.

CP20. Air pollution caused by emissions from factories and gas- and diesel-powered vehicles.

CP21. The ports of Long Beach and Los Angeles have each launched a Clean Trucks Program estimated to reduce air pollution from harbor trucks by more than 80 percent within 5 years.

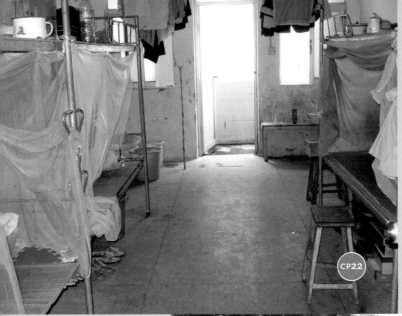

CP22. Dormitory conditions for factory workers in Guangdong Province, Dongguan, China in July 2010.

CP23. Recognized globally as a "green" factory, the MAS apparel assembly plant, in Thurulie, Sri Lanka, built in partnership with Marks & Spencer, provides pleasant working conditions in a sustainable environment, featuring roofs that reflect the sun and huge windows that let natural light in but keep heat out. The plant harvests rainwater, which reduces water consumption by 50 percent, and has an array of solar panels that reduces electricity consumption by 40 percent.

CP24. Workers making lingerie inside the MAS apparel assembly plant.

resulted in the virtual disappearance of the dinner table as a venue for discussion of family problems, including moral and ethical issues. Parents may not be strong ethical role models because of simple things like bragging about speeding or cheating on their taxes, a reflection of a weak code of morals. The presence of television in the majority of homes around the world and cell phones for every member of the family, along with access to the Internet beginning in preschool for many, means children may spend more time interacting with electronic devices than with parents, other adults, and one another.

According to a recent U.S. American Religious Identification Survey, nearly 30 million people responded "none" when asked to identify their religion—more than twice the number of respondents as in 1990 (Will, 2005). At the same time, there are reports of increasing participation in fundamentalist Christian religions. In some parts of the world, religion has a very powerful role in interpreting morality in daily life, especially in the Middle East. What is considered moral in one part of the world may be contrary to moral standards in other parts of the world. Can public beheading be shown to be a crime deterrent in Saudi Arabia? So far, capital punishment in the United States has not proven itself to be. Regardless, the United States continues the practice, with most states using lethal injection, a method of execution considered to cause less discomfort. Does this fact make capital punishment more socially responsible?

Is it the role of education to fill in the gaps in moral and ethical development? Parents may contribute to students' not valuing their educations simply by not taking their children's educations seriously. School systems in several countries—for example, South Korea—commonly send home two to three hours of homework every night, and parents expect to see that it is done. The result of these study behaviors has been a much more rapid advancement in educational outcomes

in some parts of the world, as compared with those of U.S. students, particularly in mathematics. Personal experience (antidotal information from exchange and graduate students we have encountered over the years) suggests that French and Japanese foreign exchange students studying in U.S. public high schools have been appalled at the elementary level of mathematics many children undertake here. This may carry over into other areas of endeavor.

Our education system has not effectively absorbed the challenge of imparting moral development, and we probably could not agree on the approach to the problem if it did. Reports of surveys over the past 10 years reveal that more than half of U.S. students at multiple academic levels admit to cheating to improve grades. The reasons for these statistics are difficult to determine. However, there are a number of contributing factors, including the following:

- proliferation of large survey-type classes in large auditorium-type spaces, where tests are difficult to monitor
- facilitation of improper access to information through high-tech gadgetry
- Internet access to documents that can be easily downloaded and converted into themes and research papers and presented as one's own work

Helen Moore, a professor at the University of Nebraska—Lincoln, suggested, "a consumer mentality among students encourages them to think of education as just another commodity rather than a process that will make them better human beings" ("Proliferation," 2005, p. A6).

So where do ethics come from? As early as 1989, Andrews reported that most education in business ethics occurs in the organizations where people spend their professional lives (Andrews, 1989). Ethics may be a set of standards, but if viewed only in that light, the view is limited. Cooper argued that ethics help professionals become part of a community that is clear about the overall goals

1. Business, as a force and as an impersonal entity behind which we can hide, will compromise any ethical standard if left to its own natural momentum, because there is nothing inherently ethical in a free market, in free enterprise, in the capitalistic system, or in any other system for that matter. Business competition produces and requires the will to win.

2. Ethics is a subset of morality that exists only among people—not among institutions, not among systems, not among organizations. Therefore, the code of ethics must be within every employee. If the people do not behave ethically, neither can the company.

3. A company code of ethics is valuable only to the extent that it reflects the attitudes of top management about the kind of moral judgment required of employees; for example, "be fair, sensitive, honest, trusting, and trustworthy in all our dealings among ourselves, with customers, with vendors, and with the community at large. Obey all laws, in fact and in spirit, and always do the right thing, in every situation, to the best of your abilities. And if we fail, we will do whatever is required to make amends."

4. Companies have broken out codes of ethics, many of which are primarily for public relations, to make sure no one will do what very few would ever be tempted to do anyway, and most of which are loose enough to permit what the situation requires. Therefore, there is no such thing as business ethics; there is only people ethics.

Source:

Based on Business ethics. (n.d.).Retrieved August 10, 2002, from http://www.beam-intl.com/additional_concepts/people_skills/business_ethic.htm

1. Each individual in each situation passes his or her own instant judgment.

2. Businesses devise ethical rules or codes of conduct and provide them to the employees with the expectation that they will abide by them.

3. Trade associations or professions devise codes of conduct for participants to unify ethical efforts.

4. Considering ethical rules or codes of conduct, employees or members determine relative risk or value of optional actions for themselves, for the business, and for the community.

5. Group members interpret options in light of needs of the world community (Cooper, 1982).

Source:

Based on Business ethics. (n.d.). Retrieved August 10, 2002, from http://www.beam-intl.com/additional_concepts/people_skills/business_ethic.htm

toward which it strives. When ethical standards are used to acculturate new members of a business, they can respond effectively to support directions being sought by the organization. Ethics then become an integral part of professionals' decision-making processes, allowing them to deal with not only the facts of the issues but also the values inherent to the issues (as cited in Quilling, 1998).

Making ethical decisions is easy when facts are clear and choices are black and white. More commonly, however, ethical decisions depend on both the decision-making process itself and on the experience, intelligence, and integrity of the decision maker (Andrews, 1989). Ethical decision makers need the following three qualities, which can be developed:

- competence—to recognize ethical issues and to think through the consequences of alternative resolutions
- self-confidence—to seek out different points of view and to decide what the best solution is at a given time and place
- tough-mindedness—to make decisions when all that needs to be known cannot be known and when questions have no established and incontrovertible solutions (Andrews, 1989)

Box 4.3 contains examples of perspectives on sources and applications of business ethics.

Perhaps one of the most frustrating aspects of business ethics is that there is no universal truth. For example, in some countries and in some cultures bribery and kickbacks that are technically illegal are standard practice in processing trade documents. Effective managers know who, what, and how much to pay to facilitate movement of goods. In some developing economies, particularly in countries that are transitioning from a Communist/socialist system to a market economy, essential goods may only be available in the gray or black markets. What are the appropriate ethics in these types of difficult scenarios?

Box 4.4 presents five levels of ethical judgment that may be used to resolve business questions or issues. Each sequential level requires more complex thinking and more interactive decision making. Level 1 of ethical judgment is dependent on the individual's code of ethics or morals, or both, which can vary considerably from one person to another; in a business organization the result can be frustratingly inconsistent regarding the treatment of peers, suppliers, and customers. Level 2 of ethical judgment is consistent with number 3 in the code of conduct presented in Box 4.1, in which general statements are made, but little training or follow-up is used to assure any consistency of application.

In Box 4.4, level 3 of ethical judgment represents a code of conduct imposed on a business from an exterior source, the effectiveness of which will probably depend on the level of executive leadership related to the code. Level 4 involves consideration of rules or codes of conduct in making decisions and the potential outcomes for multiple stakeholders. Level 5 requires consideration beyond the immediate stakeholders.

Ethical judgment at level 5 is required to take decision making to the *sustainability level*. In recent years, fair trade associations have become known as the organizations that are the most focused on sustainability in the global market and that perhaps come the closest to level 5 in ethical judgment. To think through all the relationships to business ethics, do Learning Activity 4.4.

Learning Activity 4.4
CONCEPTS OF BUSINESS ETHICS

1. Consider the code of conduct included in number 3 in Box 4.1. Is that statement of ethics useful in guiding business decision making? Why or why not?
2. In what ways are the fair-trade measures (Box 4.2) easier to use as a code of conduct for business decision making than the general statement in Box 4.3 (number

3)? In what ways might it be more difficult to use as a code of conduct?
3. Focus on numbers 1 and 2 in Box 4.3. Do you believe that business, in itself, has no ethics? Why or why not?
4. Consider number 4 in Box 4.3. Do you believe there are no business ethics and that there are only people ethics? Explain.
5. Considering Box 4.3, why are definitions of ethics and morals so confusing? Why is religion so often a part of a discussion of ethics or morals?
6. What are the primary differences among the five levels of ethical judgment presented in Box 4.4?
7. Choose two of your favorite apparel brands, and look them up on the Internet to see how their company statements of social, environmental, and economic corporate responsibility compare with the examples presented in Boxes 4.1 and 4.2. Are the statements broad and general, like the ones in Box 4.1, or more specific, like those in Box 4.2? What is included in the apparel companies' statements, as compared with Box 4.3? What is left out? How does the statements you found relate to sustainability?

HUMAN RIGHTS

In England, in the late 1600s, a legal statement of human rights, known as a bill of rights, was created as a guarantee of English liberty. During the late 1700s, the U.S. Congress created the first ten amendments to the Constitution, the Bill of Rights, in order to get states to approve the new constitution, which many thought did not clearly guarantee human rights. However, for many U.S. citizens the first written statement of human rights they learn of is the Ten Commandments of the Christian Bible, with its imperatives against (among other things) murder, adultery, stealing, lying, and envy.

In 1948, the United Nations General Assembly adopted a Universal Declaration of Human Rights. It asserts that all people are equal in dignity and have the right to life, liberty, and security. However, because of the multiple political, religious, and cultural perspectives on human rights around the world, no single code of **human rights** exists, and many people are deprived of life, liberty, and security as well as certain social and cultural rights. Sometimes businesses, including those engaged in textiles and apparel, contribute to the abuse of human rights, either knowingly or unknowingly, especially in the form of labor exploitation.

Labor Exploitation

Human exploitation is possible because certain segments of the population are vulnerable, allowing others to take advantage of them. Factors that contribute to vulnerability include poverty, gender, age, and ethnic or racial origin. These same factors contribute to **labor exploitation** in the context of employment.

Poverty

Previously, we defined poverty as lack of enough income and or resources, or both, to satisfy minimum needs; we also defined level of consumption as that which is experienced and a standard of consumption as that which is desired (see Chapter 2). Accurately defining what constitutes a level of poverty is very complex.

As is common, throughout this text we have used GDP per capita as an indicator of resources available. Resources available, in turn, are used as an indicator of well-being and level of industrial development. However, other resources besides GDP also contribute to well-being. For a more complete picture of the presence of poverty, the United Nations Development Programme has devised the **Human**

Development Index (HDI). The HDI incorporates three variables: GDP per capita, life expectancy at birth, and adult literacy. Life expectancy at birth is determined by a number of factors related to well-being, including nutrition and availability and quality of medical care. Adult literacy contributes to the ability to make appropriate and efficient use of whatever resources are available in a particular environment. The HDI includes 177 countries; all the countries active in textiles and apparel that we have examined are included.

The countries listed in Table 4.1 were selected because they are active in the textile and apparel business. Countries within each region are sorted by very high, high, and medium levels of human development and are listed in each category by HDI, from highest to lowest. (The annual Human Development Reports produced by the United Nations Development Programme also include countries ranked as low human development; none of those countries are active in textile and apparel trade and so are not presented here.) The index is created by converting the actual measures of GDP per capita, life expectancy, and adult literacy each to a scale of 0 to 100. The resulting three indices are averaged to create the HDI, as follows:

- very high human development has an index of 0.901 to 0.100
- high human development has an index of 0.801 to 0.900
- medium human development has an index of 0.501 to 0.800
- low human development has an index of 0.001 to 0.500

A ranking of countries based on the HDI Index differs from countries ranked by GDP per capita. For example, when a country has a relatively high GDP per capita because of oil exports but has relatively low life expectancy and literacy, the HDI ranking will be lower than the GDP ranking. If

Table 4.1 Well-Being of Populations of Countries Active in Textiles and Apparel, as Measured by the Human Development Index (HDI) in 2007

Very High Development	
Europe	
Norway	0.971
Ireland	0.965
Netherlands	0.964
Sweden	0.963
France	0.961
Luxembourg	0.960
Switzerland	0.960
Finland	0.959
Austria	0.955
Denmark	0.955
Spain	0.955
Belgium	0.953
Italy	0.951
Germany	0.947
United Kingdom	0.947
Greece	0.942
Slovenia	0.929
Portugal	0.909
Czech Republic	0.903
Malta	0.902
Oceania	
Australia	0.970
New Zealand	0.950
Americas	
Canada	0.966
United States	0.956
Asia	
Japan	0.960
Hong Kong	0.944
Singapore	0.944
Middle East	
Israel	0.935
Cyprus	0.914
United Arab Emirates	0.903

High Development	
Europe	
Estonia	0.883
Poland	0.880
Slovakia	0.880
Hungary	0.879
Croatia	0.871
Lithuania	0.870
Latvia	0.866
Bulgaria	0.840
Romania	0.837
Belarus	0.826
Russian Federation	0.817
Americas	
Chile	0.878
Argentina	0.866
Uruguay	0.865
Costa Rica	0.854
Mexico	0.854
Venezuela	0.844
Brazil	0.813
Colombia	0.807
Peru	0.806
Asia	
Korea	0.837
Republic of Malaysia	0.829

Medium Development	
Europe	
Ukraine	0.796
Asia	
Thailand	0.783
China	0.772
Sri Lanka	0.759
Philippines	0.751
Indonesia	0.734
Vietnam	0.725
India	0.612
Cambodia	0.593
Pakistan	0.572
Bangladesh	0.543
Middle East	
Yemen	0.575
Africa	
Madagascar	0.543
Kenya	0.541
Lesotho	0.514
Nigeria	0.511
Americas	
Haiti	0.532

Source: Based on Human Development Report. (2009). Overcoming barriers: Human mobility and development. Retrieved May 21, 2010, from http://hdr.undp.org/en/media/HDR_2009_EN_Complete.pdf

a country has relatively high literacy and life expectancy but low GDP per capita, the HDI ranking will be higher than the GDP ranking. The point is that there is not a perfect way to measure well-being; there are just different ways, each with its own benefits and limitations.

Compare the countries classified as developed, developing, newly developing, and least developed according to GDP per capita in Table 1.2 with the *very high*, *high*, and *medium* classifications of human development in Table 4.1. You will find several developing countries classified as having high or, in a few cases, even very high human development. This suggests that capable people are not being effectively utilized to contribute to the overall well-being of the country by making larger contributions to GDP.

The desperate search for a better life is implicit to many citizens of countries with all levels of development but particularly those living at low and moderate levels. Both legal and illegal immigration to countries with higher levels of human development are often regarded as a quick way to improve life.

Because apparel production is one of the world's lowest paying jobs, many consumer activists are now demanding that producers, particularly in developing countries, pay garment workers at least a **living wage**—that is, enough money to provide for a family's basic needs, including maintenance of good health. In 2009, activists in 11 European countries launched a series of campaigns calling for retailers to pay a living wage to all garment workers in their supply chains. The activists gave $475 a month as the amount meeting the need for a living wage. They pointed out that a living wage is regularly denied women who produce clothing for international retail chains and thus live in severe poverty (Europe, 2009). This project particularly targeted Asian apparel producers, including China.

Case 4.4 looks at the issue of migration through Mexico in order to reach the U.S. border and the promise of a better life.

Gender

In the United States it is very clear that, regardless of whether employed as executives in global corporations; faculty in schools, colleges, or universities; production floor employees; or janitors and housekeepers, men get paid approximately 20 percent more than women for doing the same jobs. (Thirty years ago men got paid closer to 30 percent more, so perhaps we have moved closer to equality.) Women are also still not rising into executive ranks at the same rate as their male counterparts, although during the economic downturn in 2009, more men lost jobs than women. Perhaps that was because the men at the same rank were paid more than women and thus provided greater savings to the company.

Women are well represented in mid-management, but only about 11 percent of corporate officers are women. Yet, women continue to head their own companies, with women-owned firms representing 38 percent of all companies. Women are most likely to pursue power by producing results or by forming relationships with teams, coworkers, or other business allies. Women are now comfortable with executive power but need to work on being willing to engage in conflict. Men always score higher on tests related to self-confidence. Another thing that holds women back is their extreme humility (Bruzzese, 2005). Even in companies in which the majority of employees are women, like retailing and apparel firms, men filter through the maze to dominate top management.

Lyn Turknett, a specialist in developing women's leadership skills, says women can help firms overcome business-leader scandals, because women score better on integrity and are more ethical leaders.

Mexico's southern border with Guatemala is supposed to be a new frontier in the war against terror. But it is economic migration that causes the problems. Hector, a Honduran in a wheelchair, lost both his legs trying to jump a freight train bound for central Mexico, the first stage of what was meant to be the long journey north to the beckoning opportunities of the United States. Like Hector, many others fall onto the track in the scramble to get any sort of toehold on the daily train. According to Olga Sanchez Martinez, the director of the refuge where Hector lives with 25 other amputees, it is the end of their American dream. Those who survive the train ride have a tough (but free) 2-week journey north.

In 2003, Mexico deported 147,000 illegal immigrants in all, some 20 percent more than in 2002. More than 90 percent came through Mexico's southern border from just three Central American countries (Guatemala, Honduras, and Nicaragua). Immigration continued to increase over the following years. In 2007, Mexico's HDI (Human Development Index) was 0.854, up from 0.802 in 2004. Even though immigrants are unlikely to be aware of HDI, they have some sense of the components that make up the HDI, like life expectancy and adult literacy. These provide the perspective of a better life.

Many of the migrants are heading for the United States; many already have families or friends and promised jobs there, where more than 500 thousand Central Americans are thought to live illegally, and another 900 thousand, legally. One Honduran said he was going to work on a building site at $13 an hour, whereas the minimum wage at home was three dollars a day. "American workers are lazy and smoke dope . . . we work." (Mexico's Immigration Problem, 2004). Roberto, from El Salvador, was preparing for his ninth journey to join his girlfriend in the United States. He says grain trucks offer the best place to hide. Even if he works in jobs illegally and is paid below minimum wage, it is relief from the poverty experienced at home (Mexico's Immigration Problem, 2004).

The underlying problem is common to Mexico's northern border too. Free trade agreements have greatly increased the flow of goods among the Americas. Immigration reform has long been discussed among political leaders, but so far no action has been taken; however, the United States has increased efforts to control illegal immigration. The number of U.S. Border Patrol guards has been doubled to 8,800, new triple fences have been built in some places, and infrared night scopes, underground sensors, and klieg lights have been implemented.

A primary response has been an increase in fees charged by those smuggling people into United States, from about $300 a few years ago, to $1,500, to $2,000. The Mexican government formed a special intelligence unit to target human smuggling. More than 50 organized smuggling bands were identified. The smugglers are also using high technology to assist in moving people across the U.S.–Mexican border illegally. The migrants risk starvation, sexual exploitation, slavery, and death at the hands of their benefactors.

California's estimated population of more than 35.5 million people includes 10 million Mexicans, 70 percent of whom are in the state illegally and 65 percent of whom have less than a high school education. Eastern Europeans, Asians, and Africans are also using the risky route through Mexico. Their goals are jobs in meat packing, construction, agriculture, tourism, and, of course, apparel manufacturing, many of which have been advertised in their native countries.

Many employers report that the migrants are hard workers who take jobs native U.S. citizens do not want. At the same time, small towns like Perry, Iowa, where a meat packing plant is the primary employer, find that 40 percent of children in its schools do not speak English as their primary language.

Sources:

Brown, S. (2003, August 20). Illegal immigration turning California into "Apartheid State," expert warns. Retrieved October 2, 2004, from http://www.cnsnews.com/viewnation

Jordon, M. (2001, May 17). People smuggling now big business in Mexico. *Washington Post Foreign Service*, p. A01. Retrieved from http://www.washingtonpost.com

Mexico's immigration problem. (2004, January 31). *The Economist*, 33–34.

Nationmaster.com. Retrieved December 23, 2009, from http://www.nationmaster.com/statistics

Her research shows that women are often more engaged with the organization, an important characteristic for top executives. "'Women go out into the field more than men, and people (employees) know who they are,' Turknett says. 'They also tend to give more feedback, both positive and negative. And that is helpful for the long-term survival of an organization'" (Bruzzese 2005).

Despite this, most women workers have little likelihood of gaining executive positions. There are many creative ways women are exploited in addition to discrimination relative to salaries or wages and promotion.

Consider Case 4.5.

Child Labor and Forced Labor
Children around the world still mine for gold and diamonds, weave carpets, sew apparel and footwear, pick cotton, and work in leather tanneries. In 2008, the International Labor Organization (ILO) estimated that more than 218 million children between the ages of 5 and 14 were working around the world, 126 million of those in hazardous forms of agriculture labor,

Figure 4.3 A child labor protest in New Delhi, India. (*Saurabh Das/ Associated Press*)

whereas 12 million people are working in some form of forced labor. In addition, although not captured in these statistics, an unknown number of children are working in drug trafficking, prostitution, and pornography (U.S. Department of Labor, 2009).

An in-depth report released by the U.S. Department of Labor (DOL) was prepared to meet one of the requirements of the Trafficking Victims Protection Reauthorization Acts of 2005 and 2008. This report details forms of child labor in 77 countries selected because initial screening showed higher incidence of child labor and forced labor, including agriculture, manufactured goods, and mined or quarried goods. Ultimately, 122 different goods were identified as being produced with forced or child labor, or both, in 58 countries. The most common goods were cotton, sugar cane, tobacco, coffee, rice, and cocoa, in agriculture; bricks, garments, carpets, and footwear, in manufacturing; and gold and coal, in mined or quarried goods (U.S. Department of Labor, 2009).

Countries cited as having child or forced labor for more than ten products include Argentina, Bangladesh, Bolivia, Brazil, China, India, Mexico, and the Philippines. India had the most, with violations 19 different products. Fifteen countries were identified as having child or forced labor in cotton industry, one in silk fabric, four in textiles, five in footwear, six in garments, and three in leather (The Department of Labor, 2009) (Figure 4.3).

U.S. child and forced labor statistics are not documented in the report, because the U.S. was not included in Acts of 2005 and 2008, which this study was designed to satisfy. However, the report noted that the DOL's Wage and Hour Division, which enforces the child labor provisions of the Fair Labor Standards Act, found 4,734 minors illegally employed in 2008. In 41 percent of the cases in which child labor

BEIJING—Wal-Mart's insistence on low prices for customers harms Chinese workers when its suppliers cut corners on health and labor standards to make the bottom line, a labor-rights group charged in a new report issued this week.

In a report that studied five of Wal-Mart's suppliers in China, New York–based China Labor Watch said the world's largest retailer places utmost importance on the cost of its products, which often hurts thousands of workers in China who make those products. Wal-Mart wasn't immediately available for comment due to the Thanksgiving holiday.

However, Reuters reported that Wal-Mart has launched an investigation into the five factories referenced in the report. "We take reports like this very seriously, and we will take prompt remedial action if our investigations confirm any of the alleged findings," Wal-Mart spokesman Richard Coyle said, according to the Reuters report.

In addition to its massive supply chain here, Wal-Mart operates 250 stores in China. "This is not about a single factory, but about Wal-Mart's inability to implement its standards," the group's executive director, Li Qiang, said in a news release that called Wal-Mart's pricing structures "unsustainable." "Wal-Mart leverages its massive product orders to purchase goods at low prices, and workers suffer the financial burden," China Labor Watch's news release said.

China Labor Watch found multiple violations of Chinese labor law in Wal-Mart's supplier factories, including unpaid overtime, with workers in all five factories studied putting in at least three hours of overtime per day to complete holiday orders. Some workers said they had their wages illegally withheld for failing to meet production quotas, the China Labor Watch report said.

"Workers' low wages are further undermined by excessive fines and unpaid days off or maternity leave, and some workers cannot even purchase social security," said China Labor Watch.

The report underscores ongoing concerns about massive supply chains in China. Retailers that conduct sourcing and manufacturing with contracted factories here often face huge hurdles in monitoring contractors for adherence to labor, safety and environmental codes. The workers in question do not work for Wal-Mart, but the company's demand to keep costs low shaves already thin profit margins.

While thousands of factories have been shuttered amid the global financial crisis, the working conditions for those who remain may have worsened amid the downturn. Workers earlier this fall in Dongguan, China's manufacturing hub, told *WWD* that more factory employees throughout the Pearl River Delta are now working without required labor contracts because factories want to save money and pay cash with no benefits.

Wal-Mart earlier this year pledged to hold its suppliers in China to high standards, vowing to end its supplier contracts with factories that did not meet strict codes of compliance on labor and environmental laws. But China Labor Watch said its investigation showed the new promise has not worked.

Such promises, it said, much be backed with financial commitments to improving factory conditions, which might mean higher prices for customers in the end.

"The case of Wal-Mart, the world's largest retailer, shows that corporate codes of conduct and factory auditing alone are not enough to strengthen workers' rights if corporations are unwilling to pay the production costs associated with such codes," the group said in its report.

Source:

McLaughlin, Kathleen E. (2009, November 26). Wal-Mart Suppliers in China Charged with Labor Abuses. *Women's Wear Daily*. Retrieved from http://wwd.com/retail-news/wal-mart-suppliers-in-China-charged-with-labor-abuses-23

violations were cited, children were working in hazardous environments or using prohibited equipment, such as paper balers and dough mixers. Other violations involving workers under 16 years of age included working too many hours and working either too late at night or too early in the morning.

The DOL report notes that there has been an increase in awareness of child labor throughout the world and that commitment to eliminating its worst forms appears to be gaining momentum. However, there are many barriers to implementation, the primary ones being poverty, lack of financial government resources, and government corruption. Governments are also reluctant to enforce laws when large numbers of a population are desperate for any source of income (U.S. Department of Labor, 2009).

Most countries have laws with a minimum work age of no less than 14. However, in many countries the laws are not enforced; in addition, when people are poor and unemployed, they will often misrepresent their age. Sometimes children are the only ones available to work and are a family's only source of income. U.S. citizens are frequently and rightly accused of inappropriately applying our standards to scenarios in which they are not appropriate. Figure 4.4 gives the minimum wage provisions required to be posted by every employer under the U.S. Fair Labor Standards Act.

How many of you worked as teenagers? How many of you worked in situations in which you had little training and unsafe conditions? Note the section in the poster under "Child Labor." How many of you worked hours that violated those standards? It is easy for us to point the finger at other cultures and other countries that seemingly exploit children and, of course, sometimes they do, but so do we; what are our standards, and what are our justifications for our violations of child labor laws?

Think through Case 4.6. It addresses the scenario you may have faced if you were a teenager growing up in Bangkok.

The activities illustrated in Case 4.6 describe abuses of human rights common to poverty-stricken people. The same people may be victims of labor exploitation in the production of apparel and other consumer goods. Some firms have codes of conduct to protect human rights, but many believe they have not been effective. Wolfe and Dickson (2002) examined codes of conduct in use in 2002 and concluded that they have largely a legal rather than ethical focus. Recommendations on how to make codes of conduct more effective included the following:

1. Apparel manufacturers and retailers should have a code of conduct that clearly states the values and goals of their businesses.

2. The code of conduct must come from the leaders of the organization and be integrated throughout the corporate culture.

3. The code of conduct should be clearly communicated to all employees and constituents.

4. An industry-wide code of conduct should be developed to lessen confusion with suppliers and allow small businesses the opportunity to adopt a code of conduct with minimal expense (Wolfe & Dickson, 2002).

Creating and implementing workable codes of conduct is clearly no small task. If it were, labor exploitation might have been resolved decades ago. However, a lot of progress has been made since 2002, and for many firms a code of conduct is being viewed as more than an effort to protect the firm's image.

Now, continue your study of human rights by doing Learning Activity 4.5.

EMPLOYEE RIGHTS
UNDER THE FAIR LABOR STANDARDS ACT
THE UNITED STATES DEPARTMENT OF LABOR WAGE AND HOUR DIVISION

FEDERAL MINIMUM WAGE
$7.25 PER HOUR
BEGINNING JULY 24, 2009

OVERTIME PAY — At least 1½ times your regular rate of pay for all hours worked over 40 in a workweek.

CHILD LABOR — An employee must be at least **16** years old to work in most non-farm jobs and at least **18** to work in non-farm jobs declared hazardous by the Secretary of Labor.

Youths **14** and **15** years old may work outside school hours in various non-manufacturing, non-mining, non-hazardous jobs under the following conditions:

No more than
- **3** hours on a school day or **18** hours in a school week;
- **8** hours on a non-school day or **40** hours in a non-school week.

Also, work may not begin before **7 a.m.** or end after **7 p.m.**, except from June 1 through Labor Day, when evening hours are extended to **9 p.m.** Different rules apply in agricultural employment.

TIP CREDIT — Employers of "tipped employees" must pay a cash wage of at least $2.13 per hour if they claim a tip credit against their minimum wage obligation. If an employee's tips combined with the employer's cash wage of at least $2.13 per hour do not equal the minimum hourly wage, the employer must make up the difference. Certain other conditions must also be met.

ENFORCEMENT — The Department of Labor may recover back wages either administratively or through court action, for the employees that have been underpaid in violation of the law. Violations may result in civil or criminal action.

Employers may be assessed civil money penalties of up to $1,100 for each willful or repeated violation of the minimum wage or overtime pay provisions of the law and up to $11,000 for each employee who is the subject of a violation of the Act's child labor provisions. In addition, a civil money penalty of up to $50,000 may be assessed for each child labor violation that causes the death or serious injury of any minor employee, and such assessments may be doubled, up to $100,000, when the violations are determined to be willful or repeated. The law also prohibits discriminating against or discharging workers who file a complaint or participate in any proceeding under the Act.

ADDITIONAL INFORMATION
- Certain occupations and establishments are exempt from the minimum wage and/or overtime pay provisions.
- Special provisions apply to workers in American Samoa and the Commonwealth of the Northern Mariana Islands.
- Some state laws provide greater employee protections; employers must comply with both.
- The law requires employers to display this poster where employees can readily see it.
- Employees under 20 years of age may be paid $4.25 per hour during their first 90 consecutive calendar days of employment with an employer.
- Certain full-time students, student learners, apprentices, and workers with disabilities may be paid less than the minimum wage under special certificates issued by the Department of Labor.

For additional information:
1-866-4-USWAGE WHD
(1-866-487-9243)   TTY: 1-877-889-5627   U.S. Wage and Hour Division
WWW.WAGEHOUR.DOL.GOV

U.S. Department of Labor | Wage and Hour Division

Figure 4.4 Your rights are required to be posted at your place of employment, under the U.S. Fair Labor Standards Act. Have your rights been violated?
(© *US Dept. of Labor*)

At midnight on July 13, I was sipping a bottle of water in a back-alley strip club in the red-light district of Bangkok. My ears were ringing from the booming music, and my stomach was turning. I'd just watched a stripper pull from her vagina a thin, 4-foot chain with small swords attached. Just as the bar owner was holding out the length of spiked jewelry for the crowd to examine, two police officers entered the bar.

The stripper jumped off stage and ran to the back room. Another dancer, wearing a swimsuit, immediately replaced her on stage.

Dancing naked is illegal in Bangkok.

The group of editorial writers I was with moved on to another bar. It was there a writer from Minneapolis, for the sake of curiosity, negotiated the purchase of a boy for 500 Baht or 12 U.S. dollars. Had the deal been completed, it would have included "quick sex" without a condom. The boy looked about 13 years old and stood on a stage along with other young boys. All wore only white underwear with a number pinned on the hip.

Boys for sale at night in Bangkok. Young women risking their health. Our group knew it was important to see what really goes on in the city, but it was a stark contrast to how I spent my days there.

I was in Thailand to attend the XV International AIDS Conference. More than 15,000 people came from all over the world to work toward fighting the AIDS crisis that has hit Africa and Asia particularly hard. Activists, drug companies, scientists, HIV-positive people, journalists and diplomats all gathered to share information, learn and further agendas. Kofi Annan, former head of the United Nations, spoke, as did former leader of South Africa Nelson Mandela.

The conference was sophisticated.

The back alleys of Bangkok were raw.

The juxtaposition of two completely different worlds in one city told the real story about fighting AIDS: It takes science and money and health-care infrastructure. But it also takes cultural shifts, personal responsibility and the eradication of poverty.

Many sex workers in Bangkok are driven to the industry by poverty. Rampant poverty. Outside my luxurious hotel, where the bed was turned down every night, the water was clean and fresh roses adorned the room, a man with no legs dragged himself along the street with a cup in his hand.

Mostly he was ignored. By the end of the week, even I barely noticed him, because he was one of so many street people. Mothers with babies lived on corners. Toddlers wandered alone with their begging cups. So many people were missing hands. And teeth. And dignity.

Poverty in Thailand is so obvious, yet the country has been hailed as a model in the war against HIV. In the 1980s, after prostitutes were found to be testing HIV-positive, the government launched an educational campaign. Condom use increased, and the schools taught kids about the dangers of unprotected sex.

But as is frequently the case, human beings grew complacent. When the editorial writer negotiating for the boy said she didn't want a condom to be used, the bar owner replied, "No problem." Yet it is a problem. In Thailand, condom use has been falling, and HIV-infection rates are rising again with new infections largely due to the sex-worker industry. Men visit prostitutes and bring the disease home to their wives.

It's disheartening. It's dangerous.

There are 40 million adults and children living with HIV/AIDS. Of the 14,000 new infections that occur each day, about 2,000 are in children. The disease ravages countries, leaving millions of orphans in its path. Schools close when no teachers are left to instruct children in African villages. A country's economy is hurt when workers are sick. The global economy is threatened. Nations are left weak and vulnerable to become potential breeding grounds for terrorism.

That's why the conference in Bangkok, with a theme of "Access for All," was important. When people in the world are dying, the people of the world should care. They should take action.

The conference was part of that action. I learned about the science of vaccines, substances called microbicides that show promise in preventing the transmission of HIV.

I learned about drugs that reduce the transmission of HIV from a mother to a baby. There were seminars on educational campaigns, funding mechanisms for AIDS programs and debates about how countries are dedicating resources. Protests, drug-company pitches and activists were everywhere.

But my mind kept wandering back to the beggars. The swords on the chain. The boy for sale. The tag pinned to his underwear.

What can the world do to get him off stage?

Buying a boy for sex in Bangkok isn't just about AIDS funding. It's also about eradicating poverty, providing education, giving the youth of the world opportunities for a better future. It means creating a world where teens are never forced to sell themselves so they can feed themselves.

What is HIV?

HIV stands for human immunodeficiency virus, the virus that causes AIDS.

HIV destroys blood cells crucial to normal function of the immune system. It cannot be transmitted through casual contact or mosquitoes. It can be transmitted in blood, breast milk and by having unprotected sex with someone who has the virus.

20 million people have died from AIDS.

40 million people are living with HIV/AIDS.

14,000 new infections occur each day.

Nearly half of those infections occur among women.

15 million children have lost at least one parent to AIDS.

Less than 1 in 12 of those infected in developing countries receive drug therapy.

Source:

Dominick, A. (2004, August 1). Aids for sale—cheap. *The Des Moines Register*, pp. 10P, 50P. Copyright 2004, printed with permission by *The Des Moines Register*.

Learning Activity 4.5
HUMAN RIGHTS

1. Where do human rights come from?
2. Why do some people have more human rights than others?
3. Why does poverty lead to labor exploitation?
4. According to the Human Development Index (HDI), Mexico is ranked within the group of nations with a high level of human development. Why then is immigration to the United States still such a persistent problem?
5. Children on family farms in the United States still do chores, feed livestock, and work the fields. Farm children are not protected by the minimum working age of 14. Farming is rated as being one of the more dangerous occupations in the United States. Why do you think farm children continue to be excluded from the minimum age labor law? Should they continue to be excluded?
6. Considering Case 4.6, how can conditions like these exist in the modern world?

HUMAN RIGHTS ORGANIZATIONS

Human rights abuses have led to the creation of organizations that defend human rights. We are focusing here on two types: labor and trade unions and social and environmental activists.

Labor Unions

A union (*labor union* in American English; *trade union* in British English; either *labour union* or *trade union* in Canadian English) is a group of workers who act collectively to address common issues. More specifically, a **labor union** is an association of workers with the purpose, in whole or in part, of bargaining with employers on behalf of workers about terms and conditions of employment. Unions may have legal rights to negotiate with management over wages, overtime, holiday pay, timing and length of working hours, health and retirement benefits, and safety- and security-related issues, depending on laws in individual countries. Collectively, workers can threaten to strike to get the attention of employers and force them to negotiate.

Unions have three levels of organization: local, national or international, and federation. A local union represents a certain group of workers in selected occupations in a city or a county. Locals serving the same crafts or industries join together to form national or international unions. The nationals and internationals usually control their locals and supervise the union's most important job—collective bargaining. The American Federation of Labor and Congress of Industrial Organizations (AFL-CIO) is an association of national and international unions. Federations usually have at least five jobs, listed as follows:

*   work for laws favorable to general welfare
*   organize workers who are not in unions
*   settle disputes and encourage friendly relations among member unions
*   take part in the world labor movement
*   help educate members and the general public on the goals of organized labor

Power and autonomy of unions vary greatly among countries. For the most part, in North America and western Europe, unions are organized democratically, with elected officials. In other countries—China and Cuba, for example—unions may be run by the government. The members of a union might include teachers, assembly workers, construction workers, firefighters, accountants, and almost any other group, including textile and apparel workers.

Textile and Apparel Labor/Trade Unions

As shown in Table 4.2, U.S. textile and apparel labor unions have evolved through at least four phases since their start in the 1880s, during the Industrial Revolution. The influx

Table 4.2 Evolution of Textile and Apparel Labor Unions in the Americas, Reported from the Unions' Perspectives

Organizational Phase

1880	Millions of mostly Italian and Jewish immigrants provide cheap labor for garment "sweatshops" in major cities where workers toiled long hours under inhuman conditions for meager wages.
1900	International Ladies Garment Workers' Union (ILGWU) founded in New York City.
1909	A winning strike of 20,000 New York shirtwaist workers, mostly teenage girls, brought 312 shops under contract and established the growing power of ILGWU.
1911	A fire at the Triangle Shirtwaist Factory in New York City killed 146 workers, leading to the first workplace health and safety laws.
1914	Men's clothing workers form the Amalgamated Clothing Workers of America (ACWA).
1917	Five thousand men's clothing workers established ACWA in Montreal.

Growth Phase

1923	ACWA ratified unemployment insurance plan for Chicago clothing workers and established the Amalgamated Bank of New York funded by ACWA to offer free checking to working people.
1937	Five thousand Montreal dressmakers went on strike to demand 44-hour workweek, wage increases, and ILGWU recognition establishing the largest local in Canada.
1939	Southern textile workers founded the Textile Workers Union of America (TWUA).
1941	ACWA begins employer-paid health and life insurance.
1953	Over 3 years, the ILGWU won a 35-hour workweek in contracts covering 97 percent of its members.
1958	One hundred thousand striking ILGWU members in 8 states won requiring use of the union label.

Mergers Begin

1965	The American Federation of Hosiery Workers merged with TWUA.
1968	ACWA opened the first labor-sponsored day care center.
1974	Canadian ACWA won wage increases, a fourth week of paid vacation, a pension increase, bereavement pay, and other benefits.
1975	Americans first see commercial "Look for the Union Label"; ILGWU educates consumers about the export of American jobs.
1976	ACWA and TWUA merge and create the Amalgamated Clothing and Textiles Workers Union (ACTWU).
1979	Sally Field wins an Oscar for her title role in *Norma Rae*, a movie depicting the ACTWU JP Stevens organizing drive.
1979	The United Shoe Workers merge with ACTWU.

Focus Turns to Recent Immigrants and Exporting Countries

1986	ILGWU established a nationwide Immigration Project to legalize union members eligible for amnesty from Caribbean Basin, South America, and East Asia.
1990	ILGWU launched an innovative community-based effort aimed at organizing emigrant workers in sweatshops.
1992	ACTWU exposed the use of U.S. taxpayers' dollars promoting Free Trade Zones in foreign countries.
1993	ILGWU and ACTWU collaborate on the first union contracts for workers in the Free Trade Zones of the Dominican Republic and other workers in the Third World.
1993	ACTWU negotiated a Code of Conduct with the Clothing Manufacturers' Association requiring employers to respect international workers rights.
1995	Union of Needletrades, Industrial, and Textile Employees (UNITE!) formed from merger of ILGWU and ACTWU.

Table 4.2 (CONTINUED)

	Social Activism Phase
1996	Revelations that Kathie Lee Gifford's clothing line was being made in sweatshops in New York and Central America brings labor exploitation into the national spotlight.
1998	College students, many who did summer internships with UNITE!, founded United Students Against Sweatshops to push their universities to take responsibility for working conditions for people around the world who make $ 2.5 billion of college-logo apparel each year.
2002	UNITE! formed partnership with NAACP and the Sierra Club to further civil and workers' rights and bring the environmental and labor movements together.
2004	UNITE! merged with HERE (Hotel Employees and Restaurant Employees International Union that had already joined with the Laundry and Dry Cleaning International Union) to form UNITE HERE!
2009	Apparel workers left UNITE HERE! to form Workers United Union of US and Canada.

Source: Based on UNITEHERE! (n.d.). Our history. Retrieved November 15, 2009, from http://www.unitehere.org/about/history.asp

of immigrants seeking jobs in the industrializing northeastern United States created a huge, low-cost labor force. Demand for ready-to-wear apparel exploded, and textile mills and sewing factories responded.

The first phase of union development was an *organizational phase* that lasted approximately from 1880 to 1920. Locals soon learned that they had more power if they joined together to influence employers. The International Ladies' Garment Workers Union (ILGWU) was organized first, followed by, for menswear, the Amalgamated Clothing Workers of America (ACWA), which also established locals in Canada. U.S. labor unions, especially the ILGWU (formed in 1900) and the Amalgated Clothing and Textile Union (ACTWU), were credited with upgrading the sweatshop conditions of weavers and garment workers during the early 1900s.

The *growth phase*, from 1920 to 1960, was dependent on effective collective bargaining for improved working conditions as well as wages and benefits. An unemployment insurance program was established, and the first employer-paid health and life insurance policies were initiated. First working hours were reduced to 44 hours in Montreal; then, late in the period, the ILGWU won a 35-hour work week. In addition, the Textile Workers Union of America was established. Recognition of the need to promote union services was implemented in the form union labels sewn into garments. Membership in ILGWU topped out in the late 1940s, with nearly 500 thousand members. Beginning in the 1950s, large numbers of apparel manufacturing firms moved away from urban areas in the northeastern United States, and the grip of unions on apparel factories was broken.

The third phase of union development, *mergers begin*, from 1960 to 1980, which involved continued improvement of working conditions and added benefits, including day care, retirement, and bereavement pay. Unions continued to raise public awareness of the importance of their existence, using paid television commercials telling viewers to "Look for the Union Label." The film *Norma Rae* increased the knowledge of the general population about working conditions in textile and apparel factories. However, union membership declined, and the power of unions began to decrease, because manufacturers began exporting production jobs for lower labor costs, while immigrants flooded the U.S. labor market, taking jobs in nonunion shops. Unions responded by mergers with other unions serving similar audiences. Hosiery workers, menswear workers, and shoe workers merged with textile workers to form Amalgamated Clothing and Textiles Workers Union (ACTWU).

When the fourth phase began, from 1980 to 1995, *attention turned to immigrants*. By then, because of mergers there were only two primary textile and apparel unions: the ILGWU and the ACTWU. The ILGWU was first to recognize that its future was tied to supporting and organizing immigrant labor. The ILGWU's first effort was the legalization of illegal immigrants who had become union members, while the ACTWU politicized the federal government's practice of subsidizing free trade zones in developing countries. Both unions responded by organizing workers in developing countries and by establishing codes of conduct to protect worker rights. However, union membership declined until, in 1995, the ILGWU, with 125 thousand members, and the ACTWU, with 175 thousand members, merged to form UNITE! UNITE! adopted a social activist perspective to provide workers with numerous services available to all, regardless of union membership. A **social activist** is a person or organization that endorses a doctrine or policy of taking positive, direct action to achieve an end, especially a political or social end.

The fifth phase (which carries into the present), *social and environmental activism phase*, joined UNITE! with members of the public who were active in the movement to eliminate labor abuse in factory situations as well as waste of resources. Mergers continued, including broader-based social activist organizations that included both labor and environment. In 2004, after rapid decline in apparel production in the United States, UNITE! merged with HERE (Hotel Employees & Restaurant Employees), whose members were also both legal and illegal immigrants, to form UNITE HERE! However, the UNITE HERE! merger did not work out, and in 2009 garment workers split from UNITE HERE! to form **Workers United Union**. It is unclear at the time of this writing how stable the new union will be.

However, it is very clear how active unionization is around the world in textiles and apparel as well as in nearly every other industry sector. By 2009, there were ten global union federations representing different industry sectors, including one for textiles and apparel, the **International Textile, Garment, and Leather Workers' Federation (ITGLWF)**, which represents 217 affiliated organizations in 110 countries. Textile and apparel unions have evolved from being locally based, to nationally and internationally based, to a federation of unions in a global context. Apply your enhanced understanding of labor unions by completing Learning Activity 4.6.

Learning Activity 4.6
THE ROLES OF LABOR UNIONS

1. Do you think of a labor union as a human rights organization? Explain.
2. Give three reasons why many textile and apparel companies might prefer to operate nonunion shops.
3. Why have unions experienced multiple mergers at the same time that textile and apparel firms are also merging?
4. Why was it to the advantage of the labor unions to join with the social activists during the 1990s?

SUMMARY

Business ethics are human ethics, because human beings make business decisions. Ultimately, if business ethics are to improve, human ethics must improve. Corporate social and environmental responsibility is dependent on business ethics and the influence of activists to force businesses to act in a socially responsible manner. Human exploitation occurs because certain segments of the population are vulnerable, while others are ready and able to take advantage of them. Sustainability incorporates multiple forms of corporate responsibility to assure the future of the human race.

Three primary factors that contribute to making people vulnerable to exploitation are poverty, gender, and age. Women and children are the elements of the labor force most frequently abused. As is common, throughout this text GDP per capita has been used as a measure of well-being. The World Bank has defined poverty as a level of income of less than two dollars per day per person, but it also measures poverty using the Human Development Index (HDI). HDI considers not only GDP per capita but also adult literacy and life expectancy at birth. The countries actively engaged in the textile and apparel business now rank in the very high, high, and moderate categories of HDI. Thus, HDI presents a different perspective on overall well-being than GDP.

Labor and trade unions have long sought to empower workers with the ability to protect themselves against labor exploitation through collective bargaining. In recent years, unions have joined with social and environmental activist organizations to pressure businesses into responsible labor and resource management. Trade associations, such as AAFA, have also joined in to promote the sustainable activities of their business members.

REFERENCES

American Apparel and Footwear Association. (2005). Excellence in social responsibility award 2006. News release.

Andrews, R.N.L. (1989, February 10). Climate and human values. Paper presented at the University of North Carolina at Chapel Hill Humanities Weekend.

Apparel industry and codes of conduct: A solution to the international child labor problem? (1996). U.S. Department of Labor.

Brown, S. (2003, August 20). Illegal immigration turning California into "Apartheid State," expert warns. Retrieved October 4, 2004, from http://www.cnsnews.com/viewnation

Bruzzese, A. (2005). Parenting skills spill over into the workplace. Retrieved April 18, 2006, from http://www.thejournalnews.gannettoline.com

Business ethics. (n.d.). Retrieved August 10, 2002, from http://www.beam-intl.com/additional_concepts/people_skills/business_ethic.htm

Callimachi, R. (2005, April 14). Nike discloses location to all its factories. *The Des Moines Register*, p. 3D.

Campaigners against clothing sweatshops go to the Olympics. (2004, August 19). *The Economist*. Retrieved from http://www.economist.com

Company reduces energy use by 20% over 5 years as a part of overall climate action plan. (2009, December 2). Press release. Retrieved from http://www.gap.com

Dominick, A. (2004, August 1). Aids for sale—cheap. *The Des Moines Register*, pp. 10P, 50P.

Ellis, K. (2003, June 3). DOL report: Child labor still abounds. *Women's Wear Daily*, 2, 4.

Europe: Garment retailers urged to pay Asian living wage. (2009, October 5). Retrieved October 10, 2009, from http://www.just-style.com

European Fair Trade Association. (n.d.). What is fair trade? Retrieved on May 21, 2010, from http://european-fair-trade-association.org/obervatory/index.php/fairtrade

Emerging green intelligence: Business analytics and corporate sustainability. (2009). White paper. *BusinessWeek* Research Services. Retrieved June 15, 2010, from http://hbp.hbr.org/pdf-dep/200810/sas/WP4_Green_Intelligence.pdf

The Fair Labor Association (n.d.). Workplace code of conduct. Retrieved December 2, 2009, from http://www.fairlabor.org/about_us_code_conduct_el.html

Fair Trade Federation. Principles for the Fair Trade Federation members (n.d.). Retrieved from http://www.fairtradefederation.org/ht/d/sp/i/8447/pid/8447

Human Development Report. (2009). Overcoming barriers: Human mobility and development. Retrieved May 21, 2010, from http://hdr.undp.org/en/media/HDR_2009_EN_Complete.pdf

Jordon, M. (2001, May 17). People smuggling now big business in Mexico. *Washington Post Foreign Service*, p. A01. Retrieved from http://www.washingtonpost.com

Line, V. L. (2004). Corporate reputation in Asia: Looking beyond bottom-line performance. *Journal of Communication Management, 8*(3), 233–245.

Littrell, M. A., & Dickson, M. A. (1999). *Social responsibility in the global market: Fair trade of cultural products.* Thousand Oaks, CA: Sage Publications.

McLaughlin, K. E. (2009, November 26). Walmart suppliers in China accused of labor abuses.

Women's Wear Daily. Retrieved from http://wwd.com/retail-news/wal-mart-suppliers-in-China-charged-with-labor-abuses-23

Meeting the environmental challenge in the apparel industry: Management briefing. (2009, July–August). Worcestershire, UK: Aroq.

Merrick, A. (2004, May 12). Gap offers unusual look at factory conditions. *Wall Street Journal*, p. A1. Retrieved from http://www.wsj.com

Mexico's immigration problem. (2004, January 31). *The Economist*, 33–34.

Nationmaster.com. Retrieved December 23, 2009, from http://www.nationmaster.com/statistics

Nike. (2009). *Corporate responsibility report.* Retrieved January 10, 2010, from http://www.Nikebiz.com/crreport/

Parker, M. (2009). *Nike, Inc., corporate responsibility report.* Retrieved May 23, 2010, from http://www.nikebiz.com/crreport

No sweat: Campaigners against clothing sweatshops go to the Olympics. (2004, August 19). *The Economist*, n.p.

Office of Child Labor, Forced Labor, and Human Trafficking. (2009). *The Department of Labor's list of goods produced by child labor of forced labor.* Bureau of International Labor Affairs. Retrieved November 2009 from http://www.dol.gov/ilab/programs/ocft/PDF/2009TUPRA.pdf

Proliferation of cheaters in our schools. (2005, May 4). *The Tribune* (Ames, Iowa), p. A6.

Quilling, J. (1998, Winter). Ethics: The hidden dimensions of home economics. *Journal of Home Economics*, 33–36.

Ransom, D. (2001). *The no-nonsense guide to fair trade.* Oxford, UK: New International Publications.

UNITEHERE! (n.d.). Our history. Retrieved May 8, 2010, from http://www.unitehere.org/about/history.asp

U.S. Department of Labor. (2009). Department of Labor's list of goods produced by child labor or forced labor. Retrieved May 23, 2010, from http://www.dol.gov/ilab/programs/ocft/pdf/2009tvpra.pdf

Victory for workers Russell Athletic in Honduras. (2009, November 19). Clean Clothes Campaign. Retrieved from http://www.cleanclothes.org/news/victory-for-workers-russell-athletic-in-honduras

Will, G. (2005, May 5). Religion not required. *The Des Moines Register*, p. 15A.

Wolfe, J. H., & Dickson, M. A. (2002). Apparel manufacturer and retailer efforts to reduce child labor: An ethics of virtue perspective on codes of conduct. *Clothing and Textiles Research Journal*, (4), 183–195.

Worldwide Responsible Accredited Production (WRAP). Retrieved December 12, 2009, from http://www.wrapcompliance.org

World Bank Institute. (n.d.). Corporate Social Responsibility. Retrieved November 24, 2004, from http://www.worldbank.org/wbi/corpgov/csr

World Fair Trade Organization. (2009, November 7). What is fair trade? Retrieved May 29, 2010, from http://wfto.com/index.php?option-com_content&task=view&id=11

Zager, M. (2009, August 13). Doing well by doing good: Gap Inc's social responsibility program. *Apparel.* http://www.apparelmag.com/ME2/dirmod.asp?sid=&nm=&type=MultiPublishing&mod=PublishingTitles&mid=CD746117C0BB4828857A1831CE707DBE&tier=4&id=83AD30069F4D447092D27E4AED84C87F

Linen
正宗麻料

2 THE GLOBAL SUPPLY CHAIN

5 Global Sourcing

In the early 1960s, President Kennedy approved importing up to 5 percent of apparel sold in the United States; today the United States imports more than 95 percent of its apparel and 99 percent of its shoes from other nations (*Trends*, 2009).

FUN FACT

FIFTY YEARS AGO, when the majority of merchandise sold to consumers in a particular country was manufactured domestically, supply chains were much simpler. An apparel manufacturer assessed customer needs; planned, designed, and developed products; purchased materials, the majority of which were made domestically; produced garments in its own factories; and sold the finished goods to retailers at wholesale markets. That process seems pretty straightforward compared with today's global supply chain. Today, the supply chain requires attention to many complex components linked to the sourcing of materials and production explored in this chapter, to trade barriers and regulation (Chapter 6), to illegal and unethical trade activity (Chapter 7), and to politics and political positioning within and among countries (Chapter 8).

This chapter focuses on exploration of the supply chain components that support the processes required to produce and deliver finished textile and apparel products and utilize today's expanded global sourcing options, including design, product development, vendor compliance, materials and factory sourcing, manufacturing control, and logistics (see Figure 1.8). Some firms manage all the needed supply chain components themselves; other firms may contract with

Objectives

- Examine the processes for locating and evaluating alternative sources of textiles and findings needed for the production of apparel products.

- Identify and evaluate potential sources of apparel product development.

- Locate and evaluate potential alternative sources of finished apparel products, both domestic and foreign.

- Understand how to evaluate vendors who can provide appropriate apparel production capacity for desired products.

- Analyze the costs, overt and hidden, of purchasing from a cross-section of domestic and offshore sources.

- Introduce the types of government regulations that impact sourcing decisions.

outside sourcing specialists who can provide needed services, such as design, product development, and vendor compliance, when expertise in these areas is not available within the firm. Somewhere between the merchandise plans and the arrival of finished styles at a retail store near you, an incredibly complex set of tasks and processes occur. This chapter is designed to clarify the broad categories of these tasks and processes, exploring the competencies essential to survive in the multifaceted world of global sourcing.

ROLE OF GLOBAL SOURCING

One only has to consider the growth in the percentage of apparel imported into the United States from approximately 5 percent 50 years ago to more than 95 percent today to recognize that significant changes have occurred in the merchandise acquisition process over the last few decades. Similar trends are in place for other developed countries in the world. Since the founding of the United States, textile and apparel products have been brought into the country from Europe. Settlers requested fabrics and looked to European suppliers for accessories and fashion ideas, but they were soon producing cotton fabrics and apparel domestically. The concept of sourcing has been a part of the business environment for centuries for both domestic and international acquisition of goods and services. Our purpose here is to examine the role of sourcing in the supply chain.

From the outset we know that a minimum of two firms will be involved in any sourcing process. One entity desires some material, product, or service (the **customer**), while the other provides it (the **vendor**). Retail merchandise buyers (the customer) have traditionally purchased finished goods directly from manufacturers (the vendors) at wholesale. In addition to that traditional

method of sourcing, an exploration of the rapidly emerging discipline of apparel sourcing also includes numerous other methods of acquiring products.

To comprehend the complexity of the sourcing process today we must

- acquire an understanding of the structure of all the interconnected, yet flexible components of the merchandise planning, product development, production, and distribution pipelines
- consider the criteria for identifying appropriate sourcing partners, from individual suppliers to international contractors and sourcing agents
- gain awareness of the myriad processes that impact garment production and distribution decisions
- comprehend the multitude of legal, political, and economic barriers that restrict sourcing activity
- recognize current technologies that facilitate these processes

Although some parts of this list have already been introduced, it will take this chapter, the rest of this text, and beyond to understand fully the decision making that is involved in carrying out the sourcing process as a part of a firm's supply chain.

One simple definition of sourcing is researching and obtaining materials, trimmings, and finished garments. Another straightforward definition of sourcing that only addresses the beginning of the sourcing process is choosing the suppliers, domestic or international, that will deliver desired goods and services. This text defines sourcing as *determining the most cost-efficient vendor(s) of services, materials, production, or finished goods, or a combination of these, at a specified quality and service level for delivery within an identified time frame.*

Today, most apparel firms employ specialists whose job is to make sourcing-related decisions. These sourcing specialist positions exist in addition to the more traditional

agile manufacturing an operational strategy focused on inducing velocity and flexibility in a make-to-order production process with minimal changeover time and interruptions (Rockford Consulting Group, n.d.)

consolidator a person or firm that combines cargo from a number of shippers going to the same destination into one container for the purpose of reducing shipping rates

cost, insurance, freight (CIF) reflects the cost of goods as well as shipping and insurance to the requested port

customer in the sourcing world, the sourcing company that contracts for delivery of services, materials, product development, or finished goods

EDI electronic data interchange; a means of passing document information between companies

free on board (FOB) covers price to produce, pack, and load goods onboard a vessel at the foreign port of export

joint venture shared ownership of a business or facility by two or more firms

lean manufacturing a philosophy of production that emphasizes efficiency and strives to eliminate waste throughout the process, while improving quality

letter of credit a guarantee to the seller that the buyer has the funds to complete the purchase and that they are reserved for the seller

licensing contract a means of transferring intellectual property rights; extending the value of a brand without having to produce the product; putting a brand name on a product produced by someone else for a contracted percentage of the sales

manufacturing the entire process of transforming raw materials into finished goods for use or sale, using machines, tools, and labor

manufacturing control a process in which expected performance is compared with planned performance

private brand a label owned and marketed exclusively by a brand manager or retailer

private brand importer a brand manager or retailer who sources private brand products in foreign countries for import into the domestic economy

quality assurance a commitment to product quality that utilizes the concept of error prevention as integral to the entire product development process

sourcing agents firms or entities that provide services necessary to procure and deliver products and services to wholesale customers

sourcing calendar a time line related to the sequence of design, product development, production, and delivery to the retail sales floor

specifications detailed graphic and written descriptions of styling, materials, dimensions, production procedures, and finishing instructions for a garment style (Keiser & Garner, 2008)

standards basic characteristics used to determine acceptability of products and services

vendor a company that supplies services or products to other companies commonly known as customers

vendor compliance performance standards or rules established by the customer that a vendor must follow in order to do business with that customer

---

positions of merchandisers, designers, and quality assurance specialists. In some large firms with expanded sourcing needs and responsibilities there may be teams of sourcing specialists responsible for acquiring diverse product categories, all working under someone in a leadership position with a title such as vice president of sourcing. The sourcing responsibilities for a small firm may fall to an individual designated the product manager or sourcing manager. These individuals or teams make the purchasing decisions for a firm after weighing all the criteria—what to buy; from where and from whom; importance to how much it will cost; and, ultimately, when and how finished goods will be delivered.

According to *just-style*, researchers have found that students graduating with technical design proficiency and sourcing competencies are being employed within the industry at higher rates and at significantly higher salaries than creative designers ("Apparel Industry Training," 2008). Retail merchandisers also benefit from sourcing competencies, because the merchandising divisions of many retailers include product development and global sourcing components. One goal of this text is to facilitate preparation for expanded avenues of employment within the textile and apparel industry, going beyond the traditional roles by examining competencies and opportunities as sourcing specialists.

SOURCING OPTIONS FOR APPAREL

Informed decisions regarding whether to develop and produce materials and garments in-house, purchase finished garments, or contract a vendor to develop and produce the garments cannot be made without a basic understanding of what each of these sourcing avenues entails, including

- identifying all the specific product development tasks that must be accomplished and who is to do them
- determining how to evaluate and contract vendors of materials, product development services, and production, including evaluating their quality and output capabilities
- deciding who will be responsible for specific sourcing tasks, including vendor compliance, logistics, and customs clearance
- assessing and comparing the factors that impact the final costs of sourcing option decisions

As we look to methods of sourcing apparel products we begin with the two basic *factory direct* models used for contracting production of finished garments: CMT and full package. There are many variations of these models, dependent on business conditions and product needs. However, the primary differences between the models are as follows:

- with *CMT* the customer (sourcing firm) is responsible for the merchandise plan, design, product development, and materials sourcing; the vendor is responsible for garment production

- with *full package* the customer is responsible for the merchandise plan and product line concept; depending on the sourcing agreement, the vendor may provide product development, materials sourcing, and garment production

Clearly, a vendor providing full-package services must employ people with a much greater variety of technical expertise than a CMT vendor and will require more access to computerized product development systems and additional equipment.

CMT

One prevalent view for determining a vendor from which to purchase specific products is to seek the lowest product price offered by a contractor or supplier of that product. That has been the strategy utilized over several decades for CMT (cut-make-trim) sourcing of textiles and apparel in less developed nations for importation into developed countries. With CMT sourcing, the original sourcing company (the customer, in sourcing language), whether a manufacturer or retailer, bears all the costs, and the production contractor (vendor) provides the expertise and equipment for the actual production of the garments. The customer does the product development, sources the fabric for the product line, delivers the fabric to the vendor, and pays duties and transportation costs. The CMT vendor does not own the garments; it simply contracts to produce them and is paid for that service.

CMT sourcing enables the customer (the retailer, wholesaler, or brand manager) to control many of the product development processes, but the customer also must bear most of the responsibility and cost. This method of sourcing became more complex as sourcing customers began to use multiple CMT contractors in increasingly varied international locations. As the amount of offshore trading increased, the complexity of government regulations and the costs of logistics and importation escalated; thus, labor cost became a smaller part of overall product cost. Sourcing customers then sought ways to push more and more of the costs and responsibilities onto the vendors.

Full Package

At the other end of the sourcing spectrum for contracted goods is full-package sourcing, in which the vendor must contribute to and finance most of the **manufacturing** process, including product development and materials sourcing. The sourcing customer requests price quotes from vendors covering all the specific product materials and procedures the customer will require. A price quote from a full-package vendor reflects a much more comprehensive view of the overall cost of the product, but each final contract must be very specific, with all the criteria firmly established in advance of production, to ensure **vendor compliance**, that is, that performance standards established by the customer are followed in the process of developing and producing the quality and quantity of the merchandise ordered.

The following are some of the terms that must be established prior to signing a contract to ascertain the true full-package cost of the product from a vendor and to achieve satisfactory products delivered on time:

- How much of the overall product development process is covered by the vendor's quoted price? design? pattern making? grading? packaging? fabrics? findings? shipping floor ready (tagged and hung or bagged)?
- Does the vendor have the technology and expertise to perform the specified product development processes?
- Does the vendor have the technical expertise to write the materials specifications necessary to source the fabrics the customer prefers?

- Does the vendor have the necessary equipment and production capacity to produce the needed assortment of styles, sizes, and colors and the specified quantities of each?
- What quantity of product must be purchased at the given price to secure the actual quantity of product needed? Does the vendor require minimums? Are maximums limited by available materials? Is there reorder capability?
- Does the quality level match the specifications? Will the quality level be adequate to warrant the cost? What percentage of production can be expected to be first quality? What happens to seconds and overruns produced in the process necessary to achieve the appropriate number of acceptable products?
- What are the shipping costs from the location to the destination? According to the terms of the contract, are they part of the price?
- What are the tariffs? Who pays for them, and are they part of the quote?
- Does the country's infrastructure support the manufacture and delivery of the desired products? Are trained operators available? electricity and water for requested production? necessary equipment? transportation to docks? warehouse facilities? dock facilities?
- Are adequate technology and communication means available?
- What about security for the products? intellectual property rights to first quality and seconds? safety in transit?
- How long will it take not only to construct products, but also to get them to their destination?
- Can the vendor be depended upon to deliver on time? What happens if the vendor is late or can only provide partial orders?
- Is the country's government politically stable enough to sustain this transaction to its completion?

- Do the country and vendor support the humanitarian and environmental conditions that are considered appropriate by the sourcing customer and the ultimate consumers?

This list is extensive, but concise compared with the magnitude of specific information that must be evaluated by sourcing customers to ensure timely acquisition of desired end products. No purchase decision should be made until all these components are identified and compared with alternative vendor options for the same or similar product. It should be clear by now that deciding in what country to source has become almost as much of a driving force in this business as deciding what to buy. Make no mistake, successful firms address all the questions posed above and include vendor compliance terms in contracts. Many sourcing companies are also demanding that responsibility for more and more of these activities be borne by vendors. It has become a priority for sourcing companies to select suppliers based on criteria far beyond the lowest labor costs.

Many manufacturers and retailers have been shifting product sourcing from lowest-labor-cost CMT production in developing countries to full-package sourcing facilities, especially in China and other distant locales, in part because the dollar sometimes buys more abroad than in domestic locations. Efficient full-package production requires higher levels of management expertise, the latest technology, more fully developed infrastructure, and the financial resources to assume the majority of manufacturing expenses.

In contrast, many developing countries in the Americas, including Mexico, have not yet invested in the training and technology necessary to compete fully in a full-package market, although they are trying to work in that direction. Chinese producers have become full-fledged manufacturers, even establishing immense wholesale markets to display their product lines. Chinese producers have

- efficient supply chain strategies, including frequent introduction of new styles
- huge production capacity, both domestically and via outsourcing to other lower-wage countries
- an immense labor force that is willing to work very hard
- availability of a wide variety of materials

However, China does not necessarily have the lowest labor costs. Instead, it currently manages an undervalued currency, making products from China comparatively less expensive to both manufacturers and retailers in the developed world. Should China revalue its currency upward, as demanded by political pressure from several developed countries, its products could become more expensive, but the market would become more favorable for China to purchase and import product categories from developed nations, such as the United States and the EU. It will also be very instructive to see if China's current number one status as the world's largest apparel exporter can be maintained as its own consumer population prospers and makes further demands for access to the world's products.

There was some evidence of deglobalization, resulting from the worldwide recession, during the first decade of the 2000s. Some sourcing experts were looking toward more regional sourcing in which smaller, more frequent shipments could be available, with lower shipping costs and less shipping time. This may contribute to a decrease in China's dominance.

Private Brand Importer

Many retailers have expanded their merchandising activities to include development of their own products. Traditionally, a retailer would seek out and purchase finished apparel products directly from a branded manufacturer or through a wholesale market. Today, it is not unusual for large retailers to do part or all of their own product development and source full-package production to put their exclusive private brand on these products. **Private brand** reflects the ownership of an exclusive label by a brand manager or retailer. By owning their own brands, retailers may be able to reduce merchandise costs by bypassing the manufacturer or brand manager and sourcing directly with a full-package production contractor for finished apparel products. Should the retailer contract production of these products offshore, it becomes a **private brand importer**. Listed among the top global private brand retailers are H&M, of Sweden; Zara, of Spain; and The Gap Stores Inc., of the United States ("Best Global Brands," 2009).

Most national U.S. retailers today, whether a department store, specialty store chain, or mass merchant, are active private brand importers. The department store Macy's has private brand merchandise matched to customer lifestyles, including Alfani, for a "versatile and polished wardrobe"; American Rag, for the "young fashion-forward" customer; Charter Club, for "contemporary, all-American style"; Epic Threads, for "tweens"; and First Impressions, for "newborns and infants" (Macy's Inc., 2010). Victoria's Secret is a specialty chain that carries the Victoria's Secret brand. No other firm can legally sell Victoria's Secret products, and most of its lingerie is imported from other nations, including such far-flung locations as Jordan.

One example of a mass merchant is Walmart. Walmart's merchandise mix includes many private brands, including its George and Faded Glory apparel products, which are imported and exclusive to Walmart stores. Walmart has its own sourcing offices, including facilities in Shenzhen, China. Shenzhen is just over the border from Hong Kong, in close proximity to many apparel production facilities found in the Pearl River region between Shenzhen and Guangzhou. It is an excellent location for sourcing professionals to oversee the production of Walmart products.

Branded Importer

Many apparel manufacturers began by producing and distributing their products under their own brands. Today, especially in the United States, many traditional manufacturers practice the process of outsourcing much of their production to offshore facilities that they either own wholly or operate as joint ventures. They also source production of their branded goods through sourcing agents or other contractors. This may be for the simple reason that the products can be manufactured more easily in other locations or that materials are more readily available in distant locations, or that the costs associated with production are less when the manufacturing is completed offshore. Perhaps the most visible example of this sourcing practice, to U.S. consumers, is Levi Strauss & Co., whose headquarters are in San Francisco, California. For more than a century Levi jeans were manufactured in production facilities within the United States. Then production was gradually moved into Mexico. Today, all of their own U.S. domestic production facilities have been closed, and most Levi jeans are now produced outside both the United States and Mexico and imported into the Americas from other locations. Levi's are also sold in many other countries around the world, because Levi's has registered copyrights to all its brands and labels in more than 80 countries.

Some firms that began as manufacturers have outsourced so much of their production that they are now considered brand managers rather than manufacturers. VF Corporation, the owner of JanSport, Lee, Nautica, The North Face, Wrangler, 7 for All Mankind, and many other brands, is one such firm.

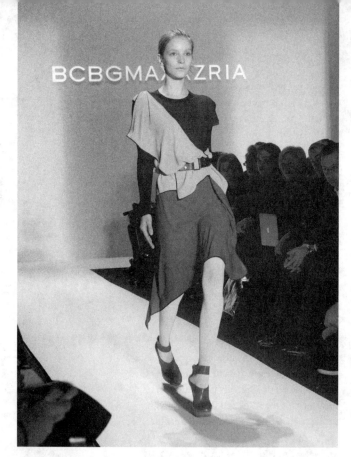

BCBGMAXAZRIA

Figure 5.1a Fashion show presentations are a major part of apparel markets.

(Courtesy of WWD/ Steve Eichner)

Now, further your understanding of sourcing options for apparel by completing Learning Activity 5.1.

Learning Activity 5.1
SOURCING OPTIONS FOR APPAREL

1. What are the primary reasons for going offshore for apparel production?
2. Compare the services required for CMT and full-package apparel sourcing. Explain which form of sourcing requires the most technical expertise from the vendor.
3. Why are sourcing firms tending to lean more toward full-package contracts?
4. What changes in apparel sourcing options explain the trend toward increases in private label products and importation of branded products?

Additional Sourcing Venues

Numerous other venues for sourcing textile materials and apparel products have long been in existence, and others continue to evolve. These methods of sourcing include trade shows and trade fairs, joint ventures, licensing agreements, and hiring of sourcing agents.

Trade Fairs and Trade Shows
Trade fairs and shows are designed to get textile and apparel producers, manufacturers, and retailers together with potential customers to facilitate efficient transfer of ownership of products and services. These events are closed to ultimate consumers but are the primary lifeblood for participants in the textile and apparel business. The shows serve as the conduit for locating fabrics and other materials and for identifying locations and firms that provide CMT and full-package vendor services as well as for selling apparel product lines at wholesale to retailers. These scheduled markets or market weeks are held periodically throughout the year to showcase new products and services to the trade. Consumers may become aware of these trade fairs when fashion show photos from these events are distributed through the Internet and other media. However, the real business of these market events occurs on the floor of the market itself, where vendors present their wares to their customers, including retail buyers and other trade representatives, to generate orders for materials, technology, machinery, finished products, and services. The calendars and locations for trade fairs and shows are readily available online and published regularly in trade papers, such as *Women's Wear Daily*. We have endeavored to identify a representative sample of some of the biggest and most productive of these trade shows from throughout the globe.

In the United States seasonal markets are scheduled throughout the year in most of the major cities, from New York and Chicago to Atlanta, Dallas, and Los Angeles. Perhaps the most visible trade shows in the United States are in New York City, where upscale women's fashion wear is presented and reported heavily in the media. Mercedes-Benz Fashion Week is held in February and September; Fashion Avenue Market Expo (FAME) is held in January, May, and August. For many years, Material World was the major U.S. textile show devoted to marketing textile materials and related products, particularly emphasizing those products produced in the United States, but in 2009 domestic business had dropped off to the point that this market was discontinued.

The biggest trade show in the United States now is MAGIC, held in Las Vegas in February and August each year. This show began as a venue featuring men's sportswear produced in California back in the 1980s, when manufacturers in California became leaders in men's sportswear. The acronym for the Men's Apparel Guild in California (MAGIC) became the name of this market event, and with the growth of the industry and the addition of new categories of merchandise, the location was changed to Las Vegas. MAGIC now consists of four individual markets: MAGIC, for men's categories; WWDMAGIC, for women's categories; MAGIC kids, for children's categories; and Sourcing at MAGIC, for private brand developers and brand managers to find vendors (Figure 5.1a–d).

The number of international trade fairs has mushroomed since the mid 1990s, keeping pace with the overall market trend of purchasing materials, products, and services from offshore locations. There are too many to cover here, but some stand out. The prêt-à-porter and couture shows in Paris, Milan, and London are notable, because they have been traditionally scheduled to introduce retailers and the consumer market to the newest

Figure 5.1b Textile buyers at Interstoff Asia. (*Courtesy of WWD/Graham Uden*)

Figure 5.1c Booths on the market floor at MAGIC. (*Courtesy of WWD*)

Figure 5.1d Vendor showing accessories to buyer at MAGIC.
(*Courtesy of WWD/Tyler Boye*)

trends in ready-to-wear products coming from the major designers of Europe. But even long-established European shows, such as the lingerie market Mode City, have found that in order to stabilize their position they have had to move from Lyon, France, into Paris.

In terms of volume of product sold for breadth of distribution, today's buyers are being enticed to travel to other areas of the world to conduct business. For example, China's longest running trade fair is the Canton Fair in Guangzhou, China. This marketplace is enormous and, when in session, is teeming with activity as buyers from all over the world gather to order all manner of products produced in China, including apparel (Table 5.1).

Offshore Facilities and Joint Ventures
Some domestic firms in developed countries have found that shutting down domestic production plants and moving their facilities to locations in another country that has lower labor costs or fewer restrictions on their activities is good for their overall businesses. Offshore facilities can improve control over some activities, but they also carry considerable risk. Even though a firm may find labor costs and taxes are lower, the investment in facilities and equipment can be high, and locking capital into a fixed asset in another nation can be risky if the political or business climate in that nation changes rapidly. There are, however, ways to avoid some of the potential hazards of ownership of offshore production facilities. One is to locate the new plant in a free trade zone, which is an area within a country that enables the duty-free movement of goods and equipment from one country to another. Free trade zones are discussed further in Chapter 6.

A less risky alternative to owning offshore production plants is a joint venture. A **joint venture** is shared ownership of a facility with a business based in another country. The positive aspects of joint ventures include a sharing of the financial risks and the better understanding of the culture and business legalities that local offshore partners can provide. Also, the initial investment can be lower.

Licensing
Licensing is a means of extending the value of a brand without actually having to produce the new product (Keiser and Garner, 2008). Typically, the name of a brand, sports team, cartoon character, or celebrity is placed on the product of another firm, and the owner of the brand or name is paid a percentage of the sale of any items sold under its name. This is how Ralph Lauren can have his name on a perfume made by someone else, or a cartoon character can appear on children's pajamas. Licensing contracts specify the responsibilities of each partner involved, and strict guidelines and product specifications are generally a part of the agreement.

International licensing is an alternative to exporting that enables well-known brands to establish a presence in another country without having to manufacture or distribute there. A brand owner contracts (as the licensor) with an offshore producer (the licensee); the licensee then produces and may distribute the branded product styles. This is how some designers gain a presence in a distant nation.

Sourcing Agents
The concept of sourcing agents is not new, but their role is typically not apparent to the retail consumer. Because of the exceptional growth of international sourcing in the apparel business since 1990, the importance of sourcing agents has increased significantly as a critical link in the overall supply chain. **Sourcing agents** provide services related to finding materials vendors, product development services and production capacity, and finished products for other firms.

Table 5.1 SAMPLING OF MAJOR TEXTILE AND APPAREL TRADE FAIRS FROM AROUND THE GLOBE

Trade Fair	Location	Show Focus	Dates
Dubai Fashion Week http://www.dfw.ae/	Dubai City, UAE	Enables local and regional designers and fashion houses to present their collections to global and regional buyers, media, fashion professionals; also have an event to connect U.S. brands with Middle Eastern buyers	October and March
Hong Kong Fashion Week http://www.hkfashionweekfw.hktdc.com/	Hong Kong, China	Asia's biggest fashion event, sponsored by the Hong Kong Trade Development Council (HKTDC); showcases wide array of garments, fabrics, and accessories	January and July
Intermoda http://www.intermoda.com.mx/	Guadalajara, Mexico	Mexico's premier apparel/fashion event	January and July
Interstoff http://www.interstoff.messefrankfurt.com/	Frankfurt, Germany	Germany's major textile event producer; mounts major shows in Paris, New York, China, and elsewhere	January (New York) and February (Paris)
Interstoff—Asia http://www.biztradeshows.com/trade-events/interstoff-asia.html	Hong Kong, China	Textiles from Asia	Spring and fall
Lakmé Fashion Week http://www.lakmefashionweek.co.in/	Mumbai and New Delhi, India	Platforms for Indian fashion industry	March and October
Mercedes-Benz Fashion Week http://www.mbfashionweek.com/	New York and Berlin, Germany	IMG is the world's largest fashion show producer and mounts trade fashion shows throughout the globe, including New York, Berlin, and Moscow	January (New York), February (Berlin), March (Moscow)
Pitti Immagine Filati http://www.pittimmagine.com/	Florence, Italy	Premiere showing of collections for the knitting industry, including yarns and finished apparel	January
Première Vision http://www.premierevision.fr/	Paris, France	Europe's number one fashion textile event for color trends, fabrications, and technological news	Spring and fall
Texworld USA http://www.texworldusa.com/	New York	Largest sourcing event in North America for apparel fabrics	January

Li & Fung Limited is a leading consumer goods sourcing company, managing the supply chain for retailers and brands worldwide. Headquartered in Hong Kong, the company manages a global sourcing network of about 15 thousand international suppliers via its offices in more than 40 economies across North America, Europe, and Asia.

In 2005, Li & Fung USA, a subsidiary of the Hong Kong–based Li & Fung Limited, opened its U.S. corporate headquarters and showrooms at 1359 Broadway, in New York City. The facility houses its global brands business, design studios, logistics operations, and showrooms. Teams of product specialists focus on each customer segment to manage the entire supply chain, from product design and development, to raw material and factory sourcing, to production planning and management, to quality assurance and export documentation, to shipping control.

In January of 2010, Li & Fung Limited opened a new hub in Istanbul, Turkey, for the firm's sourcing business in Europe, the Mediterranean, Middle East, Northern Africa, and the former Soviet republics. The firm will serve as the interface between suppliers in Turkey and the firm's worldwide customers in the fields of textile export, logistics, merchandising, and quality assurance.

Li & Fung has evolved from a sourcing agent to a global supply chain manager through innovation in the development of supply chain management. In 2009, Li & Fung began supporting its extensive supplier network with a new online portal to boost collaboration between vendors and agents. The Web-based, role-based applications serve as a common platform to standardize trade and customs documents and consolidate shipment data. Included is an online system for scheduling quality inspectors and reporting results back to Li & Fung.

Currently, Li & Fung manages the entire sourcing and distribution from Asia for many multinationals, including Walmart, Tesco, Nike, and Tommy Hilfiger. The firm also has a buying agency agreement with Talbots and orchestrates sourcing activities for Liz Claiborne, Inc., and Levi Strauss & Co.

Sources:

Li & Fung. Retrieved January 26, 2010, from http://www.lifung.com

Li & Fung Group. Retrieved January 10, 2010, from http://www.lifunggroup.com

Li & Fung Group purchases stakes in future logistics. (2009, July 21). *Logistics Business Review*. Retrieved from http://www.logistics-business-review.com/news/li__fung_group_purchases_stakes_in_future_logistics_090721

Talley, K. (2009, February 25). Liz Claiborne hires agent for sourcing operations—Li & Fung of Hong Kong will handle negotiations with vendors and monitor quality, with air of smoothing supply chain. *The Wall Street Journal*.

U.S.: Li & Fung grows supply chain with online trade tool. (2009, June 9).Retrieved January 4, 2010, from http://www.just-style.com

The role of the agent is to facilitate all the needs that exist between a sourcing firm and a vendor of the services required. Often, familiarity with a different language and knowledge of distant factories are the primary reasons to enlist the service of an agent, but agents can do many things, from finding vendors, to negotiating contracts between a firm and a vendor, to guiding the customer through importing procedures. Sourcing agents are usually paid a commission, based on a percentage of the amount of the total purchase.

One U.S. firm that previously provided sourcing services for numerous retail establishments throughout the country was the Associated Merchandising Corporation (AMC). Founded in 1918, the company was acquired by Target in 1998 and now does business as Target Sourcing Services/AMC, providing apparel sourcing and product development services only for its parent company, the retail giant Target Corporation. Target Sourcing Services/AMC "spots trends; designs apparel, accessories, and house wares; arranges for their production; and oversees retail delivery of the merchandise" (The Associated Merchandising Corporation, 2010). The company operates from more than 50 offices in 40 countries worldwide.

Reflecting the importance of these sourcing firms to the global market is that the second largest supplier of apparel to the world after China is not an individual nation, but a firm—*Li & Fung*. Perhaps the distinctiveness of Li & Fung's position can best be understood when one considers that it has achieved this status without owning any factories or employing any factory workers. With current headquarters in Hong Kong, Li & Fung has been in the sourcing business for more than a century. It provides sourcing services for a multitude of U.S. apparel brands, including Gap, Liz Claiborne, and Ralph Lauren.

Read Case 5.1 to learn more about the firm Li & Fung. Follow your reading with Learning Activity 5.2.

Learning Activity 5.2
ALTERNATIVE SOURCING VENUES

1. Refer back to Table 5.1. According to the description in the table, which trade fairs focus primarily on opportunities for materials sourcing?
2. Pick one of the materials-focused trade fairs, and look it up on the Internet. What does its Web site identify as the benefits of participating in this trade fair?
3. Which trade fairs focus primarily on opportunities for apparel sourcing?
4. Pick one of the apparel-focused trade fairs, and look it up on the Internet. What does its Web site identify as the benefits of participating in this trade fair?
5. Why might it be better to call Li & Fung a supply chain agent than a sourcing agent?

FACTORS IMPACTING SOURCING DECISIONS

Determining which sourcing option is best for a business at any given time is influenced by numerous factors that are constantly in flux and dependent not only on the type and quantity of products needed, but also on the monetary costs of acquisition and the time required to produce and deliver the products. Other factors that have to be considered concern the customs requirements in different countries, manufacturing philosophies, manufacturing control, sourcing calendars, and product development systems.

Manufacturing Philosophies

During the late 1980s, Textiles and Clothing Technology Corporation (TC²) and other consultants promoted "quick response" business systems to shorten the time line from product concept to the ultimate consumer. Quick response is focused on time-based competition, agility, and partnering. The system has now evolved into the much more comprehensive concept of supply chain management, incorporating two different manufacturing philosophies: agile manufacturing and lean manufacturing.

Along the way, these two manufacturing philosophies have been integrated into the apparel industry. **Agile manufacturing** methods, as a part of quick response, were at first promoted as tools contributing to flexibility and speed on the production floor. These methods allowed quick and easy changeover from one product to another without a lot of downtime, making it possible to do much smaller but still profitable production runs. By the late 1980s, lean manufacturing had also become a popular focus. **Lean manufacturing** emphasizes efficiency and strives to eliminate waste of time and materials throughout the entire process, while also improving quality. These priorities reflect the recent trends related to corporate responsibilities. It is now recognized that both agile and lean manufacturing have a place in apparel production, because each is best suited to different types of products.

Lean manufacturing strategies lend themselves to the production of basic products, whereas agile strategies are better suited to fashion products. Refer back to Table 2.1 to review the characteristics of basic and fashion merchandise. Basic products are more functional and have longer retail selling periods and less frequent changes in styling. Fashion goods have much shorter retail selling periods and more frequent changes in styling. Demand for basic goods is more predictable; demand for fashion goods is more volatile. Assortment forecast error is also much lower for basic goods, and markdowns are much higher for fashion goods, because it is more difficult to predict exactly quantities of styles, sizes, and colors. Basic customers want to resupply their wardrobe with similar garments, causing less product variety in the assortment offered. Fashion customers want to see new products every time they shop, and so product variety is high. Menswear has a higher proportion of basic styles, and women's wear has a higher proportion of fashion merchandise. Customers of basic merchandise tend to be more price conscious than customers of fashion goods. Merchandisers compensate by taking much lower gross margins on basic goods than fashion goods, but they also get much higher turnover on basic styles. It is easy to see that if a firm is engaged in manufacturing both basic and fashion goods, applying the same manufacturing philosophy throughout will not necessarily result in the most success (Bhatia, 2004).

Sourcing Calendars

The overall result of the application of agile and lean manufacturing philosophies, including the associated changes in technology and production methods to apparel manufacturing processes, has been the opportunity for compression of the sourcing calendar. A **sourcing calendar**, as presented in Table 5.2, is based on the merchandising calendar that sets the classifications of merchandise and the retail selling periods and that provides a time line related to the sequences of merchandise development. These include design, product development, production, and delivery to the retail sales floor. As with the merchandising calendar, timing of the sourcing calendar is planned backward from the projected retail sales date. Putting the sourcing calendar into a time line is helpful for gaining understanding of the processes necessary as a product line progresses from concept to retail selling floor and also for appreciating the changes occurring today to speed up this cycle.

Table 5.2 presents three different time lines; the traditional time line is followed

by more currently recognized time lines for two different types of merchandise. The traditional sourcing time line that had been in place for more than three decades took approximately 54 weeks, from start to finish. That time line meant that making decisions about the styles, sizes, and colors to be offered at retail had to be made more than a year before the merchandise arrived at the store. This schedule was accepted as customary, yet it was burdened with considerable redundancies in processes and a somewhat overblown belief that production labor costs were where the time and money issues were centered. That concern motivated the movement of production to offshore locations in a quest for lower cost labor. Unfortunately, many did not consider that getting the finished garments delivered from these far-off locations also heavily impacted the overall time line.

As shown in Table 5.2, today's basic/ core merchandise sourcing calendar of about 25 to 35 weeks is considerably shorter, allowing styling and fabric decisions to be made much closer to point of sale to the ultimate consumer, as compared with the traditional model. Core merchandise is sometimes called staple merchandise. It is stocked continually at retail, refilling similar spaces with the same sizes and colors. Men's white underwear and socks are classic examples. Lean manufacturing is generally applied to the production of more basic/core/staple apparel products that have long selling periods at retail (26 to 56 weeks or more, with no style or color changes) and for which quality is of importance.

A major contributor to the initial shortening of the sourcing time line was innovation in product development and communications technology. These improvements made it possible to shorten the total sourcing time line, while still taking advantage of low-cost labor. However, because of competition in the business, the recent worldwide economic recession, and increases in fuel costs, the focus has begun to shift from low-cost

Table 5.2 COMPARISON OF THE TRADITIONAL SOURCING CALENDAR WITH TODAY'S MODELS, IN TOTAL WEEKS, UNTIL DELIVERY TO RETAIL STORE

Total Weeks	54	50	45	40	35	30	25	20	15	10	0

Traditional Calendar
- Trend & Color
- Design & Sampling
- Buy
- Production
- Logistics
- Set Floor

Today's Basics/Core Merchandise
- Trend and Color
- Design & Sampling
- Buy
- Production
- Logistics
- Set Floor

Today's Fashion Goods
- Trend & Color
- Design & Sampling
- Buy
- Production
- Logistics
- Set Floor

Source: Olivier, Susan. (2008).The value of fast: Speed to market through the glass pipeline. Presentation at AAFA Sourcing Conference. Retrieved from http://www.wwd.com

labor to cutting time and redundancies in other processes within the sourcing cycle.

Today's fashion goods sourcing calendar provides only 16 to 20 weeks, from merchandise plan to retail store, and a retail selling period of only 2 to 4 weeks. That is a very tight time line when global sourcing is involved, putting significant pressure on all the components of the supply chain. Problems inherent to the current "fast-fashion" calendar seem to be centered on availability of fabrics and other materials. Where this calendar has garnered criticism is in the risk of sacrificing quality in materials and garment assembly to achieve rapid fashion change, resulting in almost disposable fashion. There is some question of whether the sourcing calendar pendulum may begin to swing back closer to the middle ground of 25 to 30 weeks, in the interest of achieving better quality and greater variety of available fabrics. Some consumers may reach a point where they will not be willing to sacrifice the perceived value in quality just to change their styling every few weeks or months. It will be interesting to see how this plays out in the next few years.

Now, read Case 5.2 for a look at how the apparel retail chain Zara handles the sourcing calendar for its fast-fashion products.

Product Development Systems

Speed of product development is a primary consideration when sourcing a full-package vendor. Current **EDI (electronic data interchange)** and integrated product development systems are essential for controlling the sourcing time line. As product development computer applications became widely available in the 1980s, paperwork was computerized, utilizing EDI applications, solving much of the problem of recalculating of figures and repetitive creation of forms and of communications between a vendor and a customer. The ability to gather information on color, design, and styling trends became easier with electronic media providing new tools for information gathering and enhanced graphics. Some of the more advanced time-saving tools came in the form of CAD (computer-aided design) applications, in which sketches could be shared rather than repeatedly recreated by hand.

One of the first computer applications adopted by the apparel business was computer-engineered markers that allowed accurately scaled pattern blocks to be moved around on the screen and fit into a rectangle representing the available fabric. This application significantly shortened the time required to develop a marker, which had been one of the most time-consuming and costly processes in pattern development. Computerization of other tasks ensued, and soon grading for different sizes and production pattern making times were shortened. Today, sights are set on lessening the time required for design development by creation of styles directly on three-dimensional avatars draped on the computer, revised and altered on the computer, and translated directly into two-dimensional patterns without the time-consuming need of developing actual samples.

One nagging issue throughout the business has been that of color matching on the computer. This problem is extremely costly for the textile and apparel business because of problems encountered in the transfer of color resolution between different computers, the translating of color from computer to printer, and compounded by the need to create different dyestuffs to achieve matching colors on different fibers. The geographic distance of producers from one another exacerbates these problems. eWarna, a company from Kuala Lumpur, Malaysia, specializes in online color collaboration solutions for sewn products. In early 2005, eWarna was awarded a patent for its new Color Indexer, an application that allows automated color cross-referencing from one palette to another on the Internet ("eWarna Unveils," 2005). Being able to match colors from other palettes will free up significant time and money in the color matching tasks required in textile and apparel product development. With this new technology, waiting for costly lab dips to color match each product might become a thing of the past. This system can provide "digital samples that can be authenticated and validated against the stored digital fingerprint of any color" and enable replacement of physical samples in the color matching process (eWarna, 2005).

Apply your knowledge of factors impacting sourcing by doing Learning Activity 5.3.

Zara is owned by the Inditex Group, one of the largest fashion retailers in the world, with more than 4,500 stores in 73 countries. Zara's headquarters are in A Coruña, Galicia, Spain, where the first Zara store opened in 1975. Inditex, best known for its Zara stores, replaced Gap as the world's biggest fashion retailer by sales (Keeley & Clark, 2008). One of its newer Zara stores opened in Chicago, Illinois, in October 2009, offering Zara's latest apparel collections for women, men, and children.

The firm's fashion philosophy of "creativity and quality design together with a rapid response to market demands" has resulted in expansion. This firm was one of the initiators of the concept of fast-fashion as it changed its design, manufacturing, and distribution process to reduce lead times and react to new trends in a shorter time frame. "[T]hey have streamlined the cumbersome old supply chain response from 40–50 weeks down to 8–10 weeks and their customers are eagerly awaiting next week's—take note, not next season's, new fashion. . . . Small and frequent shipments keep product inventories fresh and scarce—compelling customers to frequent the store in search of what's new and to buy now . . . because it will be gone tomorrow" (Anderson, 2006).

Zara opened its largest U.S. store in Chicago, Illinois, in 2009.
(Copyright © Englewood Construction)

Zara is a vertically integrated retailer and controls most of the steps in its supply chain, as it designs, produces, and distributes its own products. Zara employs a creative team of more than 300, and 60 percent of the manufacturing processes are outsourced in countries close to the Zara headquarters in A Coruña. The more basic products come from China, where they get the typical 4- to 6-month lead times, but the fast-fashion products, which are sourced from near A Coruña, have 2- to 3-week lead times. In addition, Zara pays for air transport in order to get things to its many far-flung stores (Keeley & Clark, 2008).

Traditionally, garment design precedes fabric procurement, but Zara has turned this practice upside down. For its fast-fashion goods, Zara is fabric driven. To eliminate waiting through the long and laborious process of fabric formation, new designs are developed with available fabrics and trims. Each new style has a relatively short production run, because the styles are replaced with new merchandise every two to three weeks in Zara's retail stores around the globe.

Inditex, SA, has selected GT Nexus, Inc., to provide a platform for tracking and managing global ocean shipments. This system utilizes the Internet to provide container status reports and document management and shipment transaction capabilities between ocean carriers. Some of Zara's other strategic moves include:

- making products available online for fall 2010 in its mature markets in Europe, to be followed later by a rollout in other countries to keep pace with its fast-fashion rival H&M
- expanding into new stores under the Lefties banner in France, Portugal, and Mexico to offload unsold stock from its flagship Zara chain
- rapid expansion into Asia, with stores in Hong Kong, Korea, and India (Rigby, 2010)

Sources:

Anderson, K. (2006, August). Fast fashion evolves. *AATCC Review*, 6(8). Retrieved from http://www.techexchange.com

Baigorri (2009, August 27). Zara looks to Asia for growth. *BusinessWeek Online*, 10. Retrieved January 7, 2010, from http://web.ebscohost.com.proxy.lib.ilstu.edu/ehost

Berton, E. (2009, August 18). Zara expands off-price format. *Women's Wear Daily*, 12.

Keeley, G. and Clark, A. (2008, August 12). Retail: Zara bridges Gap to become world's biggest fashion retailer. The Guardian. Retrieved September 1, 2010 from http://www.guardian.co.uk/business/2008/aug/12/retail.spain

Rigby, E. (2010, June 10). Inditex returns to double-digit sales growth. Financial Times. Retrieved September 1, 2010 from http://ft.com/cms/s/eedf0f36-738d-11df-bc73-00144feabdco,dwp_uuid=dc15438a-a525

Learning Activity 5.3

FACTORS IMPACTING SOURCING DECISIONS

1. What are some factors a sourcing agent should consider when deciding between a production vendor engaged in lean manufacturing and one engaged in agile manufacturing?
2. What is the purpose of a sourcing calendar?
3. Why is it acceptable for a sourcing calendar for basic/core products to have a longer time line than a sourcing calendar for fashion merchandise?
4. Why is a vendor's speed of product development a primary consideration when seeking a full-package vendor's services?
5. What are the limitations of Zara's practice of using available fabrics to speed up its sourcing calendar?
6. Why are the quality issues that Zara's critics are raising less relevant in the fast-fashion market?

MANUFACTURING CONTROL AND VENDOR COMPLIANCE

The sourcing company—the customer—has to have an established set of rules by which it will do business with its vendors, whether the vendors are providing materials, product development, production, quality assurance, shipping, or customs clearance. The customer's set of rules provides **manufacturing control** and defines standards for **vendor compliance**. The standards are included in the contract that the vendor signs when hired to provide services. Communication related to vendor compliance is now set up on EDI systems, but both companies must have the EDI systems required to handle it. A vendor usually has many customers, so it may have to be prepared to deal with a wide variety of standards. The vendor compliance contract establishes the areas of manufacturing control

desired by the customer related to quality and performance of materials and finished goods as well as quantities and timing of delivery.

Customs Issues

Prior to signing a contract with a vendor, both the customer's and the vendor's customs agencies, as well as any other countries where merchandise will be shipped, should be consulted to avoid potential problems regarding legal issues that might exist with the product in the country of import, especially compliance with country of origin (COO) regulations. The duty levied by customs must be paid before the importer can take possession of the goods, so it is critical to know what the rate on the products will be prior to their arrival at port. Also, precise contract language will help ensure that packing regulations required at the destination country have been followed by the vendor. Most of this is about paperwork, but it must be handled properly to avoid having merchandise held offshore while customs in the importing countries accepts resolution to the problems.

For novice importers, it is recommended that a customs broker be selected early in the sourcing process to ensure that goods can ultimately enter the desired arrival port and that necessary documents will be available when needed. In the United States, customs brokers are licensed by U.S. Customs and Border Protection. The information derived from the customs broker becomes a part of the vendor compliance standards.

Quality Assurance and Safety Standards

Quality assurance is a commitment to product quality that utilizes the concept of error prevention as integral to the entire product development process. The overarching concept is that making it right the first time is more cost-effective than deciding what to do with defective garments. The issue of quality is complicated by the desire to have fabrics sourced in one part of the world but compatible with items, such as trims, sourced elsewhere. The result is the need for development of quality and product standards followed by constant monitoring of their application in product specifications and production.

Standards are the basic characteristics used to determine acceptability of the quality and resulting performance and appearance of products and services. Specific standards are usually established for thread, fabrics, findings, fit, and garment assembly for all the products sourced by a firm. These standards provide the parameters for business decisions related to development of a firm's product specifications and a baseline for consistency of product offerings. To ensure that they contribute to making a profit, product developers ultimately determine which product characteristics will be desired by their customers and yet also will comply with regulations imposed by the government. Determining the appropriate standards to apply to a particular product depends on the type and length of use a product might receive in the hands of a consumer.

The United States utilizes voluntary standards developed by industry members working within ASTM International to establish criteria related to performance of textiles, stitch and seam classifications, and measurements for sizing. Voluntary standards developed by the American Association of Textile Chemists and Colorists (AATCC) are used as criteria for evaluating product performance related to colorants (dyes) and chemical finishes.

Note that new government restrictions came into effect in the United States in 2009, stemming from application of the Consumer Product Safety Improvement Act (CPSIA) governing products sold to children. These restrictions include tighter regulations on lead content of items for children aged 12 and under and can impact the selection of findings and trims used in garments for this age group.

In recent years, lead content of consumer products has become a global safety issue.

There are also some U.S. government–mandated standards related to flammability and product safety, which are overseen by the Consumer Product Safety Commission (CPSC), within the Department of Commerce. However, in an increasingly global environment, the movement has been toward using mandates from the International Organization for Standardization (ISO) for determining product standards. Organizations in the United States and abroad have worked with the ISO to select or develop recognized methods for evaluating textile materials in numerous categories. There are now ISO standards for evaluating textiles for such properties as crocking (color transfer by rubbing), shrinkage, fading, and pilling. Methods for testing tensile strength of yarns have been developed but vary by fiber and yarn type. Standards for laboratory ovens used for drying lab dips for color matching remain an issue.

Among the few areas of standards that are mandated by governments are two categories that appear to have more overall impact on apparel producers and consumers than others: labeling standards, including COO, and product care and maintenance. Sizing standards, because of the lack of mandated oversight, have flexible application and potential ongoing annoyance to ultimate consumers.

Country of Origin Labeling

With the extinction of the Multi-Fiber Arrangement (MFA), which limited quantities of apparel that could be imported into developed countries, it was thought that COO would become less of an issue in global trade. However, today COO labeling rules are still sorely needed, because they continue to be used to help establish the tariff rate for duties charged on imported products. Also, consumers like to know where products come from. Consumers active in social responsibility often use COO as a primary selection criterion.

The complexity of international sourcing increases the difficulty in determining the COO of a product. When an apparel product's fiber comes from one country, the textile used for it is produced in another country, and the garment is constructed in still another before it is shipped to the final location for retail sale, it is not that easy to determine the actual source of that product. Moreover, as recently as 1996, the U.S. Customs and Border Protection (CBP) used different criteria from the Federal Trade Commission (FTC) for the CBP's "Made in the USA" labeling requirements, exacerbating the problem of establishing COO. Some groups used the country where the product originated, others used the country that contributed 50 percent or more of the product's transformation or construction, and still others used a monetary value of 50 percent of the product as the cutoff for qualification for "Made in USA" status. This problem exists in part because COO rules have been revised multiple times, and some groups have not kept up with the changes.

For example, during the GATT (General Agreement on Tariffs and Trade) Uruguay Round of negotiations, which became the basis of World Trade Organization (WTO) rules, international standards for determining the COO were established for apparel products: the COO became the country where the garment is assembled (Wolf, 1996). Even that simple statement requires clarification when some assembly processes on a garment are done in one location, and completion occurs in another. The descriptor that is considered definitive here is that assembly occurs wherever the product is "substantially transformed" during the assembly process. As a WTO member, the United States is now supposed to abide by that interpretation, although even that can be controversial.

WTO rules have also determined the requirement that the label stating COO be permanently attached to the garment. That permanence may be established by a sewn-in label or by marking the fabric in a manner that will not come off during wear or care.

Care Labeling

The issue of care labeling also intensified as global trade became the prevailing sourcing method—especially the issue of whether care instructions should be provided in multiple languages. (One of your authors recently bought a coat rack at IKEA that had installation instructions in 31 languages.) The ISO solved that problem by selecting a series of pictograms to express the cleaning and pressing requirements for apparel products. For the EU those diagrams eliminated the necessity of using all the different languages spoken in 27 countries on those products sold throughout Europe.

When the North American Free Trade Agreement (NAFTA) was being implemented, care labeling requirements already in place in the United States became an issue, as there were then three languages that required communication: English, French, and Spanish. On some children's clothing, spelling out the care requirements in three languages produced a label that overwhelmed the size of the garment itself.

ASTM went to the ISO and requested that it be able to use the ISO care labeling pictograms on products to be sold in the United States, Canada, and Mexico. A French company owned the rights to the ISO pictograms, and ASTM worried that it might have to pay for the privilege of using them (Dowling, 1997). Also, FTC officials indicated that some of the European care labels included water temperature, and U.S. washing machine controls only indicate hot, warm, and cold. The result was that ASTM developed its own set of pictograms that are similar to but not exactly the same as the ISO care label standards. The care label issue persists in that the ASTM symbols used in North America are not compatible with the symbol system developed by the ISO and required of products sold elsewhere. The dilemma continues.

Tackling Sizing Issues

One of the most persistent issues in the apparel business continues to be consumers' difficulties in finding garments that fit their bodies. Because sizing standards for apparel products in the United States are voluntary, the marketplace generates significant variation and can be extremely difficult for consumers to navigate. The problem is compounded when purchasing apparel through catalog, television, or the Internet.

In the United States the voluntary sizing standard that is monitored by ASTM provides tables of body measurements, giving designers and manufacturers a basic blueprint they may use as a starting point for sizing apparel they produce. The ASTM standards originated from U.S. government army measurement data analyzed after World War II and were massaged by entering measurement recommendations, not actual body measurement data, from a variety of industry members to produce standard updates in the 1970s and again in the 1990s. The revised standards were still in place at the end of the 20th century but were severely compromised by lack of body measurement data evidence. The result was that clothing companies increased the measurements they used and continued to "relax" their sizes to achieve approximate fit for the "growing" population.

Zernike wrote of a national survey done in 2002–2003: "The survey—called SizeUSA and sponsored by clothing and textile companies, the Army, Navy and several universities—measured more than 10,000 people in 13 cities nationwide using a light-pulsing 3-D scanner" (2004). Zernike went on to explain: "Over all, the new measurements shake up

what have long been considered the average outlines of the American body." The SizeUSA study determined that at that time the median height of U.S. women was 5 feet 4 inches and of U.S. men was 5 feet 9 inches, with a median weight for women of 148 pounds and for men of 180 pounds. The numbers suggested that

- people have not simply gotten larger, but rather rounder in the middle
- the measurements did not differ much by region or by education
- the differences were between race, ethnicity, and age group (Zernike, 2004)

The study also identified several measurements that are important to the consumer's idea of adequate fit but easy to miss using more traditional grading practices. Adults can understand that their arms do not get longer as they gain weight and as they age; instead, their girth increases, so the extension of their arms and legs might actually be shorter. However, standard grading practices make the sleeves longer as the body get wider. Manufacturers and retail product developers are being encouraged to use the findings of the SizeUSA study to establish more logical grade rule tables, thereby improving product fit.

The ISO developed ISO/TC133, a set of ten size designation standards for size labeling of ready-to-wear garments in Europe. In 1992, TC133 was implemented in Europe to provide a single apparel sizing system, using Mondoform labeling. This method for indicating the appropriate body size used "the wordless pictogram, which consists of a standard body outline with body dimensions shown" (Minks, 1992, p. iii). The method was used in conjunction with a numbering system for factory and retail in-house use. For example, a woman's body size 92AS was the codification for

- bust girth, "92" [centimeters]—the preferred number within the range 90 to 93 centimeters, inclusive
- "A," representing hips larger than bust
- "S," indicating the short height range— 156 to 163 centimeters (Minks, 1992)

Human Solutions has launched its new "body dimension portal"—believed to be a world's first—which should help apparel firms tailor their garments to shoppers in new markets by enabling them to check their ready-made size tables against international databases. The iSize portal includes international data pools on body shapes in different countries, and manufacturers will be able to interactively modify their size tables in line with the databases.

"Customers only buy what suits them," points out Dr. Andreas Seidl, managing director of Human Solutions GmbH. "Any company can increase its market share by modifying its garment cuts. iSize plainly shows the correlation between fit and market success." Information is currently available on body shapes in key export markets including Germany, France, Eastern Europe, the Ukraine, Belarus, Austria (men's wear only), Switzerland (men's wear), the U.S., China and Korea. But there are also plans to integrate data from other countries over the next few months.

Companies can input their own size tables to obtain a ranking of the most suitable export markets for their products—including the percentage of each size that needs to be produced for each export country. Human Solutions says the information in the databases has been obtained from size surveys based on up to 140 different body measurements as well as criteria such as age and gender.

Source:

Germany: Body size portal goes live. (2009, October 9). Retrieved from http://www.just-style.com/article.aspx?id=105560

However, the EU has still been troubled with sizing and fit issues, similar to the United States. In 2001, Great Britain completed a sizing study much like the SizeUSA project, using a three-dimensional scanner to collect body measurement data, but in 2009 the EU was still trying to cope with sizing variations between different firms and even within companies. The EU requires nations exporting apparel products to be sold in EU countries to use metric measurements and European labeling standards. This is not a problem for nations that use metric measurements, but U.S. companies must convert to those labeling and measurement standards on any apparel they sell in the EU.

Some countries with less diversity in their population do not seem to have difficulty with sizing. For example, Japan has only six sizes for women's apparel, whereas there are currently at least 55 recognized numbered sizes for women in the United States. Case 5.3 discusses the 2009 launch by the German firm Human Solutions of an international data pool that may provide some solutions to sizing issues in global trade. For another solution to the sizing challenge, see Case 5.4. Finally, following your reading with Learning Activity 5.4.

Learning Activity 5.4
Manufacturing Control and Vendor Compliance

1. What are some of the aspects of manufacturing a sourcing company needs to control?
2. Why are apparel products required to have COO labels?
3. Give three reasons why there are no widely accepted standards for apparel sizing.
4. Do you think Intellifit will replace fitting rooms in retail stores? Why or why not?
5. What is the purpose of vendor compliance contracts

MATERIALS AND PRODUCTION SOURCING OPTIONS

We are ready to explore the options and processes required for acquisition of necessary materials and to consider selection of vendors for production. We also must take into account all the costs involved as a product moves through the supply chain from concept to completion and explore the logistics required to get the product from the vendor to the point of sale.

Intellifit helps you quickly find clothes that fit—while it also helps clothing brands and manufacturers create clothes that fit more people. Finding what fits saves time and money for you, your favorite stores, and your favorite online clothing source, because you know the fit before you even take the time to try on the clothes.

Using holographic imaging technology created to detect weapons in airports, Intellifit's body scanners size you up in about fifteen seconds. The body scanner, a transparent glass booth, is equipped with a vertical wand that encircles the shopper and emits harmless radio waves. Those waves collect more than 200 accurate measurements of the body. During the process, shoppers remain clothed and comfortable. Previous white-light or laser scanners required customers to don cycling shorts for their scans.

Intellifit body scanner used for collection of body measurements.

(Copyright © The Intellifit Virtual Fitting Room™ [VFR])

Once you have been scanned, you can quickly find what fits by searching Intellifit's database for brands and sizes that fit you best in the categories in its files (jeans, swimsuits, dresses, suits, sportswear, dress shirts, lingerie, and so on). In 2008, Intellifit was piloting a program in Philadelphia, in which consumers could have jeans custom made, based on their personal measurements.

In addition, Intellifit compiles the anonymous, aggregated data about all the bodies measured to help clothing manufacturers and retailers improve their fit and their operations so that they can create and stock clothes to fit real people. The early adopter David's Bridal revamped its plus-size dresses, based on information gathered through Intellifit scanning data. To date, Intellifit has measured more than 230 thousand individuals, representing the largest sizing database of its kind in the world.

Sources:

Bilal, M. (2005, April 8). Fashion, technology mesh at Levi's store. *The Chicago Tribune*. Retrieved from http://articles.chicagotribune.com/2005-04-08/news/0504090008_1_body-scanners-intellifit-convenience

Boyle, M. (2005, May 16). 25 Breakout companies. *Fortune*. Retrieved from http://money.cnn.com/magazines/fortune/fortune_archive/2005/05/16/8260133/index.htm

Intellifit offers custom-made jeans with a high-tech twist (2008, February 11). Retrieved from http://www.it-fits.info/INTELLIFIT-offers-custom-made-jeans-with-a-high-tech-twist.asp

Materials Sourcing Options

The materials used in garment production are produced on a somewhat different time line than that used for apparel production. The traditional schedule for production of textile fabrics tended to begin almost a year ahead of when apparel designers/product developers were making decisions about fabric preferences for the next product line. Fabrics were produced in stock quantities so that they would be available to apparel designers/product developers to use as a source of inspiration in developing new styles. This resulted in considerable unpredictability for textile firms, as they were often caught with excess inventory of items not selected by designers and shortages in items they had not predicted would sell well.

Then the textile industry moved to a calendar where fabrics were typically not produced in production-run quantities until after they were ordered by apparel firms from samples marketed at trade shows during the design phase of the merchandising calendar. Delaying full production until they knew which of the fabric choices offered were desired was less stressful for textile producers. However, then the problem became the time lag between when garments were designed and when production run quantities of the selected fabrics would be available for garment production.

Fast-fashion firms, such as Zara, have shortened their sourcing calendars by focusing on utilizing available fabrics to cut the waiting time for fabric production, a practice that, in effect, goes back to the procedures in place 30 or 40 years ago. However, for apparel firms that insist on having unique fabrics or specific quality specifications, Zara's practice is not an option. For these firms, there must be time to analyze trends in colors, patterns, and textures to forecast types and quantities of fabrics for coming retail selling periods and to design the garments that will use them.

Findings and trims are also now designed and produced as samples and sold in markets scheduled to coincide with the trending and designing phases of the merchandising calendar. Basic findings are typically produced in anticipation of sales at textile trade fairs, but the production calendar of trims varies significantly. The prices of fabrics and trims can fluctuate radically, depending on the materials and labor involved and where the products are produced. If they have to be shipped, there will be further time constraints and the potential for additional tariff costs. Also, because the variety of trims is nearly infinite, their availability often will impact not only production schedules, but also what finished products will look like if substitutions must be made during production in order to complete garments on a contract schedule.

Apparel contractors sometimes establish minimums as to the size of the orders they will produce, and this is also an issue when sourcing materials. If you are going to produce garments that require 1,500 yards of fabric, and the textile firm has an order minimum of 1,800 meters, you must recognize that first, meters are longer than yards, and second, you are going to have significant amount of leftover fabric that must either be factored into your overall cost as waste or used to produce additional garments. Both factors are going to make the overall contract cost of the garments go up.

In the fashion apparel business there are also issues of exclusivity. If you purchase a fabric or trim and do not want anyone else to have it, you will have to pay the textile or trim supplier for the privilege. Sometimes, the sourcing firm will purchase an original fabric under the condition that it will have exclusive rights to the fabric's production for a specified period of time (such as a year) and that the textile producer may sell the fabric to someone else after that time period has elapsed. All these things have to be spelled out in the contracts with the vendor.

Read Case 5.5 to learn the duties involved with being a fabric sourcing manager.

JOB TITLE: FABRIC SOURCING MANAGER

Position Objective:

Contribute to the sourcing decision-making process, from product development, to vendor selection, to product delivery.

Basic Functions:

Provides fabric leadership and expertise on fabric development and sourcing.

Uses technical knowledge of fabric structure to communicate designers' intent into clear, executable direction for Fabric Managers and mills.

Ensures the development of new fabrics in a timely and professional manner to meet the expectations established by merchandise plans as well as the Design and Product Development Departments.

Principle Responsibilities:

Attends seasonal color, fabric, and trend meetings, and textile fabric fairs, to provide input on mill performance and to understand the desired fashion direction and new fabric development needed by the planned product line.

Evaluates current textile vendors (manufacturers/mills) and researches potential new vendors regarding processes, technologies, materials, and finishes, considering cost saving, competitive advantages, and potential customer satisfaction related to the assigned product categories.

Collaborates with Design Directors, Designers, Product Development, and Testing Lab Managers to ensure all new fabrics are completed in a timely and professional manner and to meet the needs and expectations for each department.

Travels as required to visit textile mills and vendors to research, identify, and/or develop new fabrics reflecting designers' intentions for styles submitted by Product Development teams.

Based on a thorough understanding of current brand strategies, as well as pricing and quality objectives, examines, develops, and selects appropriate textile vendors (yarn sources, mills, converters) for each product category.

Participates in the vendor negotiation process by providing expert evaluation and guidance regarding cost comparisons, delivery estimates, mill status, and any other pertinent fabric information.

Skills and Requirements

Bachelor's degree in textiles and apparel

5+ years of apparel industry experience

Technical knowledge of cost, fabric, and fabric mills

Successful track record leading a team

Strong negotiation and communication skills

Sources:

JCPenney. (2010). Careers. Retrieved January 16, 2010, from http://jobs.jcpenney.com/USA/Fabric_Sourcing_Director_Product_Development_amp_Design_Wovens/012911581/job

LF USA. (2008). Careers at LF USA. Retrieved July 23, 2010, from http://careers-lfusa.icims.com/jobs/1838/job?&?mode=apply&iis=Indeed ?iisn

Selection of Production Facilities

Selecting a vendor for a production, whether for fabric or garments, involves a lot more than choosing the least expensive bid. Despite vendor compliance contracts, the conduct of vendor firms may need to be monitored throughout a production cycle to ensure that they are meeting their contractual obligations. Before making a decision among vendors, the sourcing firm should consider prior experience with them and reliability in meeting contract deadlines for delivery of goods. Knowing the factory conditions where the products are to be produced is also of importance to ensure that employees are being paid a reasonable wage and are not working under sweatshop conditions and that the vendor's record of ethical practices is appropriate.

Other areas of consideration are whether the vendor has the necessary equipment, available capacity, trained operators, and expertise to produce the garments in question. This type of evaluation may need to be made on site to confirm the suitability of the potential vendor and requires a thorough knowledge of manufacturing methods. Many apparel firms have standardized forms that evaluators fill out to be sure all the appropriate questions are asked and answered. If the sourcing firm is unfamiliar with production methods or with assessing the capacity of vendors, an alternative sourcing option, such as going through a sourcing agent, might be more appropriate than direct-to-factory sourcing. Carefully comparing bids from alternative sources helps ensure a competent, economical final decision.

Now, further your knowledge of materials and production sourcing with Learning Activity 5.5.

Learning Activity 5.5
BASICS OF MATERIALS AND PRODUCTION SOURCING

1. What are two types of apparel products for which product developers might rely on textile firms to develop and present fabrics that would be purchased finished and ready to cut? Why?
2. What are two types of apparel products for which product developers might want to engage in their own fabric development? Why?
3. Compare the types of expertise a materials sourcing manager would need if responsible for the products you chose for question 2 as compared with question 1?
4. Identify three areas of expertise (in addition to what you identified in question 3 that are fundamental to becoming a materials sourcing manager.
5. What are three things that should *always* be investigated when choosing a production facility, and why?

COSTING

Because the basic purpose of a business is to make money for the firm, it follows that in order to remain in business, the firm must acquire its goods for less than the price they will ultimately charge their customers. Remember that the firm will also be paying for numerous business expenses in addition to the cost of the goods it sells, so the overall anticipated markup is definitely not just profit. We will leave the explanation of overall accounting practices of wholesale and retail apparel firms to others and focus here only on the cost factors involved in the acquisition of finished products. These macrocost categories are inherent to all apparel production, but the actual costs will vary significantly by type of garment, number of garments ordered, materials and construction methods used, where the garments are sourced, and how the product development processes are to be allotted between the sourcing firm and the contractor. Table 5.3 identifies the macrofactors that impact the cost of goods and identifies the typical percentages of the cost of apparel production that are borne by these factors.

Fabric Costs

The single largest cost of apparel production is the fabric, which is usually between 40 and 50 percent of the total cost of goods. The basic price will be dependent on the fiber content, the type of fabric, and the quality and quantity required for the style. In some products this cost may be as high as 70 percent when

- the fabric is unique
- the fabric has to be acquired some distance from the garment production site and requires additional transportation and tariff charges
- there is significant fallout (wasted fabric), owing to large fabric design motifs or garment styling requirements
- the size range includes more large sizes

Vendors contracted to make the garments may supply the fabrics for the customer, or the customer may need to source the fabric from another location and ship it to the vendor, depending on the cost and availability of the fabrics. Fabrics are purchased by the total amount of yardage needed for production of the entire order. Note that the costs on the preliminary cost sheet are for only one garment and that the total yardage required will be dependent on the overall number of garments to be constructed plus the addition of approximately 6 percent to allow for potential seconds or irregulars, that is, garments that are not first quality when they come off the production line. The overall cost of fabrics can also be affected by textile producers who require a minimum order for a fabric, creating the

Table 5.3 Macrocost Factors for Apparel Production and the Typical Percentage of Total Garment Cost for Each Factor

Factors Included in the Cost of Apparel Goods	
Fabric	40%–50%
Cut-make-trim (CMT)	20%–30%
Labor portion of CMT	(15%–20%)
Trim percentage of CMT	(5%–10%)
Logistics and transportation	18%–31.5%
Tariffs	Average, 9%
Total costs	100%

Sources: Based on Keiser, S. J., & Garner, M. B. (2008). *Beyond design: The synergy of apparel product development* (2nd ed.). New York: Fairchild Publications. Reamy, D. W., & Steele, C. W. (2006). *Perry's department store: An importing simulation*. New York: Fairchild Publications.

potential that the sourcing firm will have to purchase yardage beyond its primary needs in order to secure the fabric.

Production Costs

Full-package costs include product development costs and fabric costs, plus CMT costs. CMT costs cover all the actual production processes. CMT is typically 20 to 30 percent of the cost of the product and can be broken down into labor costs and trim. Complicated styles will of necessity result in higher labor costs, whereas a simple style may keep labor costs low enough to permit spending more on the fabric or trims. These types of decisions usually depend on the target market for the finished goods.

The size of the order can also impact costs. For example, if the production run is small (few in number), the costs will escalate per item because of the time and effort involved in setting up, which may require adding or removing machines from the production line, changing their sequence, or adjusting machines for different types of fabrics or assembly methods. Conversely, if the order is large, the setup costs can be spread over more garments, and the cost of each garment will go down. For those who source at the factories in China, it is not unusual to have minimums placed on orders requiring 100 thousand units of one style. Should a sourcing firm require a smaller order, it may be in the firm's best interest to do business through a sourcing agent who can find a vendor willing to do smaller orders or who can consolidate the order with those of other firms in order to qualify for a factory that has the bigger minimum requirements.

Labor costs will also vary significantly, depending on how the contracts are written and what parts of the overall process are to be completed by the vendor. The more steps that are to be done by the vendor, the more costs will be included in this figure. Thus, if the vendor is a full-service contractor, the cost of goods will seem to escalate, but if the sourcing firm does much of the product development steps, the labor costs will appear to go down. However, the sourcing firm must then provide a larger margin within its own overhead or markup to cover these shifts in product development costs. Everything must be paid for, but the amounts vary, depending on which firm takes responsibility for each task and how the accounting is handled within the company.

Some of the production costs that may either be part of the vendor's price or be borne by the sourcing firm include designing and grading patterns for different sizes, making samples of the garment for approval, and producing markers (pattern layouts of all the sizes). The production labor costs will almost always include spreading the fabric, cutting the pattern pieces, sewing the garments, applying finishes and trims, pressing and packaging, and inspection. The vendor will also add in a percentage to cover overhead and administrative expenses and profit as part of the production contract.

The trim portion of CMT refers to all the materials needed to construct the garment besides the fabric. Trim usually includes garment labels, hangtags, price ticketing, and packaging, such as plastic bags and hangers. Trims and findings are purchased by the yard, gross, or dozen but are listed on the preliminary cost sheet by unit price to establish individual garment costs. The availability of fabrics, trims, and other findings can become a significant issue if they must be secured from additional vendors in distant locations, for this not only affects the time required to get the fabrics, but also creates transportation and potential additional tariffs costs.

It is critical that the specification packages provided by the sourcing firm and the contract bids provided by the potential vendor contain all the information needed for completion of the garment and that they spell out who will be responsible for each of the identified functions related to production to ensure that the products that are received are the ones the sourcing firm expects. The trend is for the customer to push as much of the cost and responsibility onto the vendor as possible, and, in doing so, it becomes ever more critical for all tasks to be accounted for in the bid contracts.

Logistics and Transportation Costs

We previously defined logistics as the science of moving products through the manufacturing and distribution system to their final destinations in a timely manner (see Chapter 3), but we need a comprehensive view of the overall process. Many transformations in logistics have occurred since handwritten transactions accompanied textiles transported on the Silk Road out of Xian, China. Centuries later, typed transactions sent by telegraph and undersea cables in the form of telex communications directed loading cartons or barrels of products onto trains, steamships, and trucks.

Today, the logistics process is controlled and monitored by complex computer networks

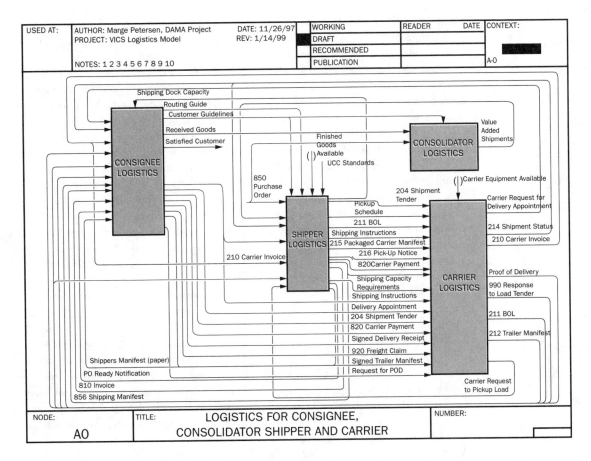

involving inputs from consignees, shippers, carriers, consolidators, and external sources as well as government agencies. To comprehend the complexity of today's logistics information flow, we suggest you look at the Voluntary Interindustry Commerce Standards Association's VICS Logistics Model, which was developed as part of the DAMA project. Figure 5.2 provides a model of one phase in the complex logistics process. Keep in mind that any component of the process could be located anywhere in the world. To view the entire logistics model, go to http://www.vics.org/docs/committees/logistics/LogisticsModel.pdf.

The technological options regarding logistics seem astonishing by previous standards: containers of garments are packed by machines, moved on conveyor belts controlled by computers, and placed onboard trucks destined for distribution points, where they are then loaded aboard a ship or plane headed for delivery anywhere in the world. The new system inputs we discussed previously, including the new bar codes and radio frequency identification (RFID) tags, are scanned into a computer network. Containers and their contents can be tracked at each stage of the trip by scanning the bar code labels or RFID tags; a person rarely handles the package during the entire trip.

Importing goods from distant locations complicates the overall costing process, but the WTO estimates that each day in shipping adds 0.5% to the cost of an item (Zarocostas, 2004). It is intuitive that costs

Figure 5.2 One page of the VICS Logistics Model, reflecting part of the interlocking decision-making processes required to achieve movement of goods from one location to another. To view the entire model, go to http://www.vics.org/docs/committees/logistics/LogisticsModel.pdf. (*www.vics.org*)

for transportation of products coming to the United States from Asia will take longer than goods coming from the Caribbean, so shipping costs will vary significantly, depending on the location of the production facilities and the types of access available. It becomes imperative that logistics costs be factored into final contract decisions and that the overall cost of goods from diverse contractors be compared, rather than incomplete quotes.

Port-to-port shipping times from Hong Kong to Los Angeles average 12 days, whereas Hong Kong to New York takes 26 days, and Hong Kong to Europe averages 21 to 23 days ("Manufacturing Sourcing," 2001). Note that these shipping times do not include loading, unloading, customs clearance, or transferring shipments to a warehouse for consolidation with other orders before shipping, which, taken together, typically add another 3 or 4 days.

Most international shipping is now done in 20- or 40-foot shipping containers. Filling the container is the most cost-effective overall, as per unit shipping costs are lower when the container is full. Overall container freight costs are divided among the items in the container; for example, if the price is based on 3,600 garments in a 40-foot container from Hong Kong, the price is $0.725 per garment, but only if 2,400 garments are in the container; if there are fewer, the cost per garment goes up to $1.09 (Reamy & Steele, 2006).

Sometimes, garments are shipped by air. The containers for air travel are smaller, and the costs are significantly higher, but it is much faster, so which form of transport is best depends on the type of sourcing calendar in use. Not having garments available for sale according to the merchandise plan is very costly for a

retailer. Air transport is more likely to be used for fast fashion or high-price-point products. Occasionally, air transport is used when the contractor is behind schedule on part of a production run; a vendor will risk losing money for the entire contract if he or she does not get all the completed goods to the sourcing firm by the delivery date on the contract.

Under normal circumstances it is common practice for the vendor to pay for transport to the ship or airplane (FOB); the customer pays for transportation to the new port, although other arrangements are available. The transportation costs must be factored into the overall product costs beyond labor and materials to determine which contractor will provide the sourcing firm with the best overall cost advantage. It is also critical that one take into consideration the infrastructure of the country where the production is to take place, for if roads are bad and some distance from the port, or there is political upheaval in the area, additional delays will ensue, and it should be abundantly clear by now that time is money in this business.

Tariff Costs

Tariffs are the rates of duty charged on products to gain their entry into a country. In the United States the average tariff cost is 9 percent of the cost of goods (Keiser & Garner, 2008). However, these rates vary significantly, depending on the type of garment and the COO. Tariff costs are commonly born by the buyer.

The tariff rates applied by U.S. Customs are established by application of the Harmonized Tariff Schedule (HTS). Each classification of garments is given a ten-digit HTS code, and calculation of the duty may be closely estimated. However, the final approval of entry of the products into the country and the amount of duty ultimately assessed is at the discretion of the customs officer at the port of entry.

Try your hand at learning Activity 5.6 to extend your knowledge of costing.

Learning Activity 5.6
COSTING

1. Why is it important to choose a production vendor that has production capacity that will accommodate the quantity of production desired?
2. What is a possible problem if the vendor is accustomed to doing larger orders?
3. What is a possible problem if the vendor is accustomed to doing smaller orders?
4. Examine the macrocosts presented in Table 5.3. Compare potential CMT costs with logistics and transportation costs. Do these costs justify using a global search for production instead of a regional one? Explain.
5. If you were going to ship apparel from Hong Kong to the United States, would you send it to Los Angeles or New York? Would you use air or water? Explain.

SOURCING FORMS AND CONTRACTUAL CHOICES

Original garment costs evolve from estimates of the cost of materials and an understanding of all the processes involved in producing an individual garment style. The sourcing process then moves to bids prepared by potential vendors containing projections of costs for production of the entire order and to selection of the appropriate vendor.

Product Specifications, Cost Sheets, and Vendor Bids

Specifications are the detailed graphic and written descriptions of styling, materials, dimensions, production procedures, and finishing instructions for a garment style. Written specifications for garment styles are used not only to ensure that final products will meet overall company quality standards, but also to provide the detailed criteria necessary for the production and ultimate acceptance of individual products. Specifications are used by everyone involved with a product, including those that develop, produce, promote, and sell the product and those suppliers and vendors that will provide materials and distribution. Specifications are an integral part of the contracts between a sourcing firm and production contractors.

Language is often an issue, so great care must be taken that specification sheets are clear and easily understood. Remember that sending photos, technical sketches, or actual samples can prevent many misunderstandings. Textile and apparel firms take great care in the development of their company specifications, for incomplete instructions or mistakes in communication can be disastrous in terms of cost. The specification (spec) sheet package for a garment style is usually prepared by technical designers who are most familiar with translating apparel designs from either sketches or samples into written instructions.

The detail of written specs will vary significantly, depending on the sourcing option selected. However, the more meticulous the spec package is, the more likely the final products will satisfactorily meet the requirements of the buyer. At a minimum a specification package should have a style summary sheet, including a drawing of the garment and a brief written description, and a preliminary cost sheet for comparing bids provided by potential contractors. More detailed instructions become part of the compliance standards discussed earlier in this chapter. Figure 5.3 shows a preliminary cost sheet for a single garment.

The cost sheet, and any other available specification information for the garment style, provides the stepping-off point for a vendor to prepare a bid quotation for consideration by the customer. The bidding process moves the cost quotations from a single sample garment to the costs of an entire production run for a specified number of garments. Negotiations continue until vendors provide all the information needed by the customer to make the final decision.

Reamy and Steele (2006) suggested that the quotation from the vendor should include the following:

- item number
- total quantity of units
- item description and specifications
- unit type (each, dozen, set)
- FOB (Free on Board) price
- case dimensions and cubic feet measurement
- item weight
- gross weight
- net weight
- FOB port
- country of origin (COO)
- minimum order quantity (MOQ)
- quantity to fill container
- production time (p. 80)

Some of the information in the above list requires further explanation. For example, the **FOB (free on board)** price reflects the amount it costs to produce, pack, and load the goods on board a vessel at the foreign port of export. The customer takes responsibility for all remaining costs for duty, shipping charges, and transportation to the final destination.

An alternative to FOB is **CIF (cost, insurance, freight)**, which reflects the cost of goods as well as shipping and insurance to the requested port. For example, CIF Los Angeles is the price for the cost of the garments, shipping, and insurance until the goods reach the port of Los Angeles. Another alternative is to quote the POE (point of entry) cost, which includes the ocean freight and duty and means the customer takes possession of the merchandise at the U.S. point of entry, but it does not include insurance. Remember that the goods still have to get from the port to the firm's distribution center, so there are still some additional transportation costs.

At this point, bids from potential vendors, including all factors that might impact the final selection, may be considered, and additional paperwork and contracts may be initiated. Certainly, the overall product costs will be of great importance in the final selection of vendor, but other considerations must also be weighed.

Alex Cameron

New York, NY 10012
212-555-7367
Cost Sheet

Style #: <u>9807</u>   Description: <u>tailored, pleated front slacks</u>   Date: <u>1/10/2010</u>
Division: <u>Women's Sportswear</u>   Size Category: <u>Miss</u>   Season: <u>F2010</u>
Sample Size: <u>10</u>   Technical Designer: <u>Beth Hale</u>
Fabric: <u>12 oz. Polyester/rayon blend suiting</u>   Color: <u>Heather gray</u>

Size	6	8	10	12	14	16
Size Set	1	2	3	3	2	1

Fabric	Yardage	Price	Cost
Suiting, 60" wide	1.5	3.90	$5.85
Lining, 60" wide	1.5	1.20	$1.80
Interfacing	.125	.90	$ .11
Total Fabric			$7.76

Trim/Findings	Quantity	Price	Cost
Zipper, 7"	1	.45	$ .45
Button	1	.09	.09
Thread	1	.20	.20
Brand Label	1	.08	.08
Care Label	1	.02	.02
Hang tag/price ticket	1	.06	.06
Packaging	1	.17	.17
Total Trim			$1.07

Labor	Cost
Cutting	$1.10
Sewing	$1.85
Total Labor	$2.95

	Description	Cost
Shipping	$10.00 per dozen	$ .83
Duty	16% of labor/material	$1.88
Overhead	18% of cost	$2.61

Total Manufacturing Cost: <u>$17.10</u>
Markup: <u>62%</u>
Retail Price: <u>$45.00</u>

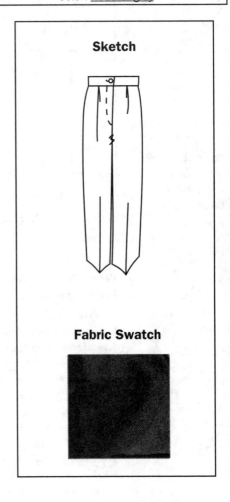

Sketch

Fabric Swatch

Figure 5.3 Cost sheet used to establish garment design and CMT cost estimates for a pair of women's slacks. (*Developed by Myrna Garner*)

Pearl River Enterprise Salisbury Road Kowloon, Hong Kong Tel: 852 5555 00000 Email: Kwon@pearlriver.com		Bankers: Bank of China Admiralty Center Hong Kong

Buyer: Alex Cameron New York, NY 10012 USA	Pro Forma No.: 201 Order No.: PDS1-2010 Payment Mode: LC Terms: FOB	Date: 15/Feb/10 Date: 15/Feb/10 Port: Hong Kong

Ref. No.	Description	Packing	Quantity	Port	Ship Date	Rate US$	Amount
9807	Tailored, pleated front slacks	12/24	3,600 Ea	Hong Kong		14.39	51,804.00

TOTAL CBM: 131.25   TOTAL FOB: $51,804.00

Figure 5.4 Example of a pro forma invoice, for Alex Cameron slacks. (*Myrna Garner*)

Vendor Selection and Payment for Goods

After receiving the quotes and deciding which bid to accept, the customer requests a **pro forma invoice** from the selected vendor that includes all information for the sale; this serves as confirmation of the total cost of the goods (Figure 5.4). A final invoice is provided by the vendor when the merchandise is shipped.

Payment for imported merchandise is often done by a **letter of credit,** which is a guarantee to the vendor that the customer has the funds to complete the purchase and that they are reserved for the seller by the buyer's bank. This letter usually has an expiration date close to the date of expected delivery in the contract; if the delivery date is not met, the letter of credit may need to be amended or in extreme cases allowed to expire, preventing payment. Other methods of payment include wire transfers, whereby the customer's bank sends money electronically to the vendor's bank when confirmation is received that the order has been shipped.

Shipping Consolidators

If a customer runs a relatively small business and thus is involved with relatively small orders, the firm might benefit from the use of a consolidator at the port where the goods are to be loaded. A **consolidator** is a person or firm that combines cargo from a number of shippers going to the same destination into one container for the purpose of reducing shipping rates. As previously mentioned, a partially filled shipping container costs more per unit to ship than does a full container—hence the need for a consolidator.

Insurance

Another area of consideration is making decisions about insurance. International business has risks, and insurance coverage can ameliorate problems the importer might encounter should anything happen to merchandise while it is en route to its destination. The two basic types are marine insurance, which protects the merchandise when it is in port or being shipped, and inland marine insurance, which covers the shipment at other times, such as on a truck, airline, or other conveyance used to get the goods to their final destination. Depending on a customer's needs, policies are available to cover loss from fire, bad weather, or theft, but coverage is not available for political instability or war.

Clearing Customs

Clearing customs is mostly about paperwork, and different goods can require different types of documentation, but the three forms the shipper must provide include

- a *bill of lading*, which is issued by the carrier or shipper, is basically a receipt of the goods, acknowledging they have been received on the vessel for shipment and spelling out their destination and the terms for transporting them to their final destination
- a *commercial invoice*, which is used as a customs declaration by the vendor that is exporting the goods and is required to determine their value for assessment of duties and taxes
- a *packing list*, which provides an itemized listing of the merchandise in the shipment and is attached to the outside of the shipping container

Having these forms available facilitates the process of getting the goods cleared. To avoid storage fees at the dock, arrangements can be made for a freight forwarder or other transporter, such as a trucking firm, to facilitate the shipment of goods to the final destination.

Do Learning Activity 5.7 to enhance your understanding of sourcing forms and contractual choices.

Learning Activity 5.7
SOURCING FORMS AND CONTRACTUAL CHOICES

1. What are the relationships among product specifications, cost sheets, and vendor bids?
2. Could the missing ship date on the pro forma invoice be an issue?
3. What is the role of a letter of credit in the sourcing process?
4. Under what conditions are consolidators essential participants in the sourcing process?

SUMMARY

This chapter focuses on sourcing as supply chain management and explores the components that support sourcing of textile and apparel products in the global marketplace. Direct factory sourcing options for apparel include CMT and full-package manufacturers, private brand importers, and branded importers. Other sourcing venues include trade fairs and trade shows, offshore facilities and joint ventures, licensing, and the utilization of sourcing agents.

Sourcing involves much more than simply finding the vendor that has the lowest labor costs. Much depends on what types of merchandise are needed as well as on whether the vendor has the capability to make merchandise to quality specifications in the volume required and in an ethical manner. In addition, attention must be paid to the level and degree of sophistication of communication capabilities and to potential variations in the time line for delivery, dependent upon the types of desired end products and the distance between production and final distribution to consumers. Determining the overall cost of textile materials and apparel, including logistics, transportation, and tariffs, is also more complex in the current global sourcing environment than when products were produced domestically.

Determining the overall cost of an apparel garment can be far more complex in global sourcing environments than when it is produced domestically. The buyer must consider macrocost areas, such as fabric and materials, production, logistics and transportation, and tariffs.

Much of the sourcing process itself is embodied in the paperwork involved in its financial forms and contracts, beginning with product specification and cost sheets. Vendor selection is made through a bidding process, using pro forma invoices and identification of forms of payment for vendor services. The logistics and transportation process may be supported through the use of consolidators. Protection of the merchandise is secured through the purchase of insurance.

Sourcing concludes with getting the products cleared through customs, a process that is largely dependent on additional paperwork and collection of duties and that can be facilitated by employing a customs broker, and with providing transportation for the products from the port of entry to their final destination.

REFERENCES

Anderson, K. (2006, August). Fast fashion evolves. *AATCC Review*, 6(8). Retrieved from http://www.techexchange.com

Apparel industry training falls short on sourcing skills (2008, July 15). just-style.com. Retrieved December 20, 2008, from http://www.just-style.com/article.aspx?id=101361

The Associated Merchandising Corporation Company Profile. (2010). Retrieved January 6, 2010, from http://biz.yahoo.com/ic/47/47224.html

Baigorri, M. (2009, August 27). Zara looks to Asia for growth. *BusinessWeek Online*, Retrieved January 7, 2010, from http://web.ebscohost.com.proxy.lib.ilstu.edu/ehost

Berton, E. (2009, August 18). Zara expands off-price format. *Women's Wear Daily*, 12.

Best Global brands, 2009 ranking. Retrieved May 8, 2010, from http://www.interbrand.com_global_brands.aspx

Bhatia, S. (2004, January 1) "Lean" vs. "agile" considerations shape supply chain strategies. *Apparel*. Retrieved from http://www.apparelmag.com

Bilal, M. (2005, April 8). Fashion, technology mesh at Levi's store. *The Chicago Tribune*. Retrieved from http://articles.chicagotribune.com/2005-04-08/news/0504090008_1_body-scanners-intellifit-convenience

Boyle, M. (2005, May 16). 25 Breakout companies. *Fortune*. Retrieved from http://money.cnn.com/magazines/fortune/fortune_archive/2005/05/16/8260133/index.htm

Dowling, M. (1997, July). New care labels for textiles. *Catalog Age*, 14(7), 18.

eWarna. About us. (2005). Retrieved April 29, 2004, from http://www.ewarna.com

eWarna unveils Color Indexer. (2005, April 5). TextileWeb. Retrieved May 7, 2010, from http://www.textileweb.com/article.mvc/eWarna-Unveils-Color-Indexer-0001

Germany: Body size portal goes live. (2009, October 9). just-style.com. Retrieved from http://www.just-style.com/article.aspx?id=105560

Inditex. (2009, December 11). *Financial Times*, p. 14. Retrieved January 7, 2010 from http://proquest.umi.com/pqdweb?did=1919585391&sid=1&Fmt=3&cl

Inditex. Our group. (n.d.). Retrieved January 7, 2010, from http://www.inditex.com/en/who_we_are/our_group

Intellifit offers custom-made jeans with a high-tech twist. (2008, February 11.) Retrieved from http://www.it-fits.info/INTELLIFIT-offers-custom-made-jeans-with-a-high-tech-twist.asp

JCPenney. (2010). Careers. Retrieved January 16, 2010, from http://jobs.jcpenney.com/USA/Fabric_Sourcing_Director_Product_Development_amp_Design_Wovens/012911581/job

Keeley, G. & Clark, A. (2008, August 12). Retail: Zara bridges Gap to become world's biggest fashion retailer. *The Guardian*. Retrieved September 1, 2010 from http://www.guardian.co.uk/business/2008/aug/12/retail.spain

Keiser, S. J., & Garner, M. B. (2008). *Beyond design: The synergy of apparel product development* (2nd ed.) New York: Fairchild Publications.

Kelleher, K. (2004, September). Bar codes get one better. Retrieved September 22, 2004, from http://www.business2.com

Li & Fung. (2010). Retrieved January 26, 2010, from http://www.lifung.com

Li & Fung Group. (2003). Retrieved January 10, 2010, from http://www.lifunggroup.com

Li & Fung Group purchases stakes in future logistics. (2009, July 21). *Logistics Business Review*. Retrieved from http://www.logistics-business-review.com/news/li__fung_group_purchases_stakes_in_future_logistics_090721

Macy's Inc. (2010). Private Brands. Retrieved May 8, 2010, from http://www.federated-fds.com/Macys/PrivateBrands.aspx

Manufacturing Sourcing. (2001). Retrieved November 11, 2009, from http://manufacturingsourcing.com/category/shipping

Minks, J. W. (1992). The sizing of clothes. *International Journal of Clothing Science and Technology*, 4(1), iii.

Olivier, Susan. (2008). The value of Fast: Speed to market through the glass pipeline. Presentation at AAFA Sourcing Conference. Retrieved December 22, 2009, from http://www.wwd.com

Reamy, D. W., & Steele, C. W. (2006) *Perry's department store: An importing simulation*. New York: Fairchild Publications.

Rigby, E. (2010, June 10). Inditex returns to double-digit sales growth. *Financial Times*. Retrieved September 1, 2010, from http://ft.com/cms/s/eedf0f36-738d-11df-bc73-00144feabdc0,dwp_uuid=dc15438a-a525

Rockford Consulting Group. (n.d.). Retrieved January 12, 2010, from http://www.rockfordconsulting.com/agile-manufacturing.htm

Talley, K. (2009, February 25). Liz Claiborne hires agent for sourcing operations—Li & Fung of Hong Kong will handle negotiations with vendors and monitor quality, with air of smoothing supply chain. *The Wall Street Journal*.

Trends: An annual statistical analysis of the U.S. apparel and footwear industries. (2009, August). Arlington, VA: American Apparel and Footwear Association.

U.S.: Li & Fung grows supply chain with online trade tool. (2009, June 9). just-style.com. Retrieved January 4, 2010, from http://www.just-style.com

Wolf, A. W. (1996, May). Labeling changes afoot. *Bobbin*, 37(9), 88–89.

Zarocostas, J. (2004, September 21) Study: Shipping costs key. *Women's Wear Daily*, 22.

Zernike, K. (2004, March 1). Sizing up American: Signs of expansion. *The New York Times*. Retrieved from http://www.nytimes.com/2004/03/01/national/01SIZE.html?pagewanted=all

6 Trade Barriers and Regulation

"Quota and tariff [trade] policies, in place for 40 years, now add as much as $80 billion a year to the retail cost of clothes and shoes" (Gresser, 2004, p. 1).

PROTECTED TRADE, FREE trade, or fair trade? Apparel professionals are challenged by all these forms of trade. Trade has many meanings in general usage—it can mean a living, an occupation, a line of business; skilled work, as distinguished from unskilled work; a craft; or an act of bargaining or exchanging. In this text the term **trade** means the buying and selling or bartering of goods and services. Trade takes place among individuals, groups, organizations, business firms, and the governments of cities, counties, states, and countries. Trade in the international and global context involves the exchange of goods and services across political boundaries. This is where protected trade, free trade, and fair trade become relevant. On the surface it seems that protected trade prevents harm, free trade does not cost anything, and fair trade provides equal value to those involved; however, that reading is much too simplistic.

THE EVOLUTION OF TRADE

"The entanglement of cultures and economies now known as globalization has been spreading for centuries and the world is smaller as

Objectives

- Explore the evolution of the textile and apparel trade.

- Examine how trade barriers protect trade.

- Discuss major international trade agreements and their intrinsic trade barriers, relevant to textiles and apparel.

ad valorem tariff a tax set as a fixed percent of the value of an imported product

Agreement on Textiles and Clothing (ATC) a World Trade Organization (WTO) trade agreement that replaced the GATT Multifiber Arrangement (MFA)

Customs and Border Protection (CBP) the U.S. customs service

customs service a government agency responsible for monitoring imported goods, assessing and collecting duties, and reporting imports against quotas

effective tariff the economic impact of a nominal tariff

exchange rates determine the ratio at which one currency can be traded for another

export policy a set of political determinations designed to regulate which types of products can leave a country for another market, and when and under what conditions those products can leave

foreign trade zone a free trade zone that allows manufacturing for export, but no domestic distribution of finished goods

free trade the unrestricted exchange of goods among nations

free trade zone a port or other site within a nation designated for duty-free entry of selected goods to be displayed, stored, and/or used for manufacturing

General Agreement on Tariffs and Trade (GATT) a multilateral trade agreement whose fundamental purpose was to promote free trade of goods and equalize trade among countries; has been absorbed by the WTO

import policy a political institution that determines what types of products and services can enter the domestic economy from another country, when, and under what conditions

international trade regulation barriers and limits on types and quantities of goods and services that cross political boundaries

most-favored nation (MFN) a very confusing term that means all nations engaged in the same trade agreement should be treated the same

Multifiber Arrangement (MFA) an international trade agreement that allowed the quantity of textile and apparel trade to be regulated through quotas established in bilateral agreements between nations

multilateral trade agreement involves more than two countries

nominal tariff rates published in each country's tariffs schedule

nontariff trade barriers the quota, quality standards, or other regulations or conditions that restrict the flow of goods between countries, not including taxes on imports or exports

normal trade relations (NTR) a term intended to replace *most-favored nation (MFN)* because it is more descriptive of the actual meaning

protectionism uses trade barriers to minimize imports

quota a method used to restrict quantities of goods that can be imported or exported

rate of duty the amount of tax to be assessed on imported or exported goods, usually according to a tariff schedule

specific tariff a fixed amount of tax per physical unit of imported product

trade policy a political institution designed to stimulate or control the exchange of goods between nations

transaction value the price actually paid or payable for goods when sold for export

Uruguay Round the final multilateral trade negotiations of GATT, which resulted in the WTO and ATC

voluntary export restraint a "gentlemen's agreement" between countries limiting trade

World Customs Organization (WCO) a global organization whose purpose is to improve the operations and efficiency of customs services

---

a result" (Elwood, 2001, p. 8). As mentioned previously, globalization has at least three dimensions: social, political, and economic. The primary focus of this discussion is the economic aspect, or, more specifically, trade among countries and companies that are located in different countries. Comments related to the political and cultural dimensions are integrated to support and explain the development of global trade. Box 6.1 lists the three phases of globalization and each phase's key components.

Friedman (2000) argued that the first era of globalization took place from 1400 to 1914, with intensive changes taking place between 1868 and 1914. The intense period of globalization following the Civil War has some similarities with the one we are currently experiencing. Great Britain was the dominant global power in the 19th

Box 6.1 KEY TIME FRAMES IN THE PROCESS OF GLOBALIZATION OF TRADE

Globalization 1.0. Globalization of Countries

1400–1865

Christopher Columbus discovered America while looking for Asia

Four hundred years of European colonization in Asia, Africa, Australia, and America

Native cultures destroyed and their peoples enslaved

David Ricardo developed the Theory of Comparative Advantage

Revolutionary War and Civil War in the United States

1866–1914

Connection of the transatlantic cable

Invention of the steamship, telegraph, railroads, and telephone

A "golden era" of international commerce

Globalization 2.0. Globalization of Companies

1915–1945

World War I, the Great Depression, and World War II

Keynesian economics led the world out of Depression

1946–1989

World divided by the cold war led by the United States and the Soviet Union

International Monetary Fund (IMF) established to manage a system of fixed monetary exchange rates

World Bank created to rebuild countries and economies destroyed in World War II

GATT (General Agreement on Tariffs and Trade) created to reduce trade barriers

Multifiber Arrangement (MFA) protected textile and apparel companies in developed countries, by using quotas on low-cost imports

Invention and use of computers, satellites, microcomputers, fiber optics

Political support of free market economy in the United States and Great Britain

Fall of the Berlin Wall

1990–2000

Conversion from the Cold War System to the Globalized System

Deregulation of financial markets

GATT integrated into World Trade Organization (WTO)

MFA integrated into Agreement on Textiles and Clothing (ATC)

Outsourcing blue collar jobs became common

Miniaturization of electronics

Explosion of microelectronics communication

Collapse of East Asian currencies

MFA's quota system scheduled to be phased out

Box 6.1 (CONTINUED)

Globalization 3.0. Globalization of Individuals

2001—2009

Giant corporations dominated global commerce with more economic power than many countries

Outsourcing white collar jobs became common

Regionalization of trade grew

Continuing education became essential

Corporate social responsibility became a priority

Creative corporate approaches to environmental responsibility produced economic benefits

Economic downturn challenged the world market

2010 . . .

Innovative approaches to developing sustainable supply chains paid dividends

Long-term trends became a foundation for economic recovery

Coalitions of business, governments, and the private sector provided leadership to link public policy and corporate responsibility

Sources:

Based on

BSR Report 2008. Retrieved January 5, 2010, from http://www.bsr.org/report

Chanda, N. (2004, March 25). Globalization 3.0 has shrunk the world: An interview with Thomas L. Friedman. *Global Envision*. Retrieved June 22, 2004, from http://globalenvision.org/library/3/601/6/

Cohen, S. D., Blecker, R. A., & Whitney, P. D. (2003). *Fundamentals of U.S. foreign trade policy* (2nd ed.). Boulder, CO: Westview Press.

Elwood, W. (2001). *The no-nonsense guide to globalization.* Oxford, UK: New Internationalist Publications.

Friedman, T. L. (2000, April). *The Lexus and the olive tree.* New York: Anchor Books.

century; the United States was the dominant global power in the 20th century. The trans-Atlantic cable, connected in 1866, linked banking and financial activities from New York, to London, to Paris, stimulating an era of "global finance capitalism." Topics on the agenda for the British parliament included dealing with competition from the Asian colonies and matching education and training standards with the United States and Germany. In that time, people freely migrated across political boundaries without passports. The invention of the steamship, the railroad, the telegraph, and the telephone were drawing the world together. According to Friedman (2000), the era of globalization before World War I (Globalization 1.0) was fundamentally a globalization of countries in which the world shrank from a size large to a size medium.

The 19th century era of globalization was shattered in the 20th century by World War I, but despite the Russian Revolution, the Great Depression, and World War II, the second era of globalization emerged (Globalization 2.0), and with it, the cold war, an international system of ideology and etiquette between the United States and the Soviet Union that lasted until 1989, when the Berlin Wall came down. Friedman (2000) described the 20th-century era of globalization as the globalization of companies that moved the world toward a single marketplace. The world changed from size medium to size small, especially from 1980 to 2000, because of the development of electronic communication and the Internet (Chanda, 2004; Friedman, 2000).

"Globalization 3.0 is [the] intensification of everything that was invented in Globalization 2.0—the bandwidths, the fiber-optics, the PCs, and the software capabilities that connected them. Now globalization is moving the world from size 'small' to size 'tiny' because of [the] globalization of individuals" (Chanda, 2004, p. 2). Individuals around the world are being manipulated, shifted, hired, and fired because global corporations are merging. Today, many global corporations have more economic power in the world market than do entire nations. Of the largest 100 economies in the world, 50 are run by multinational corporations, not countries. General Motors is larger than Greece, Thailand, or Norway; Mitsubishi is larger than Saudi Arabia; Walmart is larger than Malaysia, Israel, or Colombia. The global competition for market share over the past two decades has been the catalyst for the greatest shift toward monopoly in the last century (Elwood, 2001).

Over the past 50 years, there has been a strong movement toward eliminating trade barriers and increasing free trade. Three major categories of products remain that have relatively high levels of trade protection:

- agriculture
- steel
- textiles and apparel

Although our primary focus is on textiles and apparel, agriculture and steel may also be addressed, because they are intimately linked in the development of trade policy and practices.

Not everyone supports the goal of free trade. An old law of trade theory says people who are harmed by free trade know exactly who they are and that people who benefit have no idea. An increasing number of white collar workers are suffering because their jobs are being outsourced. Many blue collar workers have already been displaced. The stress created by this process has been offset by innovations like Google, Yahoo!, eBay, and Amazon. These new forms of business communication compensate for changes in established companies and provide new forms of employment. Countries such as India and China want jobs from the developed world, and we have to find ways for them to be able to have our products, in exchange. To do that, both tariff and nontariff barriers must come down (Chanda, 2004).

Throughout history, a country's **trade policy** has consisted mainly of a constantly evolving series of official objectives, laws, and actions designed to influence the flow of exports and imports of goods and services (Cohen, Blecker, & Whitney, 2003). Trade policy has been primarily determined by a combination of economic perspectives and political positions; it has two primary components: export policy and import policy. **Export policy** relates to efforts to sell domestically produced goods and services in foreign markets. Export policy may include government-sponsored personnel and funds to promote foreign sales as well as domestic laws that restrict the export of selected goods to unfriendly countries. **Import policy** determines the relative availability of foreign-made goods and services in domestic markets.

Protectionism seeks to use trade barriers to minimize imports, whereas **free trade** relies on market forces to determine the volume and variety of imports (Cohen et al., 2003). Each of these strategies is fraught with controversy, because there is frequent conflict between economic logic and political necessity:

- there is an intricate and ever-changing relationship between trade and other economic and political policy sectors
- there is diffusion of authority between executive and legislative branches of government (Cohen et al., 2003)
- social and cultural dimensions of trade have been frequently neglected

Now, expand your learning of the evolution of trade with Learning Activity 6.1.

Learning Activity 6.1
EVOLUTION OF TRADE

1. What is the fundamental meaning of *international*?
2. What is the fundamental meaning of *global*?
3. Why did Friedman describe globalization as three phases?
4. What do the first two phases of globalization have in common?
5. Do you think the third phase of globalization will have the same commonalities?
6. Why is a country's trade policy constantly evolving?

PROTECTED TRADE

Fundamentally, the purpose of trade protection is to prevent domestic companies from having to compete with foreign companies in their own domestic markets. A second rationale is to make competition fairer in international markets. Trade barriers allow the domestic companies to charge higher prices, grow and increase the number of jobs offered, and make a greater contribution to the domestic economy. Some types of trade barriers are also used as an important source of government revenue. Obviously, this means that consumers pay higher prices and have a more limited selection of goods from which to choose. When countries erect trade barriers, the barriers have to be monitored; thus, the need for customs services.

Customs Services

The government of nearly every country in the world has a **customs service**. The names of the service may vary slightly, as shown below:

- Australian Customs Service
- Ghana Customs Excise and Preventive Service
- Korea Customs Service
- United States Customs and Border Protection (CBP)

However, the primary responsibilities of customs in each country are similar:

- monitor imports and exports
- assess and collect duties
- report imports and exports against quota
- protect the country's borders against illegal entry

Concepts, issues, and processes related to the first three customs responsibilities are discussed in this chapter. Protecting a country's borders is discussed in Chapter 7.

Monitoring Imports and Exports

To figure out the what, when, and who of trading, a detailed accounting system is needed to record systematically the passage of products, and recording the amounts of specific types of products is a great challenge. As previously mentioned, until 1994 the United States used the English system of measurements, while the rest of the world used the metric system. When the United States joined the North American Free Trade Agreement (NAFTA), the United States government converted to the metric system, because the three countries had to agree on a common system of measurement for recording trade.

As discussed earlier, the development of the NAICS (North American Industry Classification System) was part of the changeover to the metric system (see Chapter 3). Measurements within the United States are still recorded in the English system, and the English system is still the primary system taught in schools (the rest of the world uses the metric system). However, serious trade protection requires accounting for products that cross international borders. The Tariff Schedules of the United States, based on the English system, was converted to the Harmonized Tariff Schedule (HTS) of the United States, based on the metric system and on the Harmonized Commodity Description and Coding System. Commonly known as the Harmonized System (HS), the Harmonized Commodity Description and Coding System is a global classification system used to describe most trade in goods. The HS is based on 97 product classifications called chapters. The product classifications break down into more than 5 thousand product categories, with classification numbers of up to ten digits, a brief description, the standard unit of measurement, and the rates of duty applicable to each category.

Classifying an article under the HS is not as straightforward as it may seem. There are many rulings on HS classification. For example, a knit shirt is not necessarily a knit T-shirt or a knit blouse. Classification of textile and apparel articles is generally determined by fiber content, weight, type of product or garment, and gender and age of the end user.

The **World Customs Organization (WCO)** describes the HS as the "language of international trade." The WCO's mission is to improve the effectiveness and efficiency of customs administrators. Approximately 80 percent of the 176 customs administrations that are members of the WCO represent developing countries or countries that are in transition to a market economy. Custom duties are an important source of revenue for these countries. Trade barriers that restrict trade and generate revenues are commonly classified as tariff and nontariff barriers.

Continue your exploration of protected trade by doing Learning Activity 6.2.

Learning Activity 6.2
PROTECTED TRADE

1. What are the possible reasons the export and import policies of a nation may be different?
2. Given the commonality of global trade and travel, do you think the United States should take up using the metric system, like the rest of the world? What might be major barriers to the change-over to metric?
3. Why is the Harmonized System (HS) so important in keeping track of the types and amounts of exchange in international trade?
4. If you have traveled internationally, you probably had to go through customs when you entered the foreign country and also when you returned. Which of the four functions of customs were carried out in those situations?

Tariffs and Duties

The most common form of trade protection is a **tariff** schedule establishing the taxes that are collected as duties on imported or exported goods. Paying duty increases the cost of acquiring the goods and therefore increases the selling price in the importing country. **Nominal tariffs**, which are the rates published in each country's tariff schedule, are the basis of determining how much duty has to be paid for specified products. Nominal tariffs have two forms: specific and ad valorem.

Specific tariffs
- are a fixed amount of money per physical unit of product
- are easy to apply and administer, especially on standardized goods
- provide a degree of protection that varies inversely with changes in import prices

Table 6.1 Examples of Specific and Ad Valorem Tariffs That Might Be Applied to Different Products

Product	Rates of Duty
Specific tariffs	
Chickens, ducks, turkeys	$ 0.02 each
Cattle, 1,550 kg or more	$ 0.007 per kg
Ad valorem tariffs	
Reptile leather luggage	8.5% ad valorem
Women's raincoats	8.9% ad valorem
Combined tariffs	
Baby sweaters of wool	$ 0.318 per kg + 14.4% ad valorem
Men's ties of man-made fibers	$ 0.248 per kg + 12.7% ad valorem

In other words, because the tariff does not change, if the import value goes up, the tariffs is a smaller proportion of the revenue gained from sale of the product in the foreign country; if the import value goes down, the tariff is a larger proportion of the revenue from the sale of the goods. Thus, when the import value goes down, the tariff provides more protection from competition with low-priced imported goods for domestic goods of the same type than when the import value goes up. When the value goes down, it will cost the exporter proportionally more to sell the lowest-value product in the foreign country.

Ad valorem tariffs are like a sales tax; they

- are a fixed percentage of the value of the product
- can be applied to products with a wide range of product variation
- maintain a constant degree of protection, even when prices vary

Sometimes, one type of tariff is applied to a single product; other times, both specific and ad valorem tariffs are applied (Table 6.1).

Determining the amount of duty that will have to be paid to import a product can be more complex than it looks. Duty is the payment due to import or export goods, usually based on a tariff schedule. Specific tariffs are relatively straightforward, because the amount of duty is dependent on physical measurements, usually the number of products or the weight of the product. The duty based on a specific tariff is calculated by multiplying the number of units of goods times the specific **rate of duty**.

Looking at Table 6.1, if 10 thousand ducks are imported, the duty due on the flock is

duty due =
physical units of goods × specific duty rate

$200 = 10,000 ducks × $0.02 each

According to the table, if cows are imported, the duty due is based on the total weight of the shipment rather than the number of cows. For example, if 60 cows are imported, and they weigh an average of 316.25 kilograms, the total weight of the shipment must be determined by multiplying the number of cows by the value of one cow and then multiplying the total by the tariff rate.

duty due =
physical units of goods × specific duty rate

= (60 cows × 316.25 kilogram) ×
$0.007 per kilogram

$132.83 = 18,975 kilogram ×
$ 0.007 per kilogram

If reptile leather luggage is imported, then an ad valorem tariff is applied. Remember, ad valorem tariffs are based on the value of the product rather than the number of units of the product. For example, if 1,250 pieces of reptile leather luggage were imported at a value of $340 each, the duty due would be

duty due = total value of the product ×
ad valorem duty rate

$36,125 =
($340 × 1,250 pieces of luggage) × 8.5 percent

When combinations of specific and ad valorem tariffs are applied to the same product, each duty has to be calculated separately and then added together. Applying both types of tariffs helps balance the inequities associated with specific tariffs. The basic calculation is

total duty due = specific duty + ad valorem duty

An example of a combined tariff, again based on Table 6.1, is the import of 60 dozen men's man-made fiber ties at $28 a dozen. The 3 dozen ties weigh 1 kilogram. To calculate the total tariff

specific duty due = physical units of goods × specific tariff rate

$4.96 = (60 dozen ties ÷
3 dozen per kilogram) × $0.248 per kilogram

ad valorem duty due = value of the product × ad valorem duty rate

$213.36 = (60 dozen ties × $28 per dozen) × 12.7 percent

combined duty due = specific duty + ad valorem duty

$218.32 = $4.96 + $213.36

These examples of tariffs and their related duties seem fairly straightforward, but a number of questions remain. For example, how is product value determined for ad valorem tariffs? According to GATT 1994, Article VII, the customs' value of a product used as a base for ad valorem tariffs is the transaction value. The **transaction value** is the price that is actually paid or payable for the goods when sold for export. However, customs evaluators in different countries use different criteria for when the transaction value applies to the tariff.

For example, the U.S. **Customs and Border Protection** (**CBP**) evaluators in the United States have traditionally used the FOB (free on board) import values, or the value when the product is loaded onto the carrier to leave the exporting country. The term FOB is misleading, because it sounds like there is no charge for freight to get the products to the carrier. There is always a cost related to transport to the carrier—it is just a matter of who pays it. With FOB the seller initially pays the freight to the carrier. Yet, from a practical, financial perspective, the cost of the freight is included in the product cost rather than listed separately. However, despite the confusing nature of FOB, for the customs product valuation the product cost is the FOB import value.

The European Union (EU) uses CIF (cost, insurance, freight) import values, the value as the product arrives in the importing country. CIF means

- C = merchandise cost
- I = transport insurance
- F = freight

The transaction value includes merchandise cost plus transport insurance and freight. Thus, even if the importing firms in the EU face the same nominal tariffs, the duty paid will be higher, because the transaction value is higher. Consequently, retail prices on imported goods will be higher in the EU than retail prices for the same goods with the same markup in the United States. The result is that U.S. manufacturers may be less likely to export to EU, whereas EU manufacturers may be more likely to ship to the United States. Firms in the EU have a greater protection from the same nominal ad valorem duty rate because of a difference in product valuation.

Let us go back to the luggage example in Table 6.1; when 1,250 pieces of luggage are imported at a value of $340 each, with 8.5 percent ad valorem, the total FOB duty for the United States is the same as previously calculated.

FOB ad valorem duty due = FOB value of the product × ad valorem tariff duty

$36,125 = ($340 × 1,250 pieces) × 8.5 percent

To determine CIF ad valorem duty for the EU, insurance and freight have to be added to FOB value. Assume each suitcase weighs 11 pounds, for a total shipment weight of 13,750 pounds (1,250 suitcases × 11 pounds). The freight costs $4.49 per pound, and the insurance is $2 per suitcase, making a total of $2,500 (1,250 × $2).

CIF ad valorem duty due = [FOB value + freight + insurance] × ad valorem duty rate

CIF ad valorem duty due = [($340 × 1,250) + (13,750 lbs × $4.49 per lb) + $2,500] × 8.5 percent

$41,585 = [$425,000 + $61,738 + $2,500] × 8.5 percent

Thus, the suitcase manufacturers in EU have $5,460 more tariff protection on the shipment of luggage than U.S. manufacturers just because of a difference in the way the transaction value is determined by customs in the two countries.

Another key question is what the effective rate of tariff protection is. The **effective tariff** determines how much more expensive domestic production can be, relative to foreign production, and still compete in the market. The effective tariff also demonstrates the real impact of the nominal tariff on the prices paid by customers in the domestic market.

For example, (refer back to Table 6.1 again) if you were a duck importer, would you be better off if you imported large ducks or little ducks, given a specific tariff of $.02 per duck? If you imported ducks that weighed 8 kilograms, the effective duty rate is $.0025 per kilogram (2 cents ÷ 8 kilograms). If you imported ducks that weighed 1 kilogram, the effective duty rate is $.02 per kilogram. Clearly, the effective rate of tariff protection is much less on large ducks than little ducks. The little ducks obviously have to be fed large amounts of grain to become large ducks, but that is another story. The point here is that the effective protection pro-

vided by a specific tariff can vary, depending on size or the value of the product imported.

What is the effective rate of tariff protection on a finished product when a tariff is applied to imported materials? Assume that three pounds of cotton are imported to make a pair of jeans. The cost of the cotton is $.43 a pound, and the duty rate is the maximum allowed according to WTO at 56 percent. Assume also that the value of the product doubles each time it is sold from the fiber importer, through the product development and production process to the ultimate consumer.

When the cotton is imported, that cost of the duty becomes part of the cotton cost, so although the cotton cost is $1.29, the importer regarded the cotton cost as $1.29 plus the duty (56 percent of the cost), a total of $2.01. The cost of the tariff is forever incorporated into the product cost when the product is priced for sale. As a result, the value of the tariff gets paid again and again, each time the product is sold (Table 6.2).

At the point of retail sale, where you buy the jeans, one third of the retail price can be attributed to the cost of the tariff. If there were no tariff on the cotton, with all the rest of the same assumptions, the retail price on the jeans would have been $41.28. This simplistic example demonstrates the concern about the burden put on consumers by tariffs that are intended to protect domestic industry.

In sum, import tariffs reduce the volume of trade and raise the domestic prices of imported goods. In the country that imposes the tariffs, producing firms gain, and consumers lose, because the producing firms can charge more for their products, and consumers have to pay higher prices. In the world as a whole, tariffs decrease the volume of trade and thus decrease the benefits of trade. The opposing argument is that there would be no consumers to buy the merchandise if there were no jobs to support domestic spending and that such jobs should therefore be protected by trade barriers.

Table 6.2 Effective Rate of Protection on Jeans Made from Three Pounds of Imported Cotton with a 56 Percent Duty Rate, Assuming the Price Doubles Each Time the Product Is Sold

Transaction	Total Cost		
	Product + Duty	Product	Duty
Import cotton	$ 2.01	$ 0.43 × 3 lbs = $ 1.29	$ 1.29 × 56% = $ 0.72
Yarn mill buys cotton	$ 4.02	$ 2.58	$ 1.44
Fabric mill buys yarn	$ 8.04	$ 5.16	$ 2.88
Apparel manufacturer buys fabric	$ 16.08	$ 10.32	$ 5.76
Retailer buys jeans	$ 20.64	$ 11.52	$ 32.16
You buy jeans	$ 64.32	$ 41.28	$ 23.04

Free Trade Zones

Free trade zones, in their various formats, represent provisions within trade agreements between countries that are designed to reduce trade barriers and facilitate trade. A **free trade zone** is defined as a port or other site within a nation designated for duty-free entry of selected goods to be displayed, stored, or used for manufacturing. The goods imported into the free trade zone may be stored or undergo repackaging or other minor operations before they are exported to another country. The products imported into the zone are not subject to duties assessed on similar imported goods that enter commerce in the country.

Free trade zones are often established within individual nations that are just entering into competitive participation in the global market. Their primary suppliers are sourcing companies representing firms from developed countries that seek low-cost labor and avoidance of duties on imports. At the same time, the zones provide jobs for people in developing countries who are desperately in need of employment and lower costs to people in developed countries in which the goods are ultimately consumed.

A **foreign trade zone** is a free trade zone that allows manufacturing for export. Materials can be imported into the zone duty free, remain under the control of customs or in a bonded warehouse (a government-supervised storage facility), and undergo processing/manufacturing within the zone before being exported as finished goods. The goods produced do not compete in the developing country's domestic market, because everything stored and processed in the zone is required to be exported. Free and foreign trade zones are located in a single country, and goods move between countries with special treatment, including no duty assessed, thus eliminating the increasing costs associated with effective tariffs. In the trade press the terms *free trade zone* and *foreign trade zone* are sometimes used interchangeably.

A qualified industrial zone (QIZ) is a very specialized type of foreign trade zone that involves more than one nation, specifically Jordan and Israel or Egypt and Israel, where manufacturing can take place, similar to a foreign trade zone. QIZs are discussed further in Chapter 12. A *free trade area* is a region made up of two or more countries that have a comprehensive free trade agreement eliminating or reducing trade barriers on products traded among the countries. For example, Canada, Mexico, and United States make up NAFTA, a free trade area. Free and foreign trade zones and free trade areas require agreements between the nations involved to reduce trade barriers.

Further your study of tariffs with Learning Activity 6.3.

Learning Activity 6.3
THE EFFECT OF TARIFFS

1. Why are there inequities associated with specific tariffs?
2. A poultry importer has made a deal to import 1,500 young turkeys weighing 2.7 kilograms (6 pounds) each and 1,500 young chickens weighing 0.9 kilo-grams (1 pound) each. Considering the duty rates in Table 6.1, determine how much total duty has to be paid on the turkeys and the chickens.
3. Considering your calculations for question 2, how much increase in price per kilogram will the importer have to charge to cover the duty on the turkeys? on the chickens?
4. Considering your calculations for question 3, which domestic producers have the most trade protection—the producers of turkeys or of chickens? What realities do these numbers demonstrate, relative to the effectiveness of specific tariffs?
5. According to Table 6.1, is the tariff on cattle more or less fair than the tariff on poultry? Explain.
6. You are a U.S. importer of baseball gloves, and you want to import two groups of baseball gloves: 500 dozen, with a cost of $8.50 each, and 100 dozen, at a cost of $14.00 each. Considering a 15 percent ad valorem tariff, what is the total duty due on each group? What is the duty due on one unit in each group?

7. You did not do well with baseball gloves, so you switched over to importing designer neckties from Italy. Fourteen ties equal one kilogram. Considering potential duties of $0.0265 per kilogram and 13.5 percent ad valorem, calculate the total duty due on 900 dozen ties, at $19 each.
8. In what way does a free trade zone reduce trade barriers?
9. Look up the Harmonized Tariff Schedule (HTS) on the Internet. Search out the chapter on textiles and apparel. What key components of information are presented to help identify appropriate tariff rates?

Nontariff Trade Barriers

Nontariff trade barriers restrict trade by some means other than applying a tax on import or export of products. These barriers may take the following forms:

- customs procedures
- distribution limits and restrictions
- exchange rates
- export quotas
- government procurement restrictions' lack of transparency
- import licensing
- import quotas
- infrastructure related to transport
- internal taxes and charges
- investment requirements affecting trade
- lack of intellectual property protection (copyrights, trademarks, production processes)
- minimum, or reference, prices
- price controls
- price support programs
- standards, technical regulations, certification procedures
- subsidies for domestic firms
- tariff rate quotas
- trade preference programs
- voluntary export restraints

Of this intimidating list, exchange rates, import quotas, price support programs, subsidies for domestic firms, and voluntary export restraints are the most common nontariff trade barriers that affect textiles and apparel.

Exchange rates determine the ratio at which one currency can be traded for another (Figure 6.1). The terms *strong dollar* and *weak dollar* are sometimes used to describe exchange rates in the United States. During most of the past decade, the U.S. dollar has been weak against other currencies, such as the Euro. Imports are commonly priced in the exporting country's currency and then quoted to a buyer in his or her domestic currency, based on the exchange rate at the time. A currency that is depreciating in value causes imports to be more expensive. Sometimes, an exporter acknowledges a depreciating currency by giving a special price to encourage importation of goods. An appreciating currency causes foreign goods to be less expensive and becomes an incentive to import goods or travel to foreign countries. There is usually a lag time between appreciation of currency and surge of imports, because new contracts have to be developed and merchandise produced, based on the change in exchange rate.

Beginning in 1944, countries that belonged to the International Monetary Fund (IMF) kept their exchange rates fixed relative to the U.S. dollar, and the dollar was fixed relative to the price of gold. The dollar became overvalued on the gold standard, and since 1973, exchange rates have been floating and flexible. A technical explanation of the operation of exchange rates is beyond the scope of this text—other than that exchange rates are a factor in determining the relative cost of imports and domestic production.

Read Case 6.1 to see how global exchange rates are affecting U.S. tourism.

Quotas restrict quantities of goods that can be imported or exported but are most often applied to imports. Quotas are intended

Figure 6.1 Some of the major currencies of the world, including the U.S. dollar, the EU euro, and the Japanese yen.
(*Courtesy of WWD*)

to restrict the quantities of goods that enter a country without imposing a tax that has to be paid by the ultimate consumer, sometimes after it has been multiplied many times over in the production or marketing process (as is the case with tariffs). Quotas are often administered by a government that issues import licenses up to the quantity of imports that will be allowed. The licenses may be given away or sold. If the government gives the licenses away, it sacrifices the revenue that would have been accrued if tariffs had been applied. However, if the quota is sold to importing firms, it does generate governmental revenue. Once the entire quota for a particular category of products is distributed, the quota may become a market in itself.

Textile and apparel quotas were limits set by bilateral agreements within the Multifiber Arrangement (MFA). The exporting country allocated the quantity of goods allowed by the agreement and issued the visas (licenses) for entry into the importing country. The importing country regulated the level of imports, based on the amount entered using the visas. The importing country did not allocate the quota or issue the license for entry.

A favorable exchange rate could help reverse a slide in the number of visitors to the United States. In 2004, Nicola Ross held up a sneaker for her husband, Ian, to examine in a Puma store at an Orlando outlet mall.

Ross, a tourist from Liverpool, England, was stunned by the $40 price tag and by her purchasing power, which came in no small part from a currency exchange rate that had the British pound approaching twice the value of the U.S. dollar. Ian Ross said that they could not have timed their visit better.

U.S. tourism officials expected more European and Canadian visitors to follow the Ross's example, in part because of the weak U.S. dollar. They hoped the exchange rate would help reverse the decline in the number of visitors to the United States in the late 1990s.

By 2004, the dollar hit a low against the Euro and an 11-year low against the pound. The Euro was worth about $1.22, compared with $1.07 at the same time a year earlier; a British pound was worth about $1.80, up from approximately $1.58 at the same time in 2003; and the Canadian dollar was worth about 75 cents, up from approximately 67 cents.

In 2007, the even weaker dollar had Americans packing for anywhere but Europe. A euro cost $1.37, and a British pound, $2, for the first time in 26 years. For Americans, that made meals, entertainment, and lodging extra pricey. Some European hotels were offering specials that guaranteed room rates in U.S. dollars, shifting the currency exchange risk to the hotels.

In early 2010, the dollar had gained back some value, relative to the British pound, but the euro cost even more than in 2004, at $1.63. However, a Canadian dollar in 2010 only cost $1.02, so for planning the most economical summer vacation away from the United States, Canada was recommended.

However, retailers in the state of New Jersey were well prepared when, in April 2010, the Euro began to drop in value. They recognized there was always strong demand from foreign tourists looking for world-class bargains and American brands. For example, The Jersey Gardens Mall installed a concierge desk where all foreign tourists had to do was show their passports to receive and send faxes, obtain airport shuttle information, and get shopping vouchers. One Irish tourist reported she would not even think of stepping into a Juicy Couture store back home in Ireland because of the prohibitive prices, but at the Jersey Gardens she waltzed right into the sea of leopard print and hot pink handbags. Across the mall, at the Converse store, a tourist picked up a pair of leather high-top sneakers for $50; back home in Portugal a similar pair would have cost $120.

From the U.S. apparel import perspective, the exchange rate with the Chinese yuan is of primary interest, because the United States received nearly 35 percent of imported apparel from China in 2009. The exchange rate for a Chinese yuan was $8.28 in 2004, $7.71 in 2007, and, by January 2010, $6.82. These numbers would seem to discourage imports from China, but the reality is that the dollar was losing value in relation to many currencies around the world and that China, by then, had become known as the manufacturer for the world.

Sources:

Juri, C. (2010, January 25). N.J. outlet mall lures international shoppers with bargains on U.S. brands, weak dollar. *The Star-Ledger*. Retrieved from http://www.nj.com/news/index.ssf/2010/01/nj_outlet_mall_lures_internati.html

Lollis, B. D. (2007, May 1). Exchange rates cut into U.S. travelers' fun in Europe. *USA Today*. Retrieved from http://www.usatoday.com/travel/news/2007-04-30-euro-travel-usat_N.htm

Schneider, M. (2004, March 18). Weak dollar is a big hit with foreign tourists. *The Des Moines Register*, p. 3D.

The exporting firm that holds the visas gains revenue even when it has issued more visas than it can fill (also depriving other exporting firms of needed visas). The ultimate consumers who buy the products pay for the products, the quota, and tariffs as well as the production and retailing processes. Thus, the quota system may reward firms that have done nothing to contribute to the product and causes the customer to pay substantially higher prices. Nontariff barriers tend to be controversial and divisive in trade relations because of the gap between reality and intent.

When the terms of the MFA expired at the beginning of 2005, the importation of apparel from China into developed countries exploded. China had already produced thousands of dozens of apparel garments and had them stored in containers loaded on ships, ready to arrive in port when the MFA quotas expired. For example, as a result of China's preparation, exports from China to the United States increased from 2004 to 2005, as follows:

- cotton knit shirts increased 1,277 percent
- cotton trousers increased 1,573 percent
- cotton underwear increased 318 percent
- man-made fiber shirts and trousers increased 300 percent (Zagaroli, 2008).

A similar explosion of imports in the EU caused it to move quickly to impose new import quotas on selected categories of apparel from China in June 2005. Following extensive negotiations between trade representatives, in November 2005 the United States signed a Memorandum of Understanding with China, limiting imports from China on 34 selected categories of apparel products. The agreement allowed 10 percent increases in 2006, another 12.5 percent increase in 2007, and a 15 to 16 percent increase in 2008.

When the U.S. export limit agreement with China expired in 2008, there were ship-loads of apparel sitting offshore, waiting to be unloaded, that were included in retailers' merchandise plans to supply inventories for the spring 2009 selling period. However, the CBP did not allow the merchandise to be unloaded. Instead, it imposed "staged entry procedures" for textile and apparel goods shipped from China in 2008 that exceeded the applicable quotas. At the direction of the Committee for Implementation of Textile Agreements, the CBP limited the entry of goods as follows:

- for all shipments exported in 2008 that exceeded 2008 quotas, entry was not permitted until February 1, 2009
- from February 1 through February 28, 5 percent of the applicable quota could be imported
- entry for any remaining goods was then permitted at the rate of 5 percent per month, until all shipments in excess of applicable quotas had been entered ("USA: Over-Quota Apparel Imports," 2009)

To understand the difficulty these sorts of interruptions of trade can cause, here is an example. Assume you are a retail buyer of infants' apparel for Macy's. Among the thousands of dozens of garments sitting offshore are 50 thousand pairs of infants' socks that are scheduled to be for sale in Macy's stores all across the country during the month of February 2008. There are going to be a lot of Macy's customers' babies going barefoot or perhaps going to Walmart to get their socks, assuming, of course, that Walmart's socks are not also sitting offshore onboard the same ship.

Voluntary export restraints have commonly been regarded as "gentlemen's agreements" to restrict trade, because the agreements are not formalized into international law (and because women are not likely to be involved). When serious regulation of the textile and apparel trade began early in the 20th century, British textiles dominated the industry internationally. However, the United States had also become a major producer. From the perspective of national security, the textile industry was regarded as critical for clothing the armed forces, but it was perceived as being unable to survive in the international market without trade protection. Therefore, by 1930 the U.S. tariff was 46 percent on cotton goods and 60 percent on woolen goods. Japan, the major low-cost exporter in that era, faced quotas as well as high tariffs but was still shipping increasing quantities to developed countries. The United States induced Japan to enter a voluntary export restraint agreement restricting exports. This was the first stage of a trade agreement that in the 1950s became the more structured.

MFA. The MFA limited textiles and apparel imports into developed countries until the 1990s, when the Agreement on Textiles and Clothing (ATC) was created. Many trade preference agreements are in effect around the world. These will be discussed further in Chapters 9 to 12.

Now, continue to explore trade barriers with Learning Activity 6.4.

Learning Activity 6.4
ESTABLISHING TRADE BARRIERS

1. Among the nontariff barriers, what are the means of trade restraint affecting textiles and apparel?
2. Why are foreign tourists to the United States so happy about the weak dollar?
3. What does the weak dollar mean for U.S. exporters?
4. What problem does the weak dollar create for U.S. importers?
5. Considering the exchange rates discussed in Case 6.1, if you wanted to travel internationally, where would you get the best exchange rates—Canada or Great Britain? Why?
6. How does a quota reduce trade?

TRADE AGREEMENTS

There are thousands of trade agreements that impact trade in textiles and apparel. With more than 200 countries in the world, each country only has to have five trade agreements to make up a thousand. We cannot deal with thousands here, even if we wanted to; instead, this chapter gives an overview of the primary agreements that have been relevant to the textile and apparel trade during the 20th and 21st centuries.

Implementation of Tariffs in the United States

Tariffs have two purposes: to restrict trade and to accumulate revenue for the government. In fact, the first substantive piece of legislation passed by the U.S. Congress following the Revolutionary War was a tariff act. The tariff rate was low, an average of 5 percent, so it provided little protection to domestic industry but was an important source of revenue for the government of a fledgling country that had not yet established a tax system (Cohen et al., 2003).

The battle over U.S. trade protection had begun. Over the next 50 years, tariff rates increased in fits and starts, until they became an issue between the North and South prior to the Civil War. Some tariff rates ranged from 50 to 100 percent of the value of imports, particularly on agricultural products. States in the South thought their economies and social systems were being marginalized, because high tariffs on U.S. imports angered countries such as Great Britain, which was the primary customer of the southern states' exports of cotton and tobacco. By 1846, Great Britain was already largely industrialized and recognized lower tariffs as a means of expanding world markets (Cohen et al., 2003).

Following the Civil War, tariffs were politicized in the United States, with one political party advocating lower tariffs, and the other supporting higher tariffs; however, a protectionist perspective remained firmly in place, for the most part. Other countries regarded the United States as isolationist. In 1930, with the Depression in progress, the Smoot-Hawley Tariff Act raised the average tariff rate to 53 percent, an all-time high. In 1932, President Franklin Roosevelt and Secretary of State Cordell Hull "deeply believed that an open trading system fostered a peaceful cooperation, and stable international political order, whereas a closed trading system produced international tension and conflict" (Cohen et al., 2003, p. 33). Hull negotiated the Reciprocal Trade Agreements Act of 1934, which became a turning point in international trade relations for the United States. The act allowed the executive branch of the U.S. government to negotiate up to a 50 percent reduction in tariff rates as long as the other countries reciprocated the reductions. By the early 1940s, 25 bilateral agreements were in place, mostly with countries in the Western Hemisphere. Because the most-favored nation (MFN) principle was included in the act, the United States offered the tariff rate reductions to other countries as more bilateral agreements were developed.

General Agreement on Tariffs and Trade (GATT) (1947 to 1994)

After World War II, the United States became the leader in the advocacy of free trade, 100 years after Great Britain initiated the policy. After extended negotiations among major countries, in 1947 the **General Agreement on Tariffs and Trade (GATT)** was established. GATT provided an international framework that established the ground rules for worldwide trade among its members, called contracting parties. GATT's primary purpose was to reduce trade barriers, particularly tariffs

and quotas, among its members, but it also dealt with a wide range of commercial policies. GATT rules specify that a party granting a trade advantage to one country must grant the same advantage to all contracting parties—the **most-favored nation (MFN)** clause. Therefore, *most-favored nation* means that another nation will be treated the same, not better, than other member nations. For that reason, the United States declared that MFN should now be known as **normal trade relations (NTR)**. The term was changed legally in 1998, but use of MFN still persists.

A council of representatives elected by GATT members dealt with urgent work between sessions. The GATT secretariat consisted of international trade specialists and an administrative staff. Tariff conferences and sessions were usually held at GATT's headquarters, in Geneva, Switzerland. Most decisions were made by simple majority vote; each contracting party had one vote. GATT granted special privileges to developing nations without requiring those nations to obey all of GATT's rules, which included limited use of nontariff trade barriers, such as import quotas and other restrictions on the flow of goods. Fundamentally, GATT established ground rules for worldwide trade among it signatories.

By the early 1970s, approximately 80 countries had signed GATT agreements. Several other countries had applied for membership or participated in the agreement in some manner. Contracting parties held business sessions at least once a year. Frequently topics included removal of trade barriers. These meetings reduced tariffs and other trade obstacles on thousands of products.

The greatest achievements in trade liberalization were accomplished through GATT's multilateral negotiations, known as trade rounds. The trade rounds were time–consuming, lasting from 3 to 7 years. The trade rounds were referred to as the Kennedy Round during the 1960s, the Tokyo Round during the 1970s, and the Uruguay Round during the late

1980s and early 1990s. The **Uruguay Round** created a new trade management system, the World Trade Organization (WTO).

Multifiber Arrangement (MFA) (1974 to 1994)

Following World War II, trade restraints between the United States and Great Britain eased somewhat but continued with Japan, Eastern Europe, and other developing countries. Japan joined GATT in 1955 and should have gained MFN status, but developed countries found ways to continue to restrict textile trade. The source of legal authority to control imports in the United States came from Section 204 of the Agricultural Act of 1956, which gave the president the authority to enter into agreements with countries, limiting textile and apparel imports from those countries through the introduction of quota limits.

Formal textile and apparel trade regulation through GATT began in 1961, with the Short-Term Arrangement, followed by the Long-Term Arrangement, to limit imports of cotton and cotton materials. However, between 1960 and 1970, as imports of cotton were being restricted, U.S. imports of man-made fiber textiles rose from 31 million pounds to 329 million pounds. The United States then initiated bilateral agreements extending the Long Term Arrangement to also cover man-made textile materials from Hong Kong, Japan, Korea, and Taiwan, the primary suppliers, who became known as the big four. The excess products not allowed to enter the United States were diverted to European countries, driving down prices there. The result was the negotiation of the **Multifiber Arrangement (MFA)**, which took effect in 1974 (Cline, 1990). The Short- and Long-Term Arrangements and the MFA were basically exceptions to the GATT and contrary to its primary purpose of reducing trade barriers since they involved implementing quota restraints on trade.

The MFA was a general framework for determining the conditions under which the textile and apparel trade could be controlled. The MFA defined a language for describing and limiting textile and apparel trade:

- bilateral agreement—a written agreement governing textile and apparel trade, usually between a developing exporting country and a developed importing country
- category—an apparel or textile product or aggregation of similar products for import control purposes; the several thousand textile and apparel products covered by the MFA were aggregated into 104 categories: 39 for cotton, 24 for wool, and 41 for man-made fiber; Sixty-one of those categories covered apparel products
- SYE (now SME)—the square yard equivalent (now square meter equivalent) was an overall measure of trade in physical terms; limits within bilaterals were set in SYEs, and with the exception of fabric, all apparel and textile products were assigned a conversion factor that converts units (number of garments) into SYEs; for example, a dozen men's and boy's woven shirts represented 24 SYE
- aggregate ceiling—the total amount of SYEs a country could export to the developed country in any given year under the terms of its bilateral agreement

The MFA provided for unilateral trade restraints in the absence of bilateral trade agreements, so there was pressure on developing/producing countries to establish bilateral agreements with the developed/consuming countries. The MFA also established the norms for the bilateral export-restraint agreements, and it provided for annual growth in imports of 6 percent. However, considerable flexibility was built into the MFA, via the following:

Table 6.3 DIFFERENCES BETWEEN THE GENERAL AGREEMENT ON TARIFFS AND TRADE (GATT) AND THE WORLD TRADE ORGANIZATION (WTO)

GATT	WTO
—A set of rules; a multilateral agreement	—A permanent institution with its own secretariat
—Applied on a provisional basis	—Commitments are full and permanent
—Rules applied to trade in goods	—Covers trade in goods, services, and issues related to intellectual property
—Rules selectively applied	—Commitment of the entire membership
—Disputes slow to settle, and settlements difficult to implement	—Settlement system is faster, more automatic, swift to implement
—System dependent on GATT 1947 until 1994	—GATT 1994 is foundation of the merchandise trade system

Source: Based on Roots of the WTO. (n.d.). Retrieved August 8, 2004, from http://econ2.econ.iastate.edu/classes/econ355/choi/wtoroots.htm

- swing—the ability to use a portion of the unfilled ceiling of one category for another category
- carry over—an exporting country was allowed to use some of any unused ceiling from one agreement year to apply to the subsequent year's ceiling
- carry forward—an exporting country was allowed to borrow from next year's ceiling to apply to the present year's level

Interestingly, exporting countries seldom monitored quantity of exports, so little happened until popular categories were massively overshipped, and the United States or other developed countries called the exporting countries' attention to the problem.

The MFA created the Textiles Surveillance Body to administer the MFA, and there was no lack of work because of the nature of the agreement. The MFA was renewed in 1977, 1981, and 1986, each time increasing trade restraint with bilateral agreements involving more countries.

Interestingly, the MFA really did not work. By 1980, the United States had 18 bilateral agreements; by 1990, the United States had more than 60 bilaterals, and textile and apparel imports were growing at an unprecedented rate. The MFA did limit trade with countries that were major exporters where bilaterals were created.

However, the primary effect of MFA was in driving apparel production around the world. The challenge was to find the next undeveloped, low-labor-cost country where apparel production could be established and where no bilateral agreement was in effect. The apparel industry was up to the task. Despite the MFA, U.S. imports of textiles and apparel increased from $2.3 billion in 1973 to $83.3 billion in 2004, just before the expiration of MFA in early 2005.

World Trade Organization (WTO) (1994–present)

In 1994, following the 7 years of GATT trade negotiations known as the Uruguay Round, the WTO absorbed the GATT, and the MFA was replaced by the Agreement on Textiles and Clothing (ATC), whose assigned task was to phase out the MFA, and thereby its quota system, by 2005. The WTO was directed to operate on the same fundamental assumptions as GATT:

1. Trade protection weakens the global economy.
2. Freer trade strengthens the global economy.

Over the years, these core principles of the 1947 GATT were updated and became GATT 1994, the trade rules for the new WTO (Table 6.3).

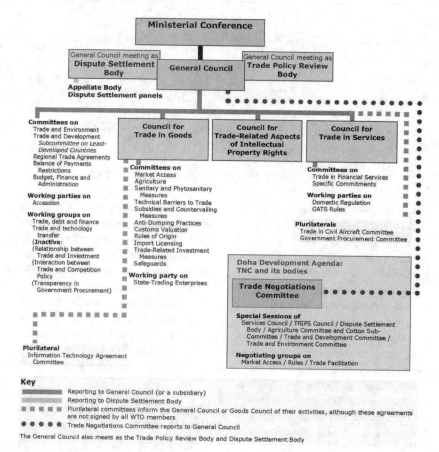

WTO structure

All WTO members may participate in all councils, committees, etc, except Appellate Body, Dispute Settlement panels, and plurilateral committees.

Ministerial Conference

General Council meeting as **Dispute Settlement Body**

General Council

General Council meeting as **Trade Policy Review Body**

Appellate Body
Dispute Settlement panels

Committees on
Trade and Environment
Trade and Development
Subcommittee on Least-Developed Countries
Regional Trade Agreements
Balance of Payments Restrictions
Budget, Finance and Administration

Working parties on
Accession

Working groups on
Trade, debt and finance
Trade and technology transfer
(Inactive:
(Relationship between Trade and Investment
(Interaction between Trade and Competition Policy
(Transparency in Government Procurement)

Council for Trade in Goods

Committees on
Market Access
Agriculture
Sanitary and Phytosanitary Measures
Technical Barriers to Trade
Subsidies and Countervailing Measures
Anti-Dumping Practices
Customs Valuation
Rules of Origin
Import Licensing
Trade-Related Investment Measures
Safeguards

Working party on
State-Trading Enterprises

Council for Trade-Related Aspects of Intellectual Property Rights

Council for Trade in Services

Committees on
Trade in Financial Services
Specific Commitments

Working parties on
Domestic Regulation
GATS Rules

Plurilaterals
Trade in Civil Aircraft Committee
Government Procurement Committee

Doha Development Agenda: TNC and its bodies

Trade Negotiations Committee

Special Sessions of
Services Council / TRIPS Council / Dispute Settlement Body / Agriculture Committee and Cotton Sub-Committee / Trade and Development Committee / Trade and Environment Committee

Negotiating groups on
Market Access / Rules / Trade Facilitation

Plurilateral
Information Technology Agreement Committee

Key

Reporting to General Council (or a subsidiary)
Reporting to Dispute Settlement Body
Plurilateral committees inform the General Council or Goods Council of their activities, although these agreements are not signed by all WTO members
Trade Negotiations Committee reports to General Council

The General Council also meets as the Trade Policy Review Body and Dispute Settlement Body

Figure 6.2 World Trade Organization (WTO) structure reflects the complexity of achieving and monitoring global trade agreements. The Textiles Monitoring Body is included under the Council for Trade of Goods.

(Copyright © World Trade Organization)

The WTO provides a permanent forum for member governments to address their multilateral trade relations and facilitates the implementation of trade agreements. As with GATT, the WTO is primarily concerned with **multilateral trade agreements,** agreements that involve more than two countries. The highest authority of the WTO is the Ministerial Conference, which is composed of representatives of all WTO member countries and is required to meet at the ministerial level at least every 2 years (Figure 6.2). The General Council is the highest authority when a Ministerial Conference is not in session and thus directs the daily work of the WTO. Three councils and one committee group report to the General Council. Our primary interest is in the Council for Trade in Goods, which includes committees addressing subsidies, customs valuation, rules of origin, and import licensing. The Textiles Monitoring Body oversees the Agreement on Textile and Apparel and also reports to the Council for Trade in Goods. In April 2008, there were 153 member countries and 31 observer countries in the WTO. All WTO decisions are made by 100 percent consensus.

Table 6.4 THE PHASEOUT OF IMPORT QUOTAS FOR WORLD TRADE ORGANIZATION (WTO) MEMBERS, ACCORDING TO THE AGREEMENT ON TEXTILES AND CLOTHING (ATC)

Stage	Time Frame	Percentage of Quota Free
1	1995–1997	16%
2	1998–2001	17%
3	2002–2003	18%
4	2004	49%
	Total	100%

Source: Gelb, B. A. (2005, June 10). Textile and apparel quota phaseout: Some economic implications (CRS-2). Retrieved June 3, 2010, from http://policyarchive.org/handle/10207/bitstreams/3465.pdf

WTO Agreement on Textiles and Clothing (1995 to 2004)

The Uruguay Round of trade negotiations created the WTO, the **Agreement on Textiles and Clothing (ATC),** and the **Textiles Monitoring Body,** which were effective January 1, 1995. The primary purpose of the ATC was to complete the following:

1. Phase out the MFA quota system.
2. Complete the MFA phase out process over a 10-year period, to be completed by December 31, 2004.
3. Reintegrate the textile and clothing sector into the WTO, the new world trading system.

During the operation of GATT, textiles and apparel was covered by the MFA and therefore was treated differently from other goods, specifically, with many imports into developed countries restricted by a system of bilateral quotas. The Uruguay Round determined that it was in the best interest of the world market to phase out the MFA. The ATC included the ground rules for the phaseout, and the Textiles Monitoring Body was created as a group within the WTO Council for Trade in Goods to monitor the process.

The ATC established a four-stage system to guide countries through the phaseout. This system included time lines for categories and percentages of textile and apparel trade to be quota free. It also specified the categories of goods that had to be phased out in each stage. The import quantity for each country in 1990 was used as a base (Table 6.4).

During the first two stages of the phaseout of the quota system, the U.S. textile and apparel industry mostly ignored its existence, while the EU moved ahead quickly. For the United States most of the categories specified for early phaseout were not covered by quota, so the requirements of that early period were not a problem, and, as new developing countries became significant producers, more bilateral agreements were created with quota restraints. However, as the world moved into a new century, the reality of the complete phaseout became clear to U.S. companies, and the majority of products under quota had to be phased out during the fourth stage.

Under the MFA developing countries producing textiles wanted phaseout, because they wanted to ship unrestricted quantities of textiles to developed countries. Then, becoming WTO members along with China, developing countries began to realize that, under MFA, they actually had an artificial advantage in the guise of guaranteed market share in their negotiated quota and that they might not be capable of competing in an unrestricted market, particularly in products like apparel, for which price is a major competitive factor.

Many firms in developed countries, including the United States, feared losing their domestic production altogether. Some firms started to panic, others started to plan, and still others started to beg. The firms in panic looked for mergers and takeovers, based on the assumption that bigger is better. The planners asked the question, If we could get product anywhere in the world without the quota barrier, where would that be? and proceeded with arrangements to make that possible. The firms that started to beg, and some countries as well, began lobbying for extension of the quota system beyond 2005.

During 2004, there were probably more articles written about the end of the quota system and the need to extend it than any other topic in textiles and apparel. Even so, there was a lack of understanding about what it would take to compete in a nonquota market as well as about the differences associated with China's becoming a WTO member. Some prognosticators insisted that China would become the primary world supplier; it was already the largest exporter. The newly developing countries that had recently became suppliers—because the quota system prevented adequate imports from countries that were the preferred sources—feared that they would be forgotten as suppliers.

There was little industrial development in the newly developing countries to provide jobs if textiles and apparel left. Sub-Saharan African countries were among those that

had few other opportunities. The textile and apparel industries in many of these countries were financed by China and by foreign investment from countries in which there was insufficient quota. After 2005, some of these investors decided to return to their home countries rather than continue their foreign investment.

Although the textile and apparel trade had been relatively stable during MFA, it was not uncommon for apparel producers to pack up and move across a border if lower costs or greater convenience existed on the other side. In other words, there was no commitment to sustainability. Textile producers tend to be less mobile than apparel producers because of the machinery required. At the same time, sourcing companies required a steady supply of goods that satisfied design, performance, and quality standards.

In a post-MFA world some countries tried to beef up their production capabilities and increase speed to market by

- creating more free trade zones to reduce costs
- producing higher quality at lower cost
- lowering import duties on materials and inputs
- aligning labor regulations with worldwide standards
- improving productivity through worker training
- improving physical infrastructure (electricity, transportation, communication, water, and so on)
- using air freight instead of ocean freight

There were some cruel and crude adjustments made in the textile and apparel supply before adjustments could be made to the quota phaseout. The ATC specifically stated that the agreement would not be extended.

Memorandum of Understanding by both the United States and the EU with China, 2005 to 2008

However, as explained earlier, both the EU and the United States did extend textile and apparel quotas on a limited basis, via the Memorandum of Understanding approach to limiting trade in some product categories. These agreements expired in 2008.

Now, extend your learning with Learning Activity 6.5.

Learning Activity 6.5
TRADE REGULATIONS

1. What was the fundamental purpose of GATT?
2. What was the MFA intended to do?
3. Why was the textile and apparel trade allowed to operate under the MFA in ways that were contrary to GATT rules?
4. Why were tariffs unable to control the textile and apparel trade?
5. What do quotas do that tariffs cannot?
6. Why did the MFA not work?
7. What was the purpose of the WTO Agreement on Textiles and Clothing (ATC)?
8. If you were now a sourcing professional, what kind of plan would you need to deal with all the trade regulations in the global market?

SUMMARY

Trade has many meanings, but the focus in this chapter is the exchange of goods among nations. Globalization of trade has evolved in at least three phases: the globalization of countries, the globalization of companies, and, most recently, the globalization of individuals. Protecting domestic industry from foreign competition and using trade to generate government revenue have been priorities since trade began. To operate a trade protection system, countries create customs services to monitor levels of trade and administer trade agreements. Because the WTO has supported reduction in trade barriers, customs services in some countries have moved their focus away from collection of duty and toward other issues, such as border protection.

Trade protection is initiated by erecting trade barriers. Trade barriers have two forms: tariff and nontariff barriers. Tariffs are taxes imposed on imported or exported goods. Tariffs increase the prices of imported goods, cause domestic industry to be less efficient, raise consumer prices, and generate revenue for governments. Nontariff trade barriers take many forms, including exchange rates, price support programs, quotas, and voluntary restraints. Quotas were a critical component of the textile and apparel trade for more than 40 years. Quotas restrict trade by limiting the quantity of goods that can be imported or exported.

The General Agreement on Tariffs and Trade (GATT) originated with the primary purpose of reducing trade barriers. However, the textile and apparel industry created the Multifiber Arrangement (MFA), a quota system to protect firms in developed countries from products made with low-cost labor in developing countries. Through multilateral trade negotiations, the World Trade Organization (WTO) absorbed the GATT in 1994. The WTO included the Textiles Monitoring body, to supervise the operation of the Agreement on Textiles and Clothing (ATC), which phased out the MFA and its quota system in 2005. Quota extension agreements between China and the United States, and China and the EU, expired in 2008.

REFERENCES

BSR Report 2008. Retrieved January 5, 2010, from http://www.bsr.org/report

Chanda, N. (2004, March 25). Globalization 3.0 has shrunk the world: An interview with Thomas L. Friedman. Global Envision. Retrieved June 22, 2004, from http://globalenvision.org/library/3/601/6/

Cohen, S. D., Blecker, R. A., & Whitney, P. D. (2003). *Fundamentals of U.S. foreign trade policy* (2nd ed.). Boulder, CO: Westview Press.

Elwood, W. (2001). *The no-nonsense guide to globalization*. Oxford, UK: New Internationalist Publications.

Friedman, T. L. (2000, April). *The Lexus and the olive tree*. New York: Anchor Books.

Gelb, B. A. (2005, June 10). Textile and apparel quota phaseout: Some economic implications (CRS-2). Retrieved June 3, 2010, from http://policyarchive.org/handle/10207/bitstreams/3465.pdf

Gresser, E. (2004). *The big bang: Ending quota and tariff policies.* Sponsored by the American Import Shippers Association (AISA), the U.S. Association of Importers of Textiles and Apparel (USA-ITA), the National Retail Federation (NRF), the International Mass Retail Association (IMRA), and the American Apparel and Footwear Association (AAFA).

Juri, C. (2010, January 25). N.J. outlet mall lures international shoppers with bargains on U.S. brands, weak dollar. *The Star-Ledger*. Retrieved from http://www.nj.com/starledger/

Lollis, B. D. (2007, May 1). Exchange rates cut into U.S. traveler's fun in Europe. *USA Today*. Retrieved from http://www.usatoday.com/travel/news/2007-04-30-euro-travel-usat_N.htm

Roots of the WTO. (n.d.). Retrieved August 8, 2004, from http://econ2.econ.iastate.edu/classes/econ355/choi/wtoroots.htm

Schneider, M. (2004, March 18). Weak dollar is a big hit with foreign tourists. *The Des Moines Register*, p. 3D.

Structure of WTO. (n.d.). Retrieved from http://www.wt.org/english/thewto_e/whatis_e/org2_e.html

USA: Over-Quota apparel imports from China subject to staged entry procedures. (2009, April 22). Hong Kong Trade Development Council. Retrieved from http://news.alibaba.com/article/detail/apparel-news/100044187-1-usa%253A-over-quota-apparel-imports-from.html

World Bank. (2001). Global economic prospects and the developing countries—2002. Washington, DC: The International Bank for Reconstruction and Development.

World Trade Organization Secretariat. (2004, January 16). Trade policy review: United States. Retrieved January 29, 2004, from http://www.wto.org/english/tratop_e/tpr_e/tp226.e.htm

7 Illegal and Unethical Trade Activity

Eighty percent of consumers admit that they buy fake or pirated goods regularly, with little remorse or concern for the consequences (World Customs Organization, 2009).

As SHOWN EARLIER, regulated trade is frequently unfair; however, free trade in the global market may also be unfair. Trade regulations, lack of trade regulations, and lack of enforcement of trade regulations are all blamed for illegal and unethical activities associated with the exchange of goods between nations. Conflicting cultural traditions and standards and opportunistic human tendencies toward exploitation intensify the sometimes horrifying results.

The roles of customs services around the world have been addressed briefly in previous chapters, but the complexity of being customs compliant has not. The supply chain model presented previously (see Figure 1.8) identifies customs clearance as one of the primary segments of the supply chain. To get timely customs clearance, the merchandise and the presenting of it must be customs compliant. Anytime a product is imported, the customs service of that country has to be dealt with, and every country has slightly different processes and standards to be met. The purposes and activities of customs services in each country include the following:

- protecting intellectual property rights
- monitoring and documenting identities and quantities of imports and exports

Objectives

- Apply concepts related to trade barriers and regulation as a framework for customs compliance.

- Examine intellectual property rights from the perspective of intellectual property law.

- Examine violations of intellectual property rights.

- Explore the many other violations of customs compliance and prevention methods.

- reporting imports and exports against quota
- assessing, collecting, and documenting duties
- protecting the country's borders against illegal entry

To be **customs compliant**, exporters must prepare and present the merchandise appropriately labeled and prepare and submit customs' forms and reports according to customs rules and regulations in each importing country. The customs services of the World Trade Organization (WTO) member countries use the Harmonized Commodity Description and Classification System (HS) to monitor and document imports and exports. Nonmember countries may or may not use HS, but countries that aspire to become WTO members *will* use it. The many types of trade agreements around the world often require preparing reports about imports and exports among countries as well as reports to WTO. Using HS helps make customs' shared data useable and comparable. From these reports, WTO documents trade of all member countries and assesses trends and comparisons among countries, including scenarios in which customs compliance is missing.

GLOBAL LEXICON

copyright a legal right gained by an author, composer, playwright, publisher, or distributor to exclusive publication, production, sale, or distribution of a literary, musical, dramatic, or artistic work

counterfeit an imitation of what is genuine, with the intent to defraud the customer

counterfeiting the act of making an imitation of an original, with the intent to defraud

country of origin (COO) the location where an article was wholly obtained; when more than one country is involved, the location where the last substantial transformation was carried out; the location where there is a change in the product designation number, according to the Harmonized Commodity Code and Designation System (HS)

customs compliant to act in accordance with customs rules and regulations

gray (grey) market goods original goods (they are not knockoffs) that are sold by unauthorized vendors

human trafficking facilitating the emigration of people for monetary gain

illegal transshipment shipping goods through a port or country to facilitate the change of country of origin or to avoid quota limitations or import duties, or both, in the destination country

intellectual property (IP) copyrights, trademarks, patents, trade secrets, and semiconductor chips; inventions or other discoveries that have been registered with government authorities for the sale and use by their owner

intellectual property rights (IPR) legal protection for exclusive use by owners of copyright, trademarks, patents, trade secrets, and semiconductor chips

knockoff an imitation of an original that does not carry the original brand, made with lower-cost materials and production methods and sold at a lower price

licensee the buyer of the right to use a merchandising property

licenser the owner of a merchandising property

licensing contract a means of transferring intellectual property rights

merchandising property the primary means of product differentiation and a source of customer loyalty

pirated a term used in the EU; an imitation of the original; counterfeit

rules of origin criteria used to determine the national source of a product

substantial transformation occurs when the processing of an article results in a new and different article having a distinct name, character, or use; occurs when an HS classification changes

trademark a word, phase, logo, or other graphic symbol used to distinguish one firm's products or services from those of other firms

trademark infringement the act of misleading the public into believing the items bearing the trademark/brand name are produced and sold by the owner of the trademark, when they are not

transshipment to transfer or be transferred from one conveyance to another in order to continue shipment

transshipment center a port where merchandise can be imported and then exported, without paying import duties

undocumented immigrant workers (UIWs) individuals from foreign countries without legal identification papers

INTELLECTUAL PROPERTY LAW

Intellectual property (IP) is a wide range of creations that are products of human intellect and that have commercial value, including copyrights, trademarks, patents, trade secrets, and semiconductor chips. Intellectual property law protects **intellectual property rights** (IPR) of creators/owners by ensuring exclusive use of these creations. According to Elias and Stim (2003), the many dimensions of intellectual property law that protect IPR include the following:

- Copyright law covers literary, musical, and artistic works and software and gives the owner of the creative work the right to keep others from using it without permission. To be copyrightable, a creative work must be original and expressed on paper, audio- or videotape, clay, canvas, or some other medium, and it must reflect some creativity.
- Trademark law covers words, pictures, symbols, industrial designs, and other forms of intellectual property used to distinguish a product from the competition.
- Patent law grants a monopoly for a limited period of time for the use and development of inventions.
- Trade secret law addresses any formula, pattern, physical device, idea, or process that provides the owner a competitive advantage and is treated in a manner to keep competitors from learning about it.

A **copyright** is a legal right gained by an author, composer, playwright, publisher, or distributor to exclusive publication, production, sale, or distribution of a literary, musical, dramatic, or artistic work. A **trademark** is a word, phrase, logo, or other graphic symbol used to distinguish one firm's products or services from those of others. A trademark is the expression of the identity of the owner of the brand. A combination of copyright

law and trademark law is what protects the ownership of brands, symbols, and logos representing brands in textiles and apparel as well as all other industries.

Consumers use trademarks as an indicator of quality, status, beauty, durability, or desirability, or a combination of these, and therefore they can have a great deal of market value. In the United States, trademark ownership is established through use; in many other countries ownership is established through registration. Global companies have to register their trademarks in each country in which their products are sold to protect their intellectual property rights.

Trademark infringement is taking advantage of the value of a brand by applying a trademark to products without permission of the owner of the brand. The resulting products are counterfeit, described as **pirated** in EU countries. Trademark infringement is the most common violation of intellectual property rights in the textile and apparel industry as well as for consumer products in general. Trademark infringement results in counterfeit merchandise that, because the counterfeit products are often made with inferior materials and production processes, weakens the market value of original products bearing the trademark.

Table 7.1 shows the relationship between intellectual property rights and the different types of creative work related to textiles and apparel. Unfair competition is also included in the table. Unfair competition is a body of law related to, but separate from, intellectual property law. The sources of U.S. intellectual property law include federal and state legislation, statutes, and court cases. Copyright and patent laws originate in the U.S. Constitution. The primary law related to trademarks is the Lanham Act, which was passed in 1946 and amended many times since. The Lanham Act addresses procedures for registering trademarks and lists the types of appropriate remedies when

Table 7.1 GUIDE TO USE OF INTELLECTUAL PROPERTY PROTECTION AND UNFAIR COMPETITION LAW RELATED TO TEXTILES AND APPAREL

Creative Work	Trade Secret	Copyright	Patent	Trademark	Unfair Competition	No Rights
Advertisement (billboard, card, flyer, sign)		x		x		
Advertising copy		x				
Carpet design			x	x		
Clothing accessories and designs (belts, hats, scarves, suspenders)			x			
Comic strips		x		x		
Commercial names				x	x	
Cosmetics	x		x			
Drawings		x				
Fabric	x		x			
Fabric design		x	x	x		
Furniture design			x	x		
Garment design			rarely			x
Jewelry		x	x	x		
Labels				x		
Logos				x	x	
Manufacturing process			x			
Method of doing business	x		x			
Names of businesses				x	x	
Names of entertainers or celebrities				x	x	
Names of famous animals				x		
Names of products or services				x	x	
Odors used in marketing				x		
Packaging			x	x		
Project designs	x	x				
Shoes			x	x		
Signs		x		x	x	
Slogans				x	x	
Songs and jingles for marketing		x		x	x	
Sporting goods designs		x	x	x		
Videotape		x				
Wallpaper design		x				
Weavings		x				
Web pages		x				
Writing articles, essays, poems, novels, short stories, nonfiction books		x				

Source: Based on Elias, S., & Stim, R. (2003). *Patent, copyright, and trademark: An intellectual property desk reference* (6th ed.). Berkeley, CA: Nolo.

trademark infringement has occurred; it also lists remedies for unfair competition (Elias & Stim, 2003).

There is no one set of international laws that address intellectual property. However, the WTO has a council called Trade-Related Aspects of Intellectual Property Rights (TRIPS). TRIPS is responsible for monitoring the TRIPS agreement, which originated with the WTO in 1994. WTO members are expected to honor the agreement, which addresses categories similar to those presented in Table 7.1, including copyrights, trademarks, patents, trade secrets, and semiconductor chips. However, different countries and cultures have different laws as well as expectations for complying with laws. TRIPS is looking to the challenges associated with developing universal standards related to intellectual property rights by organizing and presenting workshops and training sessions for leaders in member countries as well as countries aspiring to become WTO members. Protection of intellectual property has become a pressing problem as globalization has increased. It was a primary issue when the admission of China to the WTO was negotiated. As you will see, China is repeatedly identified as the country that most frequently violates intellectual property rights.

Case 7.1 is a description of a course on intellectual property for government officials organized in 2009 by the World Intellectual Property Organization (WIPO) and the World Trade Organization (WTO).

Legal Transfer of Intellectual Property Rights

Intellectual property rights are legally transferred from the owner to another legal user via a **licensing contract**. Many intellectual properties related to apparel, in addition to trademarks, are actually

---

Case 7.1 WTO-WIPO Advanced Course IPR for Government Officials

On October 5, 2009, Dr. Francis Gurry, Director-General WIPO, welcomed twenty government officials from developing countries, least-developed countries and countries with economies in transition, and three from developed countries and one from the European Union who begin their participation in the first joint WIPO-WTO Advanced Course on Intellectual Property (IP) organized by the World Intellectual Property Organization (WIPO) and the World Trade Organization (WTO). On October 5 and 6, 2009, the government officials will be at the WIPO headquarters and from October 7 to 9, 2009, at the WTO headquarters in Geneva.

Participants are from the following countries: Albania, Argentina, Bahrain, Bangladesh, Botswana, China, Colombia, Costa Rica, Egypt, El Salvador, Fiji, Georgia, Germany, Jordan, Kenya, Malta, Mauritius, Mozambique, Nepal, Netherlands, Nigeria, Peru, Sri Lanka and the European Union.

The main objective of the course is to update participating government officials on the activities and instruments of the WIPO and the WTO and to provide a forum for an exchange of information and ideas between them and the two secretariats on these matters. The course addresses a range of topics, including: an overview of international policy and law in intellectual property; the negotiating background of the TRIPS Agreement and an overview on subsequent developments; intellectual property and economic development; the WIPO development agenda; overviews of the current international landscape in copyrights, trademarks, industrial designs, geographical indications and patents; WTO Dispute Settlement and TRIPS; IP Global issues; TRIPS and public health; innovation and intellectual property; intellectual property and genetic resources, traditional knowledge and folklore; the relationship between the TRIPS Agreement and the Convention on Biological Diversity; and enforcement of intellectual property rights.

The WIPO-WTO Advanced Course on IP represents a significant step in work-sharing on a global scale and extends the growing need of IP knowledge, which will increase quality knowledge in IP management on global IP issues while building economic growth in the countries concerned. With the IP knowledge imparted to them in this advanced course, the participants will work with their IP officials and other stakeholders to attain efficiency and higher use and management of IP.

Source:

WIPO-WTO Advanced Course on IPR for Government Officials. (n.d.). Retrieved from http://www.wipo.int/academy/en/events/2009/docs/wipo_wto_ipr.html

merchandising properties, including brand names, logos, designer names, celebrity names, and cartoon characters. **Merchandising properties** are a primary means of product differentiation and a source of customer loyalty (Glock & Kunz, 2005). For example, go to http://www.vfc.com, and click on "Our Brands." You should see a list of brands and trademarks owned or licensed by the U.S.-based global company VF Corporation. Note that the brands are classified into categories to correspond with VF's lifestyle philosophy. It is not immediately apparent which are owned and which are licensed, as the company describes itself as the largest apparel company in the world. Through its growth cycle over the last 20 years, it was common for VF to buy licensing contracts for sound brands that, for one reason or another, were in financial trouble and then, after getting it reestablished, buy the brand.

In a licensing contract, the **licenser** (the owner of the merchandising property) grants the **licensee,** the buyer of the right to use the merchandising property, the right to produce or source merchandise that will carry the merchandising property. The licensee pays the licenser a **royalty** or fee for the privilege, usually between 1 and 15 percent of wholesale value. A licensing contract includes the following:

- a description of the merchandising property
- a definition of the product or products that can bear the property
- the time frame for the agreement
- the responsibilities for the licenser
- the responsibilities for the licensee
- the basis of the royalty
- the amount of the royalty
- the guarantee, or minimum royalty

When a merchandising property is used without permission of the owner, via a licensing contract, it is infringement of intellectual property rights, and the product is a counterfeit.

Further your exploration of intellectual property law with Learning Activity 7.1.

Learning Activity 7.1
INTELLECTUAL PROPERTY LAW

1. What does intellectual property law protect?
2. How does a firm or a person get intellectual property rights?
3. According to Table 7.1, what forms of protection are available for IPR?
4. According to Case 7.1, what is the goal of WTO/WIPO in holding IPR workshops for government leaders?
5. What is the purpose of a licensing contract?
   a. How does the licensee benefit?
   b. How does the licenser benefit?

Protecting Intellectual Property Rights

One of the important functions of customs services in each country is protecting the intellectual property rights of the citizens it represents. Table 7.2 compares the value of products seized by the U.S. CBP for violation of IPR in 2003 and 2009 from the countries that were the primary suppliers. Table 7.3 presents the types of consumer products that had the most IPR violations in 2003 and 2009. Look carefully at the changes that occurred between 2003 and 2009 for differences in the countries and types of products involved.

As you examine the tables, take note of which countries and products have been added and dropped from 2003 to 2009. Consider which countries and products have increased and decreased in value and which have increased and decreased in terms of percentage. Think about what types of events in the world over this time period might have influenced these changes for these countries. Also consider how those two measures of quantity (total value and

Table 7.2 SOURCES OF PRODUCTS SEIZED BY U.S. CUSTOMS AND BORDER PROTECTION (CBP) FOR VIOLATION OF INTELLECTUAL PROPERTY RIGHTS (IPR), REPORTED ACCORDING TO DOMESTIC VALUE AND PERCENTAGE OF TOTAL SEIZURES FOR 2003 AND 2008

Trading Partner	2009 Total Value (in Millions of U.S. Dollars)	2003 Total Value (in Millions of U.S. Dollars)	2009 Percentage of Total	2003 Percentage of Total
China	$ 204.7	$ 62.5	79%	66%
Hong Kong	$ 26.9	$ 10.2	5%	9%
India	$ 3.1	—	1%	—
Taiwan	$ 2.5	—	Less than 1%	—
South Korea	$ 1.5	$ 3.2	Less than 1%	3%
Mexico	—	$ 2.0	—	2%
Paraguay	$ 1.5	—	Less than 1%	—
Malaysia	—	$ 1.3	—	1%
Philippines	$ 1.5	$ 1.2	Less than 1%	1%
Canada	—	$ 1.2	—	1%
Pakistan	—	$ 0.8	—	1%
Switzerland	$ 1.3	$ 0.7	Less than 1%	Less than 1%
Dominican Republic	$ 0.9	—	Less than 1%	—
Pakistan	$ 0.7	—	Less than 1%	—
Vietnam	$ 0.6	—	Less than 1%	—
Thailand	—	$ 0.7	—	Less than 1%
All other countries	$ 16.6	$ 11.0	6%	12%
Total	$ 260.7	$ 94.0	100%	100%
Number of seizures	14,841	6,500		

Source: U.S. Customs and Border Protection (CBP), Intellectual Property Rights Seizure Statistics. (n.d.). Retrieved May 17, 2010, from http://cbp.gov/linkhandler/cgov/trade/priority_trade/ipr/pubs/seizure

percent of total) for each product and country relate to each other. What do you know about changes in technology and fashion in a broad sense (not only in relation to apparel)? How might those changes have influenced the producers of illegitimate goods?

The strongest trend that is obvious in Table 7.2 is the explosion in value of CBP-seized products from China. In Table 7.3, the most dramatic changes are the disappearance of cigarettes from the list and the upsurge in the amount of footwear. During the past decade, in which China became established as the "world's manufacturer," it has also been established as the world's leading violator of IPR. There have been ongoing reports from customs services in the EU, the United States, and other developed countries of IPR violations for apparel and other merchandise that has been traced to origin in China. One EU report described an incident of smuggling that involved 600 thousand tons of smuggled jeans, T-shirts, and other apparel as well as

Table 7.3 Types, Values, and Percentages of Imported Products Seized in Fiscal Years 2003 and 2009 by U.S. Customs and Border Production (CBP) because the Products Infringed on or Violated Intellectual Property Rights (IPR)

Types of Products	2009 Total Value (in Millions)	2009 Percentage of Total Value	2003 Total Value (in Millions)	2003 Percentage of Total Value
Cigarettes	—	—	$ 41.7	44%
Footwear	$ 99.8	38%	$ 2.6	3%
Consumer electronics	$ 31.8	12%	$ 3.8	4%
Handbags, wallets, and backpacks	$ 21.5	8%	$ 11.5	12%
Wearing apparel	$ 21.5	8%	$ 14.0	15%
Watches and watch parts	$ 15.5	6%	$ 3.4	4%
Computers/Hardware	$ 12.6	5%	—	—
Media (DVDs, movies on tape, laser discs)	$ 11.1	4%	$ 7.3	8%
Pharmaceuticals	$ 11.1	4%		
Jewelry	$ 10.5	4%	—	—
Toys and games	$ 5.5	2%	$ 1.5	2%
Sunglasses/Parts	—	—	$ 1.3	1%
Headwear	—	—	$ 1.3	1%
All other commodities	$ 19.9	8%	$ 5.7	6%
Total	$ 260.7	100%	$ 94.0	100%

Source: U.S. Customs and Border Protection (CBP), Intellectual Property Rights Seizure Statistics. (n.d.). Retrieved May 17, 2010, from http://cbp.gov/linkhandler/cgov/trade/priority_trade/ipr/pubs/seizure

sport and casual shoes originating in China (European Anti-Fraud Office, 2007). By using a country of origin of a developing country recently admitted to the EU, Chinese smugglers could avoid both a value-added tax and the quota limitations imposed on Chinese goods by the EU. However, there are also reports of violations of Chinese trademarks related to merchandise being sold within China.

More recently, the U.S. CBP seized 15 thousand pairs of fake Gucci shoes worth an estimated $3.85 million at retail. The shipment originated in China, and customs officers in Norfolk, VA, seized 472 cartons of the shoes. The total domestic value of the shoes was $1.96 million (Casabona, 2009b).

Patent Infringement

Patent law grants a monopoly for a limited period of time for the use and development of inventions. Although garment designs are usually not patentable, in the book *Uplift: The Bra in America*, Farrell-Beck & Gau (2001) documented inventions relative to brassieres that were patented between the mid-1800s and the mid-1900s. Patentable garment designs tend to be those that require creative engineering for assembly.

Case 7.2 is an example of a recently patented apparel product that may have suffered infringement from a competing apparel firm. You may recognize the names of some of the firms involved. The image of the garment helps clarify the nature of the "creative engineering" required for the "body profile enhancement." If the company that owns the patent wins the case, the company is likely to be awarded damages plus a portion of the revenue from sale of the illegal merchandise, somewhat similar to what a licensee pays a licenser in a licensing agreement. Also, the competing firm will be banned from future use of the design without permission of the patent owner.

Follow your reading with Learning Activity 7.2.

Learning Activity 7.2
PROTECTING INTELLECTUAL PROPERTY RIGHTS

1. What is the most common violation of IPR in the textile and apparel industry?
2. According to Table 7.2, which country had the largest increase in both value of seized goods and percentage of total goods from 2003 to 2009?
3. According to Table 7.3, how would you explain how seized apparel could increase in value by approximately one third from 2003 to 2008 but have the percentage of total in 2008 be only half that of 2003?
4. What are some possible reasons for the dramatic increase in the value of goods seized in 2008 as compared with 2003?
5. How many of the categories listed in Table 7.3 could be regarded as relating to appearance or fashion? Why might these concepts be so closely related to trends in violation of IPR?
6. What is the purpose of a patent?
7. Why is it unusual for apparel to be patented?

Case 7.2 APPAREL PATENT INFRINGEMENT CASE— CENTRAL DISTRICT OF CALIFORNIA PATENT INFRINGEMENT LAWSUIT FILED OVER PANTS GARMENT DESIGN PRODUCT

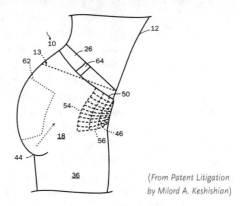

(From Patent Litigation by Milord A. Keshishian)

Los Angeles, CA—Corporation's patent attorneys filed a patent infringement lawsuit in the Central District of California (Los Angeles Division), accusing Charming Shoppes and Lane Bryant of patent infringement. U.S. Patent No. 6,543,062 entitled "Pants Garment with Body Profile Enhancement Features" was duly issued by the U.S. Patent & Trademark Office on April 8, 2003. After the '062 patent's issuance, it was assigned to plaintiff Corporation.

The '062 patent covers a pants garment with elastic components built therein to allow for an improved anatomical fit: "the pants garment is provided with a unique cut and assembly that lifts and accentuates the wearer's buttocks. In another preferred aspect of the invention, the pants garment additionally reduces the wearer's stomach." Defendants sell jeans and pants under the "Secret Slimmer" trademark, which are accused of infringing the '062 patent: "[t]he Secret Slimmer products are not staple articles of commerce, and Defendants know or should know that these products have no substantial non-infringing uses. Defendants engage in these acts despite their actual notice and knowledge of the '062 patent." In addition to monetary damages, which Plaintiff asks the Court to treble based on the alleged intentional infringement by Defendants, the Plaintiff also seeks preliminary and permanent injunctions. The case is titled *Corporacion 1466, C.A. v. Charming Shoppes, Inc. et al.*, CV 08-04693 MMM (Central District of California 2008).

Source:

Keshishian, M. A. (2008, August 1). Central District of California patent infringement lawsuit filed over pants garment design product. Retrieved May 16, 2010, from http://www.iptrademarkattorney.com/2008/08/central-district-of-california-patent-attorney-garment-pants-patent-infringement-lawsuit.html

COUNTERFEITING/ PIRATING PRACTICES

The U.S. Federal Bureau of Investigation (FBI) reported that intellectual property crime costs $200 to $250 billion a year in U.S. business losses (FBI, 2002). Counterfeiting/pirating is a primary cause of those losses. A **counterfeit** is something that a perpetrator forges, copies, or imitates without having the right to do so and with the purpose of deceiving or defrauding. **Counterfeiting** is the act of making or selling look-alike goods or services bearing fake trademarks. Counterfeiting is an age-old practice that began before the 17th century. The past quarter century, however, has experienced a remarkable rise in the practice. According to the U.S. CBP, counterfeit goods cost brand owners around the world more than $720 billion every year. It was estimated in 2003 by the Counterfeiting Intelligence Bureau (part of the International Chamber of Commerce) that 7 to 9 percent of all world trade was counterfeits ("Special Report," 2003). The International Anti-Counterfeiting Coalition, based in Washington, D.C., reported counterfeiting has tripled in the last decade and, in 2009, cost U.S. companies more than $250 billion, almost 2 percent of world trade (World Customs Organization, 2009).

Globalization of production of all kinds of goods has resulted in worldwide access to popular products and technology. At the same time, ingenious marketing and receptive consumers have exploded the demand for "brands." Much of a product's worth is now tied up in the brand, a form of intellectual property, rather than in the product's quality or serviceability. It is possible to sell a product with a brand name at five or ten times the price of a similar product without one; this is what attracts counterfeiters. Here are eight reasons why owners should file for registrations of brands/trademarks with the governments of the countries in which properties will be distributed:

1. "Valuable Asset"—federal registration of brand names/trademarks in all countries that are potential distribution sites provides national rights to the property.

2. "Nationwide Priority"—gain the right to expand business into new geographic areas without the threat of someone else's registering as the owner of what you have claimed as your property.

3. "Tool against Cybersquatters"—if a Web site claims your registered property, federal registration is an element considered in legal proceedings to determine the rightful owner and allows a hold to be placed on the use of the property until the case is settled.

4. "Advantages in Court"—provides the legal presumption of who is the legitimate owner of the property.

5. "Enhanced Remedies for Infringement"—acts as a deterrent to potential infringers and triples the potential damages suffered by the owner.

6. "Prevent Importation"—property can be filed with customs services to prevent importation and allow seizure of infringing foreign goods.

7. "Incontestable Trademark"—after 5 years of continuous registration, certain grounds for cancellation of the ownership of the property are foreclosed, saving litigation expenses.

8. Cost is low—nominal costs of registration are far outweighed by significant financial and legal advantages (Milord and Associates, 2009).

Counterfeiting/pirating is as diverse as any legal business, ranging from back-street sweatshops to full-scale factories. Counterfeiters often get their goods by bribing employees in a company with a valuable brand to hand over manufacturing moulds or master discs for them to copy. One of the most infuriating problems for brand owners, including apparel, is when their licensed vendors "overrun" production lines (produce more than was ordered by the customer) without permission and then sell the extra goods on the side.

Production overruns sold on the side are sometimes called the gray market. **Gray market goods** are the original goods (not knockoffs) but are sold by unauthorized vendors. Because they are not sold by the owner of the brand the goods carry or by one of the owner's representatives, these goods are technically counterfeit. For example, during the 1990s, Target Stores stocked and sold some Calvin Klein Jeans. Calvin Klein sued Target because his company had never sold any jeans to Target. It turned out that the source of the jeans was a Calvin Klein CMT (cut-make-trim) vendor located in Florida that created production overruns to supply the Target order.

Owners of brands often try to control the quantity of goods produced by supplying vendors with only the number of labels and signature snaps or buttons to cover the number of legitimate orders. In the Calvin Klein case the vendor either managed to acquire extra labels and snaps or had copies made for the additional garments; the Target buyer probably did not know the goods were not legal. The sale to Target was very profitable for the vendor, because all it had invested in the jeans was the labor for assembly and possibly some extra fabric, probably less than 20 percent of the wholesale price. Thus, counterfeiting is profitable, even when goods

are sold at a much lower price, because there is little investment in product development, and no advertising is required—the owner of the brand covers those expenses.

Distribution of counterfeit goods may involve street vendors, flea markets, or shops anywhere in the world. The Internet is now believed to be the vehicle for more than $25 billion in counterfeit goods a year. Organized crime has also become involved in complex distribution networks that support large counterfeiters. There is evidence that counterfeiting is one of the funding sources used by terrorists. Sale of counterfeit T-shirts and videos in New York City are believed to be part of the funding sources for the bombing of the World Trade Center in 1993 and for its destruction in 2001. Drug dealers have turned their attention to counterfeiting, because they regard it as lucrative and low risk ("Hitting the Pirates," 2003).

Consumers also contribute to the counterfeiting problem. Increasingly, shopping for fakes is cool. People want the latest gear but can't afford or choose not to pay for the genuine article. Designer bags, designer shoes, and other accessories, as shown by the data in Table 7.3, have been favorite counterfeited products in the United States in recent years. Every major city has its favorite faux haunts. In the United States, these include the sidewalks of Georgetown; Baltimore's Inner Harbor; Santee Street, in Los Angeles; and Chinatown, in New York. Other countries also have areas known for counterfeit merchandise: Tokyo's Shibuya and Shinjuku districts; Silk Alley, in Beijing, China; Bangkok; Hong Kong; and London have too many to list. Customer demand is a primary reason for the huge market and the ongoing vigorous activity of counterfeiters. Consumers both knowingly and unknowingly purchase counterfeit goods, because they want the brand, price, memory,

Figure 7.1a

Counterfeit bags are a favorite of shoppers in New York, Hong Kong, and other cities. The bags can be purchased for a fraction of the cost of the originals, but producers and sellers, when caught, are subject to criminal penalties.

(Courtesy of WWD)

Figure 7.1b

Customs officials sorting through counterfeit goods.

(Lionel Cironneau/ Associated Press)

or image, unaware of or unconcerned about the damage the practice causes legitimate businesses (Figures 7.1a and 7.1b).

Legitimate businesses lose sales, and their brands lose value, because of counterfeiting. In 2001, in the EU the counterfeit brands most frequently confiscated were Nintendo, Nike, Adidas, Nokia, and Louis Vuitton. "A study in 2000 by the Centre for Economics and Business Research estimated that the counterfeiting of clothing, cosmetics, toys, sports equipment, and pharmaceuticals within the European Union cost the region 17,120 jobs and reduced GDP by €8 billion ($7.4 billion) a year" ("Special Report," 2003, p. 53). Governments also lose revenue, because counterfeiters do not pay taxes.

The magnitude of counterfeiting worldwide has also made anticounterfeiting big business, and legitimate businesses bear the cost of implementing **anticounterfeiting** measures. Fortune 500 companies have reported that they are spending $2 to $4 million a year each on anticounterfeiting, with some spending more than $10 million. Many companies are now using hi-tech strategies similar to those used to protect dollar bills. Other strategies include unique identification numbers, holographs, and special package markings. An entire segment of business has sprung up to develop and provide anticounterfeiting technology. Anticounterfeiting experts believe that the best solution to counterfeiting is the same used to solve most other types of crime: enforcement, education, and economic growth. Illiterate and poor people are likely to be recruited to work in the production of counterfeit goods. Improving literacy and alleviating poverty reduces the opportunity for production of counterfeits as well as the customers for them. People with higher levels of living are better able to purchase branded goods than their illegal imitations.

Counterfeiting in Textiles and Apparel

Of the 80 billion garments produced annually worldwide, 16 billion are T-shirts (Speer, 2004). Because the world population is approximately 6,500,000,000, that means apparel producers make nearly three T-shirts for every man, woman, and child in the world every year. That surely makes a statement about apparel oversupply and the competitiveness of the apparel business.

Of that same 80 billion garments produced annually, up to 22 percent of all *branded* apparel and footwear sold is counterfeit. As shown in Table 7.3, more than $132 million in counterfeit fashion goods, including footwear, apparel, and jewelry, were seized in 2009 for attempted importation into the United States. And remember that the branded products are found to be counterfeit because of violation of trademark law.

The trademark may be a brand name or logo but may also be letters, numbers, package design, color, or other aspects of a product (Elias & Stim, 2003). For example, for Levi's 501 jeans, Levi's brand name plus the double-curved arcuate stitched design on the patch pockets and the folded pocket tab are trademarks that belong to Levi Strauss & Co.

Apparel companies invest millions in brand development. At the same time, legitimate tags and labels

- only cost a few cents each
- represent the brand
- bear a company's trademarks
- are key components of product presentation
- are an important source of customer loyalty
- are very easy to duplicate

In Beijing, fake fashion goods have permeated everyday life. In the Muxiyuan fabric market, merchants make a living off of fake label sales—a bag of 500 Diesel tags costs the equivalent of $6; Prada and Burberry are sold in batches of 10 thousand or more (Lowther, 2004).

Knockoffs

In the case of apparel, a counterfeit is often a knockoff of the original that illegally carries its trademark. A **knockoff** is an imitation, usually using lower-cost fabric and production methods and sold at a lower price. In the fashion business, imitation is the greatest form of flattery; therefore, knockoffs in themselves are not illegal. Without imitation, a new design idea would never become popular and thus become a fashion.

According to both U.S. and international law, most garment designs are not protected against counterfeiting, but trademarks used on the garments are protected. Unfortunately, in the trade press it is not unusual to find the term *knockoff* used interchangeably with *counterfeit*. Thus, when reading articles about this topic it is important to have your critical thinking hat on to determine exactly what the writer means. Remember that a knockoff is not counterfeit unless the knockoff is presented as the original, with the original brand name. However, laws are difficult to enforce.

Counterfeiting operations are both sophisticated and diverse, with operators keeping abreast of fashion and even ahead of consumer trends. Branded sports apparel has been a primary target, but as fashions evolve, pirating has turned to purse brands, such as Louis Vuitton, Prada, and Chanel (found at purse parties in the United States) and to knockoff athletic shoes, which are found in street markets throughout the world. The counterfeiters attend international trade fairs to steal prototypes of new products that represent heavy investment in product development but are not yet on the market. Counterfeits can then be produced so quickly that they are sometimes available before the genuine article hits the market.

Now, continue your study of counterfeiting with Learning Activity 7.3.

Learning Activity 7.3

COUNTERFEITING/PIRATING ACTIVITY

1. How can owners of intellectual property expect that customs services will be able to identify counterfeit/pirated products carrying their brands?
2. What is the legal difference between a counterfeit/pirated product and a legitimate product?
3. True or false: gray goods are the same as counterfeit goods. Explain.
4. True or false: knockoffs are legal, but counterfeits are not. Explain.

OTHER CUSTOMS VIOLATIONS

There are many customs violations beyond those covered by intellectual property law. The ones commonly found in the textile and apparel industry are addressed here, including misrepresentation of country of origin, misclassification of goods, illegal transshipment, and undocumented immigrant workers.

Misrepresentation of Country of Origin

The **country of origin (COO)** of a product is determined by rules of origin. According to WTO, **rules of origin** are used

- to implement measures and instruments of commercial policy, such as safeguard measures, including quotas, tariffs, and antidumping duties
- to determine whether imported products will receive preferential treatment, based on trade agreements
- for the application of labeling and marking requirements
- for purpose of trade statistics
- for government procurement (World Trade Organization, n.d.)

The descriptions of rules of origin have evolved over the past 35 years and still leave considerable room for interpretation to individual countries. For example, according to U.S. 1985 rules, the COO for apparel was where the fabric was cut into garment parts. During the late 1980s and early 1990s it was common practice to cut garments out of U.S.-made fabric in the United States, export cut parts to Mexico or Central America (or both), where garments were assembled, and then return the finished garments to the United States for retail sale. However, the 1985 rules allowed the garments to carry "Made in USA" labels even though they were assembled elsewhere.

The general principles now in effect for determining the COO were included in the 1994 GATT Agreement on Rules of Origin (now the WTO Rules of Origin). These rules state that the COO is the country where goods are wholly obtained or, when more than one country is involved, the country where the last **substantial transformation** is carried out. The customs service in each WTO country is responsible for establishing regulations to carry out the COO rules and the definition of "substantial transformation." Not surprisingly, customs regulations differ considerably from one country to another, particularly with regard to this definition.

To continue with the U.S. example, the U.S. CBP regulations published in 1996 (Section 102.21), based on GATT 1994, required considerable adjustment for trading partners, as compared with the 1985 rules. These regulations state that the last substantial transformation for textiles occurs where the fabric is made; for apparel, it is where the garment is assembled (except for products covered by NAFTA or originating in Israel, where other rules were in effect).

The lay interpretation of the U.S. 1996 rules was as follows: the COO for fabric was determined by where it was knitted or woven, whereas the origin for yarn was determined by where the cotton was spun or the fiber, extruded. The origin for apparel was determined by where the most important process of formation occurs, usually garment assembly (Ellis & Stim, 2003).

Despite some efforts to clarify application of the 1996 rules of origin, WTO reports that COO disputes in the global market have continued to increase. For example, in late 2007 the port of Norfolk, Virginia, announced that more than 2,900 cartons of mainland Chinese socks, with a domestic value of $1.5 million, had been imported into the United States with false COO papers. CBP determined that socks manufactured in mainland China had been mixed with socks produced in Ghana. The mainland China socks were declared to CBP not only as products of Ghana (thus evading quota restrictions), but also as eligible for duty-free treatment under the African Growth and Opportunity Act (AGOA) ("Chinese Apparel Quotas," 2007). This example supports some possible reasons why COO disputes have continued to be a serious problem in developed countries:

- increase in the number of preferential trading arrangements, including free trade areas among developed and developing countries
- bilateral agreements, customs unions, and common markets, each with different definitions of COO
- increased use of antidumping laws and subsequent claims of circumvention of antidumping laws (World Trade Organization, n.d.)

In 2008, CBP, after years of consideration and delay, proposed sweeping changes in COO rules for imported articles. CBP proposed replacing the existing system of case-by-case "substantial transformation" determinations with a uniform system of "tariff shift" rules based on the NAFTA COO marking rules codified in Part 102 of the CBP regulations. The outcomes of the application of this system to determine substantial transformation are likely to be different from those from application of the traditional rules, so serious adjustments had to be made by firms using the system (Hogan & Hartson LLP, 2008). Additional information about the progress of this proposal was unavailable at time of printing. However, it seems as if the use of change in HS classification to determine COO could produce more consistent outcomes than the traditional system of interpreting substantial transformation.

The EU, to accommodate the variety of practices inherent to its country members, has incorporated multiple options for determining COO by application of "last substantial transformation":

- "by a rule requiring a change of tariff (sub) heading in the HS nomenclature
- by a list of manufacturing or processing operations that do or do not confer on the goods the origin of the country in which these operations were carried out
- by a value added rule, where the increase of value due to assembly operations and incorporation of originating materials represents a specified level of the ex-works price of the product." (European Commission, 2010)

In any case, probably the only thing that is plain to see is that identifying COO is not necessarily a clear-cut process. Determining COO has been, and continues to be, a serious challenge for customs services. At the same time, COO is a key component for determining application of imports in relation to quota quantity limitations and collection of duties based on tariff schedules.

Misclassification of Goods

Another way to avoid quota limitations and paying of duties is misclassification of merchandise into an inappropriate HS classification. (The structure of the HS product classification system was introduced in Chapter 2). One of the important functions of HS is the classification of merchandise for export and import. The types of merchandise that are traded must be specifically matched to the appropriate description in the HS system. This allows documentation of the quantities of the numerous different classifications of merchandise that are being traded. If an exporter knows that quota for a particular classification has been exceeded in the importing country, the classification might be changed to what is known to be an open category. When import limitations are in place, it is the task of customs services to be sure that merchandise shipped for import or export is correctly classified and does not exceed quota limitations.

Customs uses a statistical, random sample selection system, such that only a few of the lots of goods are actually physically checked to see that the goods match the description. For example, in November 2007, while quota restrictions were in place on merchandise from China, CBP announced seizure of a shipment of ladies' cotton T-shirts with an estimated domestic value of $870 thousand "for violation of quota/visa restrictions from China. In this case, the importer was accused of misclassifying the merchandise and submitting incorrect entry documents to avoid quota restraints" ("Chinese Apparel Quotas," 2007).

If the category of goods being shipped is one of the quota-limited groups, a different category number might be used to allow the goods to be imported without being blocked. Sometimes, misclassification happens by accident or lack of attention to the details involved in classifying goods correctly. Other times, misclassification is a method of getting merchandise into the country illegally. Table 7.4 lists the categories of goods covered by the U.S–China 2005 Memorandum of Understanding related to quotas on textiles and apparel for 2006 to 2008. The two countries agreed on the total acceptable imports for 2006 for the identified categories and then established an acceptable growth rate based on the 2006 numbers.

For example, if you were manufacturing cotton sweaters (category 345/645/646) for the U.S. market and had them ready to ship when the agreement went into effect, you might have been tempted to change the category to ramie sweaters so that you would not have to compete for the space within the limits of the agreement. Your U.S. customers would be happy, because they would get the sweaters on time, and you would be paid for your products on time.

There are many other "creative" ways that goods move from country to country outside of the laws and regulations of

Table 7.4 CHINA–UNITED STATES BILATERAL MEMORANDUM OF UNDERSTANDING: QUOTA LIMITS, 2006–2008

HS Category	Product Description	Unit	Agreed Limit for 2006	Growth Rate for 2007	Growth Rate for 2008
200/301	Sewing thread/combed cotton yarn	Kilogram	7,529,582	15.0%	17.0%
222	Knit fabric	Kilogram	15,966,487	15.0%	17.0%
229	Special purpose fabric	Kilogram	33,162,019	16.0%	17.0%
332/432/632 T	Hosiery, including baby socks—T	Dozen pairs	64,386,841	14.9%	15.0%
332/432/632 B	Sublimit—socks and baby socks—B	Dozen pairs	61,146,461	15.0%	15.0%
338/339 pt	Cotton knit shirts and blouses	Dozen	20,822,111	12.5%	15.0%
340/640	Men's and boy's woven shirts, cotton and manmade fiber	Dozen	6,743,644	12.5%	15.0%
345/645/646	Sweaters, cotton and manmade fiber	Dozen	8,179,211	12.5%	16.0%
347/348	Cotton trousers	Dozen	19,666,049	12.5%	15.0%
349/649	Brassieres	Dozen	22,785,906	12.5%	15.0%
352/652	Underwear	Dozen	18,948,937	12.5%	15.0%
359S/659S	Swimwear	Kilogram	4,590,626	12.5%	16.0%
363	Cotton terry towels	Number	103,316,873	12.5%	16.0%
443	Men's and boy's wool suits	Number	1,346,082	12.5%	16.0%
447	Men's and boy's wool trousers	Dozen	215,004	12.5%	16.0%
619	Polyester filament fabric	Square meter	55,308,506	12.5%	16.0%
620	Other synthetic filament fabric	Square meter	80,197,248	12.5%	15.0%
622	Glass fiber fabric	Square meter	32,265,013	15.0%	17.0%
638/639 pt	Manmade fiber knitted shirts and blouses	Dozen	8,060,063	12.5%	15.0%
647/648 pt	Manmade fiber trousers	Dozen	7,960,355	12.5%	15.0%
666 pt	Window blinds/window shades	Kilogram	964,014	12.5%	17.0%
847	Silk blend and other vegetable fiber trousers	Dozen	17,647,255	12.5%	16.0%

Sources: Based on Chinese apparel quotas could be charged for recent seizures of misclassified goods. (2007, November 22).
Business Alert–U.S. Retrieved January 31, 2010, from http://info.hktdc.com/alert/us0724d.htm
ITCB (International Textiles and Clothing Bureau). New U.S.–China textile agreement.
Retrieved from http://www.itcb.org/Documents/ITCB-MI52.pdf

Figure 7.2 U.S. Customs inspector checking containers as they arrive in port.

(Joe Raedle/ Getty Images)

one or more countries. CBP issued a press release announcing that officers in New York and New Jersey seaports seized a record $60 million worth of counterfeit and pirated goods during fiscal year 2007, up from 25 million in 2006 and $18 million in 2005 (Figure 7.2).

Now, try your hand at Learning Activity 7.4.

Learning Activity 7.4
COUNTRY OF ORIGIN AND MISCLASSIFICATION OF GOODS

1. Why is it important for customs to monitor imports?
2. What makes COO such a key factor in customs compliance?
3. Why is substantial transformation an important factor in determining COO?
4. Why would an exporter purposely misclassify goods?

Legal Transshipment

Transshipment can be legal. It is when goods are moved through a third country as a result of normal shipping patterns; the goods are not modified in the third country, but simply travel into and out of it. **Transshipment** means to transfer or be transferred from one conveyance to another to continue shipment. Transshipment is a standard part of moving goods from one country to another. For example, a number of small vessels may haul apparel or textiles relatively short distances to a large **transshipment center**, such as Hong Kong, where the goods are consolidated onto larger vessels for more efficient shipment to distant port cities, such as Los Angeles.

Case 7.3 details the selection, in late 2009, of the Tokyo-based freight forwarder and consolidator MOL by the U.S. department chain Belk for transport of its private brand merchandise.

Illegal Transshipment: Benefits and Risks

Because quota limitations and import tariffs vary greatly by country, one way to avoid any quotas and duties related to tariffs is to practice illegal transshipment. **Illegal transshipment** involves shipping products to a nonquota or nontariff port or country, changing COO, and then reexporting to the intended importing country. The purpose of this activity is to use a COO where no quotas will be applied or tariffs, assessed against the goods by the importing country's customs services.

There are often significant economic benefits (and risks) to be gained by using illegal transshipment to get products into a country in a manner in which they are accepted, but not necessarily customs compliant. As discussed earlier, the level of quota available when quota limitations are in place, and the amount of duty due, is determined by COO, and with it, consideration of location of production processes; types of products, as defined by HS; relevant trade agreements in effect; and origin of materials and production processes. Once COO is determined, if quota is filled, the products may be denied admission to the country; if there is no duty, or duty is waived, an additional cost of 5 percent to more than 50 percent of the value of the products may be saved. Some exporting countries, because of preferential trade agreements, may have no quota limitations or duty due on the products.

Illegal transshipment occurs when goods are shipped through a third country or port to produce counterfeit documents that illegally change the COO to avoid tariffs or quota limitations in the actual importing country. Partly because of the new COO

Case 7.3 MOL Starts International Freight ·
Forwarding and Consolidation Services for Belk, Inc.

Dec. 18, 2009—Mitsui O.S.K. Lines, Ltd. (MOL; President: Akimitsu Ashida) today announced that Belk, Inc., the largest privately owned mainline department store company in the U.S., has selected Hong Kong–based MOL Consolidation Service Limited (MCS) as its freight forwarder and consolidator throughout China, India, Cambodia, Vietnam and other locations around the world where Belk sources the manufacturing of its private brand merchandise.

Charlotte, N.C.–based Belk, Inc., operates more than 300 fashion department stores in 16 contiguous southern states and reported sales of $3.5 billion in its past fiscal year. Belk said it selected MCS because of its track record in providing international freight forwarding and consolidation services and its global service network and cargo information service.

Diane Hartjes, Belk, Inc. director of private brands operations, said, "During a recent visit to Asia, I was very impressed with MCS's ability to work with our overseas factories and assist us in implementing critical new programs aimed at improving vendor performance. As we continue to evaluate and optimize our supply chain, MCS turned out to be the perfect fit for our overseas consolidation and freight forwarding services. We are excited about entering this new partnership." . . .

. . . MCS's buyers consolidation service transports products purchased by European and U.S. retailers and apparel companies from suppliers in China and Southeast Asia via ports in Asia. The company's STARLINK cargo information service and other value-added services such as product inspection and bar code reading are available throughout those regions.

Source:

MOL starts international freight forwarding and consolidation services for Belk, Inc. (2009). Retrieved May 15, 2010, from http://www.mol.co.jp/pr-e/2009/e-pr-2800.html

rules, illegal transshipment of goods became a serious problem during the late 1990s. When the Multifiber Agreement (MFA) was in effect, the U.S. CBP estimated that $2 to $4 billion of textiles and apparel was illegally transshipped annually, with most of it assembled in China. The goods were transshipped primarily to avoid China's MFA quota limitations in the EU and the United States.

Other countries identified as active illegal transshippers in the 1990s included Armenia, Hong Kong, Macau, Russia, and Taiwan as well as some African nations. Countries that shipped relatively little textiles and apparel to the United States were likely candidates for illegal transshipping, because they did not have bilateral agreements under MFA and therefore did not have quota limitations (Salinger, Barry, & Pandolfi, 1997). Between 1998 and 2000, approximately $50 million of imported textiles and apparel were detained by CBP annually because of falsified COO documents (Green, 2000).

The 2002 U.S. revisions of the Caribbean Basin Trade Partnership Act (CBPTA) and AGOA created new transshipping targets because they provided tangible incentives for opening their economies and building free markets. These new laws made Central American and African countries likely candidates for illegal transshipment because both import tariffs and quotas are waived (American Immigration Law Foundation, 2002).

By 2004, Los Angeles—owing to its location on the Pacific Rim—became an illegal transshipment epicenter. Ninety percent of illegal transshipped goods coming into the United States were arriving in Los Angeles, and companies set up to transship goods actively continued to recruit business. For example, the following is a fax that was received by an apparel company in Mexico from an apparel company in Hong Kong. (The English has been edited for clarity and the signature, deleted):

Dear Sirs,

We would like to introduce ourselves as an export company based in Hong Kong with offices in China manufacturing a wide range of garments of all kinds especially in jackets for men, women, and children. We are also dealing in items such as jeans, sportswear, swimming shorts, and other knitted items [that] we currently export to Central American markets. We would like to widen our business in Mexican markets.

We would also provide you services such as a certificate of Indonesian origin or even just Hong Kong certificate of origin in order to ease the importation of merchandise.

Yours faithfully,

[Signature deleted]

(American Apparel Producers' Network, 2003)

Even though MFA quotas and their extensions have now been phased out, illegal transshipment remains a significant issue, because it is also used as a tool for avoiding tariffs. Customs services have published lists of hundreds of companies (including the one that wrote the fax above), most of them Asian, that are known transshippers so that importers can avoid their services. However, the illegal transshipment problem has not been resolved. Fewer than 1 percent of all imported goods are actually examined by customs. If an item is flagged, perhaps because it came from a known transshipper, customs officials look at a container's packing list, pull a sample, and send it to an import specialist. If there is suspicion of transshipment or other violation, the agency can issue a detention notice and ask the importer to furnish production records within 30 days. A month's delay in receiving fashion goods is a disaster for a fashion retailer. If illegal transshipment is determined, customs can then make a decision whether to release the goods or exclude them from consumption in the United States. Financial penalties can be assessed after the shipment has been liquidated or returned to its COO. If the COO cannot be verified, CBP can make a decision to exclude the goods from consumption in the United States. Financial penalties can be assessed under some circumstances.

Undocumented Immigrant Workers

Customs services are responsible for border protection, including transport of drugs, weapons, and other contraband and illegal aliens. Providing international border security is a complex process relating to issues from terrorism, to immigration, to imported product safety. Thus, border security begins a long way from the border. For example,

internationally shipped cargoes travel in various conveyances on a variety of infrastructures, through a number of places, are held in custody of numerous people and organizations, and can involve up to 40 separate documents to complete the journey from source zone to the distribution zone. If the border can be envisioned not merely as a physical boundary but rather as a flexible concept that allows for the possibility that the border begins at the point where goods or people commence their U.S.-bound journey, a significantly wider array of options for border management policies becomes available. (CSR Report for Congress, 2007)

This perspective enhances our understanding of the controversy that surrounds border protection, particularly the concept of building fences around the border, as well as the inseparable role of global trade across the border. Of particular interest here is the role of legal and illegal immigrants involved in the textile and apparel industries.

Whereas developed countries have worked toward freer trade over the last 50 years, similar attention has not been paid to immigration. Legal and illegal immigrants are blamed by many for rising crime rates and for stealing jobs that would otherwise go to native workers. Immigration is restricted by government policies, and limited numbers of people have been allowed to emigrate because of military conflict or economic catastrophe, for example, from Vietnam and eastern Europe. Others must resort to illegal means of emigration.

Human trafficking, facilitating the emigration of people for monetary gain, developed in many places in the world hundreds of years ago. The slavery system in the early U.S. was certainly based on capturing people and transporting them against their will. The lure of jobs also makes poor people susceptible to gangsters dealing in human beings for forced labor and prostitution. Job seekers may pay a fee for transport, often under horrendous conditions, and end up in prisonlike environments, where they are paid little for forced labor. We still hear reports of boats sinking because they held hundreds more people than was safe, railroad cars discovered containing dozens of dead bodies, shipping containers on seagoing ships full of human beings.

Approximately 200 million standardized 40-foot and 20-foot boxes move among major ports annually; many are loaded with textiles and apparel. These shipping containers provide illicit opportunities for the transport of human beings for labor exploitation, terrorist's operatives and equipment, and other contraband. In 2004, a U.S.-based international security program, Container Security Initiative (CSI), went into effect in the United States to prevent the use of cargo containers for smuggling or terrorism. It was estimated that CSI cost $450 to $550 per shipment, but another goal of the program was to reduce costs to companies, particularly for lost merchandise (Zarocostas, 2004).

Following are three core areas of CSI:

- identify high-risk containers, based on advance information and strategic intelligence
- prescreen and evaluate containers as early in the supply chain as possible—before they are shipped
- use technology (large-scale x-ray and gamma ray machines and radiation detection devices) for prescreening to prevent the slowing of movement of trade
- achieve 100 percent container scanning by 2012

CSI offers its participating countries the opportunity to send their customs officers to major U.S. ports to target oceangoing, containerized cargo to be exported to their countries ("CSI in Brief," 2008).

Unfortunately, the progress toward having 100 percent container scanning by 2012 has been hampered by cuts in funding related to the global recession. Thus, a plan was made in late 2009 to streamline efforts to balance trade and security concerns by partnering customs with a number of U.S. government agencies to support the port security objective (Casabona, 2009a).

Undocumented workers is now the term for what historically has been referred to as *illegal aliens*. **Undocumented immigrant workers (UIWs)** are individuals from foreign countries without legal identification papers. It is estimated that about 11.6 million UIWs lived in the United States in 2008. Between 2000 and 2008, the number of undocumented immigrants increased 37 percent (Hawley, 2009). The breakdown in 2000 was as follows: 60 percent Mexican, 20 percent Central American, and 20 percent from other countries. The large number of Mexican UIWs is attributed to the common border between Mexico and the United States and a long history of Mexican migration. Employment contributions include nearly every major sector of the economy, particularly food processing, taxi services,

food service, cleaning companies, farms, and apparel production (Congress of the United States, Congressional Budget Office, 2006).

Because of the economic recession, the number of UIWs in 2008 actually declined slightly from 2007, to 11.6 million: 61 percent were from Mexico; 9 percent, from El Salvador; 4 percent, from Guatemala, and 2.5 percent, from the Philippines. Although relatively small in number, the largest increases came from Honduras (81 percent) and Brazil (72 percent) (Hart, 2009). Many of the UIWs have families in their home countries who benefit from the U.S. employment. Millions of families in Mexico had become accustomed to a comfortable life supported in part by members employed in the United States, but many had to make difficult adjustments in their consumption and lifestyle because of fewer hours worked by their financially productive UIWs (Hawley, 2009).

A recent study of the economic potential for legalizing undocumented workers found that comprehensive immigration reform would yield $1.5 trillion to the U.S. GDP over a 10-year period, generate billions in additional tax revenue and consumer spending, and support hundreds of thousands of jobs (Hinojosa-Ojeda, 2010)). Yet, the issue remains politically volatile.

The production of U.S. Social Security and green cards, for which immigrants may pay between $300 and $500, has been described as a growth industry for more than 10 years (Bonacich & Appelbaum, 2000). UIWs are the most exploitable of workers. Records show they are paid less than other workers, sometimes half of minimum wage; receive no benefits; work long hours, including 12-hour days and 7-day weeks; and do not receive overtime pay. UIWs may be hired as a "favor," in exchange for an agreement that they will not to cause trouble. They are susceptible to unreasonable demands, including sexual exploitation, because they are afraid to have their illegal status revealed.

Migrant workers, many of whom are UIWs, have long been regarded as essential to U.S. agriculture, particularly for farms that grow fresh fruits and vegetables. Migrant workers are regarded as temporary residents, people who enter during the harvest season and return to their native countries when the season is over. Often, whole families migrate, and everybody works. Child labor laws do not apply to agriculture.

The apparel business, particularly in California and Florida, employs large numbers of documented and undocumented immigrants. During the 1970s, nearly half of the apparel workers in Southern California were Asian, mostly Korean; now nearly half are Latino, mostly Mexican. The Asians gradually moved on to better paying jobs and have been replaced by Latinos (Bonacich & Appelbaum, 2000). But immigration has spread across the country. For example, in 2002 a small sewing shop in Iowa had 40 operators that spoke five different native languages. Apparel factories continue to be a site where pay is low but training periods are relatively short, and necessary communication does not require complete understanding of one language.

However, over the past decade, there has been a dramatic decline in U.S. apparel production, with most of what is left concentrated in Southern California. Migrants from Central America, as well as Asia, entering via Mexico have relatively easy access to those job opportunities. Many migrants are attracted to apparel production jobs because of their short training periods and because the plant supervisors are accustomed to working with many nationalities and languages and like to hire people who are not afraid to work very hard.

Read Case 7.4 for an interesting perspective on human trafficking from Europol (European Law Enforcement Agency). Then complete Learning Activity 7.5.

Case 7.4 FACILITATED ILLEGAL IMMIGRATION INTO THE EUROPEAN UNION

The term "facilitated illegal immigration," covers a number of serious different crimes all aimed at assisting, for financial gain, the entry into or residence in a country, in violation of the laws of that country. Facilitated illegal immigration thus covers the production and procurement of falsified travel documents or permits obtained under false pretences, the provision of clandestine transportation or other assistance in order to obtain illegal entry or stay, often connected to a number of other criminal activities.

Migration itself is not illegal: it is in fact necessary for the development of both source and destination countries. Migration, however, becomes illegal when individuals themselves, or with the assistance of others, attempt to enter a country clandestinely or by deceptive means. . . .

The reasons why migrants leave their home countries are commonly referred to as "push factors" and can include conflicts, dissolution and/or disintegration of multicultural states, natural disasters or other environmental problems, discrimination, political instability or poor economic situations. Although poverty, conflict and disasters are all powerful push factors, they tend to cause local or regional migration, not international facilitated illegal immigration. Poor and war-torn states are less interesting for the facilitators of illegal immigration since people in these states usually cannot pay the huge fees these facilitators demand.

Paired with the push factors are the so called "pull factors," those criteria that make a destination country attractive to a prospective migrant. These factors may include the need for a labor force, a positive economic situation, democratic governance with political and social stability, and various historical or cultural links between the source and destination country, but especially the presence of large communities form the source countries in the destination countries. The existence of organized crime (OC) groups, involved in the facilitation of illegal immigration and present in a destination country, tends to act as a pull factor in itself. These OC groups actively promote illegal immigration and tend to create and develop their own illicit market by encouraging people who would otherwise have had no intention of emigrating. The trend is also flourishing in transit countries or in some of the countries surrounding the EU that in some cases were the original desired destination countries of the migrants.

Source:

Europol: Facilitated illegal immigration into the European Union. (2009, September). Retrieved February 1, 2010, from http://www.europol.europa.eu/publications/Serious_Crime_Overviews/Illegal_Immigration_Fact_Sheet_2009.PDF

Learning Activity 7.5

LEGAL AND ILLEGAL TRANSSHIPPING AND UNDOCUMENTED WORKERS

1. Why do firms transship goods?
2. What makes transshipping illegal?
3. Why did Hong Kong and Los Angeles become transshipment epicenters?
4. What are the risks of illegally transshipping goods?
5. Why is changing COO the fundamental purpose of illegal transshipment of goods?
6. Why is production of Social Security cards and green cards perceived as a growth industry in the United States?
7. From the perspective of a U.S. citizen, what are the central issues related to undocumented workers?
8. From the perspective of undocumented workers, what are the central issues related to undocumented workers?
9. What special insights related to undocumented workers was gained from Case 7.4?
10. As a sourcing professional, what strategies would you implement to protect your business against illegal trade activities?

SUMMARY

Protected trade has long been regarded as unfair, but free trade is also unfair. Some people claim that with free trade the rich get richer, and the poor get poorer. However, just because trade can be unfair does not make it illegal or unethical; the illegal and unethical business practices addressed in this chapter include ignoring customs compliances, violating intellectual property rights, and engaging in unfair business practices.

Intellectual property rights protect creative innovations and merchandising properties with patents, copyrights, and trademark law. Products are counterfeit because of violation of trademark law. Counterfeiting is a huge global problem, with billions of dollars in counterfeit goods produced and sold every year. A licensing contract makes it possible to use legally intellectual property owned by someone else. In the apparel business the terms *knockoffs*, *counterfeits*, and *gray market goods* are sometimes used interchangeably, but they are technically different.

Customs compliance issues include transshipment to change illegally COO and violations of borders by undocumented workers. Transshipment has been used to avoid tariffs or other trade barriers. Undocumented workers immigrate to developed countries because of better paying or more pleasant jobs than are available in their home country.

The United States has merged immigration and customs into CBP, but in most countries these functions are covered by different agencies.

REFERENCES

American Apparel Producers' Network. (2003). Fax. Retrieved from http://www.aapnetwork.net/index.cfm

American Immigration Law Foundation. (2002, September). Mexican immigrant workers and the U.S. economy: An increasingly vital role. *Immigration Policy Focus*, 1(2). Retrieved May 16, 2010, from http://www.unityblueprint.org/_documents/research-and-policy/immigrant-workers/2.AILF-MexImmWorkers&USEcon.pdf

Bonacich, E., & Appelbaum, R. P. (2000). *Behind the label: Inequality in the Los Angeles apparel industry.* Berkeley: University of California Press.

Casabona, L. (2009a, December 15). Customs seeks strong partners as deadlines approach. *Women's Wear Daily.* Retrieved from http://www.wwd.com/business-news/customs-seeks-strong-partners-as-deadlines-approach-2396270#

Casabona, L. (2009b, September 2). Customs seizes 15,000 pairs of fake Gucci shoes. *Women's Wear Daily*. Retrieved from http://www.wwd.com/business-news/customs-seizes-15-000-pairs-of-fake-gucci-shoes-2253740

Chinese apparel quotas could be charged for recent seizures of misclassified goods. (2007, November 22). *Business Alert–U.S.* Retrieved January 31, 2010, from http://info.hktdc.com/alert/us0724d.htm

Congress of the United States, Congressional Budget Office. (2006, February). Immigration policy in the United States. Retrieved June 22, 2010, from http://www.cbo.gov/ftpdocs/70xx/doc7051/02-28-Immigration.pdf

CSR Report for Congress. (2007). *Border security The complexity of the challenge*. Retrieved from http://italy.usembassy.gov/pdf/other/RL32839.pdf

Elias, S. & Stim, R. (2003, April). *Patent, copyright, and trademark: An intellectual property desk reference*. (6th ed.). Berkeley, CA: Nolo.

European Anti-Fraud Office. (2007, October 22). *Fraudulent imports of Chinese textiles and shoes*. Retrieved May 18, 2010, from http://europa.eu/rapid/pressReleasesAction.do?reference=OLAF/07/12&type=HTML

European Commission: Taxation and Customs Union. (2010). *General aspects of non-preferential origin: Introduction*. Retrieved on June 22, 2010 from http://ec.europa.eu/taxation_customs/customs/customs_duties/rules_origin/non-preferential/article_410_en.htm

Europol: Facilitated illegal immigration into the European Union. (2009, September). Retrieved February 1, 2010, from http://www.europol.europa.eu/publications/Serious_Crime_Overviews/Illegal_Immigration_Fact_Sheet_2009.PDF

Farrell-Beck, J., & Gau, C. (2001). *Uplift: The bra in America*. Philadelphia, PA: University of Pennsylvania Press.

Federal Bureau of Investigation (FBI). (2002, July 17). Press Release. (n.p.). Retrieved from http://www.fbi.gov/pressrel/pressrelease02/outreach071092.htm

Glock, R. E., & Kunz, G. I. (2005). *Apparel manufacturing: Sewn product analysis*. (4th ed.). Upper Saddle River, NJ: Prentice Hall.

Hart, J. (2009, March 3). DHS: Decline in number of undocumented immigrants living in U.S. Retrieved January 30, 2010, from http://www.immigrateusa.us/content/view/1790/69/

Hawley, C. (2009, July 11). Dreams fade as money from U.S. dries up. *The Des Moines Register*, p. 9A.

Hinojosa-Ojeda, R. (2010, January). Raising the floor for American workers: The economic benefits of reform. Retrieved May 15, 2010, from http://www.americanprogress.org/issues/2010/01/pdf/immigrationconreport.pdf

Hitting the pirates where it hurts. (2003, October–November). *Fashion Business International*, 25, 27.

Hogan & Hartson LLP (2008, July). CBP proposes sweeping changes to country of origin rules, *Customs Update*. Retrieved February 1, 2010, from http://www.hogan-lovells.com/files/Publication/988dc1a2-0f16-4645-b97b-89b16e79af48/Presentation/PublicationAttachment/7bee5283-89fe-4351-aa12-9342d97f99d4/Customs2.pdf

ITCB (International Textiles and Clothing Bureau). New US–China Textile Agreement. Retrieved from http://www.itcb.org/Documents/ITCB-MI52.pdf

Keshishian, M.A. (2008, August 1). Central District of California patent infringement lawsuit filed over pants garment design product. Retrieved May 16, 2010, from http://www.iptrademarkattorney.com/2008/08/central-district-of-california-patent-attorney-garment-pants-patent-infringement-lawsuit.html

Littrell, M. A., & Dickson, M. A. (1999). *Social responsibility in the global market: Fair trade of cultural products*. Thousand Oaks, CA: Sage Publications.

Lowther, B. (2004, October 11). No end for China's counterfeiting contagion. *Women's Wear Daily*, 20–21.

Merrick, A. (2004, May 12). Gap offers unusual look at factory conditions. *The Wall Street Journal*, p. A1.

Milord & Associates, PC. (2009). Seven reasons to register your trademarks—NOW. Retrieved May 16, 2010, from http://www.milordlaw.com/lawyer-1294758.html

MOL starts international freight forwarding and consolidation services for Belk, Inc. (2009). Retrieved May 15, 2010, from http://www.mol.co.jp/pr-e/2009/e-pr-2800.html

Salinger, L., Barry, A. W., & Pandolfi, S. (1997, October 31). Pursuing the Africa Growth and Opportunity Act: Countering the threat of textile and apparel transshipment through Africa. Retrieved August 6, 2004, from http://www.aird.com/AIRDArticles/pursuing.htm

Special Report: Counterfeiting: Imitating property is theft. (2003, May 17). *The Economist*, 52–54.

Speer, J. K. (2004, April 1). A label-conscious world: Tagless labeling, shorter cycle times drive product ID trends. *Apparel*. Retrieved October 10, 2004, from http://www.bobbin.com/bobbin/search/seach_display.jsp?vnu_content_id51000469611

Summary of AGOA II. (2002, August 6). *African Growth and Opportunity Act*. Retrieved May 17, 2010, from http://agoa.gov/agoa_legistlation/agoa_leislation2.html

U.S. Customs and Border Protection (CBP). (2008, March 20). CSI in brief. Retrieved February 1, 2010, from http://www.cbp.gov/xp/cgov/trade/cargo_security/csi/csi_in_brief.xml

U.S. Customs and Border Protection (CBP), Intellectual Property Rights Seizure Statistics. (n.d.). Retrieved May 17, 2010, from http://cbp.gov/linkhandler/cgov/trade/priority_trade/ipr/pubs/seizure

WIPO-WTO Advanced Course on IPR for Government Officials. (n.d.). Retrieved from http://www.wipo.int/academy/en/events/2009/docs/wipo_wto_ipr.html

World Customs Organization. (2009, December 3). Counterfeiting and piracy endangers global economic recovery, say Global Congress leaders (n.p.). Retrieved June 8, 2010, from http://www.wcoomd.org/press/?v=1&lid=1&cid=6&id=201#

World Trade Organization. (n.d). Agreement on rules of origin. (209–219). Retrieved June 8, 2010, from http://www.wto.org/english/docs_e/legal_e/22-roo.pdf

Zarocostas, J. (2004, March 16). Officials warn new security will be costly. *Women's Wear Daily*, n.p.

8 Politics and Political Positioning

Instituted after the war of 1812, the first protective tariffs in the United States, intended to help boost sales of domestic goods, became a political issue when the southern states, in their resentment over having to pay more for British items, renamed Tariff 11828 the "Tariff of Abominations" ("The Road to the Civil War," n.d.).

IN A CONTROVERSIAL political climate the different segments of the textile complex often take different political positions to further the particular interests of each. For example, traditionally manufacturers and retailers held opposite positions on free trade: domestic manufacturers wanted trade protection, and retailers wanted free trade in order to be able to access imports from the world market. Trade associations and labor unions also take conflicting politically active roles to influence members' priorities as well as government policies, with trade associations representing management and labor unions representing workers.

In the United States trade in nonagricultural industrial goods accounts for more than 75 percent of total global trade in goods and more than 90 percent of total U.S. goods exports. In 2008, U.S. exports of industrial goods grew to an annualized $1.2 trillion, more than nine times the level of U.S. agricultural exports. This figure was up 16 percent from 2007 and, 166 percent from 1994 (Office of the United States Trade Representative, n.d.). In recent years, the United States has had positive trade balances with all countries where free trade agreements were in place. This occurred during a period when textile and apparel imports increased remarkably, while already low levels of exports diminished even more.

Objectives

- Introduce the role of politics in trade.

- Explore the concept of unfair competition.

- Examine political positions adopted by different segments of the textile and apparel industry, including labor activists and trade associations.

- Introduce regionalization of global trade.

Tariff assistance to domestic producers of selected products (including agriculture, steel, textiles, and clothing) has burdened consumers, taxpayers, and trade in many developing countries. For example, emerging markets, such as India and Egypt, have import tariff rates as high as 150 percent, a significant trade barrier. In the WTO's NAMA (Non-Agriculture Market Access) negotiations both the United States and the EU are seeking significant new competitive opportunities for domestic export businesses through cuts in tariff rates and reduction of nontariff barriers from potential recipients of exports. Other developed countries have similar politically motivated scenarios (Office of the United States Trade Representative, n.d.).

ECONOMIC SYSTEMS OF GOVERNMENT

The silk traders of Asia and Europe represented **totalitarian** government systems in which one family or some other entity maintained complete political and economic control under a **dictatorship**. Many, mostly developing countries, still operate under some form of totalitarian government. Current forms of successful international trade tend to be based most heavily on the Western capitalist form of economic exchange, or trade. **Capitalism** is an **economic system** in which

- private ownership of property exists
- income from business operations accrue to the individuals or firms that own it
- individuals and firms are free to compete for economic gain
- profit motive is basic to economic life

In the capitalist model, international transactions involve private businesses and the exchanges of monetary value between firms in separate countries. Capitalism tends to be associated with democratic **political systems**, but **democracy** is not necessarily required for capitalism to thrive. In contrast, with **socialism** or **communism**, resources are cooperatively or state owned. International trade transactions in these systems may take place between governments rather than between firms engaged in buying materials or producing products to be sold at retail.

When firms in the capitalist model trade with governments in the socialist/communist model, the method of valuing the transaction differs. The socialist/communist government may value a transaction in number of jobs, that is, the labor value created by engaging in trade, whereas the capitalist firm will be concerned with the monetary value of the trade (Shen & Dickson, 2002).

Political Manipulation of Trade Relationships

Politics are the methods, or tactics, involved in managing an organization, business, state, or government. Power, influence, and manipulation of people and other resources tend to be the primary motivators. Sometimes, executives in the textile and apparel industry will say that they are looking for jobs in education because they want to get away from the politics. However, many colleges and universities are at least partially publicly funded with tax dollars. What could be more political? The point is that politics are everywhere, and **political strategy** makes it possible for governments, firms, other organizations, and individuals to deal with and manipulate important and powerful components in their environments. There is always more than one way to accomplish a specified goal; the questions are, who will benefit, and who will bear the costs? The answers to those questions represent different political positions.

As mentioned previously, the textile and apparel industries in developed countries

capitalism an economic system based on freedom of owner-ship, production, exchange, acquisition, work, movement, and open competition

Caribbean Basin Initiative (CBI) an economic development program established by the U.S. government

communism an economic system in which resources are cooperatively or state owned; a classless society in which equal distribution of economic goods is the economic goal

countervailing duty a special tax that increases the price of goods to a competitive level

democracy a political system in which the people hold the rul-ing power, either directly or through elected representatives

dictatorship a political and economic system operated by a ruler with absolute power, or authority

dumping selling a product in another country at less than it is sold in the home country or less than it costs to produce

economic system a method of managing resources; produc-ing, distributing, and consuming wealth

embargo the prohibition of the entry of goods into a defined political area; the stoppage of trade until issues can be negotiated

export subsidy a payment from a government to a firm as a reward for exporting products

fabric-forward rule a trade rule that limits tariffs or provides quota-free imports, or both, for garments made of fabrics produced in the sourcing country

government subsidy a payment from a government to a busi-ness to defray business costs

import surge an unexpected or unplanned flood of imports of particular categories

Item 807 (9802) a ruling that allowed garments cut in the United States to be exported and assembled and then imported with tariff based only on value added

labor activist a person or organization that endorses a doc-trine or policy of taking positive, direct action to achieve an end, especially one that is political and employment related

lobbying the process of influencing the formation of leg-islation or the administration of rules, regulations, and policies

lobbyists paid professionals who carry the messages defined by their employers and try to influence formation or admin-istration of legislation

political strategy the general approaches used by govern-ments, firms, other organizations, and individuals in dealing with and manipulating important and powerful components in their environments

political system the principles, organization, and methods of government; the components in an organization's structure and environment that can influence its decisions, survival, and growth

preferential trade agreements a form of economic integra-tion created by reducing trade barriers

price support program purchasing and storing products from the market to reduce the supply, relative to demand, to drive up the price

production subsidy a negative trade tax; a payment of money from a government to a business to defray costs of making goods and commodities

quota avoidance strategy using transshipment, fabric blends, and other means not covered by quota

red tape unnecessary obstructions and delays in processing paperwork

regionalization reducing trade barriers in selected geographic regions to facilitate trade

socialism an economic system in which ownership, produc-tion, and distribution are operated by members of the com-munity rather than by individuals or the government

totalitarian one family or some other entity maintains abso-lute governmental control; dictatorship

trade association an organization of executives or managers, or both, that share common professional interests

trading bloc a group of countries that have created regional trade incentives and that jointly participate in trade negotiations

transnational fair trade perspective being responsive to local needs in multiple countries while simultaneously retaining global efficiency

unfair competition activities defined by legal rulings and statutes that protect against unethical business practices (Elias & Stim, 2007)

unfair competition law governs commercial activity that tends to confuse, mislead, or deceive customers and/or provide unfair business advantages

yarn-forward rule a trade rule that limits tariff and quota free imports to garments made of domestically produced yarns and fabrics

have traditionally been protected by import quotas and tariffs, whereas agriculture production has enjoyed other forms of protection (see Chapter 6). However, the U.S. subsidy of the production of cotton is one trade barrier these products hold in common. A **government subsidy** is a reverse tax; it is a payment from a government to a company rather than a payment from a company to a government. The subsidy may make it possible for the firm to sell its products at a lower price in domestic markets and still make a profit. Subsidized products also may be sold in international markets at prices below the normal cost of production. This is regarded as a form of **unfair competition** that can be addressed by unfair competition law.

Production subsidies were regarded by GATT 1994 as an unfair form of competition, in which a government makes a gift of money to firms to defray costs of production (World Trade Organization, n.d.). If for some reason a country's government regards a domestic industry as essential, import barriers (tariffs and quotas) might be imposed, but then domestic consumers would have to pay higher prices. A government subsidy might be an option to sustain the domestic industry without increasing prices; in fact, the subsidy might decrease prices. However, consumers then have to pay higher taxes to fund the subsidy program, although the cost may be less than with other forms of trade protection. A prolonged use of government subsidies tends to make an industry subsidy dependent. For example, sheep growers in the United States and other developed countries have long had a wool subsidy as part of the annual revenue related to the sale of wool from the sheep. Without this subsidy, farmers and ranchers may not find wool an economically viable crop.

Shifts in textile trade policy have altered the market for U.S. cotton since the 1990s. The expiration of the textile and apparel trade quotas has made the sale of U.S.-produced cotton dependent on global markets, reversing a 60-year trend in which domestic consumption of U.S.-produced cotton was more than 60 percent. In 2004, 35 percent of apparel consumed in the United States was produced in the United States; thus, more fabric and yarn were made in the United States and more cotton, grown in the United States. The quotas were removed in 2005 and again in 2008, and so now less than 5 percent of apparel is made domestically; correspondingly, domestic textile production has declined dramatically as well as domestic consumption of U.S.-grown cotton. As a result, from 2005 to 2010 large quantities of U.S. production–subsidized cotton were sold on the world market at what the rest of the world regards as less than market price.

According to the International Cotton Advisory Committee, U.S. total direct support to cotton production was more than $3 billion in the 2008–2009 growing season, or 50 cents per pound of actual production. Government subsidies for large-scale cotton growers in the United States are regarded as unfair to competitors in the global market and particularly hurt farmers in poor countries. A study by Oxfam, an independent, nongovernmental organization, found that with a complete removal of U.S. cotton subsidies, the world price of cotton would increase by 6 to 14 percent, resulting in additional income that could feed a million children for a year or pay school fees for at least 2 million children living in extremely poor West African cotton-growing households,

The United States, apparently, ignored a 2005 ruling by the WTO to discontinue subsidies for cotton production. However, the WTO ruled again in 2009 that the United States will face an estimated $300 million in annual sanctions as the result of failing to eliminate illegal subsidies to cotton growers. The

2009 WTO ruling confirmed that Brazil was entitled to start retaliation procedures, with the possibly of lifting intellectual property protections. The United States was pleased that the WTO later rejected Brazil's request for "unlimited" sanctions on U.S. patents and trademarks (Klapper, 2009; Kripkme, 2009).

Now, extend your understanding of the relationship between agricultural and textile trade barriers with Learning Activity 8.1.

Learning Activity 8.1
RELATIONSHIPS BETWEEN AGRICULTURAL AND TEXTILE TRADE BARRIERS

1. How do politics relate to power?
2. What are some of the ways that global trade decisions differ in the presence of a totalitarian government as compared with a capitalist government?
3. Trade negotiations are almost always in progress. Why do you think trade negotiations are never finished?
4. Why do developed countries' views tend to be opposed to those of developing countries?
5. What types of U.S. companies would have paid the cotton subsidy price if Brazil had been allowed to retaliate by lifting intellectual property protections?
6. In what ways might Brazil's retaliation have affected the global apparel industry?

GLOBAL COMPETITION

The intensity of global competition inspires the use of creative and sometimes unfair political manipulation of trade. Temporary restraints and incentives that protect fledgling industries are regarded as justifiable trade strategies, as are preservation of industries deemed vital to national security. **Unfair competition law** governs commercial activity that tends to confuse, mislead, or deceive customers and provide unfair business advan-

tages. These activities tend to include trademark or trade name infringement, deceptive advertising, simulation of packaging, false country of origin (COO), and other unethical business practices. Obviously, unfair competition addresses some of the same issues as intellectual property law, but the approach is different. Unfair competition law looks at the business practices themselves rather than protection of the intellectual property. Lifting intellectual property protection, as in the Brazil cotton subsidy example, is likely to be addressed using unfair competition law (Elias & Stim, 2007). It is also regarded as legitimate to impose trade barriers or sanctions against unfair trade practices, such as government subsidies, price support programs, and dumping (Cohen, Blecker, & Whitney, 2003).

Export Subsidies and Price Support Programs

Some governments are alleged to subsidize their export industries extensively. Exporting goods is an important source of revenue for governments, via tariffs, and for the firms (and their employees) that produce the goods or commodities. When **export subsidies** are available, a firm receives the price of the goods exported, plus a payment from the government at whatever rate is specified for the product. Governments may subsidize exports to support growth of domestic industry or to increase cash flow into the country, or both. The United States, the EU, and Australia have used agricultural export subsidies since the 1970s. These subsidies were regarded as legal as long as exports did not exceed what was considered a "reasonable" market share. Although explicit export subsidies are relatively rare, indirect subsidies, such as preferential credit terms and reduced utility rates, are used throughout the world (Cohen, Blecker, & Whitney, 2003). Both production subsidies and export subsidies may provide the opportunity to sell goods

The Chinese government has agreed to end a range of subsidies that help boost sales of Chinese-branded merchandise around the world—including apparel and textiles—rather than face a fight with the U.S. at the World Trade Organization (WTO). In a decision announced on Friday (December 18, 2009), the office of the U.S. Trade Representative said the deal marks the end of "numerous subsidies we identified as prohibited under WTO rules." The agreement between Washington and Beijing brings to a close legal action begun by the U.S. at the WTO last December.

In its case, the U.S. said it had identified more than 90 official measures "providing what appeared to be WTO-inconsistent financial support." These included cash grant rewards for exporting, preferential loans for exporters, research and development funding to develop new products for export, and payments to lower the cost of export credit insurance. The subsidies, the U.S. said, were tied to exports, "giving an unfair competitive advantage to Chinese products and denying U.S. manufacturers the chance to compete fairly with them."

Key to the case were three central government initiatives promoting famous Chinese brand merchandise: the "Famous Export Brand" initiative, the "China World Top Brand" initiative, and the "China Name Brand Products" initiative. But the U.S. also identified several other subsidy programs that appeared to benefit Chinese exports—including textiles—"regardless of whether they were famous brands."

U.S. Trade Representative Ron Kirk said: "The termination of the subsidies will level the playing field for American workers in a wide range of manufacturing and export sectors."

Source:

U.S. Wins End to Chinese Brand Export Subsidies. (2009, December 21). Retrieved from http://www.just-style.com/article.aspx?id=106263

abroad at less than the cost of production and less than the domestic sales price.

China has been accused of dominating international trade in apparel through the use of export subsidies (National Council of Textile Organizations, n.d.). Read Case 8.1 to learn the outcome of legal action the United States brought against China at the WTO in December 2008 regarding export subsidies.

Price support programs are commonly applied to agricultural products in developed countries to raise the commodity price paid to farmers. These programs commonly involve the government in purchasing and storing products from the market to reduce the supply relative to demand and drive up the price. In the United States some of the surplus goods are dispersed in the form of subsidies for school lunch programs. Payments to agriculture producers to produce less are also often a part of the subsidy program. For example, support of U.S. agricultural producers from 2008 to 2012 was set at $58 billion a year (European Commission, 2009). Whenever negotiations to reduce textile and apparel trade barriers begin, a counterpart is always reduction of agricultural subsidies. Reduction of price subsidies increases agricultural prices on the world market, but it also makes more products available to newly developing countries, where availability of adequate food is a common problem.

Dumping

The Kennedy Round of multilateral trade negotiations during the mid 1960s resulted in a GATT Anti-Dumping Agreement. The Tokyo Round, during the 1970s, after years of negotiation, tried to extend and improve the GATT system. Agreements and arrangements, relative to subsidies, and countervailing duties, import licensing, government procurement, and customs valuation were also added to the code (World Trade Organization, n.d.).

Dumping is defined as selling a product in another country at less than the domestic sales price or less than the product costs to produce. Dumping is often a companion activity to international sale of government-subsidized agriculture products. Dumping can result in an **import surge** that causes a dramatic drop in sales for domestic companies. Dumping is regarded as unfair competition by the WTO and by the governments of many countries, including United States (World Trade Organization, n.d.).

Why would a company dump products? It would appear that dumping could cause the exporting company to lose money. However, dumping can be a

- temporary strategy for establishing or maintaining market share
- form of inventory control
- result of government production to provide domestic employment
- result of export subsidies that lower the price in the world market

Price competition is a common means of establishing market share. In a highly competitive market, such as apparel, glitzy advertising and price promotion are the hallmarks of getting customers' attention. For example, assume a Hong Kong–based retailer decided to enter the United States retail market with stores in Los Angeles and San Francisco as well as an elaborate Web site. The retailer might use intensive television and Internet advertising to describe fashion-forward, upscale styling at very low promotional prices to get the attention of customers and to establish a share of the market. It may be necessary to offer products below the price that they would be sold at in Hong Kong and, at least initially, below the cost of production, to sustain customer interest.

Dumping is also used as a form of inventory control when a firm develops an oversupply because of a downturn in world demand or an unexpected increase in world production. Dumping may allow a company to generate cash flow when resources otherwise would be invested in unsalable inventory.

Dumping, by international law, is now regarded as unfair competition. More specifically, according to GATT 1994, dumping is introducing a product into commerce in another country at less than its normal value. Polyester fiber production has become a global activity that has flooded the market and driven down prices (World Trade Organization, n.d.). Case 8.2 presents a recent example.

Case 8.2 DEMAND FOR ANTI-DUMPING DUTY ON POLYESTER IMPORTS FROM CHINA

Pakistan—Since anti-dumping duties had been levied on imports of polyester from countries other than China, the local manufacturers are hopeful of having the same implemented against the Chinese exporters. . . .

In the past, China was a big importer of polyester from other Asian countries. But now over a period of time, it has built vast polyester production capacities, leading to negligible imports of the raw material. This has led to these manufacturers' seeking new markets and also selling at low rates, to the detriment of the local polyester producers, which led to a levy's being applied to imports from these countries.

China has added vast polyester capacities in the last few years and since the unfolding of the economic crisis, is looking for new markets due to the slowdown in its domestic markets. Chinese manufacturers are dumping polyester in Pakistan and other markets at prices lower than those at which they sell in the domestic markets.

This has rung alarm bells among the polyester manufacturers in Pakistan, who are struggling to keep themselves afloat. Most of the polyester units are operating below capacity since the last few months, and the Chinese polyester dumped at low prices is creating havoc among the polyester manufacturers.

fibre2fashion.com spoke to Mr. Shahid Amin, Secretary General, Polyester Staple Fibre Manufacturers Group (PSFM), to get a better understanding of the situation. He said, "Yes, PSFM has petitioned to the National Tariff Commission of Pakistan to impose anti-dumping duty on Chinese PSF exporters as they are dumping PSF in Pakistan and we have supplied substantial evidences to this effect."

According to him, the import duty on Polyester Staple Fibre was 7.5%. In the budget for the year 2008–2009 it was reduced to 4.5%. The government in the past, with the purpose to protect its domestic industry, had levied a 15% duty on imports of polyester but on expiry of the period in June last year, had reduced the duty substantially.

Source:

Demand for anti-dumping duty on polyester imports from China. (2009, January 23). Fibre2fashion.com. Retrieved February 9, 2010, from http://www.fibre-2fashion.com/news/polyester-news/newsdetails.aspx?news_id=68452

Countervailing Duties

Because subsidies and dumping are regarded as interference with free markets, countervailing duties may be used by importing countries to offset the price effect of subsidy. **Countervailing duties** are a special type of tariff designed to counteract subsidies and dumping. Countries importing subsidized products are empowered by the WTO to apply countervailing duties to raise the product price to what would be a normal level without the subsidy (Cohen, Blecker, & Whitney, 2003). The **countervailing duty** eliminates unfair competition of the subsidized low-price products' competing with nonsubsidized domestic products.

Countervailing duties are not listed in tariff schedules, but rather are determined according to the level of the subsidy or the amount below the regular selling price in the country the product came from.

In Case 8.2, the Pakistani polyester manufacturers were appealing to their government to reapply a duty that had previously been in place to compensate for dumping. To apply the countervailing duty, and have it approved on the global level, the importing country submits a complaint to the WTO against the exporting country. The WTO evaluates the situation and produces a ruling related to the issue.

Other safeguards against dumping include trade **embargoes** against import surges, in which trade is stopped until terms are negotiated. Sometimes, merchandise sits offshore, aboard ship for months while negotiations take place. Developed countries increased their charges, relative to dumping of textiles and apparel, after the MFA quota system expired. As mentioned earlier, the U.S. embargoed the apparel shipments from China in 2008 when volume exceeded the quota limits in the Memorandum of Understanding between the United States and China.

Antidumping investigations have tripled since the 1980s, involving many different types of products. For example, the United States has been accused of dumping steel. Historically, the United States and the EU have been primary users of antidumping duties, but now India and other developing countries, as demonstrated in Case 8.2, are becoming just as active.

Continue your study of unfair competition with Learning Activity 8.2.

Learning Activity 8.2
UNFAIR COMPETITION

1. What do agriculture subsidies have to do with trade barriers on textiles?
2. Why is dumping regarded as unfair competition?
3. Why was China dumping polyester fiber?
4. Why would a firm sell products at below cost?
5. What is the purpose of a countervailing duty?
6. What is the likely result of an import surge?
7. How do embargos aid negotiations related to unfair competition in the global market?

Government Red Tape Trade Barriers

A study by the World Bank shows that **red tape** is one of the chief obstacles to growth in almost all poor countries. Pointless regulations foster graft; the more irksome the rule, the greater the incentive to bribe officials not to enforce it. In some countries it appears as if there is government-endorsed corruption. The following are some examples of obstacles:

- Angola forbids the export of its banknotes even though they are worthless outside the country. Thus, the main airport in Luanda has cubicles—one for men and one for women—where people are searched by police officers before boarding. They take all the local currency and issue no receipt.

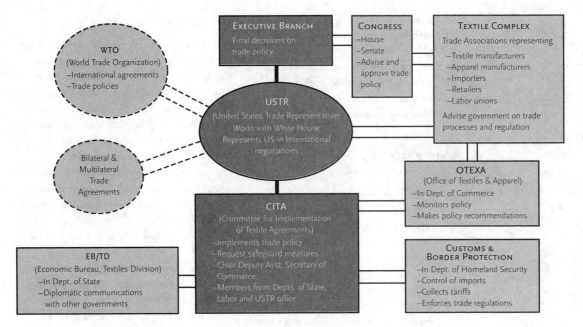

In the figure:

WTO (World Trade Organization) —International agreements —Trade policies

EXECUTIVE BRANCH Final decisions on trade policy

CONGRESS —House —Senate —Advise and approve trade policy

TEXTILE COMPLEX Trade Associations representing —Textile manufacturers —Apparel manufacturers —Importers —Retailers —Labor unions Advise government on trade processes and regulation

USTR (United States Trade Representative) Works with White House Represents US in International negotiations

Bilateral & Multilateral Trade Agreements

OTEXA (Office of Textiles & Apparel) —In Dept. of Commerce —Monitors policy —Makes policy recommendations

CITA (Committee for Implementation of Textile Agreements) —Implements trade policy —Request safeguard measures —Chair Deputy Asst. Secretary of Commerce —Members from Depts. of State, Labor and USTR office

EB/TD (Economic Bureau, Textiles Division) —In Dept. of State —Diplomatic communications with other governments

CUSTOMS & BORDER PROTECTION —In Dept. of Homeland Security —Control of imports —Collects tariffs —Enforces trade regulations

- In Haiti it takes 203 days to register a new company; in Australia it takes 2. In Sierra Leone, registration costs 1,268 percent of per capita income; in Denmark, registration costs nothing.
- In Lagos, Nigeria, to buy land to build a factory and register the purchase takes 274 days and requires 21 procedures and payment of fees that are 27 percent of the purchase price; in Norway the same procedure takes 1 day and costs 2.5 percent of the price.
- In Turkey, women who marry are allowed 1 year to decide whether to quit their jobs. Employers are required to give them a large severance package if they go. Thus, firms hire men instead; only 16 percent of Turkish women have formal jobs ("Measure First," 2004).

Politics in multiple forms influence trade every hour of every day. Change in trade policy and methods invariably improves the lot of one group, while having a negative impact on other groups. Decisions are seldom simple and are consistently multifaceted. There are two primary holders of a country's trade policy, rules, regulations, and laws: a country's government and the World Trade Organization (WTO). Negotiations may be in process for months or years within a country's government before the issue is ready to be presented to WTO.

Figure 8.1 represents the major components of the political decision-making process that creates and enforces textile and apparel trade rules, policies, and regulations for the United States. Changes in rules, policies, and regulations start in the office of the United States Trade Representative (USTR), but the final proposal has to be approved and administered by the U.S. government. To be globally accepted, approval of the WTO is important.

The U.S. textile complex frequently strives to influence the formulation and administration of trade law. This is accomplished by lobbying the U.S. Congress or the Office of Textiles and Apparel (OTEXA). OTEXA documents trade data, assists firms with exporting, and continuously updates the status of trade agreements. When Congress passes legislation that supports the wishes of the textile complex, these bills still have to

Figure 8.1 The textile complex interacts with both the executive and legislative branches of government to influence implementation, administration, and enforcement of textile and apparel trade policies, rules, and regulations. Note in particular with which functions the textile complex tends to have direct contact.

(Developed by Grace Kunz)

be signed by the president. The Committee for Implementation of Textile Agreements (CITA) is responsible for implementing trade agreements. CITA also handles requests for safeguard measures against market surges and other forms of unfair competition.

Now, try your hand at Learning Activity 8.3.

Learning Activity 8.3
GOVERNMENT RED TAPE

1. "The more irksome the rule, the greater the incentive to bribe officials to ignore it": Why aren't "irksome rules" done away with?
2. How do "irksome rules" support development of a culture in which bribery is commonplace?
3. Does the U.S. government's system for making and enforcing textile and apparel trade regulations seem efficient? Explain.
4. What are the primary sources of the rules, regulations, and laws related to the textile and apparel trade?
5. How can textile and apparel firms influence formulation of trade law that affects their businesses?

POLITICAL POSITIONING BY THE TEXTILE AND APPAREL COMPLEX

Political positioning in the business environment requires evaluating circumstances and opportunities and determining priorities in order best to serve the interests of the firm. The challenge then becomes communicating the firm's priorities to people with the power to initiate or control change. **Lobbying** is the process of influencing the formation of legislation and the administration of rules, regulations, and policies. Lobbying is commonly carried out by **lobbyists**, paid professionals who communicate the political positions defined by their employers to influence formation or administration of legislation.

Vehicles for Political Positioning

The primary vehicles for political positioning and lobbying by business and industry are labor unions and trade associations. Labor unions, as discussed previously, bargain with employers on behalf of workers about terms and conditions of employment (see Chapter 4). Labor unions also collaborate with labor activists and employ lobbyists to convey the interests of workers to legislators and policymakers, whereas trade associations represent the perspectives of management. A labor activist is similar to a social activist, but with a more defined focus. A **labor activist** is a person or organization that endorses a doctrine or policy of taking positive, direct action to achieve an end, especially one that is political and employment related.

Now, read Case 8.3 to see how Nike responded to social and labor activists to develop sustainable sourcing programs.

TRADE ASSOCIATIONS

Trade associations are to management what labor unions are to workers. Just as corporations have responded to social activists, so, too, have their trade associations. Because of the expectation by the public for evidence of corporate responsibility among consumer goods suppliers, trade associations began providing opportunities for their members to reflect their activism. For example, in the 1990s **American Apparel and Footwear Association (AAFA)** initiated the organization of WRAP (Worldwide Responsible Apparel Production) to give AAFA members a means of preventing labor exploitation by their production contractors. As mentioned previously, WRAP has now been spun off as an organization independent of the trade association to eliminate any perceived conflict of interest for their members. Many other organizations are now available with services similar to those of WRAP.

In 2000, this author was contacted by Nike about a consulting project. Nike had decided it wanted to become a "world-class merchandiser." Another consultant working for Nike had discovered my newly published merchandising textbook on Amazon.com and proposed that Nike build its merchandising program around the principles presented there. We spent several weeks in conference calls (the consultant, Nike executives, and me) discussing Nike goals, issues, and needs relative to merchandising processes. Later, I spent a few days in Beaverton, Oregon, at Nike's headquarters, conducting a workshop with 53 international Nike merchandisers and meeting with executives.

When I told my faculty colleagues and students about my consulting project, all were appalled that I would work with a company that had such a negative reputation relative to labor abuse. At that point, I had been teaching a global issues class for 15 years, so I was familiar with the charges from social activists against Nike and other companies as well as with companies' codes of conduct and business practices. There were at least two sides to the story, but the public was primarily aware only of the social activist perspective. Nike and other companies were not taking the impact of the negative reports very seriously and therefore were doing little to protect their professional image.

At the first face-to-face meeting with Nike executives, I mentioned the response I received relative to participating in the consulting project. They were amazed that people in the Midwest were aware of social activism and its resulting negative perspective on Nike and its products. Their response was, "We improve wages, working conditions, and benefits everywhere we go." I replied, "But the public doesn't know what it was like before you got there." We spent most of the following morning not talking about merchandising, but about social activism, labor exploitation, implementation of codes of conduct, and proactive behavior on the part of employers in the global market.

Some social activists have continued to try to discredit Nike and other large apparel companies, and that may be of some use, because it keeps up awareness of the importance of social responsibility and reminds company executives that they need to continue to work on maintaining positive public image and improving communication with the public regarding their social responsibility and sustainability behaviors.

Nike has embraced all dimensions of corporate responsibility with projects related to multiple aspects of the environment and human resources. In 2005, it disclosed the locations of all its factories and has since initiated projects related to human resources, climate, and the environment. For example, Nike recently designed a new shoe box. Like Nike's first recycled-content box, developed in 1995, the new box is made from 100 percent recycled fiber. But it also has a new design that reduces fiber content by 30 percent and is expected to save millions in packaging costs. The box is expected to be fully in use across the Nike brand by 2011.

Nike also has a newly developed sustainability mission that does a wonderful job of delineating the merits of their corporate goals, as shown in its 2009 corporate responsibility report. The company calls the mission Nike's North Star:

- Healthy Chemistry—minimize the impact of product ingredients throughout the life cycle.
- Climate Stability—provide leadership toward climate stability.
- Water Stewardship—borrow water responsibly and return it clean to communities.
- Closing the Loop—product creation to allow for material recovery or safe return to nature.
- Thriving Communities—enable our stakeholders along our value chain to meet their needs and lead fulfilling lives.
- Game Changers—educate, challenge, and empower athletes to join the sustainability journey.
  (Nike, 2009, p. 81)

Nike understands the meaning of the sustainability model presented in Figure 4.1.

Sources:

Kunz, G. I. (2005). Memories from a Nike experience. Unpublished paper. Iowa State University.
Nike (2009). Corporate Responsibility Report. Retrieved January 10, 2010, from http://www.nikebiz.com/crreport/</BS4>

Figure 8.2 At the Interstoff Asia textile market, merchandisers and designers are seeking design inspiration or selecting fabrics for their product lines. This trade fair is put on biannually by Messe Frankfurt GmbH at the Hong Kong Convention and Exhibition Centre. The event includes 30 seminars addressing global issues.

(*Courtesy of WWD/ Gareth Jones*)

More recently, AAFA created its annual Excellence in Social Responsibility awards, which recognize best practices in a variety of areas of social and environmental responsibility that positively impact employees, businesses, and the community. AAFA member companies apply for the award by submitting a PowerPoint presentation and an executive summary of the action or project. Presentations address preservation of the environment, community outreach, women's issues, health and safety, and general welfare (American Apparel and Footwear Association, 2005).

In 2009, AAFA held a conference titled "Sustainability: Turning Responsibility into Opportunity." The event featured speakers from 3Degrees, Brooks Sports, Ceres, The Coca-Cola Company, the Environmental Protection Agency, the Federal Trade Commission, Harvard University, Levi Strauss & Co., and Timberland.

A **trade association** is a nonprofit organization formed to serve the common needs of its members. Members are usually firms that are in business in the sector that the trade association represents and pay membership fees to support the services and activities of the association. Services may include industry research, publications, seminars, trade shows, opportunities for sharing business challenges and solutions, government relations, and lobbying. Active participants in trade associations include executives of the member firms; consultants active in the field; suppliers of technology, materials, and other services; editors and writers of industry news; and educators who are specialists in the appropriate field of study. Lobbyists employed by trade associations convey the political positions of its members to appropriate legislators.

The United States alone has more than 100 of the hundreds of textile, apparel, and retail trade associations around the world. During the past 50 years, trade associations have merged many times to form fewer but larger and more influential organizations. For example, in 2004, during the phaseout of the MFA quota system, the U.S. textile manufacturing industry joined together to form a new trade association called the National Council of Textile Organizations (NCTO) in order to lobby specifically for continued trade protection (National Council of Textile Organizations, n.d.). See Box 8.1 for more examples of trade associations around the world.

Some trade associations try to represent the entire textile and apparel complex; others are specialized and represent a single industry segment or geographic area. For example, the Computer Integrated Textile Design Association (CITDA) represents a particular type of technology for applying color and texture to fabrics. The U.S. Hosiery Association represents firms that knit socks and stockings nationwide. The

Box 8.1 TEXTILE AND APPAREL TRADE ASSOCIATIONS

Textile Manufacturing

American Association of Textile Chemists and
   Colorists
American Fiber Manufacturers Association
   (FiberSource)
American Reusable Textile Association
Association of Nonwoven Fabrics
Brazilian Textile and Apparel Industry Association
   (ABIT)
Computer Integrated Textile Design Association
   (CITDA)
Global Manufactured Fiber Association
Malaysian Knitting Manufacturers Association
National Council of Textile Organizations (United
   States)
Taiwan Textile Federation
Textile Institute (United Kingdom)
U.S. Hosiery Association
U.S. Industrial Fabrics Association International
   (IFAI)
National Textile Chamber of Mexico

Apparel Manufacturing

American Apparel and Footwear Association (AAFA)
American Apparel Producers Network (AAPN)
Apparel British Columbia Association (Canada)
Brazilian Fashion Association
Canadian Apparel Federation (CAF)
Clothing Manufacturers Association of India
Estonian Clothing and Textiles Association (ECTA)
European Apparel and Textile Organization
   (EURATEX)
Garment Contractors Association of Southern
   California
Fashion Group International (FGI) (United States)
Fashion from Spain
International Licensing Industry Merchandisers
   Association
Japan Fashion Association
Polish Federation of Apparel and Textiles (PIOT)

Textile and Apparel Exporting and Importing

Alexandria Cotton Exporters' Association (Egypt)
American Cotton Shippers Association
Bangladesh Garment Manufacturers and Exporters
   Association
Bulgarian Association of Apparel and Textile
   Exporters
Istanbul Textile and Apparel Exporters Association
Pakistan Readymade Garments Manufacturers and
   Exporters Association (PRGMEA)
Turkish Ready Wear and Garments Exporters
   Association (ITKIB Clothing)
U.S. Association of Importers of Textiles and
   Apparel (USA-ITA)

Retailing

Australian Retailers Association
British Retail Consortium
International Council of Shopping Centers
International Mass Retailers Association
International Retail Federation
Mexican Retail Consortium
National Association of Store Fixture Manufacturers
National Retail Federation (NRF)
Professional Pricing Society
Retail Industry Leaders Association (RILA)

Source:

Directory of Trade Associations, 2010.

Apparel British Columbia Association represents apparel manufacturers from only that one province in Canada. The Brazilian Textile and Apparel Industry Association appears to represent the entire textile complex for this large South American country. The Web sites for these associations are often rich sources of information about the textile or apparel industry, or both. The groups are easy to find on the Internet and frequently post daily news bulletins about activities, events, and political developments related to the industries they represent.

Continue your study of lobbying with Learning Activity 8.4.

Learning Activity 8.4
POSITIONING FOR LOBBYING

1. What are three fundamental purposes of labor unions?
2. Why might firms in the textile complex use trade associations for lobbying?
3. Identify three ways that trade associations are fundamentally different from trade unions? (Refer back to Chapter 4 for a quick review, if necessary.)
4. Why are both labor unions and trade associations likely to be engaged in lobbying?
5. In what fundamental ways would you expect the political positions of labor unions and trade associations to differ?
6. Pick one trade association from each level of the textile complex in Box 8.1. Look up each on the Internet, and identify its mission and the types of firms that are members. What types of benefits are derived from membership in each association?

Political Orientation of Firms and Their Trade Associations

Five classifications of political perspectives that may apply to firms and trade associations associated with the textile complex are as follows:

- *domestic* managers think their companies' activities are focused on obtaining domestic suppliers and customers and dealing with domestic political policies
- *international* managers source products and materials abroad but think their companies' overseas activities are primarily to support activities for the domestic parent company in increasing sales or supplying materials for the domestic market
- *global* managers of global firms view the world as their unit of analysis, source products and materials for the lowest price, and market products assuming that national tastes and preferences are more similar than different among nations; global companies produce and market standardized products for the world market
- *multinational* managers recognize and emphasize the differences among national suppliers, markets, and operating environments; accordingly, these firms design their products and strategies to meet demands in domestic as well as national markets
- *transnational* companies are responsive to local needs in multiple countries and simultaneously retain global efficiency (Ali, 2000)

These classifications evolve from the protectionist perspective in the domestic orientation, to global free trade, to a global **transnational fair trade perspective**. Table 8.1 describes the political evolution of textile, apparel, and retail firms in the U.S. textile complex from 1950 to the present and beyond. The firms that are part of the three primary components of the U.S.

textile complex see the world differently and have different pressures and priorities and different expectations of the political environments within which they operate. The different components of the textile complex seem to have similar perspectives in other parts of the world.

The 1950s and 1960s

In the 1950s, the free trade spirit was strong in the United States after the protectionist perspective of the Depression and years that followed. Prior to World War II, tariffs were raised to the highest levels ever, and world trade dropped to half of pre-Depression levels. After World War II, the economy was booming, and so was U.S. industry. Europe and Japan both had a great deal of destruction to their infrastructure and industrial production capability during the war, and the United States launched an unprecedented effort to finance reconstruction.

Multilateral negotiations were regarded as the best way to resolve international trade and financial problems. GATT (General Agreement on Tariffs and Trade) was formed in 1947, based on this free trade, multilateral perspective. By 1952, tariffs had dropped to one third the 1934 rates. Western Europe and the United States collaborated to implement freer international trading and monetary policies and developed a high level of interdependence, becoming each other's largest customers (Cohen et al, 2003).

However, the economies and the production capacities of Europe and Japan recovered very quickly, and by the late 1950s these nations began to compete with U.S. industry. The political spirit remained strongly focused on increasing free trade, and the Kennedy Round of multilateral negotiations (1963 to 1967) reduced average tariff levels by 36 percent among industrialized countries. At the same time, there

was a shift from tariff to nontariff trade barriers, beginning with the Long Term Arrangement Regarding International Trade in Cotton. This was soon followed by regulations related to meat products and woolen textiles (de la Torre, Jedel, Arpan, Ogram, & Toyne, 1978).

The textile and apparel manufacturing industries were close allies during the 1950s and 1960s. Both were focused on increasing business in the domestic economy. On average, textile firms employed approximately 150 people, and apparel firms employed approximately 50 people. The textile industry had been slowly concentrating into fewer larger firms and becoming more capital intensive, whereas the apparel industry remained labor intensive. Both industries were concentrated in northeastern United States; New York City was the fashion capital, and 80 percent of U.S. apparel was produced there (de la Torre et al., 1978). The Long Term Arrangement Regarding International Trade in Cotton protected cotton farmers and suppliers of cotton for the textile mills. Textile firms, apparel firms, and their trade associations all supported the protectionist perspective.

The retailers had entirely different priorities. Department stores dominated the retail scene, and they were focused on their domestic markets. However, the retailers had discovered the benefits of international sourcing, with a focus on Hong Kong, Japan, South Korea, and Taiwan. The retailers wanted to shop the world market to provide unique apparel for their customers. Thus, they supported the free trade perspective.

The 1970s

By 1970, protectionism was again on the rise. Clashing national policies designed to solve domestic political and social problems stalled multilateral negotiations. Free

Table 8.1 U.S. Textile and Apparel Industry Perspectives on Politics Related to World Trade Relationships and Regulations

Decade	Textile Manufacturing	Apparel Manufacturing	Textile and Apparel Retailing
Entrepreneurism/Protectionism			
1950s	Domestic focus Protected trade	Domestic focus Protected trade	International sourcing Free trade
1960s	Domestic focus Protected trade Long-term Arrangement	Domestic focus Protected trade	International sourcing Free trade
Protectionism/Internationalization			
1970s	Domestic focus Protected trade	Domestic focus Protected trade Multifiber Arrangement	International sourcing Free trade
Verticalization/Internationalization			
1980s	Trade protection with fabric-forward rules	Protected trade Stronger MFA	International sourcing Free trade
Horizontalization/Globalization/Exploitation			
1990s	Trade protection with yarn-forward rules	Free trade International sourcing U.S.–Canada Free Trade Agreement	Global sourcing International marketing NAFTA MFA phaseout Free trade
Regionalization/Multinationalism/Customization			
2000s	Actively seeking continued trade protection Moving toward international production	Global sourcing International marketing MFA expires Extend NAFTA Free trade Social responsibility	Free trade Global sourcing Multinational marketing
Sustainability/Transnationalism			
2010s?	Freer trade? Global sourcing? International marketing? No yarn-forward rule?	Free trade? Transnational sourcing? Transnational marketing?	Free trade? Transnational sourcing? Transnational marketing?

trade and high employment were not compatible policies. The United States was still the largest cotton-producing country, with 19.2 percent of world production, followed by the USSR, China, and India (Cline, 1990). Cotton imports were limited by the Long Term Arrangement. However, consumer preferences had changed, and in the United States consumption of manufactured fibers exceeded consumption of cotton. Textile and apparel manufacturing and the labor unions held firmly to their protectionist leanings and supported the development of the Multifiber Arrangement (MFA), which in 1974 established import quotas based on bilateral agreements. But the MFA did not prevent the growth of imports; it just moved the sources of imports around the world.

In the United States, the textile and apparel industries were shifting away from large urban areas into rural areas, primarily in the southeastern United States, where real estate cost less, unions were not established, and wages were lower. The number of apparel plants in the Northeast dropped to 64 percent of the total. Apparel labor unions had gained 90 percent membership in men's and boy's apparel, but with the move to the Southeast, membership in women's and girl's apparel diminished to 5 percent (Arpan, Torre, & Toyne, 1982).

By 1976 the United States was the largest employer of apparel workers in the world, with more than 1,300,000 employees (Japan had 565 thousand; Great Britain, 292 thousand). Most apparel firms were family-owned, single plant operations. The new plants were larger, modern, and more automated. However, the demand for qualified employees at the desired low wage gradually exceeded the supply in the Southeast, so wages had to rise. The result was the beginning of a westward movement by apparel manufacturers, to the Southwest and Pacific regions of the United States (de la Torre et al., 1978).

The apparel industry depended almost exclusively on research and development performed by manufactured fiber firms and textile machinery producers. The primary interest of apparel manufacturers was finding ways to increase the speed of garment assembly. The first major technical innovation in apparel production in 70 years was the laser beam cutter, introduced in the early 1970s. This helped the preproduction process, but sewing operators were still spending two thirds of their time handling the garment parts within and between sewing operations (de la Torre et al., 1978).

U.S. textile manufacturing continued to be regarded as internationally competitive, but the apparel industry was not, because textiles were less labor intensive than apparel. Meanwhile, apparel imports were on the rise. In 1961, apparel imports were about 6 percent of domestic consumption; by 1972, they were 25 percent. Many of the imports were manufactured fiber goods not covered by the Long Term Arrangement. (The MFA was established in 1974 and renewed in 1977, but it did not effectively deter imports.) Instead, the United States became the largest importer of apparel in the world, with more than $3 billion annually. Germany was ranked second, with nearly $3 billion, but at that time data were only available from developed countries (Arpan et al., 1982).

Worldwide, the leading exporters of apparel were Germany, France, Belgium, Japan, and the United States, which ranked fifth (Arpan et al., 1982). In general, European countries exported apparel to other European countries; the United States imported from Asian and Caribbean Basin countries. Hong Kong, Japan, South Korea, and Taiwan were primary contributors; Mexico and Colombia were making their mark.

The Tariff Schedules of the United States had a clause known as **Item 807**, which allowed garments cut in the United States to be exported and assembled and then imported, with tariff based only on value added. Value added was primarily dependent on labor cost, which kept the duty very low when products were assembled in Caribbean Basin countries. Pattern making and cutting operations were established in Miami to support 807 operations.

In the retail sector independent retailers were still in the majority, but department store chains were growing, and discount stores had been born. Bypassing U.S. manufacturers by sourcing apparel in Hong Kong was common. Retailers also joined in the Item 807 frenzy. Lower product cost was the primary justification. Retailers continued to stand strongly for free trade, recognizing the benefits of lower costs available abroad.

The 1980s

By the early 1980s, the MFA was in place as a global mechanism for controlling textile and apparel trade. The United States had 34 bilateral agreements, representing 80 percent of its textile and apparel imports from developing countries. The European Community (EC) had bilateral agreements with 25 countries, along with unilateral restraints on Taiwan and some Eastern European countries (Cline, 1990). Japan was a primary source of import pressure in the 1930s and the 1950s but no longer was a factor in the 1980s.

The MFA, by limiting quantities of exports, forced suppliers to upgrade the value of exports to increase sales. The MFA also encouraged diversification of supplier countries and product types, and the quota itself developed market value. For example, some U.S. retailers shifted sourcing from the quota-restricted countries, including Hong Kong, Taiwan, and South Korea, to countries where no bilateral agreements were in place (Glock & Kunz, 1995). As apparel production migrated to other developing countries, the materials supply became an issue. Some textile producers

began to establish production plants in developing countries to facilitate speed to market for the apparel plants in those locations.

Another **quota avoidance strategy** was to include fiber content in products that were not covered in the bilateral agreements. Quota restricted cotton, wool, and major manufactured fibers, primarily nylon, polyester, and acrylic. Blends, including ramie, silk, and linen, exempted products from quota limits and could be imported quota free, with tariffs as the only trade barrier. Until this time, ramie was seldom used in apparel, because it is a rough, course, stiff cellulose fiber. The MFA caused ramie to be developed as an apparel fiber to avoid the quota system. Silk and linen blends also became more common (Glock & Kunz, 1995).

Buyers from developed countries were sometimes willing to pay fees, known as quota rent, to continue to import from established suppliers because of reliable quality and time of delivery. Sometimes, the cost of the quota more than doubled the import cost of the product. Consequently, the MFA drove up the cost of imports, diversified the fiber content of products being imported, and established the apparel industry in more developing countries, rather than controlling the quantity of imports. Imports continued to increase in developed countries at an astounding rate.

In 1986, the United States and 54 other nations renewed the MFA for the fourth time. At U.S. textile and apparel industry insistence, the new agreement tightened quotas and extended product coverage to ramie, silk, and linen. The EC was initially more ambivalent; it thought the MFA should be renewed, but in a more flexible manner and with a phaseout plan in place. However, because of a downturn in the economy, the EC joined the United States to clamp down on imports with the MFA. There were also pledges to cooperate against fraud and falsification of COO. Using transshipment to avoid quotas by modifying COO had become a known practice (Cline, 1990).

At nearly the same time, the **Caribbean Basin Initiative (CBI),** known as 807a, was put in place by the United States. Guaranteed Access Levels (GALs) were established, assuring U.S. market access for Caribbean apparel products assembled from fabric formed and cut in the United States. CBI encouraged movement of apparel production out of the United States, while the MFA was restricting imports (Cline, 1990). The **fabric-forward rule** guaranteed the domestic textile manufacturers would supply the fabric, regardless of where the products were assembled. Around this time, the U.S.–Canada Free Trade Agreement was approved as well, and it also included a fabric-forward rule: to qualify for free trade, apparel had to be made of fabric produced in one of the two countries. Because Canada had very little textile manufacturing, the advantage was obvious for U.S. textile manufacturers.

On the U.S. domestic front, the size of textile manufacturing, apparel manufacturing, and retailing firms was exploding. Vertical mergers became commonplace. Small firms merged, were bought, or went out of business. Yarn spinners merged with weavers and with fabric finishers. U.S. textile manufacturers built new plants, with mass production as the primary goal. They reduced the variety of types of products produced, focused on budget- to moderate-priced goods, and increased the minimum number of yards required to make a purchase, strategies that were not necessarily in the best interest of their apparel manufacturer customers.

Apparel manufacturers bought their fabric suppliers or forward vertically integrated into the retail sector, or both. Manufacturers' outlets became the most rapidly growing form of retailing. At the same time, retailers developed their own product development divisions so that they could go directly to CMT contractors in developing countries and avoid the apparel manufacturer's role in the traditional supply matrix. Consultants and educators promoted

quick response business systems as a means of sustaining domestic production.

Major manufacturers and designers developed brands, including names such as Ralph Lauren, Calvin Klein, and Liz Claiborne, that remain powerful components of the apparel industry today. Department stores were at the mercy of their branded suppliers, who determined what, how much, and when merchandise would be shipped and how it would be displayed.

Textile manufacturers continued to advocate strongly for protectionist perspectives and succeeded in implementing the fabric-forward rule in CBI. Apparel manufacturers remained protectionist, whereas developing 807 operations throughout the Caribbean basin built their own retail stores and experimented with the retailers' practice of sourcing in the Far East.

The 1990s

GATT morphed into the World Trade Organization (WTO), continuing the global focus on free trade. MFA was scheduled to be phased out within 10 years—by 2005. Meanwhile, **regionalization,** in the form of preferential trading agreements, continued to develop. In 1994, the North American Free Trade Agreement (NAFTA) went into effect, which included a **yarn-forward rule**: to qualify for free trade, yarns, as well as fabrics, had to be produced in Canada, Mexico, or the United States. Once again the benefit of the yarn-forward rule accrued to the U.S. textile industry, because there was little textile production in Mexico. During the same time, the EEC evolved into the European Union (EU), comprising 12 western European countries (3 were later added, to form the EU-15).

Apparel manufacturers abandoned their protectionist stance and the textile manufacturers to join their retail customers in seeking the benefits of free trade (Glock & Kunz, 2000). The American Apparel

Manufacturers Association (AAMA) and the American Textile Manufacturers Institute (ATMI) had been the primary lobbying associations for trade protection from the U.S. government for more than 30 years. Many apparel manufacturers had long been operating their businesses with a global perspective but had maintained an international perspective in the political environment. The move to a free trade stance allowed them to unify their business and political goals. Their retail customers had already moved on to global sourcing.

The U.S. apparel manufacturing industry had experienced continuous decline in employment since the peak in the 1970s. However, because of increases in productivity, quantity of apparel produced continued to increase into the 1990s, with fewer sewing operators. Many domestic apparel manufacturers owned no production plants. They were product developers that sourced production in Mexico, the Caribbean Basin, or Asia. Branding was the name of the game, with a strong emphasis on brand licensing on a variety of apparel products as well as many other types of products. For firms that owned major brand names, it was common for licensing revenues to equal or exceed production revenues (Glock & Kunz, 2005).

Many retailers, through growth, mergers, and acquisitions, became huge. Walmart grew to be the largest retailer in the world. Walmart took control away from the manufacturers in the retail market place. Price promotion became the primary mode of competition. Retailers became global in product development, sourcing, and marketing. Sourcing materials and finished goods from the lowest-labor-cost developing country continued to be the primary challenge. But gradually, the inefficiencies of this strategy because apparent, and China established itself as the primary source of choice for many brand managers.

The 2000s

In 2001, the American Apparel Manufacturers Association (AAMA) merged with two other large trade associations, to form the American Apparel and Footwear Association (AAFA). As shown in Case 8.4, the political position of apparel and footwear manufacturers was made perfectly clear in a 2002 AAFA press release.

Mergers among apparel manufacturers continued, creating "batteries" of brands. The manufacturers also became known as brand managers. As smaller firms failed or owners retired, other firms bought the intellectual property rights to the brands. For example, some brand managers specialized in dress shirts, with a group of brands positioned for different target customers and price points. Some of the brands targeted specialty stores, others discount stores, and still others department stores. Similar strategies were being used for men's and women's sportswear and casual apparel and by firms in Europe. The process continued to the point that the brand managers could outfit the whole family at two or three different price and lifestyle points.

The phaseout of the MFA and its quota system created huge turmoil throughout the textile complex. Hundreds of articles were published in 2004, many predicting dire results of the phaseout. The reality was that much of the U.S. textile complex ignored the 10-year phaseout of the MFA until there were only 2 years left, putting some companies in desperate situations related to merchandise acquisition.

In the new century U.S. textile manufacturers and textile manufacturers in other developed countries experienced dramatic decline in demand for domestically produced products, owing for the most part to the dramatic decline in quantity of domestically produced apparel. Many firms went out of business, others declared bankruptcy,

AAFA's mission is to promote and enhance AAFA members' competitiveness, productivity, and profitability in the global market by minimizing regulatory, legal, commercial, and political trade restraints. To this end, AAFA will

- promote access to international markets through reduction and/or elimination of tariff and non-tariff barriers and free access to raw materials
- advocate the reduction and/or elimination of duties and quotas through trade preference programs, through bilateral free trade agreements, through regional free trade agreements, or through multilateral trade talks
- advocate rules of origin with no or minimal input requirements to minimize costly paperwork associated with trade operations
- advocate simplification and harmonization of rules of origin in all trade agreements
- discourage the use of quotas and other safeguard measures that seek to restrict market access
- promote best practices to ensure that goods are produced in a socially responsible manner
- encourage AAFA members to operate under programs that foster socially responsible production practices compliant with applicable labor and environmental laws and regulations
- encourage the U.S., other governments, and foreign trade associations to recognize and support programs that have been designed to achieve these goals
- pursue policies that encourage development of human rights and democratic values in countries in which AAFA members conduct business and discourage trade with countries that promote and support terrorism
- promote protection of brands, trademarks, and other intellectual property rights (IPR) and promote adherence to international trade rules and obligations such as Customs valuation requirements
- promote policies to expedite and facilitate Customs operations and activities and encouraging common sense measures to improve cargo and port security
- seek full funding of the U.S. Customs and Border Patrol Automated Computer Environment (ACE) by 2005
- advocate simplification and harmonization of Customs procedures, product classifications, and labeling requirements
- oppose the use of Customs user fees to fund non-Customs-oriented programs and activities
- promote best practices by AAFA members and common sense measures by the U.S. and other governments to improve cargo and port security and prevent smuggling and other illicit activities

Source:

Based on AAFA announces international trade policy: Emphasis on market access and social responsibility. (2002, June 5). Arlington, VA: American Apparel and Footwear Association.

and still others were merged or absorbed. Through it all, the textile industry maintained its protectionist perspective. However, by 2005 the largest of the U.S. textile firms, INVISTA, was expanding operations into China, recognizing that there were opportunities for textile production when it had proximity to apparel production.

The results of the initial quota phaseout, in 2005, followed by the final quota expirations in 2008, have already been addressed in a number of different contexts. The initial result was that the United States and the EU reimposed quotas on China and Vietnam until 2008. This quota system continued to shelter the rest of the world from the textile and apparel production power that had developed in China and Vietnam (Barrie & Ayling, 2010). Another obvious result was that less than 5 percent of apparel sold in the United States in 2009 was made in the United States, with 35 percent of it coming from China. The effect on the EU was not quite as dramatic, given that it had expanded from 15 to 27 countries and by doing so had incorporated a number of developing countries that provided some competitive sources for textile and apparel production. Yet, regulation of the textile and apparel trade had not gone away. Although quota-type trade regulations were in place, antidumping and countervailing duty trade remedies were rarely applied to textiles and apparel. That has changed. These strategies are expected to increase in use during the next decade (USAID, 2009).

The 2010s

At the time of this writing, we still do not know what will be the ultimate fallout of the phaseout of the MFA and the worldwide recession that plagued the last half of the last decade. However, trends are beginning to emerge. Chasing the lowest labor cost around the world resulted in long lead times, inconsistent quality, bad merchandise assortments, drastic markdowns, and huge amounts of excess inventory at retail. Several of the brand managers were not able to deal with the consequences of that many bad decisions, causing some firms to fail in the textile, manufacturing, and retail worlds, and others to become much larger, by absorbing the losers. The worldwide recession and high energy costs contributed to the impact on business operations.

In 2004, there were 28 countries that each exported more than $500 million in apparel to the United States and the EU, but over the latter half of the decade the market shifted. Primary losers included Mexico, Honduras, and the Dominican Republic. Primary winners included China, Vietnam, Indonesia, India, and Bangladesh. Among the dozens of small suppliers, there were even bigger losses in market share, with only five countries experiencing increases. Least developed and newly developing countries with preferential trade agreements with the United States and EU have struggled during this period. Relief of duty alone does not appear enough to ensure competitiveness in the new environment for textiles and apparel trade. The rules of origin rules that govern these agreements frequently dictate the sourcing of materials, increasing input costs and paperwork (USAID, 2009).

Changing priorities in supply chain operation are causing buyers (the sourcing company) to impose different expectations on potential vendors (the supplier company). The trend toward faster turnover of inventory in the retail setting drives buyers to vendors with proximity to materials; reliable infrastructure for energy, transportation, and communication; and a workforce that is skilled, flexible, and dependable. Newly developing countries seldom have these resources in place.

In early 2010, there was apparel manufacturing capacity in 130 countries (Barrie & Ayling, 2010). The trade press was full of articles related to dealing with the lasting effects of the recession, while improving the efficiency and sustainability of supply chains. A primary result of the recession was that all textile and apparel firms, large and small, were finding ways to improve efficiency and reduce costs. Not surprisingly, this meant brand managers and sourcing firms were finding ways to do more with less—fewer people and less time. Management teams were downsized, and priorities changed from sourcing goods at the lowest cost to reducing sourcing risks related to quality, assortment, and timely delivery (Barrie & Ayling, 2010), with additional considerations for continuing productive trade relationships.

It appeared that adoption of the transnational concept of companies' being responsive to local needs in multiple countries, while simultaneously retaining global efficiency (Ali, 2000), was becoming a priority. At the same time, the ongoing, growing complexity of trade preference programs, and whether they facilitated or impeded trade, had to be addressed. There will be fascinating developments evolving over the next decade.

Now, expand your knowledge of political positioning with Learning Activity 8.5.

Learning Activity 8.5
POLITICAL POSITIONING OF THE TEXTILE COMPLEX

1. Why have retailers long supported free trade, whereas textile and apparel manufacturers have held a protectionist perspective?
2. What caused apparel manufacturers to join retailers with a free trade perspective?
3. According to Case 8.4, what is the political perspective of AAFA?
4. How does the transnational perspective differ from free trade and protectionist perspectives?
5. In what way is the transnational perspective consistent with corporate responsibilities related to global sourcing?

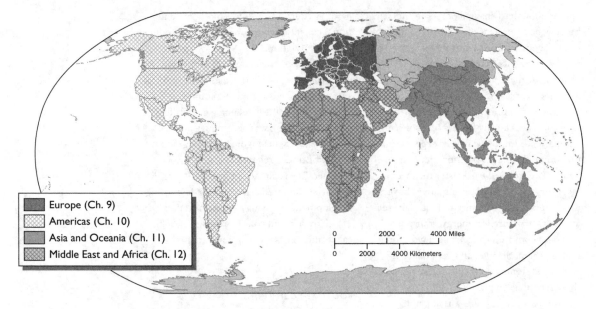

Figure 8.3 Four trading blocs are identified on this map: Europe and the European Union (EU), the Americas and the Caribbean, Asia and Oceania, and the Middle East and Africa. All have regional distinctions in the manufacture and distribution of textiles and apparel. These regions are the topic of discussion in the next four chapters. (*Courtesy Fairchild Books*)

Legend:
- Europe (Ch. 9)
- Americas (Ch. 10)
- Asia and Oceania (Ch. 11)
- Middle East and Africa (Ch. 12)

REGIONALIZATION OF GLOBAL MARKETS

The complexity of the global market and the diversity of political climates among nations have fostered a trend to regionalization of the global textile and apparel industry, using **preferential trade agreements** (PTA). A PTA, among a group of countries, extends special trading advantages by reducing trade barriers. Political unification of diverse types of governments and levels of development in a geographic region benefits participants by increasing overall economic power and rate of industrial development. Four primary regions form **trading blocs** in the textile and apparel industry:

1. Europe and the European Union
2. the Americas and Caribbean
3. Asia and Oceania
4. the Middle East and Africa

Each of these regions includes a combination of developed and developing countries. The developed countries in a region provide market demand for the products produced with low-cost labor in the developing countries. Another common characteristic of the regions is free trade practices within the area. This discussion introduces the basic characteristics of these four trading blocs. The rest of this text contains chapters addressing the nature of the textile and apparel industry in each of these four geographic regions (Figure 8.3).

We should note at this time that there is a portion of the globe that is not actively a part of these four trading blocs. This region, identified as the Commonwealth of Independent States (CIS), was created in December 1991 from those nations that previously made up the Soviet Union (Interstate Statistical Committee of the CIS, 2010). In the adopted declaration the participants of

the Commonwealth declared their interaction on the basis of sovereign equality;
in 1993 they signed an agreement for the
creation of an economic union to provide
for free movement of goods and services
among members. At present the CIS unites
Azerbaijan, Armenia, Belarus, Georgia,
Kazakhstan, Kyrgyzstan, Moldova, Russia,
Tajikistan, Turkmenistan, Uzbekistan, and
Ukraine. Although many of these nations
have not as yet made significant inroads into
global trade in textiles and apparel, in the
future we may be hearing a lot more from
them. For example, Azerbaijan is an important source of cotton and is being aided
by other governments, such as the United
States, in its quest to enter into the global
textile market more fully.

Europe and the European Union

Europe stretches from Iceland, in the
North Atlantic, to Russia, in the east, and
from Scandinavia, in the north, to Spain
and Turkey, in the south. Western Europe
includes many of the most developed countries in the world, whereas eastern Europe
includes a variety of developing countries,
many of which reemerged in the global
marketplace after the breakup of the Soviet
Union, in the 1990s. The population of western Europe is far greater than that of eastern
Europe.

Europe moved toward regionalization first, by creating the Common Market,
beginning in 1952, followed by the European
Economic Community (EEC). Then, in
1993, the EEC evolved into a 12-nation group
known as the European Union (EU). The EU
has now expanded to include 27 countries
throughout Europe.

The European trading bloc includes several western European nations—specifically,
Great Britain, France, Italy and Germany—
that have been major contributors to the
globalization of fashion apparel goods and the

technologies required to remain competitive
in the international textile and apparel market.
Several eastern European countries, including
Bulgaria, Romania, and Russia, are suppliers
of textiles and apparel to western Europe as
well as the rest of the world. This segment of
the globe is examined in Chapter 9.

The Americas and Caribbean Basin

The Americas comprise Central America
(7 countries), North America (3 countries),
South America (13 countries), and the West
Indies (13 countries). Political regionalization of the Americas started in the 1980s,
when the Reagan administration initiated
economic development legislation related to
textiles and apparel favoring the Caribbean
Basin. The U.S. **Caribbean Basin Initiative**,
in 1987, and U.S. Special Regime with Mexico
were followed by the U.S.–Canada Free
Trade Agreement.

The North American Free Trade
Agreement (NAFTA) then unified North
America in 1994. NAFTA was followed by
the U.S.–Caribbean Basin Trade Partnership
Act (CBTPA) and establishment of the
Central American Free Trade Agreement,
which ultimately added the Dominican
Republic, to become CAFTA-DR, as well as
bilateral free trade agreements with individual South American countries, including Chile and Peru. Political unrest and
economic instability in Central America
and South America have been deterrents to
their political regionalization. Nevertheless,
these areas have come together to form
Mercosur, the common market of the
south, and CARICOM, the Caribbean
Community.

With the elimination of the quota system, U.S. apparel firms moved many apparel
sourcing operations away from Central and
South America and the West Indies to Asia, but
some are now reconsidering that move. This
part of the world is examined in Chapter 10.

Asia and Oceania

This bloc is a combination of mainland and island countries, including the two most populous nations on the globe—China and India. In 1898, after serious political turmoil, China leased Hong Kong to the United Kingdom (UK) for 99 years. While a British colony, Hong Kong developed a strong free market system; in the mid-1970s, Hong Kong was the largest export processor of textiles and apparel. By the time Hong Kong reverted to Communist China, in 1997, China had become the largest apparel exporter in the world and was struggling to develop a free market system. The two political entities agreed to a one-country, two-political-system arrangement and continue to dominate world trade of textiles and apparel.

India has become a major world supplier of textiles and apparel, yet at the same time low manufacturing productivity remains a major stumbling block. When fiber, yarn, fabric, and finished goods are considered, Pakistan is one of the largest exporters of cotton and cotton goods in the world. Tiny Sri Lanka (formerly known as Ceylon), located off the coast of India, is one of the poorest island countries in the world, but it has a thriving apparel industry. Sri Lanka has a strong record of compliance with international standards in terms of labor laws, environmental protection, and human rights, especially as compared with its much larger neighbors. Sri Lanka and many other countries in the Far East hope to continue to expand their role in the global apparel market.

Regionalization in the Asia and Oceania area proceeded in 1977, with the creation of the Association of Southeast Asian Nations (ASEAN). The current member countries are Brunei, Cambodia, Indonesia, Laos, Malaysia, Myanmar, the Philippines, Singapore, Thailand, and Vietnam. The major purpose of this association has been the economic development of nations within the region. ASEAN has fostered free trade agreements among mainland and island country member nations and with other countries.

Many Asian countries, including Hong Kong, Taiwan, China, Japan, and Vietnam, are heavily involved in textile and apparel trade. Hong Kong, South Korea, and Taiwan became known as the "Big Three" apparel exporters, dominating world trade until the early 1970s, when the Nixon administration opened trade between the United States and China, leading to the explosion of export capability from China. The many changes in this region of the world are examined in Chapter 11.

Middle East and Africa

We are defining the Middle East region as an area stretching from Turkey, on the eastern shore of the Mediterranean, eastward through Iran. At this time, the region includes some of the more politically volatile portions of the globe, including Iraq, Iran, and Afghanistan. The Middle East has assumed much greater importance in the global textile and apparel market since developing some of the world's lowest-cost suppliers of finished goods, including apparel manufacturers in Jordan, and significant consumer markets in cities such as Dubai, in the United Arab Emirates (UAE).

Africa became a more significant contributor to global apparel trade through the development of CMT facilities, such as those on the island nation of Mauritius (located off the eastern coast), but Africa has had hard times since the beginning of this century. African nations have been working toward a regional presence with such international agreements as the African Growth and Opportunity Act

(AGOA). AGOA has progressed through some revisions since it was originally instituted (AGOA II, AGOA III and now AGOA IV), as refinements were made to provide incentives for African countries to continue their efforts to open their economies and build free markets, including those related to textiles and apparel. The uniqueness of this region is addressed in Chapter 12.

Deepen your understanding of world regions with Learning Activity 8.6.

Learning Activity 8.6
REGIONS OF THE WORLD

1. What are the benefits of regionalization?
2. What do the four trading bloc regions have in common?
3. Identify one aspect of the Americas region that is unique.
4. Which region benefited from the breakup of the former Soviet Union?
5. Which region involves only one continent?
6. Which region has the most convenient access to ocean transportation?
7. Which region has the world's largest textile and apparel producer?
8. Which region includes the most politically volatile countries of the world?
9. If you were now a sourcing executive, which two aspects of politics of textiles and apparel would you find the most difficult to deal with? Explain.

SUMMARY

Politics are the methods, or tactics, involved in managing an organization, business, state, or government. Power, influence, and manipulation of people and other resources may be the primary motivators. Politics exist in all organizations in which there is controversy related to objectives, use of resources, or competition for power, or a combination of these.

Unfair competition is commercial activity that tends to confuse, mislead, or deceive customers and provide unfair business advantages. Government activities, including production subsidies, export subsidies, and price support programs, are frequently regarded as unfair competition in the global market. Dumping is a form of unfair competition that involves selling products below cost of production or their normal price in the domestic market. Governments compensate for this by applying antidumping duties to reduce import surges.

Firms in the textile complex use trade associations and labor unions as vehicles for lobbying for favorable trade legislation. For many years, U.S. textile and apparel manufacturers favored protectionist legislation, and retailers favored free trade. Retailers have long recognized the value of the global market for giving their customers the best prices and a unique variety of goods. As U.S. apparel manufacturers lost garment assembly to developing countries, they also learned the value of the global market and changed their political perspective to support free trade. Textile manufacturers staunchly adhered to their protectionist stand throughout most of the 20th century.

The last 20 years has seen growth of regionalization in the global apparel market. The EU has formed a powerful political and economic unit, whereas the United States has been working toward a more unified Americas. Asia has risen to a dominant position in production of textiles and apparel. The Middle East and Africa face unique challenges for economic and industrial development. These four regions are the foundation for discussion in the next four chapters.

REFERENCES

AAFA announces international trade policy: Emphasis on market access and social responsibility. (2002, June 5). Arlington, VA: American Apparel and Footwear Association.

Ali, A. J. (2000). *Globalization of business: Practice and theory.* New York: Haworth Press.

Apparel Search Company. (2010). Apparel and textile industry associations and organizations. Retrieved May 26, 2010, from http://www.apparelsearch.com/associations.htm

Arpan, J. S., Torre, J., & Toyne, B. (1982). The U.S. apparel industry: International challenge, domestic response. *Research Monograph No. 88.* Atlanta, GA: Georgia State University.

Barrie, L., & Ayling, J. (2010, January–February). Apparel industry issues to watch in 2010: Management briefing. Bromsgrove, Worcestershire, UK: Aroq. Retrieved February 15, 2010, from http://www.just-style.com

Cline, W. C. (1990). *The future of world trade in textiles and apparel.* Washington, DC: Institute of International Economics.

Cohen, S. D., Blecker, R. A., & Whitney, P. D. (2003). Fundamentals of U.S. *Foreign Trade Policy* (2nd ed.). Boulder, CO: Westview Press.

Concept Marketing Group. Retrieved January 5, 2004, from http://www.marketingsource.com

de la Torre, J., Jedel, M. J., Arpan, J. S., Ogram, J. S., & Toyne, B. (1978). Corporate responses to import competition in the U.S. apparel industry. *Research Monograph No. 74.* Atlanta, GA.: Georgia State University.

Demand for antidumping duty on polyester imports from China. (2009, January 23). Fibre2fashion.com. Retrieved February 9, 2010, from http://www.fibre2fashion.com/news/polyester-news/newsdetails.aspx?news_id=68452

Elias, S., & Stim, R. (2003, April). *Patent, copyright, & trademark: An intellectual property desk reference* (6th ed.). Berkeley, CA: Nolo.

Elias, S., & Stim, R. (2007). *Trademark: Legal care for your business & product name.* (8th ed.). US: Stephan Elias.

Ellis, K. (2004, August 2). WTO negotiators in tariff accord. *Women's Wear Daily.* Retrieved from http://www.wwd.com

European Commission. (2009, February). The new U.S. farm bill: Zooming in on ACRE. *MAP.* Retrieved February 9, 2010, from http://ec.europa.eu/agriculture/publi/map/01_09.pdf

Feds set polyester dumping duties. (2000, May 2). *Women's Wear Daily,* 13.

Fowler, J. (2004, July 31). Negotiators continue global trade talks. *The Des Moines Register,* p. 6D.

Glock, R. E., & Kunz, G. I. (1995). *Apparel manufacturing: Sewn product analysis.* (2nd ed.). Upper Saddle River, NJ: Prentice Hall.

Glock, R. E., & Kunz, G. I. (2000). *Apparel manufacturing: Sewn product analysis.* (3rd ed.) Upper Saddle River, NJ: Prentice Hall.

Glock, R. E., & Kunz, G. I. (2005). *Apparel Manufacturing: Sewn Product Analysis.* (4th ed.). Upper Saddle River, NJ: Prentice Hall.

Interstate Statistical Committee of the CIS. (2010). About CIS. Retrieved from http://www.cisstat.com/eng/cis.htm

Irwin, D.A. (2004, August 9). Free-trade worriers. *Wall Street Journal,* p. A12.

Klapper, B. S. (2009, September 1). WTO sanctions U.S. over cotton subsidies. *The Washington Post.* Retrieved from http://www.washingtonpost.com/wp-dyn/content/article/2009/08/31/AR2009083103679.html

Kunz, G. I. (2005). Memories from a Nike experience. Unpublished paper. Iowa State University.

Kunz, G. I., Lewis, C. J., & Coffin, I. A. (1992). Opportunities for cooperation between educators and apparel and textiles trade associations. *Clothing and Textiles Research Journal, 10,* 9–16.

Measure first, then cut: The global business environment. (2004, September 8). *The Economist.* Retrieved September 14, 2004, from http://www.economist.com/agenda/Story_3172172)

National Council of Textile Organizations. (n.d.). Retrieved June 30, 2005, from http://www.ncto.org

Office of the United States Trade Representative. (n.d). Non-Agriculture Market Access (NAMA). Retrieved June 8, 2010, from http://www.ustr .gov/trade-topics/industry-manufacturing/ non-agricultural-market-access

Oxfam reaction to WTO judgment on U.S. cotton subsidies. (2009, August 31). Oxfam International. Retrieved from http://www.oxfam .org/en/pressroom/pressrelease/2009-08-31/ oxfam-reaction-wto-judgement-us-cotton-subsidies

Rising protectionism: The dumping dilemma. (2002, June 1). *The Economist*, 71.

The road to the Civil War: Sectional disagreements over import tariffs. (n.d.). Retrieved May 25, 2010, from http://www.brtprojects.org/ cyberschool/history/ch13/13answers.pdf

Shen, D., & Dickson, M.A. (2002). Apparel exports from China to the U.S.: A Marxist perspective. *Clothing and Textiles Research Journal*, 20(4), 215–226.

Stone, N. (1994). The globalization of Europe: An interview with Wisse Dekker. *Global Strategies*. Boston, MA: Harvard Business School Press.

United States Agency for International Development. (2009, May). *Post-Quota textiles and apparel in developing countries*. Nathan Associates Inc.

USAID. (2009, May). Post-quota textiles and apparel trade in developing countries. Retrieved June 8, 2009, from http://tcboostproject.com/ _resources/resource/Postquota_Textiles_and_ Apparel_Trade.pdf

U.S. Wins End to Chinese Brand Export Subsidies. (2009, December 21). Retrieved from http://www.just-style.com/ article.aspx?id=106263

World Bank. (2001). Global economic prospects and the developing countries—2002. Washington, DC: The International Bank for Reconstruction and Development.

World Trade Organization. (n.d.). WTO agreement on Implementation of Article VI of the General Agreement on Tariffs and Trade 1994. Retrieved June 8, 2010, from http://www .wto.org/english/tratop_e/adp_e/antidam2_e .htm

3 TRADING PARTNERS

9 Europe and the European Union

The EU textile and clothing industry is one of the two biggest players in the world market, representing 29 percent of the world's exports (European Commission, 2009).

THE CONTINENT OF Europe encompasses multiple ethnicities; frozen and tropical environments; diverse cultures; and miniscule-to-large developed, developing, newly developing, and least developed countries. It incorporates part of the former Soviet Union as well as part of Turkey. Throughout history, countries have struggled with ethnic conflicts and efforts to unify the territory. Europe also has a long history in textiles and apparel and includes many of the leading fashion centers in the world.

POLITICAL AND ECONOMIC OVERVIEW: EFFORTS TO UNIFY EUROPE

Examine Figure 9.1, a map of Europe. Sometimes, Europe is described as having two parts: western Europe and eastern Europe. Other times, Europe is described as having four or six geographical parts. Note the locations of large countries, and consider which might generally be described as northern, western, eastern, and southern Europe. Because geographical sources differ in how they describe the locations of countries, we are not going to pick one system; however, it is

Objectives

- Examine the evolution of economic and political organization in Europe.

- Examine the roles of producing and consuming countries, areas of expertise, and specialization.

- Explore trade and economic development regulations in the region.

- Discuss major participating countries in the textile and apparel business.

Figure 9.1 The continent of Europe was where the Industrial Revolution began and where machines for mass production of textiles and apparel were invented. *(Courtesy Fairchild Books)*

useful to know the general location of the nations on the continent and their relationships to one another. As you work your way through the following discussion, be sure to locate on the map each country as it is mentioned.

People in Europe have long sought to create economic and industrial if not political unity beginning as early as the 9th-century empire of Charlemagne, which included much of western Europe. During the early 1800s, the French empire of Napoleon I encompassed much of the European continent. During World War II, in the early 1940s, Adolph Hitler nearly succeeded in uniting Europe under Nazi domination. In between these events, many other European dynasties developed and fell. Table 9.1 provides a summary of the continuing evolution of European economic and political organization over the last 60-plus years. This evolution required dozens of years of negotiations and dozens of treaties among European countries. You can use this table as a point of reference as these countries are discussed throughout the chapter.

Early collaborations among European countries were international or intergovernmental organizations that depended on the voluntary cooperation of their members. Following World War II, requests for supranational organization became frequent. A **supranational organization** requires that members give up a portion of their control over selected policies and allows the organization to compel compliance with its mandates. European countries recognized the need to take common political positions and command resources comparable with the organization of the United States. They believed that larger markets would promote competition and lead to greater productivity and higher

Table 9.1 EVOLUTION OF EUROPEAN POLITICAL AND ECONOMIC ORGANIZATION

Year	Event	Countries Involved
1948	Benelux Customs Union free trade area formed	Belgium, Luxembourg, the Netherlands
1950	European Coal and Steel Community (ECSC) formed	Belgium, France, Italy, Luxembourg, the Netherlands, West Germany
1957	European Economic Community (EEC) Common Market formed by ECSC	Belgium, France, Italy, Luxembourg, the Netherlands, West Germany
1960	European Free Trade Association (EFTA) formed	Austria, Denmark, Norway, Portugal, Sweden, Switzerland, United Kingdom
1967	European Community (EC) formed by merger of EEC and ECSC	Belgium, France, Italy, Luxembourg, the Netherlands, West Germany
1973	EC expanded	Denmark, Ireland, United Kingdom
1981	EC expanded	Greece
1986	EC expanded	Portugal and Spain
1993	European Union (EU) officially formed when EC member legislatures ratified Maastricht Treaty, became known as European Union–12 (EU-12)	Belgium, Denmark, France, Germany, Greece, Ireland, Italy, Luxembourg, the Netherlands, Portugal, Spain, United Kingdom
1994	EU and EFTA joined to form European Economic Area (EEA)	Austria, Belgium, Denmark, France, Germany, Greece, Ireland, Italy, Luxembourg, the Netherlands, Norway, Portugal, Spain, Sweden, Switzerland, United Kingdom
1995	European Union–15 (EU-15) created by adding 3 countries to EU-12	Austria, Finland, Sweden
2001	EU-15 adopted the euro	Currency used in everyday transactions in 12 European countries
2004	EU-15 added 10 countries, became EU-25	Cyprus, Czech Republic, Estonia, Hungary, Latvia, Lithuania, Malta, Poland, Slovakia, Slovenia
2005	Countries identified for potential EU membership	Belarus, Bulgaria, Romania, Russia, Turkey
2005	EU constitution rejected by France and the Netherlands, raised questions about use of euro	France and the Netherlands
2005	EU import quotas phased out, according to the Agreement on Textiles and Clothing	EU-15 and all countries with bilateral agreements
2005	EU initiated new quotas on apparel from China	EU-25 and China
2007	EU-25 added 2 countries, to become EU-27	Romania and Bulgaria
2007	EU extended import quotas with China expired	EU-27 and China
2009	New EU constitution went into effect as the Treaty on the Functioning of the European Union (TFEU)	

Source: Data collected from the World Trade Organization (WTO) and the European Commission.

levels of living. Because countries were reluctant to surrender control over political affairs, supranational organization began with economic and industrial integration.

Belgium, Luxembourg, and the Netherlands were leaders in trade integration. In 1948, they created a free trade area encompassing the three small countries by forming the Benelux Customs Union (BCU). Trade within the area was tariff and quota free. Then France and West Germany proposed industrial unification of the coal and steel industries, creating the European Coal and Steel Community (ECSC). They invited other nations to participate, and the members of BCU responded. Many nations

adversarial relationships a common behavior between suppliers and customers in the textile complex; belief that success of one is dependent on costs to another

euro European Union common currency, initiated in 2001 by EU-15

European Commission a politically independent institution responsible for proposing EU legislation, implementing it, and monitoring compliance

European Community (EC) European Economic Community membership expanded to form this in 1967; France blocked membership of the United Kingdom until 1973

European Economic Area (EEA) a cooperative arrangement to strengthen trade and economic relations in order to create a homogenous European trade area with the support of European Union

European Economic Community (EEC) the unification of Belgium, Luxembourg, the Netherlands, France, and West Germany in 1957; became known as the Common Market

European Union (EU) an organization formed in 1993 to expand cooperation regarding trade, social issues, foreign policy, security, defense, and judicial issues

European Union–12 (EU-12) the original 12 members included Belgium, Denmark, France, Germany, Greece, Ireland, Italy, Luxembourg, the Netherlands, Portugal, Spain, and the United Kingdom

European Union–15 (EU-15) Austria, Finland, and Sweden were admitted to the EU in 1995

European Union–25 (EU-25) Cyprus, the Czech Republic, Estonia, Hungary, Latvia, Lithuania, Malta, Poland, Slovakia, and Slovenia were admitted to the EU in 2004

European Union–27 (EU-27) Bulgaria and Romania were admitted to the EU in 2007

extra EU trade with nations that are not members of the EU

industrial espionage commercial spying; made it possible for U.S spinners and weavers to use machines copied from the English inventions

intra EU trade among nations that are members of the EU

Maastricht Treaty treaty signed by 12 EC members, to form the European Union in 1991

supranational organization requires that members give up a portion of their control over selected policies and allows the organization to compel compliance with its mandates

---

were concerned about controlling the rapidly growing German steel industry, but the United Kingdom (UK) declined to join the ECSC.

In 1957, the ECSC nations carried unification one step further through formation of the **European Economic Community (EEC),** widely known as the Common Market. The EEC treaty included a gradual elimination of import duties and quota among member nations and a common external tariff system. Member nations implemented common policies regarding transportation, agriculture, and social insurance and permitted free movement of people and financial resources among the member countries. The UK and other nations wanted a free trade area instead; therefore, they formed the European Free Trade Association (EFTA), which provided for elimination of tariffs on industrial products only. However, the UK soon recognized the success of the EEC and, overcoming considerable internal resistance, sought membership but was denied twice because of vetoes by President Charles de Gaulle, of France.

In 1967, the ECSC and the EEC joined to form the **European Community (EC).** The EC gradually implemented the economic features of the EEC, but France blocked expansion of membership until 1973, when the UK, Ireland, and Denmark joined. Within the UK, considerable resistance to EEC participation continued.

European economy and European competitiveness passed through a deep recession in the late 1970s and early 1980s. The combined profit of Europe's 100 largest corporations was zero. Unemployment, especially among the young, was very high. Growth in productivity had lagged behind wage increases. Social costs (health care, unemployment and disability compensation, education, and so on) were twice that of either Canada or the United States (Stone, 1994). It was very apparent that changes had to be made to revitalize European business. The effort became focused once again on attempting to create a unified western Europe.

In 1991, the 12 EC members signed the **Maastricht Treaty** and in 1993 became the **European Union (EU).** The primary goal of EU was to expand cooperation regarding trade, social issues, foreign policy, security, defense, and judicial issues. Another major goal was to implement a single currency for EU members. In a move toward these goals, the **European Union–12 (EU-12)** (the original group of EU countries) and EFTA joined in a cooperative arrangement, to form the **European Economic Area (EEA).** EEA's purpose is to promote a continuous and balanced strengthening of trade and economic relations among the contracting parties, with a view toward creating a homogenous European trade area. Accomplishments include the development of common product standards and the reduction of trade barriers among countries, to institute a so-called single-document structure. For example, truck drivers previously had to carry more than 35 documents, which had to be processed when crossing the border from one country to another.

Another problem was that nationalistic policies within countries had created internal monopolies in services, particularly in telecommunications. These monopolies were in a position to continue to charge their customers for the inefficiencies that had become common in their operations. Monopolies were abandoned in favor of competition. Government procurement also was opened up to all countries in the group instead of being confined to individual countries. It was possible to access the whole western European market and take advantage of economies of scale (Stone, 1994).

In 1995, the EU-12 became the **European Union–15 (EU-15)** when Austria, Finland, and Sweden were admitted. In 2001,

the EU-15 implemented the use of a single currency, the **euro**, thereby accomplishing one of the EU's primary goals. Of the 15 countries, 12 adopted the Euro.

In 2004, the EU-15 was enlarged to include ten new member states, forming the **European Union–25 (EU-25).** These new nations also participate in the EEA. Some of the new nations are located in eastern Europe and include some of the newly developing countries in the world. These countries are emerging from communist rule, in part as a result of the demise of the Soviet Union. Negotiations continue as other European countries apply to become a part of the EU-25 and the EEA. The EEA could potentially control up to 40 percent of world trade, including some of the highest income countries in the world. Western Europe is not yet completely united with eastern Europe as a trading bloc, but economic power would be clearly increased if they were; western Europe provides a huge consumer base, whereas eastern Europe provides a huge, low-cost production base.

In 2007, with the admission of Bulgaria and Romania the EU-25 became the **European Union–27 (EU-27).** At this time, a revised constitution was sought, via development of the Treaty of Lisbon (which was based on a previous version, the Reform Treaty), and nations within the union began to sign the newly developed constitution. In late 2009, the Treaty of Lisbon became the Treaty on the Functioning of the European Union (TFEU), providing a new constitution for the EU.

The **European Commission**, which is the politically independent institution responsible for proposing EU legislation, implementing it, and monitoring compliance, considers the single market one of the EU's greatest achievements (European Commission, 2009).

Continue your study of the unification of Europe with Learning Activity 9.1.

1. In what ways is the EU similar in organization and purpose to the United States?
2. In what ways is the EU different in organization and purpose from the United States?
3. How is a country in the EU different from a state in the United States?
4. What are some of the reasons it has taken so long for the countries in Europe to evolve into the EU?
5. Identify the geographic location of each of the countries listed in Table 9.1 on the map in Figure 9.1 Take note of common boundaries, particularly between the EU-15 countries and newer EU-27 countries. (Table 9.1 identifies which countries were in EU-15 and which joined more recently.)

ECONOMIC AND INDUSTRIAL STANDING OF SELECTED EUROPEAN COUNTRIES

Europe includes some of the richest and poorest countries in the world. Table 9.2 itemizes characteristics of European countries that are active in the textile and apparel trade, sorted by time of EU membership and geographic location. Scan down the first two columns of data (geographic size and population). Look for the countries that are the largest and have the largest populations. Russia is by far the largest country (more than 17 million square kilometers) and has the largest population. Russia is physically nearly twice as large as the United States and spans 11 time zones. Western Russia is less than a fourth of the total country and is located east of the Ural Mountains, in

Europe. Eastern Russia makes up northern Asia. Russia is being discussed in this chapter, because its population density is concentrated in the West, it has become closely associated with the EU, and it is a potential EU member. Also, Russia is a primary participant in the textile and apparel trade with EU countries. Turkey is the second-largest country, a little bigger than Texas, and has the third-largest population. Turkey, too, is split between Europe and Asia and has been trying for many years to gain membership in the EU. We have elected to leave much of our discussion of Turkey to Chapter 12, as part of the Middle East. Germany, slightly smaller than Montana, has the second-largest population.

Examine the life expectancies listed in Table 9.2. Note that most of the countries in the EU-15 have life expectancies exceeding 78 years, whereas most of the new members of the EU have life expectancies that are considerably shorter. What does that tell you about the levels of development of these two groups of countries? Literacy is uniformly high for most countries, with the exception of Portugal.

Note, too, that Germany has the largest gross domestic product (GDP), even though Russia has by far the largest population. What does that say about the level of industrial development in each country? It is dangerous to examine GDP outside the context of the other characteristics of a country. Geographic size, population, and literacy may all contribute to GDP. That is why per capita GDP is a better measure of overall well-being in a country than is GDP alone. Per capita GDP explains the relationship between GDP and the size of the population.

In Chapter 1, based on 2009 data, we used per capita GDP as an indicator of a country's overall level of economic and industrial development (see Table 1.2). The categories broke down as follows:

- least developed countries had per capita GDP of less than $3 thousand
- newly developing countries had per capita GDP between $3 thousand and $10 thousand
- developing countries had per capita GDP between $10 thousand and $20 thousand
- developed countries had per capita GDP of more than $20 thousand

According to that distribution, none of the EU members included in Table 9.2 would be classified as least developed or newly developing. Ukraine would be described as newly developing, but it is not yet an EU member. There are European countries that could fall into the "least developed" category, but they are not included on this list, because they are not yet significantly involved in the textile and apparel trade. All the EU-15 members are well into the "developed" category. Of the 2004 and 2007 new EU members, Cyprus, the Czech Republic, Malta, Slovakia, and Slovenia are in the "developed" category (more than $20 thousand), whereas the others are in the "developing" category.

Of the European countries listed in Table 9.2 that are outside the EU, Switzerland, Norway, and Russia have remained independent of the EU by choice. Belarus, Croatia, and Ukraine are likely to wish to gain EU membership in the future.

The highest inflation rate among the EU countries is Romania, with 5 percent; the lowest is Ireland, with -3.9 percent. According to some standards, inflation of 3 percent or less is regarded as acceptable or normal. Negative inflation rates are unusual, but, in general, inflation rates were low because of the worldwide economic recession that was in place in 2009. Rapidly rising inflation is often a part of economic recovery.

The size of the labor force and the unemployment rate are of particular interest when seeking locations in which to establish apparel production facilities. Obviously, countries with larger populations have larger labor forces. Average age of population may also be of interest; it might suggest whether a large portion of the population is very young or very old and therefore unemployable. Some small countries, such as Luxembourg, which is smaller than Rhode Island, have thousands of workers who commute from surrounding countries daily to work there.

Unemployment rate is a statistic that countries do not like to report, and the numbers can be very misleading. Many footnotes tend to be attached to employment and unemployment data. For example, some countries report low unemployment rates but note that large portions of the population are "underemployed," that is, are doing jobs for low pay that do not make use of peoples' capabilities. There is a question as to whether transient labor should be counted. Thus, it is not appropriate to take employment data at face value. Seek out explanations from alternative sources.

The "Internet Users" column is included in the table as an indicator of two things. First, the number of customers that might be available as Web sites for business purposes, including retail sale of merchandise, is established. Second, the number of Internet users as a percentage of the population is an indicator of the level of overall technology development and adoption within a particular country.

Now, try your hand at Learning Activity 9.2.

Table 9.2 CHARACTERISTICS OF SELECTED EUROPEAN COUNTRIES THAT ARE ACTIVE IN THE TEXTILE AND APPAREL TRADE, SORTED BY EUROPEAN UNION MEMBERSHIP AND GEOGRAPHIC LOCATION

Country	Geographic Size (in Square Kilometers, in Thousands)	Population (in Millions)	Life Expectancy (in Years)	Adult Literacy
European Union (EU-15) (1995)				
Austria	83.9	8.2	79.5	98.0%
Belgium	30.5	10.4	79.2	99.0%
Denmark	43.1	5.5	78.3	99.0%
Finland	338.2	5.3	79.0	100.0%
France	643.4	64.1	81.0	99.0%
Germany	357.0	82.3	79.3	99.0%
Greece	131.9	10.7	79.7	96.0%
Ireland	70.3	4.2	78.2	99.0%
Italy	301.3	58.1	80.2	98.4%
Luxembourg	2.6	0.5	79.3	100.0%
The Netherlands	41.5	16.7	79.4	99.0%
Portugal	92.1	10.7	78.2	93.3%
Spain	505.4	40.5	80.1	97.9%
Sweden	450.3	9.1	80.9	99.0%
United Kingdom	243.6	61.1	79.0	99.0%
European Union (EU 25) (2004)				
Cyprus	9.3	1.1	77.5	97.6%
Czech Republic	78.9	10.2	76.8	99.0%
Estonia	45.2	1.3	72.8	99.8%
Hungary	93.0	9.9	73.4	99.4%
Latvia	64.6	2.2	72.2	99.7%
Lithuania	65.3	3.6	74.9	99.6%
Malta	0.3	0.4	79.4	92.8%
Poland	312.7	38.5	75.6	99.8%
Slovakia	49.0	5.5	75.4	99.6%
Slovenia	20.3	2.0	76.9	99.7%
European Union (EU–27) (2007)				
Bulgaria	110.9	7.2	73.0	98.2%
Romania	238.4	22.2	72.5	97.3%
European Countries Outside the European Union				
Belarus[a]	207.6	9.6	70.6	99.6%
Croatia	56.6	4.5	75.4	98.1%
Norway	323.8	4.7	80.0	100.0%
Russia[a]	17,098.2	140.0	66.0	99.4%
Switzerland	41.3	7.6	80.9	99.0%
Ukraine	603.6	45.7	68.3	99.4%

GDP[b] (in Billions of U.S. Dollars)	Per Capita GDP (in U.S. Dollars)	Inflation Rate[c]	Labor Force (in Millions)	Unemployment Rate	Internet Users (in Millions)
$ 323.1	$ 39,400	0.1%	3.62	4.9%	5.9
$ 381.4	$ 36,600	0.0%	5.01	8.3%	7.3
$ 199.1	$ 36,200	1.3%	2.85	3.6%	4.6
$ 183.1	$ 34,900	0.0%	2.69	8.6%	4.4
$ 2,113.0	$ 32,800	0.1%	27.99	9.7%	49.9
$ 2,812.0	$ 34,200	0.0%	43.51	8.2%	62.0
$ 339.3	$ 32,100	1.0%	5.01	8.9%	4.3
$ 226.8	$ 42,200	−3.9%	12.60	12.6%	2.8
$ 1,756.0	$ 32,200	0.6%	25.00	7.5%	25.0
$ 38.1	$ 77,600	0.5%	0.21	6.8%	0.4
$ 652.3	$ 39,000	0.7%	7.71	5.0%	14.3
$ 232.2	$ 21,700	−0.9%	5.6	9.2%	4.5
$ 1,367.0	$ 33,700	−0.6%	23.0	18.5%	25.2
$ 333.2	$ 36,800	−0.5%	4.9	9.3%	8.1
$ 2,165.0	$ 35,400	2.1%	31.3	8.0%	48.8
$ 22.6	$ 21,200	0.9%	0.40	4.8%	0.3
$ 256.7	$ 25,100	1.1%	5.38	9.3%	6.0
$ 24.5	$ 18,800	0.4%	0.70	14.3%	0.9
$ 186.36	$ 18,800	4.3%	4.20	11.0%	5.9
$ 32.4	$ 14,500	3.3%	1.21	16.6%	1.3
$ 53.4	$ 15,000	4.9%	1.66	15.0%	1.8
$ 9.7	$ 23,800	2.7%	0.17	6.0%	0.2
$ 686.2	$ 17,800	3.4%	17.0	11.0%	18.7
$ 115.3	$ 21,100	1.6%	2.6	11.8%	3.6
$ 56.5	$ 28,200	0.8%	0.9	9.4%	1.1
$ 90.5	$ 12,600	2.7%	2.63	9.1%	2.7
$ 256.3	$ 11,500	5.0%	9.3	7.6%	6.1
$ 111.9	$ 11,600	12.5%	4.9	1.6%	3.1
$ 78.98	$ 17,600	2.5%	1.8	15.2%	1.9
$ 276.5	$ 53,300	2.3%	2.6	3.2%	3.9
$ 2,103.0	$ 15,200	11.9%	75.8	8.9%	45.3
$ 315.1	$ 41,600	−0.6%	4.1	3.7%	5.7
$ 294.3	$ 6,400	16.5%	21.2	4.8%	10.4

Source: Based on estimates of 2009 data from Central Intelligence Agency (CIA). The world factbook.
Retrieved from https://www.cia.gov/library/publications/the-world-factbook/index.html
a. Potential additional members to EU-27.
b. Gross domestic product (GDP), in purchasing power parity.
c. Consumer prices.
d. Data not available.

Learning Activity 9.2
CHARACTERISTICS OF EUROPEAN COUNTRIES

1. Within the EU-27, which countries are likely to be importers for consumption of textiles and apparel?

2. Which countries are more likely to be the producers and exporters of textiles and apparel? Why did you select these countries?

3. Calculate the percentage of Internet users for the population of each country in Table 9.2.

4. According to your numbers, which five countries have the highest percentage of Internet users?

5. Assuming that a higher percentage of Internet users is an indicator of higher technology development throughout a country, what other indicators are available in the data for the same countries to support that assumption?

6. Which five countries have the lowest percentage of Internet users?

7. What other evidence in the table supports the conclusion that the countries with low Internet use are likely to be operating at a lower level of technological development?

8. If you were a retail telemarketer, would you be more interested in the number of Internet users or the percentage of Internet users in a country? Why?

ROLE OF THE EUROPEAN UNION IN TEXTILES AND APPAREL

In general, in Europe as well as around the world, newly developing and developing countries have used production of textiles and apparel as a means of industrialization. During the last 50 years, developed countries maximized their international competitiveness related to production and have since seen their textile and apparel industries decline, while domestic consumption became dependent on imports.

The European Commission reports that the textile and clothing industry "plays a crucial role on the economy and social well-being in numerous parts of the EU-27.... In 2006 there were 220,000 companies employing 2.5 million people." (European Commission, 2009). The textile and clothing industry in the EU comprises the following segments:

- treatment of raw materials, that is, the preparation or production of natural and man-made textile fibers and yarns
- production of knitted and woven fabrics
- finishing activities, to give fabrics visual, physical, and aesthetic properties
- transformation of fabrics into products such as garments; carpets; home textiles; and technical, or industrial, textiles

It is reported that the European textile and clothing industry is heavily based on small companies, in which those with fewer than 50 employees account for more than 90 percent of the workforce and produce almost 60 percent of the value added.

Within the EU-27, the biggest producers are in the five most populated countries: Italy, France, the UK, Germany and Spain. These five nations account for about 75 percent of EU-27 production of textiles and clothing. Clothing production tends to come from southern countries and from some of the newer member states, such as Romania and Poland, whereas textile producers tend to be the northern countries, such as the UK, Germany, and Belgium. As might be expected, based on level of development, the textile and clothing industry plays a more important role in the economy and in the employment of the new member states than in the original EU-15.

The industry has had a series of radical transformations since the early 1990s owing to a combination of technological changes, higher production costs, the emergence of significant global competition, and the elimination of the quota system. The response to these challenges has been considerable shifts in the industry's overall approach. In general, the industry has reduced its focus on mass production and fashion basics to concentrate on a wider variety of products, especially technical/industrial textiles and nonwovens and on high-quality garments with high design content.

Distribution is the last element of the textile and clothing supply chain and is made up of all the activities involved in selling the product to the final consumer through various distribution networks, including retail. This element is reported separately from the textile and apparel industry itself. To appreciate the magnitude and diversity of this process, we need to briefly explore European retail. What may be a surprise to some is that the five top retailers in the world, after the global leader, Walmart, are European:

- Carrefour—France
- Tesco—UK
- Metro—Germany
- Schwartz—Germany
- Aldi—Germany

These firms are all involved in the sale of general merchandise, with a heavy focus on food, but they also carry clothing.

The top ten fashion retailers in Europe are reported in Table 9.3. Many of these retailers are also leaders in the sourcing of their own brands and have expanded far beyond Europe to assert a global presence.

Table 9.3 Top Ten European Fashion Retailers in 2009, Ranked by Sales in Billions of Euros[a]

Rank	Retailer	Retail Sales (in Billions of Euros)	Description[b]
1	H&M	11	Sweden; 2 thousand stores around the world; concept is fashion and quality at best price
2	Inditex	8.6	Coruna, Spain headquarters for more than a hundred companies that design, manufacture, and distribute apparel in more than 4,530 stores in 73 countries; Zara, Pull and Bear, and other brands
3	C&A	6.3	Part of Swiss Cofra Group, with retail headquarters in Belgium and Germany; 1,149 clothing stores, plus 214 kids stores and other specialty formats, in Europe, Latin America and China
4	Marks & Spencer	5.3[c]	UK; more than 600 UK department stores, and expanding internationally; 51% of business in food, 49%, in clothing and home goods
5	Next	4.4	UK; 500 stores in the UK and Ireland and 170 franchise stores overseas
6	Esprit	2.8	Founded in San Francisco; managed now from Kowloon, Hong Kong, and Ratingen, Germany; 770 stores in 40 countries
7	Debenhams	2.6	UK; department store group with 153 stores in the UK and Ireland and 48 stores in 17 other nations
8	Arcadia	2.1	UK; privately owned, with 2,500 stores in 30 countries, with 7 major fashion brands, including Topshop and Miss Selfridge
9	Benetton Group	1.6	Italy; 6 thousand stores in 120 countries; major brands include United Colors of Benetton, Sisley, and Playlife
10	House of Fraser	1.2	UK; department store group with 62 stores in the UK and Ireland

Source: Fashion & Clothing Retailers in Europe, Retrieved May 28, 2010, from http://www.retail-index.com/HomeSearch/RetailersinEuropedatabaseEnglish/FashionClothingRetailersinEurope.aspx
a. In Europe it is common to use the term *turnover* instead of *sales*. The author encouraged us to change the term to *sales* for our audience.
b. Information in this column was derived from individual companies' Web sites.
c. Estimate.

At the end of the Multifiber Arrangement period, in the mid-2000s, the textile industry of Europe was still generating a surplus of exports over imports; however, EU nations as a group have recently experienced a reversal in that pattern. Much of the growth in overall textile production in the region has been attributed to the automation of the spinning and weaving processes and the development of textile products beyond those used for apparel, such as industrial applications and nonwovens.

In the first decade of the 21st century, Europe was also focusing attention on the development of automation in a number of processes within apparel manufacturing. It was felt that these technological advances would contribute to mass customization in garment production and could contribute to reclaiming some of the business being lost to imported products. The primary goal of the European apparel business has been to retain its image as a world fashion leader and contributor of high-value design.

The overall picture of import and export of EU textile and apparel products can be ascertained by an examination of Tables 9.4a and 9.4b. As mentioned previously, the quantity and value of textiles and apparel in trade are based on square meter equivalents determined by HS (Harmonized Commodity Description and Classification System) (see Chapter 3). All WTO members use this system.

However, ranking countries by dollar value of imports can be misleading, because the value per square meter equivalent varies considerably among countries. For example,

Table 9.4a IMPORTS OF TEXTILES AND APPAREL BY THE EUROPEAN UNION (EU-27) AND OTHER SELECTED EUROPEAN COUNTRIES, IN MILLIONS OF U.S. DOLLARS, AND TEXTILES AND APPAREL AS A PERCENTAGE OF EACH COUNTRY'S TOTAL MERCHANDISE IMPORTS

Country	Textile Imports (in Millions of U.S. Dollars)			Apparel Imports (in Millions of U.S. Dollars)			Percentage Share of Total Textile and Apparel Imports[a]	
	2000	2006	2008	2000	2006	2008	2000	2008
EU-27	$ 57,422	$ 76,329	$ 83,962	$ 83,191	$ 144,448	$ 177,741	5.4%	4.1%
Intra EU[b]	$ 41,200	$ 52,402	$ 56,035	$ 43,043	$ 70,078	$ 84,658	—[d]	—
Extra EU[c]	$ 16,222	$ 23,927	$ 27,927	$ 40,148	$ 74,370	$ 93,083	6.2%	5.3%
Other European Countries								
Belarus	$ 256	$ 427	$ 591	—	—	—	3.0%	1.5%
Croatia	$ 249	$ 484	$ 598	$ 278	$ 518	$ 762	8.3%	4.4%
Norway	$ 509	$ 772	$ 1,020	$ 1,287	$ 1,977	$ 2,729	5.2%	4.2%
Russia	$ 1,316	$ 3,613	$ 5,512	$ 2,688	$ 8,103	$ 21,427	8.9%	9.2%
Switzerland	$ 1,326	$ 1,800	$ 2,177	$ 3,160	$ 4,654	$ 5,804	5.4%	4.4%
Ukraine	$ 450	$ 916	$ 1,118	$ 60	$ 342	$ 877	3.6%	2.2%

Source: World Trade Organization (WTO) (2009). *International Trade Statistics 2009*. Section 2: Merchandise trade by product, 107–114. Retrieved January 16, 2010, from http://www.wto.org/english/res_e/statis_e/its2009_e/its09_merch_trade_product_e.pdf
a. Total = total textile plus apparel imports in the world.
b. Intra EU—trade among EU-27 nations.
c. Extra EU—trade with countries other than EU-27 nations.
d. Data not available.

at one point Canada had the highest dollar per square meter equivalent, more than double the lowest (Honduras, at $2.17). Hong Kong was also an upscale source; Indonesia and Pakistan were two other low-cost sources. Considering the value of square meter equivalents from Canada and Honduras, you would receive more than twice as many units from Honduras at the same total cost. That opportunity has great appeal, particularly to those retailers operating in the mass market. However, considering quantity rather than value can also be deceiving. You can get many baby garments out of a square meter, but perhaps only the sleeves for a man's parka.

Table 9.4a addresses textile and apparel imports; Table 9.4b addresses textile and apparel exports as measured by value in square meter equivalents. The tables present totals for EU-27 first, breaking those figures down into intra EU and extra EU, and finish with selected non-EU European nations. **Intra EU** refers to trade among countries that are members of the EU. **Extra EU** refers to trade with countries that are not members of the EU. The countries included in addition to EU members are those identified by the WTO as European countries ranked among the largest textile and apparel traders in the world.

The last two columns of each table identify the percentage of each nation's total merchandise trade that is textiles and apparel. These numbers are indicators of the prominence of textiles and apparel in each country's overall economy. These percentages may be associated with a number of

Table 9.4b EXPORTS OF TEXTILES AND APPAREL BY THE EUROPEAN UNION (EU-27) AND OTHER SELECTED EUROPEAN COUNTRIES, IN MILLIONS OF U.S. DOLLARS, AND TEXTILES AND APPAREL AS A PERCENTAGE OF EACH COUNTRY'S TOTAL MERCHANDISE EXPORTS

Country	Textile Exports (in Millions of U.S. Dollars)			Apparel Exports (in Millions of U.S. Dollars)			Percentage Share of Total Textile and Apparel Exports[a]	
	2000	2006	2008	2000	2006	2008	2000	2008
EU-27	$ 56,737	$ 73,846	$ 80,207	$ 56,240	$ 91,437	$ 112,375	4.6%	3.3%
Intra EU[b]	$ 41,170	$ 52,310	$ 56,035	$ 43,286	$ 70,538	$ 84,658	5.1%	3.5%
Extra EU[c]	$ 15,567	$ 21,536	$ 24,172	$ 12,954	$ 20,899	$ 27,717	3.7%	2.7%
Other European Countries								
Belarus	$ 410	$ 504	$ 588	$ 262	$ 350	$ 449	9.2%	3.2%
Croatia	$ 87	$ 113	$ 141	$ 469	$ 538	$ 604	12.6%	5.3%
Norway	$ 173	$ 233	$ 266	—[d]	—	—	0.3%	0.2%
Russia	$ 430	$ 537	$ 554	—	—	—	0.4%	0.1%
Switzerland	$ 1,503	$ 1,593	$ 1,892	$ 607	$ 1,620	$ 1,922	2.7%	1.9%
Ukraine	$ 127	$ 244	$ 289	$ 417	$ 682	$ 719	3.8%	2.1%

Source: World Trade Organization (WTO) (2009). *International Trade Statistics 2009*. Section 2: Merchandise trade by product, 107–114. Retrieved January 16, 2010, from http://www.wto.org/english/res_e/statis_e/its2009_e/its09_merch_trade_product_e.pdf
a. Total = total textile plus apparel exports in the world.
b. Intra EU —trade among EU-27 nations.
c. Extra EU—trade with countries other than EU-27 nations.
d. Data not available.

things related to dependence on the textile and apparel trade, as follows:

- level of domestic consumption
- availability of materials for domestic production
- level of economic or industrial development, or both

In Tables 9.4a and 9.4b, focus first on EU-27. Note that EU-27 had steady increases in both textile and apparel imports and exports but that the dollar value of apparel trade was higher. During the time period, the dollar value of textile imports and exports remained similar to each other, whereas the dollar value of apparel imports and exports more than doubled. Remember, this is the time period in which trade adjustments were being made to the ending of the MFA quota system, which had long limited low-cost apparel imports from developing countries. That is reflected in the $43 billion increase in apparel imports from 2006 to 2008.

Now look at Intra EU textile and apparel imports and exports. These data show steady increases in trade through the period. The data reported for imports and exports are similar to each other in each time frame, because they reflect reports of the same goods being traded across borders within the EU system of countries.

Compare intra EU and extra EU textile imports and exports. Intra EU trade in textiles is more than double extra EU trade. In other words, EU countries were acquiring more textiles for production of finished goods from countries inside the EU than from the rest of the world.

Now compare extra EU apparel imports and exports. Apparel exports were far lower than imports throughout the period. The majority of apparel being consumed was coming from outside the EU. At the beginning of the period, extra EU apparel imports were already more than double apparel exports; at the end, they were more than triple, showing a rapid increase from outside countries.

Consider the other European countries. As with the EU, both textile and apparel imports and exports increased throughout the period for those countries for which data were available. The greatest changes occurred for Russia, whose trade with the EU increased dramatically. Russia was a primary European player in the textile trade as well as a primary importer of apparel. Turn your attention to the last two columns of the tables. These columns report the country's percentage share of total textile and apparel trade in the world. This is an indicator of the dependence of a country's economy on the textile and apparel trade. Related to imports, all except Russia show the same or slight declines of participation; Russia shows a slight increase. In terms of exports all the countries show declines in participation.

The EU liberalized trade with China, based on normal trade relations principles, when China joined the WTO in 2001. Trade was also liberalized with countries in Central and Eastern Europe, many of which had previously been part of the former Soviet Union. Free trade areas were developed between the EU and Egypt, Tunisia, Morocco, Mexico, and Sub-Saharan African nations. However, many of these agreements have had to be renegotiated recently, as the EU expanded and old agreements expired. To be competitive, manufacturers and retailers in high-wage countries increasingly used outsourcing of CMT (cut-make-trim) production in eastern Europe and northern Africa to reduce garment costs because of the availability of preferential trade agreements. As a result, despite outsourcing, some EU domestic manufacturing firms went out of business, and others were gobbled up in mergers and acquisitions.

In 2003, the EU was collectively considered the largest trader of textiles and apparel in the world. In 2005, the EU faced a surge in imports from China when Multifiber Arrangement expired. As mentioned earlier, the EU immediately initiated a series of extended quotas on selected apparel categories that, to the fury of importers and retailers, resulted in a refusal to release more than 80 million Chinese-made sweaters, trousers, and bras that were being held in European ports. Importers could not fill orders, and retailers could not fill their shelves. European governments were blamed for issuing too many import licenses (Fuller, 2005). By the end of 2007, all those extended quotas on Chinese goods had expired, and the influx of goods from that country resumed.

By 2009, China provided more apparel to the world market than the EU, which is now considered the second-largest trader in the global market. However, be careful how that is interpreted, because much of the import/export data reported today includes the value of goods traded intra-EU, whereas the value of extra-EU trading is typically much smaller (as demonstrated in Table 9.4). Overall, the EU internally is still producing large quantities of these product categories,

but its members are also their own best customers, and Russia has become one of the best external customers.

The EU has trade agreements with numerous nations throughout the world. Some are with other European nations, such as Norway, Iceland, and Switzerland. Others are part of the Euro-Mediterranean Agreement, which has been signed by some of the participants but not yet entered into force. Separate agreements are in force with Chile and Mexico. Of particular interest here is that the Cotonou Agreement, which had provided for free trade in goods with numerous nations throughout Sub-Saharan Africa, expired in December 2007. Since then, the EU Trade–European Commission has established many separate interim economic partnership agreements between groups of African nations and with Pacific Island nations, such as Papua New Guinea and Fiji, until more comprehensive agreements can be negotiated.

Between the changes in the membership of the EU itself, the involvement of the WTO and ongoing negotiations, understanding the full gamut of trade agreements in force for this continent can be somewhat daunting. One of the most recent developments is that the EU renewed its Generalized System of Preferences (GSP), under the United Nations Conference on Trade and Development (UNCTAD), and in the process added three new beneficiaries: Armenia, Azerbaijan, and Paraguay ("Trade and Trade Policy, 2009). In general, these trade agreements provide for trade preferences, which may include the provision for reduced or nonexistent tariffs on goods traded between the participating nations and the EU.

Read Case 9.1 for a discussion of the increased competition from China and Vietnam that resulted from the expiration of extended quotas in the late 2000s. Follow your reading with Learning Activity 9.3.

Learning Activity 9.3
TEXTILE AND APPAREL TRADE

1. Examine Table 9.3. How many of the companies have names that you recognize? Did you associate the names you knew with the appropriate countries?
2. Pick one of the companies you did not recognize, and do a Web search. What brands do they represent? Where are their primary markets?
3. Considering Table 9.4, why is examining EU trade so complicated?
4. What is the meaning of extra-EU versus intra-EU? What difference does it make in terms of trade relationships?
5. What is the significance of the percentage of total textile and apparel exports?
6. Does the EU appear to be more dependent or independent of countries outside the EU for textiles and apparel? Explain.
7. Considering Case 9.1, what is the primary explanation for the decline in European countries' exports of textiles and apparel? Does Table 9.4 provide any support for that conclusion?

PARTICIPATION OF INDIVIDUAL COUNTRIES IN TEXTILES AND APPAREL

For the most part, in Europe the textile and apparel business is operated by companies rather than by governments. Trade regulations and economic incentives are developed and managed by governments. Manufacturing and retailing of textiles and apparel are planned and managed by companies based in individual countries and doing business in one or more countries. Labor costs and social costs are some of the primary determinants of which countries have continued to have primary roles in the textile and apparel complex.

Some of the western European countries that were early members of the EU have been leaders in the textile and apparel trade for hundreds of years. Because there is relatively little data available from the WTO about trade by individual members of the EU today, other sources of data are used to explore the roles of the European countries selected for discussion in this text. Table 9.5 demonstrates the range of labor and social costs for textile manufacturing in EU countries. Similar types of comparisons are appropriate for other dimensions of the textile complex, including apparel production and retailing.

The source of the data is Werner International, a management consulting firm that specializes in assisting firms' decision making in the global market. In its presentation of the data in Table 9.5, Werner points out that exchange rate volatility can quickly change the advantage of a low-cost labor source. A lower cost labor advantage can become a disadvantage, because even though the labor rate is less, what the importing nation has to pay as a result of the exchange rate could be more than the difference in labor costs. Transportation cost volatility has also become an issue, in part because of high energy costs. Proximity to the goods' ultimate destination may also more than compensate for lower labor costs in a distant location (Werner International Management Consultants, 2009).

The textile production costs reported in Table 9.5, and in similar tables in the following three chapters, are based on all production activities in the textile industry, including spinning, weaving, dyeing, and finishing. Apparel manufacturing labor costs

Struggling garment industries around the world are blaming the recession for their difficulties, assuring everyone there's a recovery just around the corner, and they'll be a lot better off when it comes.

But in most cases they're completely deluding themselves. In the first nine months of 2009, garment exporters outside China and Vietnam exported 12.5% fewer clothes to Western countries than in the same period of 2008.

But most of that sales loss had nothing at all to do with the recession. China's share of those exports grew from 41.3% in 2008 to 46% in 2009—and it was China's and Vietnam's growing market share, rather than falling demand, that's really damaged factories elsewhere. . . .

Double Whammy

It's not just a fall in the number of clothes being sold. Prices have also fallen throughout 2009: in October 2009, US apparel importers bought 8.8% fewer clothes than in 2008, but paid 15% less.

As the year came to an end, many manufacturers found their costs going up too, as a result of a wholly unexpected surge in cotton prices.

Businesses in countries whose currencies have fallen against the U.S. dollar (like most of Central America) were especially hit by rising raw material prices.

But even businesses in countries whose currencies have been appreciating against the dollar lately (like India) saw export income in their own money fall further.

Garment makers throughout the world have been hit by the double whammy of tougher competition from China and Vietnam at the same time as fluctuating prices and exchange rates.

This is nothing new and is completely unrelated to the recession. In fact, it's been that way in the garment industry all this decade.

But in 2009 the U.S. and EU also finally removed the last shackles on China and Vietnam that had sheltered the rest of the world from the full force of competition.

Post Post-Quota World

There was a great deal of fuss about the post-quota world in 2005, when quotas were removed from all significant garment producers except for China and Vietnam. But only in 2009 did we finally move into the real post post-quota world.

That's coincided with a—well, if we're honest, really rather small—decline in the number of clothes retailers are selling in rich countries (in total, Western countries imported just 4.2% fewer clothes in Jan–Sep 2009 than in 2008).

But far too many businesses have been concluding it's that recession that underlies garment makers' current problems. . . .

Successful garment exporters will be those that adjust to the reality of the post post-quota world. Those hanging around waiting for a government to help them won't be hanging round anywhere for long.

Source:

Flanagan, M. (2010, February 3). *China competition hits harder than recession*. just-style.com. Retrieved February 6, 2010, from http://www.just-style.com/comment/china-competition-hits-harder-than-recession_id106631.aspx

Table 9.5 Total Labor Costs per Hour for Textile Production in Selected European Countries, as Compared with U.S. Labor Costs Considering Direct Wages and Social Costs[a]

Country	Total Labor Costs (in U.S. Dollars)	Total Labor Costs as a Percentage of U.S. Labor Costs[b]	Total Labor Costs (in Local Currency)	Direct Wages (in Local Currency)	Social Costs (in Local Currency)	Social Costs as a Percentage of Direct Wages[c]
Belgium	$ 36.39	209%	25.84 €[d]	14.90 €	10.94 €	73%
France	$ 30.39	175%	21.58 €	11.10 €	10.48 €	94%
Germany	$ 25.42	146%	18.05 €	13.46 €	4.59 €	34%
Italy	$ 22.31	128%	15.84 €	9.66 €	6.18 €	64%
Spain	$ 18.39	106%	13.06 €	8.79 €	4.27 €	49%
UK	$ 17.70	102%	12.21 £[f]	9.16 £	3.05 £	33%
U.S.	$ 17.41	100%	$ 17.41	$ 13.52	$ 3.89	29%
Portugal	$ 9.45	54%	6.71 €	4.21 €	2.50 €	59%
Poland	$ 4.81	28%	14.14	10.85	3.29	30%
Bulgaria	$ 1.85	11%	2.55	1.84	0.71	39%

Source: Based on Werner International Management Consultants. (2009). *Primary textiles labor cost comparisons 2008*. Retrieved May 25, 2010, from http://texnet.ilgstudios.net/files/2009/08/Werner_International_-_Labor_Cost_Study_2008.pdf
a. Total labor cost per hour = direct wages per hour + social cost per hour.
b. In U.S. dollars, total labor cost per hour as a percentage of U.S. labor costs per hour = a country's labor cost per hour ÷ U.S. labor cost per hour × 100.
c. In local currency, social costs as a percentage of direct wages = social costs ÷ direct wages × 100.
d. € = EU euro.
f. £ = British pound.

are generally proportionally lower than textile labor costs. Production of apparel tends to be more fragmented (thousands of tiny businesses with fewer than 50 operators, up to many huge ones with thousands of operators). Apparel production is also less automated and more labor intensive than textile production, and total labor costs are very difficult to measure. That is why we do not have comparable data for apparel production.

In Table 9.5, total textile production labor costs per hour equals direct wages per hour plus social costs per hour. Direct wages are what the employee earns per hour. Social costs include additional contributions from the company to support benefits, which often include health care and retirement. European countries are listed from highest to lowest

total labor costs in U.S. dollars to provide a basis of comparison among the countries.

The total labor cost per hour in EU countries, converted to U.S. dollars, ranges from $36.39 in Belgium to $1.85 in Bulgaria. The dollar cost, of course, is based on the U.S. exchange rate for the local currency in 2008. The ratio of other countries' cost to U.S. costs—from 209 percent in Belgium to 11 percent in Bulgaria—provides important insight into overall well-being and levels of consumption and living in the EU. It would be interesting to see a similar comparison among U.S. states.

The relationship between direct wages and social costs is also indicative of levels of development. Social costs related to the production of goods and services, such as textiles and apparel, are the result of the social responsibility component of supply chain sustainability. In general, developed countries tend to provide higher rates of social costs, because standards of living include greater expectations for medical care and retirement benefits, both primary elements of social costs. Social costs also include deduction for income taxes, which varies greatly among countries. To an employer, social costs represent what it costs to have an employee beyond paying a wage. For example, according to Table 9.5, in France a firm's financial plan must include a level of sales/revenue that will support a relatively high level of wages for employees, plus nearly an equal additional amount for social costs.

Note that the U.S. social costs are not nearly as high as those of most of the EU countries listed, even though social costs are relatively high for all the countries. The difference is that, in the EU basic healthcare services are provided to citizens free of charge, and employers are responsible for providing funds to support the government program. In the United States, many employee benefits plans include some medical coverage, but employees are personally responsible for the rest—the result being that wages need to be relatively higher in the United States to provide the same level of living.

Social costs are a primary contributor to the decline of textile and apparel manufacturing in the EU and other developed countries. When products can be sourced from newly developing countries instead, not only are the wages less, but the social costs are sometimes much less as well. Unfortunately, social costs can be used for worker exploitation. Social costs are sometimes deducted from employees' salaries and used by the employers for their own benefit.

The countries that follow have been selected to represent those European nations with major participation in textiles and apparel. Some were members of EU-15, others became members of the EU in 2004 and 2007, and still others are potential members of the EU, but all are involved in textiles and apparel. Many other European countries are also important participants. We encourage you to explore their contributions on your own.

United Kingdom

The United Kingdom (UK) was formally known as the United Kingdom of Great Britain (England, Wales, and Scotland) and Northern Ireland. The Industrial Revolution that began in Great Britain during the early 1700s had, by the mid-1800s, made it the richest country in the world. By then, the British Empire controlled one fourth of the world's surface, including colonies in India, Africa, and the Americas. During the 1900s, two world wars seriously depleted British resources, and the empire was dismantled. The UK is now a member of the EU but has not adopted the euro; it has maintained the pound as its currency. Review "United Kingdom" in Table 9.2 for a demographic perspective.

Great Britain's Industrial Revolution had spread to the Americas and other parts of Europe by the early 1800s, moving production out of homes and into factories, where power-driven machines and their operators replaced handwork. Some historians argue that the greater availability of goods did more to increase levels of living than political and trade union activities. Other historians focus on the disruption of family life; crowded and unsanitary conditions in housing; and terrible working conditions for men, women, and children. The majority agree that most of the Western world was changed from a rural and agrarian society to an urban and industrial society as a result of the Industrial Revolution.

The textile and apparel industry was a major contributor to Great Britain's Industrial Revolution. For thousands of years there had been few changes in the techniques for making cloth. European spinners had borrowed and adapted the Indian spinning wheel and weaving looms, but the speed of producing yarns and cloth remained largely the same (Baity, 1942). Then, in 1733, John Kay invented the flying shuttle, which carried the filling yarn through the warp, speeding the pace of weaving. Suddenly, yarn spinners who spun by hand could not keep up with the mechanized weaving process. In the 1760s, James Hargreaves's spinning jenny allowed multiple yarns to spin at the same time, and in the 1780s a steam engine was created to drive power looms. Spinning and weaving became a thousand times faster than they had been 100 years before. Moreover, **industrial espionage** made it possible for U.S. spinners and weavers to use machines copied from the English inventions. It was not until 1840, however, after several tries by European inventors, that the sewing machine came into being, through the work of Thomas Howe. A. B. Wilson and Isaac Singer later added features to make it more efficient. Clearly, the textile industry was well established before the making of apparel became a factory system.

The wool industry was established as a cottage industry, but the explosive growth of the cotton industry in the early 1800s was dependent on import of raw cotton. With cotton from the United States and India, Great Britain became the largest producer of cotton cloth in the world, but not without conflict. Wool was domestically produced, and woolen fabrics were regarded as staples for apparel. Wool producers, spinners, and weavers demonstrated against what they regarded as unfair competition from the imported cotton fiber. But the fashion for Indian-style cotton calico prints won the day.

By 1913, Great Britain was responsible for 60 percent of world trade in cotton goods.

As recently as 1969, textiles and apparel provided 21 percent of jobs for the employed segment of the British population. Great Britain is still known for fine quality cotton and wool fabrics. Its success has been dependent on anticipating trends in the consumer market and on using international suppliers. Internationalization of the textile pipeline has always been the case in the UK (Jones, 2002). Liberty of London, originally a textile brand known for fine woolen and cotton fabrics, flourished through the middle of the 20th century, and more recently struggled through vertical mergers and takeovers, but the firm is still a factor in the London retail scene.

Adversarial relationships among specializations in the textile pipeline were established early. For example, spinners of yarn, weavers of cloth, and producers of garments developed their own trade associations, did not know one another, and had little knowledge of one another's businesses. There was little understanding that collaboration could make business better for both suppliers and customers. Instead, managers of firms believed that for a firm to make more profit, its suppliers and customers had to make less profit. These attitudes carried over well into the 20th century. Jones (2002) proposed that the failure to achieve collaboration between the UK textile manufacturing and apparel manufacturing segments was a major factor in the recent decline of those two parts of the industry. The same attitudes that have been a detriment to the growth of the textile industry are reflected in the still present adversarial relationships between apparel manufacturers and retailers. These problems suggest a dysfunctional trade matrix whose participants have not been able to engage in the collaboration necessary for effective supply chain business systems.

Today, the UK manufacturing base and employment are still eroding, with output in some segments more than halved over the last 10 years, after an already lengthy decline. Imports now account for more than half of the total UK apparel market, but with up to 90 percent in the discount and sportswear business. Activity in textile and apparel manufacturing in the UK is now focused on design and product development more than production. Potentially, the UK may also serve as a source of innovation in niche or high-quality products, such as state-of-the-art wool production. The UK is also focusing on nanotechnology coatings and smart functions, to be applied to clothing and textiles, and on the design and manufacture of technical textiles, such as those made for protective clothing and medical use ("Well Dressed?" 2009).

Table 9.6 demonstrates the relationship between UK output and employment between 1978 and 2002. The trend reflected by these statistics is also representative of apparel production trends in many other developed countries in Europe as well as the Americas. The table presents output and employment in the form of an index. The level of employment and output in 1995 is treated as 100 percent; each of the other numbers represents the difference from 100 percent. Employment has continued to decline since 2002, but new data were not available at the time of this writing.

Comparing 1995 and 1978, clothing output in 1978 was 108.8 percent of clothing output in 1995, whereas clothing industry employment was 202.8 percent of employment in 1995. In other words, in 1978 clothing employment was nearly double clothing employment of 1995 but producing nearly the same output as 1995. Note that employment declined until 1985, with a slight increase in 1985, after which declines continued. At the same time, output represents a series of business cycles, each with similar levels before dropping dramatically after 1995, but at nearly the same rate as the drop in employment. By 2003, apparel production employment was

Table 9.6 OUTPUT AND EMPLOYMENT IN THE UK CLOTHING INDUSTRY, ACCORDING TO A PRODUCTION INDEX (1995 = 100)

Year	Output	Employment
1978	108.8	202.8
1980	99.9	178.1
1985	109.4	151.9
1990	106.2	129.2
1995	100.0	100.0
2000	72.5	72.0
2001	62.6	65.6
2002	56.0	55.5

Source: Based on Jones, R. M., and Hayes, S. G. (2004). The UK clothing industry: Extinction or evolution? *Journal of Fashion Marketing and Management, 8*(3), 262–278.

only at 68,300 jobs. The decline in apparel production employment was mirrored by the dropping employment of other manufacturing jobs as well (Jones & Hayes, 2004). By 2004, the overall UK clothing and textile industry employed approximately 182,000 people, divided evenly between clothing and textiles ("Well Dressed?" 2009)

During the 1998 to 2002 time period in the UK, overall consumption expenditure increased, as did consumption expenditure on clothing and footwear. The consumer clothing market in the UK was more than £26 billion in the mid-2000s (Jones & Hayes, 2004). Clothing as a percentage of total consumption expenditure also increased, from 6.5 percent to 8 percent, so lack of demand would not seem to be an explanation for reduction in clothing production unless the garments being produced domestically were not the styles that were in demand. A minimum wage was introduced in 1999 at £4.50 and increased in 2003 to £4.85, but it also has not been shown to be a factor in the clothing industry decline (Jones & Hayes, 2004). By 2006, consumers in the UK were spending about

Figure 9.2a Marks & Spencer is one of Europe's top fashion retailers.
(Copyright © Jack Sullivan/Alamy)

Figure 9.2b UK-based Tesco is one of the top five mass merchants in the world.
(Copyright © ICP / Alamy)

£780 per person per year on textiles and apparel, £625 of which were on clothes ("Well Dressed?" 2009). Even with overall production declines, however, some textile and apparel firms continue to be successful.

Because the UK is an EU member, UK policy is subsumed in EU policy, which covers such areas as trade, innovation, competition, and employment. The EU focus on trade liberalization is reflected in UK trade practices, including the removal of barriers to imports. Overall, clothing imports have been on the increase, but not uniformly from all sources. Despite the exit of most manufacturing in clothing and textiles from the UK, the industry continues to be highly valuable in the retail and branding portion of the supply chain. In general, the UK is characterized by potential for high profit from innovation, marketing, and retailing, but low return from production.

The UK contributes heavily to the global market in high-end designer and brand recognition. UK fashion apparel designers, such as Stella McCartney and Vivienne Westwood, and UK brands, such as Burberry and Aquascutum, are known throughout the world. Burberry products—its famous raincoats, its trademarked plaid scarves, and other fashion items—are sold in stores in 50 nations. The Dewhirst Group Ltd. focuses on apparel production, and from its offices scattered across the globe, including those in the UK, Indonesia, and Morocco, it provides merchandise for such leading customers as Marks & Spencer and Nike.

Europe's previously dominant clothing retailer, the UK-based Marks & Spencer (M&S), has lost a share of its target market to other firms, such as Hennes & Mauritz (H&M), from Sweden; Inditex (Zara), from Spain; and numerous other clothing specialty stores. These specialty chains are characterized by their abilities to predict and respond to demand from fashion-conscious customers in the form of speed, from design to the retail sales floor. The UK's traditional apparel retailers are also finding their markets eroded by competition from mass merchants, such as the UK-based Tesco (rated the fourth-largest global retailer) and Asda, a division of Walmart, both of which focus on value-priced merchandise. Other dominant UK-based specialty retailers include Next (ranked the number five clothing retailer in Europe); Arcadia, known for its Topshop and Miss Selfridge brands (ranked number eight); and the department store Debenhams (ranked number seven) (Figure 9.2a–c).

Read Case 9.2 to learn about the success of the UK apparel store chain Topshop. Follow your reading with Learning Activity 9.4.

Learning Activity 9.4
TEXTILES AND APPAREL IN THE EU AND UK

1. According to Table 9.5, which two countries have the highest total labor costs? Which two countries have the highest social costs? Which two countries have the highest social costs as a percentage of direct wages?

2. How can U.S. social costs be lower than EU social costs?

3. According to Table 9.6, what makes it possible for a company to reduce employment but maintain the level of production?

4. Why is it likely the UK will use international sourcing and marketing?

5. How has the UK continued to be a world leader in fashion?

6. What are some possible reasons mass merchandiser-type retailers are making serious inroads in the clothing market in the UK?

7. Can you think of any parallel examples (e.g., supermarkets) in the United States?

Figure 9.2c Topshop and Topman are UK-based apparel specialty stores.
(*Courtesy of WWD/Kyle Ericksen*)

Case 9.2 TOPSHOP

Topshop is a specialty store chain owned by the UK-based Arcadia group. Topshop was launched in 1964 and now has more than 300 stores in the UK and more than 100 international locations, including one that opened in New York City in 2009. Topshop sells a variety of clothes, including a vintage range and collaborations with famous names in the fashion business, such as Kate Moss and Celia Birtwell, as well as shoes and accessories and, in some stores, cosmetics. The chain is a favorite for those in their early teens to late twenties.

The flagship store is located at London's Oxford Circus and, at 90 thousand square feet, is the largest fashion store on High Street. That store alone receives more than 200 thousand shoppers a week. In September 2005, Topshop became the first High Street retailer to show during London Fashion Week when it presented its own acclaimed in-house design collection, Unique (created in 2001). Topshop maintains a partnership with the print designer Jonathan Saunders, who is responsible for the store's recent denim and devore collection.

Topshop's ownership group, Arcadia Group Ltd., also operates stores under other nameplates, such as Topman, Evans, and Miss Selfridge, and sells its brands via international franchise stores in more than 30 countries across Europe, the Far East, and the Middle East. The company also has a significant e-commerce operation.

Sources:

Arcadia Group. (2010). Retrieved May 26, 2010, from http://www.arcadiagroup.co.uk/about/index.html

Ayling, J. (2010, January 26). UK: Topshop extends Jonathan Saunders partnership. just-style.com. Retrieved February 5, 2010, from http://www.just-style.com/news/topshop-extends-jonathan-saunders-partnership_id106542.aspx

Topshop. (2010). Retrieved May 26, 2010, from http://www.topshop.com/webapp/wcs/stores/servlet/StaticPageDisplay?catalogId=19551&storeId=12556&brdcrmb_trail=&identifier=ts1%20about%20story

Germany

Germany has Europe's largest economy and one of the largest populations. Modern Germany emerged after World War II, when the military zones created by the Allies were merged to form two separate states: the Federal Republic of Germany and the German Democratic Republic (known outside of the country as West Germany and East Germany, respectively). West Germany became embedded in the economics and politics of western Europe; East Germany was aligned with the communist Soviet Union. The end of the cold war allowed for the unification of Germany, in 1990. Since then, some German efforts have focused on matching the productivity, industry standards, and wages in the eastern part of Germany to those already established in the western part. Germany's affluent and technologically powerful economy is currently the fifth largest in the world (World Bank, 2009). Review Germany in Table 9.2 for a demographic perspective.

Germany has a highly regulated labor market and a skilled workforce, but unemployment is a chronic problem. This scenario

Figure 9.3a The German firm Hugo Boss, known for fine men's tailored apparel sold around the world. *(Jamie McCarthy/WireImage for HUGO BOSS)*

limited innovation and favored development of outsourcing for apparel production during the early 1980s. Low-wage markets in central Europe were the target, particularly Hungary. German apparel manufacturers used CMT contractors by exporting materials and importing the finished goods. Trade regulations were in place to reduce import tariffs, based on value added in the foreign country rather than on total product value (Taplin & Winterton, 2004). Consequently, apparel production in Germany began to decline, while the apparel firms themselves started to grow.

Effective management has resulted in rapid growth of some apparel firms, placing a few German firms among Europe's largest. Referring back to Table 9.2, two of the largest German-based fashion retail groups are C&A, ranked number three in Europe, and Esprit (originally from San Francisco, but now based in Ratingen, Germany), ranked number six. An example of a high-profile German design group known around the world is Hugo Boss AG, which has focused on lifestyle marketing avenues, including a flagship store on New York's Fifth Avenue. There, the company presents all its fashion group collections under one roof, including classic lines and leisure wear for men and women, sportswear, and tailored menswear (Hugo Boss, n.d.).

Another well-known German clothing brand is Bogner. This firm specializes in leisure wear and active sportswear and is particularly known for its skiwear. This firm was one of the first German design firms to export clothing to the United States. It was also the outfitter of the 2010 German Olympic team (Bogner, n.d.) (Figures 9.3a and 9.3b).

German textile manufacturers are focused on increasing their market share of high-quality fabrics. For decades, Italian competitors have had almost a monopoly on this market because of close collaboration with the strong brands created by Italian apparel designers. As shown in Table 9.5, Germany has higher textile manufacturing labor cost than most nations in Europe, so focusing on production of high-end, luxury products increases profitability potential. German textile manufacturers are also exploiting opportunities for the development of new innovative textiles that satisfy needs beyond traditional end uses, including health care, environmental protection, road building, packaging, and so on (Adler, 2004). Prices of these products are not limited by the high levels of competition that are common in the apparel market. Technical textiles—textiles related to thermal/mechanical performance and durability (approximately 40 percent of total textile production)—is recognized as the most promising area of the textile industry (Export Advantage, 2005).

Germany is a global leader in the development and export of textile and apparel production machinery, focusing on sewing and garment machinery, laundry and textile cleaning equipment, and machines for processing and finishing technical textiles. In 2008, production value of this equipment was EUR1bn, with exports accounting for EUR773m ("Germany: Textile," 2009). Germany is also the largest European import market for U.S. origin apparel. The high level of identification with the "American lifestyle" among German youth offers great potential for U.S. apparel manufacturers and retailers.

One of the major trade shows in Germany is the International Trade Fair for Sports Equipment and Fashion (commonly known as ISPO), held in Munich. ISPO is considered the world's largest sporting goods trade show, and it reflects industry strength in specific product lines ("Final Report," 2009). In addition to active sport apparel, especially apparel products related to winter sports, this fair also features safety products, such as helmets and protectors. In 2009, the fair featured 1,950 exhibitors, from 50 countries.

In early 2010, another mainstay of the European apparel trade shows, Bread and Butter, was moved from Barcelona, back to Berlin, where it exhibited more than 600 selected brands of apparel, representing street and urban wear for the young adult market. Organizers were pleased that attendance had grown to 90 thousand visitors for the 4-day show, reflecting a somewhat more positive view of the economic climate than a year ago.

Figure 9.3b Bogner, a German firm specializing in leisure wear and active sportswear, most notably skiwear.
(Copyright © Bogner)

Italy

A democratic republic replaced a dictatorship after Italy's alliance with Germany resulted in defeat in World War II. Economic revival followed. Italy was a charter member of EEC and has been on the forefront of European economic and political unification, including membership in the Economic and Monetary Union as of 1999. Persistent problems include illegal immigration, low income, and low technical standards in the welfare-dependent agricultural south. In contrast, the prosperous industrial north is dominated by private, prosperous companies. As shown in Table 9.5, Italy's labor costs are less than those of France and Germany, but more than those of the UK and Spain. Review Italy in Table 9.2 for a demographic perspective.

Textiles, apparel, and footwear are all regarded as essential industries in Italy. Italy employs approximately 800 thousand people and is home to 30 thousand distribution companies (Zargani, 2009). Production of high-value garments tends to be spatially concentrated around sources of high-quality fabric production within Italy, especially Milan and Florence. Manufacturers also use fabrics from other European and Asian countries.

One of Italy's largest textile trade fairs is the Pitti Immagine Filati, held in Florence. This trade show features the latest in yarns and knit fabrics produced by Italian yarn mills. In 2009, the trade show attracted 118 exhibitors showing yarn collections. International visitor numbers were down somewhat from the previous year; this was thought to be a result of the economic downturn (Epiro, 2009) (Figure 9.4).

Italy has an industrial organization model in which small firms are formed into industrial districts that support the production of certain types of finished goods. The industrial districts receive government support and have therefore proliferated.

Figure 9.4 A display at the Pitti Immagine Filati trade show, in Florence. *(Copyright © Francesco Guazzelli)*

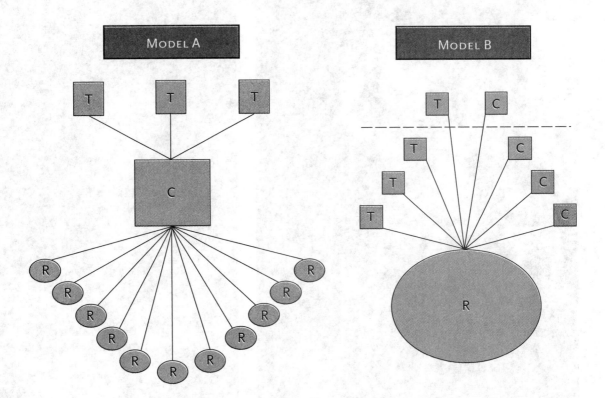

The Italian textile complex has been able to evolve into a scenario in which major clothing firms have multiple domestic textile firms supplying materials and many small domestic as well as international retailers as their customers, as indicated in Model A, in Figure 9.5. Retail distribution in Italy continues to be extremely fragmented, but the system is protected by extensive regulations and the powerful influence of shopkeepers' organizations.

The Italian strategy for competing with low-wage countries has been differentiation and niche marketing related to high-value-added products consistent with its designer image and extensive use of domestic subcontracting. Italy is now the leading exporter of upscale, fashion-forward apparel and shoes, with the United States as one of its primary customers.

The demands of sophisticated Italian consumers and the Italian fashion sense perpetuated by brands such as Giorgio Armani, Versace, Prada, Brioni, and many others have solidified Italian dominance in the high-value market. However, recognizing these brands individually as Italian in origin can be tricky; for example, the Italian firm Fendi is part of

Figure 9.5 The Italian textile and apparel industry has moved from a central manufacturer model (Model A) to the central retailer model (Model B). In the diagram, *T* represents textiles, *C* is clothing, and *R* is retailers. *(Based on Guercini, 2004, p. 331.)*

Figure 9.6b A Fendi fashion show on the Great Wall of China, near Beijing, reflects the global outreach of Italian firms. *(Courtesy of WWD)*

Figure 9.6a Giorgio Armani Privé spring couture, 2010. *(Courtesy of WWD/ Giovanni Giannoni)*

the LVMH (Moët Hennessy–Louis Vuitton) ownership group of France (Figure 9.6a–c).

Referring back to Figure 9.5, Model B shows that there has also been a strong trend toward the growth of huge, powerful retailers. This trend is making dramatic changes in the organization of the clothing business in Italy. These huge firms have come about through a combination of vertical and horizontal integration. These retailers are becoming industrial retailers by absorbing merchandising, design, and product development responsibilities that used to be the exclusive functions of apparel manufacturers. When retailers absorb these tasks, textile and apparel firms produce the materials and garments ordered by the retailers. The dot-

ted line in the model shows that pressure from industrial retailers on their suppliers to reduce wholesale prices has increased the tendency of textile and clothing manufacturers to locate production plants outside of Italy, especially in low-wage countries.

Italy has many of the largest clothing companies in Europe. Some of these companies have grown through mergers with suppliers, others through mergers with their retail customers, and still others through both. Sometimes, a company will grow by merging with a competitor. For example, the Benetton Group, known as the United Colors of Benetton and Sisley brands, remains one of Italy's and the world's primary vertically integrated apparel firms, with manufacturing and retailing in 120 countries. One of the newer fast-fashion companies in Italy is Freesoul, founded in Florence in 1994. Freesoul has an international staff of more than 60 people, and its collections are successfully marketed in 26 countries worldwide (Kitmeout. n.d.).

The transition of the EU into a common market has threatened to take away some of Italy's identity, with its strong branding and high-fashion products. Italy has been fighting hard to keep its "Made in Italy" label rather than moving to a "Made in Europe" label that could dilute its identity (Zargani, 2004). Italian industry was particularly hard hit by the economic recession of 2008–2009, but there were signs of recovery in early 2010, as wealthier consumers began to return to the luxury goods marketplace.

Read Case 9.3 to learn more about the fashion-forward company Freesoul. Then try your hand at Learning Activity 9.5.

Case 9.3 ITALY: FAST FASHION DENIM DESIGNER FREESOUL TURNS TO PLM

Italian holding company Eldo Srl is hoping to speed the introduction of new clothing lines under its Freesoul denim fashion label by turning to Product Lifecycle Management (PLM) to manage its design and development process.

The Florence-based firm has selected Dassault Systèmes' Enovia Apparel Accelerator for Design and Development to take products from concept to store—giving consumers the right products at the right time.

Launched in 1994, Freesoul creates and markets denim wear, casual pants, skirts, dresses, tops, jackets, knitwear and accessories to independent retailers and retail chains in more than 25 countries worldwide.

It will use the software to "improve global collaboration with our production centers and vendors, enabling them to stay ahead of the latest consumer trends and meet time to market requirements," explains Ernesto Barbieri, Eldo's chief executive officer.

The off-the-shelf PLM solution comes with industry-specific best practices for apparel design including pre-defined work processes, data models, reports, role-based user interfaces and document management capabilities.

This will enable Freesoul to reduce sample development time and increase seasonal options. It will also enable the company to collaborate with suppliers around the world, tracking prices to control costs and improve margins.

Source:

Fast fashion designer Freesoul turns to PLM. (2009, June 29). just-style.com. Retrieved May 26, 2010, from http://www.just-style.com/plm/ITALY-Fast-fashion-denim-designer-Freesoul-turns-to-PLM_n104594.aspx

Figure 9.6c Leather accessories from Italy are sold around the world. (*C.J. Beenenga Photo*)

1. Why is the focus on technical textiles and equipment appropriate for the German textile and apparel industry?

2. How do sporting goods and the world's largest sporting goods trade fair fit with German expertise?

3. The Italian apparel market has made a major transition from a manufacturer-focused industry to a retailer-focused market. Identify significant ways operation of individual apparel firms had to change because of this transition.

4. What forms of integration have large Italian apparel firms used to grow?

5. From your consumer perspective, does it make a difference whether a label says "Made in Europe" or "Made in Italy"? Explain your perspective.

6. How does your perspective relate to the success of the Italian textile and apparel industry?

7. How are computer applications changing the product development methods of Italian apparel firms?

France

France suffered extensive losses in its empire, including wealth, manpower, and rank among world powers despite being on the winning side in both world wars. In recent years, France's reconciliation with Germany has contributed to the economic unification of Europe. France is in the process of a transition from a socialist-led, well-to-do economy featuring extensive government intervention to one that relies more on market mechanisms. As with Germany, the government is focusing on problems of high-cost labor and an inflexible market with restrictions on layoffs in the face of an economic slowdown. Over time, textiles and apparel have been among France's major industries. Overall, the French economy is open to trade. However, through the years, U.S. exporters have complained about France's complex technical standards and lengthy testing procedures. EU policies have improved this problem, because France no longer has its own trade import and export rules; it conforms to EU practices. Review France in Table 9.2 for a demographic perspective.

In 2002, the textile and apparel industry in France employed 200 thousand people and generated sales of $30.2 billion, with exports of $13 billion. Today, this information is absorbed into EU figures, and we were only able to ascertain that overall, production has gone down and that the focus has shifted to imported goods for domestic distribution and the export of high-value-added garments. The bulk of France's fashion exports today are in prêt-à-porter (ready-to-wear) products manufactured and sold under the names of recognized designers or fashion houses in a variety of venues worldwide, such as Karl

Figure 9.7a Taking fabric orders at the Premiere Vision textile trade show in Paris.

(Copyright © Première Vision SA / Laurent Julliand, Stéphane Kossmann)

Lagerfeld, for Chanel; John Galliano, for Christian Dior; and Hermès (a brand, not a designer). The collections of these brands are sold globally in their own nameplate boutique stores and also by other retailers. The semiannual prêt-à-porter trade shows in Paris are among the marketing highlights of the fashion business calendar. The Mode City trade fair, featuring lingerie, was recently moved to Paris from Lyon, France, where it had been held for many years.

With mergers and acquisitions a consistent part of the industry, it is of interest to take a closer look at one of the more visible ownership groups. Moët Hennessey–Louis Vuitton (LVHM), with headquarters in Paris, represents not only Louis Vuitton, but also Marc Jacobs, Fendi, Céline, Kenzo, Givenchy and, a surprise to some, Donna Karan.

France also maintains leadership in the marketing of fashion-forward fabrics. Fashion fabrics are featured at the Première Vision textile trade shows held in Paris. An estimated 700 weavers present collections to some 50 thousand professional visitors from 106 different countries when they come together in Paris twice each year to view the latest in fabric designs.

Haute couture (high fashion), which was once the undisputed empress of Paris fashion, now sustains itself through hosting Hollywood celebrities and their stylists at fashion shows and through the sale of very high price, unique fashion products to individual customers. The royalties earned on sales of designer prêt-à-porter and other licensed products provide financial support for the smaller haute couture businesses. Many French designers and manufacturers have had to take action to protect their designer names and their meaning in the global marketplace (Figures 9.7a and 9.7b).

Figure 9.7b Final preparation of a model for the Chanel designer show in early 2010. *(Courtesy of WWD/Dominique Maitre)*

PARIS—A French court Friday ordered eBay, the online auction giant, to pay damages to LVMH Moët Hennessy–Louis Vuitton SA for allowing the sale on its site of counterfeits of the French luxury goods company's fragrances.

EBay has been ordered to pay 80,000 euros or $117,820 at current exchange rates, for allowing a key word search for Christian Dior, Kenzo, Givenchy and Guerlain perfumes on its site without authorization.

The ruling marks LVMH's second court victory against eBay. In June, the auction site was ordered to pay 38 million euros, or $55.7 million, for allowing the sale of fake LVMH merchandise.

EBay this week petitioned the European Union to stop luxury goods companies from blocking online sales of their products, as regulators prepare to adjust antitrust rules on distribution deals to take into account the stronger power of large retailers and the growing popularity of e-commerce.

EBay lawyers have become regular courtside fixtures on both sides of the Atlantic as the Internet auction site has locked horns not only with LVMH, but also L'Oréal and Tiffany & Co. The Internet company has had mixed results to date. In June 2008, the Web site was ordered to pay Hermès a fine of 20,000 euros, or $31,058, for failing to monitor the authenticity of goods sold on its site.

However, in July, in a case that pitted eBay against Tiffany, a U.S. court ruled eBay does not have the legal responsibility to prevent the sale of counterfeit goods. The jewelry retailer's lawyers have since presented written arguments to an appeals court asking for a reversal of the ruling. And in May, the Paris High Court ruled eBay is not accountable for the sale of counterfeit L'Oréal beauty products on its French Web site in a case brought against the online auctioneer by the beauty giant.

Source:

Berton, E. (2009, September 21). LVMH wins eBay suit. *Women's Wear Daily*. Retrieved from http://www.wwd.com/business-news/lvmh-wins-ebay-suit-2301885//

Case 9.4 details legal actions taken by a handful of luxury goods companies to protect their brands against the sale of counterfeit goods.

Many developed countries, including France, experienced a wave of mergers and acquisitions among textile and apparel manufacturers early in the 21st century. As with Italy, these mergers and acquisitions were much more intense in retailing than in manufacturing, resulting in fewer, more powerful retailers. The large vertical retailers greatly increased their outsourcing to optimize their financial resources with more favorable production terms (Taplin & Winterton, 2004). Paris is the principal import, marketing, and distribution center in France; Lyon is its primary commercial and industrial center. The Avenue des Champs-Elysées, in Paris, is the most expensive retail space in Europe. Until the late 1990s, imports came primarily from other European countries, including Italy, Germany, and Belgium; CMT production came from Turkey and northern African nations. Then, as eastern European production centers became available after the breakup of the Soviet Union, some production was sought from the new Russian Federation.

Today, China supplies much of France's moderate-priced goods. Couture houses and major retailers also develop bridge and moderate-priced lines of ready-to-wear carrying designer names to increase sales volume. Large department stores in France include the landmark Galleries Lafayette and Printemps flagship stores on the Boulevard Haussmann, in Paris. The emergence of mass merchandisers in France has paralleled their growth in other developed nations. Today, the second-largest retailer in the world is the French Carrefour (Figure 9.7c). An intriguing recent retailing development is that stores in Paris, Marseille, Lille, and some of the tourist areas across France will be able to trade on Sunday, while the rest of the nation will continue its long maintained policy of closing on Sunday (Berton, 2009).

Figure 9.7c French-based Carrefour is the second largest retailer in the world. *(Courtesy of WWD/ Vinai Dithajohn)*

Spain

Spain has been slower to embrace the Industrial Revolution than the European countries already discussed; therefore, its economic development has also been slower than that of the UK, Germany, and France. However, Spain's per capita GDP has expanded admirably in recent years. In 2004, it was second only to Portugal's in being the lowest in the EU-15; in 2009, it was higher than that of Greece, Italy, and Portugal. Apparently, Spain has weathered the recession more successfully than its neighboring countries. As shown in Table 9.6, total labor costs are also low, similar to that of eastern Germany. With relatively slow industrial development, Spain is a major producer of textiles and apparel, and the country's economy relies heavily on this industry, which provides 11 percent of the country's employment. Review Spain in Table 9.2 for a demographic perspective.

The spinning and fabric industries are highly concentrated in the Catalonia and Valencia areas, representing 67 percent of employment in those areas. Markets are joined by two major hubs: Madrid and Barcelona. Italy is their main materials supplier, and China is their largest non-European supplier. High-quality imported or locally produced foreign apparel is usually sold effectively by small, specialty chain stores (Export Advantage, 2005). However, Spain and other lower-cost apparel producers face new challenges now that the quota system has expired.

Zara is a very bright spot in the Spanish fashion scene. A member of the Inditex Group, Zara has become known as a vertical international fashion leader. The first Zara shop opened in La Coruña, Spain, Zara's headquarters; 50 percent of production is also located in Spain. Fashion forecasting is based on ongoing communication from store customers to more than 300 design professionals.

Case 9.5 discusses Inditex's expansion of Zara into the Asian market. When you have completed your reading, extend your knowledge of textiles and apparel in EU countries with Learning Activity 9.6.

Learning Activity 9.6
TEXTILES AND APPAREL IN
FRANCE AND SPAIN

1. Consider the labor and social costs for France reported in Table 9.5. How do they relate to France's current position in the textile and apparel industry?

2. Does your image of French fashion allow France to be the home of the second-largest mass merchant in the world? Explain.

3. Considering Case 9.4, do an Internet search for two of the major fashion brand names mentioned. On which Web sites did you find the merchandise? Describe your results. What might be the risk of purchasing a counterfeit on these sites?

4. Consider the labor and social costs for Spain reported in Table 9.5. How do they relate to Spain's current position in the textile and apparel industry?

5. Spain might be regarded as a late-comer to the fashion business. What advantages does Spain currently hold over France and Italy?

6. What do you see that justifies Zara's rapid growth and continuing success as a vertically integrated company?

Poland

Poland, slightly smaller than New Mexico, joined the EU in 2004 and is the most productive of the newer EU members. Poland gained its independence in 1918, after having been partitioned among Russia, Prussia, and Austria since the late 18th century. During World War II, Poland was invaded by Germany and the Soviet Union. As a Soviet satellite state after the war, Poland was relatively tolerant and progressive. Cotton, wool, and silk textile mills were important industries. During the 1990s, after the dissolution of the Soviet Union, the country transformed its economy into one of the most robust in central Europe, even though it still has low GDP, high unemployment, underdeveloped and dilapidated infrastructure, and a poor rural underclass. With its transformation into a democratic, market-oriented country largely completed, Poland is an increasingly active member of Euro-Atlantic organizations. Poland belongs to the WTO and stands as a success among the transition economies. (The Central Intelligence Agency [CIA], 2010). Review Poland in Table 9.2 for a demographic perspective.

Referring back to Table 9.1, examine the numbers for Poland. Poland's determination to join the EU shaped many aspects of its economic policy. The country spent most of the 1990s privatizing former state-owned companies and encouraging investment. Most of its trade is with other EU-27 countries. As with many eastern European countries, Poland's apparel industry is a legacy of its communist era. Apparel production within Poland was estimated at $1.5 billion, from 44 thousand small factories, in the first decade of the 21st century, and 90 percent of exports were garments based on CMT contracting (Export Advantage, 2005). The Polish apparel industry was expecting intensified competition from Asia when the quota system ended, even though, as shown in Table 9.5, Poland's labor costs were some of the lowest in the EU.

PARIS—Profits at Spain's Inditex SA climbed 4.3 percent in the third quarter as the fast-fashion giant pushed deeper into Asia with its flagship Zara banner.

"We have significant expansion plans for the market," Inditex's chief executive officer Pablo Isla said on a conference call Tuesday, noting that half of all future Zara stores are destined for Asia, underscoring the region's strategic importance to the group.

Inditex, which also owns the Massimo Dutti, Bershka and Pull and Bear chains, said it opened 90 stores in Asia in the first nine months of the year, including Zara flagships in Tokyo's Shibuya district and on Beijing's bustling pedestrian corridor, Wangfujing Street. Japan already counts 50 Zara stores, while China has more than 60.

Inditex operates 4,530 stores in 73 countries, and has added 266 locations since the beginning of the year.

Net income in the three months ending Oct. 31 totaled 456 million euros, or $663 million, from 437 million euros, or $635.4 million, a year ago, based on calculations made on the nine-month results published. Dollar figures are converted at average exchange rates for the periods to which they refer.

Sales in the quarter rose 3.8 percent to 2.9 billion euros, or $4.21 billion, from 2.79 billion euros, or $4.06 billion, as Europe's biggest fashion retailer capitalized on robust growth in China, Japan and South Korea.

Sales in local currencies rose 9 percent between Aug. 1 and Dec. 6, roughly in line with the pace in the first half.

For the nine months, net income slipped 1.2 percent to 831 million euros, or $1.15 billion, from 843 million euros, or $1.17 billion, as sales grew 5.5 percent to 7.76 billion euros, or $10.73 billion, from 7.35 billion euros, or $10.17 billion, a year earlier.

Gross margin—a key profitability indicator—slipped to 57.1 percent from 57.6 percent, but Inditex said it would likely post "stable" gross margins for the full year when it announces results on March 17.

During the call, capital market director Marcos Lopez noted that "fashionable products" are selling best. "Product with a lower fashion component is more difficult to sell in the current environment," he said.

Asked about the company's home market, which accounts for about a third of sales, Lopez cited "no further deterioration in the Spanish market" and asserted that Inditex is outperforming what "official figures" suggest about consumer confidence.

The company reiterated its target of better like-for-like sales growth in the second half than the first, and said it was on track to launch online selling next year.

In September, the Arteixo, Spain-based company said Zara would offer online sales starting with the fall–winter 2010 season, initially in Spain, France, Germany, the UK, Italy and Portugal, with a progressive rollout expected in all other markets.

The retail giant said Tuesday it would likely log square footage growth of 10 percent this year, and pursue a similar pace in 2010 as it enters India in a joint venture with the Tata Group.

Source:

Socha, M. (2009, December 10). Inditex profit up, growing Zara in Asia. *Women's Wear Daily*. Retrieved from http://www.wwd.com/business-news/inditex-profits-rise-43-percent-2391196//

Some Polish companies began moving production to Asia, Belarus, or Ukraine (Ukrainian wages were significantly lower than the Polish level). Yet, as Poland prepared to become a member of the EU, the textile and apparel industry remained an important part of the economy, representing 15 percent of manufacturing employment (Larsen, 2004). Today, many of its cotton fabric mills stand idle, but Poland is involved in providing numerous trade fair events for dissemination of information on fashion trends, new technologies, trade, and marketing.

Of note is Intermasz, the International Trade Fair of Textile, Clothes and Shoemaking Machines, which is "currently Poland's largest business platform devoted to modern machinery, devices and computer-aided production preparation systems [for apparel], as well as design and decoration studios [for upholstered products]" (Poland: Business Alongside Technologies, 2010). This trade fair and several others, such as the Fast Fashion Exhibition, reflect this nation's continuing activity as a textile and apparel producer. In 2009, Weyerhaeuser NR Company, a North American firm, announced that it intended to build a new cellulose fiber–processing plant in Gdansk, Poland, to produce cellulose for use in hygiene products, such as diapers, household wipes, and nonwoven fabrics ("Poland: Weyerhaeuser," 2009).

The growth in the economy over the past decade resulted in dramatic change in retailing. Foreign retail chains were quick to take advantage of opportunities in the market by building new, modern stores. Most of the largest retailers in Europe have established sites in Poland. Foreign retailers now hold a 50 percent market share, although there are a few hypermarkets, resulting in some decline in small domestic retailers. The largest suppliers were China, Italy, and Turkey. While U.S. sporting and denim brands are popular, they are subject to a high duty rate to get them into the EU, which results in considerable cost disadvantages.

Cyprus

A small island nation about half the size of Connecticut, Cyprus is nearly developed, with a per capita GDP of $21,200. Cyprus joined the EU in 2004. As an EU member, Cyprus occupies a unique place because it is closer in proximity to Lebanon and Israel than to Europe. The more awkward issue politically is the ongoing division between the internationally recognized Cyprus and the "Turkish Republic of Northern Cyprus," which is recognized only by Turkey. The dividing line between these two sectors has been physically patrolled by UN peacekeeping troops since the mid-1970s, and with few exceptions, permanent residents are unable to cross that line. As of early 2010, negotiations were still ongoing as UN mediators sought a solution to reunify the two sectors of this nation. Review Cyprus in Table 9.2 for a demographic perspective.

Both sectors of the country are actively involved in apparel production, although the levels of production do not seem significant, in relation to other, larger nations in the area; thus, the WTO does not report the statistics, except as part of EU-27 data. Cyprus tends to focus on CMT and knit product contracts with other EU nations, especially the UK and Germany; production of moderate-priced leather products, such as jackets and accessories; and soft-sided luggage. Cyprus must import the yarns and fabrics it uses in production, because it has no textile industry. Trained factory workers who immigrated to Cyprus from former Soviet countries, such as the Ukraine, augment the labor pool. The northern Turkish sector also produces CMT products for domestic consumption and export.

Romania

Romania, slightly smaller than Oregon, is a country in southeastern Europe bordered by Bulgaria and Ukraine. Romania is one of the newest members of the EU, gaining membership in 2007. The country was under communist control until 1996, when that system of government was overthrown. Romania had to overcome rampant corruption and lagging economic and democratic reforms before it could achieve its goal of becoming a member of the EU. Romania began the 1990s with an obsolete industrial base and patterns of output not suited to demand. As of 2010, progress had been made in privatization, deficit reduction, and curbing of inflation. However, poverty was still widespread, and government corruption and red tape hindered foreign investment into the first decade of the 21st century (CIA, 2010). Review Romania in Table 9.2 for a demographic perspective.

Romania had government-operated textile and apparel manufacturing under communist rule. Significant progress was made in privatization of these businesses, but the global recession in 2009 posed some serious setbacks to many firms that did CMT production for other brands. It was estimated that close to 20 percent of these firms would close down because it was thought that only companies that had their own brands and that were competitive in terms of quality would survive ("The Textile Industry," 2009). With the liberalization of trade in 2005, China was allowed unrestricted access to the market, and competition for Poland's export markets became brutal. From 2005 to 2009, employment steadily decreased, with more than 300 thousand Romanian textile workers losing their jobs.

Yet, in 2009 it was reported that there were still 2,100 footwear producers and 6 thousand textile and garment producers in Romania. Those firms that had been moving toward full-package methods from CMT were the firms that appeared to be meeting with the most success in surviving the competitive environment. Also, there has been movement toward Romanian companies' opening their own retail shops, initially in shopping centers in major cities, such as Bucharest.

Although Romania is considered a major producer of tailored apparel, including suits and blazers, it is a small player in the U.S. market.

Russia

Russia, formally known as the Russian Federation, is nearly twice as large as the United States, located west of the Ural Mountains, in eastern Europe, with the remainder in northern Asia, bordering the Arctic Ocean. The Russian empire was formed in the late 1600s, after nearly 500 years of gradual unification. More than 200 years of expansion followed, until 1917, when the communists seized power, and the Union of Soviet Socialist Republics (USSR; also known as the Soviet Union) came into being. Russia gradually came to dominate the Soviet Union until, in 1991, with prolonged stagnation of the economy, the Soviet Union splintered into 15 independent republics, Russia being by far the largest.

Russia is a member of the Commonwealth of Independent States (CIS), a regional organization formed during the breakup of the Soviet Union. Russia and other countries have struggled to build democratic political systems and market economies to replace the strict social, political, and economic controls of the communist period (CIA, 2004). Russia has made progress in negotiations for accession to the WTO, but at the time of this writing they had not yet been accepted into membership (WTO, 2009). Review Russia in Table 9.2 for a demographic perspective.

Figure 9.8 Ralph Lauren's Moscow flagship store on Tretyakovsky Passage near the Kremlin. (*Copyright © Miguel*)

Russia has more farmland than any other country in the world, but much of it is too cold or too dry. Cotton and wool continue to be important agricultural products. Following a financial crisis in 1998, Russia experienced economic growth averaging 7 percent annually, resulting in doubling of real disposable income and the development of a middle class, but the country was hit hard by the worldwide economic recession. Russia's manufacturing base must be modernized in order to contribute to growth (CIA, 2010). Textiles are among Russia's manufacturing industries, but according to Table 9.4 Russia is importing far more textiles and apparel than it is exporting; this indicates that a substantial portion of imports are for domestic consumption.

Retailing has undergone a profound change over the past 10 years. In Moscow alone, street markets declined significantly. Retailing experienced a significant increase in sales in the early 2000s, with the most popular retail formats being chains of discounters, supermarkets, and hypermarkets. Consumers spent freely ("Russia's Economy," 2003). In addition, these years saw the emergence of a thriving luxury market:

"Russia—in particular, Moscow—has shaped up as an El Dorado for many of Europe's leading luxury players, from Cartier and Boucheron to Giorgio Armani and Prada" ("To Russia with Love," 2007) (Figure 9.8).

For now, the overall economic picture is mixed:

Russia has fallen precipitously and could remain volatile for some time. . . . The impact of falling oil prices, from $150 a barrel in mid-2008 to about $80 today, and a collapse of domestic credit combined to hurt Russia's economy. "The other thing that exacerbated things in Russia was it alienated foreign investors by nationalizing a lot of companies. That kept a lot of foreign capital away from Russia," Suttle said. "Russia has been unique in the way its assets are distributed. A lot of wealth accumulated among the young who have an appetite for conspicuous consumption, which is why you often saw Russians spending abroad, especially in London. The Russian boon is over, but it is still an economy that has a lot of potential to grow over time." (Ellis, 2010)

Continue your study of textiles and apparel in EU countries with Learning Activity 9.7.

Learning Activity 9.7

TEXTILES AND APPAREL IN
POLAND, CYPRUS, ROMANIA, AND RUSSIA

1. What advantages and disadvantages does Poland have as a former communist country?

2. As a member of the EU, what is unique about Cyprus?

3. Romania has a history of great political and cultural turbulence, and some of that continues to the present day. Should this instability be a barrier for an apparel firm that wants to source there? Explain.

4. If you do not already know it, find the location of Moscow in Figure 9.1. Is this city situated in the European or the Asian part of Russia? Why might this matter?

5. Given what you know now, if you were in charge of sourcing for a moderate-priced, private label line of casual, young women's apparel to be imported by Macy's, would you consider a firm in a European country as a supplier? Why or why not?

6. If, as a sourcing professional, you were required to use a European country for your product line, which country would you choose? Explain.

SUMMARY

Examination of the economic and industrial standing of European countries reveals a wide range of geographical sizes, populations, and levels of economic well-being. Of those examined, Russia is the largest in size and population, but more than half is located in Asia. Malta is the smallest, smaller than twice the size of Washington, D.C., with a population of fewer than half a million people. Per capita GDP ranges from $77,600 in Luxembourg to $6,400 in the Ukraine.

The formation of the EU has profoundly changed the relationships among countries. Members of the EU-15 are the most developed countries in Europe, not counting Switzerland and Norway, which have chosen not to join. All but two of the ten countries that joined in 2004 are in the "developing" category. Their addition unifies rich and poor countries into a powerful trading organization.

In 2003, Europe was the largest trader of textiles and apparel in the world, but by 2009 it had slipped to second place, behind China. Intra EU was nearly double extra EU trade in textiles, whereas extra EU exceeded intra EU trade in apparel. The WTO reports trade numbers for all EU nations as one set of numbers, and participation of individual countries is not identified, just as trade figures for individual states within the United States are typically not treated individually.

Most countries have some form of textile and apparel manufacturing, and all have retailing. Among European countries, total costs for textile production ranged from the equivalent of $36.39 per hour, in Belgium, to $1.85, in Bulgaria. Social costs are a serious concern and range from 73 percent of labor costs, in Belgium, to 30 percent, in Poland, as compared with 29 percent in the United States. These may be a reflection of the socialist political systems that long dominated Europe.

Many of the largest clothing manufacturers are located in four western European countries: France, Germany, Italy, and Spain. These EU representatives were also historical leaders in the textile and apparel trade in Europe. In addition, Poland and Cyprus joined the EU in 2004; Romania is one of the EU's newest members, having joined in 2007. All have heavy involvement in textiles and apparel. Significant changes have occurred in Russia in recent years, and it has given a rollercoaster performance as a major market for EU-produced textiles and apparel.

REFERENCES

Adler, U. (2004). Structural change: The dominant feature of the economic development of the German textile and clothing industries. *Journal of Fashion Marketing and Management, 8*(3), 300–319.

Arcadia Group. (2010). Retrieved May 26, 2010, from http://www.arcadiagroup.co.uk/about/index.html

Ayling, J. UK: Topshop extends Jonathan Saunders partnership. (2010, January 26). just-style.com. Retrieved February 5, 2010, from http://www.just-style.com/news/topshop-extends-jonathan-saunders-partnership_id106542.aspx

Baity, E. C. (1942). *Man is a weaver.* New York: Viking Press.

Berton, E. France allows Sunday trading. (2009, August 7).*Women's Wear Daily*. Retrieved from http://www.wwd.com/retail-news/france-allows-sunday-trading-2232470//

Berton, E. (2009, September 21). LVMH wins eBay suit. *Women's Wear Daily*. Retrieved from http://www.wwd.com/business-news/lvmh-wins-ebay-suit-2301885//

Bogner, (n.d.). Retrieved February 9, 2010, from http://www.bogner.com

The Central Intelligence Agency (CIA). (n.d.) *The world factbook*. Retrieved February 6, 2010, from http://www.odci.gov/cia/publications/factbook/index.html

Ellis, K. Emerging nations: The year ahead. (2010, January 28). *Women's Wear Daily*. Retrieved from http://www.wwd.com/business-news/emerging-nations-the-year-ahead-2437851//?full=true

Epiro, S. (2009, July 14). Mills at Pitti Filati seek partners to deal with downturn. *Women's Wear Daily*. Retrieved February 7, 2010, from http://www.wwd.com/markets-news/pitti-yarn-mills-seek-partners-to-deal-with-downturn-2211049

European Commission. (2009, December 12). Textiles and Clothing, External Dimension. Retrieved January 30, 2010, from http://ec.europa.eu/enterprise/sectors/textiles/external-dimension/index_en.htm

European Commission. (2009, December 12). Textiles and Clothing. Single Market. Retrieved May 28, 2010, from http://ec.europa.eu/enterprise/sectors/textiles/single-market/index_en.htm

Export Advantage (OTEXA). (2005, January 5). EU: Local industry and market information for Member Countries. U.S. Department of Commerce—International Trade Administration, Office of Textiles and Apparel (OTEXA). Retrieved January 5, 2005, from http://web.ita.doc.gov/tacgi/overseas.nsf

Fashion and clothing retailers in Europe. Retrieved May 28, 2010, from http://www.retail-index.com/HomeSearch/RetailersinEuropedatabaseEnglish/FashionClothingRetailersinEurope.aspx

Fast fashion designer Freesoul turns to PLM. (2009, June 29). just-style.com. Retrieved May 26, 2010, from http://www.just-style.com/plm/ITALY-Fast-fashion-denim-designer-Freesoul-turns-to-PLM_n104594.aspx

Final report: World's leading sporting goods trade show ISPO winter generates positive mood in the industry. (2009, February 5). Retrieved February 10, 2010, from http://www.ispo.com/link/en/21384636

Flanagan, M. (2010, February 3). China competition hits harder than recession. just-style.com. Retrieved February 6, 2010, from http://www.just-style.com/comment/china-competition-hits-harder-than-recession_id106631.aspx

Germany. (n.d.). In *Encyclopedia Britannica online*. Retrieved from http://www.britannica.com/EBchecked/topic/231186/Germany

Germany: Textile technology firms hopeful of recovery. (2009, November 16). just-style.com. Retrieved February 5, 2010, from http://www.just-style.com/news/textile-technology-firms-hopeful-of-recovery_id105927.aspx

Guercini, S. (2004). International competitive change and strategic behavior of Italian textile-apparel firms. *Journal of Fashion Marketing and Management. 8*(3), 320–339.

Hugo Boss. (n.d.). Retrieved February 8, 2010, from http://www.hugoboss.com/de/en/indexUSA.php

Jones, N. (2004, August 2). British firms deal with global issues. *Women's Wear Daily*, 36.

Jones, R. M. (2002). *The apparel industry*. Osney Mead, UK: Blackwell Science.

Jones, R. M., & Hayes, S. G. (2004). The UK clothing industry: Extinction or evolution? *Journal of Fashion Marketing and Management, 8*(3), 262–278.

Larsen, P. E. (2004, July). Poland ready for a wild 2005. *Women's Wear Daily/Global*, 16.

Poland: Business alongside technologies alongside trends. (2010, January 18). Retrieved February 10, 2010, from http://www.fibre2fashion.com/news/fashion-news/newsdetails.aspx?news_id=81348

Poland: Weyerhaeuser to build cellulose fibers processing facility in Gdansk. (2009, November 6). Retrieved February 10, 2010, from http://www.fibre2fashion.com/news/fibre-news/newsdetails.aspx?news_id=78894

Russia's economy: Spend, spend, spend. (2003, June 21). *The Economist*, 66–67.

Socha, M. (2009, December 10). Inditex profit up, growing Zara in Asia. *Women's Wear Daily*. Retrieved from http://www.wwd.com/business-news/inditex-profits-rise-43-percent-2391196//

Stone, A. (1994). What is a supranational constitution? *The Review of Politics 56*(3), 441–474.

Taplin, I. M, & Winterton, J. (2004). The European clothing industry: Meeting the competitive challenge. *Journal of Fashion Marketing and Management. 8*(3), 256–261.

The textile industry in Romania. (2009, October 6). Radio Romania International. Retrieved February 10, 2010, from http://www.rri.ro/art.shtml?lang=1&sec=10&art=22392

Topshop. (2010). About Topshop. Retrieved May 26, 2010, from http://www.topshop.com/webapp/wcs/stores/servlet/StaticPageDisplay?catalogId=19551&storeId=12556&brdcrmb_trail=&identifier=ts1%20about%20story

To Russia with love. (2007, May 16). *Women's Wear Daily*, 12.

Trade and trade policy: The world's leading clothing exporters. (2009, July) *Textiles Intelligence*. Retrieved February 12, 2010, from http://www.researchandmarkets.co.uk/reportinfo.asp?report_id=1056320

Well dressed? The present and future sustainability of clothing and textiles in the United Kingdom. (2009). Cambridge, UK: University of Cambridge Institute for Manufacturing. Retrieved February 6, 2010, from http://www.ifm.eng.cam.ac.uk/sustainability/projects/mass/UK_textiles.pdf

Werner International Management Consultants. (2009). *Primary textiles labor cost comparisons 2008*. Retrieved May 25, 2010, from http://texnet.ilgstudios.net/files/2009/08/Werner_International_Labor_Cost_Study_2008.pdf

World Bank. (2009, September 15). World development indicators database. Retrieved February 5, 2010, from http://data.worldbank.org/indicator

World Trade Organization (WTO). (2004). *International Trade Statistics 2004*. Section 4: Trade by sector, 143–157. Retrieved November 27, 2004, from http://www.wto.org/english/res_e/statis_e/its2004_e/its04_bysector_e.pdf

World Trade Organization (WTO). (2009). *International Trade Statistics 2009*. Section 2: Merchandise trade by product, 107–114. Retrieved January 16, 2010, from http://www.wto.org/english/res_e/statis_e/its2009_e/its09_merch_trade_product_e.pdf

Zargani, L. (2004, April 9). Italy fights to keep "Made in Italy" label. *Women's Wear Daily*, 13.

Zargani, L. (2009, March 6). Italian government to boost fashion. *Women's Wear Daily*. Retrieved February 7, 2010, from http://www.wwd.com/business-news/italian-government-to-boost-fashion-2042397/

10 The Americas and the Caribbean Basin

The Americas are a great landmass that is longer from north to south than any other land area on the globe.

NORTH, CENTRAL, AND South America span the globe vertically, from the Arctic Ocean, across the equator, almost to the Antarctic continent. The combination of these continents is sometimes referred to as the New World. From the old-world perspective—that of Europe, Asia, and Africa—the Americas were unknown for thousands of years. Once the Americas were discovered, northern Europe colonized primarily the northern areas, whereas southern Europe focused more on the southern areas. The industrial technology developed in Europe migrated to the early colonies through industrial espionage. The influences of European and some Asian cultures are still reflected in different sectors throughout the Americas and in the textiles and apparel found there.

POLITICAL AND ECONOMIC OVERVIEW

Examine Figure 10.1, a map of the Americas. Many names are given to the combined land areas of North, Central, and South America as well as the West Indies. These are the primary land areas in the region of the world commonly called the Western Hemisphere or the New

Objectives

- Examine the evolution of economic and political organization in the Americas.

- Examine the roles of producing and consuming countries, areas of expertise, and specialization.

- Explore industrial development and trade regulations in the different sectors.

- Discuss major participating countries in the textile and apparel business.

Figure 10.1 Map highlighting the Western Hemisphere trading sector: North America, Central America, the West Indies, and South America.

(Courtesy Fairchild Books)

World. Sometimes, these land areas are referred to as North and Latin America, which separates Canada and the United States from the rest of the countries. Another system describes North America, inclusive of the United States and Canada; Middle America, inclusive of Mexico, Central America, and the West Indies; and South America, inclusive of all the countries located in the South American continent. In textile and apparel literature, Central America and the West Indies are commonly referred to as the Caribbean Basin countries. The terms *America* and *the Americas*, as used in this text, refer to the combination of North, Middle, and South America. All these terms are used as appropriate to the discussion that follows. As each sector or country is discussed, be sure to locate it on the map.

Efforts to Unify the Americas

In 1776, following the Revolutionary War, 13 North American colonies gained independence from Great Britain and formed the United States. During the early 1800s, while western North America was still being settled, the first Pan-American Conference was held, with the purpose of uniting new Latin American republics that had also recently gained independence from European monarchies and dictatorships. In the mid-1800s, Mexico ceded Texas to the United States, and Canada retained ties to the British crown but became self-governing. At the same time, Latin Americans believed the United States wanted to rule the Western Hemisphere. Two world wars and the Great Depression reorganized the world map during the first half of the 20th century. Table 10.1

Table 10.1 EVOLUTION OF THE POLITICAL AND ECONOMIC ORGANIZATION
OF THE AMERICAS IN THE SECOND HALF OF THE 20TH CENTURY

Year	Event	Countries/Sectors
1948	Ninth Pan-American Conference creates Organization of American States (OAS)	20 Latin-American republics and United States
1956	First bilateral agreements established to control trade in cotton	United States, Japan
1959	Alaska and Hawaii join United States, a total of 50 states	United States
1960	Economic programs begin to improve living conditions in Latin America	United States, Latin America
1961	Short-Term Arrangement (STA), first multilateral cotton agreement	United States, EEC
1962	OAS expels Cuba's communist government	OAS members
1962	Long-Term Arrangement (LTA), multilateral agreement to restrict trade; renewed in 1967 and 1972	19 major trading countries
1973	Caribbean Community and Common Market (CARICOM) formed to foster trade	17 West Indies countries
1973	Multifiber Arrangement (MFA) with import quotas to restrict textile and apparel imports in developed countries; renewed in 1978, 1981, 1986; ended in 1994	United States, EEC, and developing countries
1982	Canada becomes completely independent of Great Britain as a confederation with a parliamentary democracy	Canada and Great Britain
1983	Caribbean Basin Economic Recovery Act (CBERA) enacted to stimulate industrial development; includes Item 807	United States and Caribbean Basin countries
1988	U.S.–Canada Free Trade Agreement eliminates trade duties and quotas	United States and Canada
1988	Andean Pact, a free trade area with a common external tariff	Bolivia, Ecuador, Peru, Venezuela
1991	Andean Trade Preference Act (ATPA)	United States, Bolivia, Colombia, Ecuador, Peru
1993	World Trade Organization (WTO) emerges from Uruguay Round of GATT	Member countries
1994	North American Free Trade Agreement (NAFTA) implemented	Canada, Mexico, United States
1994	Southern Common Market (Mercosur, in Spanish, or Mercosul, in Portuguese); free internal trade; a common and external tariff	Argentina, Brazil, Paraguay, Uruguay; Bolivia, and Chile have agreement
1995	Agreement on Textiles and Clothing (ATC) replaces Multifiber Arrangement	WTO countries
2000	Caribbean Basin Trade Partnership Act (CBTPA) and African Growth and Opportunity Act (AGOA) implemented	United States, Caribbean countries, and Africa
2000	Normalized commercial relations with Vietnam	United States, Vietnam
2000	Textile and Enforcement Operation Division of U.S. Customs and Border Protection (CBP) created to control shipping contraband	United States
2001	China admitted to WTO, gaining normal trade relations (NTR) with WTO members	China and all WTO members
2001	Free Trade Area of Americas (FTAA) proposed by United States	United States, 34 democracies in Western Hemisphere
2001	September 11 bombing of World Trade Center in New York	United States and terrorists of the world
2002	Trade Act, including ANDEAN Trade Promotion and Drug Eradication Act (ATPDEA), expands ATPA	United States and Andean countries

Table 10.1 (CONTINUED)

Year	Event	Countries/Sectors
2002	Central American Free Trade Agreement (CAFTA) approved by negotiators	United States and 6 Central American countries
2003	CAFTA becomes CAFTA-DR	Dominican Republic added
2003	U.S.–Chile Free Trade Agreement	United States and Chile
2005	Textile and apparel quotas phased out, according to WTO Agreement on Textiles and Apparel	All countries with bilateral agreements
2005	U.S. approves Central American Free Trade Agreement (CAFTA)	United States and 6 Central American countries
2005	U.S. initiates new quotas on some categories of apparel from China and Vietnam	United States and China United States and Vietnam
2006	United States reaches CAFTA agreements	United States and El Salvador, Honduras, Nicaragua, Guatemala
2007	United States reaches CAFTA agreements	Dominican Republic
2009	United States reaches CAFTA agreements	Costa Rica
2009	U.S.–Peru Trade Promotion Agreement	United States and Peru
2010	United States pending free trade agreements	United States, Columbia, Panama

Source: Data collected from the World Trade Organization (WTO).

provides a list of key political and economic events that influenced the textile and apparel business in the Americas during the second half of the 20th century. Many of these agreements and trade programs are still in effect and can be drawn upon under appropriate conditions. Use this table as a point of reference as these events are discussed throughout the chapter.

A Pan-American Conference created the **Pan-American Union** in 1910, with the purpose of closer economic, cultural, and political relations within the Americas. Almost 40 years later, following World War II, while three European countries were forming their first free trade area, the ninth Pan-American Conference created the **Organization of American States (OAS)**. The original members included the United States and 20 democratic Latin American republics.

The Pan-American Union held the First Summit of the Americas in 1994. The members established broad political, economic, and social development goals and entrusted the OAS with the responsibility of advancing their shared vision:

- defending democracy through an Inter-American charter that defines essential elements of democracy and guidelines for responding effectively if it is at risk
- protecting human rights by addressing problems, including police abuse and violations of due process, by applying regional law to human rights
- strengthening security to prevent financing of terrorism, tightening border control, and increasing cooperation among law enforcement agencies
- fostering free trade by creating a hemisphere-wide trading zone, the Free Trade Area of the Americas (FTAA)
- combating illegal drugs by strengthening antidrug laws, enhancing prevention programs, and taking steps to stem trafficking of illegal narcotics, related chemicals, and firearms
- fighting corruption by adopting the Inter-American Convention against Corruption, the first treaty of its kind in the world (OAS, 2005)

There are now 35 member states in the OAS, despite the political turmoil that continued in some countries past the end of the 20th century. However, in 2009 Honduras was banned from participation in the OAS until democracy was restored. The OAS also passed a resolution to allow the Republic of Cuba to participate, at Cuba's request. One has only to check the news each day to realize that much remains to be done to meet the goals established by the OAS, but the challenge is great, given the diversity of perspectives that the goals must address.

Free Trade Area of the Americas (FTAA) is the most comprehensive free trade agreement now under discussion, involving 34 countries in North, Middle, and South America. It was hoped that negotiations on a FTAA would be completed by 2005, but there was no closure on the matter in early 2006, and little progress has been made since. The planned focus of FTAA would be industrial development through reduction of trade barriers. One of the reasons development is difficult is the number of trade agreements with conflicting terms already in existence among the participating countries. North Americans see FTAA as an extension of NAFTA, and South Americans see FTAA as an extension of **Mercosur (Common Market of the South)**.

The OAS has four official languages (English, Spanish, Portuguese, and French), reflecting the rich diversity of people and cultures that are a part of the Americas. Table 10.2 presents some of the conflicting cultural perspectives that continue to divide North and Latin America, despite the efforts of the OAS and other organizations. The roots of these ideas, customs, and skills, passed from one generation to the next and still exist in Europe and parts of Asia, the source of much of the Americas' emigrated population.

The cultural values related to time, work, frugality, education, merit, community, and ethics cannot be judged in terms of right and wrong; rather, they should be recognized as various perceived realities, judged case by case (or culture by culture).

GLOBAL LEXICON

Andean Trade Preference Act (ATPA) the primary trade agreement between the United States and northern South America, established in 1991

Andean Trade Promotion and Drug Eradication Act (ATPDEA) made the sector eligible for duty-free treatment on exports of U.S. goods for the first time, in 2002

Caribbean Basin Economic Recovery Act (CBERA) commonly known as the Caribbean Basin Initiative (CBI), a trade preference program initiated by the United States in 1983 that expanded the use of Item 807 by eliminating quota restraints

The Central America–Dominican Republic–United States Free Trade Agreement (CAFTA-DR) intended to solidify the United States as the leading supplier of goods and services to Central America and Dominican Republic and to provide them with duty-free access to the U.S. market, beginning in 2002

charge-back a financial penalty imposed by the customer on a vendor for noncompliance with established vendor compliance rules

Free Trade Area of the Americas (FTAA) the most comprehensive free trade agreement under discussion since early 2000s, involving 34 countries in North, Middle, and South America

Mercosur (Common Market of the South) free trade within, and a common external tariff for, Argentina, Brazil, Paraguay, and Uruguay, since 1994; accounts for 70 percent of South America's total economy

North American Free Trade Agreement (NAFTA) eliminated tariffs and quotas among Canada, Mexico, and the United States in 1994

Organization of American States (OAS) has continued since 1948, with the purpose of a Pan-American Union for closer economic, cultural, and political relations within the Americas

Pan-American Union created in 1910, with the purpose of closer economic, cultural, and political relations within the Americas

trading partners in EDI terminology, vendors and customers who exchange (trade) electronic documents in order to do business

Table 10.2 CULTURAL VARIABLES THAT DIVIDE NORTH AND LATIN AMERICA

Cultural Value	Progressive Societies	Traditional Societies
Time focus	Focus on the future.	Focus on the past or the present—the future is often in the other world.
Work	Work is a source of satisfaction and self-respect, the foundation of the structure of daily life, and an obligation of the individual to the broader society.	Work is a "necessary evil" and real satisfaction and pleasure are attainable only outside of the workplace.
Frugality	Save the fruit of work for investment or subsequent consumption.	Sees what one gains or saves as coming at the expense of others, thus the elaborate ceremonies and fiestas where savings are redistributed.
Education	See education as the key to progress.	See education as a frill for the masses, reserved for the elites.
Merit	Merit as the basis for advancement is a reality.	Family, friends, connections, and nepotism are what count.
Sense of community	The sense of community extends beyond the family to the broader society. It creates a broader radius of trust and spontaneous association, and it contributes to entrepreneurialism and the creation of social capital.	Identification and trust are confined to the family. Those outside the family are inconsequential, possibly hostile, and certainly outside a felt "community." The lack of a sense of community nurtures authoritarianism and is also linked to nepotism, corruption, tax evasion, lack of punctuality, and absence of traditions of philanthropy.
Ethics	Possess a more rigorous ethical code that influences economic efficiency and political performance and increases social trust, which in turn builds community.	Societies that emphasize the afterlife typically have more flexible ethical systems.
Justice	The idea of justice and fair play is nurtured by both the sense of community and a rigorous ethical code.	Justice is a highly theoretical concept and in practice a rare commodity that is undermined by money, influence, politics, and kinship.
Authority	Recognize merit and allow for specialization in government and business. Resulting in more creative, productive, and entrepreneurial organizations, and societies	Encounter difficulties in establishing pluralistic political institutions, and in the case of Latin America (but not Asia), authoritarianism stifles dissent, creativity, and entrepreneurship and ignores merit.
Secularism	Religion is confined to the spiritual sphere.	Religion intrudes into worldly affairs, including economics and politics.

Source: Based on Abbott, J. D. and Moran, R.T. (2002). *Uniting North American business: NAFTA best practices*. Burlington, MA: Elsevier Science.

Differences in the perspectives of progressive societies (North America) versus traditional societies (Latin America) are by no means exclusive, but rather predominant in the visions of the people. Both are preferred ways to live in each region but are not necessarily compatible ways to live (Abbot & Moran, 2002).

Further your understanding of American political and economic organization by doing Learning Activity 10.1.

Learning Activity 10.1

EVOLUTION OF AMERICAN POLITICAL AND ECONOMIC ORGANIZATION

1. Identify the following sectors on the map in Figure 10.1:
    *   North America, Middle America, and South America
    *   North America, Central America, the West Indies, and South America
    *   North America and Latin America

2. Which of these systems of organization do you feel most familiar with? Why?

3. Locate each of the countries listed in the right-hand column of Table 10.1 on the map in Figure 10.1. Identify the countries that share boundaries among North, Central, and South America.

4. Identify two primary ways the Organization of American States (OAS) is different from the European Union (EU).

5. Describe two primary ways the OAS and the EU are similar.

6. What is the meaning of the term *culture*, as relates to Table 10.2? Do the cultural values in the table conform to what you commonly define as culture? Explain.

7. Why is it sometimes difficult for people from different cultures to work together?

Economic and Industrial Standing of Selected American Countries

Europe includes some of the richest and poorest countries in the world, as do the Americas. Table 10.3 itemizes characteristics of countries in the Americas that are active in the textile and apparel trade, sorted by geographic sector. By scanning the first two columns of the table, it quickly becomes apparent that Canada has the largest geographic size, with nearly 10 million square kilometers, although the United States and Brazil are only a little smaller. However, the United States has by far the largest population, with an estimated 308.7 million, followed by Brazil, with 198.7 million, and Mexico, with 111.2 million. Canada, although very large in size, has a population of only 33.5 million. Argentina has a slightly higher population than Canada but is less than one third of Canada's size. Most of the West Indies, islands in and around the Caribbean Sea, are tiny in comparison with countries in North and South America.

Examine life expectancies and literacy rates in the table. Canada has the longest life expectancy, 81.2 years, followed by the United States, Costa Rica, and Chile. Haiti has by far the lowest level of life expectancy, at 60.8 years. Canada and the United States report high literacy rates, at 99 percent, followed closely by Uruguay and Argentina. Haiti has the lowest literacy rate, at 52.9 percent; Nicaragua is second lowest, at 67.5 percent. For Haiti, these data mean that many children never know their grandparents, and, given the Haitian literacy rate, very few of them will have the opportunity to experience college.

Considering gross domestic product (GDP), as with the EU, whose demographic and productivity data were not reported by country, the U.S. data are not reported by state. In 2009, when the GDP for the EU-27 was totaled, it equaled $14.52 trillion, number one in the world; here, we find the United States is second, at $14.25 trillion. The economic and industrial dominance of the EU-15 in Europe is similar to the economic and industrial dominance of the United States in the Americas. The next largest GDP in the Americas is Brazil, at $2.02 trillion, followed by Mexico, at $1.5 trillion, and Canada, at $1.3 trillion. All other countries included in the table have GDPs ranging from Argentina, at $558 billion, to Haiti, at $11.6 billion.

The United States has by far the highest per capita GDP in the Americas, at $46,400, but we know that it is not the highest in the world, because Luxembourg (in Europe) has $77,600. Canada is interesting, because it is second in the Americas, with per capita GDP of $38,400, even though it has a relatively low total GDP. The reason, of course, is the relatively small population in Canada. Thus, Canada and the United States are the only countries in the Americas that can be regarded as developed countries, according to the criteria presented in Chapter 1 (developed countries' per capita GDP: $20 thousand or more). However, if we were to consider the GDP per capita of the U.S. states individually, each state would also qualify as a developed country. Most of the countries' GDPs per capita fall within the range of Uruguay

Table 10.3 CHARACTERISTICS OF SELECTED COUNTRIES LOCATED IN THE AMERICAS THAT ARE ACTIVE IN TEXTILE AND APPAREL TRADE

Country	Geographic Size (Square Kilometers, in Thousands)	Population (in Millions)	Life Expectancy (in Years)	Adult Literacy (in Percentage)	
North America					
Canada	9,984.7	33.5	81.2	99.0%	
Mexico	1,964.4	111.2	76.1	91.0%	
United States	9,826.7	307.2	78.1	99.0%	
Caribbean Basin					
Costa Rica	51.1	4.3	77.6	94.9%	
Dominican Republic	48.7	9.7	73.7	87.0%	
El Salvador	21.0	7.2	72.3	80.2%	
Guatemala	108.9	13.3	70.3	69.1%	
Haiti	27.8	9.0	60.8	52.9%	
Honduras	112.1	7.8	70.5	79.8%	
Jamaica	11.0	2.8	73.5	87.9%	
Nicaragua	130.4	5.9	71.5	67.5%	
South America					
Argentina	2,780.4	40.9	76.6	97.2%	
Brazil	8,514.9	198.7	72.0	88.6%	
Chile	756.1	16.6	77.3	95.7%	
Columbia	1,138.9	43.7	74.1	90.4%	
Peru	1,285.2	29.6	70.7	92.9%	
Uruguay	176.2	3.5	76.4	98.0%	
Venezuela	912.1	26.8	73.6	93.0%	

	GDP[a] (in Billions of U.S. Dollars)	Per Capita GDP	Inflation Rate[b]	Labor Force (in Millions)	Unemployment Rate	Internet Users (in Millions)
	$ 1,287.0	$ 38,400	0.2%	18.4	8.5%	25.1
	$ 1,473.0	$ 13,200	5.3%	46.1	6.2%	23.3
	$ 14,250.0	$ 46,400	−0.7%	154.5	9.4%	231.0
	$ 48.2	$ 11,300	8.3%	2.1	6.4%	1.5
	$ 78.9	$ 8,200	1.4%	4.4	15.1%	2.1
	$ 42.2	$ 6,000	1.0%	2.9	7.2%	0.8
	$ 69.2	$ 5,200	2.3%	4.2	3.2%	2.0
	$ 11.6	$ 1,300	0.4%	3.6	NA	1.0
	$ 33.1	$ 4,200	5.2%	3.1	6.0%	0.7
	$ 23.4	$ 8,300	8.6%	1.3	14.5%	1.5
	$ 16.5	$ 2,800	4.0%	2.4	5.9%	0.2
	$ 558.0	$ 13,800	6.2%	16.4	9.6%	11.2
	$ 2,024.0	$ 10,200	4.2%	95.2	7.4%	65.0
	$ 244.3	$ 14,700	1.7%	7.4	10.0%	5.5
	$ 400.3	$ 9,200	3.0%	20.0	12.0%	17.1
	$ 253.4	$ 8,600	1.2%	10.3	9.0%	7.1
	$ 44.1	$ 12,600	7.3%	1.6	7.9%	1.3
	$ 355.2	$ 13,200	27.3%	12.7	10.9%	7.2

Source: Estimates of 2009 data from Central Intelligence Agency (CIA). (2010). *The World Factbook*.
Retrieved February 4, 2010, from https://www.cia.gov/library/publications/the-world-factbook/index.html
a. GDP adjusted by purchasing power parity.
b. Consumer prices.

($12,600) and Jamaica ($8,300), (developing countries' per capita GDP: $3 thousand to $20 thousand). Only Nicaragua and Haiti, with per capita GDPs of less than $3 thousand, are classified as newly developing countries in this hemisphere. Haiti is the lowest, at $1,300. Interestingly, most of the Central American countries could be defined as newly developing according to our criteria, and most of the South American countries are in the "developing" category. Where would you expect most of the apparel production to take place? You are right if you chose Central America.

Inflation rates across the Americas range from -0.7 percent, in United States, to 27.3 percent, in Nicaragua. Only ten countries reported inflation rates of less than 4 percent, suggesting a number of unstable economies. The Americas are suffering from the uncertainties of the global recession, just as Europe is. Labor force and unemployment rates are indicators of opportunities for economical labor costs, although labor pools seem relatively small. Only Brazil, Colombia, Mexico, and the United States exceed 20 million workers. Jamaica had the smallest labor force, with 1.3 million; the United States had the largest, with 154.5 million. Unemployment rates range from 3.2 percent, in Guatemala, to an unnamed amount in Haiti (in 2004 it was 66 percent). Most rates are higher than those reported by European countries. Several of the countries of the Americas have less than 2 million Internet users, so current opportunities for e-tailing are limited.

The U.S. economic and industrial dominance in the Americas and in the world is both an advantage and a responsibility. The high level of consumption in the United States parallels equally high levels of imports, to satisfy consumers, the vast majority of which have relatively large pocketbooks. As shown in Table 10.1, over the past 30 years, and especially over the past 15 years, the United States has developed free trade agreements with many of the countries in the Americas. These trade agreements have had a profound influence on

the volume of trade among these countries.

Now, extend your knowledge of the Americas with Learning Activity 10.2.

Learning Activity 10.2
CHARACTERISTICS OF AMERICAN COUNTRIES, AS REFLECTED IN TABLES 10.2 AND 10.3

1. Assume you are ready for a global adventure and are seeking a job in which you could be employed at least part of the time in a foreign country. Which of the data presented in Tables 10.2 and 10.3 would help you in deciding the countries you might like to consider?

2. Does it surprise you that Canada has the longest life expectancy of all the countries of the Americas and Europe? Explain.

3. How many American countries generate GDP that exceeds that of the United States? What is the fundamental meaning of this observation?

4. How does Canada's per capita GDP compare with the per capita GDP of developed EU countries? What is the fundamental meaning of this observation?

5. How many countries in the Americas have per capita GDP that is lower than Mexico's? What is the fundamental meaning of this observation?

6. Which country in the Americas has the lowest number of Internet users? What other information do you need to know before deciding the implications of this statistic?

TRENDS IN TEXTILE AND APPAREL TRADE IN THE AMERICAS

The overall picture of trends in textile and apparel imports and exports in the Americas can be seen by examining Tables 10.4a and 10.4b. As with the countries of Europe (see Tables 9.4a and 9.4b), the American countries selected are those identified by the

WTO as ranking among the largest textile and apparel traders in the world. The tables report the value of imports and exports of textiles and apparel in U.S. dollars for selected years from 2000 to 2008. The last two columns of each table include each country's percentage share of total world imports, plus exports of textiles or apparel. Because of recent growth and the developing nature of some of these countries, there is some missing data. You will refer to these tables frequently throughout the rest of this chapter. The tables begin with North American NAFTA countries, followed by the other sectors of the Americas.

As mentioned previously, Canada and the United States are by far the most developed countries in the Americas and in the world, and a quick scan of the numbers in Table 10.4a and 10.4b shows the dominance of the United States, Canada, and Mexico (the NAFTA countries) in the textile and apparel trade in the Americas. These numbers demonstrate the dramatic changes that have occurred within the American textile and apparel business. NAFTA was a primary player in those changes in the early years of the 21st century, but once the quota system expired, exports from Canada, Mexico, and Caribbean Basin countries to the United States decreased as imports from China and other Asian nations increased. This created some hard times for the Caribbean Basin countries, with either decrease or only small increases in exports.

For the United States, there was a huge increase of imports of both textiles and apparel between 2000 and 2008. In contrast, increase in exports of textiles was slight, and export of apparel actually decreased. Many U.S. apparel brands were being sold around the world, but few of those garments were actually produced in the United States; instead, they were being sourced and sold elsewhere by U.S. firms.

Consider the Caribbean Basin countries. Comparison of textile imports with textile exports suggests the imports are intended either for domestic consumption or for inputs into production of apparel for export. Apparel imports have even less in value than textile imports, supporting that proposition. Considering apparel exports, all but Costa Rica, in the Caribbean Basin, show increases over the time period. However, the force of China is likely to have decreased Caribbean Basin apparel exports since 2008.

South America shows considerable activity in both textile imports and exports and also in apparel imports. Brazil shows the largest quantity of textile imports and exports, although imports did not increase from 2006 to 2008. Brazil grows large quantities of cotton and manufactures denim fabric and apparel. The end of quota restraints reduced foreign demand for Brazil's jeans, although its exports are not reported. Columbia and Peru were the only countries reporting apparel exports, and they had impressive increases between 2006 and 2008. However, the totals are modest compared with the rest of the Americas.

A comparison of the labor costs for producing textiles in selected nations in the Americas provides us with some insight as to why some have met with more success than others in global trading of their textile materials. We have data for the United States and South American countries but, unfortunately, data from Caribbean Basin countries were not available, because very few textile materials are produced in the Caribbean Basin. Historically, companies here have been primarily involved with apparel production, with labor rates lower than those of the lowest South American countries. The Caribbean Basin companies originally competed for a share of the U.S. market by using 807-type production: Importing U.S. textiles, especially cottons, in the form of cut garment parts; assembling the garments, and exporting finished apparel back to the United States. With the implementation of CAFTA-DR, apparel production in most countries converted to CMT. This has been

Table 10.4a IMPORTS OF TEXTILES AND APPAREL BY SELECTED AMERICAN COUNTRIES, IN MILLIONS OF
U.S. DOLLARS, AND TEXTILES AND APPAREL AS A PERCENTAGE OF TOTAL MERCHANDISE IMPORTS

Country	Textile Imports (in Millions of U.S. Dollars)			Apparel Imports (in Millions of U.S. Dollars)			Percentage Share of Total Textile and Apparel Imports[a]	
	2000	2006	2008	2000	2006	2008	2000	2008
North America (NAFTA)								
United States	$ 15,985	$ 23,498	$ 23,128	$ 67,115	$ 82,969	$ 82,464	6.6%	4.9%
Canada	4,126	4,472	4,431	3,690	6,987	8,452	3.2	3.2
Mexico	5,822	5,951	5,366	3,602	2,517	2,544	5.4	2.5
Caribbean Basin (CBERA)								
Costa Rica	184	232	290	592	214	272	12.2	3.7
Dominican Republic	1,173	941	774	—[b]	—	—	12.4	4.8
El Salvador	325	672	693	713	217	117	21.0	8.3
Guatemala	59	1,144	990	33	190	183	1.9	8.1
Haiti	—	—	—	—	—	—	—	—
Honduras	501	1,239	1,559	1,304	423	186	45.2	16.8
South America (Andean) (Mercosur)								
Argentina	653	820	1,147	333	192	417	3.9	2.7
Brazil	1,045	1,599	2,947	173	442	883	2.2	2.2
Chile	431	522	642	501	1,003	1,348	5.0	3.2
Columbia	558	864	999	80	159	335	5.5	3.3
Peru	165	358	691	59	134	268	3.0	3.2
Venezuela	286	644	1,427	390	736	1,593	4.7	6.1

Source: World Trade Organization (WTO). (2009). *International Trade Statistics 2009*. Section 2: Merchandise trade by product, 107–114.
Retrieved January 16, 2010, from http://www.wto.org/english/res_e/statis_e/its2009_e/its09_merch_trade_product_e.pdf
a. Total—total textile plus apparel imports in the world.
b. Data not available.

Table 10.4b EXPORTS OF TEXTILES AND APPAREL BY SELECTED AMERICAN COUNTRIES, IN MILLIONS OF U.S. DOLLARS, AND TEXTILES AND APPAREL AS A PERCENTAGE OF TOTAL MERCHANDISE EXPORTS

Country	Textile Exports (in Millions of U.S. Dollars)			Apparel Exports (in Millions of U.S. Dollars)			Percentage Share of Total Textile and Apparel Exports[a]	
	2000	2006	2008	2000	2006	2008	2000	2008
North America (NAFTA)								
United States	$ 10,952	$ 12,580	$ 12,496	$ 8,629	$ 4,885	$ 4,449	2.5%	1.3%
Canada	2,204	2,369	1,988	2,077	1,798	1,308	1.6	0.7
Mexico	2,571	2,192	1,993	8,631	6,323	4,911	6.7	2.4
Caribbean Basin (CBERA)								
Costa Rica	—[b]	—	—	660	235	266	11.2	2.7
Dominican Republic	—	—	—	2,555	1,734	1,080	44.5	15.5
El Salvador	79	80	122	1,673	1,814	1,956	59.6	45.7
Guatemala	53	183	248	49	1,557	1,230	3.8	19.1
Haiti	—	—	—	245	432	421	76.9	86.0
Honduras	—	—	—	2,275	2,613	2,940	68.0	48.6
South America (Andean) (Mercosur)								
Argentina	258	219	274	—	—	—	1.0	0.4
Brazil	895	1,365	1,361	—	—	—	1.6	0.7
Chile	114	112	110	—	—	—	0.6	0.2
Columbia	268	383	858	520	962	1,222	6.1	5.5
Peru	128	199	313	504	1,204	1,635	9.0	6.2
Venezuela	—	—	—	—	—	—	—	—

Source: World Trade Organization (WTO). (2009). *International Trade Statistics 2009*. Section 2: Merchandise trade by product, 107–114. Retrieved January 16, 2010, from http://www.wto.org/english/res_e/statis_e/its2009_e/its09_merch_trade_product_e.pdf
a. Total—total textile plus apparel exports in the world.
b. Data not available.

Table 10.5 Total Labor Costs per Hour for Textile Production in Selected American Countries, as Compared with U.S. Labor Costs Considering Direct Wages and Social Costs[a]

Country	Total Labor Costs (in U.S. Dollars)	Total Labor Costs as a Percentage of U.S. Labor Costs[b]	Total Labor Costs (in Local Currency)	Direct Wages (in Local Currency)	Social Costs (in Local Currency)	Social Costs as a Percentage of Direct Wages[c]
U.S.	$ 17.41	100%	$ 17.41	$ 13.52	$ 3.89	28.8%
Uruguay	$ 6.20	36%	151.11	114.70	36.41	31.7%
Argentina	$ 4.48	26%	15.41	10.76	4.65	41.2%
Brazil	$ 3.41	20%	7.90	4.80	3.10	64.6%
Columbia	$ 2.45	14%	5,484	3,775	1,709	45.3%
Mexico	$ 2.17	12%	30.01	20.14	9.87	49.0%
Peru	$ 2.02	12%	6.32	3.41	2.91	85.3%

Source: Werner International Management Consultants. (2009). *Primary textiles labor cost comparisons 2008*.
Retrieved May 25, 2010, from http://texnet.ilgstudios.net/files/2009/08/Werner_International_-_Labor_Cost_Study_2008.pdf
a. Total labor costs per hour = direct wages per hour + social costs per hour
b. In U.S. dollars, total labor cost per hour as a percentage of U.S. labor costs per hour = a country's labor cost per hour ÷ U.S. labor cost per hour × 100.
c. In local currency, social costs as a percentage of direct wages = social costs ÷ direct wages × 100.

working to some degree for Honduras, El Salvador, and Haiti, but the Dominican Republic has been losing significant market share in recent years. Table 10.5 shows the relationships between U.S. and South American textile production costs.

All the nations in Table 10.5 have lower labor costs for fabric production than the United States. From the U.S. standpoint, however, the big question is whether those nations have the expertise and the equipment to make desired textiles of the quality and quantity needed. Unfortunately, the answer to that is often no. Low levels of technology and expertise have limited access to U.S. and other world markets.. The South American countries also show significant levels of social costs. This may contribute as well to the lack of textile and apparel export activity for these countries. Peru, the South American nation with the lowest total cost, has taken a different approach by seeking out a niche market for fine alpaca sweaters and fabrics that appeal to U.S. consumers.

Further your study of trends in the American textile and apparel trade with Learning Activity 10.3.

Learning Activity 10.3

TRENDS IN TEXTILE AND APPAREL TRADE IN THE AMERICAS

1. Considering Tables 10.4a and 10.4b, which American countries are most dependent on textile exports? apparel exports?
2. Why did textile and apparel exports for NAFTA countries decline during the first decade of the 21st century?
3. Why are Caribbean Basin countries likely to be more active in textile imports and apparel exports?
4. Why might high percentage of social costs be a factor for lack of activity in apparel manufacturing in South American countries?
5. Given the data in Table 10.5, how do total labor costs in American countries compare with total labor costs in European countries (see Table 9.5)?
6. Why is it not really possible to compare levels of social costs in the two regions, except as a percentage of total costs?

ROLE OF NORTH AMERICAN COUNTRIES IN TEXTILES AND APPAREL

The United States and Canada have one of the longest unprotected but shared borders in the world, and almost nine of every ten Canadians live within 100 miles of it. When the U.S. president Ronald Reagan and the Canadian prime minister Brian Mulroney met in 1985 to explore a free trade agreement between the two countries, 80 percent of trade was already free. Among the products that still had tariffs were textiles, apparel, and automobiles. Trilateral negotiations (among the United States, Canada, and Mexico) began for the **North American Free Trade Agreement (NAFTA)** in 1991. The U.S. president Bill Clinton finalized negotiations, and NAFTA went into effect in 1994. Three different U.S. presidents have supported implementation of NAFTA.

NAFTA focuses primarily on trade and investment matters related to goods and services rather than on political or economic unity. Based on country of origin (COO) qualification, the following went into effect following ratification of NAFTA:

- fifty percent of duty was removed from U.S.-made goods imported into Mexico
- ninety percent of goods traded among Mexico, Canada, and the United States would be tariff free within a 10-year period
- textiles and apparel had a 15-year transition period to eliminate tariffs
- nontariff barriers, such as quotas, were removed immediately
- restrictions on direct foreign investment were eliminated
- national environmental standards were to be upheld
- workplace health and safety, the minimum wage, and child labor laws were to be upheld

Average hourly wages at that time were $2.32 in Mexico, $14.31 in the United States, and $14.71 in Canada. There was fear, especially by states in which apparel manufacturing was still a major employer, that low-wage jobs would move to Mexico (Taplin, 2003).

By 2002, in part because of NAFTA, the United States was by far the largest **trading partner** of both Canada and Mexico and the largest foreign investor in both countries. Total trade between the United States and Canada was more than $450 billion a year, almost two-and-a-half times more than in the early 1990s: 70 percent of Canada's imports were from U.S. suppliers, and more than 85 percent of Canada's exports went to U.S. firms; nearly two thirds of Canada's foreign investment came from the United States (Hakim & Litan, 2002).

Trade between Canada and Mexico also increased five times, to $9 billion, nearly the same as trade between Brazil and Argentina. Despite these trade gains, the effect of NAFTA on the industrial well-being of the participating countries has been controversial ever since it was proposed. From a textile and apparel perspective, NAFTA represented a break with the protectionist perspectives that had been in effect for more than a century; quotas were immediately eliminated, tariffs were reduced over time, and trade among the NAFTA members increased. However, since the demise of the global quota system, competition from China and other nations, such as Vietnam, has become too great, and Mexico has suffered significant setbacks in its overall trade numbers in textiles and apparel.

The United States

With victories in both world wars and the end of the cold war, the United States became the world's most powerful nation. It has a market-oriented economy in which private individuals and business firms make most of the decisions, and federal and state governments buy most needed goods and services in private markets. The economy had steady growth, low unemployment and inflation, and rapid advances in technology. The September 11, 2001, terrorist attack on New York City's World Trade Center dramatically changed perspectives on safety, security, and patriotism. The subsequent war between the United States-led coalition and Iraq, and the continuing U.S.-NATO supported war in Afghanistan, shifted significant economic resources to the military. Long-term problems include rapidly rising medical costs, pension costs of the aging population, sizable trade and budget deficits, and stagnation of family income for lower-income groups. In late 2008 and early 2009, the global economic system experienced something of a meltdown and the United States was plunged into a recession, with unemployment figures rising to more than 10 percent, an increasingly heavy debt burden, and a crisis in the banking sector. As this text was being written, it appeared that the worst of this downturn was over, and there were welcome signs of a strengthening in the overall economy and in the textile complex and retail environment.

Domestic Production of Textiles and Apparel
As expected with the implementation of NAFTA, in 1994, manufacturing employment declined in textiles and apparel as well as across the manufacturing sector in general. However, the trend toward declining manufacturing employment was established long before NAFTA was implemented. Employment in the U.S. textile industry peaked in 1950, and by 1980 textile employment had decreased by 33 percent. During the same time, the number of apparel employees increased by 5 percent.

This loss of textile and apparel industry jobs is even more significant when measured against a modest growth of 11.3 percent in overall manufacturing jobs in the United States during this period. The decline in employment in textiles from 1950 to 1980 was largely related to application of new technology, resulting in increased productivity. As employment dropped, fewer people were producing more goods until production peaked, in 1997. The decline in apparel workers began after 1980; between 1980 and 2002, the workforce was cut by a total of 56.6 percent. These job losses were concentrated in the southeastern United States: North and South Carolina, Georgia, Alabama, and Virginia. U.S. production of apparel continued its decline through 2008, down to 582 million garments, and import penetration, or the percentage of the U.S. market that is supplied by imports, reached record levels in 2008, of 97 percent (*Trends,* 2009). As a result of the turmoil in the textile manufacturing industry, the highly respected American Textile Manufacturers Institute ceased to exist, and the National Council of Textile Organizations emerged in its place.

One of the most startling numbers to come out of the post-NAFTA era is that between the implementation of NAFTA in January 1994 and May of 2007, the U.S. textile and apparel manufacturing sector lost more than one million jobs, reflecting a 65 percent decrease in employment in the industry ("USA: Post-NAFTA Job Loss," 2007). This drop cannot be solely blamed on NAFTA; overall market trends, including the end of the MFA quota system among WTO members; the implementation of numerous bilateral free trade agreements between the United States and other, individual nations; and the implementation of the Central America–Dominican Republic–United States Free Trade Agreement (CAFTA-DR) all exerted an influence as well. The pattern of sourcing textile and apparel products offshore parallels similar patterns found in other fully developed nations in Europe and in Japan and should really come as no surprise, yet for those whose livelihood depended on this industry, it has been a severe blow.

Yet, there were still some bright spots in the U.S. textile industry. U.S. textile mills have spun almost five million bales of cotton into yarns on average for each of the years 2006 to 2008 ("National Cotton Council of America," 2009). According to the National Cotton Council of America, that is enough cotton to make more than one billion pairs of jeans; or, from a different perspective, each bale could make 1,217 men's T-shirts. Historically, China is the largest cotton producer globally, and India, the second, but the United States is still the third, with Texas being the leading cotton-producing state. During this 3-year time period, an average of almost half of the U.S. cotton supply was exported. Cotton that is being spun into yarns here is typically being done in smaller quantities, on newer equipment, and on quicker turns, of 4 to 6 weeks (Borneman, 2009) (Figure 10.2).

United States-based manufacturers, such as VF Corporation and Levi Strauss & Co., two of the largest apparel manufacturers in the world, have closed dozens of jeans plants in the United States and moved them to other, low-wage countries over the past 15 years. At one time Levi Strauss had moved all its production offshore, and VF Jeanswear, which makes Lee and Wrangler jeans, closed its production plants and its jeans-washing plant in El Paso, Texas. VF still produces about half of its Jeanswear in locations throughout the Americas, such as Mexico and Argentina; the remainder is produced in other locations throughout the world. Many U.S. manufacturers have out-

Figure 10.2

Harvesting cotton in San Angelo County, Texas.

(*Ken Grimm*/San Angelo Standard-Times)

sourced so much of their production that they are now considered brand managers. We have discussed many of these as examples elsewhere throughout this text.

Not all apparel production jobs have left the United States, but even New York, once the most prominent fashion center in the Americas, and the largest production center up through the mid-1900s, has been feeling a significant downturn in its role. New York seems to be maintaining its position as the marketing center for the fashion business, and it certainly has many of the finest retailers in the world, but the fashion industry in New York is finding itself in a different type of struggle. New York has great expertise in design and marketing, but so much of its manufacturing expertise is being lost that it is becoming a burden for designers in the city to find manufacturing capacity to complete their samples and custom orders. In January 2010, Mayor Bloomberg announced a yearlong initiative to study ways to ensure that the fashion industry continues to be centered in New York (Feitelberg & Moin, 2010)

Case 10.1 reports on the rally of industry workers, union members, and designers held in October 2009 to help save New York's Garment Center. Follow your reading with Learning Activity 10.4.

Learning Activity 10.4
NAFTA and U.S. Production of Textiles and Apparel

1. In what way might the EU have provided an incentive for the formation of NAFTA?

2. What do the United States and Canada have in common that provided the incentive for free trade with Mexico?

3. Identify a few fundamental ways in which NAFTA differs from the EU.

4. Identify a few fundamental ways in which NAFTA is similar to the EU.

5. What are three factors that have contributed to the decline of textile production in the United States?

6. What are three factors that have contributed to the decline of apparel production in the United States?

7. How does the United States continue to be one of the primary cotton producers in the world?

8. Considering Case 10.1, what has caused the unification of three normally combative groups?

9. Identify one issue not addressed in the case that has contributed to the decline in apparel production in New York City.

10. Do you think a "Made in New York" label help save the New York fashion district? Why or why not?

"This is the game changer."

That's how Yeohlee Teng summed up Wednesday's Save the Garment Center rally that drew 750 supporters including Michael Kors, Diane von Furstenberg, Nanette Lepore, Elie Tahari and other designers onto Seventh Avenue to raise awareness of the New York neighborhood's plight.

"This will change the conversation with the city," Teng said after the event. "It won't just be about square footage anymore. It will be about issues that are more indicative of what is going on now—saving jobs, being American, and cultural identities."

Several of the 16 speakers hammered home the need to protect American workers, to market a Made in New York label and to give domestic companies tax incentives to keep production in the city.

The Council of Fashion Designers of America's (CFDA) executive director, Steven Kolb, helped round up a battalion of designers including Marcus Wainwright, Doo-Ri Chung, Chris Benz, Maria Cornejo, Victoria Bartlett and Charles Nolan. Supporters did their part, waving "Save the Garment Center" and "It's Sew N.Y." signs, and shouting their cause when prompted by fiery leaders like Workers United's Bruce Raynor and Edgar Romney.

Before activists took to the stage set up at Seventh Avenue and 39th Street, Romney said Wednesday's rally was the first time in his 43-year tenure that industry workers, union members, and designers had come together. Today, there are 4,500 to 5,000 union workers in the New York garment center compared with five years ago when there were 12,000 to 13,000, Romney said. The apparel industry is New York City's second-largest employer behind the financial sector — a statistic not lost on City Council Speaker Christine Quinn.

"If there is one thing that we should have clearly learned this year, . . . we cannot base New York City's entire economy on two industries: Wall Street and real estate. Those industries are important—those people wear clothes" she said. "But we need a diversified economy in New York City, so when there is a Wall Street setback it doesn't become a massive problem in our city." . . .

[Michael] Bloomberg's mayoral rival, William Thompson, said, "Government needs to step up to do its part. We need to stand up and save the garment center now." . . .

Noting New York's reputation as a global fashion capital is under threat and the Garment District is facing extinction, Thompson recalled how 95 percent of clothes sold in the U.S. in the Fifties and Sixties were also made here. Today, 90 percent of clothes sold in America are manufactured in other countries.

"Top fashion designers say they depend on nearby manufacturers to fill their orders, and if there is further contraction they will leave the city, along with the fashion shows and hundreds of millions of dollars in economic activity," Thompson said. "A failure to enforce zoning rules in the garment center now threatens our city's fashion industry. The illegal conversion of hundreds of thousands of square feet of manufacturing space to offices, condos and stores in recent years is a major reason the garment center has contracted so sharply."

. . . [Designer Nanette] Lepore said she started out 20 years ago with a $5,000 loan and a dream of building a business. She now employs more than 130 people in the area and manufactures 15,000 to 30,000 units each month. "Why deny that opportunity to others?" she said. . . .

And there is no question many design students come to New York because of the garment center, according to Parsons New School for Design's dean of fashion, Simon Collins. Marc Jacobs, Narciso Rodriguez, Donna Karan and Proenza Schouler's Jack McCollough and Lazaro Hernandez are among the school's alumni who put together their first designs in the neighborhood. . . .

En route back to his office, former CFDA president Stan Herman said action is in order. "The big thing is, if we don't preserve the core of production, we could stop being a viable industry."

The scene on Seventh Avenue, in New York City, in October 2009. *(Courtesy of WWD)*

Source:

Feitelberg, R. (2009, October 22). Designers rally to save garment center. *Women's Wear Daily.* Retrieved from http://www.wwd.com/business-news/designers-out-in-force-to-save-the-garment-center-2350947//?full=true

Figure 10.3a Retail buyers from Mexico and South America visit the Silvergate market in the San Pedro Wholesale Mart, the California enclave of Korean American apparel makers. Garments can be bought at wholesale prices right off the racks. (*Donato Sardella/WWD*)

California Apparel Centers

Major manufacturers also seemed to be abandoning the San Francisco area as a production center. Levi Strauss & Co. still has headquarters there, but its products are sourced offshore. Esprit moved its financial headquarters to Hong Kong and now has its marketing arm in Germany. But we would be remiss not to mention The North Face, which is located across the Bay from San Francisco, in Berkeley, and has become a leader in performance sportswear for hiking and mountaineering. What remained was a beautiful opportunity to develop a niche market in the form of a thriving independent designer venue based in San Francisco's Mission District, with locally made and sold wares.

Learn more about the indie designers in San Francisco's Mission District in Case 10.2.

Since the mid-1980s, Los Angeles County, California, has become the largest apparel production center in the United States, specializing primarily in women's wear, specifically juniors. The area was already a main center for design and fashionable sportswear as well as home to the most visible means of presenting emerging styles: the entertainment industry. High-end fashion jeans, including Rock & Republic, 7 for All Mankind, Citizens for Humanity, and paperdenim&cloth are made in Los Angeles. Employment in the Los Angeles apparel industry nearly doubled, while textile and apparel employment in the rest of the nation declined by half. By the 1990s, Los Angeles was the nation's largest apparel employer; New York City was second. There are still many surviving pockets of apparel production in other areas throughout the country, including the Hart Schaffner Marx men's tailored suit facility near Chicago. However, Los Angeles has many advantages in today's markets.

Los Angeles is a major center for immigration, especially from Asia, Central America, and Mexico; therefore, it has a ready supply of low-cost labor as well as apparel manufacturing expertise. By 2000, Los Angeles County had 144 thousand textile and apparel jobs, 60 percent of which were held by Korean Americans. Los Angeles had the largest Korean community outside of Korea, with more than 186 thousand residents (Bowers, 2002). Many emigrating Koreans were experienced in the textile and apparel industry and were able to establish firms with relatively few resources. The result was the growth of a Korean subset of the Los Angeles textile and apparel industry that includes family-owned firms. The Koreans also have their own apparel market center, San Pedro Mart, where the first language is Korean, the second language is Spanish (because many Koreans migrated to the United States via South America), and the third language is English (Bowers, 2002). The second generation of Korean manufacturers is now assuming leadership of family companies (Figure 10.3a).

A survival guide on keeping indie fashion afloat in a sour economy could be written by designers based in San Francisco's bohemian Mission District, where their wares are made locally and sold in namesake boutiques or cooperatives.

"This is ground zero for diversity and creativity," says Julienne Weston, who since 1980 has designed and manufactured her Weston Wear wrap dresses ($135) and other knitwear in the Mission, which are sold at 600 wholesale accounts. "When I first came here, the neighborhood was real rough, but I knew it had something going on."

Weston's only retail outlet is a 2,800-square-foot space on Valencia Street, where sales now are being bolstered with thousands of samples priced from $5 to $35 that otherwise would be warehoused for an annual sale. The boutique is also where the designer goes to critique her entire collections with younger staff. "Lately, we're focusing on every garment, every style, asking, 'Why are people buying one thing and not the other?'" Weston explains.

Up the block at Dema, sportswear designer Dema Grim is having success recasting popular silhouettes from earlier seasons using new fabrics and playing with proportions. . . .

"I've also been eavesdropping on what people are looking for," says Grim, in business 12 years, who cuts fabric in the back of her 600-squarefoot store. Her clothes also are sewn by contractors in the Mission. To keep her Sixties Mod–inspired shop a destination for accessories, her sales staff scours Mission thrift stores.

Priya Saraswati, designer of the tailored sportswear label Saffron Rare Threads, credits a special sale she held for her best retail customers for helping to weather the recession's initial shock to wholesale and online sales. Sharing retail space with two designers, under the name Studio 3579, also has helped with expenses—and maintaining a high-profile location across from hipster hangout Dolores Park at Dolores and 18th Streets.

But crucial to her survival, Saraswati says, is being a San Francisco–made label, which gives her flexibility in changing orders and filling them in six weeks. Additionally, "I find that people who value a high-quality product made locally still shop here," offers Saraswati. . . .

While a strong buy-local culture is part of the Northern California ethos, the mantra is particularly ingrained in the Mission—the city's former garment-manufacturing center—as are the area's working-class and artistic roots, which are always at odds with gentrification and development.

With few exceptions, there are no chain stores in the Mission, the city's largest, sunniest and flattest neighborhood of early 19th century wooden buildings and warehouses spread across roughly 2 square miles.

"It's nice that we can keep small businesses here. If you want to go to the Gap or another big business, you can hop on BART and be downtown in a minute," says Zoe Magee, who's behind the tailored-to-fit Mission swimwear line and shop Zoe Bikini on 18th Street, with a following of large-breasted women.

"A lot of people who come to me are really psyched to buy something directly from a designer. Even in this economy, I do well because there's been a change of consciousness about where you shop, especially in San Francisco, where we advocate everything locally grown and sewn," notes Magee, who personally sells her bikinis, which ... are made of Italian fabric and fittings at a garment contractor next door. . . .

Besides her Joy O line being locally made, Mission jewelry designer Joy Opfer said consumers are responding well to her eco-conscious creations, such as her recently launched line of recycled steel and glass accessories. . . .

"The Mission is definitely suited for what I do," says men's wear designer Estrella Tadeo of The Mission Statement, whose tailored designs have a streetwear flare.

Classic sportswear designer Sunhee Moon credits customer loyalty to her San Francisco–made sportswear and its fit for pulling her business through in the down economy at her 16th Street boutique. She says her customers have kept shopping in the recession, and the store outsells her second city location on Fillmore Street in well-heeled Pacific Heights and a third spot on Union Street, before she closed it last year. Says Moon: "It's the Mission customer."

Source:

Ramey, J. (2010, January 14). Mission possible: San Francisco's thriving indie designers. *Women's Wear Daily*. Retrieved from http://www.wwd.com/fashion-news/mission-possible-san-franciscos-thriving-indie-designers-2405947//

Figure 10.3b U.S. manufacturers are facing higher costs for some textile and apparel components.

(*Ted Soqui/Corbis*)

One of the most visible apparel manufacturing companies located in the Los Angeles area today is American Apparel, which is a vertically integrated manufacturer, distributor, and retailer, based in downtown Los Angeles. The company prides itself on its American-made products. This firm employs about five thousand people in the Los Angeles area and another five thousand globally, in 281 retail stores in 20 countries throughout the United States, Europe, Asia, and Australia ("American Apparel," 2010). American Apparel also operates a wholesale business that supplies T-shirts and other casual wear to distributors and screen printers. In 2008, the firm put a garment dye facility into operation, acquired a fabric dye facility in Garden Grove, and added knitting and production capacity (Figures 10.3b and 10.3c).

And then there is Guess. It began as a small jeans manufacturer in Berkeley, California, and evolved into a global brand, doing more than $2 billion in business last year. In a 2010 interview, Jeff Streader, the senior vice president of sourcing at Guess, said his main concern as he made sourcing decisions for Guess was to keep the fashion firm from placing too much of its production in China, preferring that Guess "have 35 percent of its production in China with the remaining 65 percent split between other countries in Asia and factories in the Western Hemisphere" (Casabona, 2010b, n.p.). Streader said he expected that more companies would be diversifying their sourcing strategies in the future (Casabona, 2010b).

Read Case 10.3 to learn about how, in the first decade of the 2000s, Guess shifted its focus from wholesale to retail.

U.S. Retailing

Walmart, mergers, and the growing visibility of global fast-fashion retailers based in Europe, such as H&M and Zara, are

Figure 10.3c The American Apparel store at Carrefour Laval, in Montreal, Quebec.

(*Courtesy of WWD*)

the biggest news in U.S. retailing. It seems one can hardly pick up a newspaper or magazine without seeing some story about Walmart, the retailer that has $374.5 billion in sales annually. Walmart is ranked number one in the world, and is more than three times larger than any other retailer in the world.

Two of the largest retail mergers occurred between 2004 and 2005. After Sears took over Lands' End, in 2002, Sears merged with Kmart, in late 2004. Then Federated Department Stores, which owned Macy's and Bloomingdale's, took over May Department Stores, which in turn owned Marshall Field's, which May had acquired from Target Corporation. May Department Stores also owned nearly a dozen smaller department store groups throughout the Midwest and West. Federated put the Macy's nameplate on most of those stores, while closing some stores whose markets overlapped or were underperforming. In the process, Macy's became the first national department store group in the United States. The success of this merger plan is easily defined by the store's 2007 number one global fashion goods retailer ranking.

What were lost in these monumental mergers were the landmark department stores that were unique to every major city in the United States and the department store buyers who guided fashion for their customers. Also, department stores are in a squeeze from all sides. Mass retailer giants, such as Walmart; specialty stores, such as Gap and Victoria's Secret; and upscale retailers, such as Neiman Marcus and Nordstrom, are all encroaching on the Macy's market.

Huge retailers require huge quantities of merchandise, which limits the ability of small- and medium-sized apparel producing firms to become suppliers,

---

Case 10.3 GUESS INC.: THE YEAR AHEAD

Throughout its 29 years in business, Guess Inc. has been able to keep its pulse on pop culture and capitalize on new trends. As one of the pioneers in the American designer denim industry, it understood how customers aspired to live a glamorous lifestyle as easily attainable as slipping into a pair of sexy jeans. It rounded up the most bodacious of the bombshells—Claudia Schiffer, Anna Nicole Smith, Drew Barrymore and Paris Hilton, to name a few—to pout, smolder and wear nearly nothing in its signature ads.

Then, in the Aughts, the Los Angeles–based company began shifting its focus from a wholesale-centric business to a retail-driven one, as it sensed opportunity, not to mention fatter profit margins, outside the consolidating ranks of its retail customers. It also expanded the footprint of its Guess-branded stores in Europe and Asia.

Anticipating the growing popularity of accessories, contemporary sportswear and fast fashion appealing to younger customers, the firm unveiled Guess Accessories, Guess by Marciano and G by Guess to cater to those respective markets. As of Oct. 31, it operated 1,186 stores worldwide. In its last fiscal year, it generated revenue of $2.09 billion, compared to $551.2 million in 1996, the year it went public.

Source:

Tran, K. (2010, January 25). Guess: The year ahead. *Women's Wear Daily*. Retrieved from http://www.wwd.com/markets-news/guess-inc-the-year-ahead-2425137

---

a serious problem for apparel entrepreneurs. The landscape for acquisition of apparel products has changed significantly as the percentage of imports has increased. Merchandisers still source at the major trade fairs in the U.S., such as in New York and the MAGIC shows in Las Vegas, but they are continuing to move toward developing private label merchandise and sourcing off-shore. They have moved toward direct to factory sourcing through their own sourcing offices or electing to employ a sourcing agent, to do the job for them.

The top fashion goods retailers of 2007 are reported in Table 10.6. Six of the top ten are based in the U.S. indicating the strength of these businesses. However, note that even the biggest fashion retailers can sometimes run into trouble in a short period of time, for number nine Arcandor AG of Germany, a department store group, filed for bankruptcy in 2009.

The globalization trend for retailers has been growing over a period of several years. Many of the largest retailers from other areas of the world, such as H&M and Zara, are opening shops here, whereas many of the major stores from the United States are opening elsewhere. Walmart has expanded internationally, into Argentina, Brazil, Canada, Central America, Chile, China, Japan, India, Mexico, Puerto Rico, and the United Kingdom (UK). The Gap Stores, Inc., operates more than 3,100 stores worldwide, with stores throughout the United States as well as in Canada, the UK, France, Ireland, and Japan.

The United States has been notoriously overstored at times, with vacancies available in many malls across the nation. Specialty retailers, both independents and those from other nations, are finding themselves welcomed as tenants for some of these vacant storefronts.

One of the biggest recent trends in the apparel retail business has been the movement into Internet shopping. Most U.S. retail stores today have Web shopping sites and do a significant amount of their overall business through this venue. The marketing of fashion is also in an era of change as the nation makes its move into the online social networking environment. This is impacting the ways that designers introduce their new lines as some of them experiment with this avenue of reaching the ultimate consumer.

U.S. Role in the Textile and Apparel Trade
In addition to NAFTA, the United States has many free trade and trade preference programs with countries around the world. Table 10.7 reports the top countries that were sources of textiles and apparel for the United States in 2007 and 2008. Note that Mexico, Honduras, and El Salvador are the only major supplier countries to the United States located in the Americas. China took the top spot from

Table 10.6 TOP TEN GLOBAL FASHION GOODS RETAILERS, 2007, RANKED BY SALES IN BILLIONS OF U.S. DOLLARS

Rank	Retailer	Retail Sales (in Billions of U.S. Dollars)	Country of Origin
1	Macy's	$ 26.3	United States
2	J.C. Penney Company, Inc.	$ 19.9	United States
3	TJX (T.J.Maxx and Marshall's)	$ 18.6	United States
4	Kohl's	$ 16.5	United States
5	The Gap Stores, Inc.	$ 15.8	United States
6	Inditex (Zara)	$ 12.9	Spain
7	LVMH	$ 12.7	France
8	H&M	$ 11.6	Sweden
9	Arcandor AG	$ 11.5	Germany
10	Limited Brands, Inc.	$ 10.1	United States

Source: Deloitte. (2009). *Global powers of retailing 2009*. Retrieved February 16, 2010, from http://public.deloitte.com/media/

Mexico in 2003, and China's dominance is expected to continue, as all quota extensions between it and the United States expired in 2008. Note, too, that Mexico has now moved from being the number one supplier, in 2003, to the sixth, in 2008, with a significant drop reported in the years just after the end of all quotas. Vietnam increased its market share with the United States significantly when the quota restrictions on all its goods expired.

According to the American Apparel and Footwear Association (AAFA), the trend in apparel sourcing trade to the United States since the expiration of the quota system in 2005 has been consolidation among the top few suppliers and a loss of market share for smaller suppliers (*Trends*, 2009). Between 2004 and 2008, market share of the top ten apparel suppliers rose from 57.5 percent to 77.2 percent, whereas the next group of ten suppliers lost market share, dropping from 25.3 percent to 14.4 percent during the same time period. Preliminary data on 2009 imports indicated that China, Vietnam, Indonesia, Bangladesh, India, Pakistan, Haiti, and Sri Lanka were benefitting from trade (Birnbaum, 2009). Sufferers included Mexico, the Philippines, Jordan, Sub-Saharan Africa, Cambodia, and, unfortunately, CAFTA-DR nations.

Continue your study of the U.S. textile and apparel trade with Learning Activity 10.5.

Table 10.7 Comparison of Quantities of Market Share in U.S. Apparel Imports from Primary Suppliers for Calendar Years 2007–2008

Source of Imports	Rank	Market Share in 2008	Change from 2007
World		100.00%	−2.73%
China	1	34.32%	−3.05%
Vietnam	2	6.73%	19.95%
Bangladesh	3	6.33%	6.25%
Honduras	4	5.87%	8.85%
Indonesia	5	4.84%	3.28%
Mexico	6	4.56%	−14.48%
Cambodia	7	3.92%	2.54%
India	8	3.89%	1.71%
El Salvador	9	3.68%	3.21%
Pakistan	10	3.05%	−0.38%
Thailand	11	2.16%	−6.16%
Philippines	12	1.70%	−15.59%
Sri Lanka	13	1.67%	−7.20%
Dominican Republic	14	1.58%	−5.95%

Source: Trends: An annual statistical analysis of the U.S. apparel and footwear industries. (2009, August). Arlington, VA: American Apparel and Footwear Association.

Learning Activity 10.5
CALIFORNIA APPAREL CENTERS, U.S. RETAILING, AND TEXTILE AND APPAREL TRADE

1. What are the implications for aspiring apparel entrepreneurs, given the decline of apparel production in the United States?
2. Most of the countries that are low-cost textile and apparel suppliers have gained U.S. market share, whereas higher-cost suppliers have lost market share. What are the implications for "Made in USA"?
3. What elements of the consumer population are helping support San Francisco's Mission District–based apparel entrepreneurs?
4. Check out the Los Angeles–based company American Apparel on the Internet (http://www.americanapparel.com). Click on "About Us," and then identify three or four things that are very unusual about the organization and operation of this company. Would you like to be one of its customers? Why?
5. Some industry observers believe that the enclosed shopping mall with department store anchors will soon be history. What shopping patterns have you observed that would support or dispute this observation?

Canada

Since World War II, with vast distances and rich natural resources, Canada has been transformed from a largely rural economy into a largely industrial and urban one. Canada, with ten provinces and three territories, became completely independent of Great Britain in 1982. Economically and technologically, Canada has developed in parallel with the United States. The United States-Canada Free Trade Agreement and NAFTA resulted in a dramatic increase in trade and economic integration with the United States.

Canada also has established free trade agreements with Chile, Costa Rica, Israel, and Peru. As a result of free trade with Chile, Canada more than doubled its textile exports, but apparel imports declined in both directions. The Israeli agreement has had little impact on textile trade, but Canadian apparel exports to Israel tripled right after the agreement was signed. Canada also participates in the European Free Trade Agreement (EFTA). Canada requires all apparel to have all labeling and marking in both English and French, and imported products must have COO labels.

A number of other trade agreements are under discussion, but the largest is the 34-nation Free Trade Area of the Americas (FTAA). Canadian textile and apparel companies have hoped FTAA will resolve inequities implicit in the United States–Caribbean Basin Trade Partnership Act (CBTPA). As presently written, CBTPA requires use of U.S.-made yarns and fabrics; it is a yarn-forward rule. This precludes participation from the Canadian textile industry. However, no progress has been made on FTAA, and CBTPA is set to expire at the end of 2010 (Barrie, 2009).

Today, Canada is very similar to the United States' market-oriented economic system, patterns of production, and high living standards. The two countries are so closely aligned that a downturn in the U.S. economy has an immediate effect on Canada's. A key strength of the Canadian economy is a substantial trade surplus, something the United States does not have. One of Canada's internal political issues continues to be the relationship with the province of Quebec, with its French-speaking residents and unique culture.

Textiles and Apparel in Canada

Canada has three very active trade associations: the Canadian Textiles Institute, the Canadian Apparel Federation, and the Retail Council of Canada. All have fine Web sites, and the Canadian Apparel Federation has a journal, *Canadian Apparel*, with articles that are available online. Fashion forecasting is one of *Canadian Apparel*'s features, along with global fashion markets and trade issues.

In the mid-1990s the Canadian textile industry included about 1,100 plants and employed 62 thousand people. The apparel industry was producing industrial applications, military uniforms, and a range of garments for consumers. The latest available data indicate that 75 percent of the firms have fewer than 50 employees accounting for one third of all shipments, leaving some large, technologically advanced firms. Overall, the apparel industry had 94,850 employees in 2002, but that number had decreased to about 65 thousand by 2006 (Industry Canada, 2009). The apparel industry has been highly fragmented; Quebec accounted for 61.3 percent of Canada's apparel production, with other key areas being Ontario, Manitoba and British Columbia.

The majority of apparel exports from Canada, almost 90 percent, are destined for the United States, but the overall amount has been declining steadily as Canada competes for market share with Asian powerhouses. At the same time, imports have been increasing. China continues to be the largest source of import increases, reaching 50 percent in 2006, followed by Bangladesh and the United

States, with contributions of a mere 7 percent each (Industry Canada, 2009).

According to the Canadian Apparel Federation, the Canadian apparel industry also has many things that, compared with the U.S. industry, are unique:

Canada . . . has [only] about 10 percent of the U.S. population. Canadians believe they have a stronger sense of regional identity whereas the United States subscribes to the "melting pot" theory. They believe their regional identities influence the way they dress. Canadian apparel often reflects a "mid-Atlantic/Western European" influence in its textile and apparel design, in part because Canadian manufacturers do a lot of research in international markets; they believe that influence is not present in the U.S. market.

Canadian garment makers have become experts at producing small runs of their products because the domestic market is small. U.S. firms are experts at supplying mass retailers because their domestic markets are huge. Canadian apparel firms have the systems in place to effectively produce and market small runs, and that gives them a leg up on American companies when it comes to filling niche markets. Canadian apparel firms are already operating in a niche market environment by American standards. Canadian apparel manufacturers are fast. They deliver quality and they are accountable. (Industry Canada, 2009)

Canada's textile and apparel manufacturers have faced pressures similar to those that have decimated European and U.S. industries, prompting Canadian survivors to focus on high-end products and highly automated systems. Among Canadian firms that are doing well at this time are

- lululemon athletica—headquarters in Vancouver, British Columbia, with more than 100 stores across Canada, the United States, Australia, and Hong Kong; specializes in active sportswear, including yoga wear

- Roots—headquarters in Toronto; product lines focus on active sportswear and leather goods, including footwear, bags, jackets, accessories, and natural fiber clothing
- Tribal Sportswear—a Montreal-based company known for its superior quality pants, jackets, tops, sweaters, and other sportswear for women.

Retailing in Canada

There has been massive retail consolidation in Canada over the past two decades, leading to fewer, larger retailers. In the process, these large retailers have tended to augment their global sourcing capabilities and eliminate many Canadian apparel suppliers from their supply chain. These larger retailers are exerting tremendous price and performance pressures on traditionally smaller Canadian apparel companies, increasingly levying **charge-backs** on suppliers and requiring sharing in advertising costs (co-op advertising) and other discounts (Industry Canada, 2009). To compete, midsize retailers have been going to these methods also.

Twenty years ago the apparel retail community was made up of department and specialty stores; discount retailing was not yet established. Then Walmart arrived in 1994, spread rapidly, and consumers began to understand the concept of everyday low prices. Costco and Sam's Club are now also well established. Internet shopping is a growing retail channel, with consumers buying goods and services online. Both the population and 60 percent of retail sales are concentrated in Ontario and Quebec. The retail consolidation trend that is strong in the United States and in Europe is also on the march in Canada.

We would be remiss if we did not include Canada's best-known retail department store in this discussion: Hudson's Bay Company. Affectionately referred to by locals as the Bay, this department store has been a part of Canadian history for more than three centuries (Hudson's Bay Company, 2010):

Its first century of operation found Hbc firmly ensconced in a few forts and posts around the shores of James and Hudson Bays. Natives brought furs annually to these locations to barter for manufactured goods such as knives, kettles, beads, needles, and blankets. . . . A string of posts grew up along the great river networks of the west foreshadowing the modern cities that would succeed them: Winnipeg, Calgary, and Edmonton.

In 1821, Hbc merged with its most successful rival, the North West Company, based in Montreal. . . .

In 1912 . . . Hbc began an aggressive modernization program. The resulting "original six" Hudson's Bay Company department stores, in Victoria, Vancouver, Edmonton, Calgary, Saskatoon and Winnipeg, are the legacy of this period. . . .

The 21st century finds Hbc well into its fourth century of retailing in Canada. Its major retail channels—the Bay, Zellers, Home Outfitters, and Fields—together provide more than two-thirds of the retail needs of Canadians. (Hudson's Bay Company, 2010)

Mexico

The site of advanced Amerindian civilizations, the area that would become Mexico gained independence in the early 1800s, following three centuries of Spanish reign. Mexico is a federal republic with 31 states. It has a mixture of modern and outmoded industry and agriculture, with a growing private sector. Infrastructure has improved, particularly in the north, because of increased trade with the United States and Canada since NAFTA. "'You trust your blood, and that's it'," reflects the Mexican perspective on the advantages of family-owned businesses and a lack of faith in other institutions, including academic and financial ("Still Keeping It," 2004, pp. 63–64). It is estimated that 95 percent of Mexican businesses are still wholly family owned and run.

The Mexican government is aware of the need to modernize the tax system and labor laws, but progress is slow. Government eradication efforts to control cultivation of opium poppy and cannabis, production of heroin and methamphetamine, and trans-shipment of cocaine from Central America have been essential for keeping levels low. However, in 2004 it was estimated that 70 percent of the U.S. cocaine supply came through Mexico; in 2007, it was the largest foreign supplier of marijuana and methamphetamine (Central Intelligence Agency [CIA], 2010). One has only to check the news to hear of trouble on the U.S.–Mexico border related to the drug trade.

According to the World Bank's vice president for Latin America, NAFTA has had positive effects in Mexico, but they could have been better. The benefits across the country were unequal. The most developed and competitive sectors, of the north and central regions, clearly gained from trade liberalization, whereas less developed areas in the south, with largely Amerindian populations, have not. Moreover, large firms benefited from access to U.S. capital markets, whereas small- and medium-sized firms did not. In addition to NAFTA, Mexico has negotiated 13 free trade treaties with more than 40 nations, making more than 90 percent of its exports and imports under free trade agreements (Workman, 2007). Mexican per capita GDP is the highest in Middle America, but per capita income is about 35 percent of the United States', with highly unequal income distribution and high levels of underemployment.

Free trade created demand for a more skilled Mexican workforce, a challenge the educational system was not prepared to meet (NAFTA, 2003). Mexican business schools are catering to a rising demand for courses specifically focused on the problems and exigencies of running a family-owned business, including conflict resolution and familism, which results in having too many family members who do not serve a real purpose on the payroll ("Still Keeping It," 2004).

Free trade brought new economic opportunities, but the lessons from NAFTA, for other countries negotiating with the United States, are that free trade alone is not enough without significant policy and institutional reform. A World Bank study says that without NAFTA, Mexican global exports would be roughly 25 percent lower, direct foreign investment would be approximately 40 percent less, and per capita income would be approximately 5 percent lower. The modest gains in per capita income were attributed to underinvestment in education, innovation, and infrastructure. Institutional failures in improving accountability, regulatory effectiveness, and control of corruption have moderated the gains provided by NAFTA (NAFTA, 2003).

Textiles and Apparel in Mexico
Following implementation of NAFTA, in 1994, Mexico's share of the U.S. textile and apparel market grew dramatically, but China became dominant in 2003, and Mexico has lost market share ever since.

Some of the textile jobs that were added after NAFTA was instituted were at plants owned by U.S.-based firms, including Burlington, Cone Mills, Dan River, DuPont, Guilford, and Tarrant. These companies, as well as some major apparel companies, established ultramodern production plants in Mexico. The apparel plants were established first, and textile production followed because efficiency increases when textile plants are located close to apparel plants. The goal was to reduce the established 34- to 40-week apparel supply chain to 15 to 20 weeks in order to compete with escalating imports from Asia (Kurt Salmon Associates, 1999). It appeared that NAFTA was working well for Mexico. But then the world began to feel the influx of China into the global market and the results of the expiration of the quota system.

There were 563 thousand people employed in apparel manufacturing in 2004. However, by 2009 the textile and apparel sector only generated approximately 300 thousand direct jobs in Mexico, which was about 2 percent of national employment (Maquila, 2009). The majority of these jobs were held by women, with the key states for textile and garment production being State of Mexico, the Federal District, Puebla, and Guanajuato. Within Latin America, Mexico remained the largest exporter of apparel to the U.S. market. However, by 2008 Mexico had dropped to sixth place as a supplier to U.S. market, a drop of more than 14 percent just in the previous year. Today, Mexico supplies only 4.5 percent of U.S. textile and apparel imports.

The results of economic and industry changes during this period were that in early 2009 thousands of additional jobs were lost and 666 more businesses closed. Labor groups were reporting the following:

- more production is destined for the national market with declining orders from international brands
- more precarious employment conditions, production slowdowns and withholding of salaries
- extended work hours and intensified production goals to make up for decrease in personnel
- plant closures (Maquila, 2009)

The Mexican federal government instituted measures to help the industry cope with the downturn in the form of a fiscal stimulus package, but it has been heavily criticized. Of the business that remains, the United States still receives more than 90 percent of Mexico's textile and apparel exports. Mexican textile and apparel exporters are now almost entirely dependent on U.S. retail market demand.

The World Bank reports the belief that NAFTA would be more effective with certain modifications in the agreement itself, with regard to COO: Mexican industries, such as textiles and clothing, should have easier access to the U.S. market; COO rules should be less of a barrier (NAFTA, 2003). Many U.S. apparel firms disagree strongly because of the essential need to control transshipment and counterfeiting.

Retailing in Mexico
From 1999 to 2003, both the manufacturing and retailing sectors suffered lack of growth because of the flat economy in the United States. Nonetheless, retailing in Mexico developed two distinct parts. One part is a growing, modern retail sector with specific target markets, operational efficiencies, and advanced technology. Many retail formats are available, from limited selection warehouses to more service-oriented hypermarkets, which stock more than 30 thousand SKUs.

The other part is the traditional retail sector, a sizable segment of which is in the informal economy, with open markets in which prices are bartered, and taxes are not paid. Traditional, owner-operated, neighborhood stores and markets now rely on extensive distribution networks for merchandise, similar to convenience stores in the United States. Shopping patterns have also changed. More women are employed, so men take on some shopping responsibilities. Working families are more likely to shop once a week instead of every day, as their parents still do. Cash payments are predominant, as most consumers do not have credit cards.

Walmart became a big retail factor in 1997, when it bought a chain of stores in Mexico. Walmart is now Mexico's largest retailer and is Mexico's largest private sector employer, with 105 thousand employees on the payroll. Walmart is able to sell at lower prices because of its centralized distribution system and technology. The rest of Mexico's retail industry is rushing to adopt Walmart's cost-cutting techniques. Domestic producers and retailers are feel-

ing the pressure from the abundance of Chinese and Indian imports that are being carried in the stores. It is not surprising that Walmart has put many small, family-owned retailers out of business. Sam's Club is also very successful in Mexico.

Walmart raised the fury of activists by planning to build a store next to two-thousand-year-old, pre-Columbian treasures, just north of Mexico City. There were marches and protests, similar to events related to the building of Walmart stores in the United States. However, there were already several other businesses in the same area, and Walmart was eventually granted the permits to build (Case, 2004).

Now, further your study of Canada and Mexico with Learning Activity 10.6.

Learning Activity 10.6
TEXTILES AND APPAREL IN CANADA AND MEXICO

1. Do you agree that the United States subscribes to a "melting pot" theory? Explain.
2. Why might Canada be more closely involved in European culture than the United States?
3. Like in the United States, Canadian retail is becoming more concentrated. Why might this trend be more difficult for Canadian customers?
4. How has NAFTA contributed to the development of textiles and apparel in Mexico?
5. How has NAFTA impaired the development of textiles and apparel in Mexico?
6. Why did U.S. textile firms move production plants to Mexico? Did they stay?
7. What kinds of problems continue to impair business development in Mexico?
8. Why has Walmart been able to become the largest retailer in Mexico?

CARIBBEAN BASIN (CBERA) COUNTRIES

Caribbean Basin countries include countries that are located in Central America and the West Indies. The earliest residents of what is now Central America were the Mayan Indians, who built one of the earliest known civilizations in the Western Hemisphere more than two thousand years ago. Spanish invasions in the 1500s destroyed the Indian societies. In 1821, the Central American area was freed from Spain, and five states were formed: Costa Rica, El Salvador, Guatemala, Honduras, and Nicaragua. One hundred years of efforts toward unification of the states resulted in the formation of Central American Union, in 1923. The Central American Union nations became members of OAS and in the 1960s formed the Central American Common Market. Shortly thereafter, political and military conflicts broke out and continued sporadically well into the 1980s, at times with U.S. intervention.

The West Indies is a two-thousand-mile chain of dozens of islands that separate the Caribbean Sea from the Atlantic Ocean. The West Indies consists of three major groups of islands: the Bahamas, in the north; the Greater Antilles, near the center; and the Lesser Antilles, in the southeast. The islands are actually the peaks of an underwater chain of mountains. Their mild winters make the islands some of the world's most popular resort areas.

Some islands are independent countries, such as Barbados, Cuba, Haiti, the Dominican Republic, and Jamaica. Others are territorial possessions of the United States or several European countries. The people represent many races and nationalities. Most people speak English, French, or Spanish, along with many local dialects.

Caribbean Basin countries are transshipment points for cocaine and heroin from South America as well as for arms for drug dealing. Illicit production of opium poppy and cannabis is mostly for local consumption. For the most part, poverty still prevails because of unequal distribution of income. Review the locations of the countries in Figure 10.1 and the descriptive demographics in Table 10.3.

The growth of the textile and apparel industry in the Caribbean Basin is largely the result of U.S. economic development legislation and trade preference programs.

Table 10.8 U.S. TRADE PROGRAMS THAT FAVOR CARIBBEAN BASIN COUNTRIES

Program	Benefits
Tariff Schedules of the U.S. (1963), Harmonized Tariff Schedules of the U.S. (HTSUS) (1989)	U.S. fabric-forward rule of origin for cut garments parts to be exported, assembled, and imported, with tariff based only on value added
Caribbean Basin Economic Recovery Act (CBERA or CBI) (1983)	U.S. fabric-forward rule of origin for duty-free access to U.S. markets
Caribbean Basin Trade Partnership Act (CBTPA) (2000)	U.S. yarn-forward rule of origin for duty-free access to U.S. market
The Central America–Dominican Republic–United States Free Trade Agreement (CAFTA-DR) (negotiated 2002; rolling implementation until all countries approved, January 2009)	Sectoral rule of origin for yarns and fabrics for products cut and sewn in the sector, for duty-free access to regional markets

Table 10.8 provides summaries of some of the recent programs. Many other trade programs are also in existence, including numerous free trade agreements among different Caribbean Basin countries.

The United States has had trade economic incentive programs with Caribbean Basin countries for more than 40 years. For example, Item 807 of the United States Tariff Schedules was established in 1963 and replicated as Chapter 9802 of the Harmonized Tariff Schedules of the United States in 1989. When referring to the program, textile and apparel professionals still use the term 807. Item 807 has a fabric-forward rule that allows cut parts of garments to be exported, assembled in a foreign country, and imported with tariff assessed only on value added if the parts were cut from U.S.-made fabric. Item 807 allows U.S. apparel production to leave the country but benefits U.S. textile production, because use of U.S.-made fabrics is a requirement.

Many Caribbean Basin countries established apparel industries because of the demand for sewing services for 807 by U.S. manufacturers and retailers. The use of 807 exploded during the 1980s because of escalating apparel production costs in the United States. Huge cutting services developed in Miami to process cut parts for export to Caribbean Basin countries, where they were assembled.

In 1983, the United States initiated the **Caribbean Basin Economic Recovery Act (CBERA)** (commonly known as the Caribbean Basin Initiative [CBI]), a trade preference program intended to stimulate industrial growth in initially 22, and later 27, Caribbean countries in Central America and the West Indies. CBERA expanded the use of 807 by eliminating quota restraints.

The Central America–Dominican Republic–United States Free Trade Agreement (CAFTA-DR) includes seven signatories: the United States, Costa Rica, the Dominican Republic, El Salvador, Guatemala, Honduras, and Nicaragua. The U.S. Congress approved the CAFTA-DR in July 2005. The United States implemented the CAFTA-DR on a rolling basis as countries made sufficient progress to complete their commitments under the agreement. The agreement first entered into force between the United States and El Salvador on March 1, 2006, followed by Honduras and Nicaragua, on April 1, 2006; Guatemala, on July 1, 2006; and the Dominican Republic, on March 1, 2007. The agreement finally entered into force between the United States and Costa Rica on January 1, 2009, and is now fully implemented ("U.S.–CAFTA-DR," n.d.). However, the controversy over CAFTA-DR has been significant, and many continue to question its efficacy in light of other economic issues in the marketplace and the massive competition for market share coming from Asia.

If you are in the textile and apparel business and want to source products from the Caribbean Basin, the greatest challenge is to decide which trade preference program is most appropriate for your products. The second most difficult thing is to decide which country is the best source. The following discussion provides basic information about many of the countries and their roles in textiles and apparel. Apparel professionals were expecting the elimination of the quota system to reduce demand for textiles and apparel from Mexico and Caribbean Basin Countries, and this proved to be the case. The Dominican Republic and Costa Rica are WTO members.

Central American Countries

Costa Rica is a Central American success story. Since the late 1800s, only two brief periods of violence have interrupted its democratic development. Although still a largely agricultural country with land ownership widespread, Costa Rica has expanded its relatively stable economy to include strong technology and tourism industries. As shown in Table 10.3, Costa Rica's level of living, as measured by per capita GDP, is the highest in the sector. Foreign investors are attracted by the country's political stability and its high education levels; in addition, tourism brings in foreign exchange.

Costa Rica was ranked number 21 among the top 25 countries exporting apparel to the United States in 2003, but the amount has declined significantly for several years, especially when quotas were removed globally. Costa Rica also lost market share to CAFTA-DR members as they implemented the agreement gaining access to the U.S. market (Costa Rica did not sign until early 2009). In the interim numerous factories closed. Also, because of Costa Rica's economic and industrial success in other areas, production costs have increased, so sourcing companies looked elsewhere. Costa Rica is a member of Central American Common Market (CACM).

El Salvador, Guatemala, Honduras, and Nicaragua have continued to be relatively unstable politically and economically. The governments are striving to open new export markets, encourage foreign investment, modernize the tax and health care systems, and stimulate their sluggish economies. El Salvador adopted the U.S. dollar as its currency and now concentrates on maintaining a disciplined fiscal policy, as reflected in its low inflation rate. Embracing the dollar has benefits but also caused problems, because it was common practice for Latin American countries to devalue their currencies against the dollar regularly in order to take business away from neighboring countries and the United States (Lyons, 2005). As shown in Table 10.7, in 2009 El Salvador ranked ninth in apparel imports into the United States.

Guatemala is the largest and most populous country in Central America but has a per capita GDP less than half of Costa Rica's. Textiles and apparel is the second largest source of export earnings. Guatemalan apparel producers were concerned about the U.S. 2002 legislation requiring that fabrics be dyed and finished in the United States to qualify for CBTPA preferences. The producers believed it would make it more difficult to change over to full-package production. Korean-based investors accounted for about 65 percent of Guatemala's apparel production during the middle of the first decade of the 21st century. They made some significant inroads in apparel trade with the United States with the implementation of CAFTA-DR, but when China and Asia unleashed their competitive blitz at the end of quotas, the Guatemalan industry began a downward spiral.

One of the success stories in Guatemala has been Denimatrix, which has been focusing on the high-fashion jeans market. The firm was formed when Carlos Arias teamed with the Texan cotton-making cooperative Plains Cotton Cooperative (PCCA) to purchase the family-owned Koramsa; and in early 2010, the firm was producing 140 thousand garments a week (Freeman, 2010). Denimatrix is a leaner firm than those in the past, but it has a faster turn-around time, which makes it highly competitive in its niche market.

Honduras is one of the poorest countries in the Americas, with extraordinarily unequal distribution of income and massive unemployment. Honduras is the leading apparel producer in Central America by sales, and apparel is its largest source of export earnings. Implementing CBTPA is changing Honduras from being an 807/9802 supplier to importing U.S. fabrics (instead of cut garment parts). Production of knit fabrics and apparel is also an important part of its business. Despite its problems, Honduras has attracted investment both by U.S. companies looking for cheaper offshore

The Kattan Group is a family enterprise founded in 1920 that had a pioneering presence in the economic, political, and social development of Honduras. One of the group's main pillars is its garment-manufacturing export business, with which it serves clients in the Americas and Europe. In 1965, the company obtained a license to produce and sell garments under the "Van Heusen" label in Central America.

Kattan Group is committed to sustainability, social responsibility compliance, and a host of benefits that solve the problems of more than 4,500 people. Kattan has established alliances with government institutions for improvement of education, health, and the environment in Honduras. The Cleaner Production Project has developed activities to save energy, water, and supplies with practices that positively impact the environment.

The Kattan group offers a wide range of products, including knitwear, woven tops and bottoms, shirts, and uniforms. It provides full-package service as well as 806/807 programs, with the benefit of sourcing fabric and trims to customer specs. Facilities also include screen printing and embroidery, cutting, and wet processing, using technologies such as tinting, tie-dying, sandblasting, and spraying. The following operations are ongoing:

Protexsa—manufacturing of dress shirts; more than two thousand specialists; capacity of 15 thousand dozen per week; experience includes CK, Geoffrey Beene, Kenneth Cole, DKNY, Izod, PVH, Arrow, Chaps

Finessa—high-end, high-needle garment production with 500 skilled operators, including a custom production line; capacity of 2,400 dozen per week; experience includes Brooks Brothers, Benetton, Polo RL, Zara, Tommy, Macy's, Men's Warehouse, Lands' End, Casual Male, Overton, JCPenney, May Company, and the award-winning original designer Carlos Campos

Unisa—production of uniforms, including chef coats, chef shirts, lab coats, scrubs, patient gowns, airline pilot shirts, and hotel housekeeping, with a capacity of 3,500 dozen per week; experience includes VF, Clipper, Landau, Pinnacle, Kazoo, Coppel, and Carhartt.

Dragon Maya—knits, including basic Ts, pocket Ts, fleece tops and bottoms, placket shirts, and women's casual, with a capacity of 3,500 dozen per week; experience includes Hanes, Fruit of the Loom, Gildan, and Russell.

Source:

Kattan Group of Honduras joins AAPN. (2010). Retrieved March 11, 2010, from http://todaro.posterous.com/kattan-group-of-honduras-joins-aapn

opportunities and by Asian firms seeking a spot for speed-to-market production for the Americas. As shown in Table 10.7, in 2009 Honduras secured the rank of fourth in U.S. apparel imports.

Honduras was engulfed in a political crisis after its president was forced into exile, in 2009, but business has largely gone on as usual, according to industry sources. Factories continue to work without disruption, and orders are going out on time.

Case 10.4 presents an example of a successful, Honduran-based apparel company.

Nicaragua, the poorest Central American country, slowly rebuilt its economy through the 1990s but was hard hit by Hurricane Mitch in 1998. Nicaragua continues to be dependent on international aid and debt relief. The textile and apparel sector consists mostly of assembly operations in government-sponsored free trade zones. Growth of the industry is largely attributed to the low-cost and high-quality workforce (Figure 10.4). In 2003, Nicaragua was 25th among the top 25 apparel exporters to the United States, having shown increases 3 years in a row. (Nicaragua was not in the top 25 in 2001.)

The West Indies

The Dominican Republic shares one of the larger islands with Haiti. Its economy, however, is more developed than Haiti's. The Dominican Republic had one of the fastest growth rates in the Western Hemisphere, although political problems have persisted. The service sector, which includes tourism and free trade zones, has taken over as the nation's largest employer. Growth slowed in the early 2000s, largely because of the sluggish U.S. economy. In 2004, the unequal

distribution of income meant that the poorest half of the population received less than 10 percent of national income, while the richest 10 percent received nearly 40 percent of the national income. The Dominican Republic was the 7th largest exporter to the United States in 2003; however, the end of quotas brought much stronger competition for the U.S. market, which, combined with a weakened global economy in 2008 and 2009, greatly affected the country's U.S. market share. In 2009, the Dominican Republic had dropped to 14th in imports into the United States.

Haiti, in a space slightly smaller than Maryland, is the poorest country in the Western Hemisphere. Early in its colonization, it was a French colony dedicated to forestry and sugar-related industries that became the richest in the Caribbean through heavy importation of African slaves and environmental degradation. In the late 1700s, half a million slaves revolted. After a prolonged struggle, independence was gained, but political violence continues to the present day. Despite the turmoil, Haiti has a small but vital apparel industry. In 2001, Haiti exported $217 million in apparel to the United States, but production was reduced after that because of political unrest. Efforts in U.S. Congress to provide additional aid to Haiti have proven to be uneven. At the time of this writing, the United States was making a significant effort to impact the local economy, especially in light of the devastating earthquake that hit in January 2010, and encouraging U.S. firms to select this nation for CMT activities.

Case 10.5 outlines the efforts being made in the wake of the January 2010 earthquake in Haiti to get that country's apparel industry up and running. Follow your reading with Learning Activity 10.7.

Learning Activity 10.7
TEXTILES AND APPAREL IN
CENTRAL AMERICA AND WEST INDIES

1. What factors have contributed to the slow development of Caribbean Basin countries?
2. Why have U.S. trade programs been essential to the development of Caribbean Basin countries?
3. Considering the turmoil in many Caribbean Basin countries, why are U.S. companies sourcing apparel production there?
4. Why were the Caribbean Basin countries expected to lose apparel production business when quotas were eliminated?
5. Considering Case 10.4, what advantages does the Kattan Group have over some other Middle American companies?
6. What do North American apparel producers need to do to compensate for the loss of quota protection?
7. How might sourcing a company's commitment to sustainability result in assistance in restoring production during situations such as Haiti's earthquake?

Figure 10.4 Skilled sewing machine operators attach a band to a sheer gown in a Nicaraguan co-op factory. Nicaragua is very dependent on apparel production as a legitimate source of economic growth. (*Courtesy of WWD*)

Apparel manufacturers in Haiti are rushing to get operating again in the face of significant challenges for workers and supply chains.

The apparel industry in Haiti was a mainstay of the country's economy, accounting for two-thirds of exports and nearly 10 percent of gross domestic product. As the country struggles to recover from the devastating Jan. 12 earthquake, the garment sector will be an important tool in helping it get back on its feet.

Most factories operating in and around Port-au-Prince escaped the earthquake and its aftershocks with little damage, said Georges Sassine, president of the Association of Industries of Haiti, which represents the country's manufacturers. He predicts apparel production will be fully back online by the end of February.

However, the industry faces some daunting hurdles, including getting safety certifications for all factory buildings, even those without visible damage, so production can begin in earnest. Starting Thursday, engineers from the U.S. and France began visiting factories with Haiti's Minister of Public Works to start the certification process, Sassine said.

Prior to the quake, 28 apparel and textile companies operated in Haiti. They employed 28,000 workers at last count, Sassine said. In one of the largest tragedies caused by the earthquake, the Palm Apparel factory, which manufactured T-shirts for companies such as Gildan Activewear Inc., collapsed, killing an estimated 500 workers.

Four other factories, including Sassine's, sustained damages that will take about a month to fix. At least six factories that initially shut down their production have resumed operations, and one denim factory near the border with the Dominican Republic was unaffected by the quake, Sassine said. He is worried companies who worked with contractors in Haiti will be forced to make business decisions that will pull production out of the country.

Gildan implemented a contingency plan to replace production lost in Haiti after the earthquake by moving it to facilities in the Dominican Republic and Central America, said Laurence Sellyn, executive vice president, chief financial officer and administrative officer for Gildan.

"We continue to be committed to our long-term presence in Haiti, and we are pleased our contractors are advising us they're able to start up more quickly than we originally anticipated in the circumstances," Sellyn said.

The devastation faced by Haitian workers is also a challenge. Sassine said increasing numbers of workers have returned to work in the factories, but it's hard to predict the long-term effects, as many were forced to leave the capital city to find shelter or check on their families. As early as Monday, attendance at the factories able to resume production was at 30 percent, and that number climbed to 60 percent by the middle of the week, he said.

"Every day, more and more are returning," Sassine said. "If we reach 80 percent [attendance] we will consider ourselves very lucky." Mobile meal trucks supplied by the Dominican Republic helped some factories feed workers two meals a day, Sassine said, but shelter remains challenging. Sassine said he was working to get 25,000 to 50,000 tents from the U.S. Agency for International Development to offer shelter to workers who returned to the factories.

U.S. companies are working to gather information and get production going, as well. Gildan employs 40 people in Haiti to oversee social responsibility compliance and quality control at its contract factories, Sellyn said. The company is working with its employees to meet

A worker looks over the devastation at the Palm Apparel T-shirt factory, in Haiti.
(*Chris Hondros/ Getty Images*)

their needs and established a staging area in the Dominican Republic to provide food and water to employees of Gildan and its contractors.

A spokeswoman for Gap Inc. said the company's two contractors in Haiti were up and running, including one inside the earthquake zone. Initially the factory had shut down due to some minimal damage, she said, but the company was able to come back online relatively quickly.

"Gap sources a limited amount of product in Haiti, and we're committed to continuing to do business there," the spokeswoman said. "We're working directly with our vendors to make sure things are resumed as quickly as humanly possible."

Hanesbrands Inc. said at least partial production had resumed at all three of its T-shirt sewing contractors. Hanes also said it set up an operation in the Dominican Republic to provide food, water and other aid for its workers. Hanes said it expected production in Haiti to return to pre-earthquake levels by mid-February.

"We are very thankful that our major contract partners have the wherewithal to resume production, providing critical jobs for employees who are seeking to recover from the aftermath of the earthquake," said Gerald Evans, president of international business and global supply chain for Hanesbrands.

According to sources in Haiti and in the U.S., the Dominican Republic opened use of its port to companies to ship goods. The seaport in Port-au-Prince was badly damaged in the disaster, but partial operations started this week, according to some reports. Before the disaster, Haiti, the poorest country in the Western Hemisphere with 80 percent of its population living below the poverty line, was poised to emerge as a success story for international trade proponents. Following the extension of duty free apparel benefits to the country under the Haitian Hemispheric Opportunity through Partnership Encouragement Act, or HOPE, in 2006 and its successor, HOPE II, in 2008, the country's apparel manufacturing garment sector had grown significantly.

In the first 11 months of 2009, apparel and textile imports to the U.S. from Haiti grew 24.3 percent to $468 million. On a volume basis, imports to the U.S. advanced 6.8 percent to 217.1 million square meter equivalents.

Source:

Casabona, L. (2010a, January 29). Haitian industry coming back slowly. *Women's Wear Daily*. Retrieved from http://www.wwd.com/business-news/haitian-industry-coming-back-slowly-2440677//

SOUTH AMERICA

South America's political history is similar to that of the Caribbean Basin: through most of the 1500s, South America was occupied by Spain or Portugal, and the continent has struggled with military dictatorships and rebellions ever since. Some countries are further along than others in developing market economies. South America has huge deposits of natural resources, including minerals and petroleum that are not fully commercialized, but some resources are being exploited in ways that are highly destructive to the environment. These natural resources, along with agriculture, are responsible for the majority of GDP. Both oil and agriculture are subject to wide fluctuations in world market prices. The countries suffered through the U.S. and global recessions from 1999 to 2003 and again from 2008 to 2010 but are persevering.

For most countries, privatization of utilities, banking, and trade is still in progress. In general, the less developed the market economy, the greater the poverty level and the more unequal the distribution of income. Many of the countries have the same problems as the Caribbean Basin, with trafficking of drugs and money laundering. Colombia, Peru, and Bolivia are the world's largest cultivators of coca and cocaine, which are exported mostly through Argentina, Brazil, and Chile to European and U.S. drug markets. Promotion of alternative crop programs has been unable to keep pace with farmers' attempts to increase cultivation of products for the drug market.

South American countries fall into two trade groups: Andean countries, in the north, and Mercosur countries, in the south. The term *Andean*, a reference to the Andes Mountains, includes Bolivia, Colombia, Ecuador, and Peru. The United States established the Andean Pact, a trade preference program, in 1960 and updated it in 1991 and 2002. Mercosur is a trade name for the Southern Cone Common Market, which includes Argentina, Brazil, Paraguay, and Uruguay. Mercosur countries account for 70 percent of South America's total economy. The EU is developing more trade agreements with South America.

Andean Countries

The Andean countries are a relatively small source of U.S. imports of textiles and apparel. The Andean sector became eligible for duty-free treatment for the first time with enactment of the **Andean Trade Promotion and Drug Eradication Act** (**ATPDEA**), Division D of the Trade Act of 2002. Peru and Colombia account for most of the U.S. textile and apparel imports from Andean countries. The two countries were considered price competitive by sourcing countries when the quota system increased the costs of sourcing from Asian countries, but both found themselves affected by the rise in Asian competition after quotas were removed. However, the allowance in ATPDEA for use of sectoral yarns and fabrics was expected to help keep Andean products competitive, by qualifying them for tariff reductions. These nations have been having a bumpy ride between the demise of quotas and the recent global economic downturn.

Colombia suffered a 40-year insurgent campaign to overthrow the government, supported in part by funds from the drug trade that escalated during the 1990s. Colombia has been negotiating with the United States for a free trade agreement, but there has been little more than a vague commitment from President Barack Obama to complete it. Nonetheless, Colombia's textile and clothing industry is persevering (Tait, 2008). Colombia is one of the more successful apparel producers in South America; key products are knits, denims and T-shirts. Colombia's textile and apparel sector is concentrated in two major cities: Medellín focuses on apparel production and some textiles, and Bogotá generates more in textiles, especially knitted fabrics and knit apparel. Much of Bogotá's knitwear companies are family run and vertically integrated, producing for exports on a full-package basis (Figure 10.5).

Colombia produces a range of fabrics but has to make up for shortfalls with imported fabrics from China and the United States. Venezuela had been Colombia's biggest customer, receiving more than half its exports from there (the United States was the second-largest customer, Mexico, third). However, Venezuela's president, Hugo Chavez, froze trade ties with the country in August 2009, resulting in a sharp fall in trade and loss of jobs in Colombia. Read Case 10.6 to learn more about the effects of Venezuela's trade freeze with Colombia.

Even in the wake of a turbulent global economy, and issues with its neighbors, Colombia has become one of the main fashion centers in Latin America with its successful trade shows Colombiatex and Colombiamoda. These are international trade shows with hundreds of exhibitors from throughout the Americas, from Brazil to the United States, and thousands of international buyers and visitors. Colombiatex features everything from fiber innovations to finished textiles and supplies, from buttons and zippers to machinery. Colombia specializes in high-quality fashion apparel and jeans, and its facilities meet ISO 9000 and ISO 9002-4 certification, internationally recognized standards for world-class production. Colombia is a good source for quick-turn business, for which customers are willing to pay a premium.

Ancient Peru was the seat of Andean civilizations, most notably that of the Incas, whose empire was captured by the Spanish in 1533. Peruvian independence was declared in 1821. After many years of military rule, Peru returned to democratic

Figure 10.5 A worker fabricates textiles in Textiles Romanos factory in Bogotá, Colombia. *(Alejandra Parra/Bloomberg via Getty Images)*

Case 10.6 COLOMBIA: TEXTILES SUFFERING FROM VENEZUELAN POLITICAL ROW

Colombia's textiles industry is suffering from the country's poor diplomatic relations with neighbor Venezuela, with trade falling sharply and 50,000 job losses this year.

"We can't hide the fact that many jobs are being lost in the labor-intensive textiles sector while exports fall and factories continue to close," Gillermo Valencia Jaramillo, boss at leading industry lobby Inexmoda, said in a statement.

Valencia said more job losses are expected as exports continue to falter amid the political stalemate.

The row has been triggered by Venezuela's president Hugo Chavez's protest against a recent high-stakes Colombian military cooperation agreement with the U.S., which has resulted in him freezing trade ties with the country.

Venezuela and Ecuador buy roughly 40% of Colombia's textiles output.

Valencia said the Venezuelan quarrel is dealing the sector a heavy blow at a time when it is already struggling from weaker U.S. exports and a rising peso.

The political impasse is hurting both small and large players.

In recent days, top textiles firm Tejicondor was reported to be seeking 150 layoffs to survive the crisis while many others are mulling redundancies.

Source:

Freeman, I. C. (2009, November 10). Colombia: Textiles suffering from Venezuelan political row. just-style.com. Retrieved February 21, 2010, from http://www.just-style.com/news/textiles-suffering-from-venezuelan-political-row_id105863.aspx

Figure 10.6 Women doing repair work on alpaca sweaters at Art Atlas, in Arequipa, Peru. (*Sandra Keiser*)

leadership in 1980. A decade of dramatic turnaround in the economy was followed by significant progress in curtailing guerrilla activity.

Despite its internal problems, Peru developed an integrated textile and apparel sector, from the production of raw material inputs (cotton, alpaca, llama, and vicuña) and textile processing through apparel manufacturing. The Zarate Industrial Zone, in Lima, is the center of several leading clothing makers and suppliers of textile inputs. Peru produces high-quality apparel products, including combed cotton knit tops. Some suppliers believe Peru could compete in high-end knit shirts.

After years of uneven performance, Peru's economy grew rapidly in 2002 and 2003, but allegations of government corruption continued to arise. Textile and apparel exports from Peru to the United States rose 21.54 percent in 2003. Those positive export results were primarily due to a spike in trade under the ATPDEA. However, lack of infrastructure has deterred continued expansion in trade and investment.

Southern South American and Mercosur Countries

Chile is the Costa Rica of South America, and yet it is not a member of Mercosur. Sound economic policies maintained consistently since the 1980s have contributed to Chile's steady growth and have helped secure the country's commitment to a democratic system of government. Chile has increasingly assumed sectoral and international leadership roles benefiting its status as a stable, democratic nation. Chile is considered the most stable economy in Latin America (Hall, 2009).

Chile and the United States signed a free trade agreement in 2003, the first such pact with a South American country. Chile already had free trade agreements with Bolivia, Canada, CACM, Colombia, EFTA, Ecuador, the EU, Mercosur, Mexico, South Korea, and Venezuela. Chile's retail sector has been very active. Walmart, Topshop, and Zara all have a presence there.

After Argentina gained independence from Spain, in 1816, periods of political conflict limited growth until a return to democracy, in 1983. Argentina began to build on rich natural resources, a highly literate population, an export-oriented agricultural sector, and a diversified industrial base. Rapid-growth economic problems have persisted in the form of inflation, external debt, and budget deficits. After intense problems in 2001, recovery was in place by 2003 (CIA, n.d.). Argentina is a member of Mercosur, which supports duty-free trade of apparel among member countries. Textile and apparel companies are located mainly in the city of Buenos Aires and in the surrounding area. The Argentinean textile market is heavily dependent upon import of synthetic fibers, fabrics, and novelty items, such as accessories. Argentina is one of the fastest growing markets for Indian textiles. It also concentrates heavily on niche products. Argentina's apparel industry is fragmented, and more than 65 percent is run by small family units employing, on an average, 50 people.

Argentina has become a fashion-conscious nation and is a magnet for international retailers. Zara, Harrods, Calvin Klein, Lacoste, Nike, and Yves Saint Laurent have locations here. The leading retailer in Argentina is the French retailing giant Carrefour-Promodes. Forecasts are optimistic for the near future.

Brazil is by far the largest country with the largest population in South America. Brazil became independent of Portugal in 1822 and has recently overcome 50 years of military rule to pursue industrial and agricultural growth. Today, Brazil is South America's leading economic power and regional leader. Its economy outweighs all the other South American countries, and it is expanding its presence in world markets. Brazil's strong economy is based on a floating exchange rate, an inflation-targeting regime, and tight fiscal policy. Problems include increasing domestic and foreign debt and the challenges of increasing employment. Strength in the textile and apparel sector had made Brazil the sixth largest textile and clothing producer in the world by 2006, but achieving that status had been an uneven road. The major strength of its textile market has been cotton, but there has been expansion into production of polyester. Unifi has operations in Brazil, and Santana Textiles is a Brazilian fabric giant that has launched an eco-friendly stretch denim, with Creora elastane.

One issue that had been brewing for several years between the United States and Brazil was settled by WTO arbitration in 2009. Case 10.7 presents this dispute, and the ramifications of the outcome for the United States.

Case 10.7 U.S.: WTO Approves $295M Sanctions in Cotton Row

The U.S. faces millions of dollars worth of retaliatory trade sanctions against its products after a World Trade Organization (WTO) arbitration panel upheld last year's ruling that it paid illegal subsidies to its cotton farmers.

In a decision on Monday (31 August), the WTO panel agreed that Brazil could take retaliatory action against the U.S. totaling around US$295m after deciding the subsidies breach global commerce agreements.

However, this was far less than the $2.7bn requested by Brazil, which launched the initial complaint against the U.S.

"While we remain disappointed with the outcome of this dispute, we are pleased that the arbitrators awarded Brazil far below the amount of countermeasures it asked for," said Carol Guthrie, spokesperson for the United States Trade Representative (USTR).

The arbitrators also denied Brazil's request for an additional one-time $350m in countermeasures in connection with the so-called Step 2 payment program, which gave U.S. exporters and manufacturers an incentive for buying higher-priced cotton from U.S. cotton growers.

The WTO ruled that Brazil can suspend concessions ("impose countermeasures") against U.S. trade but may not impose cross-sectoral countermeasures.

However, the National Cotton Council of America said the ruling doesn't reflect the current market since it was based "almost exclusively on 2005," the peak of U.S. cotton production.

"The U.S. cotton program and export credit guarantee programs have changed considerably since 2005, with U.S. cotton production down 45% and the export credit guarantee program operating at no net cost," said NCC chairman Jon Hardwick. "Today's programs cannot possibly be determined to be causing injury in the world market."

The dispute goes back to 2002, when Brazil accused the U.S. of paying out $12.5bn in subsidies and export credit guarantees to its farmers.

It also alleged the U.S. kept its position as the world's second-biggest cotton producer because of the subsidies.

The U.S., however, maintains it has made the changes necessary and that it has been complying with all WTO rules since 2004.

Source:

U.S.: WTO approves $295m sanctions in cotton row. (2009, September 2). just-style.com. Retrieved February 21, 2010, from http://www.just-style.com/news/wto-approves-295m-sanctions-in-cotton-row_id105222.aspx

Brazil has been leading South America out of the economic crisis and is considered one of the fastest-growing consumer economies in the world. *Women's Wear Daily* identified Brazil, with its $94 billion apparel market, as the top-ranked nation with potential for retail expansion (Hall, 2009). There is a high level of fashion consciousness here, compared with other emerging markets. International retailers currently in Brazil are Zara, 7 for All Mankind, C&A, and Timberland, while luxury firms are working to enter this market. Walmart also has a significant presence here.

Further your understanding of South American trade and apparel with Learning Activity 10.8.

Learning Activity 10.8
SOUTH AMERICA AND ANDEAN PACT

1. In some ways, South America seems more closely tied to Europe than to the United States. Why might that be?
2. What advantages might Colombia have over Caribbean Basin countries because it specializes in fashion rather than basic goods?
3. Why have Costa Rica and Chile been able to develop at a more rapid rate than other Latin American countries?
4. What is the significance of the WTO ruling against the United States, relating to cotton subsidies?
5. What should be done about the Latin American drug problem?
6. Put on your Macy's sourcing professional hat again. Given what you know now, if you were in charge of sourcing for the same moderate-priced, private label line of casual young women's apparel to be imported by Macy's, would you prefer a firm based in Europe or in the Americas. Explain.
7. Which country would you choose for #6? Explain your choice.

SUMMARY

The Americas consist of four primary land areas: North America, Central America, the West Indies, and South America. The United States economically dominates the area, much as the EU dominates Europe. The ranges of measures that describe the economic and industrial standing of countries in the Americas also have much in common with countries in Europe: countries are very large and very small, very rich and very poor.

The Organization of American States (OAS), formed in 1948, was the first effort to unify the political, social, and economic goals of the Americas. The challenge, in part, is the numerous agreements, all with different terms, already in place among countries in the Americas. Another challenge is the difference in cultural values between North American progressive and Latin American traditional cultures. Little action has taken place since 2005.

From a textile and apparel perspective, Canada and the United States have negative trade balances in both textiles and apparel, because they are importing for production and consumption more than they are producing for export. Los Angeles County is the largest apparel production center that remains in the United States. Imports of less expensive Asian textiles have made serious inroads into apparel production in the Americas.

The North American Free Trade Agreement (NAFTA) initially increased the flow of textile and apparel production to Mexico, but some of that growth has almost evaporated, owing to the end of quotas and the poor economy in 2008 and 2009, and Mexico has dropped to sixth in rank of importers into the United States. NAFTA also rapidly increased trade among the three countries, such that they are each other's largest customers and suppliers.

Apparel production in Central America and the Caribbean was developed and continues to be supported by U.S.-initiated trade programs, but some of these countries have also been hard hit with the end of the quota system. The Dominican Republic and Honduras remain major suppliers. The tropical environment of the Caribbean Basin—the combination of Central America and West Indies—represents some of the most famous tourist areas of the world.

South America has two politically unified areas: the Andean sector, in the north, and the Mercosur sector, in the south. Colombia is in the Andean sector and is a major apparel supplier, especially to neighboring nations; it is also the site of a primary apparel trade show. The Mercosur sector represents 70 percent of South America's GDP. Brazil now has one of the world's strongest economies.

REFERENCES

Abbott, J. D., & Moran, R. T. (2002). *Uniting North American business: NAFTA best practices.* Burlington, MA: Elsevier Science.

American Apparel is an industrial revolution. (2009). Retrieved February 19, 2010, from http://www.americanapparel.net/contact/profile/html

Birnbaum, D. (2009, March 10). Economic headwinds take toll on U.S. apparel imports. just-style.com. Retrieved October 14, 2009, from http://www.just-style.com/comment/economic-headwinds-take-toll-on-us-apparel-imports_id103541.aspx

Borneman, J. (2009, September/October). Manufacturing on the move. *Textile World.* Retrieved September 22, 2009, from http://www.textileworld.com

Casabona, L. (2010a, January 29). Haitian industry coming back slowly. *Women's Wear Daily.* Retrieved from http://www.wwd.com/business-news/haitian-industry-coming-back-slowly-2440677//

Casabona, L. (2010b, January 28). People to watch: Jeff Streader. *Women's Wear Daily.* Retrieved from http://www.wwd.com/business-news/people-to-watch-jeff-streader-2438008?gnewsid=af3e60c4ee3592bcc4f676625bdf24a9

Case, B. M. (2004, November 9). Welcoming Wal-Mart to Mexico. *Dallas Morning News.* Retrieved from http://www.dallasnews.com

The Central Intelligence Agency (CIA). (n.d.) *The world factbook.* Retrieved February 6, 2010, from http://www.odci.gov/cia/publications/factbook/index.html.

Deloitte. (2009). *Global powers of retailing 2009.* Retrieved February 16, 2010, from http://public.deloitte.com/media/0460/2009GlobalPowersofRetail_FINAL2.pdf

Feitelberg, R. (2009, October 22). Designers rally to save garment center. *Women's Wear Daily.* Retrieved from http://www.wwd.com/business-news/designers-out-in-force-to-save-the-garment-center-2350947//?full=true

Feitelberg, R., & Moin, D. (2010, January 11). Mayor's office to kick off fashion initiative. *Women's Wear Daily.* Retrieved from http://www.wwd.com/business-news/mayors-office-to-kick-off-fashion-initiative-2406953//?full=true

Freeman, I. C. (2009, November 10). Colombia: Textiles suffering from Venezuelan political row. just-style.com. Retrieved February 21, 2010, from http://www.just-style.com/news/textiles-suffering-from-venezuelan-political-row_id105863.aspx

Freemen, I. C. (2010, January 19). Speaking with style: Carlos Arias, president, Denimatrix. just-style.com. Retrieved February 21, 2010, from http://www.just-style.com/interview/carlos-arias-president-denimatrix_id106466.aspx

Hall, C. (2009, July 2). *WWD* List: Windows of opportunity. *Women's Wear Daily.* Retrieved from http://www.wwd.com

Honduras apparel industry says business as usual. (2009, July 23). just-style.com. Retrieved February 19, 2010, from http://www.just-style.com/comment/honduras-apparel-industry-says-business-as-usual_id104815.aspx

Hudson's Bay Company. (2010). Our history. Retrieved May 31, 2010, from http://www.hbc.com/hbcheritage/history/overview.asp

Industry Canada. (2009). Overview of the Canadian apparel industry: Industry profile. (2009, July 9). Retrieved February 18, 2010, from http://www.ic.gc.ca/eic/site/apparel-vetements.nsf/eng/ap03295.html

Kattan Group of Honduras joins AAPN. (2010). Retrieved March 11, 2010, from http://todaro.posterous.com/kattan-group-of-honduras-joins-aapn

Kurt Salmon Associates. (1999, summer). *Moving to Mexico—The battle against low cost Asian imports.* New York, NY: Author.

Lyons, J. (2005, March 8). El Salvador faces costs of taking the U.S. currency as its own. *The Wall Street Journal.* Retrieved March 8, 2005, from http://www.wsj.com

Maquila Solidarity Network. (2009, October). The crisis and its effect on Mexico's textile and apparel industry. Retrieved June 3, 2010, from http://en.maquilasolidarity.org/sites/maquilasolidarity.org/files/MSN-Crisis_and-Garment_Sector_in_Mexico-2009-10.pdf

NAFTA is positive for Mexico but not enough, says World Bank report. (2003, December 17). The World Bank Group. Retrieved June 1, 2010, from http://web.worldbank.org/WBSITE/EXTERNAL/NEWS/0,,contentMDK:20146245~menuPK:34463~pagePK:64003015~piPK:64003012~theSitePK:4607,00.html

National Cotton Council of America. (2009, March). Frequently asked questions. Retrieved February 18, 2010, from www.cotton.org/edu/faq/

Organization of American States. (n.d.). About the OAS. Retrieved February 15, 2005, from http://www.oas.org/documents/eng/oasinbrief.asp

Ramey, J. (2010, January 14). Mission possible: San Francisco's thriving indie designers. *Women's Wear Daily.* Retrieved from http://www.wwd.com/fashion-news/mission-possible-san-franciscos-thriving-indie-designers-2405947//

Still keeping it in the family. (2004, March 20). *The Economist.* 63–64.

Tait, N. C. (2008, September 8). Colombia hopes to attract more clothing business. just-style.com. Retrieved February 21, 2010, from http://www.just-style.com/analysis/colombia-hopes-to-attract-more-clothing-business_id101720.aspx

Taplin, I. M. (2003). The politics of industrial restructuring: NAFTA and beyond. *Journal of Fashion Marketing and Management, 7*(2), 111–118.

Tran, K. (2010, January 25). Guess: The year ahead. *Women's Wear Daily.* Retrieved from http://www.wwd.com/markets-news/guess-inc-the-year-ahead-2425137

Trends: An annual statistical analysis of the U.S. apparel and footwear industries. (2009, August). Arlington, VA: American Apparel and Footwear Association.

United States textile and apparel industries: An industrial base assessment. (2003, October). U.S. Bureau of Industry and Security and U.S. Department of Commerce. Retrieved from http://www.bis.gov/defenseindustrialbaseprograms/osies/defmarketresearchrpts/textileexecsum03.htm

USA: Post-NAFTA job loss in textiles and apparel exceeds 1mm. (2007, June 2). Retrieved from http://www.fibre2fashion.com/news/daily-textile-industries-news/newsdetails.aspx?news_id=35976

U.S.–CAFTA-DR Trade Agreement: How U.S. companies can benefit. (n.d.). Export.gov. Retrieved June 1, 2010, from http://www.export.gov/FTA/cafta-dr/index.asp

U.S. free trade agreements. (n.d.) Export.gov. Retrieved February 18, 2010, from http://www.export.gov/fta/

U.S.: WTO approves $295m sanctions in cotton row. (2009, September 2). just-style.com. Retrieved February 21, 2010, from http://www.just-style.com/news/wto-approves-295m-sanctions-in-cotton-row_id105222.aspx

VF Corporation. (2010). About VF—Global presence. Retrieved June 2010 from http://www.vfc.com/about/global-presence

Werner International Management Consultants. (2009). *Primary textiles labor cost comparisons 2008.* Retrieved May 25, 2010, from http://texnet.ilgstudios.net/files/2009/08/Werner_International_-_Labor_Cost_Study_2008.pdf

Workman, D. (2007, February 7). World's top free trade country: Mexico leading nation with most privileged export-import deals. Retrieved June 3, 2010, from http://free-trade.suite101.com/article.cfm/worlds_top_free_trade_country

World Trade Organization (WTO. (2009). *International Trade Statistics 2009.* Section 2: Merchandise trade by product, 107–114. Retrieved January 16, 2010, from http://www.wto.org/english/res_e/statis_e/its2009_e/its09_merch_trade_product_e.pdf

11 Asia and Oceania

Keqiao Town, in the Shaoxing region of China, produces 15 billion meters of textiles per year—that's almost 3 meters per capita for the entire world population (Movius, 2009).

ASIA IS THE largest continent, both in terms of size and population, covering almost one third of the world's landmass, with countries ranging from fully developed to least developed. Oceania, located in the Southern Hemisphere, is small by comparison but is closely connected to Asia economically. The world's highest mountains, longest rivers, largest deserts, and thickest jungles are all in Asia. Political systems in the regions range from democratic and communist governments to those ruled by kings, sheiks, and sultans. The civilization in Asia is ancient compared with those of Europe, the Americas, and Oceania. Yet, when the Industrial Revolution occurred in the Western Hemisphere, the result was rapid economic development that left Asia's traditional cultures intact. China, the country with the greatest population in the world, is now the largest trading nation in the world (value of imports plus value of exports), followed by the United States, Japan, and Germany (World Trade Organization [WTO], 2009).

The world's two most populous nations, China and India, each with more than a billion individuals living within their borders, are located in Asia. Half of the Asian continent's countries have populations smaller than that of New York City, including Macau, which is an apparel supplier country with a population of fewer than one million

Objectives

- Comprehend the magnitude of Asia as a political and economic trading bloc.

- Appreciate the economic and political positions of individual countries within Asia.

- Examine the status of the textile and apparel business in selected Asian countries.

- Project textile and apparel trading trends for Asian countries into the period following the phaseout of the quota system.

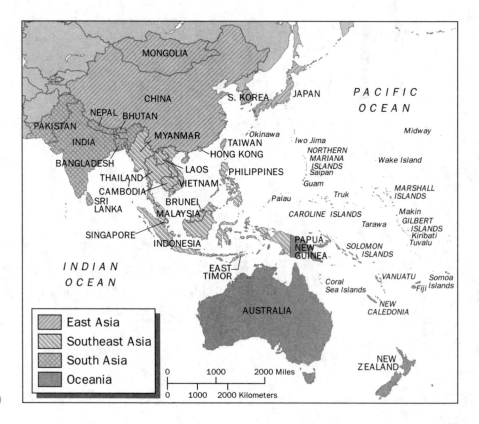

Figure 11.1 This map highlights the four subsectors of the Asian trade region: East Asia, Southeast Asia, South Asia, and Oceania.

(Courtesy Fairchild Books)

people. In contrast, Oceania is made up primarily of two developed island countries, Australia and New Zealand, with a total population comparable to only one of Asia's smaller countries.

POLITICAL AND ECONOMIC OVERVIEW

Figure 11.1 is a map of the geographic regions, and their subsectors, that are discussed in this chapter. For our purposes, Asia and Oceania have been subdivided into the following four groups of nations:

- East Asia, represented by China, South Korea, Taiwan, and Japan
- Southeast Asia, including Hong Kong and eight of the ten ASEAN (Association of Southeast Asian Nations) countries
- South Asia, from Pakistan to Bangladesh
- Oceania, made up of Australia and New Zealand

Table 11.1 MEMBERSHIP IN ASIA-PACIFIC ECONOMIC COOPERATION (APEC)—
THE "PACIFIC RIM" COUNTRIES

East Asia	Southeast Asia
China	Singapore
Japan	Brunei
South Korea	Hong Kong, China
Taiwan (Chinese Taipei)	Indonesia
North Asia	Malaysia
Russia	Papua New Guinea
North America	The Philippines
Canada	Thailand
Mexico	Vietnam
United States	**Oceania**
South America	Australia
Chile	New Zealand
Peru	

Russia and Turkey have land areas in both Europe and Asia. (Russia was discussed with Europe, because most of the population of Russia is located primarily in Europe; Turkey is discussed with the Middle East; see Chapters 9 and 12.) As we progress through this chapter, please refer back to the map (Figure 11.1) as each region or nation is introduced, to clarify its location in your mind and identify its neighbors.

Asian Regional Collaboration

The **Asia-Pacific Economic Cooperation (APEC)** was established in 1989 as a forum for facilitating economic growth, cooperation, trade, and investment in the Asia-Pacific region. APEC has 21 member nations that extend beyond Asia, to North and South America and Oceania. Table 11.1 provides a list of member nations. The region served by APEC is sometimes called the Pacific Rim, an area very deeply involved in the trade of textiles and apparel. APEC's member econo-

mies account for more than 41 percent of the global population, 54 percent of the world GDP, and about 44 percent of global trade (Asia-Pacific Economic Cooperation, n.d.).

Read Case 11.1 for a presentation by APEC leaders, in November 2009, of a growth and supply chain paradigm for the Asia-Pacific region.

APEC is similar to the OAS (Organization of American States), in that dialogue among APEC members does not produce treaty obligations or binding commitments; rather, members reach consensus and make commitments on a voluntary basis. APEC's first efforts were to increase trade by reducing trade barriers, including tariffs in countries located on the Pacific Rim. APEC's goal of free and open trade and investment not only fosters economic growth, but also creates jobs and helps lower costs of goods and services. Furthermore, this goal helps create an environment for the safe and efficient movement of goods, services, and people across borders in the region. However, many

We, the Leaders of APEC, gathered in Singapore to chart a new growth paradigm for the Asia-Pacific region that meets the needs of the 21st-century global economy.

The global economy has begun to recover, with the Asia-Pacific region taking the lead. But we cannot go back to "growth as usual" or "trade as usual." The post-crisis landscape will be different. We need a new growth paradigm. We need a fresh model of economic integration. . . .

We endorse the goals of the G-20 Framework for Strong, Sustainable and Balanced Growth. Representing the economically most dynamic region in the world and accounting for half of global trade and output, APEC is well placed to provide the momentum necessary to achieve these goals:

Balanced Growth. Strong and sustained economic growth will require structural reforms to gradually unwind global imbalances and raise the potential output of our economies. . . .

Inclusive Growth. To achieve inclusive growth, we must broaden access to economic opportunities and build the resilience of the most vulnerable against economic shocks. . . .

Sustainable Growth. Future growth must be compatible with global efforts to protect the environment and mitigate climate change. At the same time, efforts to address climate change must be consistent with our international trade obligations. . . .

We will take a comprehensive approach to build a 21st century model of economic integration that will combine trade liberalisation *"at the border,"* improve the business environment *"behind the border,"* and enhance supply chain connectivity *"across the border."*

"At the Border" Liberalisation. We will continue to explore building blocks toward a possible Free Trade Area of the Asia-Pacific in the future. . . .

"Behind the Border" Structural Reforms. A key component of our structural reform efforts to reduce regulatory impediments is the Ease of Doing Business Action Plan.

We will strive to achieve by 2015 a collective 25% reduction in the cost, time, and number of procedures that our businesses face when starting a business, getting credit, enforcing contracts, dealing with permits, and trading across borders.

We will reduce business transaction costs by 5% by 2010, having already achieved a cost reduction of 3.2% between 2006 and 2008 through the Trade Facilitation Action Plan II.

"Across the Border" Connectivity. APEC's Supply Chain Connectivity Initiative has identified eight key chokepoints in regional supply chains and actions to address them.

We will explore how to enhance multi-modal connectivity by air, sea, and land, to facilitate a more seamless flow of goods and services and business travelers throughout the Asia-Pacific.

Source:

APEC: A new growth paradigm for a connected Asia-Pacific in the 21st century. Retrieved February 10, 2010, from http://www.whitehouse.gov/the-press-office/statement-apec-leaders

countries still resist a comprehensive agreement that extends across the regions and that could greatly simplify the trade process.

Among Asian and Oceania countries, across-the-border connectivity in the form of regional and bilateral trade agreements is already in place, with many more on the horizon. By one count, in 1991, there were just 6 regional/bilateral agreements; in 1999, there were 42; in 2009 there were 166, with more than 60 others in various stages of negotiation. However, this multitude of trade agreements did not generate the increases in trade that were anticipated. Trade barriers (primarily in the form of tariffs) within Asia were, for the most part, already relatively low, and many of the new trade agreements conflict with each other. Because of the conflicts, these trade agreements may be used only about 20 percent of the time (WTO, 2009).

Economic and Industrial Standing of Countries in Regions of Asia and Oceania

Focus on the first two columns of Table 11.2, geographic size and population. China wins the world size race, with by far the largest population. India is second to China in population. Russia is the largest nation geographically, but since part of its area is in Europe, we look to China as being the largest Asian nation discussed here. Australia is second in size but has a comparatively small population, somewhat similar to Canada in both measures. Two of these nations are very tiny: Hong Kong, in East Asia, and Singapore, in South Asia.

Focus on columns 3, life expectancy, and 4, adult literacy. Note that, as with other parts of the world, longer life expectancies tend to be associated with higher levels of literacy. In general, East Asia and Oceania have longer life expectancies and higher literacy rates than do Southeast Asia and South Asia. Less than 50 percent of the population is literate in

three of the five countries in South Asia, the exceptions being India and Sri Lanka. Oceania and Japan have the highest literacy rates among the countries in the table, comparable to developed countries in the Northern Hemisphere in other parts of the world.

Consider column 5, gross domestic product (GDP). Based on GDP, China has the second largest economy in the world (the United States has the largest), followed by Japan, Germany, and India. A study comparing the evolving economies of India and China indicates some significant differences between them. Industry makes up only 4 percent of India's overall GDP, reflecting an economy that sort of jumped over industrialization, going directly from an agriculturally based economy to a service-based economy ("Survey of India and China," 2005). At the same time China shows a pattern of change from farming to labor-intensive manufacturing. Some economists find China to be an oddity, in that its service sector seems "stunted" compared with other growing economies, but its industrial economy certainly is not.

Recall the system presented previously for ranking countries according to level of development, using per capita GDP (see Chapter 1). Each of the regions of the world reviewed so far exhibit different patterns of economic development and overall well-being. Most of the European countries examined are relatively rich developed countries, some are relatively well-off developing countries, and a few are relatively poor developing countries. Only two American/Caribbean Basin countries are very rich and only two are very poor; most are relatively poor developing countries.

Within the Asian/Oceania region, according to the per capita GDP presented in column 6, there are three countries that are among the most fully developed nations on the planet: Japan, Australia, and New Zealand. All the countries of East Asia are in the "developed" category, with per capita GDPs

Table 11.2 CHARACTERISTICS OF SELECTED COUNTRIES IN ASIA AND OCEANIA
THAT ARE ACTIVE IN THE TEXTILE AND APPAREL TRADE

Country	Geographic Size (Square Kilometers, in Thousands)	Population (in Millions)	Life Expectancy (in Years)	Adult Literacy (in Percentages)
East Asia				
China	9,569.9	1,338.6	73.5	90.9%
Hong Kong	1.1	7.1	81.7	93.5%
Japan	377.9	127.1	82.1	99.0%
Macao	0.03	0.6	84.4	91.3%
South Korea	99.7	48.5	78.7	97.9%
Taiwan/Taipei	36.0	23.0	78.0	96.1%
Southeast Asia				
Cambodia	181.0	14.5	62.1	73.6%
Indonesia	1,904.6	240.3	70.8	90.4%
Malaysia	329.8	25.7	73.3	88.7%
Philippines	300.0	98.0	71.1	92.6%
Singapore	0.7	4.6	82.0	92.5%
Thailand	513.1	66.0	73.1	92.6%
Vietnam	331.2	88.6	71.7	90.3%
South Asia				
Bangladesh	144.0	156.1	60.3	47.9%
India	3,287.3	1,157.9	66.1	73.4%
Nepal	147.2	28.6	65.5	48.6%
Pakistan	796.1	174.6	65.3	49.9%
Sri Lanka	65.6	21.3	75.1	90.7%
Oceania				
Australia	7,741.2	21.3	81.6	99.0%
New Zealand	267.7	4.2	80.4	99.0%

GDP (in Billions U.S. Dollars)[a]	Per Capita GDP[b]	Inflation Rate (in Percentage)[c]	Labor Force (in Millions)	Unemployment Rate (in Percentage)	Internet Users (in Millions)
$ 8,767.0	$ 6,500	−0.8%	812.7	4.3%	298.0
$ 301.3	$ 42,700	−0.3%	3.7	5.9%	4.1
$ 4,141.0	$ 32,600	−1.3%	66.0	5.6%	90.9
$ 18.1	$ 30,000	6.2%	0.3	3.0%	0.3
$ 1,343.0	$ 27,700	2.8%	24.4	4.1%	37.5
$ 693.3	$ 30,200	0.7%	10.9	6.4%	15.1
$ 27.9	$ 1,900	−1.2%	8.6	3.5%	0.07
$ 514.9	$ 4,000	5.0%	113.3	7.7%	30.0
$ 378.9	$ 14,700	0.4%	11.3	5.0%	16.9
$ 327.2	$ 3,300	3.0%	37.7	8.0%	5.6
$ 234.5	$ 50,300	0.5%	2.9	3.4%	3.4
$ 535.8	$ 8,100	−0.9%	38.1	2.7%	16.1
$ 256.0	$ 2,900	7.3%	47.7	6.5%	20.8
$ 242.2	$ 1,600	5.1%	72.5	2.5%	0.6
$ 3,548.0	$ 3,100	9.8%	467.0	9.5%	81.0
$ 33.3	$ 1,200	13.2%	18.0	46.0%	0.5
$ 448.1	$ 2,600	14.2%	55.9	15.2%	18.5
$ 96.8	$ 4,500	3.3%	7.6	7.0%	1.2
$ 819.0	$ 38,500	1.9%	11.4	5.7%	15.2
$ 116.5	$ 27,700	1.8%	2.3	7.3%	3.1

Source: Estimates of 2009 data from Central Intelligence Agency (CIA). (2010). *The world factbook.*
Retrieved February 2010 from http://www.odci.gov/cia/publications/factbook/index.ht
a. GDP, in purchasing power parity.
b. Official data for urban areas only; considerable underemployment and unemployment in rural areas.
c. Consumer prices.

of more than 20 thousand dollars, except China, which is in the "newly developing" category, well under 10 thousand dollars. Except for Singapore (developed) and Malaysia and Sri Lanka (developing), Southeast Asia and South Asia have a combination of five newly developing and five least developed countries, with per capita GDPs of less than 3 thousand dollars. There were two least developed countries in the Americas and none among the countries considered in Europe.

Considering Columns 8, 9, and 10, unemployment rates appear similar to what we have seen for other parts of the world, with higher rates for some of the poorest countries. Labor force displays the number of people available to generate the GDP. China's 800 million potential laborers make it easy to see how it has become the manufacturer to the world. Unemployment rates are also similar to what we have seen in other parts of the world, although the reports for China are likely to include only the urban unemployment, excluding what could be millions of additional unemployed workers in rural areas. Note what a small proportion of the population uses the Internet, a sure sign of a lower level of development. For example, China has 298 million Internet users, of more than 1 billion in population. When you look at the other three parts of the world together (Europe, the Americas, and Asia), it is easy to see that only a few developed countries are in the Americas and Asia; most are in Europe, but their combined GDP is less than that of the United States.

Overall, for Asia and Oceania, Oceania is rich; East Asia is relatively rich, except for China; Southeast Asia is relatively poor, except for Singapore; and South Asia is poor. In fact, comparing the world regions we have examined so far, South Asia is by far the poorest. Most of the newly developing countries are in the Americas and Asia, and that is where most apparel production is now based.

Complete this political and economic overview of Asia and Oceania with Learning Activity 11.1.

Learning Activity 11.1
POLITICAL AND ECONOMIC
SCENARIO IN ASIA AND OCEANIA

1. What are the four major sectors within the Asian trading region? Locate them on the map shown in Figure 11.1.
2. What are the major countries located in each of the sectors identified in question 1? Which countries have common boundaries?
3. Compare the overall functions of the EU, OAS, and APEC. Which one contributes to the opportunities for development of the textile and apparel business?
4. In Table 11.2, choose two countries in the "least developed" category. For each country, answer the following questions:
5. What criteria did you use to choose these countries?
6. What other information presented for these countries convinces you that these are least developed countries?
7. Calculate the percentage of Internet users for the population of each country listed in Table 11.2.
8. According to your numbers, which five countries have the highest percentage of Internet users?
9. Assuming that a higher percentage of Internet users is an indicator of higher technology development throughout a country, what other indicators are available in the data for the same countries to support that assumption?
10. How do the percentages of Internet users compare with the percentages of Internet users in European countries?
11. If you were a retail telemarketer, would you be more interested in developing your business in Europe, the Americas, or Asia? Which region would be your first target? Why?

OVERVIEW OF ASIAN
TEXTILE AND APPAREL TRADE

As discussed previously, a significant portion of production capacity in textiles and apparel has moved from developed nations, countries in western Europe and the Americas, to developing countries (see Chapters 9 and 10). The migration of textile and apparel production to areas with lower labor costs in Asia began more than 60 years ago, when Japan first assumed the role of low-cost producer of many products, including textiles and apparel. During the 1970s, as Japan developed, and production costs increased, Hong Kong, Taiwan, and South Korea (as newly developing countries) took over the position of leading exporters of low-cost apparel. At the same time, the United Kingdom (UK) and the United States initiated the Multifiber Arrangement (MFA) to protect domestic production, but the trend of moving apparel production to newly developing countries continued. Japan progressed rapidly and turned to other, more technical and lucrative forms of industrialization in place of textile and apparel production.

At their peak in the early 1980s, despite quotas, Hong Kong, Taiwan, and South Korea (the "big three") supplied almost 30 percent of world exports of textile and apparel products. However, wages began to increase in the big three as these countries developed, again making room for production in nations with lower labor costs. Then a new generation of low-cost exporting countries emerged. China was the leader, teaming with the big three, to make it the "big four." India, Pakistan, Indonesia, the Philippines, and Thailand also became major suppliers.

More quotas were imposed by importing nations on the new exporters, creating opportunities for another wave of emerging suppliers, including Bangladesh, Macau, and Sri Lanka. This movement toward lower-labor-cost nations is referred to by economists, such

as Pietra Rivoli, as the "race to the bottom," that is, the bottom of labor costs (Rivoli, 2009). For many newly developing and developing Asian nations, their textile and apparel industries are a significant source of employment and export earnings. However, when China gained membership in the WTO, in 2001, that nation became the dominant apparel supplier in the world. In 2005, the WTO-mandated termination of the MFA brought the end to most quotas, and caused considerable apprehension among participating nations. The EU and the United States fought for extensions on some categories of apparel from China and got them, but by the end of 2008 those quota extensions also ran out. Vietnam entered the picture during the decade, and as a new WTO member in 2007 benefited from the end of quota restrictions on their textile and apparel products.

Tables 11.3a and 11.3b are similar in structure to those presented in Chapters 9 and 10 (see Tables 9.4a, 9.4b, 10.4a, and 10.4b). They show, for 2000, 2006, and 2008, textile and apparel imports (Table 11.3a) and textile and apparel exports (Table 11.3b). The last two columns of each table present the share of total textile and apparel imports or exports in each country's total merchandise trade. These tables are organized by region: East Asia, Southeast Asia, South Asia, and Oceania.

Consider the countries in East Asia. Between 2000 and 2008, China increased both its textile and apparel imports, but the quantity for textile imports slightly decreased in 2008. Over the previous 10 years, China built its internal textile production capacity, so when the economy slowed down, China decreased its imports of textiles in order to keep its domestic plants running. Chinese textile exports reflect the buildup of production capacity that results from supplying fabrics for many other countries. Textile imports and exports of other East Asian countries are relatively level, with some increases and decreases. It is important to remember that business success is measured by increases.

Table 11.3a IMPORTS OF TEXTILES AND APPAREL BY ASIAN COUNTRIES, IN MILLIONS OF U.S. DOLLARS, AND TEXTILES AND APPAREL AS A PERCENTAGE OF EACH COUNTRY'S TOTAL MERCHANDISE IMPORTS

Region and Country	Textile Imports (in Millions of U.S. Dollars)			Apparel Imports (in Millions of U.S. Dollars)			Percentage Share of Total Textile and Apparel Imports	
	2000	2006	2008	2000	2006	2008	2000	2008
East Asia								
China[b]	$ 12,832	$ 16,358	$ 16,228	$ 1,192	$ 1,724	$ 2,282	6.2%	1.6%
Hong Kong[b]	$ 13,716	$ 13,975	$ 12,313	$ 16,008	$ 18,852	$ 18,546	13.4%	8.1%
Japan	$ 4,935	$ 6,176	$ 6,297	$ 19,709	$ 23,831	$ 25,866	6.5%	4.3%
Macao	$ 902	$ 618	$ 310	$ 214	$ 1,056	$ 872	49.5%	22.1%
South Korea	$ 3,359	$ 4,909	$ 4,112	$ 1,307	$ 3,744	$ 4,223	2.9%	1.9%
Taiwan/Taipei	$ 1,630	$ 2,059	$ 2,444	$ 978	$ 1,223	$ 1,171	3.3%	1.9%
Southeast Asia								
Cambodia	$ 432	$ 1,202	—[c]	—	—	—	22.3%	24.9%
Indonesia	$ 1,251	$ 730	$ 3,262	—	—	—	2.9%	2.6%
Malaysia[b]	$ 1,114	$ 1,063	$ 1,121	$ 148	$ 359	$ 492	1.6%	1.0%
Philippines[b]	$ 1,250	$ 1,244	$ 873	—	—	—	3.4%	1.4%
Singapore[b]	$ 1,275	$ 1,101	$ 1,193	$ 1,881	$ 2,497	$ 2,224	2.3%	1.1%
Thailand	$ 1,630	$ 2,059	$ 2,444	$ 131	$ 276	$ 392	2.8%	1.6%
Vietnam	$ 1,379	$ 3,988	$ 6,048	$ 450	$ 271	$ 446	11.7%	8.1%
South Asia								
Bangladesh	$ 1,350	$ 1,538	$ 1,546	$ 174	$ 168	$ 252	17.2%	7.6%
India	$ 578	$ 1,972	$ 2,322	—	—	—	1.1%	0.8%
Nepal	—	—	—	—	—	—	—	—
Pakistan	$ 130	$ 551	$ 589	—	—	—	1.2%	1.4%
Sri Lanka	$ 1,483	$ 1,540	$ 1,694	—	—	—	20.7%	12.1%
Oceania								
Australia	$ 1,632	$ 2,051	$ 2,210	$ 1,858	$ 3,279	$ 4,280	4.9%	3.4%
New Zealand	$ 369	$ 506	$ 537	$ 401	$ 740	$ 914	5.6%	4.3%

Source: World Trade Organization (WTO). (2009). International Trade Statistics 2009. Section 2: Merchandise trade by product (107–114). Retrieved January 16, 2010, from http://www.wto.org/english/res_e/statis_e/its2009_e/its09_merch_trade_product_e.pdf
a. Data not available.
b. Includes imports into processing zones.

Table 11.3b Exports of Textiles and Apparel by Asian Countries, in Millions of U.S. Dollars, and Textiles and Apparel as a Percentage of Each Country's Total Merchandise Exports

Region and Country	Textile Exports (in Millions of U.S. Dollars)			Apparel Exports (in Millions of U.S. Dollars)			Percentage Share of Textile and Apparel Exports	
	2000	2006	2008	2000	2006	2008	2000	2008
East Asia								
China[b]	$ 16,135	$ 48,678	$ 65,256	$ 36,071	$ 95,579	$ 119,978	21.0%	13%
Hong Kong[b]	$ 13,441	$ 13,910	$ 12,256	$ 24,214	$ 28,391	$ 27,908	18.5%	10.8%
Japan	$ 7,023	$ 6,934	$ 7,340	$ 534	$ 485	$ 591	1.6%	1.0%
Macao	$ 272	$ 242	$ 107	$ 1,849	$ 1,610	$ 1,053	83.5%	58.1%
South Korea	$ 12,710	$ 10,110	$ 10,371	$ 5,027	$ 2,183	$ 1,741	10.3%	2.9%
Taiwan/Taipei	$ 11,891	$ 9,780	$ 9,220	$ 3,015	$ 1,410	$ 1,190	7.1%	3.8%
Southeast Asia								
Cambodia	—[c]	—	—	$ 970	$ 1,798	$ 3,645	69.8%	84.8%
Indonesia	$ 3,505	$ 3,614	$ 3,675	$ 4,734	$ 5,760	$ 6,285	9.9%	4.9%
Malaysia[b]	$ 1,270	$ 1,437	$ 1,549	$ 2,257	$ 2,842	$ 3,624	3.6%	2.6%
Philippines[b]	$ 297	$ 239	$ 554	$ 2,536	$ 2,624	$ 1,979	.7%	5.4%
Singapore[b]	$ 907	$ 911	$ 885	$ 1,825	$ 1,983	$ 1,557	2.0%	.8%
Thailand	$ 1,958	$ 2,873	$ 3,211	$ 3,759	$ 4,247	$ 4,241	8.2%	4.2%
Vietnam	$ 299	$ 1,058	$ 1,639	$ 1,821	$ 5,579	$ 8,971	14.7%	16.9%
South Asia								
Bangladesh	$ 393	$ 1,494	$ 1,090	$ 5,967	$ 8,318	$ 10,920	85.5%	78.2%
India	$ 5,570	$ 3,614	$ 10,267	$ 5,960	$ 9,499	$ 10,854	27.1%	11.9%
Nepal	$ 182	$ 157	$ 185	—	—	—	22.7%	17.6%
Pakistan	$ 4,532	$ 7,469	$ 7,186	$ 2,144	$ 3,907	$ 3,906	74.0%	54.6%
Sri Lanka	$ 244	$ 154	$ 188	$ 2,812	$ 3,046	$ 3,460	56.3%	43.1%
Oceania								
Australia	$ 347	$ 312	$ 319	—	—	—	.5%	.2%
New Zealand	$ 142	$ 262	$ 280	—	—	—	1.1%	.9%

Source: World Trade Organization (WTO). (2009). International Trade Statistics 2009. Section 2: Merchandise trade by product (107–114). Retrieved January 16, 2010, from http://www.wto.org/english/res_e/statis_e/its2009_e/its09_merch_trade_product_e.pdf
a. Data not available.
b. Includes imports into processing zones.

China apparel imports increased slightly, but exports tripled to nearly $120 billion, overtaking the EU, with "only" $112 billion (keeping in mind that almost $85 billion of that was among EU members). No other countries in the world exceeded $10 billion in apparel exports, except Hong Kong, with about $28 billion, and Bangladesh and India, with about $11 billion. All the East Asian countries show increases in apparel imports, whereas exports for Macao, South Korea, and Taiwan decreased rather dramatically. The growth of their economies had increased production costs, so these countries could not compete with China.

Among Southeast Asian nations, Singapore is unique, a tiny developed country actively engaged in the textile and apparel trade. Singapore has increases in textile and apparel imports but decreases in textile and apparel exports, a pattern consistent with other developed countries. For other Southeast Asian nations, textile trade was erratic; some countries had increases and others, decreases in both apparel imports and exports. Cambodia and Vietnam were the growing kids on the block. Vietnam shows dramatic increases in textile imports and exports as well as a quadrupling of apparel exports. Southeast Asian countries had increases in textile imports, but only Bangladesh had data reflecting an increase in imports of apparel. Nepal shows no data, which may be due to political unrest. Textile exporting was a growing industry, except in Sri Lanka. Apparel exports for Bangladesh and India nearly doubled whereas Pakistan and Sri Lanka had some increase.

Oceania is represented by a pair of developed countries, Australia and New Zealand. Both have increasing textile and apparel imports. These countries are exporting textile products, primarily in the form of wool, but reflect no exports of apparel in amounts comparable to the other nations included here. Both countries exhibit the typical import and export patterns of developed countries.

Considering percentage share of textile and apparel imports, look at the exports table first. Numbers indicate the level of economic dependence a country has on the textile and apparel industries. All the countries in East Asia are less dependent on textiles and apparel in 2008 than they were in 2000. This suggests that industries in those countries have become more diversified. In Southeast Asia, four countries are less dependent, three are more dependent. Dependence on these exports in South Asia is the highest for the region but had lessened somewhat by 2008, even though exports were increasing.

Apparel manufacturers and retailers in many developed countries, including the United States, are expected to consolidate their purchasing activity to fewer nations as a way of simplifying their task and achieving benefits of economy of scale. For example, at one point a few years ago Liz Claiborne was sourcing from more than 60 countries. That number was reduced to about 30 as quota restrictions were lifted. However, today the firm is using Li & Fung and JC Penney for much of its sourcing activities, so we are unable to determine easily its current pattern of sourcing.

Adjustments are still being made to sourcing patterns since the elimination of MFA quotas. As we enter the second decade of the 21st century, we can observe that the big three turned into the big four, and now there is the "big one." Each of the earlier production powerhouses was dominant for at least a decade before growing out of the role. It will be very interesting to see how long China will maintain its completely dominant status as the world's major apparel producer. In sum, in the foreseeable future China (in the short term) and Asia (in the long term) are likely to remain the world's largest producers and exporters of textiles and apparel.

Now, complete your overview of the Asian textile and apparel trade with Learning Activity 11.2.

Learning Activity 11.2
OVERVIEW OF ASIAN TEXTILE AND APPAREL TRADE

1. Using the Tables 11.1 to 11.3, identify which nations are primarily consumer/importer nations within each region of Asia and Oceania. What criteria did you use to make your choices?
2. Identify which nations are primarily exporting nations economically dependent on textiles or apparel, or both, within each region. What criteria did you use to make your choices?
3. In Table 11.3, for cases in which both textile imports and apparel exports are high, what does that indicate, in terms of vertical integration of the industry?
4. Considering the data presented in Tables 11.2 and 11.3, which three or four Asian countries will take the lead in assuming some of China's responsibilities in the textile and apparel business?
5. On what bits of data did you base your decision for question 4? Why did you choose those criteria?

PARTICIPATION OF ASIAN COUNTRIES IN TEXTILES AND APPAREL
....

The WTO's elimination of quotas between MFA member nations fostered changes in the patterns of production, trade, and consumption of textile and apparel products for Asian nations and in other parts of the globe. Perhaps the following statement can communicate the impact of the elimination of quotas:

Quota rights were traded like a commodity in China, and at times represented half the cost of a garment or more. The expiration of those quota charges has been one factor causing importer executives to predict that garment prices could drop by 15% to 30% the following year (Malone & Ellis, 2004, pp. 10–11).

By early 2005, some minor reductions in prices had manifested themselves in China, along with an explosion of its exports into developed country markets. Then, of course, quota was reinstated on many categories until 2008, delaying the impact of elimination of the costs involved in the quota market.

With quota system eliminated, competitiveness of nations as sources of textile and apparel production was expected to shift from quota-based restrictions to other factors, including the following:

- tariff structures
- social responsibility
- security of shipping
- a country's overall business climate
- infrastructure conditions and logistics
- proximity and access to major import markets
- availability of low-cost, skilled workers
- effective management
- appropriateness of product quality
- access to reliable supply of competitively priced materials
- reliability of delivery, according to specifications
- levels of supplier service (*Textiles and Apparel*, 2004)

Obviously, there are many ways to influence levels of trade besides the quota system.

Among the expectations listed, several have already become priorities. Many of those items contribute to the sustainability of supply chains, which in 2010 was the most frequently mentioned priority of textile and apparel firms. Several items have been discussed at appropriate times earlier in

Table 11.4 LABOR COSTS PER HOUR FOR TEXTILE PRODUCTION IN SELECTED ASIAN AND OCEANIAN COUNTRIES, COMPARED WITH U.S. LABOR COSTS CONSIDERING DIRECT WAGES AND SOCIAL COSTS[a]

Country	Total Labor Costs (in U.S. Dollars)	Total Labor Costs as a Percentage of U.S. Labor Costs[b]	Total Labor Costs (in Local Currency)	Direct Wages (in Local Currency)	Social Costs (in Local Currency)	Social Costs as a Percentage of Direct Wages[c]
Asia						
Japan	$ 30.81	177%	2,760	1,650	1,110	67%
United States	$ 17.41	100%	$ 17.41	$ 13.52	$ 3.89	29%
Taiwan/Taipei	$ 7.89	45%	257	183	74	40%
South Korea	$ 6.31	36%	8,420	7,400	1,020	14%
China—Coastal	$ 1.88	11%	12.77	8.93	3.84	39%
Thailand	$ 1.80	10%	62	55.98	6.02	11%
Malaysia	$ 1.57	9%	5	3.64	1.36	37%
China—Inland	$ 1.44	8%	9.81	6.74	3.07	46%
India	$ 0.85	5%	40.97	31.34	9.63	31%
Indonesia	$ 0.83	5%	9,160	7,000	2,160	31%
Vietnam	$ 0.57	3%	9,912	7,812	2,100	27%
Pakistan	$ 0.56	3%	44	34.18	9.82	29%
Bangladesh	$ 0.31	2%	21.18	19.08	2.10	11%
Oceania						
Australia	$ 23.13	139%	34.75	25.60	9.15	36%
United States	$ 17.41	100%	$ 17.41	$ 13.52	$ 3.89	29%
New Zealand	$ 11.21	64%	19.40	15.20	4.20	27%

Source: Werner International Management Consultants. (2009). *Primary textiles labor cost comparisons 2008.*
Retrieved May 25, 2010, from http://texnet.ilgstudios.net/files/2009/08/Werner_International_-_Labor_Cost_Study_2008.pdf
a. Total labor costs per hour = direct wages per hour + social costs per hour.
b. In U.S. dollars, total labor costs per hour as a percentage of U.S. labor costs per hour = a country's labor cost per hour ÷ U.S. labor cost per hour x 100.
c. In local currency, social costs as a percentage of direct wages = social costs ÷ direct wages x 100.

this text and they will continue to come up. Right now, regarding Asia and Oceania, we will focus on two: availability of low-cost skilled workers and social responsibility, as represented by social costs. Note that total labor costs in China are divided to show the difference between coastal and inland China workers (Table 11.4).

High domestic labor costs have forced many firms in developed nations to seek production or finished products in countries with lower labor costs. As you now know, looking only at wage rates severely underestimates total labor costs and distorts actual perception of labor costs. Social responsibility costs also have to be considered. In Table 11.4, when expressed in U.S. dollars, some of these labor costs seem unreasonably low and not at a level that could be regarded as a living wage. It is important to remember that many people in the United States are paid the U.S. minimum wage for work (that sometimes includes apparel production processes and retail sales), and that is not a living wage either.

Total labor costs per hour in Asia range from $30.81 in Japan to $0.31 in Bangladesh. Oceania labor costs rank within the top three in Asia. Total labor costs in Japan are almost double those of the United States, and the United States is almost double those of Taiwan and South Korea (whose costs are quite close to the U.S. minimum wage). From there on, costs are less than $2 an hour. Look at the center column, "Total Labor Costs as a Percentage of U.S. Labor Costs." Japan's wages are 177 percent of the United States'; only four other countries are more than 4 percent of U.S. wages.

Social costs range from 67 percent of total costs, in Japan, down to 11 percent, in Thailand and Bangladesh. That means that in Japan take-home pay is $10.17 an hour; in Bangladesh it is $.30 (one penny is held back for insurance and medical care or for any other costs the employer wishes to impose).

Beyond the wage rates and social costs, many other things factor into the cost of production. Rates of productivity, including sewing skills, culturally influenced work patterns, and availability of viable production equipment are also factors contributing to labor costs. These factors vary significantly among countries and influence not only the amount, but also the types and quality, of products that can be produced. Asia, most particularly China, is considered to have a highly skilled labor force that can provide complex sewing and construction details appropriate for diverse apparel goods. This makes a nation a highly desirable source for export products.

Availability of cost-competitive and high-quality fabrics and trim within a country or region is expected to become a more important factor in determining where importing nations will go to secure finished apparel in the competitive postquota era. China seems to have the advantage in avail-

ability of fabrics, trims, and findings, because most materials needed to construct garments are produced there. If the fabrics must be imported, most are available in surrounding Asian countries. However, shipping times and other logistics issues, such as customs service practices, especially tariff rates, can affect the lead time required for delivery and the costs of finished apparel products.

Several Asian nations have also improved their capabilities by seeking capital and technical assistance from more advanced economies. The result is improved competitiveness in critical areas, such as providing one's own materials, coordinating production to improve quality and time to market, and wholesale marketing of finished goods.

The level of service required by suppliers is also a consideration in the selection of a country for procuring products. Countries in East Asia, in particular, seem to have high levels of some of the services that encourage others to source there, including more comprehensive product development and pattern making services, customized packaging, and more reliable quality control and logistics arrangements. At the other end of the spectrum are nations in which political unrest and security issues have become increasing threats to doing business.

The textile and apparel industry is a key source of output and job growth in many developing countries and provides them with capital to foster further economic gains in other areas. One of the by-products of innovation within the industry as a whole has been that in some developing countries, employment figures may have dropped, but productivity has increased because of technical advancements, just as it did years ago in developed countries. Even with these advancements, however, the apparel industry remains a largely labor-intensive sector and a major employer in many developing nations.

As the effects of the economic downturn began to become known in 2009 and

Table 11.5 SUMMARY OF WORLD VIEWS BETWEEN EASTERN AND WESTERN CULTURES

World Views	Eastern Culture	Western Culture
Thinking patterns	Spiral (holistic)	Linear
Communication	Implied and subtle	Explicit and direct
Goals/Success	We/Us-oriented; meeting group goals and working for group success	I/Me-oriented; focusing on individual achievement
Self-Expression	Subtle and nonverbal	Overt; people are asked to "speak their mind"
Time sense for meetings	Appointments less driven by exact start and end times	Arrive on time, and end on time
Business relationships	Taking time to develop sound relationships; hard to form but usually long lasting	Written agreement is important; easy to form but not necessarily long lasting

Source: Jung, J. (2009, February). Doing business the Chinese way: Eastern and Western world view and business practices in China. *Fiber: Online Journal of the International Fashion and Apparel Industry.* Retrieved February 16, 2009, from http://www.udel.edu/fiber/issue3/researchbriefs

early 2010, some generalizations could be drawn about the overall impact of the final end of quotas. David Birnbaum (2009) indicated that the export industries of this area could now be divided into three groups. At the top were the strategic suppliers, the inner critical core, which he identified as China, Vietnam, and Indonesia. Below the favored few are the second line suppliers, still preferred, but not at the same level of support. This group includes India, Pakistan, and Sri Lanka. At the bottom are the marginal suppliers, the national equivalents of subcontractors. When business is good, this group does well, but when business goes bad, they feel a sense of crisis. Birnbaum goes on to identify the marginal suppliers as CAFTA-DR (see Chapter 10) and Cambodia.

There are many differences in the viewpoints of Eastern and Western cultures, from the type of logic used for self-expression to the sense of time. Table 11.5 gives a brief summary of these contrasting views and may provide readers with a platform for understanding the two contrasting viewpoints that may be present when seeking sourcing agreements between firms from these different cultures.

Tony Liu, the director of external relations and international programs at Beijing University, indicates that respect for authority carries over into business negotiations and that "just call me James" when introducing oneself will not work in China, where formality is embedded in business practices (Jung, 2009). In addition, it is helpful for foreign businesses to utilize *guanxi,* or the importance of connections and personal relationships, when working within China. The goal of being considered a part of the group, and not an outsider, may be achieved through informal dinner meetings and the exchange of favors. These behaviors often lead to long-term business relationships within this culture.

Now, try your hand at Learning Activity 11.3.

Learning Activity 11.3
PARTICIPATION OF ASIAN COUNTRIES IN TEXTILES AND APPAREL

1. Consider the list of factors that relate to competitiveness of sources of textiles and apparel at the beginning of this section. Pick two from the list on page 351, and describe how each one could contribute to the sustainability of supply chains.

2. Using Table 11.5, identify in which regions of Asia wages are highest and lowest. What does this tell us about the overall economies of the nations involved?

3. Put on your sourcing manager hat. Considering Tables 11.4, 10.5, and 9.5, what column of information do you regard as the most insightful when making decisions about where to source merchandise? Explain.

4. How do total wages in Asia compare with total wages in regions of the Americas?

5. Do import and export data support your observation in question 4?

6. What aspects of Asian countries might have put CAFTA-DR countries third in line, with the title of "marginal suppliers"?

7. Which cultural orientation (Eastern or Western) would seem to contribute most to supply chain sustainability? Explain.

EAST ASIA

East Asian nations are diverse in their political and economic structure, ranging from Japan, a nation that is developed economically and enjoys one of the higher per person GDPs in the world, to China, one of the largest and most populous nations on the planet and a communist country that is moving toward a more open economy. We begin with a discus-sion of China, owing to its role as the largest producer of textile and apparel products in the world; followed by three East Asian nations that have developed beyond their apparel pro-duction peak, Japan, South Korea, and Taiwan; and complete the discussion of East Asia with the contributions of Hong Kong and Macao.

China

U.S. trade with China began in 1785, when a ship carrying Chinese products landed in New York with tea, porcelain, and 3,200 pounds of nankeen, a cotton fabric used to make men's trousers ("The Story of Porcelain," 2005). In the late 1800s, China withdrew from trade with much of the world and stayed shut off until the Nixon administration reopened trade with China in the late 1970s. A sleeping giant with 1.3 billion people that constitutes about one fifth of the world's population, China has been awaken-ing and undergoing enormous change in recent years. After decades under a sluggish, centrally planned communist system, China began moving into a "socialist-capitalist" economy in 1978, under the leadership of Deng Xiaoping. This revised system is a more privatized market-oriented economy that promotes trade and growth, while still restricting the freedoms of individuals. As the current global leader in the export of textile and apparel products, the country has gained its competitive edge because of a favorable economic environment, govern-ment support through tariffs and tax incen-tives, and low labor and raw materials costs.

China is not only a big producer, but also a big new market. In 2004, China had more than 100 million people who were considered middle class. A Chinese family could live a life comparable to a U.S. middle-class family for a fraction of the cost, when measured in U.S. dollars (Fishman, 2004). The number of people living in urban centers in China rose dramatically, from 19 percent in 1976 to

30 percent in 1996 (China, 2004). As part of the population continued to shift away from rural lifestyles, the number of urban centers rose, from 223 to 666. There were 100 cities with more than a million in population in China (Fishman, 2004). In 2009, Shanghai was the largest city in the world, with more than 13 million people. The capital, Beijing, had a population of more than 7 million, just a million shy of New York City's population of approximately 8 million people.

Through direct foreign investment from Hong Kong alone, more than 11 million Chinese were employed in apparel factories at the beginning of the 21st century, many of them in the Pearl River Delta region between Guangzhou and Shenzhen, near the border of the Hong Kong territories. However, years of economic expansion have placed enormous pressures in some of these areas, not only on the economy, but also on the infrastructure. Foreign investors were dealing with issues such as energy shortages, escalating raw material and labor costs, and limited availability of land. As the pressures increased, growth of urbanization began shifting from the southern region to the north, spreading from the Guangzhou area (formerly Canton), in Guangdong province, to the coastal provinces, to the northeast, including Fujian, Shanghai, Jiangsu, and Zhejiang. China is also developing the Yangtze River from Shanghai into its heartland.

Although China's leaders have been trying to move away from manufacturing, toward an economy based on innovation, basic production remains very strong in this economy, with the textile industry one of the significant contributors. To counteract the growing tensions with the United States and EU markets late in 2009, China became intent upon developing its domestic consumer market. Consumption has risen steadily in recent years, but China is still a nation in which the consumer consistently saves more than it spends ("Country Focus: China," 2010).

Textile Manufacturing in China
China has become a significant importer of textiles. In 2008, China was the world's third-largest importer of textiles, after the EU and the United States, reflecting its use of these products not only for producing the apparel it makes for export, but also for serving its domestic market. China imports cotton when the domestic supply is insufficient to meet demand but has abundant supplies of other natural fibers, such as ramie, silk, and Angora rabbit hair. In recent years, China has focused heavily on improving its textile production capabilities. By 2003 it was exporting about two times more textiles than it was importing; by 2008 it was exporting four times more textiles than it was importing, while still remaining a significant global importer. Considering the dominance of China's apparel exports provides further evidence of the magnitude of this country's textile business. China is now the world's largest producer of man-made fibers, and it is competitive in supplying not only fibers, but also yarns, fabrics, and trim (Figure 11.2).

Figure 11.2 Fountain Set's Jiangyin Fuhui textile mill, in Jiangsu province, reflects the technological advances now employed in Chinese textile production. (*Courtesy of WWD*)

Read about one of China's largest textile-producing regions in Case 11.2.

Apparel Manufacturing in China

There are about 110 thousand apparel companies in China, 10 percent of which are very large and employ more than 5 thousand workers each. Much of the country's production is regarded as high quality, high enough to satisfy critical sourcing managers from around the world. The WTO reports that between 2000 and 2008, market share of clothing exports from China into other nations shifted, as shown in Table 11.6. We know that Chinese production increased significantly over this period, but what is of interest here is that the EU-27 began to absorb a significantly larger portion of the overall exports, whereas Japan may have maintained the amount it was purchasing, but this was a much smaller proportion of the overall Chinese export market than in the past. Also, CIS (Commonwealth of Independent States) nations increased their impact on the Chinese market by a very significant percentage, which may reflect improvement in their own economies. Table 11.7 identifies some of the largest textile and apparel companies currently operating in China and their major strengths. Examine the descriptions of the companies, their business strategies, the variety of types of goods, and the quantities they produce.

There has been a trend for larger China-based companies to consolidate their production within self-contained cities, in which factory buildings that employ several thousand people are combined with accommodation blocks (including housing) for both workers and management. "There are also design rooms, research and development facilities, finishing plants, printing and embroidery, even company hotels for visitors" (Tait, 2004a, p. 32). Hong Kong–based Pacific Textiles, Luen Thai, and TAL operate examples of these

KEQIAO, China—Whether the garment label reads Made in China, France or the USA, there's a good chance the fabric originated in a relatively unknown textile region: Shaoxing.

In the 20 years since Keqiao Town in Shaoxing County was designated China Textile City, tax breaks and political support have helped boost its development as the main textile hub in the world's largest fabric-producing country. However, its standing remains under the radar, especially to the West. . . .

Keqiao manufactures 10 percent of all the cloth in China, and dyes or prints, one-third. It is home to 19,000 trading companies, more than 10,000 textile producers, 3,500 international purchasers and scores of other players in the textile supply chain. . . .

About 40 percent of that output is exported. Other nearby towns in Shaoxing Country, such as Anchang and Qianqing, also boast formidable material outputs and Shaoxing City, like Keqiao, hosts a substantial concentration of textile offices. In 2008, Shaoxing County had a gross domestic product of 60.83 billion yuan, or about $8.92 billion, at current exchange. The textile industry generated 65 percent of the total.

Shaoxing proper is one of Eastern China's ancient cultural centers, known for its yellow wine, pungent tofu, tea houses and literati, in addition to its textiles. Its historic celebrities include King Yu, a legendary founder of Chinese civilization dating to 2200 B.C., and Ming poet and painter Xu Wei. . . .

The area's textile heritage is no less distinctive. Coastal Zhejiang's history of producing and exporting cloth dates to China's Spring and Autumn Period (770 to 476 B.C.). The region's reputation as a textile center continued through subsequent dynasties and millennia, abating only during the political upheavals of the 19th and 20th centuries.

Table 11.6 PERCENTAGE OF CHINESE APPAREL EXPORTS, BY DESTINATION, 2000 AND 2008

	Market Share in 2000	Market Share in 2008
EU-27	12%	25%
United States	13%	15%
Japan	32%	15%
CIS	3%	13%
Others	40%	32%

Source: World Trade Organization (WTO). (2009). International Trade Statistics. Section 2: Merchandise trade by product (36). Retrieved January 16, 2010, from http://www.wto.org/english/res_e/statis_e/its2009_e/its09_merch_trade_product_e.pdf

Textile City is now divided into three sectors—manufacturing, trade and design—and employs some 200,000 migrant laborers. Zhou claims that work conditions are among the best in China, providing top-notch education, housing, medical care, insurance, benefits and pensions.

In 1999, Keqiao launched its own trade fair. The event, which used to be held annually, became biannual last year. The most recent four-day edition of the China Keqiao International Textile Expo wrapped up Oct. 28. Although the infrastructure and government support give it an edge, Keqiao is one giant among many, and faces competition from other textile hubs in Zhejiang and neighboring Jiangsu.

One way that Textile City has sought to consolidate its position is through a huge expansion of physical infrastructure. Driving to Keqiao from downtown Shaoxing, a gleaming new city of half-built office high-rises and luxury villas emerges Oz-like from the surrounding landscape of boxy factories and markets enveloped in smog. It recalls Beijing in 2006 or 2007, at the height of the pre-Olympics building boom. There is a sickly brown shade to the air and repetition of ultra-modern, half-finished towers along extra wide roads.

A benefactor of China's stimulus spending on infrastructure and high local tax revenues, Keqiao seems emblematic of the build-it-first, make-it-work later approach typical of development in China. Of the smart new market facilities, the first floors showcased to visitors are usually occupied, but their upper stories are mostly vacant. . . .

Along with infrastructure construction, Keqiao is looking to shift from cheap manufacturing to higher-end, value-added products by investing in what China calls "creative industries." To this end, the Zhejiang Textile Industry Institute invites dozens of South Korean textile designers to teach in Keqiao and participate in the city's trade fair.

Jin said Keqiao needs to put more emphasis on design to broaden its textile client base beyond Asia to Europe and North America. China Textile City's Zhou also stressed the importance of creativity and finding people to take the region forward.

"Beijing and Shanghai have such people, but they have no place to be creative or no opportunities," he said. "So we bring them together, like in Milan and London. We are cooperating with the Shanghai fashion industry, so that we can be a place where good ideas come to fruition."

Source:

Movius, L. (2009, November 24). China's textile city grows in stature. *Women's Wear Daily*. Retrieved February 17, 2010, from http://www.movius.us/articles/WWD-ShaoxingKeqiao.html

"cities," and are being copied by domestic companies such as Youngor. According to Tait (2004a), Youngor has taken the idea even further to include spinning, weaving, and fabric finishing in its city, making it a total vertically integrated operation, from yarn to finished garment, in one location.

Read Case 11.3 to learn more about the expansion of factory towns throughout China.

Labor has become an increasing problem in some of the areas supporting factory towns. As shown in Table 11.2, China reported an unemployment rate in urban areas of about 4.3 percent in 2008, but, according to *The World Factbook*, those data do not represent the rural population, in which there is a great deal of under- and unemployment. The rural population is attracted to entry level positions; thus, the migration of people from rural areas into cities, in search of work, is continuing, but at an unpredictable pace. Workers are not reliably available at the time and place in which needs arise, and then they must be trained before becoming productive.

At the same time, wage rates are rising, exceeding those in newly developing countries, including Bangladesh and Indonesia, as are turnover rates of employees. Skilled workers are attracted to higher-paying positions elsewhere in the industry or in other sectors, such as electronics. Chinese apparel manufacturers are now addressing the same economic challenges that have been faced by firms in the rest of the world: how to maintain an appealing selling price while meeting time lines and covering all costs. Because of lower labor costs elsewhere, China is now outsourcing production to other countries to meet demand for finished goods from the rest of the world.

China alone represented 23 percent of total global trade in textiles and apparel in 2003, but by 2008 that percentage had risen to a staggering 33 percent (WTO, 2009). To expand on the significance of that statement, in 2008 China exported $65,256 million in textiles (up

Table 11.7 MAJOR APPAREL PRODUCERS IN CHINA

Company	Date Established	Business Strategy	Output per Year
Jiangsu Sunshine Group	1986	Largest wool textile producer in Asia Imports much of wool fiber from Australia Produces own power for spinning weaving, dying, finishing, and garment production Uses Integrated system of advanced technology Retail shops in Shanghai and Qingdao	350,000 men's suits 20 million meters of worsted wool fabrics 20 million meters of denim 15,000 tons of tops 2 million meters of roving fabrics and cashmere 1.5 million suits $ 785 million in sales in 2003
Youngor Group Co.	1979	Fully vertically integrated, from yarn to finished garments, in one "city" Market leader in shirts and business suits Mostly men's and women's wear; children's wear is ancillary	2 million suits 10 million shirts 30 million knitted leisure wear and children's wear $ 1.2 billion in sales; 50:50 textiles and apparel 50% exported
Dalian Dayang Trands Co.	1979	Better men's suits, women's fashion, casual and sportswear One suit factory a joint venture with Israel's Bagir One of largest garment manufacturers in China	10 million pieces per year, including 450,000 suits from joint venture with UK's Marks & Spencer $ 2 billion in sales; 95% exported
Baoxiniao Group	1996	Moderate men's suits Operates out of 550 retail stores in China Pioneered franchise operations in China	800,000 suits, 90% domestic $ 120 million in sales
Bosideng Group	—	World market leader in down wear One of China's biggest clothing manufacturers and retailers	Products sold around the world, majority domestic Has stores in UK Exports $ 40 million annually
EverGlory International Group	1993	High- to middle-priced casual wear and sportswear for men, women, children Joint-venture factories in Cambodia and Vietnam Operates three wholly owned subsidiaries: Goldenway Nanjing Garment Co. New-Tailun Garments Co. Nanjing Catch-Luck Garments Co.	18 million garments per year $ 80 million in sales Traded on NASDAQ in the United States
Zhejiang Shouwang Group	—	Based in Hangzhou, the world's largest production base for leather and fur garments Produces cashmere sweaters Has 12 garment factories 360 company–owned retail shops in China	4 million fur and leather garments $ 120 million in sales, 95% exported
Shenzhen H&S Garment Co.	1990	Casual clothing, sportswear, casual clothes, uniforms Use state-of-the-art CAD/CAM systems	Gross production capacity more than $ 5 million

Source: Based on Tait, N. (2004, June–July). China: This giant is not sleeping. *Fashion Business International*, 28–35; updated via company Web sites March 3, 2010.

DATANG, China—You probably have never heard of this factory town in coastal China, and there is no reason why you should have. But it fills your sock drawer.

Datang produces an astonishing nine billion pairs of socks each year—more than one set for every person on the planet. People here fondly call it Socks City, and its annual socks festival attracts 100,000 buyers from around the world. . . .

. . . They produce over a third of the world's [socks] output, and the government has nothing but praise for such entrepreneurs and their domination of the sock business. . . .

Dong Ying Hong, who in the 1970s gave up a $9-a-month job as an elementary-school teacher to make socks at home. Now, she is the owner of Zhejiang Socks—and a sock millionaire.

Hai Yun Shi, the 41-year-old founder of Hongyun Socks, has a similar tale.

"I started out making socks by hand when I was 18," he said at the company's headquarters. "In '96 we founded this company. Now, we have a contract with Wal-Mart."

These kinds of gains have sharply eroded America's old sock-making might. . . .

Textile and apparel makers in China have long been preparing for the boom. In recent years, they have invested billions of dollars in new factories along the country's eastern seaboard, particularly here in the Yangtze River Delta.

Many of the old government-owned operations are gone. Private enterprises are importing high-end machinery and luring millions of peasants from the countryside.

Since the early 1980s, when China began moving to a market economy, much of its competitive advantage was built on low-cost labor. . . .

Investors from Hong Kong, Taiwan, Japan and South Korea were among the first to come. But in recent years, Chinese entrepreneurs set up their own shops, starting out with small stitching operations and quickly expanding into gigantic factories.

For instance, Shengzhou, now popularly known in Chinese as International Necktie City, developed after a Hong Kong investor moved his necktie operations there in 1985 and brought modern tie-making techniques to the city. That was only a few years after China opened itself to capitalism when Deng Xiaoping in 1978 declared, "To get rich is glorious."

Later, some of the company's managers broke away to start their own tie companies. And within a decade, Shengzhou was awash in tie makers and suppliers.

Similar stories can be heard throughout the province of Zhejiang, which is considered one of this country's most enterprising regions.

But textile specialists say China's boom is not simply the product of the newfound entrepreneurialism that is sweeping this country; it is also the nation's ability to form what are called lump economies, focused on one product. . . .

"The clusters are getting more and more specialized," says Qingliang Gu, a professor of textile economics at Donghua University in Shanghai. "It's a little like Italy, where you have the city of Como making silk fabric, Vicenza with fine wool and Veneto for knitting."

The Chinese government has also played a crucial role, opening huge swaths of land for development, forming giant industrial parks, doling out tax benefits and developing the infrastructure and transportation networks needed to move products quickly to market.

"The textile cities started initially from the spontaneous development of private companies," said Chunyi Xie, an economist at the Shanghai Garment Trade Association. "But when it reached certain dimensions it drew attention from the government."

Private companies, with the support of the government, now build huge textile factory complexes, complete with dormitories, hospitals and even curfews to replace the state role in providing food, shelter and health care, along with close supervision. Many textile companies in the province of Jiangsu house and feed thousands of migrant workers who are bused in from the countryside, often for three- or four-year factory stints.

The campus of the Huafang Group, one of China's largest textile companies, has over 100 factory buildings, 30,000 employees and round-the-clock operations.

On any day, it teems with more than 20,000 workers, who live free of charge in Huafang's dormitories. Conditions are hardly heavenly, but they are often a step up for these workers, who are mostly young women from poorer inland provinces like Anhui or Henan. Many of them come here after high school, intending to stay for a few years before returning home to be married. . . .

"When we need new workers," said Wei Xin Shi, a Huafang Group executive, "we just announce it and people here call home and tell their friends to come to work at our factories." . . .

"In terms of vertical supply chain, China has no competition," says Ruizhe Sun, president of the China Textile Information Center, a government-sponsored agency in Beijing. "We have button makers, fabric makers, thread makers, zipper makers, you name it."

That situation is luring investors and competitors from other parts of the world. . . .

Chinese textile executives, however, are well aware of the risks of overexpansion. And there are other problems looming as well. The market for labor has tightened in the past year, pushing up wages. . . .

"We feel labor costs are going up," Jianhong Gu, vice general manager of Pukun Textile, a Zhangjiagang suit maker whose factories operate 24 hours a day. "There's tremendous competition."

Moreover, foreign designers and retailers are keen to keep a network of business ties with other countries with relatively modern factories, like India, Pakistan and Bangladesh.

Fred Abernathy, a researcher at the Center for Textile and Apparel Research at Harvard, says retailers in the United States will continue to buy quantities of textiles and apparel close to home, particularly in Latin America and the Caribbean. . . . But, he concedes, "China will gain over the long run."

Jinfei Wang, the chairman of the Jiangsu Diao Garment factory in Tongzhou, just outside Nantong, says there's no doubt about that.

"I've been to factories all over the world," he said in a recent interview while walking his own bustling factory floor, observing women's suits destined for JCPenney stores. "And we can compete with any of them. Without restrictions, certainly China is going to be No. 1."

Source:

Barboza, D. (2004, December 24). In roaring China, sweaters are west of socks city. *The New York Times*. Retrieved from http://www.nytimes.com/2004/12/24/business/worldbusiness/24china.html

Figure 11.3 Workers manufacture down jackets at the Quanli Garment Factory in Pinghu, Zhejiang Province, China. (*Qilai Shen/Bloomberg News/Getty Images*)

Figure 11.4a The Seven for All Mankind store in Beijing. (*Courtesy 7 For All Mankind*)

Figure 11.4b A Walmart Supercenter in China. (*Courtesy of Walmart*)

from \$26,901 million in 2003) and \$119,978 million in apparel products worldwide (up from \$52,061 million in 2003), totaling \$185,234 million (remember, that is more than \$185 billion) in exports (refer back to Table 11.3b).

Such significant growth in a short time frame caused considerable concern among struggling nations, such as Bangladesh, in which 85.5 percent of merchandise exports in 2000 were apparel products; in 2004 those figures had dropped to 62.3 percent of total merchandise exports; but by 2008 they had recovered some, to 78.2 percent of overall merchandise exports. This single comparison reflects the threat China has posed to other nations in the global supply of textiles and apparel. In the middle of the first decade of the 21st century, some countries were beginning to raise concerns that China was on the verge of overcapacity, literally threatening to saturate the world in products, but by 2008 things had settled down somewhat, and, despite the general global economy's downturn, China was still producing and exporting massive amounts of textile and apparel products throughout the world.

Rontex International represents one example of the movement of business into China from outside sources ("Shaping Up to Share," 2004). After years of successful operations in Chile, the chairman, Ronald Cheung, chose to move the company's production operations to China. Rontex went into partnerships and set up four factories, in different locations. The company's facilities were located in areas that specialize in the item that each produces.

- Beijing—suit production (approximately 300 thousand pieces per year)
- Ningbo—knitwear (1.8 million pieces per year)
- Nanjing—wovens (1.32 million trousers and 660 thousand jackets per year)
- Huzhou—sweaters (approximately 450 thousand pieces per year) ("Shaping Up to Share," 2004)

Of additional interest, Rontex was launching its own brand and opening retail shops in Beijing to expand beyond production.

China has proven itself to be a supplier of choice for many U.S. retailers, but it has also proven itself a formidable competitor in other developed markets (Figure 11.3). Review Table 11.6 to appreciate China's recent expansion into the EU and Japan.

Retailing in China

Changes in China have not all taken place in its manufacturing sector. Over the last few years, especially with the surge in the size of its middle-class, China has become an advantageous retail market. There has been a significant increase in retail offerings, further facilitated by changes in government regulations. Restrictions were lifted in December 2004 on foreign-invested companies with retail interests in China, allowing China to enter and expand into the market much more easily. Today, many upscale retailers from around the globe have opened stores in China's major cities, especially Shanghai and Beijing. Mass-market retailers from the EU and the United States have made their presence known. In fact, Walmart's overall trade activities with China were so immense that by the early 2000s this company accounted for 1 percent of China's overall GDP (Fishman, 2004).

Another recent change is in the visibility of Chinese apparel designers in the retail scene. They are working toward increased input into the overall design of apparel products, by moving into technical design and creative design areas. To this end, enrollment in apparel programs in China's universities has increased the supply of trained personnel in these fields. One apparel firm of note is Li Ning Co., Ltd., a leading sports brand enterprise. Li Ning focuses on the midmarket consumer and is a vertically integrated company that manufactures, distributes, and retails its own products related to sport and leisure uses (Figures 11.4a and 11.4b).

Read Case 11.4 for a list of key Chinese retail trends.

Case 11.4 TEN KEY TRENDS IN CHINA'S FASHION RETAIL MARKET

Here is a list of ten important considerations for international retailers looking to do business in the emerging Chinese retail market. The trends were presented by Brenda Wang, the managing director of Brandxcel, at the recent UKFT Seminar "China: Today's Source; Tomorrow's Market."

Chinese clothing [domestic] sales increased 21.2% in 2008, with branded fashion and fast fashion leading the way. Around 80% of clothing is bought for Chinese consumers above the age of 20.

71% of China's wealth is concentrated in southern and coastal areas. The highest monthly household budgets are held by those living in the four 1st-tier cities of Beijing, Shanghai, Guangzhou and Shenzen.

Key shopping destinations in Beijing include Shin Kong Place, Joy City, Sogo, The Village, and Scitech Outlet Mall. In Shanghai, meanwhile, the most popular malls include Plaza 66, Raffles City, Parkson, and Xintiandi.

Department stores represent 54% of the main distribution channels for fashion in China, with clothing and footwear stores selling 29% and Internet retailing comprising 4%.

Clothing is China's biggest online purchased category, representing over half of the country's e-commerce transactions.

Men's apparel is the highest growth clothing product category in China, growing at a rate of nearly 20%, trailed by women's and children's wear.

China has a population of 1.3bn, and the spending power of Chinese women alone is expected to reach U.S.$216bn during the next decade.

International brands still dominate the high-end market in China, while domestic brands like Li Ning have a bigger share of the mid- to low-end market, more driven by function. Household brand names include Louis Vuitton, Dunhill, Zara, Nike, Coach, Vero Moda, Li Ning and Belle.

Options for retailers expanding to China include directly operated stores, selling direct to retailers, going through a distributor, franchising, wholesaling, and e-commerce.

Wang believes the key consideration for entering the Chinese retail market is to have a long-term commitment. She says there is no point in just opening five stores, as that's what everyone else is doing. She also says that "guanxi"—meaning relationships—is key to success.

Source:

Ayling, J. (2009, December 15). Ten key trends in Chinese's fashion retail market. just-style.com. Retrieved June 3, 2010, from http://www.just-style.com/comment/10-key-trends-in-chinas-fashion-retail-market_id106204.aspx

Shanghai, China's largest port city, expanded its port facilities to meet the needs of huge increases in imports and exports to service the retail expansion and export of manufactured goods. Major shipping lines, including Maersk, APL, and P&O Nedlloyd, all operate offices in Shanghai. During the first half of 2004, exports of textiles and apparel from Shanghai's port were worth $17.6 billion, up more than 35 percent from the same period the year before (Zarocostas, 2005b). Although there was some grumbling of reduced exports going through the ports in 2008 and 2009, it would appear that a recovery is well underway. Certainly, the overall export numbers reflect continuing activity.

One final note about this giant nation. For many years its currency, the yuan, was regulated by the government and considered undervalued, by being pegged to a percentage of the U.S. dollar. (This makes exports to the United States lower in price than they would be otherwise.) In 2005, the government was reported to be considering some deregulation of its currency, which, many believed would cause the costs of purchasing apparel in China to escalate considerably. After assurances that it was not going to make any large changes, the government did devalue the yuan by 2.2 percent, in mid-2005. This appeared to have little impact on overall trade. China's currency valuation will bear close monitoring as the world recovers from the economic downturn, and currency values of the EU and elsewhere continue in a state of flux.

Now, further your study of textiles and apparel in China by doing Learning Activity 11.4.

Learning Activity 11.4
TEXTILES AND APPAREL IN CHINA

1. Identify and describe two strategies China is using to maintain the competitive position of its textile industry.
2. Why might you expect that rapid growth in urbanization would parallel rapid growth of the apparel industry in other countries, as it has in China?
3. Of China's largest apparel companies (Table 11.7), only one, Ever-Glory, makes casual and sportswear for men, women, and children. Four of those large companies specialize in men's suits. In what ways is the suit business more consistent with being made by very large companies than men's and women's sportswear?
4. Considering Case 11.3, imagine that you are a sock buyer for Walmart. You buy millions of dollars in socks several times a year. What would be the advantages and disadvantages of buying at Socks City?
5. Pick a country from Table 11.2. Search the Internet for information about textile and apparel trade for that country. Evaluate whether the prediction of effects of quota removal came true.

Textile-Producing Countries in East Asia

Japan, South Korea, and Taiwan have developed their economies beyond the point at which low-cost apparel production is feasible, so they have turned to outsourcing most apparel production and developing technical textiles. See Table 11.2 to review the demographics of these countries and Tables 11.3a and 11.3b for a review of their textile and apparel trade. These countries have no domestic supply of natural fibers, so some firms have focused on research and development of synthetic materials.

Japan

Japan's rapid economic development after World War II moved it through the "developing country category" into a developed nation. Japan has matured and shifted its industrial focus to high technology on a wide range of products, including specialized textiles and apparel. Japan's apparel imports have increased dramatically throughout the last 10 years. Tariff and nontariff barriers have virtually disappeared. According to Table 11.3, Japan imported $19.5 billion in apparel in 2008. Japanese consumers demand high-quality products and fashionable apparel, and European luxury brands continue to open flagships there. It was estimated that Japanese citizens consumed "41 percent of the world's luxury goods" earlier in the decade (Socha, 2004, p. 14).

During the recent economic downturn, rather than discontinue shopping, the Japanese consumer tended to move toward inexpensive fast-fashion purchases at an array of new stores, including Japan's own Uniqlo, a subsidiary of Fast Retailing Co., Ltd. Uniqlo has research centers in Tokyo and New York; 90 percent of its products are manufactured in China; and it has quality assurance offices in Shanghai, Shenzhen, and Ho Chi Minh City, Vietnam. Because of the large scale of operations, the company negotiates directly with textile manufacturers, including Toray Industries, of Japan and the United States (Uniqlo, 2009).

Currently, Japan's textile industry focuses on the production of high-tech synthetic fibers and fabrics, including microfibers. In 2008, Japan was ranked by the WTO as number nine in global exports of textiles and number three in global imports of clothing, after the EU and the United States (Figure 11.5a–c).

Read Case 11.5 to explore the role of fast fashion in Japan.

Figure 11.5a Japanese shoppers in the trendy Harijuku area of Tokyo reflect the consumption orientation of this developed nation. *(Yukie Kasuga/WWD)*

Figure 11.5b The striking ultramodern Prada retail facility in Tokyo, Japan. Prada began nearly a century ago in Italian leather goods and now has designer goods sold in nearly every country in the world. *(Courtesy of WWD)*

Figure 11.5c Uniqlo is Japan's entrant into the fast fashion market. *(www.uniqlo.com)*

Tokyo's Harajuku district is where to find Japan's fashion-forward youth. Every weekend, sidewalks disappear under a frenzy of shoppers looking for new trends. The latest: fast-fashion retailing. During the Golden Week holiday in early May, typically a shopping extravaganza, Los Angeles–based chain Forever 21 debuted its flagship store in Japan. Harajuku girls lined up on five floors full of clothes, shoes and accessories in enough of a dizzying array to make any young woman swoon. It wasn't the first time the giants of cheap chic had stormed Tokyo. Last November about 2,500 shoppers jammed the very same sidewalk for the opening of Swedish H&M, the world's third largest casual-clothing retailer, located next door. And that was just one month after the launch of British retailer Topshop a few stores down.

This is the new Harajuku. The once super-stylish district is rapidly transforming into an outdoor mall of the titans of casual clothing—H&M, Uniqlo, Topshop, Gap, Zara and now Forever 21—all competing for wardrobe space within a few hundred meters of one another. Expensive Japanese boutique stores are receding to the backstreets. Retail analysts say that Japanese consumers are continuing to spend in the recession, but have gone considerably down-market to less costly items. As a result, fast fashion "is a hot issue in Japan's fashion industry, especially after the entry of H&M," says Dairo Murata, a retail analyst at Credit Suisse in Tokyo. Luxury-brand sales in Japan are expected to decline 10% in the first half of the year compared with sales in the same period in 2008.

But though branded luxury may be out, style is still in, and sales at inexpensive fast-fashion and casual-clothing stores have picked up. That's the kind of market that Forever 21 expects will help it reach $2.4 billion in global sales this year, up 40% over 2008's figure. The company thinks that its retail offering, where $100 buys an outfit, a bag, shoes and accessories, fits the Japanese mood right now.

Forever 21 stores are big (they need to be to stock the variety of merchandise they do and to refresh it so often) and big parcels of real estate aren't easy to find in Japanese cities. Forever 21 president Alex Ok said that the search for the site, which at 19,000 sq. ft. (1,800 sq. m.) is still just one-fifth of the size of a store planned for New York City's Times Square, began a year ago. But he found what he was looking for, and is confident he can tap into the new Japanese frugality. "A Gucci handbag and a Forever 21 top," says Ok. "It's a way for [consumers] to think, 'I'm smart about how to shop.'"

Forever 21 hopes the new store is just the beginning. The chain now has 460 stores in 13 countries, after launching last year in Thailand, South Korea, and China. Lawrence Meyer, Forever 21's executive vice president, says the firm plans to open more than 100 stores in Japan. The recession isn't a deterrent. "Woman always wants to shop," says Wedda Uyeda, an adviser to Forever 21 on the Japanese market. "You want to have the fun of shopping, like in a candy store. I don't think that any of the Japanese companies really realize that."

Up to a point: Uniqlo, the local entry in the segment, seems to be doing just fine. Tadashi Yanai, a cheap-chic guru and head of Fast Retailing, which owns Uniqlo, is now Japan's richest man, according to *Forbes* magazine. While most retailers are seeing same-store sales drop between 5% and 15%, Uniqlo's same-store sales rose 2.9% for fiscal year 2008 and 12.9% in the six months to February this year. "Uniqlo is the only big winner so far," says Murata of Credit Suisse, who thinks that for non-Japanese fast-fashion companies such as Forever 21 and H&M to succeed against Uniqlo they will have to pay more attention to quality. But Forever 21's Ok is confident that his brand can grow, and he has the tenor of the times on his side: the soft property market is making it easier to find large retail spaces in metropolitan areas.

Granted, you don't normally associate the word *cheap* with Japan. But cheap land, cheap chic; something's going on.

Source:

Masters, C. (2009, May 18). In Japan, fast fashion rules in slow times, *Time*, Retrieved from http://www.time.com/time/world/article/0,8599,1895240,00.htm

South Korea

South Korea did not follow the more traditional corporate, private business path of industrialization as a means of improving its economy after the Korean War, in the 1950s. Instead, South Korea followed a path blending government–business relationships with corporatist ties that Dennis McNamara labeled "syncretic capitalism." This system is based on a framework of relationships between the state and the *chaebol* (Korea's business conglomerates) and led to rapid economic growth (Kang, 2003). The government regularly intervened in the marketplace, yet the country achieved rapid industrialization. A full examination of how this economic philosophy influenced South Korea's textile and apparel industry is beyond the scope of this text; suffice it to say that there has been more recognized government intervention in the textile and apparel business and trade issues in South Korea than in most other nations.

Figure 11.6a A crowd outside the new H&M store in Seoul, South Korea. *(Courtesy of DK Park/HM)*

Because of the strength of its economy, South Korea has turned much of its attention to the marketing of fashion and the retail sector. Sungjoo Group has met with success as a fashion franchising industry, beginning in the business in the 1990s and now operating stores in South Korea for Marks & Spencer, Lulu Guinness, and Billy Bag. Kim Sungjoo, the CEO of Sungjoo Group, has talked about Westerners' making the mistake of believing that Asia is focused on the past. She claims that "recent developments . . . have created a generation of younger consumers who are currently driving Asia's markets. . . . [W]omen are behind 70 to 80 percent of all purchases made by Asian households every year" (Cambie, 2007, p. 2) (Figures 11.6a and 11.6b).

Figure 11.6b The South Korean designer Kuho Jung's designs for Hexa proved intriguing, with a focus on draping. *(Courtesy of WWD/Pasha Antonov)*

"As the nation has turned into a signifi-cant economic power, the wages and costs in its garment factories have risen steadily, caus-ing some of its manufacturers to focus on higher-end, higher-value products" (Malone, 2004, p. 11). South Korean firms have moved much of their textile and apparel production to factories they own and manage in other parts of the developing world, shifting their focus to the marketing and domestic con-sumption of these products.

Textile firms in South Korea are still a major supplier of fabrics, attributable mainly to its large man-made fiber industry. South Korea has large spinning and weaving sectors, and despite rising labor costs, has remained competitive in the relatively capital-intensive production of synthetic fibers and fabrics. However, exports have diminished somewhat in recent years. As with Japan, South Korea's strength is in its technical innovations and its focus on research and development.

Innovations in the use of natural fibers are also in progress. Jungwoo Biotecs, a Seoul-based knitter, is focusing on fabrics made of cellulosic fibers, such as rayon, acetate, lyocell, and bamboo-based rayon. All these fibers are derived from natural materials, but bamboo is a newer product for fabric use. One of South Korea's particular strengths is in the yarns produced for use in the knit-to-shape garments it continues to make in large quantities. One of the more visible manufacturers is the South Korea–based high-density synthetic fabrics specialist Goldlon Worldwide.

Taiwan (Taipei)

Along with South Korea, Taiwan is a major supplier of man-made fiber and fabrics and yarns for the knit-to-shape garments it pro-duces. Taiwan is currently ranked eighth world-wide in textile exports, down from second in 1999, with exports valued at $9.2 billion in 2008.

However, Taiwan's textile industry has developed into a major seat of manufacturing in the region. With little access to local natural fibers, Taiwan has focused on becoming the synthetics capital. Companies are attracted to the country's innovative textiles as it focuses more on production of the newest of tech-nological performance fabrics. Companies in Taiwan make many of the materials that are needed to produce Nike and other firms' athletic shoes. Taiwan also has expanded its emphasis on high-tech products in other man-ufacturing sectors, paralleling growth of its overall economy. Taiwan is also concentrating more on higher-end fashion in its marketing and consumer perspectives (Table 11.8).

The Taiwan Textile Federation (TTF) held its Taipei Innovative Textile Application Show (TITAS) at the Taipei World Trade Center in 2009, with 325 exhibitors and more than 20 thousand visitors. TITAS has been focusing on innovative technology, environ-mental protection, and fashion-forward prod-ucts. Companies from Taiwan that exhibited at TITAS included Asiatic Fiber Corporation (AFC), Joyoung Knitting, and Taroko Textile.

Close to a hundred sourcing representatives from globally renowned brands visited TITAS 2009 despite the fact that the world economy remained on its way to a slow recovery. Eighty percent of these buyers came from Europe and North America. French brand Lafuma, O'Neill from the Netherlands, Italian brand BAILO, German's Vaude, Helly Hansen from Norway, Marmot, Under Armour, SCOTT, Patagonia and L.L. Bean from U.S., Lolë from Canada, Nikko from H.K., Kailas from Australia and Toread from Beijing, China, were among many important visitors at this year's event. The majority of the names on the long list was from outdoor cloth-ing and sportswear sectors and was targeting at advanced and innovative textiles from Taiwan. Four hundred forty one-on-one trade meetings were therefore arranged to serve as the match-making platform for suppliers and buyers. Both sides expressed their appreciation for this effi-cient and fruitful arrangement. (TITAS, 2009)

Table 11.8 Taiwan's Export and Import Values/Trade Surplus of Textile and Apparel Industry, 2000–2008, in Billions of U.S. Dollars

Year	Export Values	Import Values	Trade Surplus Textiles and Apparel	Trade Surplus of Total Trade
2000	15.22	2.89	12.32	8.37
2002	12.14	2.47	9.68	22.07
2004	12.53	2.68	9.85	13.61
2006	11.76	2.70	9.06	21.32
2008	10.90	2.70	8.20	14.83

Source: Taiwan Textile Federation. (2009). *Overview of Taiwan's textile industry–2009*. Retrieved from http://ttf.textiles. org.tw/Textile/TTFroot/overview-english.pdf

This final report, *TITAS 2009*, provides an excellent picture of the professional benefits of attending global trade shows. What is not mentioned in the report are the dozens of parties that also occurred to help attendees meet each other and enjoy the experience.

It must be noted that Taiwan lives in the shadow of China, because China does not recognize it as a sovereign nation, but rather, considers it one of its territories. The United States also does not officially recognize the government of Taiwan as a separate nation; however, the United States and most of the world treats it as such. The WTO keeps Taiwan's trade figures separate from China's, under the Chinese-recognized name Taipei.

Apparel-Producing Countries in East Asia

Hong Kong and Macau have a number of things in common, in that they are both tiny nations located along China's shore. Macau is about one tenth the size of Washington, D.C., and Hong Kong is about six times the size. Hong Kong and Macau have free market economies that are heavily dependent on international trade. Macau was the first European settlement in the Far East, settled by the Portuguese; Hong Kong was occupied by the UK in 1841. Both nations

developed under European occupation, and both nations became a special administrative region (SAR) of China during the last 15 years. Hong Kong and Macau were promised they would enjoy a high degree of autonomy in all matters, except foreign and defense affairs, for the next 50 years. Therefore, their free market economies continue as well as their extensive roles in the textile and apparel business.

Hong Kong

Hong Kong is one of the leading global exporters of textiles and clothing, right behind the EU and China. Over the past half century, Hong Kong's industry experienced four development stages of production migration and embarked on another, related to the MFA quota system. The four completed stages are as follows:

1. In the late 1950s, as Hong Kong's economy prospered, Hong Kong apparel firms established subsidiaries in neighboring countries in which exports were less restrictive.

2. During the 1970s, Hong Kong moved production to Southeast Asian countries, and as far as Mauritius, to gain preferential export access to the European market and was already beginning to provide sourcing services to U.S. department stores.

3. In the late 1970s, as China opened up to global trade, Hong Kong intensified its efforts into the United States and other developed countries, seeking additional export markets for its products.

4. In the late 1980s, when textile and apparel export quotas were introduced in many additional nations, Hong Kong, which had entered into these arrangements early and therefore had larger quota allotments than many newer entries into the market, was able to continue to expand overall production (Au & Yeung, 1999).

During the phaseout of the quota system in the early 2000s, a fifth stage evolved. Competition from other nations throughout Asia increased, and Hong Kong had to make numerous adjustments, owing not only to the WTO quota issues, but also to its return to Chinese jurisdiction after 100 years of British rule.

During much of its industry development, Hong Kong initiated considerable direct foreign investment (DFI) into other countries, including ASEAN nations and China. Hong Kong especially sought production capacity in the Guangdong Province of China, focusing on the Pearl River Delta region. By investing heavily in production facilities in areas where low-cost labor was readily available, garments destined for the United States were initiated with origin-conferring operations in Hong Kong but frequently moved to Chinese factories for minor assembly or labor-intensive operations. The products were then reexported through Hong Kong, under quota. With the end of quotas, Hong Kong had to compete directly with Chinese factories that were no longer hampered by quota limitations. On first examination, one might expect this to cause great upheaval, but because Hong Kong often owned the Chinese facilities, its involvement was actually simplified: the reexport factor was eliminated, and Hong Kong could construct and ship products directly from its Chinese factories.

Two firms with headquarters in Hong Kong are Fountain Set Limited and TAL Group. These successful firms are very different in their organization. Fountain Set is recognized as one of the world's largest circular knitted fabric manufacturers and has vertically integrated operations, from spinning through finishing. Fountain Set's product range includes dyed yarns, sewing threads, and knit garments. It is a public firm, listed on the stock exchange in Hong Kong, and has facilities in China, Sri Lanka, and Indonesia. The TAL Group has been a private, family-owned firm and one of the world's largest clothing manufacturers (Tait, 2004b). It produces a variety of garments for a number of global brands and is considered the world's largest dress shirt manufacturer. Although it makes fabric in the United States, TAL considers its strength to be contract garment manufacture. The firm employs approximately 23 thousand people in garment plants in China, Hong Kong, Indonesia, Malaysia, Mexico, Taiwan, and Thailand.

Much of Hong Kong's attention in textiles and apparel is now being redirected to broker activities. Many apparel firms are shifting their focus by turning all or at least part of their sourcing functions to outside vendors, better known as export trading companies or sourcing agents. They can coordinate everything from product development to shipping. As has been discussed, businesses such as Li & Fung excel in this venue. As early as 2006, Li & Fung was using Southeast

Asia and Bangladesh for sourcing rather than China. The goal has been to use management of materials and borderless manufacturing to reach its value-added sourcing goals, and the measure of the company's success can be seen almost daily as updates of its activities are reported in the industry trade papers. (See Chapter 1 to review the Li & Fung supply chain model and Chapter 5 for further information on Li & Fung).

Other supply chain management or sourcing firms of note include Connor (officially listed on the business information Web site Hoover's as William E. Connor & Associates), which began as a small purchasing office in Tokyo but has since moved to Hong Kong, and two other Hong Kong–based firms, Linmark and Newtimes International Trading, which have headquarters in Hong Kong and Taipei. Newtimes sources production for everything from bridge-priced knitwear to moderate-priced jeans. Hong Kong may now be recognized for having one of the largest global trade shows, Hong Kong Fashion Week, which ran concurrent with the World Boutique trade show in early 2010, all put on by the Hong Kong Trade Development Council (HKTDC) (Figure 11.7).

Macau

The textile and apparel industries of Macau followed patterns of growth similar to those of Hong Kong, although Portuguese settlers, rather than the British, exerted an influence. Macau developed outward processing arrangements with China, in which some production took place in Macau to establish the country of origin (COO) for trade purposes during quota restrictions, but the remainder of the sewing and packaging was done in China, where labor is cheaper. Unfortunately, Macau

was not included in the Werner Labor Cost Study, the source of data for Table 11.4, so we cannot offer 2008 labor cost comparisons.

In 2000, the value of apparel exported from Macau was more than $1.8 billion. For such a small nation, this figure was especially significant because, as shown in Table 11.3b, those exports represented more than 83 percent of the total merchandise exported from the nation. The need for establishment of COO became less significant with the demise of quota restrictions, placing Macau in the very vulnerable position of competing directly with China, unless new quota restrictions with that country were established. Note that by 2008, Macau's apparel exports had decreased to just over $1 billion, a significant drop.

Now, try your hand at Learning Activity 11.5.

Figure 11.7 The Hong Kong designer Dorian Ho showed his work at Hong Kong Fashion Week in January 2010. (*Victor Fraile/ Getty Images*)

Learning Activity 11.5
EAST ASIA

1. Considering the data in Table 11.2, which country is more developed— Hong Kong, Japan, Macao, South Korea, or Taiwan? Which data did you use to make your decision?

2. Identify three ways Hong Kong and Macau are unique, as compared with South Korea, Taiwan, and Japan.

3. According to Table 11.8, based on Taiwan's Department of Statistics, why might Taiwan be proud of its trade balance in the face of declining export values?

4. Why are South Korea's apparel manufacturing firms now going offshore to other developing countries for apparel production?

5. Why are Japan, South Korea, and Taiwan focused on technological development of synthetic fibers and fabrics rather than other aspects of the textile and apparel business?

6. How has Hong Kong been able to maintain active participation in apparel manufacturing? What presently threatens that hold?

7. Japan has become a nation of consumers of imported luxury goods. Would you rather run an apparel-manufacturing business or a retailing business in Japan? Explain.

SOUTHEAST ASIA (ASEAN COUNTRIES)

....

The nations to be explored here are countries selected from members of the **Association of Southeast Asian Nations (ASEAN).** The ASEAN members are Brunei, Cambodia, Indonesia, Laos, Malaysia, Myanmar (formerly Burma), the Philippines, Singapore, Thailand, and Vietnam.

A major function of ASEAN is to enhance trade options for its ten member countries. A significant decision announced at its summit conference in Bali, in October 2003, was the intention to "establish an ASEAN Economic Community as a single market and production base with free flow of goods, services, investment, and skilled labor as well as freer flow of capital by 2020" ("Joint Press Statement," 2004). In early 2010, a new free trade agreement between ASEAN nations and China came into full effect. This new "ASEAN plus one" agreement means that 94 percent of the products traded in the area will be tariff free ("Asia," 2010). It was anticipated that this agreement might encourage more Chinese companies to set up factories in Cambodia.

The United States began some discussion of an area-wide trade agreement with ASEAN, but because of a breaking off of trade with Myanmar, a member of ASEAN, that did not progress. (U.S. trade with Myanmar is the topic of Case 1.1.) Instead, the United States has proceeded with trade agreements on a nation-by-nation basis.

In the middle of the first decade of the 21st century, specific description of the textile and apparel business in South Asia was difficult. For example, as the potential threat of China's takeover of some of the textile and apparel business loomed, another threat intervened, this time a natural disaster. The **International Labor Organization (ILO)** estimated that one million people lost their jobs in Indonesia and Sri Lanka because of the tsunami of December 26, 2004, and a significant number of those were related in some way to the textile and apparel industry (Zarocostas, 2005a). Unfortunately, Southeast Asia also had been proving itself to be home to terrorist activities. Attacks occurred in the Philippines (Manila) and Indonesia, including Bali and the Marriott hotel bombing in Jakarta. Such behavior gave pause to companies desirous of doing continued business in the area.

The following discussion begins with island countries and Malaysia—countries on a peninsula and surrounding islands in the South China Sea—including Singapore, Malaysia, Indonesia, and the Philippines. Southeast Asian countries share the Southeast Asian peninsula; for example, Thailand, Vietnam, and Cambodia share the area bordered by the Gulf of Tonkin and the Gulf of Thailand.

Island Countries and Malaysia

Singapore, Malaysia, Indonesia, and the Philippines were all colonized by European countries at about the same time that Hong Kong and Macau were colonized. These countries were occupied during World War II, and their economies were greatly disrupted. Recovery was accomplished sporadically and at different rates.

Singapore

A small island nation about three times the size of Washington, D.C., Singapore is located at the end of the Malay Peninsula. As shown in Table 11.2, Singapore is one of the wealthier nations in Asia, with the highest per capita GDP ($50,300) in the trading block, low unemployment, and a high literacy rate. Since the return of Hong Kong to the Chinese, some of the financial and marketing activities of Southeast Asia have shifted to Singapore. Because of its strong economy, much of the emphasis is on marketing and consumption of apparel products rather than the production of them. Singapore has become a significant fashion capital for the region, actively marketing products to buyers around the globe through international trade fairs.

In May 2003, Singapore and the United States entered into an ambitious free trade agreement, breaking new ground in emerging areas, such as e-commerce, and establishing high standards for intellectual property,

transparency, and customs. This agreement included a yarn-forward rule that enables Singapore to use some cotton and man-made fiber from any other country and still receive trade breaks on tariffs. There are also no tariffs on apparel made with U.S. or Singapore yarn and fabric.

Malaysia

Malaysia, slightly larger than New Mexico, shares with Thailand a peninsula off the western edge of the South China Sea. Malaysia's largest city is Kuala Lumpur. The nation has transformed itself since the 1970s from a producer of raw materials into an emerging multisector economy. The Malaysian Textile Manufacturers Association has been active in promoting the nation's textile industry since 1973 (The Malaysian Textile Manufacturers Association [MTMA], 2006).

Malaysia has been working toward providing more diverse product development services and the creation of indigenous brands. Industry is focusing its efforts on producing for the higher, value-added upscale market and on licensing branded goods to improve its competitiveness. Because it produces petrochemicals, Malaysia also exports quantities of synthetic fibers and yarns. One distinct advantage for Malaysia is its use of electronic data interchange (EDI) to improve the timely clearance of cargo at several of its ports.

The industry now employs more than 68 thousand workers in 662 licensed companies—fewer workers than earlier in the decade (Textiles, 2009). It was believed that the industry had been hurt by the employment of substantial numbers of illegal foreign workers, including thousands of Indonesians, many of whom have been deported. The textile and apparel industry has declined in relative importance during recent years, owing to buildup of other industries, especially in high-tech and other capital-intensive industries. These changes are reflected in higher labor costs than in many other Asian nations (Table 11.4). Although Malaysia has slightly increased exports during the past decade, it is expected that its textile and apparel industry will continue to decline in coming years.

Indonesia

Indonesia is a group of dozens of islands between the Indian and Pacific Oceans. The total landmass is about three times the size of Texas. Indonesia is the world's third-largest democracy, after the United States and India, and had its most ambitious election, in which a parliament and president were elected ("Business as Usual," 2004). However, Indonesia suffers from significant political and social instability, so doing business can be a challenge. There are sometimes problems with counterfeiters within the nation, and foreign companies are warned to be vigilant to protect their products from copyright infringement. One of the major reasons for concern is Indonesia's unpredictable court system.

Despite these problems, the WTO data ranks Indonesia number 12 globally in textile exports and number 8 in apparel exports by dollar value (WTO, 2009, p. 112). Indonesia is the largest producer of textiles and apparel in the ASEAN region. Overall, Indonesia had approximately 8 thousand manufacturers of textiles and apparel in 2004, most of which were in West Java and Jakarta, and was producing quantities of woven, knit, and nonwoven fabrics. It was estimated that there were 1.2 million people working directly in textiles and apparel and an additional 3.5 million workers in related areas, such as distribution (*Textiles and Apparel*, 2004). Cotton fabric accounted for the largest part of the country's textile production, although its domestic cotton was generally viewed as inferior to imported cotton.

Although Indonesia enjoyed a healthy industry previously, recently production capacity in the textiles sector has been declining somewhat as aging machinery has gradually worn out. However, there is potential for revitalization as financial backing for newer machinery is secured. In 2010, Sae-A Trading Co., of South Korea, was reported to be building a new textile plant in Jatiluhur, West Java, which will have dying and knitting units and which could employ up to 15 thousand workers. This firm already operates two factories in Indonesia and others in Vietnam and Latin America.

One of the more secret assets of this country is its center for artists and designers, in Bali. They produce some unique and well-received textile and apparel designs. According to Birnbaum (2000), "Bali will never be a major garment producer, but there are some well-known importers who use Bali as a little mine from which each season a little gold is extracted" (p. 89).

The Philippines

The United States established military bases in the Philippines during World War II; the last ones were finally closed in 1992. The Philippines has had a difficult time sustaining continued economic growth to alleviate poverty; it has a high annual population growth rate and unequal distribution of income.

Textiles and apparel trade has declined in importance in the Philippines during the last decade. Its textile sector remained small, but the apparel sector became quite large, with 1,200 factories employing about 400 thousand workers in the middle of the decade (*Textiles and Apparel*, 2004). There also appeared to be an abundant supply of skilled production workers. Yet, by 2009 apparel exports had dropped significantly from 2000, reflecting the competition from China.

The Philippines is appreciably closer to markets in the Americas than other ASEAN nations; however, this advantage was tempered by manufacturing costs, which were much higher in the Philippines than in China. In addition, the Philippines has no locally produced raw materials, making production lead times longer than those of other nations in the region.

This does not mean that the nation has been neglecting modernization. One of the more timely innovations is a Web site. This online service, TUKAweb.com, has teamed up with FedEx to accelerate the time needed for getting plotted patterns or markers from anywhere in the world to anywhere in Asia. The patterns or markers are sent to the TUKAweb hub electronically, printed, and rolled into a mailing tube, and FedEx delivers the parcel to a site in Asia within 24 hours ("Markers for Asia," 2004). This process eliminates problems incurred by lack of technical services in less developed areas and speeds overall turnaround time from remote sites in the region.

The government has encouraged active enhancement of the sector, especially in stemming the declining export market. The sector is encouraged especially to participate in apparel trade fairs in Europe and Shanghai to promote its producers. It is noted, however, that security has become an increasing issue, in terms of doing business in the Philippines.

South China Peninsula Countries

Vietnam was seriously disrupted by both the Vietnam War, in the 1970s, and the conservative government that followed. Thailand is the only Southeast Asian nation never to be taken over by a European power. Cambodia was invaded by Vietnam during the war and occupied for 30 years afterward. Political disruption continues to the present day. The three countries are all about the same size, similar to New Mexico. As shown in Table 11.2, Thailand's per capita GDP is more than double the combined per capita GDP of Vietnam and Cambodia, at $8,100.

Vietnam

Vietnam took advantage of the low capital investment requirements and availability of low-cost labor within its country, establishing a significant garment industry during the final decade of the 20th century. The country saw this avenue of industrialization as a means of gaining a more sound economic footing, after several decades of political unrest. Vietnam began by supplying cheap T-shirts and other low-quality garments to the Soviet Union and Eastern Europe. Through trade relations with Europe, Vietnamese textile and apparel manufacturing flourished, with shipments to Europe and development of skilled laborers. Today, Vietnam's producers have significantly upgraded their production capabilities. In doing so, the nation has become an attractive source of exports to the EU and the United States.

Vietnam's success is evident, with export of $2.1 billion in textiles and garments in 2000 (refer back to Table 11.3b). By 2008, that figure increased significantly, to $10.6 billion, ranking Vietnam number seven globally in apparel exports, when compared with other producers around the globe (WTO, 2009, p. 112).

Vietnam entered into a bilateral free trade agreement with the United States to encourage trade between the two nations; however, non-MFA quota limits were imposed in 2003 to slow Vietnam's rapid acquisition of U.S. market share. When Vietnam became a WTO member, in early 2007, all quotas disappeared.

Vietnam's textile and apparel industry has three components. In the early 2000s, all state-owned textile and apparel companies belonged to Vinatex (Hayes, 2004). By the end of 2008, Vinatex completed its privatization, and the company had five big subsidiary companies; Phong Phu Textile, Dong Xuan Knitting, 8.3 Knitting, Dong Phuong Garment, and Vietnam Fashion (Tuan, 2008). Other enterprises were privately owned and family run, some

Figure 11.8 Sewing shirts at a factory in Hanoi, Vietnam. (*Andrew Holbrooke/ Corbis*)

belonging to municipal government agencies. The third group of companies consists of foreign-owned companies (Figure 11.8).

Case 11.6 explores the growth of Vietnam's textile and apparel industry.

Vietnam's plan to increase market share has been extremely successful. In the beginning, the two objectives were to shift the focus from CMT to full-package production and to increase domestic content of garment production by investing in cotton production and in spinning and weaving. By 2009, it was reported that Vietnam was supporting the development of cotton farming in the Central Highland area; and in early 2010 Vinatex announced plans to build two new industrial parks, specializing in textile and dyeing, in the Mekong Delta province of Tra Vinh and in the northern province of Thai Binh.

Thailand

Thailand has a free enterprise economy and welcomes foreign investment. A popular government had pushed expansionist policy, including support for village economic development until late 2009, when citizen unrest resulted in protests and riots. Thailand also has multiple ongoing border conflicts and serious problems with cultivation and production as well as illicit transit of drugs (see Case 4.6).

Thailand has a well-developed textile industry, but, because of increased costs and product quality that was not high enough to compete with some advanced nations, a decline in the industry's importance was anticipated. Yet, in 2008 Thailand's textile exports had increased more than 50 percent from 2000. In addition, apparel production seemed to be of better quality than that of some neighboring countries, with lead times that were shorter, owing to the use of locally produced materials. Although its apparel exports did not grow as much as in the textile market, Thailand was exporting more apparel in 2008 than in 2000 (refer back to Table 11.3b).

Thailand maintains a full spectrum of operations, from spinning yarns and making fabrics, through apparel design and production. The country has a larger export market in greige product than in finished goods. The apparel industry has a large number of firms, ranging in size from small, ten-person operations to those with a thousand machine stations; about half of these are large integrated operations.

The textile and apparel sector is concentrated mainly in Bangkok, but that industry has not been well supported. For example, as shown in Table 11.4, there was an abundance of labor, but hourly wages were higher than those of competing nations throughout southern Asia, causing loss of market share to Cambodia and Bangladesh. When the Triumph International plant laid off over 1,900 workers in 2009, workers protested for 8 months, but by the end of the strike many of those workers had started up their own undergarment business, under a new brand name. There was also a need for upper-level employees in management and technologically advanced areas, because wages in these positions were lower than in surrounding areas, such as coastal China, Korea, and Taiwan. In effect, the contracts were going to those with lower construction costs or who had more expertise, putting Thailand's businesses under stress to maintain market share. Also, the infrastructure for moving production out of the area was heavily overtaxed, compared with the more affluent Malaysia and Singapore. Shipments from Thailand to the United States have been declining in recent years, and their overall trade surplus has been declining. The country had put some hope in negotiations for a free trade agreement with the United States, but at the time of this writing, no agreement had been reached.

The Bangkok International Fashion Fair (BIFF) and Bangkok International Leather Fair (BIL) showcase the ASEAN fashion industry (Figure 11.9).

Cambodia

Mirroring the history of many other nations, Cambodia established a significant garment industry during the 1990s. Cambodia saw this avenue to industrialization as a method of putting its nation on sounder economic footing, after several decades of political unrest.

Cambodia negotiated a trade agreement with the United States, based on Cambodia's commitment to improving labor conditions, such that they conformed to international labor standards, in exchange for liberalized quota in the nation's textile and apparel sector. The growth in Cambodia's apparel business over the last few years has been significant. In 2000, apparel exports were less than $1 billion and represented almost 75 percent of the entire country's merchandise exports; by 2008 apparel exports had risen to $3.6 billion, but this reflected

Figure 11.9 The Bangkok International Fashion Fair (BIFF) and Bangkok International Leather Fair (BIL) showcase the ASEAN fashion industry.
(Photo by Bill Hutchinson)

Case 11.6 VIETNAM EYES SOARING TEXTILE AND CLOTHING EXPORTS BY 2010

Vietnam plans to double the value of its textile and clothing exports from US$4.8bn in 2005 to US$10bn by 2010, according to a new report by *Textiles Intelligence*. At the same time it hopes to double the number of people working in the industry from 2m to 4m.

Vietnam's textile and clothing industry plans to achieve these targets by streamlining production and thereby reducing unit costs to boost international competitiveness. . . .

Export growth since 2000 has been steep. It was particularly strong in 2002 at 40% and in 2003 at 33%.

But growth in 2005 slowed to just 9.4%. This was due mainly to the fact that quotas restricting imports from other Asian countries were eliminated at the beginning of the year but imports from Vietnam into the USA—Vietnam's largest export market—were still subject to quotas. U.S. retail buyers therefore turned to countries such as China and India for their clothing.

In 2006, however, the USA implemented safeguard quotas on several categories of Chinese textiles and clothing, with the result that buyers returned to Vietnam. As a result, Vietnamese exports soared by 20.8% to US$5.8bn.

Another milestone was reached on January 11, 2007, when Vietnam joined the World Trade Organization (WTO) and the USA was obliged to remove all quotas on textile and clothing imports from the country.

This removal of quotas is widely expected to boost U.S. demand for Vietnamese clothing, especially for lower-end products. . . .

Investment Plans for Increased Exports

In order to achieve its goal, the Vietnamese government . . . plans to increase the domestic content of garment production by investing in cotton production, and in spinning and weaving facilities.

The government has also identified three other aims for the industry.

One aim is for the industry to build on its existing reputation for high quality by moving from the lower end of the market to the mid-range and the high end of the market. A second aim is for the industry to become more efficient in the sourcing of materials. This is to be achieved by:

- increasing Vietnamese textile production;
- implementing more efficient import sourcing methods; and
- achieving further vertical integration by adding upstream capacity.

A third aim is to increase the competency and productivity of the industry by enhancing research, training and development. . . .

Import Trends

Vietnam currently relies on substantial imports of fibers, yarns, fabrics and garment accessories to feed its expanding apparel industry. . . .

The most important import item is fabric, upon which Vietnam's garment industry is heavily dependent. . . .

The government has a clear strategy of increasing the supply of domestically produced inputs such as raw cotton, yarns, fabrics and garment accessories. Its overall aim is to reduce the import content to less than 25% by 2010.

Machinery Investments

Investment in modern machinery has soared in recent years. . . .

The Vietnamese textile and clothing industry has also managed to attract a substantial amount of foreign investment. The largest foreign investor in the Vietnamese textile and clothing industry is Taiwan, followed by South Korea and Hong Kong.

Source:

Vietnam eyes soaring textile and clothing exports by 2010. (2007, 8 August). just-style.com. Retrieved February 25, 2010, from http://www.just-style.com/analy-sis/vietnam-eyes-soaring-textile-and-clothing-exports-by-2010_id98051.aspx

almost 85 percent of overall exports (refer back to Table 11.3b). This heavy dependence on apparel exports during a volatile economy can be quite risky, yet indications are that China may outsource some of its CMT here, when its factories are overextended.

Further your study of Southeast Asia with Learning Activity 11.6.

Learning Activity 11.6
SOUTHEAST ASIA

1. In what ways are the ASEAN countries different from the East Asian countries?
2. Pick the two Southeast Asia countries that you think will be most active in textiles and apparel in 10 years. Explain your choices.
3. Identify two things that seem to be the largest barriers to industrial development in these regions. Why are the things you chose such a problem?
4. What advantages has Singapore had that allowed it to develop so much more rapidly than other countries in the same region?

SOUTH ASIA

The textile and apparel sector is believed to be the largest source of manufacturing jobs in South Asia, and its labor costs for textile and apparel production are among the lowest in the world. India has by far the most invested in the textile and apparel industry in this region. However, there are concerns that the productivity rates of laborers in India, Pakistan, and Bangladesh are about 20 to 25 percent below those in China. One of the most difficult issues in securing products from South Asia is the distance from major markets. It takes about 45 to 60 days to ship from India to the East Coast of the United States. The EU is considerably closer and provides India with its biggest market for products.

India

India's population reached one billion in 2000 and is growing at a startling rate of 2 percent per year. At this rate, it could soon surpass China in total population. One of India's strengths in global trade is competency in the English language, initiated in part by a long history as a part of the British Empire. India was a major provider of raw cotton to the British long before much of Asia was focused on the global market. Cotton is such a significant part of Indian culture that when the nation gained independence from Britain, in 1947, it placed a blue spinning wheel on its flag—appropriate for a country that derives 30 percent of its export earnings from the textile sector (Krznaric & Schmidt-Whitley, 2003).

India's intent is to build on its ranking as one of the world's largest cotton exporters. In 2010, India was the world's top organic cotton producer, ranking in the top three in overall cotton production, along with China and the United States. In the past, the industry also relied heavily on production of other natural fibers, such as wool, silk, and jute. Production of man-made fibers has been increasing in recent years, and man-made fibers now constitute 25 percent of all yarn produced. "Textiles has always played a crucial role in Indian history and today this sector is the second largest employer in the country" (Krznaric and Schmidt-Whitley, 2003, p. 31).

Read Case 11.7 for a discussion of efforts to advance the textile and apparel industry in the Indian state of Tirupur.

Although India has a long tradition of textile production, much of its apparel industry previously placed the greatest emphasis on domestic consumption. The middle class is increasing remarkably in size, and tastes are turning away from the traditional sari or shalwar kamiz forms of dress to Western tastes in apparel design. Overall, however, the nation is still considered a Third World country, in terms of per person GDP. Many

people cannot afford branded clothing, still preferring to go to a local tailor for custom-made suits and trousers. Yet, even with its domestic emphasis, India's sheer size enabled it to secure a global apparel export ranking of sixth in 2008, by dollar value (WTO, 2009). In recent decades, India has begun to focus its attention on challenging China in the global marketplace.

Production facilities are scattered throughout the country, but the headquarters of India's most powerful companies are divided among three locations: Mumbai (Bombay), considered the economic heart of India; New Delhi, the capital; and Bangalore (considered the nation's Silicon Valley), where the more temperate weather has lured manufacturers seeking to modernize their

Figure 11.10a Apparel workers in India preparing bundles for the production line. Traditional apparel for women is more pervasive in India than in China.
(Courtesy of WWD)

production processes. These firms cater to the mass-produced market (Figure 11.10a).

A lesser-known benefit of India's industry is its fashion culture. India's apparel producers seem to have the ability to make things that do not look ethnic; "they simply look special" (Birnbaum, 2000, p. 90). One of the serendipitous outcomes of having rather antiquated loom capabilities in some locations is that they can turn out unique fabrics that are used by couture designers throughout the world (Figure 11.10b).

One local firm, TCNS, decided to capitalize on decades of experience manufacturing for export to customers such as JCPenney, Target, Levi Strauss & Co., Gap, and Banana Republic, to cater to a promising local market. To this end, TCNS focused on more traditional clothes for its domestic brand W but incorporated Western influences (Krznaric & Schmidt-Whitley, 2003). Foreign brands are coming to India, not only to manufacture for their own markets, but also to establish a commercial presence in the retail market.

To enable Indian firms to compete with China, the government provides them with some assistance by allowing import of raw materials at zero customs duty or tariff. India's duties on other products range from 15 to 35 percent. Infrastructure problems at ports and procedural delays must be addressed. Also, India's rigid labor laws, which prevent companies from laying off workers if business slows, are a major worry. In response to these industry concerns, the government is setting up China-style special economic zones in various parts of the country, where factories are expected to have somewhat greater flexibility in their hiring and firing practices.

Although India is considered a major alternative source to China for apparel products,

Figure 11.10b Nikasha Tawadey showing at Lakme Fashion Week, in Mumbai, India.
(Gautam Singh/AP Photo)

the nation is also seen as suffering from a weaker infrastructure and inefficiencies posed by the country's bureaucracy. Some firms indicated difficulty working with India because of a lack of transparency in legal requirements and complicated paperwork that increase costs and necessitate the use of a broker, rather than dealing directly with manufacturers. These factors affect timely deliveries and may impact India's competitiveness. However, India has a very large pool of workers, and Indian firms tend to have well-educated management and technicians.

Volume is no longer seen as the main goal of the Indian garment exporter community, which is now focusing on higher-value products, including more fashionable items and accessories. Because India is known for its capability for providing labor-intensive embellishments on apparel, such as hand embroidery and beading, "Indians think that they should capitalize on designs, embellishments, embroideries, and details" (Krznaric & Schmidt-Whitley, 2003, p. 35). The Indian fashion industry is globally competitive on price and quality and has the added dimension of being able to provide innovative design.

Bangladesh

Bangladesh appeared to be a nation that was vulnerable to the pressures of China. In 2004, there were "3,200 export-oriented factories in Bangladesh, but only 1,200 were actively exporting. Of the remaining 2,000 factories, 700 were inactive and 1,300 mainly did subcontracting for the exporters" ("Export Advantage," 2004). This source went on to report that the garment industry was performing at efficiency levels well below those of other key competitors, partially due to wasteful methods, ill-managed production, and lack of modernized machinery.

Bangladesh's major port, Dhaka, is easily accessible, but its communications network was considered substandard and its roads, poor; frequent power outages were considered another hardship. In addition, there was concern regarding child labor, although there were indications the country was working to get its factories certified for international labor standards. Bangladesh also has suffered from low literacy levels, and it was dealing with frequent labor unrest.

Despite all these issues, figures from the WTO indicate that Bangladesh imports large quantities of fabrics and uses them to produce the garments that it exports. In 2000, Bangladesh was importing $1.3 billion in fabrics; in 2008 that had risen to $1.5 billion. Of great interest is that during that same time period, Bangladesh's apparel exports almost doubled, from $5.9 billion, in 2000, to $10.9 billion, in 2008 (refer back to Tables 11.3a and 11.3b).

It was anticipated that Bangladesh would suffer greatly when quotas were lifted on China, but the country seems to have weathered that threat reasonably well. In 2008, Bangladesh was ranked fifth in the world in apparel exports (WTO, 2009). The biggest concern is that 78.2 percent of Bangladesh's total merchandise exports are currently textile and apparel products, and when the global economy fluctuates, it could be in trouble. As shown in Table 11.2, Bangladesh already suffers from high unemployment and has the second lowest per capita GDP in Asia, after Nepal.

Sri Lanka

Sri Lanka (formerly Ceylon) is an island nation located off the southeast tip of India. Sri Lanka won its independence from Britain in 1948. The country maintains strong links with the UK, and many people continue to speak English. Sri Lanka suffered a prolonged civil war for more than 25 years, but in 2009 it finally appeared to be drawing to a close as the last Tamil group was taken over.

Nonetheless, the garment industry became an engine for Sri Lanka's economy, providing more than 300 thousand jobs and almost half of the nation's foreign earnings (Burtin & Ergüney, 2003). One of Sri Lanka's particular product strengths is lingerie. Sri Lanka lacks a significant textile industry and depends on textile imports to supply much of its apparel production, causing lead times of 90 days rather than the 60-day standard of many Asian neighbors. Sri Lanka imports most of its fabrics and yarns from Hong Kong, China, and India. To ensure quick delivery times of these materials, the country has focused on closer links with India and Pakistan. To that end, Sri Lanka instituted a free trade agreement with India in 2000 that was to provide local suppliers with tariff-free fabrics (Roy, 2004). A similar agreement was developed with Pakistan, but it did not take effect until later. Sri Lanka produces only 10 percent of its textile needs locally and hopes to increase that level. Its processing facilities are technologically advanced.

During the application of the quota system, the garment industry grew significantly between the mid-1980s and mid-2000s, and it was anticipated that many of the 850 major companies active in the apparel-manufacturing sector would disappear with the dismantling of WTO quotas (Burtin & Ergüney, 2003). However, as shown in Table 11.3b, when you look at the figures for apparel exports during the period from 2000 to 2008, they continued to reflect a slow but steady climb. Much of Sri Lanka's production was for discount stores, and its present goal is to increase their presence in the higher-end market.

The garment industry has given rise to an impressive accessory industry. Among these firms is Mainetti, one of the largest garment hanger suppliers in the world, with operations in 25 countries. The company's local facility, Mainettech, is the island's lead-ing supplier of hangers and is the regional hub for supplying these to the Indian sub-continent. In 1998, Mainettech became the first local hanger producer to obtain ISO 9002 certification. This certification indicates a high level of management and quality of products.

In the past, Sri Lanka was known for compliance with international standards in labor, environmental protection, and respect for human rights. However, in February 2010 the EU withdrew the country's GSP (Generalized System of Preferences) trade benefits for 6 months to encourage Sri Lanka to address problems with its poor human rights record. This meant apparel exports would have tariffs added to some apparel categories of up to 9.6 percent, effectively a price hike on products imported into the EU (Barrie, 2010). Although this could prove critical to the industry here, it was also reported that between 40 and 45 percent of Sri Lanka's exports were already headed to the United States.

Sri Lanka suffered greatly from the tsunami that affected much of southern Asia on December 26, 2004. The factories, which are largely clustered inland, near the capital of Colombo, experienced little damage, but the railways and roads on which they relied for supplies and shipping of finished goods were battered. Because the waves hit on Boxing Day, a holiday, workers were at home.

Pakistan

Pakistan provides a more limited range of products than India but is considered a good source of cotton goods, especially home textile products and fabrics. Pakistan is the world's fourth largest producer of cotton after China, the United States, and India. The country is recognized as providing consistent quality and having large capacity for producing spun yarn and unfinished cotton fabrics. In 2008, Pakistan ranked tenth in textile exports and twelfth in apparel exports globally (WTO, 2009).

The business climate in Pakistan can be more difficult than in India, according to some industry sources, and there has been concern expressed that, unless the mill is known to be funded by World Bank loans, purchasing from some private mills increases the possibility that financing comes from drug money profits (*Textile and Apparel*, 2004). Terrorist activity in the region near the Afghanistan border causes some trepidation in doing business here but does not seem to affect the industry.

In late 2009, the government of Pakistan began to intervene in industry activities by monitoring, and finally, blocking, some of the country's cotton yarn exports (Abdullah, 2010). The rationale was that this would ensure availability of raw materials for value-added textile and apparel industry activities within the country. Cotton yarn exports had been increasing from year to year and were making it difficult for the producers of ready-made cotton garments to secure raw materials for their work.

The garment cities in Pakistan are Karachi, Lahore, and Faisalabad. In early 2010, plans were announced for setting up the nation's largest garment city at Hyderabad, in Sindh province, in the hope of attracting foreign investors.

Labor issues have been surfacing in early 2010, as textile workers have been staging protests calling for workers' rights and an increase in minimum wages. It is estimated that approximately 3.5 million people are employed as textile workers in Pakistan, and most work on daily wages, without job security or social security benefits (Abdullah, 2010).

OCEANIA

Oceania, which is made up of Australia and New Zealand, is unique because of its location as an economically developed set of island nations in the Southern Hemisphere that also has strong ties to Europe. Until now, all the developed countries we have looked at have been in the Northern Hemisphere. The British, first following the U.S. Revolutionary War and later, World War II, populated Oceania with immigrants. Before the Revolutionary War, Great Britain had sent many convicts to the American colonies; after losing those colonies, it shipped prisoners to Australia instead. The prisoners included criminals, but also political prisoners, petty lawbreakers, and poor people who had been imprisoned for not being able to pay their debt. They first established a settlement in Sydney, in 1788, and during the 80 years that Australia served as a penal colony, nearly 200 thousand people were sent there. Free settlers also migrated to the colony, most often family members of the convicts.

Following World War II, the governments began a program to encourage people to migrate to Oceania and, throughout a 30-year period, generated more than 3.5 million additional immigrants. Japanese investors soon enhanced development of Oceania's natural and industrial resources. Signage in Sydney reflects the role of the Japanese in its development, as street signs are bilingual, in English and Japanese. Today, after a long flight from the United States to Australia, one can turn on the TV and not miss a single day of the "soaps"; however, when conducting business in this area, it is important to remember that it is on the other side of the international dateline, a day ahead of the United States—be sure to check your calendar.

Australia

Australia is a developed nation with the third-highest per capita GDP in Asia, after Singapore and Hong Kong (refer back to Table 11.2). Australia's textile and apparel industry has moved its focus from production to consumption, following the pattern of developed nations in other parts of the globe. Following World War II, Australian policy was to support the process of the WTO and avoid bilateral free trade agreements. However, since the mid-1990s the country has moved in the opposite direction, negotiating free trade agreements with Singapore and Thailand. A free trade agreement with the United States was implemented in 2004. This seeming turnaround focuses attention on the possibility that some nations are concerned about the trajectory the WTO is taking with trade issues.

Australia remains the world's top producer and exporter of wool fiber and fabric. In 2004 Australia's 106 million sheep produced more than 1.05 billion pounds of wool, accounting for almost 50 percent of the global total (Tucker, 2005). There has been a slow decline in wool output for several years, but this appeared to be steadying in late 2009. The two largest wool-producing states are New South Wales and Western Australia. Tasmania also produces wool. The wool industry has formed the Wool Carbon Alliance to work with the Australian government to research the role wool can play in the future. The premise is that a household can reduce its carbon emissions by living with wool products, a planet-friendly fiber that is renewable, biodegradable, and recyclable and that takes less energy to produce than man-made fiber products.

Australia is also researching the use of insect silk and is moving a step closer to making lightweight fabrics from this biomimetic material. The nation's scientists have managed to produce an artificial version of threads made by honeybee larvae and are currently looking at potential applications for these fine threads, including medical use (sutures and artificial tendons and ligaments).

Australia's apparel industry is relatively small and focused on fashion goods, and just a few apparel lines are produced for export. One apparel manufacturer here is Pacific Brands. This firm has found very difficult market conditions in the past few years that have affected its international sales. The firm has had to cut its work force and close several of its factories since the end of the quota system, yet its top-performing brands have maintained market share. Its key brands include Mossimo, Clarks, and Volley. The Oroton Group has extended its Ralph Lauren licensing agreement for another 3 years and looks forward to elevating the brand in this territory by opening new stores, including a factory outlet, in 2010.

Like most developed nations, the majority of apparel sold within the country is imported. However, we would be remiss if we did not mention UGG boots, for they are distributed throughout the world. Australia has been credited with their origin, but their earliest identification was with pilots in World War I, who were said to have worn them for warmth in unpressurized airplanes. Reportedly, sheep shearers in rural Australia wore the boots during shearing season in the 1920s, surfers and competitive swimmers wore them during the 1960s and 1970s for keeping warm while out of the water. The boots are made from sheepskin tanned with the wool attached, and assembled with the wool side inside (imitations are made of synthetic materials). The wool provides warmth and comfort by absorbing moisture and retaining heat. The boots also have a sensible rubber sole. The brand has a long and complicated history involving multiple ownerships in several countries. In the early 2000s, UGGS became a fashion trend in the United States, leading to increased global production and sales. Now, most people cannot tell the difference between those made in Australia and imitations made in China.

New Zealand

New Zealand consists mainly of two islands in the Pacific Ocean located east of Australia. The center of the domestic apparel industry is Auckland, the capital. Domestic production within the country is increasingly limited but of very high quality and mostly for domestic consumption. Like Australia, New Zealand has moved into the realm of consumption of textile and apparel products, rather than production. New Zealand imports a large portion of its apparel. The retail market operates approximately a season behind Europe and the United States, and local importers use this to their advantage, purchasing end-of-season surplus goods and selling them at the start of the season in New Zealand. Residents are heavy users of the Internet, and online shopping is gaining popularity. However, some consumers remain hesitant to purchase clothing in this way because of sizing issues.

Now, extend your understanding of textiles and apparel in South Asia and Oceania with Learning Activity 11.7.

Learning Activity 11.7
TEXTILES AND APPAREL IN
SOUTH ASIA AND OCEANIA

1. What pattern of economic development was taken by those individual nations within the region that now enjoy the highest per person GDPs?

2. From question 1, what pattern of future activity can be projected for those newly developing nations that are now aggressively pursuing the production and exporting of apparel products to jumpstart their economies?

3. What are some of the major obstacles identified in this chapter for achieving overall economic growth?

4. What are some of the major obstacles identified in this chapter for achieving growth in the textile and apparel industries?

5. Of the obstacles identified in questions 3 and 4, identify those that are
   • political
   • economic
   • social/cultural

6. Compare the mission of ASEAN with those of the WTO, the OAS, APEC and the EU.

7. What is the likelihood that Australia will become a major apparel exporter? Give several reasons to support your response.

8. Put on your Macy's sourcing hat. You are still sourcing a moderate-priced, private brand line of casual young women's apparel. Given what you now know, which region would you select—Europe, the Americas, Asia, or Oceania? Why?

9. If you were required to use an Asian country for sourcing, what country would you use? Why?

SUMMARY

Asia is the largest trading bloc of the global textile and apparel industry. Taken individually, China and India produce massive quantities of textile and apparel products for their own huge populations, but also for export to the rest of the world. Some of the poorest nations, Bangladesh and Cambodia, are also in this bloc. Some perceive these two nations as the most vulnerable in the region to changes in trade patterns brought about by the disappearance of apparel quotas, but so far they have been holding on to their market share. Although Malaysia was seen as suffering industry setbacks from the termination of quotas, the country is moving toward a more diversified economy.

The pattern of growth for textile and apparel industries has reflected the overall economic development of the individual nations. Beginning with a population in which the labor force was needed to fill basic survival needs, attention has shifted to more advanced technologies and, finally, to consumption as overall economies grew. Japan and Australia were producing nations after World War II, and as they developed, other locations, including Taiwan, South Korea, and Hong Kong, took up the production banner.

The pattern continues today as each nation repeats the cycle by participating in basic apparel production, followed by rising wage demands and shifting production to more advanced products that bring about a higher overall economic productivity, and, ultimately, predominance of marketing and consumption of textile and apparel products over production. Today, China is riding the pinnacle of the production wave, but Vietnam and other nations, such as India, are poised to take advantage if China's economy heats up and costs accelerate there. The demise of quotas fueled some changes, but a serious issue is how more sophisticated technologies and more effective management systems can improve the efficiencies of supply chains while doing a better job of meeting and exceeding consumer needs and wants.

REFERENCES

Abdullah, A. (2010a, February 12). Pakistan: Customs authorities block cotton yarn shipments. just-style.com. Retrieved March 5, 2010, from http://www.just-style.com/news/customs-authorities-block-cotton-yarn-shipments_id106725.aspx

Abdullah, A. (2010b, February 23). Pakistan: Protests held over workers' rights. just-style.com. Retrieved March 5, 2010, http://www.just-style.com/news/protests-held-over-workers-rights_id106841.aspx?lk=rap

APEC: A new growth paradigm for a connected Asia-Pacific in the 21st century. (2009, November 15). Retrieved February 10, 2010, from http://www.whitehouse.gov/the-press-office/statement-apec-leaders

Asia-Pacific Economic Cooperation. (n.d.). About APEC. Retrieved January 24, 2005, from http://www.apec.org/content/apec/about_apec.html

Asia: Region awaits effects of new China trade deal. (2010, January 5). just-style.com. Retrieved February 25, 2010, from http://www.just-style.com/pap.aspx?id=106309

Au, K., & Yeung, K. (1999). Production shift for the Hong Kong clothing industry. *Journal of Fashion Marketing and Management, 3*(2), 166–178.

Ayling, J. (2009, December 15). Ten key trends in Chinese's fashion retail market. just-style.com. Retrieved June 3, 2010, from http://www.just-style.com/comment/10-key-trends-in-chinas-fashion-retail-market_id106204.aspx

Barboza, D. (2004, December 24). In roaring China, sweaters are west of socks city. *The New York Times.* Retrieved from http://www.nytimes.com/2004/12/24/business/worldbusiness/24china.html

Barrie, L. (2010, February 17). EU: Retailers brace as Sri Lanka loses trade benefit. just-style.com. Retrieved March 5, 2010, from http://www.just-style.com/news/retailers-brace-as-sri-lanka-loses-trade-benefit_id106786.aspx

Birnbaum, D. (2000). *Birnbaum's global guide to winning the great garment war*. Hong Kong: Third Horizon Press.

Birnbaum, D. (2009, August 21). Sourcing: Marginal suppliers need a radical re-think. just-style.com. Retrieved February 25, 2010, from http://www.just-style.com/comment/marginal-suppliers-need-a-radical-re-think_id105103.aspx

Burtin, A., & Ergüney, Ö. (2003, April–May). Sri Lanka: A prospect of peace. Special report. *Fashion Business International*, 24–35.

Business as usual. (2004, March 20). *The Economist*, p. 44.

Cambie, S. (2007, March 1). Brand rehab: How Sungjoo Group CEO Kin Sunghoo bagged an ailing German luxury brand and resuscitated it for the Asian market. *Communication World*. Retrieved March 4, 2010, from http://www.thefreelibrary.com/Brand+rehab:+how+Sungjoo+Group+CEO+Kim+Sungjoo+bagged+an+ailing...-a0160166934

Cardenas, J. (2010, January 27). Hong Kong fashion week grows. *Women's Wear Daily*. Retrieved from http://www.wwd.com/fashion-news/hong-kong-fashion-week-grows-2436114

Central Intelligence Agency (CIA). (2010). *The world factbook*. Retrieved February 2010 from http://www.odci.gov/cia/publications/factbook/index.html

China: The world's factory. (2004, October–November). *Fashion Business International*, 30–32.

Country focus: China. (2010, January 28). *Women's Wear Daily*. Retrieved from http://www.wwd.com/business-news/country-focus-china-2437560?navSection=package&navId=2438328

Export Advantage. (2004, August 11). Bangladesh: Local Industry and Market. U.S. Department of Commerce—International Trade Administration, Office of Textiles and Apparel (OTEXA). Retrieved January 5, 2005, from http://www.ita.doc.gov/tacgi/overseas.nsf

Fishman, T. C. (2004, July 4) The Chinese century. *The New York Times Magazine*. Retrieved from http://www.nytimes.com/2004/07/04/magazine/04CHINA.html?pagewanted=all

Hayes, D. (February–March, 2004). Vietnam export acceleration. *Fashion Business International*, 22–26.

India aims to be sourcing hotspot. (2004, April–May). *Fashion Business International*, 18.

INDIA: Knitwear Technology Center Launched in Tirupur. (2010, January 10). just-style.com. Retrieved June 2, 2010, from http://www.just-style.com/news/knitwear-technology-centre-launched-in-tirupur_id106340.aspx

Joint press statement: 17th ASEAN-US Dialog. Association of Southeast Asian Nations. (2004, January 30). Retrieved February 5, 2004, from http://www.aseasnsec.org/15982.htm

Jung, J. (2009, February). Doing business the Chinese way: Eastern and Western world view and business practices in China. *Fiber: Online Journal of the International Fashion and Apparel Industry*. Retrieved from http://www.udel.edu/fiber/issue3/researchbriefs

Kang, D. (2003, spring). Market and society in Korea: Interest, institution and the textile industry. *Business History Review*, 77(1), 203. Retrieved January 24, 2005, from http://www.firstsearch.oclc.org.proxy.lib.ilstu.edu

Krznaric, A., & Schmidt-Whitley, J. (2003, October–November). India: Millions in the making. Special report. *Fashion Business International*, 30–37.

Largest cities of the world—by population. (n.d.). worldatlas.com. Retrieved June 2010 from http://www.worldatlas.com/citypops.htm

Malaysian Industrial Development Authority (MIDA). (2009, April 2). Industries in Malaysia: Textiles and apparels industry. Retrieved June 4, 2010, from http://www.mida.gov.my/en_v2/index.php?page=textiles-and-apparel-industr

The Malaysian Textile Manufacturers Association (MTMA). (2006). About us. Retrieved June 4, 2010, from http://www.fashion-asia.com/page.cfm?name=aboutus

Malone, S. (2004, September 28). Sourcing horizons: Winners and losers. *Women's Wear Daily*, 10–11.

Malone, S., & Ellis, K. (2004, December 14). China to impose export tariffs in trade reversal. *Women's Wear Daily*, 10–11.

Markers for Asia. (2004, August–September). *Fashion Business International*, 66.

Masters, C. (2009, May 18). In Japan, fast fashion rules in slow times. *Time*. Retrieved from http://www.time.com/time/world/article/0,8599,1895240,00.html

Movius, L. (2009, November 24) China's textile city grows in stature. *Women's Wear Daily*. Retrieved from http://www.movius.us/articles/WWD-ShaoxingKeqiao.html

Rivoli, Pietra. (2009). *The travels of a T-shirt in the global economy: An economist examines the markets, power, and politics of world trade*. Hoboken, NJ: John Wiley.

Roy, D. (2004). Indi-Sri Lanka trade: Hype and reality. *Asia Times Online*. Retrieved June 4, 2010, from http://www.atimes.com/atimes/South_Asia/FC12Df05.html

Shaping up to share the boom. (2004, October–November). *Fashion Business International*, 38.

Socha, M. (2004, December 8). Big brands opening bigger Tokyo stores. *Women's Wear Daily*, 14.

The story of porcelain. (2005). Retrieved January 25, 2005, from http://www.cnn/com/2004/TRAVEL/12/21chinaware.ap/index.html

Survey of India and China: The Tiger in front: Sweatshops and technocoolies. (2005, March 5). *The Economist*, Special Section, 9–11.

Tait, N. (2004a, June–July) China: This giant is not sleeping. *Fashion Business International*, 28–35.

Tait, N. (2004b, August 2). TAL sews up the Asian clothing market. just-style.com. Retrieved June 4, 2010, from http://www.just-style.com/analysis/tal-apparel-sews-up-asian-clothing-market_id92380.aspx

Taiwan Textile Federation. (2009). *Overview of Taiwan's textile industry–2009*. Retrieved from http://ttf.textiles.org.tw/Textile/TTFroot/overview-english.pdf

Textiles and Apparel: Assessment of the competitiveness of certain foreign suppliers to the U.S. market. (2004, January). U.S. ITC investigation no. 332-448; Publication 3671. Retrieved March 16, 2005, from http://www.otexta.ita.doc.gov.default.htm

TITAS 2009 final report. (2009). Retrieved March 7, 2010, from http://www.titas.com.tw/pdf/titas2009-finalreport-1-4.pdf

Tuan, N. (2008, January 25). Vietnam: Vinatex to complete privatisation this year. just-style.com. Retrieved February 25, 2010, from http://www.just-style.com/news/vinatex-to-complete-privatisation-this-year_id99709.aspx

Tucker, R. (2005, July 27). Australian wool industry in two-sided tangle. *Women's Wear Daily*, 8.

Uniqlo. (2009). About Uniqlo. Retrieved June 3, 2010, from http://www.uniqlo.com/us/corp/

Vietnam eyes soaring textile and clothing exports by 2010. (2007, August 8). just-style.com. Retrieved February 25, 2010, from http://www.just-style.com/analysis/vietnam-eyes-soaring-textile-and-clothing-exports-by-2010_id98051.aspx

Werner International Management Consultants. (2009). *Primary textiles labor cost comparisons 2008*. Retrieved May 25, 2010, from http://texnet.ilgstudios.net/files/2009/08/Werner_International_-_Labor_Cost_Study_2008.pdf

World Trade Organization (WTO). (2009). International Trade Statistics 2009. Section 2: Merchandise trade by product (107–114). Retrieved January 16, 2010, from http://www.wto.org/english/res_e/statis_e/its2009_e/its09_merch_trade_product_e.pdf

Zarocostas, J. (2005a, January 20). ILO study finds 1M jobs lost as result of tsunami. *Women's Wear Daily*, 19.

Zarocostas, J. (2005b, January). Shanghai in major port expansion push. *Women's Wear Daily/Global*, 9.

12 The Middle East and Africa

• • • •• • • • •• • • • • •• • • • • •• • • • •• • • • •• • • • •• • • • • •• • • • •• • • •• • • • •• • • • •• •

Muslin fabric originally
came from the Iraqi city of Mosul
(Progressive Policy Institute, 2005)

ALL PHASES OF life in the Middle East and Africa, including
the textile and apparel business, are impacted heavily by the cultural
patterns rooted in religious affiliations. Three of the world's major religions were initiated here: Judaism, Christianity, and Islam. The tensions
flourish among those who focus on a faith-based culture anchored in
religious beliefs versus those who espouse a more secular orientation
based on economic and political behaviors. Followers of the Islamic
faith, Muslims, constitute the largest representative group throughout
much of this trading bloc that stretches from sub-Saharan Africa (SSA),
up to the Mediterranean Rim, and eastward through Iran. Doing business here requires recognition of some basic patterns of behavior, such
as Sunday is a business day, Friday is the day of faith, and the workweek
therefore becomes Sunday through Thursday. There are exceptions to
this pattern, but it can be somewhat disconcerting to those coming
from more secularly based cultures in Europe and the Americas.

Sensitivity to cultural differences must also extend to perceptions
of the role of women in some of these societies. For many Muslim
women, the ability to work outside the home is often restricted by
male relatives. This may include discouraging activities such as working for male supervisors. Two geographic areas within the region,

Objectives

- Understand the economic and political
  strengths of organizations in individual
  countries within the Middle East and Africa.

- Explore religious and cultural influences
  on the role of women and the operation of
  businesses.

- Examine textile and apparel trading trends
  for Middle Eastern and African countries.

Figure 12.1

Map highlighting the Middle East, North Africa, and Sub-Saharan Africa.

(Courtesy Fairchild Books)

the Nile valley of Egypt and the Mesopotamian region we now know as Iraq, are major cultural centers of the region and are foundations of their civilizations. See the Global Lexicon.

POLITICAL AND ECONOMIC OVERVIEW

Figure 12.1 is a map of the Middle East and Africa. This trading bloc encompasses some of the very richest and the very poorest people in the world. We will discuss this region as three commonly used sectors: the Middle East, North Africa, and Sub-Saharan Africa (SSA). As with the other chapters in this part of this text, the countries selected for discussion from each sector are those most prominently involved in the textile and apparel industry. We will approach discussion of the region as follows:

- Middle East—the countries lying east of the Mediterranean and Red Seas, south through the Arabian Peninsula, and eastward, toward South Asia; includes Turkey, which straddles Europe and Asia
- North Africa—the countries on the northern border of the continent, adjacent to the Mediterranean Sea; includes Morocco, Tunisia, and Egypt
- SSA—including Ghana and Nigeria, on the Gold Coast; Kenya and Uganda, in the central region; South Africa and Lesotho, in the south; and the island nations of Madagascar and Mauritius, off the eastern shore.

As we progress through this chapter, please refer back to the map in Figure 12.1 to appreciate each nation's location in relation to other countries in the region.

World Bank

The **World Bank** has been mentioned numerous times throughout this text, but it is particularly important to this region. It is not actually a "bank," but rather a specialized agency of the United Nations, made up of 184 member nations. The term *World Bank* is used to refer to the International Bank for Reconstruction and Development and the International Development Association. The mission of the World Bank Group is to improve the living standards of people in the developing world. It is a development institution that collaborates with many other related organizations.

The world's least developed nations typically cannot borrow money in international markets or have to pay high interest rates to do so. The World Bank is able to provide them with interest-free loans and direct contributions or loans from developed countries, along with policy advice, technical assistance, and knowledge-sharing services. In fiscal 2009, the World Bank provided $58.8 billion in financing for 767 projects worldwide, while, in 2009 the International Development Association (IDA) provided $14 billion for 176 new operations in 63 low-income countries. Africa received 56 percent of this assistance—$7.84 billion (World Bank, 2010). In addition, the World Bank, in partnership with the European Investment Bank, and in collaboration with the governments of France, Lebanon, Morocco, Tunisia, Egypt, and Jordan, launched The Marseille Center for Mediterranean Integration (MCMI), to facilitate access to knowledge and improve cooperation for enhanced, sustainable development and greater integration and trade within the Mediterranean region. MCMI offers a new approach to integration and trade partnership among Middle Eastern and northern Africa countries (World Bank, 2010).

The **International Monetary Fund (IMF)** also works in tandem with the World Bank, but its role is different. The purpose of the IMF is to help integrate countries into the global economy. IMF does this through advising and assisting member countries in implementing economic and financial policies that promote stability, reduce vulnerability to crisis, and encourage sustained growth and high living standards. Because international trade and investments cross national borders, countries must buy and sell currencies to finance imports and exports. The IMF monitors these transactions and helps member nations work within the global monetary system. Any of the 184 IMF member nations (rich or poor) may call on their services.

Background and Current Conditions in the Sectors of the Region

Political tensions in and among some of the countries in the sectors of the region are often very pronounced and result in difficult conditions for doing business. Nevertheless, the importance of the area to our understanding of the overall global marketplace is underscored by their tradition of centuries of trade with other nations. Active textile and apparel trade has extended from the ancient camel caravans traversing the Middle East and African deserts to and from India and China, to the ships that plied the Mediterranean, carrying products to Europe. Southern Africa also has a long history of significant cotton production and trade with other nations. Many areas of these trading regions, both in the Middle East and in Africa, were repeatedly colonized by European nations, most recently by the United Kingdom (UK) and France, in the 1800s. These areas did not gain full independence until after World War II, in the mid-20th century.

There is some confusion as to which countries to include in which sector, because there are nations that are perceived to be European, Asian, or African but that are located in the area generally considered to be the Middle East. The countries included for the purposes of this text may prove to be controversial, but we are including Turkey in our discussion of the Middle East, even though Turkey is actively seeking EU membership. Turkey's largest city, Istanbul, is in Europe, but the bulk of the nation, including its capital, Ankara, is in continental Asia, in the region commonly described as the Middle East. Cyprus, Turkey's near neighbor, has been admitted to the EU on a contingency basis and so was discussed earlier (see Chapter 10).

According to the United Nations Conference on Trade Development, despite a long history of regional integration, internal trade among countries in the Middle East and Africa remains low, compared with other parts of the world. The two countries most active in intrasectional trade are South Africa and Nigeria, responsible for about half of total internal trade. Reasons for the extremely low internal trade include time-consuming and high transport cost, a result of poor transport and communications infrastructure, and lack of skilled labor. Political instability and low levels of domestic investment result in multiple inefficient, costly, and unpredictable border procedures, hampering trade in and among the Middle Eastern, North African, and SSA sectors (*Statement by H. E. Ambassador*, 2009).

Internal trade is made up of a diversified set of manufactured goods, whereas exports to the rest of the world are concentrated primarily in a few types of commodities, including ores, minerals, and agricultural products, such as cotton. There appear to be real opportunities for developing systems to facilitate internal trade as well as export of manufactured goods. Recent bilateral and multilateral trade agreements among countries in the Middle East, as well as with China and the United States, are expected to provide opportunities for both intraregional trade and exports to other parts of the world (*Statement by H. E. Ambassador*, 2009).

Table 12.1 provides an overview of the primary countries in the Middle East and Africa that are involved in the textile and apparel industry. From the standpoint of geographic size, Saudi Arabia, nearly one fifth the size of the United States, is by far the largest, followed by Ethiopia and South Africa. The smallest countries in the trading bloc are Lebanon and Mauritius, both of which are somewhat smaller than Rhode Island. Nigeria has the largest population, followed by Ethiopia, Egypt, and Turkey. With a few exceptions, life expectancy and literacy are among the world's lowest, compared with the other regions of the world we have examined.

Factors such as oil reserves heavily influence the overall economic health of some nations within the region, including Saudi Arabia and the United Arab Emirates (UAE); this is reflected in their GDPs (gross domestic product). According to Table 12.1, the most developed nations in the region, in terms of annual per capita GDP, are the UAE (with $41,800) and Israel (with $28,400). At the other end of the spectrum, seven nations are considered among the least developed in the world, with per capita GDPs of less than $3 thousand. Six of them are located in SSA, whereas Yemen is located on the Arabian Peninsula. High inflation rates and unemployment rates in the same countries provide additional dimensions of the levels of poverty. The miniscule number of Internet users, in relation to the population, is a strong indicator of lack of technological development.

Extend your learning about trade in the Middle East and Africa with Learning Activity 12.1.

Learning Activity 12.1
GEOGRAPHICS AND DEMOGRAPHICS OF THE MIDDLE EAST AND AFRICA

1. Identify the Middle East and Africa on the map in Figure 12.1. What forms the borders of these regions?
2. Locate each of the countries in Table 12.1. Which ones share boundaries?
3. What cultural issues are likely to create problems with trade in the Middle East?
4. What cultural issues are likely to create problems with trade in Africa?
5. Which countries in Table 12.1 are the most developed? What criteria did you use to make your choices?
6. Which countries are least developed? What criteria did you use to make your choices?
7. Based on the data in Table 12.1, if you were a sourcing manager responsible for identifying the next country that will become successful in low-cost apparel production, which country would you choose? What criteria did you use to make your choice?

TEXTILE AND APPAREL TRADE ACTIVITY

As we discovered with the other geographic regions discussed (see Chapters 9 through 11), developed nations, such as the UAE, tend to focus on the consumption of textile and apparel products; developing nations, such as Turkey, Mauritius, and South Africa, tend to use the textile and apparel industry as an industrial engine to fuel their development; and newly developing nations such as Jordan, and least developed nations, such as Nigeria, are looking to make use of apparel production as an avenue to economic development.

Tables 12.2a and 12.2b present nations that are tracked by the World Trade Organization (WTO) for activity in textiles and apparel. We take a closer look at these nations and choose a few others that are just now initiating expansion into this business but that may not have WTO membership.

Between 2000 and 2008, the dominant textile traders in both imports and exports were Turkey and the UAE, located in the Middle East. Morocco and Tunisia, in North Africa, also had substantial textile imports, but relatively low textile exports. Apparently, the textile imports were supporting their rather substantial apparel exports. Most of the reporting nations had increases in textile imports, and all the nations for which data were available had increases in apparel imports. Syria had big increases in both textile and apparel exports, suggesting increases in domestic production of textiles, along with a rapidly developing apparel industry.

The dominant countries involved in apparel imports are the developed countries in the Middle East: Israel, Saudi Arabia, and the UAE. Turkey also shows a relatively high level of apparel imports, although some of those may not be intended for domestic consumption, but rather for transshipment. The

Table 12.1 CHARACTERISTICS OF SELECTED COUNTRIES IN THE MIDDLE EAST AND AFRICA THAT ARE ACTIVE IN THE TEXTILE AND APPAREL TRADE

Country	Geographic Size (in Square Kilometers, in Thousands)	Population (in Millions)	Life Expectancy (in Years)	Adult Literacy	
Middle East					
Israel	22.1	7.2	80.7	97.1%	
Jordan	89.3	6.3	79.9	89.9%	
Saudi Arabia	2,149.7	28.7	76.3	78.8%	
Syria	185.2	21.8	47.2	79.6%	
Turkey[a]	783.6	76.8	72.0	87.4%	
UAE	83.6	4.8	76.1	77.9%	
Yemen	528.0	22.9	63.0	50.2%	
North Africa					
Egypt	1,002	78.9	72.2	71.4%	
Morocco	446.6	31.3	75.5	52.3%	
Tunisia	163.6	10.5	75.8	73.4%	
Sub-Saharan Africa					
Ethiopia	1,104.3	85.2	55.4	42.7%	
Ghana	238.5	23.9	60.1	57.9%	
Kenya	580.4	39.0	57.9	85.1%	
Lesotho	30.4	2.1	40.4	84.8%	
Madagascar	587.0	20.7	62.9	68.9%	
Mauritius	2.0	1.3	74.0	84.4%	
Nigeria	923.7	149.3	46.9	68.0%	
South Africa	1,219.1	49.0	49.1	86.4%	

GDP (in Billions of U.S. Dollars)[b]	Per Capita GDP	Inflation Rate[c]	Labor Force (in Millions)	Unemployment Rate	Internet Users (in Millions)
$ 205.2	$ 28,400	3.4%	3.0	8.0%	2.1
$ 33.6	$ 5,300	1.7%	1.7	13.5%	1.5
$ 581.3	$ 20,300	5.0%	6.9	11.6%	7.7
$ 102.5	$ 4,700	3.8%	5.8	9.2%	3.6
$ 861.6	$ 11,200	5.9%	24.2	14.6%	24.5
$ 200.4	$ 41,800	1.5%	3.2	2.4%	2.9
$ 58.2	$ 2,500	3.6%	6.6	35.0%	0.4
$ 470.4	$ 6,000	10.1%	25.8	9.7%	11.4
$ 145.2	$ 4,600	2.0%	11.5	9.1%	10.3
$ 83.6	$ 8,000	3.4%	3.7	15.7%	2.8
$ 75.9	$ 900	11.0%	37.9	NA	0.4
$ 36.6	$ 1,500	19.6%	10.3	11.0%	1.0
$ 63.6	$ 1,600	20.5%	17.5	40.0%	3.4
$ 3.3	$ 1,500	8.5%	0.9	45.0%	0.07
$ 20.5	$ 1,000	8.0%	9.5	NA	0.3
$ 15.9	$ 12,400	3.4%	0.6	7.8%	0.4
$ 353.2	$ 2,400	11.5%	47.3	4.9%	11.0
$ 488.6	$ 10,000	7.2%	17.3	24.0%	4.2

Source: Estimates of 2009 data from Central Intelligence Agency (CIA), *The world factbook*. (2010). Retrieved February 2010 from http://www.odci.gov/cia/publications/factbook/index.html
a. Potential additional member to the EU-27.
b. GDP, in purchasing power parity.
c. Consumer prices.

reason for transshipment of those imports might be apparel that was sourced from firms in Turkey, but those firms subcontracted production to firms in other countries, where free trade was available. The garments produced were then shipped to Turkey to be exported with Turkey's domestically produced goods.

The other countries representing the total trading bloc also show increases in imports of apparel between 2000 and 2008, and most of them show increases in exports, suggesting their domestic production is growing faster than domestic consumption. All the countries, except Israel, the UAE,

Saudi Arabia, and South Africa, show a positive trade balance in apparel, which suggests they produce more than they consume. Having a negative trade balance, in which apparel imports exceed exports, is a common condition for developed countries.

There is a higher proportion of nations within this geographic region that are much more dependent upon textile and apparel products as a major share of their total merchandise exports than are other nations we have explored. Tables 12.2a and 12.2b show that in 2008, textile and apparel imports and exports have largely declined as a proportion of total merchandise imports and exports. The decline

Table 12.2a IMPORTS OF TEXTILES AND APPAREL BY MIDDLE EASTERN AND AFRICAN COUNTRIES, IN MILLIONS OF U.S. DOLLARS, AND TEXTILES AND APPAREL AS A PERCENTAGE OF EACH COUNTRY'S TOTAL MERCHANDISE IMPORTS

Country	Textile Imports (in Millions of U.S. Dollars)			Apparel Imports (in Millions of U.S. Dollars)			Imports as a Percentage Share of Total Trade	
	2000	2006	2008	2000	2006	2008	2000	2008
Middle East								
Iran	$ 298	$ 730	$ 428	—[a]	—	—	2.9%	2.6%
Israel	$ 759	$ 718	$ 801	$ 471	$ 788	$ 1,123	3.3%	2.4%
Jordan	$ 172	$ 725	$ 651	$ 61	$ 247	$ 326	5.0%	5.8%
Saudi Arabia	$ 986	$ 1,204	$ 1,655	$ 813	$ 1,649	$ 2,018	13.2%	3.8%
Syria	$ 399	$ 353	$ 358	—	—	—	10.5%	2.0%
Turkey	$ 2,124	$ 4,686	$ 5,646	$ 264	$ 1,098	$ 2,216	4.4%	3.9%
UAE[b]	$ 2,055	$ 3,567	$ 4,771	$ 832	$ 3,055	$ 5,503	3.7%	4.4%
North Africa								
Egypt	$ 526	$ 1,094	$ 1,628	$ 404	$ 411	$ 622	6.7%	4.7%
Morocco	$ 1,364	$ 1,945	$ 2,296	$ 232	$ 274	$ 337	12.8%	6.3%
Tunisia	$ 1,207	$ 1,594	$ 2,088	$ 438	$ 550	$ 635	14.6%	9.6%
Sub-Saharan Africa								
Mauritius	$ 411	$ 266	$ 264	—	—	—	19.6%	5.7%
Lesotho	—	—	—	—	—	—	—	—
South Africa	$ 570	$ 975	$ 1,015	$ 223	$ 1,123	$ 993	2.9%	2.3%

Source: World Trade Organization (WTO). (2009). International Trade Statistics 2009. Section 2: Merchandise trade by product (107–114). Retrieved January 16, 2010, from http://www.wto.org/english/res_e/statis_e/its2009_e/its09_merch_trade_product_e.pdf
a. Data not available.
b. United Arab Emirates.

as a proportion of imports suggests that the countries have improved in their ability to support domestic textile and apparel consumption.

The dependence of the economy on apparel exports was extremely high for some countries in these sectors in 2000 and was still high for many in 2008:

- Lesotho, at 73.1%, down to 69.2%
- Mauritius, at 66.1%, down to 39.4%
- Turkey, at 46.7%, down to 17.4%
- Tunisia, at 40.7%, down to 22.0%

Lesotho reported in 1995 that 94 percent of its total merchandise trade was in export of textile and apparel products (*Textiles and Apparel*, 2004), indicating there was little industry there besides textile and apparel production. One would like to think that the dependence on the textile and apparel industry declined because the economy in the country improved and diversified. However, two factors have probably made greater contribution to this decline: the worldwide recession, which slowed up demand for textiles and apparel in developed countries, and the end of the MFA quota system, which abolished limits on imports from Asia's big exporting countries. These developments have greatly affected the textile and apparel industry throughout this trading bloc; development of trade over the next decade will be very interesting to watch.

Table 12.2b EXPORTS OF TEXTILES AND APPAREL BY MIDDLE EASTERN AND AFRICAN COUNTRIES, IN MILLIONS OF U.S. DOLLARS, AND TEXTILES AND APPAREL PERCENTAGE OF EACH COUNTRY'S TOTAL MERCHANDISE EXPORTS

Country	Textile Exports (in Millions of U.S. Dollars)			Apparel Exports (in Millions of U.S. Dollars)			Exports as a Percentage Share of Total Trade	
	2000	2006	2008	2000	2006	2008	2000	2008
Middle East								
Iran	$ 766	$ 766	$ 498	—ᵃ	—	—	2.7%	0.4%
Israel	$ 490	$ 744	$ 651	—	—	—	1.6%	1.1%
Jordan	—	—	—	$ 115	$ 1,257	$ 1,041	6.1%	13.4%
Saudi Arabia	$ 114	$ 315	$ 419	—	—	—	0.1%	0.1%
Syria	$ 158	$ 820	$ 1,016	$ 129	$ 864	$ 962	6.2%	13.8%
Turkey	$ 3,672	$ 7,585	$ 9,399	$ 6,533	$ 12,052	$ 13,591	46.7%	17.4%
UAEᵇ	$ 3,137	$ 4,567	$ 5,751	$ 971	$ 2,400	$ 2,631	8.2%	3.6%
North Africa								
Egypt	$ 412	$ 650	$ 762	$ 710	$ 1,138	$ 1,551	23.9%	6.4%
Morocco	$ 123	$ 242	$ 324	$ 2,401	$ 3,238	$ 3,334	34.0%	18.2%
Tunisia	$ 154	$ 349	$ 478	$ 2,227	$ 3,018	$ 3,766	40.7%	22.0%
Sub-Saharan Africa								
Mauritius	$ 81	$ 78	$ 80	$ 948	$ 772	$ 845	66.1%	39.4%
Lesotho	—	—	—	$ 161	$ 478	—	73.1%	69.2%
South Africa	$ 240	$ 306	$ 301	—	—	—	0.8%	0.4%

Source: World Trade Organization (WTO). (2009). International Trade Statistics 2009. Section 2: Merchandise trade by product (107–114). Retrieved January 16, 2010, from http://www.wto.org/english/res_e/statis_e/its2009_e/its09_merch_trade_product_e.pdf
a. Data not available. Some of these nations are very dependent on textiles and apparel, but the volume of trade is so small it is not reported by WTO.
b. United Arab Emirates.

PARTICIPATION OF INDIVIDUAL COUNTRIES IN TEXTILES AND APPAREL

In 2008, quota restrictions lifted, which should have opened up opportunities, but the Middle East–Africa trading bloc experienced considerable stress, owing to the threat of the Chinese juggernaut. The poorest countries, the SSA sector, appeared to be the most vulnerable to the Chinese threat. China has the combination of moderately low wages and high efficiency that is very difficult to duplicate in least developed and newly developing countries, yet many people believed that Egypt and Syria could gain overall market share because of their strength as cotton and yarn producers. The postquota outlook for Morocco and Tunisia was also considered good because of the proximity of these countries to the EU markets. The recent focus on sustainability of supply chains has also decreased emphasis on lowest labor cost available because of priorities related to social and environmental responsibility, travel costs and time, and related factors.

The Mediterranean Rim nations have specific advantages for production and export of products that should put them on the right path for protecting their competitive edge, including the following:

- availability of indigenous raw material supplies, such as Turkish cotton
- an abundant supply of low-cost labor
- close proximity to important markets in the EU

Table 12.3 reflects the hourly wages in nations in the Middle Eastern–African trading bloc that are active in textile production. Several of the countries included in Table 12.2 do not appear in 12.3, because their level of textile production was below the cutoff point established by the source of the study; they import textiles and focus on the production of finished apparel products for export. Although not evidenced

Table 12.3 Labor Costs, in U.S. Dollars per Hour, for Textile Production in Selected Middle Eastern and African Countries, Compared with U.S. Labor Costs Considering Direct Wages and Social Costs[a]

Country	Total Labor Cost in U.S. Dollars	Total Labor Cost as a Percentage of U.S. Labor Cost[b]	Total Labor Cost in Local Currency	Direct Wages in Local Currency	Social Costs in Local Currency	Social Costs as a % of Direct Wages[c]
U.S.	$ 17.41	100%	$ 17.41	$ 13.52	$ 3.89	29%
Israel	$ 11.31	65%	42.20	32.80	9.40	29%
Turkey	$ 4.27	25%	6.48	4.00	2.48	62%
Morocco	$ 2.89	17%	22.99	16.55	6.44	39%
South Africa	$ 2.58	15%	24.02	17.94	6.08	34%
Tunisia	$ 2.12	12%	2.75	2.13	0.62	29%
Egypt	$ 1.12	6%	6.16	4.72	1.64	34%

Source: Werner International Management Consultants. (2009). *Primary textiles labor cost comparisons 2008.*
Retrieved May 25, 2010, from http://texnet.ilgstudios.net/files/2009/08/Werner_International_-_Labor_Cost_Study_2008.pdf
a. Total labor costs per hour = direct wages per hour + social costs per hour.
b. In U.S. dollars, total labor costs per hour as a percentage of U.S. labor costs per hour = a country's labor cost per hour ÷ U.S. labor cost per hour × 100.
c. In local currency, social costs as a percentage of direct wages = social costs ÷ direct wages × 100.

in the research that supports this table, according to other sources, the wages for textile workers are consistently higher than those of apparel workers in this region.

To get a sense of levels of textile production wages in this region, compare Table 12.3 with Table 11.4 (see Chapter 11). It should be evident that the total labor costs per hour are higher in the Middle East and Africa than in much of Asia. Compare the second columns of the tables, "Total Labor Cost as a Percentage of U.S. Labor Costs." In Asia only South Korea, Taiwan, and Japan have higher labor costs than five of the six countries located in Middle East and Africa. Social costs as a percentage of direct wages are also comparatively high.

For example, since 2004 China has tripled textile production wages, to $1.88 per hour, whereas Turkey doubled wages, to $4.27. Turkey desperately wants to continue to develop its textile and apparel industries, which have contributed greatly to the well-being of thousands of citizens in the last decade but is finding competition from Asia for the EU market to be very strong. The poorer countries in Asia are also primary competitors for contracting CMT apparel production, although Jordan has benefited some from CMT activity. With primitive infrastructure, higher wages, and lower levels of literacy, growth in some of these nations continues to be very slow.

As we discuss individual nations within the Middle East–Africa trading bloc, we explore how some have recently sought and achieved significant concessions, in the form of bilateral agreements with the EU and the United States for tariff reductions, which they hope will finesse their industries into more favorable competitive positions for market share against China. Some of these trade agreements and preference programs with the United States include the following:

- African Growth and Opportunity Act (AGOA)
- Bahrain Free Trade Agreement (FTA)
- Israel Free Trade Agreement
- Jordan Free Trade Agreement
- Morocco Free Trade Agreement
- Oman Free Trade Agreement
- Qualifying Industrial Zones (QIZ) in Jordan and Egypt

The **African Growth and Opportunity Act (AGOA)** has gone through four updates since its inception in 2002, most recently in 2006, and it is scheduled to run until 2012. A **Qualified Industrial Zone (QIZ)** is any area that has been specified as such by the U.S. government. These areas have to be designated by local authorities as an enclave where a product that is manufactured in the zone may enter U.S. markets without duty or excise taxes and without requirement of any reciprocal benefits ("Qualifying Industrial Zones," 2000). In addition, a free trade agreement between the United States and the UAE is under negotiation.

Egyptian industries were dominated by large state-owned and -controlled enterprises throughout the 1980s, but Egypt has significantly opened up its industries to the private sector and foreign investment since that time. Tunisia and Morocco have been highly dependent on foreign investment to finance their industries, and today Jordan is also heavily dependent on direct foreign investment in factories built within its QIZ areas. Some of the small entrepreneurial business activities and manufacturing start-ups being initiated in least developed nations, especially in Africa, are being supplemented by financial assistance from the World Bank and the IMF. As mentioned previously, these two global institutions provide key resources to many of the poverty-stricken countries of the Middle East and Africa as well as other parts of the world.

Continue to explore the Middle East and Africa with Learning Activity 12.2.

Learning Activity 12.2
MIDDLE EASTERN AND AFRICAN OVERVIEW

1. What is the purpose of the World Bank? What is the purpose of the IMF? Why are these organizations so important to the Middle East–Africa trading bloc?
2. What countries in this trading bloc are too economically dependent on apparel exports to have a sound economy?
3. Why might it be desirable for many Middle Eastern and African countries to have positive trade balances in apparel?
4. Compare labor costs among Europe, the Americas, Asia, and the Middle East–Africa, using Tables 9.5, 10.5, 11.4, and 12.3. How would you rank the regions from highest to lowest? Which trading bloc do you regard as the highest, and which is the lowest? What criteria did you use as the basis of your answer?
5. Put on your sourcing hat. What four criteria, in addition to total labor costs, need to be considered when making sourcing decisions?

THE MIDDLE EAST

The Middle East is a region that stretches from Turkey, south, throughout the Arabian Peninsula, and east, through Iran. Much of the Middle East is desert. People live crowded along the seacoasts and in river and mountain valleys that have enough water to grow crops. When oil was discovered in several of the Middle Eastern countries, industrial development began, creating a great dichotomy between the rich and poor. Ongoing economic, political, and religious struggles continue between the Palestinians and Israelis. Conflicts also continue within Arab monarchies, such as Saudi Arabia, and Arab republics, such as Iraq and Syria. Other conflicts continue between people who want to keep traditional ways of life and those who want to change in order to keep up with a more secular, modern world. Despite this dissension, some people in these countries benefit from higher per capita GDP from industrial sectors, such as oil, and the countries themselves are considered more as market for textile and apparel products than as producer.

With the war in Iraq, unstable politics in Iran and the ongoing unrest in the occupied territories bordering Israel, luxury retailing may not be the first thing that comes to mind when thinking of the Middle East. However, for the six Persian Gulf states that comprise the Gulf Cooperation Council—Saudi Arabia, Kuwait, United Arab Emirates, Bahrain, Oman and Qatar—huge oil riches, relative sociopolitical stability and recent drives to modernize and diversify their economies have led to growing pools of wealthy consumers and a booming demand for status brands (Lipke, 2007).

The Middle East has a long and colorful history of trade in textile and apparel products, but current information on many nations within this region is somewhat limited, owing to the ongoing political and economic unrest. However, it is believed that some of these nations, including Turkey, Oman, Qatar, and the UAE—countries that benefited from restrictions under the quota system—found their textile and apparel industries threatened by the demise of quotas and the recent economic downturn. To compensate for potential losses in trade, the

Gulf Cooperation Council (GCC), a trade organization that confers special trade and investment privileges among the member nations (Bahrain, Kuwait, Oman, Qatar, Saudi Arabia, and the UAE), had set 2003 as the target date for the elimination of tariffs and establishment of common customs regulations and procedures among member nations (*The Economic Agreement*, 2001).

A few of the nations in the Middle East are major textile and apparel traders in the world market. The WTO reported that, in terms of endeavors in the textile and apparel business, Turkey had moved up globally in textile exports, from a ranking of 10th, in 2003, to 7th, in 2008. Turkey also ranked 7th in textile imports in 2008, whereas the UAE moved up from 13th, in 2003, to 10th, in 2008 (WTO, 2009). Nations in the Middle East–Africa trading bloc that achieved world rank as top exporters of apparel products in 2008 included Turkey, at number 4, whereas the UAE moved up from 12th, in 2003, to 8th, in 2008, among top apparel importers. That these nations are ranked within the top 15 nations in the world reflects significant activity as importers and exporters of textiles and apparel even in the face of recent vulnerability.

Developed Countries of the Middle East

Despite a "wealth" of oil in many Middle Eastern countries, only a few approach the status of developed country, based on per capita GDP. Three have per capita GDP of more than $20 thousand, placing them as developed nations. The UAE, Israel, and Saudi Arabia are discussed here.

The United Arab Emirates (UAE)

During the early 1970s, seven small states formerly under protection of the UK joined to form the United Arab Emirates (UAE), a country about the size of Maine, located on the edge of the Persian Gulf. The UAE's prosperity is due to generosity with oil revenues, a moderate foreign policy, and a trade surplus that has allowed it to play a vital role in the affairs of the region. The country's oil and gas reserves are expected to last another 100 years. As shown by the imports and exports of textiles and apparel in Tables 12.2a and 12.2b, firms in the UAE are importing fewer textiles than they are exporting, indicating activity in production of textiles. On the other hand, today these firms are importing more than twice as much apparel as they are exporting and they are importing more than five times as much as they were importing in 2000. These increases indicate a booming consumer market during this time period. There were some difficulties during the global economic downturn in 2009, but at the time of this writing, they seem to be smoothing out.

Even though the UAE is considered to have a relatively small apparel manufacturing component, it does produce some woven and knitted apparel for export. Most labor in these factories is foreign. Because of its high per capita GDP—up from $23,200, in 2003, to $41,800, in 2009—the UAE has become a target market for upscale apparel retailers from around the globe, especially from the EU. Some have even labeled Dubai the Hong Kong of the Middle East because of the strength of presence of fashion retailers from Europe and other markets, including the United States (Moin, 2004). The UAE, along with Bahrain, is a major customer of U.S. industry in the area of fashion goods and industrial fabrics. In 2009, Tom Ford opened a store in Dubai, joining another he had opened earlier in Abu Dhabi, UAE. The made-to-measure suiting salon within the store is a testament to the level of the

Figure 12.2a The first Bloomingdale's store on foreign soil opened in Dubai, United Arab Emirates (UAE). (*Gabriela Maj/Getty Images*)

Figure 12.2b The Versace store in the Dubai Mall reflects the availability of designer apparel in the UAE. (*Andrew Parsons/Bloomberg via Getty Images*)

Figure 12.2c The Dubai Mall features the largest aquarium in the world. (*Kamran Jebreili/AP Photo*)

consumer experience for men in this area. European designer boutiques have thrived here (Figure 12.2a–c).

Saudi Arabia

Most of the industrial wealth of this nation comes from oil rather than from textile and apparel production. However, Saudi Arabia is a major market for women's and children's clothing. With a relatively high overall per person GDP of $20,300, in 2008 (up from $11,800, in 2003), the apparel market is distinctly divided between the upper, high-end consumer market and the lower-priced apparel sector. The growth in this economy is probably a solid reflection of oil prices in the late 2000s. The high-end sector is dominated by imports from Europe and the United States. Retailers from around the globe, including Gap, Banana Republic, and Cole Haan, are among U.S. brands that have already opened here. H&M and Zara have entered the fast-fashion market here and seem to be doing well, owing to size of the youth market. The lower end of the market is dominated by imports from Asia and by small tailor shops.

Saudi Arabia's retail apparel sales calendar tends to follow a seasonal pattern paralleling Saudi religious holidays and summer breaks, when sales are highest. The mall in the capital city of Riyadh is a testament to Western retailing. In public the women are covered by the abaya, and everyday women's dress for inside the home tends to be somewhat conservative. However, in private many of these consumers, especially the young and those from the higher end of the market, dress in the latest global fashions (Figure 12.3).

Israel

Despite an ongoing Israeli–Palestinian conflict and limited natural resources, Israel has intensively developed its agricultural and industrial sectors over the last 25 years. It is also considered a developed country, because

its per capita GDP has reached $28,400 (up from $19,800, in 2003). Substantial transfer payments and foreign loans, particularly from the United States, are major sources of economic and military aid. A considerable portion of Israel's population is concentrated in the metropolitan areas of Tel Aviv and Haifa. The transportation system in Israel is considered excellent, and most imported and exported goods pass through the Mediterranean port Haifa. As might be expected of its higher per capita GDP, Israel is home to considerable retail activity—shopping malls, specialized chain stores, and franchises.

Israel's textile and apparel industry is ongoing, despite relatively high labor costs. Israel's labor force is highly educated and trained, which partially offsets the higher labor costs. Israel is known for its use of advanced technology and production of high-quality products. Industry is highly automated and has a reputation for offering good service and rapid turnaround of orders.

However, terrorism, in the form of the ongoing intifada with the Palestinians (*intifada* is a term used to define the overt conflict between the Palestinians and Israelis), makes for an intimidating atmosphere at times. As a result, some firms have moved much of their production to more cost-competitive countries, including Jordan and Egypt, which have QIZ programs. Qualified Industrial Zones (QIZ) are areas in Jordan and Egypt that receive duty- and quota-free trade status with the United States on the condition of Israeli participation in at least part of the production process.

For example, the Israeli firm Bagir Ltd. is a maker of technologically innovative men's and women's suits. Its headquarters are in Kiryat Gat, close to the Gaza Strip, where conflicts often arise. Kiryat Gat's economy was initially based on processing the locally produced cotton and wool (Steinberg, 2009). Today, the firm maintains offices there but has shifted manufacturing to nearby Jordan and Egypt and to China. Bagir now

Figure 12.4 Retail display in Israel for the Israeli shape wear manufacturer Delta Galil. Lingerie produced in Israel is sold throughout the Middle East as well as in Western Europe and the Americas. (*Courtesy of WWD*)

employs 200 people in Kiryat Gat and about 2,700 worldwide.

Delta Galil is a firm that specializes in shape wear. Utilization of molding and seamless technology is Delta Galil's specialty in men's underwear and women's intimate apparel and related products. Delta Galil has its headquarters in northern Israel, employing about 200 Israeli Arabs among its 600 workers there (Steinberg, 2004, 2009). The firm also directly employs four thousand people in Egypt, and ten thousand Egyptians through subcontractors, with another 400 in Jordan. The products that come from these plants qualify for duty-free entry into the United States, as they meet qualifications of QIZ participation. Key clients include Marks & Spencer, Target, Walmart, Kmart, and JC Penney (Figure 12.4).

Case 12.1 presents some of the difficulties faced by Delta Galil, and the business decisions made by its chief executive officer, in the wake of terrorism and armed conflict.

Developing and Newly Developing Countries in the Middle East

One country in the Middle East falls in the "developing country" category—Turkey which in 2009 had a per person GDP of $11,200 (up from $6,700, in 2003). Jordan is a newly developing nation, with a per person GDP of $5,300, in 2009 (up from $4,300, in 2003). Each has some unique aspects to the operation of its textile and apparel industry. Syria is also a newly developing country in this area, with a per person GDP of $4,700, in 2009 (refer back to Table 12.1 for the status of these nations).

Turkey
Turkey outclassed all other countries, except China, in its speed in developing a highly effective global textile and apparel business. Turkey is a country slightly larger than Texas that lies with its western extension, including Istanbul, in southeastern Europe; the larger portion of the country, including the capital, Ankara, is in Asia, between the Black Sea

As the war in Iraq was about to begin in March 2003, a customer asked Arnon Tiberg, chief executive officer of Israeli intimate apparel maker Delta Galil, to create a contingency plan in case there were disruptions at Delta's plant in Jordan.

Tiberg arranged to use the company's Thailand plant, and though there were in fact no interruptions, the proposal for outsourcing production provided a sense of comfort.

"You have to scatter your risk—not political risk, but business risk," Tiberg said. "In the end, it's all about the business, and luckily our business can withstand the political situation."

Doing business amid terrorism and armed conflict changes the business rules, both for manufacturers in Israel seeking to keep product flowing and for customers who have been reluctant to travel to Israel.

For Delta Galil—a $25 million private label intimate apparel maker that produces underwear, bras and socks for Calvin Klein, Donna Karan, and Tommy Hilfiger, as well as Victoria's Secret, JCPenney, J. Crew, the Gap and Banana Republic—the name of the game has always been vertical production. The company has factories in Israel, Jordan, Egypt, Turkey, Romania, Bulgaria, Hungary, Thailand, China, Honduras and the Caribbean Basin. When the company considers risks that might interfere with production and distribution, it believes its Middle Eastern factories to be the most vulnerable, he said.

Still, with four sewing plants in Cairo and 10 in Irbid, Jordan, Delta has never had a political or security issue that stopped or prevented exports or shipments. The flow of bras, underwear and socks has been smooth during the almost four years of the latest intifada, with the Jordanian wares making their way to the U.S. and the Egyptian products to Europe.

"In Egypt we have over 4,000 employees and another 5,000 that work for us through outsourcing," Tiberg said. "But there's a limit to the number you can employ in one place. That's why we have the spread of production in the Far East and Central America that can offer backup if we need it."

It's a similar story for Tefron, an Israeli manufacturer of seamless and cut-and-sew undergarments and activewear. With annual sales of about $200 million, Tefron's customers include Victoria's Secret, athletic wear manufacturers Nike and Adidas, the Gap, Banana Republic and Calvin Klein, as well as Target and Wal-Mart.

Tefron has a logistics and customer service plant in North Carolina, and research and development and production facilities in Israel, Madagascar, and Jordan. Its production and distribution channels have continued to function without disruption, CEO Yoss Shiran said.

Terrorism has meant that both Delta and Tefron's clients have been less willing to come to Israel, particularly after any U.S. State Department advisory warning against travel to the Middle East.

. . . Tefron . . . has two salespeople in New York who work with the company's U.S. customers.

. . . Like the Tefron executives, Delta Galil employees also are traveling more to the U.S. and Europe. . . .

In the recent few months, clients have begun returning to Israel, perhaps because "they've gotten used to the situation," Tiberg said.

Source:

Steinberg, J. (2004, June 21). Keeping business flowing in a volatile climate. *Women's Wear Daily*, 13.

Figure 12.5a The Altinyildiz textiles factory, in Turkey.

(Kerem Uzel/ NARPHOTOS)

and the Mediterranean. Because of a complex and turbulent history, Turkey reflects the influence of Greek, Roman, Byzantine, Arabic, and Turkish cultures. Some political turmoil continues as a result of cultural conflicts. Turkey has a close trade relationship with western European countries and is negotiating admission into the EU, but at the time of this writing, conflicts with the west were escalating. Turkey provides an example of the benefits of trade liberalization to developing countries.

Despite accelerating inflation, rising unemployment, labor unrest, and political violence, beginning in the mid-1980s Turkey became a successful apparel exporter, with production centralized in Istanbul; by 2001 Turkey was the seventh largest apparel exporter in the world as well as the top apparel exporter to the EU, with production concentrated in its Asian region. Here, skilled labor was available at wages lower than those of urban Istanbul, and there was less competition for labor among employers. Turkey's apparel industry benefited from Turkey's export-led industrialization

strategy and close association with the EU. A custom's union, established with the EU in 1996, removed barriers to EU imports from Turkey and to Turkey's imports from the EU (Neidik, 2004). In 2008, Turkey's rank as an apparel exporter had risen to number four, even in the face of serious competition from Asia, especially China, for the EU market and the global economic downturn (WTO, 2009).

Another key benefit to Turkey's apparel industry, not available to many developing European countries, is a strong domestic textiles industry. Turkey, a major producer of cotton yarns and fabrics since the 1960s, is also a leading producer of wool and the third-largest mohair producer in the world. In addition, Turkey is reported to have the sixth-largest synthetic textile production capacity in the world. Because of domestic textile availability in the 1980s, Turkey became one of the few low-wage, full-package apparel vendor countries that evolved into branded manufacturing capabilities. Apparel plants became larger with cutting, sewing, and finishing in the same facility. Quality control was improved to meet standards of moderate and better manufacturers and retailers around the world. By the end of the 20th century, Turkey's major apparel producers were outsourcing production in eastern European countries, where labor costs were lower (Neidik, 2004) (Figures 12.5a and 12.5b).

In the late 1990s, foreign direct investment, particularly from the United States, made major contributions to upgrading and specializing both textile and apparel production facilities (Table 12.4). The two largest U.S. jeans makers (VF Corporation and Levi Strauss & Co.) are prominently represented here in their efforts to globalize their brands. VF is the largest apparel firm in the world and the maker of Lee, Wrangler, and Rustler jeans, among its many branded products.

Questions remained as to whether the Turkish textile and apparel industry would be able to sustain growth over the

Figure 12.5b A customer tries on a pair of Cons jeans, a Turkish label, at the brand's store in Istanbul.
(*Kerem Uzel/ NARPHOTOS*)

Table 12.4 EXAMPLES OF DIRECT FOREIGN INVESTMENT IN TEXTILES AND APPAREL IN TURKEY

Year	Foriegn Investor	Turkish Partner	Type/Amount of Investment	Sector	Goal
1997	Levi Strauss (U.S.)	Karamanci Holding ("Denimko")	Strategic partnership (U.S.$ 20 million)	Apparel	Exclusive production of 501 jeans for Levi Strauss Europe
1998	VF (U.S.)	Mavi Ege ("VF Ege")	Acquisition of former licensee; VF's third factory in Europe	Apparel	Production of Lee and Wrangler brands for local market, eastern Europe, and the Middle East
1999	Hugo Boss (Germany)	—	Greenfield (DM 25m); Boss's third factory in world	Apparel	Production of men's clothing for Europe with imported input
2000	DuPont (now INVISTA) (U.S.)	Sabanci Holding ("Du PontSA")	Joint venture (50–50)	Synthetic Fibers	Development, production, and sales of polyester, resins, fibers, and related materials
2001	Polgat (Israel)	Guney Sanayi ("Guney-Polgat")	Merger (55% Turkish ownership)	Apparel and Textiles	Gain access to U.S. market
2002	Cone Mills (U.S.)	Isko ("IsKone")	Joint venture (51–49)	Textiles	Supply denim for 501 jeans for Levi Strauss Europe
2003	Hugo Boss (Germany)	—	Expansion (details not available)	Apparel	Production of women's apparel and sportswear
2003	VF (U.S.)	—	Expansion (U.S$ 15 million in current plant)		Launch of "VF Ege" brand; production of H.I.S. and The North Face brands

Source: Based on Neidik, B. (2004). Organization foundations of export performance: The case of the Turkish apparel industry. *Journal of Fashion Marketing and Management 8*(3), 294.

next decade, but, as shown in Table 12.2b, as of 2008 textile exports had almost tripled since 2000, and apparel exports had more than doubled. Direct foreign investment had positioned Turkey for a stronger position, relative to other European countries. It could continue to be a hub for foreign brand access as eastern Europe develops. Textiles represented 46.7 percent of Turkey's overall merchandise exports in 2000 but had dropped to 17.4 percent of overall exports in 2008, even though the volume of exports had increased significantly. This reflected a general strengthening of other segments of the nation's economy.

As a reflection of the continued strength of Turkish industry, in January 2010 Li & Fung opened a new hub in Istanbul. This hub is to enable the firm to do sourcing business in Europe, the Mediterranean, the Middle East, northern Africa, and the former republics of the Soviet Union. Li & Fung will serve as the interface between suppliers in Turkey and the company's worldwide customers, collaborating closely with Turkish vendors and supporting them in the fields of textile export, logistics, merchandising, and quality assurance.

In addition to its production expertise, Turkey is now seen for its potential as a retail market. For example, to broaden its worldwide business, Kenneth Cole Productions, Inc., entered a retail licensing agreement with The Park Bravo Group, the Turkey-based firm that operates Park Bravo and Park's stores and that has licensing partnerships with other brands, including Nine West, Enzo Angiolini, AK Anne Klein, and La Senza, for the Turkish market. Park Bravo will distribute and market Kenneth Cole New York men's and women's clothing, footwear, and accessories in Turkey. Jill Granoff, the chief executive officer of Kenneth Cole Productions, emphasized that "'Turkey has a young, dynamic population and is one of

the leading emerging markets of the world'" (Karimzadeh, 2010, n.p.). The Kenneth Cole store is set to open in the Akmerkez mall, in Instanbul's popular Etiler neighborhood, in early 2010.

Jordan

"'Jordan is the eye of a hurricane,' says Constanzi Yaghnam, a Jordanian apparel factory owner. 'We're surrounded by turmoil, but then you have an oasis that's calm and beautiful'" (Greene, 2003, p. 10). With Israel on one side and Iraq on the other, Jordan is indeed in the center of unrest. Yet, as shown in Table 12.2b, for the year ending June 2003 Jordan exported $483.4 million in textiles and apparel, an 89.2 percent increase over the previous year; by 2006 that figure had risen to $1,257 million. When the import quotas came off of Asian goods, there was a noticeable dip in exports, between 2006 and 2008, and according to latest figures the numbers have continued to drop, to $900 million, and are expected to contract further as the faltering economy and competition for market share continue (Casabona, 2009c). Also, 13.4 percent of Jordan's exports now come from apparel exports, a significant drop from earlier in the decade and a reflection that Jordan is beginning to branch into forms of economic development beyond CMT activities.

Jordan has a free trade agreement with the United States. Much of the impetus for growth in CMT activities came in the QIZs, in collaboration with Israel. The Jordan–Israel trade zone is somewhat unique, in that it combines the production activities of two nations of rather dissimilar development levels in a trade scenario with the United States. Jordan's per capita GDP is now $5,300; Israel's is $28,400. Jordan has a higher unemployment rate, higher percentage of poverty, and higher infant mortality rate than Israel, but male literacy and life expectancies are quite similar. The operation of this trade zone is interesting to examine because of the cultural and economic differences between the two nations.

According to the QIZ trade initiative, garments manufactured in Jordan using some Israeli content receive preferential treatment. "Roughly 27 percent of a garment's fob cost has to be generated in Jordan, and about 8 percent, often trimming, has to come from Israel, while the remaining percentage value come [sic] from other countries" (Greene, 2003, p. 10). An example of this process is when U.S. firms "buy synthetic fleece garments that are made in the QIZs in Jordan from Asian fabrics, using the required minimum amount of content from Israel and enter the goods free of duty and quota into the United States, thereby avoiding payment of about 30 percent normal trade relations tariff rate" (Textiles and Apparel, 2004, p. 3). The QIZ concept was also used in development of the Egypt–Israel QIZ trade provision with the United States.

Most of the factories in the QIZ zones have been built with foreign investment funds, from countries such as Hong Kong, Israel, and South Korea, and the management and production expertise needed to initiate production is sent from the originating country. Jordan also has had to import workers from Bangladesh, India, and Sri Lanka to function at the line management level, since Jordan does not have a prior history of maintaining a pool of trained garment workers. Jordan is trying to develop a pool of Jordanian workers, specifically to improve employment opportunities and so it can send offshore workers back home. In addition to the U.S.–Jordan Free Trade Agreement and the QIZ program, Jordan has a free trade agreement with EU.

Shipping times to the United States are better than from many Asian countries. Jordan has low overall manufacturing costs because of low wages, no income tax, and inexpensive rent and electricity. Persistent problems with adequate water supply prevent the develop-ment of a textile industry, but Jordan is close to regional fabric suppliers, such as Egypt, Turkey, Israel, and Pakistan.

Case 12.2 discusses some of the issues faced by those producing apparel in the QIZ program.

There was great concern that the lifting of quotas would wreak havoc with the labor pool in Jordan, but between 2000 and 2008 apparel exports increased from $115 million to $1,014 million per year (refer back to Table 12.2b). Jordan felt that its firm stance on ethical employment and human rights issues would hold it in good stead. "These are not sweatshops. . . . They're fully equipped garment manu-facturing facilities, and they have very strict requirements regarding human rights standards. Jordan is a great place to make garments right now" (Greene, 2003, p. 10). Unfortunately, some rather grievous labor issues surfaced at a few of the plants within the QIZ zones, especially related to migrant workers from outside of Jordan, and it has since been working diligently to correct these problems. In October 2009, officials from the U.S. trade representative's office, the U.S. Labor Department, and the U.S. State Department convened a meeting in Jordan with the labor subcommittee of the US–Jordan Free Trade Agreement to discuss labor issues, including alleged child labor, forced labor, trafficking of migrant workers from Asia, and enforcement of the rules written into existing agreements. Representatives visited garment factories in the QIZ zone to observe and assess local working conditions (Casabona, 2009b). It is believed that many of the labor abuses can be attributed to a combination of factors, including heavy dependence on migrant labor (resulting from a lack of sufficiently trained local labor), rapid expansion of foreign-owned factories within the QIZ zone, and rapid increases in CMT orders. The sector simply became a magnet for

The development of Jordanian human resources, including women, to world-class levels is the key to its economic survival and growth in a competitive marketplace. However, employing Jordanian women involves a number of cultural challenges. In Jordan, female higher education is valued, but work outside the home is treated with more caution. There is some resistance to technical and scientific fields of study for women; preferred fields of study relate to hearth and home. It is not common practice for a woman to work outside the home; therefore, perceptions of the marketplace and the culture of work are limited to reports they receive from family and friends. Yet, there is great need for female employment outside the home to increase per capita GDP from $4,800 and to alleviate the poverty of 30 percent of the population.

The United Nations Development Program (UNDP) administered a comprehensive project for the express purpose of developing a program for improving the technical training and employment opportunities of underemployed Jordanian women. The project evolved in four stages.

Stage 1—Demand for Human Resources. Data were collected from Jordanian industrial firms, including apparel manufacturers, to identify skills that are needed in the marketplace. There was repeated mention of trained sewing machine operators that were cognizant of quality control and had knowledge of English. A comprehensive list of technical and behavioral skills was proposed; many centered on behavioral skills, such as punctuality, teamwork, and safety (Ayoubi, 1998).

Stage 2—Jordanian Female Students' Attitudes toward Work outside the Home. Jordanian female community college students preferred to work in the public sector in government and education, but they were willing to work in the private sector, including business-related activities. They were also interested in entrepreneurship. They were willing to travel to work if transportation was available. Thus, it was strongly recommended that community colleges develop new programs of study, including economics, management, and analytical skills, to prepare women to enter business occupations (Ghoseh, 2000).

Stage 3—Enhancing Technical Education Opportunities for Jordanian Women. Around the world, women are the predominant employees in apparel manufacturing. Technical training in community colleges could help Jordanian women gain employment. Two community colleges were identified as being suitable to provide training to meet labor market needs. Employees needed to be able to read specification sheets, maintain productivity levels via good time management skills, and maintain good overall work ethic. Because of the nature of the global market, the ability to read in English was critical. A basic course in business was recommended, and an internship program would be beneficial to ease a student's transition from education to work (Kharouf, 2001).

Stage 4—Curriculum Development for Technical Education in Apparel Manufacturing. To make use of the background research and develop appropriate curriculum for the community colleges, Myrna Garner was brought in as a consultant by UNDP. Additional information about specific market needs was collected during visits to the director or general manager of seven major apparel manufacturers in a Qualified Industrial Zone (QIZ) near Amman.

Al Tajamouat Industrial City is one of these manufacturing zones set up in Jordan to take advantage of free trade with the United States. The sector contains many apparel production facilities, built with investment funding from other nations, providing employment opportunities for thousands of women in the area. These manufacturing plants focus on CMT (cut-make-trim) activities related to the production of garments. To qualify for no-tariff status into the United States, garments produced in Jordan's QIZ must have a percentage of their production take place in Israel. Frequently, the portion of the process handled in Israel is the marker-making or grading, so actual design activities were not often needed in Jordan at that time. The general areas of most need include the following:

- Middle management positions, including line supervisors requiring background experience in sewing on industrial sewing machines, and enough pattern skills to communicate with other line workers about the requirements of each sewing task.
- Quality control focusing on the evaluation of individual garment construction techniques, identifying any problems with the materials being used and evaluating the individual line operators' contributions to the overall production process.
- Merchandisers, in this setting. tracking the orders through the manufacturing plant, scheduling the production lines, and securing all the findings and fabrics in the correct amounts to produce the garments in the contract.
- Pattern makers focusing on flat-pattern techniques and some grading and marker making; related computer skills are beneficial for future advancement.

Discussions were held with the trainers and administrators of the Fashion Design program at Ajloun Community College. Its program focused almost entirely on home production skills and clearly was not meeting the needs of business and industry. As a model for the industrialized Jordanian program, a visit was made to the apparel facilities in the Home Economics Department at Helwan University, in Cairo, Egypt. Changes were identified that had to be implemented to increase the viability of the Jordanian program for industry applications.

Throughout this UNDP project, considerable attention was given to the needs expressed by the apparel industry, the desires of the educational administration, and the availability of resources. An advisory group of manufacturers and local educational administrators was established, and it was concluded that a 2-year associate degree program would be the most viable plan. An inclusive curriculum package was presented with a detailed budget plan for its implementation (Garner, 2001).

The first steps to implementing this curriculum were taken: equipment was purchased, a new staff member was hired, and courses were initiated at Ajloun Community College, in fall 2001.

Ayoubi, Z. (1998, June). *Identifying the "demand" by the private industrial sector in Jordan for human resources knowledge, skills, abilities and attitudes.* Canada–Jordan economic development through technical skills project. Amman, Jordan.

Garner, M. B. (2001, June 27). *Enhancing Technical Training and Employment Opportunities for Jordanian Women: Fashion and Clothing Technology Program.* Final report to the United Nations Development Program. Amman, Jordan.

Ghoseh, H. (2000, July 23). *Stage II Report.*

Kharouf, A. (2001, January). *Enhancing Technical Education Opportunities for Jordanian Women: Labor Market.*

Source:

Garner, M. B. (2010, June 13). *Enhancing Technical Training and Employment Opportunities for Jordanian Women.* Summary of final report to UNDP.

these problems as firms overreached in their quest to complete more orders. Continuing diligence on the part of the local government to monitor these factories, and efforts to train local workers to replace migrant laborers, should resolve most of these issues.

Syria

According to the WTO data reported in Table 12.1, Syria's per person GDP puts it in the "newly developing" category. We are including Syria in this text because it has an important textile and apparel industry that exports significant quantities of textile products, including cotton fiber, textiles, carpets, and clothing. However, Syria is unique because the United States currently bans U.S. businesses from operating or investing in Syria. There is significant tension between the United States and Syria; although it supported the first Gulf War, it opposed the Iraqi war that began in 2003, and bilateral relations with the United States swiftly deteriorated; disagreements intensified, from 2004 to early 2009, primarily over issues relating to Iraq and Lebanon ("Background Note: Syria," n.d.).

Nonetheless, the textile and apparel industry accounts for 30 percent of Syria's industrial employment and is a vehicle for the nation's growth and enterprise. The government has invested heavily in new production facilities in recent years ("Profile," 2006). Between 2000 and 2004, apparel production increased from 35.1 million pieces to 54.7 million pieces, and cotton yarn output also increased significantly. In 2007, Syria's major markets were Italy, France, Saudi Arabia, Iraq, Egypt and Jordan ("Background Note: Syria," n.d.).

The state slowed technological development by placing heavy taxes on the private textile sector. It is estimated that 4 thousand of Syria's 15 thousand looms are still powered by shuttles. Exports of carpets, yarns and thread, and home textiles to the EU declined at about the time the Iraq War began and the competition from Asia began to heat up. In November 2005, the government agreed to allow garments to be imported from elsewhere, but with a 47.5 percent tariff ("Profile," 2006).

Now, further your understanding of the Middle East textile and apparel business with Learning Activity 12.3.

Learning Activity 12.3
OVERVIEW ON TEXTILE AND APPAREL BUSINESS ACTIVITY IN THE MIDDLE EAST

1. What types of things encourage economic growth in the Middle East?
2. What factors are detrimental to economic growth in the Middle East?
3. What effect does the high per capita GDP in the UAE and Israel seem to have on their participation in the textile and apparel business? Is this different from other countries in the world at similar levels of development? Explain.
4. According to Case 12.1, what kinds of strategies make it possible to operate successfully an apparel production business in locations where the political climate is unsettled?
5. What factors make Turkey a textile and apparel powerhouse within the Middle Eastern region and globally?
6. How is the apparel production sector in Israel, Jordan, and Egypt treated differently by the United States from most other free trade agreement areas?
7. According to Case 12.2, what are the key challenges involved in assisting the participation of Jordanian women in the apparel business?

NORTH AFRICA

On a continent incorporating many contrasts in culture and level of development, North African nations benefit from close proximity, across the Mediterranean Sea, to the developed countries of Europe. We are limiting our discussion of this sector to the newly developing countries of Tunisia, with an eight-thousand-dollar per capita GDP; Egypt, with a six-thousand-dollar per capita GDP; and Morocco, with a $4,600 per capita GDP.

Tunisia

Tunisia went through a 30-year period with a one-party political system in which the president repressed Islamic fundamentalism and established rights for women unmatched by any other Arab nation. Tunisia had a diverse economy and, over the past decade, the government moved toward increasing privatization. The result has been growth in GDP at a faster rate than most other African nations (Central Intelligence Agency [CIA], 2010). Tunisia's secular system of government means there is a greater openness toward Western ways of doing business than in many other countries in the region. Arabic is the primary language. Tunisia has been a WTO member since its inception.

The textile and apparel industry has been a prominent contributor to Tunisia's economy in recent years, accounting for 40.7 percent of the country's total industrial goods exports in 2000 and 22.0 percent of exports in 2008 (refer back to Table 12.2b). This indicates that even though the value of those exports was increasing, other changes were occurring in the economy to decrease the dependence on this industry and increase overall exports. Tunisia built its apparel export market on its outward processing

trade with the EU, where companies in developed countries export fabrics or parts of garments to Tunisia, then reimport them as fully formed garments, similar to the U.S. 807 system. By the end of quotas, Tunisia had become the fourth-largest clothing supplier to the EU, with the EU accounting for 80 percent of Tunisia's clothing trade.

Tunisia's major customers were France, Italy, Germany, and Belgium (Arora, 2004). But it became very hard to compete with Asian countries such as Bangladesh, whose wages in 2009 were as much as six times lower than those in Tunisia (Flanagan, 2009). The recent campaign in Asia to increase the minimum wage is being watched very carefully in nations such as Tunisia and Bulgaria, because if those nations succeed in getting higher wages, competition from that area will weaken as proximity to the EU market resurfaces as a prime sourcing factor.

Tunisia was looking for ways to safeguard its industry from Asian competition; the apparel industry provided 210 thousand jobs in more than 2 thousand companies in 2003, and there was a need for Tunisia to improve productivity in order to maintain its position (Arora, 2004). The industry embraced newer technology, such as computer-aided design (CAD), computer-aided manufacturing (CAM), and computer-integrated manufacturing (CIM), to reduce costs per unit, and had developed quick response (QR) strategies, including just-in-time (JIT) methods. In 2009, OptiTex released an Arabic version of its design software to expand its reach into countries such as Tunisia and elsewhere in the Middle East, making another tool available for use in Tunisia's quest to maintain market share. As shown in Table 12.2b, the overall export figures for textiles went up, from $154 million to $478 million between 2000 and 2008, while apparel exports increased from

$2,227 to $3,766, indicating production has definitely improved (see Table 12.2b).

If one examines the year-to-year textile and apparel export data, there was a dip in 2007, but the overall trajectory continued in an upward pattern the following year, so Tunisia seems to be weathering the downturn in the global economy and influx of Asian competition reasonably well. One of Tunisia's largest employers is the denim wear maker Satex, based in Tunis. This firm had ten thousand workers in the middle of the first decade of the 21st century, and customers included Gap and Levi Strauss and Co.

Tunisia has many trade agreements with its neighboring nations and is a driving force in the Union of Arab Maghred (UAM), which aims to strengthen cooperation among Algeria, Morocco, Tunisia, Libya, and Mauritania. Broader privatization and further liberalization of foreign investment are among the challenges for the future.

Egypt

The regular flooding of the Nile River, providing fertilizer and water to the region, and the semi-isolation created by surrounding deserts set a scene for the development of one of the world's greatest civilizations. Over nearly 2,000 years, Egypt was repeatedly overrun and seized by legions of jealous neighbors, including Greeks, Romans, Byzantines, and Arabs. It was not until after World War II that Egypt acquired full sovereignty. The government has struggled since then because of a rapidly growing population and overtaxed resources. Lack of substantial progress on economic reform limited foreign direct investment in Egypt and limited growth of GDP, until recently. The Egyptian per person GDP increased from four thousand dollars to six thousand dollars between 2003 and 2008 (CIA, 2004, 2009).

Egypt is the producer of the finest long-staple cotton in the world. The textile complex includes the full spectrum of cotton processing operations, including spinning, weaving, converting, knitting, and garment manufacture. It also has some linen production from domestic flax crops. The textile and apparel industry has been considered very important to the Egyptian economy, providing 25 percent of its manufacturing employment, 3 percent of its GDP, and 23 percent of its total exports in 2000 (*Textiles and Apparel,* 2004). Between 2000 to 2008, as shown in Table 12.2a and 12.2b, Egypt increased its textile exports from $412 million per year to $762 million per year, but its textile imports were more than tripled, indicating that the country required more than it was able to produce itself. During this same period, apparel exports more than doubled, from $710 million to $1.55 billion; overall, however, dependence on this industry decreased, as the percentage of total exports attributed to textiles and apparel dropped to 6.4 percent, signifying improvement in overall exports in other areas.

Late in 2004, the United States and Egypt signed a QIZ agreement that gave duty-free access to the U.S. market if textile and apparel products included some Israeli content ("Let My Textiles Go," 2004). This forced Egypt and Israel to work together, similar to the Jordanian QIZ agreement with the United States. The provision established free trade areas in Cairo, Alexandria, and the Suez Canal zone. Egypt and Israel began shipping cotton underwear, knit shirts, and pants to the United States duty free through this arrangement. Hard-liners in Cairo complained that they had to work with the Zionists but seemed to accept the plan as they saw Egyptian exports and incomes increase. A unique aspect of Egypt's involvement is that a 10-percent cap was placed on foreign workers to ensure that Egyptians would benefit from the creation of new jobs (Tucker, 2008). This strategy helped Egypt avoid the types of labor abuses that were alleged at factories in

Jordan, which has a similar QIZ trade agreement but relied more on foreign workers. One impediment to continued growth in these production facilities has been the lack of skilled local labor.

Egypt's foreign trade ministry reported that there were 547 textile companies operating in the QIZ zones in late 2007, but the pool of viable factories actually exporting to the United States was closer to 200 (Tucker, 2008). It appeared that operational efficiency and record-keeping capabilities to meet the needs of U.S. clients were at issue, and the government established teams to work with smaller factories to help them get up to speed.

By 2008, medium- to large-scale companies dominated the industry, with a strong public sector in spinning and weaving ("Egypt Textiles and Clothing," 2009). Textile production had been decreasing, but the value of textile exports began going up during the first decade of this century. The textile sector had been lagging behind in application of new technology; however, the latest technologies—CAD, electronic data interchange (EDI), supply chain management (SCM), Product Data Management (PDM)—were adopted for apparel production, including pattern making, spreading, cutting, sewing, and packaging. They produce a complete range of apparel products from simple T-shirts to tailored suits.

Delta Textile Egypt, which is a vertically integrated underwear manufacturer, and a unit of Israel's Delta Galil Industries, does business with Marks & Spencer, Calvin Klein, Tommy Hilfiger, Hugo Boss, Victoria's Secret, and Walmart ("Egypt: New Planning System," 2010). Delta Textile's production facilities in Egypt employ approximately 3 thousand people in four factories and produce an average of 80 thousand to 85 thousand pieces per day. Much of this production is destined for the United States under QIZ tariff-free provisions.

The Italian menswear firm Forall Group, 35 percent of which is owned by the Egyptian firm Arafa Holding, has a new licensing agreement for the Cerruti 1881 brand, covering 33 countries in the Middle East, East Asia, and Latin America. The agreement will allow Al Arafa Group to increase production of wool and wool-blend fabrics, as well as men's suits, beyond their current levels, in its local facilities in Egypt ("Egypt: Forall Menswear," 2009).

There has been an influx of multinational retailers into Egypt in recent years, as its large population provides a considerable retail market, even though the overall per person GDP is within the level of newly developing country. Egypt is home to one of the largest shopping malls in the Middle East–North Africa region (*Retailing in Egypt*, 2004).

Morocco

Morocco faces many of the challenges typical of newly developing countries: restraining government spending, reducing constraints on private activity and foreign trade, and achieving sustainable economic growth. Since winning its independence in the mid-1950s, the Kingdom of Morocco has endorsed a vigorous program to promote foreign investment in order to develop a strong textile and apparel industry. Despite programs supported by IMF and the World Bank, only modest gains have been made.

The garment industry became the country's single most crucial industrial sector, fundamental in maintaining the economic balance of the kingdom. Today, the WTO reports that Morocco is importing five times more textiles than it exports and exporting ten times more apparel than it imports (refer back to Tables 12.2a and 12.2b). This is a strong indicator that Morocco is doing a significant business in CMT production of apparel. Textile and apparel factories were considered essential for employment in the country, providing jobs for more than 60 percent of employed women, but the dependence on textile and apparel exports has decreased almost by half since 2000, and so reliance on this avenue of employment seems to be going down.

Morocco also has a long tradition of production of small leather accessory products, handicrafts, and cotton apparel production. The cities in which most industry activity occurs are Marrakech and Casablanca. Their proximity to the EU bodes well for maintaining some market share, although their trade numbers in textiles did suffer some lack of sustained growth in recent years, owing to escalating competition from Asia. The most commonly mentioned impediments to the industry include limited diversification of products, underdeveloped yarn and fabric sectors, the high price of energy, and dependence on three markets (France, Spain, and the UK) that had been receiving 82 percent of their exports but that were trending toward Asian imports at the time of this writing. The industry anticipated employment cutbacks as quotas disappeared but instituted other agreements to attempt to compensate for those losses (Sutorius & Vigneron, 2005).

Among those agreements was the U.S.–Morocco Free Trade Agreement, which entered into force on January 1, 2006 ("U.S.–Morocco Free Trade Agreement, n.d."). It was anticipated that this agreement would open up Morocco's economy to greater exports to the United States and make Morocco a more investment-friendly area to foreign direct investment, for upgrading production facilities. Another effort being attempted was to attract Spanish and Portuguese textile companies to relocate to Morocco to take advantage of lower-cost labor (Sutorius & Vigneron, 2005).

In early 2005, France and Morocco called for development of a cooperative venture in the textile sector to adapt this industry to globalization and to face competition through "a strategic euro-Mediterranean partnership" ("Morocco: Tie-up with France," 2005). The goal was to create consortiums for exports among small companies so that they would be in a better position to appeal to the large, developed markets of the world. However, participants found that only a few companies were ready to make the compromises and disclosures necessary for working together. "The Moroccan mentality is not ready yet" (Sutorius & Vigneron, 2005). Other long-term challenges include making additional efforts to prepare for freer trade with the United States and the EU, improving education, and attracting more foreign investment. Morocco also experienced some setbacks, owing to the demise of quotas on goods from Asia into the EU and the recent downturn in the global economy.

OVERVIEW OF SUB-SAHARAN AFRICA (SSA)

There are 37 nations involved in the Sub-Saharan Africa (SSA) geographic sector, many of them among the most economically disadvantaged nations in the world. Unfortunately, much of this area is also home to one of the world's worst health pandemics: HIV/AIDS. SSA accounted for 67 percent of all people living with HIV/AIDS and for 72 percent of HIV/AIDS deaths in 2007 (United Nations Programme on AIDS [UNAIDS], 2008, p. 5). With poverty and health issues a focus in this area, much of it must seek help from outside agencies for survival, let alone industrialization and overall economic development.

From a textile and apparel industry perspective, less than 1 percent of world exports came from the SSA region in 2001. What was produced tended to be done in long production runs of basic products, such as trousers, T-shirts, and woven shirts. With the exception of Mauritius, Madagascar, and South Africa, the sub-Saharan textile industry was found to remain in a largely embryonic state, when evaluating overall exports (Wise, 2005b). Most of the area's factory ownership and management are controlled by foreign interests. Much of that investment is from Asia.

SSA countries had received trade benefits from the EU under the Cotonou Agreement, which provided duty-free and quota-free access for textiles and apparel from Africa, the Caribbean, and some Pacific countries. This agreement was initiated in 2000 and subsequently renewed, but the original format expired late in the decade. At the time of this writing, participants were holding meetings for development of a revision, but the outcomes were not clear, and they were depending on interim bilateral or regional agreements until an overarching document could be completed.

The SSA region was also linked to the United States in 2002 by AGOA, which provides incentives to trade in several product areas, including textiles and apparel.

See Case 12.3 to learn more about the impact of AGOA on SSA.

Since Case 12.3 was written, AGOA has undergone yet another revision: The Africa Investment Incentive Act of 2006 (signed by President Bush on December 20, 2006) amends portions of the African Growth and Opportunity Act (AGOA) and is referred to as "AGOA IV." The legislation extends the third country fabric provision for five years, from September 2007 until September 2012; adds an abundant supply provision; designates certain denim articles as being in

Case 12.3 AGOA: GATEWAY TO OPPORTUNITY, TRUNCATED OPPORTUNITY, OR LOST OPPORTUNITY?

The main goal of the African Growth and Opportunity Act (AGOA), a component of the U.S. Trade and Development Act of 2000, is to assist sub-Saharan Africa (SSA) in achieving economic self-reliance through an overhaul and expansion of its private sector. AGOA aims to help integrate SSA into the global economy and to create a new and improved partnership between SSA and United States. To that end, the act provides duty-free and quota preferences in the U.S. market for various goods, including textiles and apparel, from eligible SSA countries. The determinants of criteria for eligibility relate to each country's orientation and practices in three main domains:
- human and intellectual rights
- free and fair trade
- U.S. foreign policy and national security

In 2004, there were 37 AGOA eligible countries pooled into two groups, based on the country's per capita GNP. All but Mauritius and South Africa had the status of Lesser Developed Beneficiary Countries (with a per capita GNP below U.S. $1,500) and are thus eligible for a special provision of the act referred to as the Special Apparel Provision. Garments manufactured in these countries from fabrics produced in non-SSA countries are still eligible for the duty-free treatment under the set caps.

Further legislation, consisting of the Trade Act of 2002, AGOA II, and the AGOA Acceleration Act of 2004, or AGOA III, have resulted in the extension of AGOA until 2015. However, the Special Apparel Provision was extended by only 4 years, until 2008.

Since its inception, AGOA has had a positive impact. A total of 150 thousand jobs were created, concentrated mostly in the textile and apparel sector in southern and southeastern SSA. In 2003, SSA apparel exports to the United States were second to those of its hydrocarbons and were valued at U.S.$1.2 billion, which corresponds to 40 percent of all SSA AGOA-related exports to the United States, less the export of oil. AGOA has improved the collaboration between governments and the business community as well as promoted intra-SSA cooperation and investments. In addition, the circle of investing countries has grown to include several Asian countries, including China, Taiwan, Malaysia, Hong Kong, and Singapore.

However, despite its positive economic impact on the continent, AGOA suffers from several severe limitations, including the following:

The third-party fabric issue. This provision may have alienated the more economically advanced SSA countries of Mauritius and South Africa and prevented their taking full advantage of AGOA. This provision discourages investment in the more capital-intensive areas of textiles, such as fabric production. Low capacity, little variety, limited styles, and relatively high costs place local producers at a disadvantage, compared with their Asian competitors, as well as making almost obsolete any prior investments in preparation for AGOA I.

Concentration of investments and trade in the energy sector. In 2003, total SSA AGOA exports to the United States were valued at U.S. $14 billion. However, only 21 percent, or one fifth of all exports to the United States, came from products other than oil, with a mere 8.6 percent coming from the textile and apparel area. This last sector is known to have a high employment absorption rate, and a low capital investment level, and has been the first step toward industrialization and economic development in many countries. Besides the jobs created, it is the multiplier effect (for example, the 28 thousand jobs created in Swaziland benefited 100 thousand people) and the indirect job creation (in Kenya each textile and apparel related job generates five other jobs) that make the textile and apparel industry a critical piece of the AGOA.

A quota-free world factor. Reducing the level of investment in the textile and apparel sector, especially the infrastructure, is more likely to hamper the readiness to compete effectively at the global level for most African countries. In fact, overall U.S. investments in SSA in 2002 were valued at U.S. $800 million, representing only 0.1 percent of U.S. global investment. Consequently, a need for safeguards has been expressed within the institutions of AGOA and by extension, through the Global Alliance for Fair Textile Trade (GAFTT).

AGOA skewed toward southern and eastern SSA. Of all AGOA eligible countries, 70 percent are located in eastern and southern Africa. Although that region benefits from being more integrated economically and politically, having better infrastructure and facilities and more highly developed business and legal institutions, and being mostly an English-speaking zone, the perception is that there is disguised favoritism toward that region. Moreover, this is perceived as a blunt form of nepotism, which has widened the gap between eligible AGOA countries and which may have prevented the full participation of the majority of non-English-speaking SSA countries.

A general lack of knowledge about U.S. markets. Most SSA producers suffer from a disconnection from the U.S. imports market. Hence, they are not able to take full advantage of the market or of the provisions of AGOA.

Each institution has its flaws, inefficiencies, and limitations. AGOA is no exception. However, in the short period since its inception, AGOA has already had a positive impact on the lives of a significant section of the population of SSA, especially women in the textile and apparel sector, enhancing their subsequent participation in the economic development process of SSA. Even though ending the quota system has created fresh challenges, the stage is set. It is now up to the SSA countries and their private sectors to take advantage of the opportunities provided by AGOA to utilize the textile and apparel industry as a stepping-stone to industrialization and economic growth.

Anson, R. (2004, January–February). Thinking the unthinkable: Will the textile and apparel quota phase-out be postponed? *Textile Outlook International*, 3–9.

Colette, E. (2003, Janvier – Fevrier). L'AGOA, un contrat à efficacité limitée. *Jeune Afrique L'intelligent*, 2194, 77–79.

Dlamini, A. T. (2004). AGOA Day on the Hill. Retrieved January 10, 2005, from http://www.gov.sz/home.asp?pid54126

Larson, A. P. (2004). AGOA III: The United States Africa Partnership Act of 2003.
Retrieved December 15, 2004, from http://www.state.gov/e/rls/rm/2004/30777.htm

Traore, M. K. (2004). International textile trading regime and textile industry development in developing countries. (Doctoral dissertation, Auburn University, 2004). *Dissertation Abstracts International*, 65(2), 630.

Source:

Based on a case developed by Moussa Traore.

abundant supply; and allows lesser developed beneficiary SSA countries export certain textile articles under AGOA. ("Summary of Africa Investment," n.d.)

In 2009, representatives from the United States and SSA met in Nairobi. The subject that dominated the deliberations was how to achieve the full potential of AGOA. At issue were the eligibility criteria, some of which had led Madagascar, Niger, and Guinea to lose their eligibility in 2009, the same year Mauritania regained eligibility for AGOA benefits, and Uganda was admonished that it could lose its eligibility if "gross violations of internationally recognized human rights" continued ("U.S.: Senator Calls for Review," 2010). Also at issue was erosion of the progress the industry had made earlier in the decade resulting from Asian competition for textile and apparel market share.

One of the primary agricultural exports from nations in SSA is cotton. The cotton-growing region stretches from Côte d'Ivoire, eastward, through Chad. Especially fine-quality cotton comes from the area near Lake Victoria, in Uganda. Côte d'Ivoire is a good example of textile activity in this area, especially since it is identified as the fourth-largest African producer of cotton and one of the leading textile exporters in West and Central Africa (Export Advantage, 2004). Privatization of textile companies increased and enabled extension of production facilities, yet it was estimated that Côte d'Ivoire still only processed 20 percent of its cotton fiber production into yarn and fabric. There is potential for growth in this area under the benefits of AGOA, but the nation has other, politically motivated issues with which to deal.

The SSA area has higher costs to produce cotton yarn and fabrics than do China, India, and other Asian nations, such as Bangladesh. For this reason, SSA lost market share when the quota system expired. It was estimated that Uganda alone showed a reduction in shipments of 68 percent from 2006 to 2008 ("U.S.: Senator Calls for Review," 2010). When compared with Asia, there also were concerns about the lack of variety of fabrics that could be produced. Because fashion dictates the types of fabrics used, these factors seem to put the region at an additional disadvantage over other trading regions. Despite these issues, SSA nations exported $1,520 million of woven and knit apparel to the United States in 2003 (Robinson-Morgan, Diemond, & Erkul, 2004). Since then, much of the industry has fallen on hard times from stronger global competition and the general economic downturn. Another practice that is prevalent in many regions of this trading area is the import and distribution of used apparel products (review Case 2.1).

Now, try your hand at Learning Activity 12.4.

Learning Activity 12.4
NORTH AFRICA AND OVERVIEW OF SUB-SAHARAN AFRICA (SSA)

1. What are the key differences between countries in North Africa and SSA, from the perspective of operating a textile business? (Tables 12.1 and 12.3 will be helpful.)
2. What are the key differences between countries in North Africa and SSA from the perspective of operating an apparel business? (Tables 12.1 and 12.3 will be helpful.)
3. Why has the textile industry not developed in SSA despite a ready supply of cotton?
4. According to Case 12.3, what are the desired economic and industry effects of AGOA on the textile and apparel businesses in SSA nations? Why does this not seem to be happening?
5. In what ways does the used clothing trade interfere with cultural continuity?
6. Considering Case 2.1, identify the primary participants in the international supply chain for secondhand clothing.

Developing Countries in Sub-Saharan Africa

Since there are no developed countries in SSA, we are focused on developing countries first. Mauritius and South Africa are among the economically strong of SSA with per capita GDPs of $12,400 and $10,000, respectively (See Table 12.1). As with countries developing to this level in other parts of the world, the textile and apparel industries are being threatened by production opportunities in lower-wage countries.

Mauritius

The small island of Mauritius, in the Southern Indian Ocean, to the east of Madagascar, seems at first an unlikely spot to discover one of the world's leading clothing industries. Historically, the island had been a port of call for ships on the East Indies trade route as far back as the 1590s. A stable democracy, with regular free elections and a positive human rights record, contributed to Mauritius's rank as Africa's largest textile producer, the world's second-largest producer of fully fashioned knitwear, and the third-largest exporter of pure new wool products in the early 2000s (Smith & Pelit, 2003). At that time, the domestic workforce in Mauritius was limited, and it was believed that about one third were foreign workers, largely from Asia (*Textiles and Apparel*, 2004).

Mauritius had been a large center for apparel production for some time, but political setbacks created difficulties for the tiny nation in 2001 and 2002. These setbacks caused a drop in overall economic conditions, and the United States reclassified the nation as "least developed," qualifying it for full eligibility in trade breaks through the provisions of AGOA. Previously, per person GDP was just high enough to make Mauritius ineligible for those incentives. This island nation has lost thousands of jobs in recent years as customers have moved their production needs to lesser-developed nations.

According to Tables 12.2a and 12.2b, since 2003 textile imports into Mauritius declined and apparel exports have also declined; thus, employment in apparel has not improved in recent years. The United States has been encouraging Mauritius to seek growth in other sectors of the industry, such as jewelry and accessories. These efforts to diversify will increase trade and investment potential with the United States and has already led to a 700 percent increase in U.S. investment in the last 5 years (Casabona, 2009a).

South Africa

After the Union of South Africa gained independence in 1902, it operated under apartheid, a policy of segregation and economic discrimination against the country's nonwhite majority. The 1990s saw the end of apartheid and the establishment of black majority rule. By African standards, South Africa is a middle-income country; as shown in Table 12.1, per person GDP in 2009 was ten thousand dollars. South Africa has an abundant supply of natural resources and well-developed infrastructure to support major urban centers throughout the region. South Africa has the most advanced transportation, telecommunications, and utilities infrastructure in SSA (*Textiles and Apparel*, 2004). However, growth has not been strong enough to lower South Africa's high unemployment rate or poverty remaining from the apartheid era.

When international antiapartheid trade sanctions were lifted, the textile and apparel business in South Africa underwent restructuring. There was a good-sized industry, but most production was for domestic use, causing a trade deficit in textiles and apparel. The government encouraged foreign direct investment, but investors were torn between lower wages in other SSA nations and the developed export infrastructure and skilled labor found in South Africa.

South Africa "produces cotton and man-made fibers, exports surplus wool, and is the world's leading producer of mohair" (*Textiles and Apparel*, 2004, n.p.). The country produces short-staple cotton (lower in quality than that produced in Egypt) and relies on imports from Zimbabwe, Zambia, and Mozambique to meet its long-staple requirements. South Africa is the only SSA nation producing synthetic filament yarn, a highly capital-intensive industry.

There appear to be four labor–management patterns in the South African apparel industry, based on the size of the firm, as follows:

1. Small firms have low-cost, unskilled, nonunion labor.
2. Medium-sized firms have high-cost, skilled, unionized labor.
3. Large firms also have high-cost, skilled labor, but competitiveness relies on collaborative labor–management relations and commensurate economies of scale in production. These are the only firms considered capable of meeting volume requirements for U.S. customers.
4. Transnational firms have low-cost, unskilled, nonunion labor. They set up large-scale operations in decentralized regions outside of the urban areas to take advantage of lower wages. These firms are often from Hong Kong and Taiwan and use Chinese methods and pay on a piecework basis rather than hourly wages (*Textiles and Apparel*, 2004).

One example of apparel production is Levi Strauss & Co., which manufacturers some clothing in South Africa and sells locally at retail in its own stores. Levi Strauss increased its retail footprint when it increased its stores from 6 to 12 in 2004 (Bolin, 2004). It appears however, that South Africa has found itself in the position today of importing far more than it exports (refer back to Tables 12.2a and 12.2b). Currently, export of textiles and apparel from this nation is less than 1 percent of overall trade.

Global competition and a downturn in the economy have taken their toll here. SA Fine Worsted announced it would close two of its factories, in Cape Town and Atlantis, in February 2010, bringing the overall loss of jobs in the industry in the past year to approximately 13,400, according to the South African Clothing and Textile Workers' Union ("South Africa: SA Worsted," 2010). The union also indicates that an estimated 1,500 factories were forced to close in 2009. These closures have put the nation on a "slippery slope to de-industrialization" (South Africa: Clothing Sector," 2010, n.p.).

The retail market of South Africa is deeply divided between those of better economic means and those who are very poor. Said Andre Kriel, general secretary of the Southern African Clothing and Textile Workers Union (SACTWU), "'Despite years of economic growth, our unemployment is the highest in the world amongst developed and large developing countries and we have the most unequal society in the world'" (South Africa: Clothing Sector, 2010, n.p.). Yet, the retail market in the more prosperous cities, such as Johannesburg, had been thriving. In this sector, buoyed by a strong currency, low interest rates, and unabated consumer spending, international brands were rushing to establish a presence. D&G, the secondary line of Dolce & Gabbana, opened its Johannesburg store in the Sandton City Mall and a freestanding boutique in Cape Town, in 2004 (Wise, 2005a). The D&G shops are owned by the Diesel Group, based in Italy, which had established a presence in South Africa 12 years before these openings. Woolworths is a South African retailer (different from the U.S. Woolworth's) founded in Cape Town, in 1931, that by 2006 had hundreds of stores in South Africa and franchise partners throughout Africa and the Middle East. The company has made considerable efforts toward sustainability in recent years and was the first South African retailer to sponsor organically grown cotton.

Figure 12.6a

Water pollution in
Lesotho, from denim
production runoff.

(*Robin Hammond/
Panos Pictures*)

Least Developed Countries in Sub-Saharan Africa

Lesotho, Kenya, and Madagascar, with a per capita GDP of $1,500 in 2008 (down from $3 thousand in 2003), $1,600 and, $800, respectively, represent some of the least developed countries of SSA and the world. As with least developed countries in other parts of the world, development is retarded in these countries because of government and business corruption, racial and cultural discrimination, and drug trafficking.

Lesotho

Lesotho is a small, mountainous, landlocked nation surrounded by South Africa. One of Lesotho's greatest plights today is the prevalence of HIV/AIDS. It was estimated that 23.2 percent of the adult population of Lesotho was infected, and in 2008, 18 thousand deaths

were attributed to the disease (Lesotho, 2008). Because of AIDS and other issues inherent to poverty, the average life expectancy is just 40.4 years (refer back to Table 12.1).

Lesotho raises jute, manufactures jute products, and produces mohair fibers, but of greater importance is the country's rapidly growing apparel assembly sector. From almost nothing a few years previous, Lesotho exported $234 million dollars of textile and apparel products in 2001, representing 94 percent of the nation's total merchandise exports that year (*Textiles and Apparel*, 2004). In 2001, per capita GDP was just $558, yet by 2004, it was estimated at $3 thousand, even with an unemployment rate of 45 percent (CIA, 2004). Unfortunately, things have deteriorated in recent years, owing to competition from Asia and the global economic downturn, and today per person GDP is down to $1,500 (refer back to Table 12.1). Exports have dropped below the level reported by the WTO, and we can only estimate their trajectory as downward.

In 2008, Lesotho was the largest AGOA apparel supplier to the United States, yet it posted a drop of 11 percent in a 5-month period in early 2009 (Ellis, 2009). One of the reasons for this drop may be attributed to reports of chemical dumping and pollution of the water supply by a factory allegedly owned by the Taiwanese firm Nien Hsing ("Update: U.S.," 2009). Gap and Levi Strauss and Co. both contracted this factory to produce jeans for them and launched supply chain investigations in Lesotho after the pollution was exposed by a UK newspaper. The Gap Stores, Inc. stated that it would sever ties with factories that did not meet its standards, which include requirements related to management and oversight of the workplace and environmental conduct, but that it hoped the problems would be corrected to prevent local workers from losing their jobs.

For Lesotho the main issue has become the disparity between those who are improving their lives economically and those who remain destitute. In the long run, the problem may become too heavy a dependence on apparel production to solve their economic ills and the potential for ultimate failure to industrialize (Figures 12.6a and 12.6b).

Kenya

Kenya is the regional hub for trade and finance in East Africa, but it has been hampered by corruption in its judicial system, resulting in cancellation of support from the IMF, in 1997. IMF support resumed in 2000, but so did corruption. One of the poorest countries in the world, Kenya is largely an agrarian society with a large incidence of HIV/AIDS that has affected the availability of trained labor in recent years.

Kenya's previously active cotton-processing industry deteriorated in the 1990s to the point that it almost collapsed from a

Figure 12.6b A man monitoring denim looms in Sub-Saharan Africa. Apparel and textile imports from Sub-Saharan Africa fell 11.5 percent through May 2009. (*Per-Anders Pettersson/ Getty Images*)

combination of bad weather and competition from foreign suppliers. There was rising unemployment during that time, causing considerable civil unrest. There was also an influx of imported used clothing, for domestic use.

Following implementation of AGOA, in 2000, Kenya began to attract some foreign direct investment in apparel production for export. Fabric imports increased as needed to make apparel for export. Industry utilized the third-party fabric provision from AGOA that enabled it to seek lower-cost fabrics from Asia. Some apparel factories that had closed in the 1990s reopened. The sector created much needed alternative employment opportunities for residents, reaching 30 thousand people, in 2003. Export of goods to the United States from Kenya tripled from 2000 to 2002, to $125 million. These numbers are small when compared with many powerhouse producers but much needed in this least developed economy. Then competition for U.S. markets increased with the end of quotas and the economic downturn, and Kenya found itself in a world of hurt.

Today, Kenyan cotton is being marketed by the International Trade Center (ITC), an associate of the WTO and the United Nations ("Kenya: Cotton Finds Saviour," 2010). Kenya has become a marginal performer, and the goal is to revitalize its sector and make progress toward reentering the market. In 2009, the U.S. Department of Agriculture reported that Kenya's cotton production had dropped to about 20 thousand bales, from a high of 70 thousand bales, in 1986. This decrease in production was blamed on inferior farming techniques, substandard seeds, and pests' contaminating the plants in the field. It is hoped that introduction of pest-resistant varieties and help from the United Nations will lead to increased production and Kenya's return to the international market.

Madagascar

A large island off the eastern coast of Africa about twice the size of Arizona, Madagascar had a growing apparel industry, fueled by AGOA participation, until political turmoil erupted, in 2002. Before the problems, there were 140 apparel companies in Madagascar's export-processing zone (EPZ) employing between 80 thousand and 100 thousand workers (*Textiles and Apparel*, 2004). The main apparel product, accounting for almost half of output, was fully fashioned knitwear. The industry was relatively low-tech by international standards, as about 90 percent of the fully fashioned knitwear was made on hand-knitting machines. Most other products were done CMT.

A primary example of the kinds of setbacks plaguing the industry following the 2001 election was a blockade of the ports and roads, which halted clothing production for most of 2002. It was anticipated at that time that the political turmoil would inhibit future investment in the area and that competition from other markets would also inhibit recovery. Although some progress was made in the late 2000s, in 2009 the government was overthrown in a military coup. Madagascar was deemed to be failing to meet the requirements necessary to continue AGOA participation in early 2010, resulting in the termination by President Barack Obama, of the United States, of their benefits of duty-free concessions under AGOA (Madagascar: Loses AGOA," 2010). Less than 2 months later Madagascar's garment industry was preparing for sanctions by the EU, owing to lack of success in meeting human rights needs and following the rule of law.

The paradox of economic development via textiles and apparel, in which labor exploitation often goes hand in hand with success and industry decline may occur for dozens of reasons, is a puzzling and frustrating phenomenon replayed in dozens of countries around the world. What is the social responsibility of the businesses involved? And what is the role of textiles and apparel as the global market evolves? These are some of the primary questions that must be answered in order to have sustainable supply chains.

Now, continue the discussion of developing and least developed SSA countries with Learning Activity 12.5.

Learning Activity 12.5
TEXTILE AND APPAREL INDUSTRY ACTIVITY IN DEVELOPING AND LEAST DEVELOPED COUNTRIES IN SUB-SAHARAN AFRICA

1. Identify four key things that contribute to the inability of countries of SSA to develop.
2. What resources are available that should contribute to textile and apparel industry development?
3. Which SSA nations are considered most vulnerable to Asian competition? What factors make them most vulnerable?
4. Now where are you going to source your Macy's moderate-priced, private label line of casual young women's apparel? Explain.
5. If you were required to source in the Middle East–Africa trading bloc, what country would you select? Why?

SUMMARY
....

The Middle East–Africa trading region is linked by a centuries-old tradition of trade with other regions, an emphasis on the use of Arabic language, and the widespread practice of Islam. The region is home to many of the least economically developed nations on the globe, averaging approximately $1,500 per capita GDP. Currently, Yemen has a per person GDP of $2,500 and Ethiopia, a per person GDP of only $900. The average life expectancy in several of the sub-Saharan nations is fewer than 50 years, largely because of poverty and the high incidence of HIV/AIDS and other diseases.

Conversely, this region is also home to some of the wealthier nations in the world, including the United Arab Emirates (UAE) and Saudi Arabia, which enjoy high per capita GDPs from the production of oil and which focus more on consumption of apparel than on its production.

This region is also where some of the world's finest cotton is grown, especially in Egypt and Uganda. Production and export of cotton textiles and apparel in Turkey places it in the top ten in world rankings for export of these products. Many other nations in the area are looking to apparel production as a means of improving their economic station in life, via either foreign investment in production facilities, such as in Mauritius and Lesotho, or entrepreneurial startup factories, such as those in Ghana, funded by the World Bank.

Regional trade agreements with the EU and the United States and preference programs provide free access to markets for exports to many nations in this region. One example of such a program is AGOA, affecting most SSA nations. The QIZ agreements between the United States and Jordan and Egypt also provide the incentive of tariff-free access to the U.S. market. Nonetheless, many of these nations are truly struggling and vulnerable. At this point, we can only wait and see how they fare.

REFERENCES

Anson, R. (2004, January–February). Thinking the unthinkable: Will the textile and apparel quota phaseout be postponed? *Textile Outlook International*, 3–9.

Arora, S. (2004, October 18). Tunisia turns to the EU for post-quota support. just-style.com. Retrieved October 20, 2004, from http://www.just-style.com/analysis/tunisia-turns-to-the-eu-for-post-quota-support_id92402.aspx

Background note: Syria. (n.d.). Retrieved March 7, 2010, from http://www.state.gov/r/pa/ei/bgn/3580.htm

Bolin, L. (2004, August 2). Levi's to expand operations in South Africa. *Mail & Guardian online*. Retrieved from http://www.mg.za/Content/I3.asp?ao5118822

Casabona, L. (2009a, August 6). U.S. and Mauritius to begin trade talks. *Women's Wear Daily*. Retrieved from http://www.wwd.com/business-news/u-s-and-mauritius-to-begin-trade-talks-2230949

Casabona, L. (2009b, October 1). U.S. sends delegation to Jordan to discuss labor issues. *Women's Wear Daily*. Retrieved from http://www.wwd.com/business-news/u-s-sends-delegation-to-jordan-to-discuss-labor-issues-2322534

Casabona, L. (2009c, November 3). Jordan addresses alleged abuses in garment sector. *Women's Wear Daily*. Retrieved from http://www.wwd.com/business-news/jordan-addresses-alleged-abuses-in-garment-sector-2360224

Central Intelligence Agency (CIA). (2004). *The world factbook*. Dulles, VA: Brassey's.

Central Intelligence Agency (CIA). (2010). *The world factbook*. Retrieved February 4, 2010, from http://www.odci.gov/cia/publications/factbook/index.html

Colette, E. (2003, January–February). L'AGOA, un contrat à efficacité limitée. *Jeune Afrique L'intelligent 2194*, 77–79.

Dlamini, A. T. (2004). AGOA Day on the Hill. Retrieved January 10, 2005, from http://www.gov.sz/home.asp?pid=4126

The economic agreement between the GGC states. (2001, December 31). 22nd Session of the GCC Council. Retrieved June 10, 2010 from http://library.gcc-sg.org/English/Books/econagree2004.htm

Egypt: Forall menswear group secures Cerruti 1881 license. (2009, August 4). just-style.com. Retrieved March 9, 2010 from http://www.just-style.com/news/forall-menswear-group-secures-cerruti-1881-license_id104907.aspx

Egypt: New planning system boosts Delta Textile (2010, February 16). just-style.com. Retrieved March 9, 2010, from http://www.just-style.com/news/new-planning-system-boosts-delta-textile_id106766.aspx

Egypt textiles and clothing report Q3 2009. (2009, July). just-style.com. Retrieved July 24, 2009, from http://www.just-style.com/market-research/egypt-textiles-and-clothing-report-q3-2009_id79155.aspx

Ellis, K. (2009, August 4). USTR Kirk to urge African nations to diversify. *Women's Wear Daily*. Retrieved from http://www.wwd.com/wwd-publications/wwd/2009-08-04/#/article/business-news/usta-kirk-to-urge-african-nations-to-diversify-2229136?navSection=issues&navId=2229021

Export Advantage. *Côte d'Ivoire: Local industry and market*. U.S. Department of Commerce—International Trade Administration, Office of Textiles and Apparel (OTEXA). Retrieved December 22, 2004, from http://www.ita.doc.gov

Flanagan, M. (2009, November 12). Comment: Lack of solidarity hinders Asian wage campaign. just-style.com. Retrieved March 10, 2010, from http://www.just-style.com/comment/lack-of-solidarity-hinders-asian-wage-campaign_id105900.aspx

Garner, M. B. (2010, June 13). *Enhancing technical training and employment opportunities for Jordanian women*. Summary of final report to United Nations Development Program. Amman, Jordan.

Greene, J. (2003, September 2). Jordan trades on stability. *Women's Wear Daily*, 10.

Karimzadeh, M. (2010, February 8). Kenneth Cole to reach Turkey in new deal. *Women's Wear Daily*. Retrieved March 7, 2010, from http://www.wwd.com/markets-news/kenneth-cole-to-reach-turkey-in-new-deal-2450238

Kenya: Cotton finds a saviour in UN body. (2010, February 9). Retrieved March 10, 2010, from http://www.fibre2fashion.com/news/textiles-association-organization-news/newsdetails.aspx?news_id=82190

Larson, A. P. (2004). AGOA III: The United States Africa Partnership Act of 2003. Retrieved December 15, 2004, from http://www.state.gov/e/rls/rm/2004/30777

Lesotho. (2008). Retrieved June 11, 2010, from http://www.unaids.org/en/CountryResponses/Countries/lesotho.asp

Let my textiles go. (2004, December 16). *The New York Times.* Retrieved December 21, 2004, from http://www.nytimes.com

Lipke, D. (2007, November 14). Growth region: Many Middle East states offer an unexpected and seemingly insatiable market for luxury goods. *Women's Wear Daily*, 26.

Madagascar: Loses AGOA benefits. (2010, January 4). just-style.com. Retrieved June 28, 2010, from http://www.just-style.com/pap.aspx?id=106296

Moin, D. (2004, July 6). Harvey Nichols headed to Dubai. *Women's Wear Daily*, 23.

Morocco: Tie-up with France to promote textile sector. (2005, February 12). *Morocco Textile News Summaries.* Retrieved March 13, 2005, from http://www.morocco.textilenews.org

Neidik, B. (2004). Organization foundations of export performance: The case of the Turkish apparel industry. *Journal of Fashion Marketing and Management, 8*(3), 294.

Profile of the textile and clothing industry in Syria. (2006, May 1). *Textiles Intelligence.* Retrieved March 7, 2010, from http://www.marketresearch.com/product/display.asp?productid=1317721

Progressive Policy Institute. (2005, February 23) *Papua New Guinea has four times as many languages as Europe.* Retrieved June 22, 2010, from http://www.ppionline.org/search_results_ppi.cfm

Qualifying industrial zones. (2000, December 21). Retrieved March 23, 2005, from http://www.jordaninvestment.com/5.htm

Retailing in Egypt. (2004, September). *Report of Euromonitor International.* Retrieved October 9, 2004, from http://www.the-infoshop.com/study/e023381_retailing_in_egypt.html

Robinson-Morgan, A., Diemond, J., & Erkul, B. (2004, April). *U.S.-African trade profile.* Market Access and Compliance, Office of Africa, U.S. Department of Commerce, International Trade Administration.

South Africa: Clothing sector key to new industrial policy. (2010, February 19). just-style.com. Retrieved June 11, 2010, from http://www.just-style.com/news/clothing-sector-key-to-new-industrial-policy_id106820.aspx

South Africa: SA Fine Worsted shuts two wool factories. (2010, January 20). iust-style.com. Retrieved March 9, 2010, from http://www.just-style.com/news/sa-fine-worsted-shuts-two-wool-factories_id106476.aspx

Statement by H. E. Ambassador Dian Triansyah Djani. (2009). United Nations Conference on Trade and Development, Trade and Development Board, 56th Session, September 14–15, 2009. Retrieved February 16, 2009, from http://www.unctad.org/sections/wcmu/docs/tdb56stat_Indonesia_en.pdf

Steinberg, J. (2004, June 21). Keeping business flowing in a volatile climate. *Women's Wear Daily*, 13.

Steinberg, J. (2009, January 13). Israeli companies undeterred by Gaza conflict. *Women's Wear Daily*, 14.

Summary of Africa Investment Incentive Act of 2006—AGOA IV. (n.d.). Export.gov. Retrieved June 7, 2010, from http://www.agoa.gov/agoa_legislation/agoa_legislation4.html

Sutorius, N., & Vigneron, G. (2005, February–March). Morocco in need of partners. *Fashion Business International*, 28–31.

Textiles and Apparel: Assessment of the competitiveness of certain foreign suppliers to the U.S. market. (2004, January). U.S. ITC investigation no. 332-448; Publication 3671. Retrieved March 16, 2005, from http://www.otexta.ita.doc.gov.default.htm

Traore, M. K. (2004). International textile trading regime and textile industry development in developing countries (Doctoral dissertation, Auburn University, 2004). *Dissertation Abstracts International, 65*(2), 630.

Tucker, R. (2008, January 8). Egypt hunts new growth paths. *Women's Wear Daily*, 16.

United Nations Programme on AIDS (UNAIDS). *Report on the global AIDS epidemic: Executive summary.* (2008). Geneva, Switzerland: Retrieved June 11, 2010, from http:// data.unaids.org/pub/GlobalReport/2008/ JC1511_GR08_ExecutiveSummary_en.pdf

Update: U.S.: Gap and Levi probe Lesotho factory scandal. (2009, August 3). just-style.com. Retrieved June 11, 2010, from http:// www.just-style.com/news/gap-and-levi-probe-lesotho-factory-scandal_id104897.aspx

U.S.–Morocco Free Trade Agreement: How U.S. companies can benefit. (n.d.). Export.gov. Retrieved March 10, 2010, from http:// www.export.gov/FTA/morocco/index.asp

U.S.: Senator calls for review of Uganda's AGOA trade status. (2010, January 15). just-style.com. Retrieved March 10, 2010, from http://www.just-style.com/news/senator-calls-for-review-of-ugandas-agoa-trade-status_id106432.aspx

Werner International Management Consultants. (2009). *Primary textiles labor cost comparisons 2008.* Retrieved February 4, 2010, from http:// texnet.ilgstudios.net/files/2009/08/Werner_International_-_Labor_Cost_Study_2008.pdf

Wise, B. (2005a, January 21). D&G store flourishing in Johannesburg. *Women's Wear Daily*, 17.

Wise, B. (2005b, September 28). Africa tries to adapt. *Women's Wear Daily*, 18.

The World Bank. (2010). Retrieved February 16, 2010, from http://go.worldbank.org/3QT2P1GNH0

World Trade Organization (WTO). (2004). International Trade Statistics 2004. Section 4: Trade by sector (143–157). Retrieved November 27, 2004, from http://www.wto.org/english/res_e/ statis_e/its2004_e/its04_bysector_e.pdf

World Trade Organization (WTO), (2009). International Trade Statistics. 2009. Section 2: Merchandise trade by product (107–114). Retrieved January 16, 2010, from http:// www.wto.org/english/res_e/statis_e/its2009_e/ its09_merch_trade_product_e.pdf

Glossary

acquisition act of making garments available for personal use; increases inventory

ad valorem tariff a tax set as a fixed percent of value of an imported product

adversarial relationships a common behavior between suppliers and customers in the textile complex; belief that success of one is dependent on costs to another

African Growth and Opportunity Act (AGOA) a component of the U.S. Trade and Development Act of 2000; the purpose is to assist sub-Saharan Africa (SSA) in achieving economic self-reliance

agile manufacturing an operational strategy focused on inducing velocity and flexibility in a make-to-order production process with minimal changeover time and interruptions (Rockford Consulting Group, n.d.)

Agreement on Textiles and Clothing (ATC) World Trade Organization trade agreement that replaced the GATT Multifiber Arrangement

American Apparel and Footwear Association (AAFA) a predominant U.S.-based apparel related trade association in the Americas

Andean Trade Preference Act (ATPA) the primary trade agreement between the United States and northern South America, established in 1991

Andean Trade Promotion and Drug Eradication Act (ATPDEA) made the sector eligible for duty-free treatment on exports of U.S. goods for the first time, in 2002

apparel firm the term currently used to describe a vertically integrated firm engaged in a combination of product development, sourcing, and retailing of garments

apparel knitting mill manufacturing facility that interloops yarns to produce garments without producing fabric first; some sweaters, tops, scarves, hats, and underwear

apparel manufacturer traditionally, a firm engaged in the entire process of apparel manufacturing

apparel manufacturing processes involved with merchandising, design, product development, production, and often wholesale marketing

apparel production part of the process of apparel manufacturing that actually converts materials—including fabrics, findings, trims, and usually thread—into a consumable good

apparel production vendor firm that takes orders for apparel products from other firms and that either produce or arrange for the production of those specific garments; historically called production contractors

apparel sourcing identifying appropriate countries of origin and contracting with cost-efficient vendors for services, production, or finished goods, or a combination of these; for delivery of a specified quantity and quality within an identified time frame

apparent consumption estimation of domestic consumption based on levels of domestic production, imports, and exports (production + imports − exports)

Asia-Pacific Economic Cooperation (APEC) established in 1989 as a forum for 21 member nations to facilitate economic growth, cooperation, trade, and investment in the Asia-Pacific region

Association of Southeast Asian Nations (ASEAN) established to enhance the trade options for its 10 member countries, with a goal of establishing an ASEAN economic community

basic goods tend to be standardized and utilitarian with infrequent demand for changes in styling

brand manager another name for a vertically integrated apparel firm whose business is based on a stable of valuable product names/brands

buying office company that provided sourcing services to retail buyers primarily from the 1950s through the 1980s

buying power the amount of goods that can be purchased with a given amount of money at a given place and time

capitalism an economic system based on freedoms of ownership, production, exchange, acquisition, work, movement, and open competition

Caribbean Basin Economic Recovery Act (CBERA) commonly known as the Caribbean Basin Initiative (CBI), a trade preference program initiated by the United States in 1983 that expanded the use of Item 807 by eliminating quota restraints

Caribbean Basin Initiative an economic development program established by the U.S. government

The Central America–Dominican Republic–United States Free Trade Agreement (CAFTA-DR) intended to solidify the United States as the leading supplier of goods and services to Central America and Dominican Republic and to provide them with duty-free access to the U.S. market, beginning in 2002

charge-back a financial penalty imposed by the customer on a vendor for noncompliance with established vendor compliance rules

CMT (cut-make-trim) apparel contractors who commonly provide apparel assembly as their primary service

code of conduct a statement of principles and standards by which business decisions are made

communism an economic system in which resources are cooperatively or state-owned; a classless society, in which equal distribution of economic goods is the economic goal

complement a product purchased and used along with another; example, shoes and socks

conglomerate a business formed when firms serving unrelated markets join together for common ownership

consolidator a person or firm that combines cargo from a number of shippers going to the same destination into one container for the purpose of reducing shipping rates

consumer obsolescence discard of products owing to a lack of interest in them rather than the lack of their usability

Consumer Price Index (CPI) a measure of the impact of inflation on consumer buying power in the United States

consumption commodities (goods and services), their uses, and services consumed

consumption expenditure money used to support the level of consumption during a specified period

contractor a firm that provides services for other businesses; often used for selected apparel manufacturing processes; in today's sourcing language these firms are called vendors

converters fabric mills that specialize in application of yarn and fabric finishes

copyright a legal right gained by an author, composer, playwright, publisher, or distributor, to exclusive publication, production, sale, or distribution of a literary, musical, dramatic or artistic work

corporate, social, economic, environmental, and political responsibilities the ethical obligation of businesses to value and support the well-being of their employees, customers, and suppliers and the resources, environments, and laws in countries in which they operate; essential for sustainability of supply chains

cost, insurance, freight (CIF) reflects the cost of goods, as well as shipping and insurance to the requested port

counterfeit an imitation of what is genuine with the intent to defraud the customer

counterfeiting the act of making an imitation of an original with the intent to defraud

countervailing duty a special tax that increases the price of goods to a competitive level

country of origin (COO) the location where an article was wholly obtained; when more than one country is involved, the location where the last substantial transformation was carried out; the location where there is a change in the product designation number according to the Harmonized Commodity Code and Designation System (HS)

current dollars buying power at specified time, numbers not adjusted to account for inflation

customer in the sourcing world, the sourcing company that contracts for delivery of services, materials, product development, or finished goods

Customs and Border Protection (CBP) U.S. customs service

customs compliant to act in accordance with Customs rules and regulations

customs service government agency responsible for monitoring imported goods, assessing and collecting duties, and reporting imports against quotas

cut-and-sew apparel manufacturing apparel production plant that performs both preproduction and production processes

democracy a political system in which the people hold the ruling power either directly or through elected representatives

department store a retailer that provides a variety of product lines, including apparel for men, women, and children; soft goods for the home; and home furnishings usually at moderate-to-higher-price levels

developed country a nation whose gross domestic product per capita and other measures of well-being fall well above the world average

developing country a nation whose gross domestic product per capita and other measures of well-being fall near or slightly below the world average based on the benefits of industrial growth

dictatorship a political and economic system operated by a ruler with absolute power or authority

discard the act of giving up possession and ownership of a garment; reduces inventory

discretionary income amount of money available after all current obligations are covered

disposable income take-home pay; the amount available to an individual or family to support the level of consumption, savings, and investment at a particular time

distressed goods merchandise that is not salable at the intended price; seconds, overruns, samples, last season's goods, retailer returns, and so on

domestic production products made in the home country

domestic trade exchange of goods, services, or both within the boundaries of a specified state or country

dumping selling a product in another country at less than it is sold in the home country or less than it costs to produce

dyeing the process of combining fibers, yarns, or fabrics with a coloring substance and creating a bond

e-commerce electronic business transactions conducted by systems such as the Internet

economic luxury superior good

economic necessity normal good

economic responsibility the obligations of an individual, group, or general population for assuming responsibility for the value of materials, services, and resources consumed and for using them efficiently with a minimum of waste

economic system a method of managing resources; producing, distributing, and consuming wealth

EDI electronic data interchange; a means of passing document information between companies

effective tariff economic impact of nominal tariff

elastic demand expenditure increases more rapidly than income increases; ratio of percent expenditure increase to percent income increase is greater than 1; a superior good

embargo the prohibition of the entry of goods into a defined political area; the stoppage of trade until issues can be negotiated

environmental responsibility the obligations of an individual, group, or general population for the physical conditions, circumstances, and related resources influencing the health and comfort of current and future generations

e-tailing retailers' providing opportunities for ultimate consumers to purchase products or services, using electronic systems such as the Internet; non-store retailing

ethics a system or code of morals of a particular person, group, or profession and its application to decisions or particular problems of conduct

euro European Union common currency, initiated in 2001 by EU-15

European Commission politically independent institution responsible for proposing EU legislation, implementing it, and monitoring compliance

European Community (EC) European Economic Community membership expanded to form this in 1967; France blocked membership of the United Kingdom until 1973

European Economic Area (EEA) a cooperative arrangement to strengthen trade and economic relations in order to create a homogenous European trade area with the support of European Union

European Economic Community (EEC) the unification of Belgium, Luxembourg, the Netherlands, France, and West Germany in 1957; became known as the Common Market

European Union (EU) an organization formed in 1993 to expand cooperation regarding trade, social issues, foreign policy, security, defense, and judicial issues

European Union (EU-12) the original 12 members included Belgium, Denmark, France, Germany, Greece, Ireland, Italy, Luxembourg, the Netherlands, Portugal, Spain, and the United Kingdom

European Union-15 (EU-15) Austria, Finland, and Sweden were admitted to the EU in 1995

European Union-25 (EU-25) Cyprus, Czech Republic, Estonia, Hungary, Latvia, Lithuania, Malta, Poland, Slovakia, and Slovenia were admitted to the European Union in 2004

European Union-27 (EU-27) Bulgaria and Romania were admitted to the EU in 2007

exchange rates determine the ratio at which one currency can be traded for another

export policy a set of political determinations designed to regulate which types of products can leave a domestic country for another market, and when and under what conditions those products can leave

export subsidy a payment from a government to a firm as a reward for exporting products

export trading and sourcing company provides services related to the entire global apparel manufacturing and distribution process

exports goods shipped to another country for import in exchange for money, other goods, or jobs

extra EU trade with nations that are not members of the EU

fabric finishing processes that convert greige goods into completed fabric

fabric-forward rule a trade rule that limits tariffs or provides quota-free imports, or both, for garments made of fabrics produced in the sourcing country

fair trade a trading partnership, based on dialogue, transparency and respect, that contributes to sustainable development by supporting trading conditions that secure the rights of marginalized producers and workers (World Fair Trade Association [WFTO], 2009)

fair trade associations known as the most socially responsible groups in the global market with concerns for human rights, business relationships, and the larger environment

fashion a style of dress accepted by the majority of a group at a particular time

fashion goods individualized, differentiated by style and color

fiberweb fabrics made directly from fibers; traditionally called nonwovens

findings materials other than face fabric used to construct garments; interlinings, pocket bags, linings, closures, and trims

firm any business, corporation, proprietorship, or partnership

flexible production system quickly and efficiently producing a variety of styles at low volume per style with zero defects; often uses single-ply cutters and modular systems with stand-up sewing

floor ready garment producers attach retailer specified tickets and labels to garments that are ready for display before shipping them out

foreign trade zone a free trade zone that allows manufacturing for export, but no domestic distribution of finished goods

free on board (FOB) covers price to produce, pack and load goods onboard a vessel at the foreign port of export

Free Trade Area of the Americas (FTAA) the most comprehensive free-trade agreement under discussion since early 2000s, involving 34 countries in North, Middle, and South America

free trade unrestricted exchange of goods between or among nations

free trade zone a port or other site within a nation designated for duty-free entry of selected goods to be displayed, stored, and/or used for manufacturing

full-package vendor apparel contractor that not only provides production services but also assists with and finances materials sourcing and sometimes some phases of product development

General Agreement on Tariffs and Trade (GATT) multilateral trade agreement whose fundamental purpose was to promote free trade of goods and equalize trade among countries; has been absorbed by the World Trade Organization

global trade includes the potential interactive participation of many groups, cultures, and nations in the merchandising, design, development, production, and distribution of products

globalization the process whereby the world's people, their firms, and their countries become increasingly interconnected in all facets of their lives

government subsidy a payment from a government to a business to defray business costs

gray (grey) market goods original goods (they are not knockoffs) that are sold by unauthorized vendors

greige (grey) goods fabrics whose fibers are still in their natural color and texture; usually require additional processes to improve aesthetics and performance

gross domestic product (GDP) the market value of the output of products and services produced within a country in a year

gross domestic product (GDP) per capita gross domestic product of a country divided by the number of people in the population, after GDP has been adjusted by purchasing power parity

gross national product (GNP) the value of the average output produced by domestic residents of a nation as they labor within that nation

gross national product (GNP) per capita gross national product of a country divided by the number of people in the population

Harmonized System (HS) international Harmonized Commodity Description and Classification System, developed by the World Customs Organization

Harmonized Tariff Schedule of the United States (HTS) classification of goods used to determine tariffs on specific products imported into the United States

horizontal integration joining together under a single management organization, previously competitive enterprises engaged in offering similar goods or services

Human Development Index (HDI) an indicator of well-being, incorporating measures of gross domestic product, life expectancy at birth, and adult -literacy

human rights the ability to experience dignity, life, liberty, and security

human trafficking facilitating the emigration of people for monetary gain

illegal transshipment shipping goods through a port or country to facilitate the change of country of origin or to avoid quota limitations and/or import duties in the destination country

import and export trading a recently developed type of enterprise that assists textile and apparel firms in satisfying customer demand for goods and services from the global market

import penetration the amount of consumption that is provided by imports (imports ÷ consumption)

import policy political institution that determines what type of products and services, when, and under what conditions goods and services from another country can enter the domestic economy

import surge an unexpected or unplanned flood of imports of particular categories

imports goods available for domestic consumption or materials available for domestic production because of exports of other countries' income elasticity of demand determined by relative changes in income and expenditures; percentage change in expenditure ÷ percentage change in income

income elasticity of demand determined by relative changes in income and expenditures over a defined period; percentage change in expenditure ÷ percentage change in income

industrial espionage commercial spying made it possible for U.S. spinners and weavers to use machines copied from the English inventions

inelastic demand expenditure increases as income increases but not as fast as income increases; ratio of percent expenditure increase to percent income increase is positive but less than 1; a normal good

inferior good product consumed out of necessity but not preferred according to the standard of consumption; the amount spent decreases when income increases and increases when income decreases

inflation an increase of general price level causing a decline in purchasing power

intellectual property (IP) copyrights, trademarks, patents, trade secrets, and semiconductor chips; inventions, or other discoveries that have been registered with government authorities for the sale and use by their owner

intellectual property rights (IPR) legal protection for exclusive use by owners of copyright, trademarks, patents, trade secrets, and semiconductor chips

International Labor Organization (ILO) a specialized United Nations agency that promotes social justice and internationally recognized human labor rights

International Monetary Fund (IMF) works in tandem with the World Bank; helps integrate countries into the global economy by assisting member countries; monitors international currency transactions

International Textile, Garment, and Leather Workers' Federation (ITGLW) a global association bringing together unions associated with the textile complex

international trade any exchange of goods involving two or more countries

international trade regulation barriers and limits on types and quantities of goods and services that cross political boundaries

intra EU trade among nations that are members of the EU

inventory the entire stock of garments owned by the individual or group that could be used as clothing at a given time

Item 807 (9802) a ruling that allowed garments cut in the United States to be exported and assembled and then imported with tariff based only on value added

joint venture shared ownership of a business or facility by two or more firms

knit fabric fabric made by intertwining yarn or thread in a series of connected loops rather than by weaving

knit outerwear sweaters (jumpers), jackets, and coats

knockoff an imitation of an original that does not carry the original brand, made with lower-cost materials and production methods, and sold at a lower price

labor activist a person or organization that endorses a doctrine or policy of taking positive, direct action to achieve an end, especially one that is political and employment related

labor exploitation taking advantage of employees because of poverty, gender, age, or opportunity, or a combination of these

labor union an organization that bargains with employers on behalf of workers about terms and conditions of employment; lobbies for the interests of workers

layette apparel that is specially designed and produced for children from birth until they begin walking

lean manufacturing a philosophy of production that emphasizes efficiency and strives to eliminate waste throughout the process while improving quality

lean retailing effective management of inventory based on accurate and timely information and frequent resupply

least developed country a nation whose gross domestic product per capita and other economic measures are among the lowest in the world; has little involvement in industrial development, which often involves production of apparel

letter of credit a guarantee to the seller that the buyer has the funds to complete the purchase and that they are reserved for the seller

level of consumption or living that which is actually experienced, enjoyed, or suffered by an individual or group during a given time period

licensee the buyer of the right to use a merchandising property

licenser the owner of a merchandising property

licensing contract a means of transferring intellectual property rights

living consumption and other dimensions of life, including levels of remuneration, comfort, job security, and working conditions, and related factors

living wage the level of income that cover a family's basic needs, including maintenance of good health

lobbying the process of influencing the formation of legislation and/or the administration of rules, regulations, and policies

lobbyists paid professionals who carry the messages defined by their employers and try to influence formation or administration of legislation

logistics science of moving products through the supply chain to their final destinations in a timely manner

Maastricht Treaty treaty signed by 12 EC members, to form the European Union in 1991

manufactured fibers made from chemical compounds; examples include nylon, polyester, acrylic, polypropylene, and spandex; also known as man-made fibers

manufacturer's identification number (RN)
number assigned by the U.S. Federal Trade
Commission to identify a product's producer

manufacturing the entire process of transforming raw
materials into finished goods for use or sale, using
machines, tools and labor

manufacturing control a process in which expected
performance is compared with planned performance

market week calendar time set aside for trade shows
featuring manufacturers' and brand managers' lines
of textile materials, apparel, or machinery, presented
at wholesale to other manufacturers or retail buyers

mass customization integration of information
technology, automation, and team-based flexible
manufacturing to produce a variety of products and
services based on individual customer demand

mass retailer a firm that offers a wide variety of consumer goods in a self-service environment with
broad appeal across income ranges, ethnic groups,
occupations, and lifestyles

merchandising property primary means of product
differentiation and a source of customer loyalty

Mercosur (Common Market of the South) free trade
within, and a common external tariff for, Argentina,
Brazil, Paraguay, and Uruguay, since 1994; accounts
for 70 percent of South America's total economy

merger combining two business entities into one larger
business

minimum needs essentials of life defined by levels and
standards of consumption and living; vary according
to place and time

morals the degree of conformity with generally
accepted or prescribed standards of goodness or
rightness in character or conduct

most-favored nation (MFN) a very confusing term that
means all nations engaged in the same trade agreement should be treated the same

Multifiber Arrangement (MFA) international trade
agreement that allowed the quantity of textile and
apparel trade to be regulated through quotas established in bilateral agreements between nations

multilateral trade agreement involves more than two
countries

natural fibers cotton, wool, silk, and linen as well as
other vegetable and animal fibers

newly developing country a nation whose gross
domestic product per capita and other measures of
well-being fall well below the world average but that
is beginning to be engaged in industrial development probably related to apparel production

nominal tariff rates published in each country's tariffs
schedule

nonstore retailer firms that sell goods to the ultimate
consumer without use of traditional "brick-and-
mortar" store presentation

nontariff trade barriers quota, quality standards, or
other regulations or conditions that restrict the flow
of goods between countries, not including taxes on
imports or exports

nonverbal communication uses appearance to communicate perspective, identity, age, sexual orientation, educational level, occupation, economic status,
or marital status

normal good spending pattern reflects an economic
necessity; the amount spent increases as income
increases and decreases when income decreases
but at a slower rate than the income increase or
decrease

normal trade relations (NTR) a term intended to
replace most-favored nation (MFN) because it is
more descriptive of the actual meaning

North American Free Trade Agreement (NAFTA) eliminated tariffs and quotas among Canada, Mexico, and
the United States in 1994

**North American Industry Classification System
(NAICS)** introduced in 1997 to standardize the identification of textiles and apparel for Canada, Mexico,
and the United States in a manner consistent with
the world market

Office of Textiles and Apparel (OTEXA) Division of
U.S. Department of Commerce that monitors textile
trade throughout the globe in both quantity and
value

Organization of American States (OAS) has continued
since 1948, with the purpose of a Pan-American
Union for closer economic, cultural, and political
relations within the Americas

origin-conferring operations processes that determine
what a label on a product will state as country of
origin

outsourcing shifting specific operations outside the
country in which the origin-conferring operations
are performed; the process of acquiring technical
services in foreign countries; sometimes used interchangeably with sourcing

outward processing outsourcing non-origin-conferring
operations to a country with a lower wage rate

Pan American Union created in 1910, with the purpose
of closer economic, cultural, and political relations
within the Americas

per capita by or for each individual; total is divided by
the number of individuals involved; all share equally

per capita expenditure average spending per person in
a given population

pirated a term used in the EU; an imitation of the
original; the same as counterfeit

political strategy the general approaches used by governments, firms, other organizations, and individuals in dealing with and manipulating important and
powerful components in their environments

political system the principles, organization, and methods of government; the components in an organization's structure and environment that can influence its decisions, survival, and growth

politics the methods or tactics involved in managing an organization, business, state, or government; sometimes includes crafty or unprincipled methods, or both

poverty lack of enough income or resources, or both, to satisfy minimum needs

poverty line the point at which income and wealth are inadequate to maintain life and health at a subsistence level

preferential trade agreements a form of economic integration created by reducing trade barriers

price elasticity of clothing expenditure inelastic, positive but less than one; defined as a normal good

price elasticity of demand determined by relative changes in prices and expenditures; percentage change in price ÷ percentage change in income

price support program purchasing and storing products from the market to reduce the supply relative to demand to drive up the price

primary source most frequent means of clothing acquisition; purchased new ready-to-wear in developed countries; purchased second-hand or handed down in least developed countries

printing localized application of color to the surface of a yarn or fabric

private brand a label owned and marketed exclusively by a brand manager or retailer

private brand importer a brand manager or retailer who sources private brand products in foreign countries for import into the domestic economy

product development the design and engineering of products to be serviceable, producible, salable, and profitable (Glock & Kunz, 1995)

production subsidy a negative trade tax; a payment of money from a government to a business to defray costs of making goods and commodities

productivity ratio of the outputs of a production process to the inputs; a measure of performance toward an established goal

progressive tax has an increase in tax rate as income rises

protectionism uses trade barriers to minimize imports

purchased secondhand money paid for garments that have been used by someone else, inferior good in the economic perspective of clothing consumption

purchasing power the amount of goods or services that can be acquired with a specified amount of currency at a certain time

purchasing power parity (PPP) measure that allows comparison of well being among populations in different countries as indicated to GDP; determined by adjusting GDP of a country by the buying power of its currency using a system like the Consumer Price Index

Qualified Industrial Zone (QIZ) geographical areas within Jordan and Egypt that receive duty- and quota-free trade status with the United States on the condition of Israeli participation in at least part of the production process

quality assurance a commitment to product quality that utilizes the concept of error prevention as integral to the entire product development process

quota method used to restrict quantities of certain types of goods that can be imported or exported; limit on the quantity of products allowed to enter or exit a country

quota avoidance strategy using transshipment, fabric blends, or other means not covered by quota

radio frequency identification (RFID) new generation of wireless bar code systems; being used for identifying and tracking products, cartons, and containers

rate of duty amount of tax to be assessed on imported or exported goods, usually according to a tariff schedule

real expenditure outlay adjusted to reflect buying power considering rate of inflation

real income earnings adjusted to reflect buying power considering rate of inflation

real-time immediately available when data are collected

red tape unnecessary obstructions and delays in processing paperwork

regionalization reducing trade barriers in selected geographic regions to facilitate trade

regressive tax requires lower-income people to pay higher rates than higher-income people

retail product developer an individual who or team that creates the product designs and develops the merchandise plans and specifications for a retailer's private brands, which are ultimately sourced from production

retailing sale of merchandise or services, or both, to ultimate consumers

rules of origin criteria used to determine the national source of a product

secondary source means of acquiring clothing other than the primary source; gifts, purchased used, handed down, rental, home sewing, custom-made, and others

social activist a person or organization that endorses a doctrine or policy of taking positive, direct action to achieve an end, especially a political or social end

social responsibility obligations of an individual, group, and/or general population for its well-being including fair treatment of human beings, related resources, and the law

socialism an economic system in which ownership, production, and distribution are operated by members of the community rather than by individuals or the government

soft goods products made of textiles or other flexible materials; fabrics, apparel, linens, towels, upholstery, and small fashion accessories

sourcing determining the most cost efficient vendor of services, materials, production, or finished goods, or a combination of these, at a specified quality and service level, for delivery within an identified time frame

sourcing agents firms or entities that provide services necessary to procure and deliver products and services to wholesale customers

sourcing calendar a timeline related to the sequence of design, product development, production, and delivery to the retail sales floor

specialty stores retailers that focus on specific classes of merchandise to the exclusion of other products

specific tariff fixed amount of tax per physical unit of imported product

specifications detailed graphic and written descriptions of styling, materials, dimensions, production procedures, and finishing instructions for a garment style (Keiser and Garner, 2008)

square meter equivalent (SME) a means of measuring quantities of fabric and garments that are being exported or imported

Standard Industrial Classification System (SIC) Replaced by North American Industrial Classification System (NAICS)

standard of consumption or living level that is urgently desired and strived for, substantial success yielding special gratification and substantial failure yielding bitter frustration (Davis, 1945)

standards basic characteristics used to determine acceptability of products and services

state trading the involvement of governments in the business environment

substantial transformation occurs when the processing of an article results in a new and different article having a distinct name, character, or use; occurs when a HS classification changes

substitute a product purchased and used in place of another; example, pants rather than skirts

superior good preferred product according to standards of consumption and living; the amount spent increases as income increases and decreases when income decreases but at a faster rate than the income increases or decreases; economic luxury

supply chain a total sequence of business processes involving single or multiple businesses and countries that enables demand for products or services to be satisfied

supranational organization requires that members give up a portion of their control over selected policies and allows the organization to compel compliance with its mandates

sustainability a corporate responsibility strategy that integrates economic, political, environmental, and cultural dimensions to promote cooperation and solidarity among people and generations

sweatshop firm with poor working conditions, very low pay, safety violations, and often inhumane treatment of employees

takeover the absorption of a weaker firm into a more successful operation

tariff tax on imports or exports; duty

temporary possession a means of momentary clothing acquisition from sources such as rental, borrowing, and perhaps clothing provided by an employer

textile materials sourcing identifying appropriate countries of origin and contracting with cost-efficient vendors of fabric, thread, or findings at a specified quantity, quality, and service level, for delivery within a designated time frame

textile complex the combination of textile-related industries that supply soft goods to the world population

textile mill manufacturing facility where yarns or fabrics are produced

textile product mill manufacturing facility that produces fabric and uses it to create consumable goods, including carpets, rugs, curtains, draperies, and bed and bath products

thread a special form of yarn designed for use in sewing cut fabric pieces together to form garments or other products

total income gross income or personal income

totalitarian one family or some other entity maintains absolute governmental control; dictatorship

trade agreement a means of encouraging, regulating, or restricting elements of trade between countries

trade association an organization of executives or managers, or both, that share common professional interests

trade balance the quantitative relationship between exports and imports of a country

trade barriers means of regulating or restricting trade; examples include state trading, tariffs, quotas, and limits on foreign investment

trade deficit a negative trade balance; value of imports exceeds value of exports

trade policy political institution designed to stimulate and or control exchange of goods between nations

trade surplus a positive trade balance; value of exports exceeds value of imports

trademark a word, phase, logo, or other graphic symbol used to distinguish one firm's product(s) or service(s) from another firm's product(s) or services

trademark infringement the act of misleading the public into believing the items bearing the trademark/brand name are produced and sold by the owner of the trademark when they are not

trading bloc a group of countries that have created regional trade incentives and that jointly participate in trade negotiations

trading partners in EDI terminology, vendors and customers who exchange (trade) electronic documents in order to do business

transaction value the price that is actually paid or payable for the goods when sold for export

transnational fair trade perspective being responsive to local needs in multiple countries while simultaneously retaining global efficiency

transparency of information open communication among all participants within a system

transshipment to transfer or be transferred from one conveyance to another to continue shipment

transshipment center a port where merchandise can be imported and then exported without paying import duties

trims a major category of findings that includes embellishments used to enhance the aesthetics of finished garments

underwear and sleepwear knitting mill a manufacturing facility in which products are produced by cutting and sewing knit fabrics

undocumented immigrant workers (UIW) individuals from foreign countries without *legal* identification papers

unfair competition activities defined by legal rulings and statutes that protect against unethical business practices (Elias & Stim, 2007)

unfair competition law governs commercial activity that tends to confuse, mislead, or deceive customers and/or provide unfair business advantages

Universal Product Code (UPC) bar code system for identifying and tracking products or containers

Uruguay Round final multilateral trade negotiations of GATT that resulted in the WTO and ATC

vendor a company who supplies services and/or products to other companies commonly known as customers

vendor compliance performance standards or rules established by the customer that a vendor must follow in order to do business with them

vertical integration combining firms that perform different stages of the production of the same type of products

voluntary export restraint a "gentlemen's agreement" between countries limiting trade

well-being a good or satisfactory condition of existence

World Bank a specialized agency of the United Nations, made up of 184 member nations, with the mission of improving the living standards of people in the developing world; term is used to refer to the International Bank for Reconstruction and Development and the International Development Association

World Customs Organization (WCO) global organization whose purpose is to improve operation and efficiency of Customs services

World Trade Organization (WTO) an organization with more than 153 countries as members; deals with the global rules of trade among nations

Worldwide Responsible Accredited Production (WRAP) an independent nonprofit corporation dedicated to the promotion and certification of lawful, humane, and ethical manufacturing throughout the world

woven fabrics produced by interlocking two or more sets of yarns at right angles

yarn a continuous strand produced by twisting fibers together

yarn-forward rule a trade rule that limits tariff and quota free imports to garments made of domestically produced yarns and fabrics

Index

Page numbers in italics refer to images or tables.